SURVEY of FINANCIAL ACCOUNTING

SIXTH EDITION

SURVEY OF

FINANCIAL ACCOUNTING

Sixth Edition

Gary L. Schugart

University of Houston

Arthur J. Francia

University of Houston

James J. Benjamin

Texas A&M University

Robert H. Strawser

Texas A&M University

1998

DAME
PUBLICATIONS, INC.

Cover Design: Andrea P. Leggett

Cover Photo: © **Corel Professional Photos.** Images may have
been combined and/or modified to produce final
cover art.

Desktop Publishing: Sheryl New

© **DAME PUBLICATIONS, INC.—1998**
7800 Bissonnet—Suite 415
Houston, TX 77074
713/995-1000
713/995-9637—FAX
800/364-9757
E-mail: dame.publications@worldnet.att.net
Website: http://www.damepub.com

ISBN 0-87393-782-1

Library of Congress Catalog Card No. 98-70893

Printed in the United States of America.

PREFACE

Survey of Financial Accounting (SFA) is a unique textbook which has been prepared for the introductory or survey course in accounting. It is ideal for use in either a one or a two-term first course (depending on the material selected and the depth of coverage desired) at the undergraduate or graduate level.

SFA has been written to provide a broad overview of all aspects of accounting from basic concepts, through the accounting information system to financial statements and special reports, emphasizing the interpretation of these statements and reports. Considerations of theory and practice are blended, and numerous illustrations and examples are included, all to enhance student understanding. Learning objectives provide an overview of what should be achieved after studying each chapter. A mini-component (described below) introduces the student to each chapter. A wealth of end-of-chapter materials (Summaries, Key Definitions, Questions, and Problems) are available to reinforce student comprehension.

The initial chapter is the annual report of Wal-Mart, Inc. No doubt everyone is familiar with many aspects of Wal-Mart's operations: its more than nineteen hundred Wal-Mart discount department stores, Wal-Mart Supercenters and Sam's Clubs. The Wal-Mart Annual Report is presented as Chapter 1 to provide students with a broad overview of accounting as communications—the language of business!

The basic approach used in SFA is illustrated by the second chapter which describes the activities of a small business in the initial month of its operations. A complete set of financial statements, including a balance sheet, income statement, statement of owner's equity, and statement of cash flows, is prepared without use (or mention) of debits, credits, accounts, or journal entries. In subsequent chapters, this illustration is again used to consider transaction analysis and the accounting cycle after basic concepts and principles have been illustrated and explained.

Eighteen comprehensive chapters have been prepared to permit maximum flexibility in topic selection without any loss of continuity or instructional benefit. The material has been prepared and is presented in a manner that allows the instructor to "pick and choose" individual topics and/or reorder subject matter without detracting from the usefulness of the text. Most, if not all, of the financial accounting material presented in all introductory principles, survey, and/or financial texts is included.

SFA presents a balanced perspective of practice and theory emphasizing decision-making using accounting information. A direct, straightforward approach achieves completeness of coverage using simple but accurate terms, examples and illustrations. SFA is a usable text geared to the understanding of basic concepts, principles, and practices. It emphasizes financial statement understanding and analysis, and decision-making using financial information. The basic intention is to address the needs and requirements of the users of financial data. Again, the analysis of this data by financial statement users is the primary focus.

A brief descriptive outline of the text and its contents follows:

1. Presents the annual report of a major U.S. corporation, Wal-Mart, Inc.
2. Discusses and illustrates the preparation of a complete set of financial statements for a small company without mentioning (or using) debits and credits.
3. Introduces the basic accounting concepts and discusses the basic financial statements, including the balance sheet, income statement, and statement of cash flows.
4. Discusses the basic financial statements and introduces the accounting equation.
5. Traces and explains the process of recording transactions, end of period adjustments and the preparation of financial statements.
6. Discusses adjusting entries and uses the worksheet as an overview of the accounting process.

v

7. Discusses the different types of organizations that engage in business activities and focuses on the analysis of corporate financial statements.

8. Illustrates the operational differences among companies with special emphasis on the differences between retailing and service organizations and considers the alternative methods for accounting for inventories.

9. Discusses the procedures used for recording, allocating and disposing of long-term assets and the accounting for intangibles and natural resources, including oil and gas accounting. MACRS procedures for computing depreciation for tax purposes are discussed.

10. Discusses the accounting procedures which are used to record and control cash accounts and notes receivable and current liabilities.

11. Discusses the accounting for bonds payable and investments in corporate securities and explains and illustrates the preparation and use of consolidated financial statements.

12. Considers the issues related to the accounting for firms organized as sole proprietorships, partnerships, and corporations. Discusses the issues related to the formation of a corporation, the issuance of capital stock, the retained earnings and the dividends of a corporation.

13. Discusses and illustrates alternative methods of revenue recognition.

14. Discusses and illustrates the basic techniques of analyzing and using the information presented in financial statements.

15. Explains and illustrates the procedures employed in preparing the statement of cash flows.

16. Presents a general discussion of the federal income tax. Explanation and illustration of both interperiod and intraperiod tax allocation are included.

17. Discusses the accounting for foreign currency transactions and foreign currency translation, as well as efforts to achieve uniform international accounting standards.

18. Presents a discussion of disclosures for pensions, other postretirement benefits, leases, segment reporting, interim reporting, management's discussion and analysis, and the auditor's report.

We are indebted to many students and colleagues for their assistance, comments, and constructive criticisms which assisted in making SFA a reality. A necessary ingredient in the writing of any text is the environment in which the effort took place. Our special thanks to John M. Ivancevich and Sarah A. Friedman of the University of Houston, A. Benton Cocanougher, William H. Mobley, William V. Muse and the late John E. Pearson of Texas A&M University for providing us with encouragement in our efforts and with environments in which this book could be created.

July, 1998

Gary L. Schugart
James J. Benjamin
Arthur J. Francia
Robert H. Strawser

Table of Contents

LEARNING Objectives

Chapter 1 presents an annual report to shareholders of a major U.S. corporation. Studying this chapter should enable you to:

1. Describe the general content of an annual report to shareholders.

2. List and briefly describe the major financial statements included in an annual report.

3. Describe and compare the financial and other information and disclosures contained in an annual report to shareholders.

CHAPTER 1

AN ANNUAL REPORT TO SHAREHOLDERS

Chapter 1 of this text presents the annual report to the shareholders of Wal-Mart, Inc., a major U.S. corporation doing business not only in the United States, but also in Puerto Rico, Mexico, Argentina, Brazil, China and Indonesia in the global mass marketplace. Of course, you are no doubt familiar with Wal-Mart, America's largest retailer with over nineteen hundred Wal-Mart discount department stores and the other stores that it operates—Wal-Mart Supercenters, combination full-time supermarkets, and Sam's Clubs, warehouse membership clubs.

This informative report contains a wealth of information—narrative and descriptive as well as quantitative—concerning every aspect of Wal-Mart's operations. The Annual Report for Wal-Mart is an excellent example of the information U.S. businesses, both large and small, make available to their owners and interested others. While much of this information is accumulated and prepared by accountants, the report is intended to meet the needs of a wide variety of users ranging from sophisticated financial analysts to individuals who know very little, or perhaps even nothing, about accounting and accountants.

The Wal-Mart, Inc. Annual Report is included as Chapter 1 of this text so you can read through it now and obtain a broad, overall perspective of the nature of the information dealt with by both accountants and users of accounting information. Throughout your accounting course, you will, no doubt, return to consider various aspects of the details included in this report and you will learn that accounting is communications—the language of business!

PRESIDENT'S LETTER

CEO David Glass looks forward to a world of future prospects.

FUTURE STOCK
Building shareholder value

Wal-Mart has a history of rising to the challenge. After a disappointing year in fiscal 1996, our associates responded with a solid performance in fiscal 1997. Sales for the fiscal year approached $105 billion and earnings topped $3 billion. Each operating division generated higher comparable sales growth and improved operating margins. Our Wal-Mart operations experienced some of the best customer approval scores in our history and SAM'S Club showed solid improvement in comparable sales, membership, merchandise selection and income.

Asset management and cash flow were key themes this year. We generated over $3 billion in free cash flow and increased our return on assets. With the growth in the Company's cash flow, we now can finance our aggressive capital expenditures program internally and still have excess cash available for distribution to our shareholders.

This strong sustainable cash flow allowed us to announce two actions to enhance shareholder value. The first was to increase our dividend by 29% and the second was to increase the size of our share repurchase program with the intent to repurchase up to $2 billion worth of stock over the next 12 to 18 months.

Our first priority remains profitable internal growth. Future increases in the dividend and repurchase program will depend on the availability of our growth opportunities.

The significant increase in both the dividend and the share repurchase program demonstrate our confidence in the Company's future earnings and cash flow growth. We believe our double digit earnings growth combined with the new shareholder initiatives will allow us to achieve our targeted annual total shareholder return of 15%.

In June of 1990, at our annual shareholder's meeting, Sam Walton predicted Wal-Mart would reach $100 billion in sales by the year 2000. At that time, we thought the goal was quite a stretch. After all, it took us 10 years to reach $100 million and another 7 to reach our first billion. But our strength has always been our dedicated associates, their ability to work together, and the support of our loyal customers. So 3 years ahead of schedule, we reached that goal.

Even though we exceeded that lofty goal, there is still plenty of room left to grow. In the United States, Wal-Mart holds only 7% of a $1.4 trillion retail market. That leaves a tremendous opportunity for future growth.

The supermarket industry, amounting to $425 billion a year, is a great opportunity for continued growth. It's almost three times the size of the discount store industry, where Wal-Mart is one of the three retailers that, combined, hold almost 85 percent of the market. Yet in the grocery segment, the top five players constitute less than 25%.

Then there is the rest of the world. Our international division reported sales in excess of $5 billion and these operations could represent 10 percent of our total sales in the next 5 years.

The international division was profitable for the year with

In June of 1990, Sam Walton predicted Wal-Mart would reach $100 billion in sales by the year 2000. At that time, we thought the goal was quite a stretch.

Canada and Puerto Rico showing excellent results and Mexico achieving profitability in a difficult economy.

Only three years after acquiring the Woolco stores in Canada, Wal-Mart has become Canada's highest volume discount retailer and in Mexico our joint venture is also the country's largest retailer.

The value our customers respond to in the United States is enthusiastically received wherever we go. In China, where we recently opened our first units, the people already know what Wal-Mart is all about. Our three story Supercenter had 80,000 visitors on its first Saturday.

With over 300 locations and more than 50,000 associates outside the United States, Wal-Mart has become a true global brand name, with worldwide appeal resembling Coca-Cola or McDonald's. The Wal-Mart way of doing business makes us one of the world's most recognizable companies - which translates to loyal customers and steady profitable growth.

Wal-Mart associates have every right to be proud of what we've built, from our very first store to today's worldwide network of nearly 3,000 stores and clubs. We're the company that works because of our people - the associates who make it happen every day.

So if anyone wonders where our next $100 billion will come from – it will come from customers who recognize value throughout the world and from our associates who will deliver it with a smile.

I am really excited about the next year. We have so much opportunity and our team is focused on continuing to serve our customers in such a way that clearly indicates they are the boss. But more importantly, they are focused on value. Value to our customers and value to our shareholders.

11-YEAR FINANCIAL SUMMARY

(Dollar amounts in millions except per share data)	1997	1996	1995
Operating Results			
Net sales	$ 104,859	$ 93,627	$ 82,494
Net sales increase	12%	13%	22%
Comparative store sales increase	5%	4%	7%
Other income-net	1,287	1,122	918
Cost of sales	83,663	74,564	65,586
Operating, selling and general and administrative expenses	16,788	14,951	12,858
Interest costs:			
Debt	629	692	520
Capital leases	216	196	186
Provision for income taxes	1,794	1,606	1,581
Net income	3,056	2,740	2,681
Per share of common stock:			
Net income	$1.33	1.19	1.17
Dividends	0.21	.20	.17
Financial Position			
Current assets	$ 17,993	$ 17,331	$ 15,338
Inventories at replacement cost	16,193	16,300	14,415
Less LIFO reserve	296	311	351
Inventories at LIFO cost	15,897	15,989	14,064
Net property, plant and equipment and capital leases	20,324	18,894	15,874
Total assets	39,604	37,541	32,819
Current liabilities	10,957	11,454	9,973
Long-term debt	7,709	8,508	7,871
Long-term obligations under capital leases	2,307	2,092	1,838
Shareholders' equity	17,143	14,756	12,726
Financial Ratios			
Current ratio	1.6	1.5	1.5
Inventories/working capital	2.3	2.7	2.6
Return on assets*	7.9%	7.8%	9.0%
Return on shareholders' equity*	19.2%	19.9%	22.8%
Other Year-End Data			
Number of Domestic Wal-Mart stores	1,960	1,995	1,985
Number of Domestic Supercenters	344	239	147
Number of Domestic SAM'S Clubs	436	433	426
International units	314	276	226
Average Wal-Mart store size	92,600	91,100	87,600
Number of Associates	728,000	675,000	622,000
Number of Shareholders of Record	257,215	244,483	259,286

* On average balances.

FINANCIALS

1994	1993	1992	1991	1990	1989	1988	1987
$ 67,344	$ 55,484	$ 43,887	$ 32,602	$ 25,811	$ 20,649	$ 15,959	$ 11,909
21%	26%	35%	26%	25%	29%	34%	41%
6%	11%	10%	10%	11%	12%	11%	13%
641	501	403	262	175	137	105	85
53,444	44,175	34,786	25,500	20,070	16,057	12,282	9,053
10,333	8,321	6,684	5,152	4,070	3,268	2,599	2,008
331	143	113	43	20	36	25	10
186	180	153	126	118	99	89	76
1,358	1,171	945	752	632	488	441	396
2,333	1,995	1,609	1,291	1,076	838	628	451
1.02	.87	.70	.57	.48	.37	.28	.20
.13	.11	.09	.07	.06	.04	.03	.02
$ 12,114	$ 10,198	$ 8,575	$ 6,415	$ 4,713	$ 3,631	$ 2,905	$ 2,353
11,483	9,780	7,857	6,207	4,751	3,642	2,855	2,185
469	512	473	399	323	291	203	154
11,014	9,268	7,384	5,808	4,428	3,351	2,652	2,031
13,176	9,793	6,434	4,712	3,430	2,662	2,145	1,676
26,441	20,565	15,443	11,389	8,198	6,360	5,132	4,049
7,406	6,754	5,004	3,990	2,845	2,066	1,744	1,340
6,156	3,073	1,722	740	185	184	186	179
1,804	1,772	1,556	1,159	1,087	1,009	867	764
10,753	8,759	6,990	5,366	3,966	3,008	2,257	1,690
1.6	1.5	1.7	1.6	1.7	1.8	1.7	1.8
2.3	2.7	2.1	2.4	2.4	2.1	2.3	2.0
9.9%	11.1%	12.0%	13.2%	14.8%	14.6%	13.7%	12.6%
23.9%	25.3%	26.0%	27.7%	30.9%	31.8%	31.8%	30.4%
1,950	1,848	1,714	1,568	1,399	1,259	1,114	980
72	34	10	9	6	3	2	
417	256	208	148	123	105	84	49
24	10						
83,900	79,800	74,700	70,700	66,400	63,500	61,500	59,000
528,000	434,000	371,000	328,000	271,000	223,000	183,000	141,000
257,946	180,584	150,242	122,414	79,929	80,270	79,777	32,896

MANAGEMENT'S DISCUSSION AND ANALYSIS

Results of Operations

Increases (Decreases) In Consolidated Operating Results Over Prior Year				
	1997		1996	
(Dollars in millions, except per share data)	Amount	%	Amount	%
Revenues:				
Net sales	$ 11,232	12%	$ 11,133	13%
Other income-net	165	15%	204	22%
	11,397	12%	11,337	14%
Costs and Expenses:				
Cost of sales	9,099	12%	8,978	14%
Operating, selling and general and administrative expenses	1,837	12%	2,093	16%
Interest Costs:				
Debt	(63)	(9%)	172	33%
Capital leases	20	10%	10	5%
	10,893	12%	11,253	14%
Income Before Income Taxes	504	12%	84	2%
Provision for Income Taxes	188	12%	25	2%
Net Income	$ 316	12%	$ 59	2%
Net Income Per Share	$.14	12%	$.02	2%

Net Sales

The sales increase in fiscal 1997 was attributable to the Company's expansion program and comparative store sales increases of 5%. Expansion for fiscal 1997 included the opening of 59 Wal-Mart stores, 105 Supercenters (including the conversion of 92 Wal-Mart stores), 9 SAM'S Clubs, and 38 international units. The majority of the sales increase resulted from Wal-Mart stores and Supercenters while International sales grew to approximately 4.8% of the total sales in fiscal 1997 from 4.0% in fiscal 1996. SAM'S Club sales as a percentage of total sales decreased from 20.4% in fiscal 1996 to 18.9% in fiscal 1997.

The sales increase of 13% in fiscal 1996 was attributable to the Company's expansion program and comparative store sales increases of 4%. Expansion for fiscal 1996 included the opening of 92 Wal-Mart stores, 92 Supercenters (including the conversion of 80 Wal-Mart stores), 9 SAM'S Clubs and 50 International units. International sales accounted for approximately 2.1% of the sales increase with the remainder primarily attributable to Wal-Mart stores and Supercenters. SAM'S Club sales as a percentage of total sales decreased from 22.9% in fiscal 1995 to 20.4% in fiscal 1996.

Costs and Expenses

Cost of sales as a percentage of sales increased .2% in fiscal 1997 and .1% in fiscal 1996 when compared to the preceding year. The increase in fiscal 1997 is due in part to one-time markdowns in the third quarter resulting from a strategic decision to reduce the merchandise assortment in selected categories. Cost of sales also increased approximately .3% due to a larger

percentage of consolidated sales from departments within Wal-Mart stores which have lower markon percents, and to the Company's continuing commitment of always providing low prices. These increases were offset by approximately .2% because SAM'S Club comprised a lower percentage of consolidated sales in 1997 at a lower contribution to gross margin than the stores. The increase in fiscal 1996 was due to lower initial markons and a larger percentage of consolidated sales from departments within Wal-Mart stores which have lower markon percents. This increase is offset by approximately .3% because SAM'S Club comprised a lower percentage of consolidated sales in 1996 at a lower contribution to gross margin than the stores.

Operating, selling and general and administrative expenses as a percentage of sales were flat in fiscal 1997 when compared to fiscal 1996 and increased .4% in fiscal 1996 when compared to fiscal 1995. As sales in SAM'S Club decreased as a percentage of total sales, the Company's operating, selling and general and administrative expenses as a percentage of sales increased approximately .1% due to a lower expense to sales percentage at SAM'S Club compared to the stores and Supercenters. This increase was offset through expense control in all of the operating formats. Approximately .2% of the increase in fiscal 1996 was due to increases in payroll and related benefit costs. The remainder of the increase resulted primarily from a lower percentage of sales attributable to SAM'S Club and a higher percentage of sales attributable to international operations. SAM'S Club operating, selling and general and administrative expenses as a percentage of sales were lower than the Wal-Mart stores and Supercenters while international expenses were slightly higher.

The Company adopted Statement of Financial Accounting Standard (SFAS) No. 121 "Accounting for the Impairment of Long-Lived Assets and for Long-Lived Assets to be Disposed Of" in fiscal 1997. The statement requires entities to review long-lived assets and certain intangible assets in certain circumstances, and if the value of the assets is impaired, an impairment loss shall be recognized. The Company's existing accounting policies were such that this pronouncement did not materially affect the Company's financial position or results of operations.

Interest Cost

Interest cost decreased in fiscal 1997 compared to fiscal 1996 due to lower average daily short-term borrowings and through retirement of maturing debt. The Company was able to reduce short-term debt through enhanced operating cash flows and lower capital spending. Interest cost increased in fiscal 1996 compared to 1995 due to increased indebtedness and increased average short-term borrowing rates. The increased indebtedness was primarily due to the Company's expansion program. See Note 2 of Notes to Consolidated Financial Statements for additional information on interest and debt.

International Operations

The Company has wholly owned operations in Argentina, Canada and Puerto Rico, and through joint ventures in Brazil, China and Mexico. International operations remain immaterial to total Company operations. However, their sales growth in fiscal 1997 exceeded all other operating formats. As a group, the international operations were profitable in fiscal 1997.

Liquidity and Capital Resources
Cash Flow Information

Cash flow provided from operations was $5.9 billion in fiscal 1997, up from $2.4 billion in fiscal 1996. The increase was primarily due to a greater emphasis on inventory management that resulted in lowering unit inventory levels. Although consolidated net sales increased by 12% in fiscal 1997, consolidated inventories decreased slightly from the prior year end. After funding capital expenditures of more than $2.6 billion, operating cash flow provided an excess of almost $3.3 billion. This enabled the Company to reduce short-term borrowings, retire maturing debt and pay dividends. At January 31, 1997, the Company eliminated short term borrowings and had $883 million invested in cash and cash equivalents. The Company anticipates that cash flows from operations will continue to exceed future capital expenditures. The excess cash flows generated may be used to purchase Company stock, pay dividends or for other investing or financing needs.

Company Stock Purchases and Common Stock Dividends

In fiscal 1997, the Company purchased over 8 million shares of its common stock for $208 million. Subsequent to January 31, 1997, the Company announced plans to purchase up to $2 billion of its common stock over the next 18 months. Additionally, the Company increased the dividend 29% to $.27 per share for fiscal 1998.

Expansion

Domestically, the Company plans to open approximately 50 new Wal-Mart stores, and 100 Supercenters. Approximately 70 of the Supercenters will come from relocations or expansions of existing Wal-Mart stores. The Company also plans to open 5 to 10 new SAM'S Clubs and 4 distribution centers. International expansion includes 30 to 35 new Wal-Mart stores, Supercenters, and SAM'S Clubs in Argentina, Brazil, Canada, China, Mexico and Puerto Rico.

Total planned capital expenditures for 1998 approximates $3 billion. The Company plans to primarily finance expansion with operating cash flows.

Borrowing Information

The Company had committed lines of credit of $2,450 million with 34 banks and informal lines with various banks totaling an additional $2,450 million which were used to support short-term borrowing and commercial paper. These lines of credit and their anticipated cyclical increases will be sufficient to finance the seasonal buildups in merchandise inventories and for other cash requirements.

The Company anticipates generating sufficient operating cash flow to fund all capital expenditures and accordingly, does not plan to finance future capital expenditures with debt. However, the Company may desire to obtain long-term financing for other uses of cash or for strategic reasons. The Company foresees no difficulty in obtaining long-term financing in view of its excellent credit rating and favorable experiences in the debt market in the past few years. In addition to the available credit lines mentioned above, the Company may sell up to $751 million of public debt under shelf registration statements previously filed with the Securities and Exchange Commission.

Foreign Currency Translation

All foreign operations are measured in their local currencies with the exception of Brazil, operating in a highly inflationary economy, which reports operations using U.S. dollars. Beginning in fiscal 1998, Mexico will report as a highly inflationary economy. All foreign operations as a group are immaterial to the Company's consolidated results of operations and financial position. In fiscal 1997, the foreign currency translation adjustment decreased by $12 million to $400 million primarily due to a favorable exchange rate in Canada. The cumulative foreign currency translation adjustments of $412 and $256 million in fiscal 1996 and 1995, respectively, were primarily due to operations in Mexico. The Company periodically purchases forward contracts on firm commitments to minimize the risk of foreign currency fluctuations. None of these contracts were significant during the year, and those outstanding at January 31, 1997 were insignificant to the Company's financial position. The Company minimizes its exposure to the risk of devaluation of foreign currencies by operating in local currencies and through buying forward contracts on some known transactions.

Forward-Looking Statements

Certain statements contained in Management's Discussion and Analysis and elsewhere in this annual report are forward-looking statements. These statements discuss, among other things, expected growth, future revenues and future performance. The forward-looking statements are subject to risks and uncertainties, including, but not limited to, competitive pressures, inflation, consumer debt levels, currency exchange fluctuations, trade restrictions, changes in tariff and freight rates, capital market conditions and other risks indicated in the Company's filings with the Securities and Exchange Commission. Actual results may materially differ from anticipated results described in these statements.

CONSOLIDATED STATEMENTS OF INCOME

(Amounts in millions except per share data)

Fiscal years ended January 31,	1997	1996	1995
Revenues:			
Net sales	$ 104,859	$ 93,627	$ 82,494
Other income-net	1,287	1,122	918
	106,146	94,749	83,412
Costs and Expenses:			
Cost of sales	83,663	74,564	65,586
Operating, selling and general and administrative expenses	16,788	14,951	12,858
Interest Costs:			
Debt	629	692	520
Capital leases	216	196	186
	101,296	90,403	79,150
Income Before Income Taxes	4,850	4,346	4,262
Provision for Income Taxes			
Current	1,974	1,530	1,572
Deferred	(180)	76	9
	1,794	1,606	1,581
Net Income	$ 3,056	$ 2,740	$ 2,681
Net Income Per Share	$ 1.33	$ 1.19	$ 1.17

See accompanying notes.

CONSOLIDATED BALANCE SHEETS

(Amounts in millions)

January 31,	1997	1996
Assets		
Current Assets:		
Cash and cash equivalents	$ 883	$ 83
Receivables	845	853
Inventories		
At replacement cost	16,193	16,300
Less LIFO reserve	296	311
Inventories at LIFO cost	15,897	15,989
Prepaid expenses and other	368	406
Total Current Assets	17,993	17,331
Property, Plant and Equipment, at Cost:		
Land	3,689	3,559
Building and improvements	12,724	11,290
Fixtures and equipment	6,390	5,665
Transportation equipment	379	336
	23,182	20,850
Less accumulated depreciation	4,849	3,752
Net property, plant and equipment	18,333	17,098
Property under capital lease	2,782	2,476
Less accumulated amortization	791	680
Net property under capital leases	1,991	1,796
Other Assets and Deferred Charges	1,287	1,316
Total Assets	$ 39,604	$ 37,541
Liabilities and Shareholders' Equity		
Current Liabilities:		
Commercial paper	$ –	$ 2,458
Accounts payable	7,628	6,442
Accrued liabilities	2,413	2,091
Accrued income taxes	298	123
Long-term debt due within one year	523	271
Obligations under capital leases due within one year	95	69
Total Current Liabilities	10,957	11,454
Long-Term Debt	7,709	8,508
Long-Term Obligations Under Capital Leases	2,307	2,092
Deferred Income Taxes and Other	463	400
Minority Interest	1,025	331
Shareholders' Equity		
Preferred stock ($.10 par value; 100 shares authorized, none issued)		
Common stock ($.10 par value; 5,500 shares authorized, 2,285 and 2,293 issued and outstanding in 1997 and 1996, respectively)	228	229
Capital in excess of par value	547	545
Retained earnings	16,768	14,394
Foreign currency translation adjustment	(400)	(412)
Total Shareholders' Equity	17,143	14,756
Total Liabilities and Shareholders' Equity	$ 39,604	$ 37,541

See accompanying notes.

CONSOLIDATED STATEMENTS OF SHAREHOLDERS' EQUITY

(Amounts in millions except per share data)	Number of shares	Common stock	Capital in excess of par value	Retained earnings	Foreign currency translation adjustment	Total
Balance - January 31, 1994	2,299	$ 230	$ 536	$ 9,987	$ –	$ 10,753
Net income				2,681		2,681
Cash dividends ($.17 per share)				(391)		(391)
Purchase of Company stock	(3)		(4)	(64)		(68)
Foreign currency translation adjustment					(256)	(256)
Other	1		7			7
Balance - January 31, 1995	2,297	230	539	12,213	(256)	12,726
Net income				2,740		2,740
Cash dividends ($.20 per share)				(458)		(458)
Purchase of Company stock	(5)		(4)	(101)		(105)
Foreign currency translation adjustment					(156)	(156)
Other	1	(1)	10			9
Balance - January 31, 1996	2,293	229	545	14,394	(412)	14,756
Net income				3,056		3,056
Cash dividends ($.21 per share)				(481)		(481)
Purchase of Company stock	(8)		(7)	(201)		(208)
Foreign currency translation adjustment					12	12
Other		(1)	9			8
Balance - January 31, 1997	2,285	$ 228	$ 547	$ 16,768	$ (400)	$ 17,143

See accompanying notes.

FINANCIALS

CONSOLIDATED STATEMENTS OF CASH FLOWS

(Amounts in millions)			
Fiscal years ended January 31,	**1997**	1996	1995
Cash flows from operating activities			
Net income	**$ 3,056**	$ 2,740	$ 2,681
Adjustments to reconcile net income to net cash			
provided by operating activities:			
Depreciation and amortization	**1,463**	1,304	1,070
Increase in accounts receivable	**(58)**	(61)	(84)
Decrease/(increase) in inventories	**99**	(1,850)	(3,053)
Increase in accounts payable	**1,208**	448	1,914
Increase in accrued liabilities	**430**	29	496
Deferred income taxes	**(180)**	76	9
Other	**(88)**	(303)	(127)
Net cash provided by operating activities	**5,930**	2,383	2,906
Cash flows from investing activities			
Payments for property, plant and equipment	**(2,643)**	(3,566)	(3,734)
Proceeds from sale of photo finishing plants	**464**		
Acquisition of assets from Woolworth Canada, Inc.			(352)
Sale/leaseback arrangements			502
Other investing activities	**111**	234	(208)
Net cash used in investing activities	**(2,068)**	(3,332)	(3,792)
Cash flows from financing activities			
(Decrease)/increase in commercial paper	**(2,458)**	660	220
Proceeds from issuance of long-term debt		1,004	1,250
Net proceeds from formation of real estate			
investment trust (REIT)	**632**		
Purchase of Company stock	**(208)**	(105)	(68)
Dividends paid	**(481)**	(458)	(391)
Payment of long-term debt	**(541)**	(126)	(37)
Payment of capital lease obligations	**(74)**	(81)	(70)
Other financing activities	**68**	93	7
Net cash (used in)/provided by financing activities	**(3,062)**	987	911
Net increase in cash and cash equivalents	**800**	38	25
Cash and cash equivalents at beginning of year	**83**	45	20
Cash and cash equivalents at end of year	**$ 883**	$ 83	$ 45
Supplemental disclosure of cash flow information			
Income tax paid	**$ 1,791**	$ 1,785	$ 1,390
Interest paid	**851**	866	658
Capital lease obligations incurred	**326**	365	193

See accompanying notes.

NOTES TO CONSOLIDATED FINANCIAL STATEMENTS

1 Summary of Significant Accounting Policies

Consolidation
The consolidated financial statements include the accounts of subsidiaries. Significant intercompany transactions have been eliminated in consolidation.

Segment Information
The Company and its subsidiaries are principally engaged in the operation of mass merchandising stores located in all 50 states, Argentina, Canada and Puerto Rico, and through joint ventures in Brazil, China and Mexico.

Cash and Cash Equivalents
The Company considers investments with a maturity of three months or less when purchased to be cash equivalents.

Inventories
Inventories are stated principally at cost (last-in, first-out), which is not in excess of market, using the retail method for inventories in Wal-Mart stores and Supercenters.

Pre-opening Costs
Costs associated with the opening of stores are expensed during the first full month of operations. The costs are carried as prepaid expenses prior to the store opening.

Interest during Construction
In order that interest costs properly reflect only that portion relating to current operations, interest on borrowed funds during the construction of property, plant and equipment is capitalized. Interest costs capitalized were $44 million, $50 million and $70 million in 1997, 1996 and 1995, respectively.

Depreciation and Amortization
Depreciation and amortization for financial statement purposes is provided on the straight-line method over the estimated useful lives of the various assets. For income tax purposes, accelerated methods are used with recognition of deferred income taxes for the resulting temporary differences.

Long-Lived Assets
In fiscal 1997, the Company adopted Statement of Financial Accounting Standards No. 121, "Accounting for the Impairment of Long-Lived Assets and for Long-Lived Assets to be Disposed Of." The statement requires entities to review long-lived assets and certain intangible assets in certain circumstances, and if the value of the assets is impaired, an impairment loss shall be recognized. Due to the Company's previous accounting policies, this pronouncement had no material effect on the Company's financial position or results of operations.

Operating, Selling and General and Administrative Expenses
Buying, warehousing and occupancy costs are included in operating, selling and general and administrative expenses.

Net Income per Share
Net income per share is based on the weighted average outstanding common shares. The dilutive effect of stock options is insignificant and consequently has been excluded from the earnings per share computations.

Stock Options
Proceeds from the sale of common stock issued under the stock option plans and related tax benefits which accrue to the Company are accounted for as capital transactions, and no charges or credits are made to income in connection with the plans.

Estimates and Assumptions
The preparation of consolidated financial statements in conformity with generally accepted accounting principles requires management to make estimates and assumptions. These estimates and assumptions affect the reported amounts of assets and liabilities and disclosure of contingent assets and liabilities at the date of the consolidated financial statements and the reported amounts of revenues and expenses during the reporting period. Actual results could differ from those estimates.

2 Commercial Paper and Long-Term Debt

Information on short-term borrowings and interest rates is as follows (dollar amounts in millions):

Fiscal years ended January 31,	1997	1996	1995
Maximum amount outstanding at month-end	$ 2,209	$ 3,686	$ 2,729
Average daily short-term borrowings	1,091	2,106	1,693
Weighted average interest rate	5.3%	5.9%	4.4%

At January 31, 1997, the Company had committed lines of credit of $2,450 million with 34 banks and informal lines of credit with various banks totaling an additional $2,450 million, which were used to support short-term borrowings and commercial paper. Short-term borrowings under these lines of credit bear interest at or below the prime rate.

Long-term debt at January 31, 1997, consist of (amounts in millions):

		1997	1996
8 5/8%	Notes due April 2001	$ 750	$ 750
5 7/8%	Notes due October 2005	597	750
7 1/2%	Notes due May 2004	500	500
9 1/10%	Notes due July 2000	500	500
6 1/8%	Notes due October 1999	500	500
5 1/2%	Notes due March 1998	500	500
7 8/10%-8 1/4%	Obligations from sale/leaseback transactions due 2014	466	478
6 1/2%	Notes due June 2003	454	500
7 1/4%	Notes due June 2013	445	500
7% - 8%	Obligations from sale/leaseback transactions due 2013	314	318
6 3/4%	Notes due May 2002	300	300
8 1/2%	Notes due September 2024	250	250
6 3/4%	Notes due October 2023	250	250
8%	Notes due September 2006	250	250
6 1/8%	Eurobond due November 2000	250	250
6 7/8%	Eurobond due June 1999	250	250
5 1/8%	Eurobond due October 1998	250	250
7 %	Eurobond due April 1998	250	250
6 3/8%	Notes due March 2003	228	250
6 3/4%	Eurobond due May 2002	200	200
5 1/2%	Notes due September 1997		500
	Other	205	212
		$ 7,709	$ 8,508

Long-term debt is unsecured except for $206 million which is collateralized by property with an aggregate carrying value of approximately $347 million. Annual maturities of long-term debt during the next 5 years are (in millions):

Fiscal year ending January 31,	Annual maturity
1998	$ 523
1999	1,024
2000	806
2001	2,018
2002	52
Thereafter	3,809

The Company has agreed to observe certain covenants under the terms of its note and debenture agreements, the most restrictive of which relates to amounts of additional secured debt and long-term leases.

The Company has entered into sale/leaseback transactions involving buildings while retaining title to the underlying land.

These transactions were accounted for as financings and are included in long-term debt and the annual maturities schedules above. The resulting obligations are amortized over the lease terms. Future minimum lease payments for each of the five succeeding years as of January 31, 1997 are (in millions):

Fiscal years ending January 31,	Minimum rentals
1998	$ 76
1999	76
2000	104
2001	100
2002	94
Thereafter	915

The fair value of the Company's long-term debt approximates $7,836 million based on the Company's current incremental borrowing rate for similar types of borrowing arrangements.

At January 31, 1997 and 1996, the Company had letters of credit outstanding totaling $811 million and $551 million, respectively. These letters of credit were issued primarily for the purchase of inventory.

Under shelf registration statements previously filed with the Securities and Exchange Commission the Company may issue debt securities aggregating $751 million.

The Company has entered into an interest rate swap on an obligation which amortizes through 2006.

The Company swapped a fixed rate of 6.97% for a variable short-term rate on a notional amount of $630 million amortizing down to $203 million with semi annual settlements. The variable rate was 5.45% at the last settlement. This interest rate swap is accounted for by recording the net interest received or paid as an adjustment to interest expense on a current basis. Gains or losses resulting from market movements are not recognized. An increase in short term rates would cause the Company an insignificant additional interest cost.

3 Defined Contribution Plan

The Company maintains a profit sharing plan under which most full and many part-time Associates become participants following one year of employment. Annual contributions, based on the profitability of the Company, are made at the sole discretion of the Company. Contributions were $247 million, $204 million and $175 million in 1997, 1996 and 1995, respectively.

4 Income Taxes

The income tax provision consists of the following (in millions):

	1997	1996	1995
Current			
Federal	$ 1,769	$ 1,342	$ 1,394
State and local	201	188	178
International	4		
Total current tax provision	1,974	1,530	1,572
Deferred			
Federal	(97)	119	7
State and local	(9)	15	2
International	(74)	(58)	
Total deferred tax (benefit) provision	(180)	76	9
Total provision for income taxes	$ 1,794	$ 1,606	$ 1,581

Items that give rise to significant portions of the deferred tax accounts at January 31, 1997, are as follows (in millions):

	1997	1996	1995
Deferred tax liabilities:			
Property, plant and equipment	$ 721	$ 617	$ 518
Inventory	145	135	88
Other	45	19	8
Total deferred tax liabilities	911	771	614
Deferred tax assets:			
Amounts accrued for financial reporting purposes not yet deductible for tax purposes	295	204	230
International, principally asset basis difference	231	101	
Capital leases	169	147	114
Deferred revenue	113		
Other	68	49	33
Total deferred tax assets	876	501	377
Net deferred tax liabilities	$ 35	$ 270	$ 237

A reconciliation of the significant differences between the effective income tax rate and the federal statutory rate on pretax income follows:

	1997	1996	1995
Statutory tax rate	35.0%	35.0%	35.0%
State income taxes, net of federal income tax benefit	2.2%	3.1%	2.7%
International	(1.3%)	(0.8%)	
Other	1.1%	(0.3%)	(0.6%)
	37.0%	37.0%	37.1%

5 Acquisitions

In fiscal 1995, the Company acquired selected assets related to 122 Woolco stores in Canada from Woolworth Canada, Inc., a subsidiary of Woolworth Corporation, for approximately $352 million, recording $221 million of leasehold and location value which is being amortized over 20 years.

This transaction has been accounted for as a purchase. The results of operations for the acquired units since the dates of their acquisitions have been included in the Company's results. Pro forma results of operations are not presented due to the insignificant differences from the historical results.

6 Stock Option Plans

At January 31, 1997, 74 million shares of common stock were reserved for issuance under stock option plans. The options granted under the stock option plans expire 10 years from the date of grant. Options granted prior to November 17, 1995, may be exercised in nine annual installments. Options granted on or after November 17, 1995, may be exercised in seven annual installments. The Company has elected to follow Accounting Principles Board Opinion No. 25, "Accounting for Stock Issued to Employees" (APB 25) and related Interpretations in accounting for its employee stock options because the alternative fair value accounting provided under FASB Statement 123, "Accounting for Stock-Based Compensation," requires

the use of option valuation models that were not developed for use in valuing employee stock options. Under APB 25, because the exercise price of the Company's employee stock options equals the market price of the underlying stock on the date of the grant, no compensation expense is recognized. The effect of applying the fair value method of Statement 123 to the Company's option plan would result in net income and net income per share that are not materially different from the amounts reported in the Company's consolidated financial statements.

Further information concerning the options is as follows:

	Shares	Option price per share	Total
Shares under option			
January 31, 1994	15,876,000	$ 1.43-30.82	$ 298,248,000
Options granted	4,125,000	21.63-26.75	95,689,000
Options canceled	(1,013,000)	1.43-30.82	(23,127,000)
Options exercised	(1,019,000)	2.08-27.25	(7,829,000)
January 31, 1995	17,969,000	2.78-30.82	362,981,000
Options granted	7,114,000	23.50-24.75	167,959,000
Options canceled	(1,953,000)	3.75-30.82	(43,873,000)
Options exercised	(1,101,000)	2.78-25.38	(9,678,000)
January 31, 1996	22,029,000	4.94-30.82	477,389,000
Options granted	11,466,000	22.25-25.25	265,931,000
Options canceled	(2,110,000)	5.78-30.82	(49,109,000)
Options exercised	(999,000)	4.94-25.75	(10,327,000)
January 31, 1997	30,386,000	$ 6.50-30.82	$ 683,884,000
(6,448,000 shares exerciseable)			
Shares available for option			
January 31, 1996	52,946,000		
January 31 1997	43,590,000		

7 Long-term Lease Obligations

The Company and certain of its subsidiaries have long-term leases for stores and equipment. Rentals (including, for certain leases, amounts applicable to taxes, insurance, maintenance, other operating expenses, and contingent rentals) under all operating leases were $561 million, $531 million and $479 million in 1997, 1996 and 1995. Aggregate minimum annual rentals at January 31, 1997, under non-cancelable leases are as follows (in millions):

Fiscal year	Operating leases	Capital leases
1998	$ 435	$ 317
1999	379	316
2000	364	314
2001	332	311
2002	321	311
Thereafter	2,913	3,245
Total minimum rentals	$ 4,744	4,814
Less estimated executory costs		79
Net minimum lease payments		4,735
Less imputed interest at rates ranging from 6.1% to 14.0%		2,333
Present value of minimum lease payments		$ 2,402

Certain of the leases provide for contingent additional rentals based on percentage of sales. Such additional rentals amounted to $51 million, $41 million and $42 million in 1997, 1996 and 1995, respectively. Substantially all of the store leases have renewal options for additional terms from five to 25 years at comparable rentals.

The Company has entered into lease commitments for land and buildings for 30 future locations. These lease commitments with real estate developers provide for minimum rentals for 20 years, excluding renewal options. If consummated based on current cost estimates, they will approximate $27 million annually over the lease terms.

8 Quarterly Financial Data (Unaudited)

Amounts in millions (except per share information)	Quarters ended			
	April 30,	July 31,	October 31,	January 31,
1997				
Net sales	$ 22,772	$ 25,587	$ 25,644	$ 30,856
Cost of sales	18,064	20,376	20,450	24,773
Net income	571	706	684	1,095
Net income per share	$.25	$.31	$.30	$.48
1996				
Net sales	$ 20,440	$ 22,723	$ 22,913	$ 27,551
Cost of sales	16,196	18,095	18,176	22,097
Net income	553	633	612	942
Net income per share	$.24	$.28	$.27	$.41

REPORT OF INDEPENDENT AUDITORS

The Board of Directors and Shareholders
Wal-Mart Stores, Inc.

We have audited the accompanying consolidated balance sheets of Wal-Mart Stores, Inc. and Subsidiaries as of January 31, 1997 and 1996, and the related consolidated statements of income, shareholders' equity, and cash flows for each of the three years in the period ended January 31, 1997. These financial statements are the responsibility of the Company's management. Our responsibility is to express an opinion on these financial statements based on our audits.

We conducted our audits in accordance with generally accepted auditing standards. Those standards require that we plan and perform the audit to obtain reasonable assurance about whether the financial statements are free of material misstatement. An audit includes examining, on a test basis, evidence supporting the amounts and disclosures in the financial statements. An audit also includes assessing the accounting principles used and significant estimates made by management, as well as evaluating the overall financial statement presentation. We believe that our audits provide a reasonable basis for our opinion.

In our opinion, the financial statements referred to above present fairly, in all material respects, the consolidated financial position of Wal-Mart Stores, Inc. and Subsidiaries at January 31, 1997 and 1996, and the consolidated results of their operations and their cash flows for each of the three years in the period ended January 31, 1997, in conformity with generally accepted accounting principles.

Ernst & Young LLP

Tulsa, Oklahoma
March 21, 1997

RESPONSIBILITY FOR FINANCIAL STATEMENTS

The financial statements and information of Wal-Mart Stores, Inc. and Subsidiaries presented in this Report have been prepared by management which has responsibility for their integrity and objectivity. These financial statements have been prepared in conformity with generally accepted accounting principles, applying certain estimates and judgments based upon currently available information and management's view of current conditions and circumstances.

Management has developed and maintains a system of accounting and controls, including an extensive internal audit program, designed to provide reasonable assurance that the Company's assets are protected from improper use and that accounting records provide a reliable basis for the preparation of financial statements. This system is continually reviewed, improved, and modified in response to changing business conditions and operations and to recommendations made by the independent auditors and the internal auditors. Management believes that the accounting and control systems provide reasonable assurance that assets are safeguarded and financial information is reliable.

The Company has adopted a Statement of Ethics to guide our management in the continued observance of high ethical standards of honesty, integrity and fairness in the conduct of the business and in accordance with the law. Compliance with the guidelines and standards is periodically reviewed and is acknowledged in writing by all management associates.

The Board of Directors, through the activities of its Audit Committee consisting solely of outside Directors, participates in the process of reporting financial information. The duties of the Committee include keeping informed of the financial condition of the Company and reviewing its financial policies and procedures, its internal accounting controls, and the objectivity of its financial reporting. Both the Company's independent auditors and the internal auditors have free access to the Audit Committee and meet with the Committee periodically, with and without management present.

John B. Menzer
Executive Vice President and Chief Financial Officer

Registrar and Transfer Agent
1st Chicago Trust Company of New York
PO Box 2540
Jersey City, NJ 07303-2540
1-800-438-6278 (GET-MART)

TDD for hearing impaired: 1-202-222-4955

Internet: http://www.fctc.com

Dividend Reinvestment and Stock Purchase available through 1st Chicago Trust Company of New York

Listings **Stock Symbol: WMT**
New York Stock Exchange
Pacific Stock Exchange
Toronto Stock Exchange

Annual Meeting
Our Annual Meeting of Shareholders will be held on Friday, June 6, 1997 at 8:30 AM (with pre-meeting activities at 7:30 AM) in Bud Walton Arena on the University of Arkansas campus, Fayetteville, Arkansas.

Independent Auditors
Ernst & Young LLP
3900 One Williams Center
Tulsa, Oklahoma 74172

Corporate Address
Wal-Mart Stores, Inc.
Bentonville, AR 72716-8611
Telephone: 501-273-4000
Internet: http://www.wal-mart.com

10 K and Other Information
The following reports are available upon request by writing the company or by calling 501-273-8446.

Annual Report on Form 10K*
Quarterly Financial Information*
Current Press Releases*
Diversity Programs Report
Copy of Proxy Statement

* These reports are also available via fax.

Market Price of Common Stock

| | Fiscal years ended January 31, | | | |
| | 1997 | | 1996 | |
Quarter	Hi	Low	Hi	Low
April 30	$24.50	$20.88	$26.00	$23.13
July 31	$26.25	$22.88	$27.50	$23.00
October 31	$28.13	$24.50	$26.00	$21.63
January 31	$27.00	$22.13	$24.75	$19.25

Dividends Paid Per Share

| Fiscal years ended January 31, | | | |
| Quarterly | | | |
1997		1996	
April 8	$0.0525	April 14	$0.05
July 8	$0.0525	July 10	$0.05
October 7	$0.0525	October 3	$0.05
January 17	$0.0525	January 5	$0.05

Trustees

5 1/2 %, 5 7/8%, 6 1/8%,
6 3/8%, 6 1/2%, 6 3/4%,
7 1/4%, 8%, 8 1/2%
Notes, and $107,000,000
of the Mortgage Notes
First National Bank
of Chicago
One First National Plaza
Suite 126
Chicago, Illinois 60670

9 1/10% Notes
Harris Trust and
Savings Bank
111 West Monroe Street
Chicago, Illinois 60690

Obligations from
Sale/Leaseback
Transaction (Wal-Mart
Retail Trust I, II, III)
State Street Bank &
Trust Company of
Connecticut
750 Main Street
Suite 1114
Hartford, Connecticut
06103

5 1/8% Eurobonds
Royal Bank of Canada
71 Queen Victoria Street
London, England
EC4V4DE
United Kingdom

6 1/8%, 6 3/4%, 6 7/8%
Eurobonds
First National Bank
of Chicago
First Chicago House
90 Long Acre
London, England
WC2E9RB
United Kingdom

Participating Mortgage
Certificates I & II
Boatmen's Trust
Company
510 Locust Street
P.O. Box 14737
St. Louis, Missouri
63178

Pass Through
Certificates
1992-A-1-7.49%
First Security Bank
of Utah, N.A.
Corporate Trust
Department
79 South Main Street
P.O. Box 30007
Salt Lake City, Utah
84130

Pass Through
Certificates
1992-A-2-8.07%
First Security Bank
of Idaho, N.A.
1119 North 9th Street
Boise, Idaho 83701

Pass Through
Certificates
1994-A-1-8.57%
1994-A-1-8.85%
1994-B-1-8.45%
1994-B-2-8.62%
First National Bank
of Chicago
One First National Plaza
Suite 126
Chicago, Illinois 60670

Outline

LEARNING OBJECTIVES

Chapter 2 introduces the basic financial statements. Studying this chapter should enable you to:

1. Describe the information needed to show the current status of a company and its history of business operations.

2. Explain which cash items should not be included in a statement that shows the history of a company's operations.

3. Explain how revenue differs from cash receipts.

4. Explain how expenses differ from cash payments.

Chapter 2
Prologue: An Introduction to Accounting

Introduction

One of your friends, Bill Kilmer, had been paying for his college education by working at various construction jobs on a part-time basis while going to school. Just before the end of the spring semester, Bill decided to form his own small business, Kilmer Contractors. He began the business by using his small savings and by obtaining an interest-free loan from his parents for the balance of the money he needed to start the business. Bill was quite pleased with his initial month's operations. He painted several houses with the help of two classmates who worked with him on a part-time basis. In addition, the prospects for additional future work seemed to be excellent. Bill was able to repay a part of the money that he had borrowed from his parents and was also able to withdraw enough money from the business to pay his tuition for the forthcoming summer semester.

Bill decided to go to the local bank and apply for a loan. He planned to use the money he would obtain from the bank loan to repay the balance of the loan he had made from his parents and also to maintain enough cash to continue and, hopefully, even expand his business operations over the summer months. He felt he would be able to devote more time to his business during the summer since he planned to take only a single course during the summer session.

The loan officer at the bank asked Bill to complete an application form and, after a brief discussion of the business, its operations and its future prospects, she also asked Bill to prepare a set of financial statements for Kilmer Contractors.

Although Bill had no formal system of keeping records, he had recorded all of the activities of Kilmer Contractors using a diary-calendar. With this source and his bank statement for the month of May, he prepared the following financial statement for the loan officer.

Kilmer Contractors
Financial Statement
For the Month Ending May 19X1

Cash received	$9,500
Cash paid out	7,100
Cash balance	$2,400

Bill left the statement and his application with the loan officer's secretary. He was told that he would receive a response from the bank the next day.

The loan officer called Bill, as she had promised, but stated that she would need additional (and more detailed) information about Kilmer Contractors and its business operations before she could make a final decision on the loan.

Bill took copies of his calendar-diary and his May bank statement to the loan officer, hoping that this would satisfy the loan officer's request for more detailed information.

After reviewing the additional information provided by Bill and making a few quick calculations, the loan officer told Bill that she could not approve a loan to Bill (and Kilmer Contractors). She explained that the results of the company's operations for May simply did not justify the loan request.

KILMER'S DIARY-CALENDAR

MAY 19X1

1 began painting business with savings of $500	2 borrowed $5,000 from Mom & Dad	3	4	5 bought supplies for $3,000	6	7
8	9 agreed to paint 3 houses — received $3,300 paid in full 10		11	12	13	14
15 repaid $2,000 to Mom & Dad	16 painted house $700 17		18	19 painted — house will receive $900 later	20	21
22	23 received $700 24		25 paid employees $1,500	26	27 took $600 from business for tuition	28
29	30 painted 1 of the 3 houses above (see 5/10) 31					

Bank Statement						
				CUSTOMER NUMBER		
				02020769 00		
				STATEMENT PERIOD		
				FROM		TO
Bill Kilmer 919 Park Lane Lincoln, NE 68588				05/01/X1		05/31/X1
				PAGE NUMBER		1
				ENCLOSURES		

ACCOUNT NUMBER	**TOTAL DEBITS**		**TOTAL CREDITS**		**FEE**	**CLOSING**
PREVIOUS BALANCE	**NO.**	**AMOUNT**	**NO.**	**AMOUNT**		**BALANCE**
.00	4	7,100.00	4	9,500.00	.00	2,400.00

```
* * * * * * *          CHECKING ACCOUNT ACTIVITY          * * * * * * * * *

                        PREVIOUS BALANCE --                          .00

------------------------------------------DEPOSITS----------------------------------------------

DATE              NUMBER            AMOUNT

05/01             001               500.00
05/02             002             5,000.00
05/10             003             3,300.00
05/17             004               700.00

-------------------------------------------CHECKS-----------------------------------------------

DATE              NUMBER            AMOUNT

05/05             001             3,000.00
05/15             002             2,000.00
05/25             003             1,500.00
05/27             004               600.00

------------------------------------------DAILY BALANCE-----------------------------------------

DATE              BALANCE

05/01               500.00
05/02             5,500.00
05/05             2,500.00
05/10             5,800.00
05/15             3,800.00
05/17             4,500.00
05/25             3,000.00
05/27             2,400.00
```

Bill is both upset and confused by the loan officer's decision. He had been confident that the loan would be quickly approved by the bank. After all, he had asked for a loan of only $3,000 and Kilmer Contractors had "made" a total of $2,400 in cash during May. At that rate, and given its future prospects, he believes that his company will easily make at least 12 times $2,400 or $28,800 in its first year of operations.

Knowing that you plan to major in business administration, Bill comes to you for your advice and help. He outlines his company's success to date and recounts for you his disappointing experience with the loan officer. Bill also provides you with a copy of both his calendar-diary and his bank statement for the month of May.

You want to help your friend Bill. Unfortunately, as you explain to him, you have not yet taken any course work in business, much less in accounting.

After talking further with Bill, reviewing the information that he provides to you, and talking briefly with the loan officer at the bank, you decide that what should be done is to assemble the information in a format that shows, in detail, both the current status of the company, Kilmer Contractors, as well as a history of its business operations to date. But, where to begin?

TO THE STUDENT: *Trace the cash received figure of $9,500 and the cash paid figure of $7,100 from the financial statement to the bank statement. Next, trace the four deposits made by Bill and the four checks Bill wrote from the bank statement to the diary-calendar.*

Details of Cash Received and Paid

As a starting point, you decide to examine the details underlying the "Financial Statement" for May 19X1, prepared by Bill Kilmer and previously submitted to the loan officer. This statement, along with the diary-calendar and the bank statement for the month of May 19X1, is used to obtain the details of the cash received and paid for May 19X1 by Kilmer Contractors. This analysis is presented below.

Cash received:		
Bill Kilmer's investment on May 1		$ 500
Loan from Mr. and Mrs. Kilmer on May 2		5,000
Received from customers:		
Agreed to paint 3 houses on May 10	$3,300	
Painted house on May 17	700	4,000
Total cash received in May		$9,500
Cash payments:		
For supplies on May 5		$3,000
To repay loan on May 15		2,000
To employees on May 25		1,500
To owner on May 27		600
Total cash disbursements		$7,100
Excess of cash received over cash payments		$2,400

TO THE STUDENT: *Analyze the cash received by Kilmer Contractors. What is the total loan amount that still must be repaid? How much cash was spent for painting-related items?*[1]

Tentative Income Statement

A careful review of the cash receipts and disbursements of Kilmer Contractors indicates that several items probably should be excluded from the statement intended to show the history of the company's operations to

---

[1] Answers to the "To the Student" activities throughout this chapter are presented at the end of the chapter.

date. These items, with a brief explanation of the reason(s) for excluding them from the statement of the company's operations, called an income statement, follow:

RECEIPTS:

1. Bill Kilmer's investment on May 1 of $500. Since this was money "put up" or invested by the owner to start the business (hopefully, a one-time item) rather than money earned by Kilmer Contractors during the month of May, it is inappropriate to include this item in the income statement.
2. An interest-free loan from Mr. and Mrs. Kilmer on May 2 of $5,000. Because this is a loan (again, hopefully, a one-time item) rather than money earned by the business during May, it is inappropriate to include this item in the income statement.

PAYMENTS:

1. Payment on loan on May 15 of $2,000. Because this is a partial repayment of the loan to the business made by Mr. and Mrs. Kilmer rather than an expense of the business for May, it is inappropriate to include this item in the income statement.
2. Payment to owner on May 12 of $600. Since this is a withdrawal made by the owner to pay a non-business item (summer school tuition) rather than an expense of the business for May, it is inappropriate to include this item in the income statement.

After excluding the above items, the tentative income statement is as follows:

Kilmer Contractors
Tentative Income Statement
For the Month of May 19X1

Received from customers		$4,000
Paid for supplies	$3,000	
Paid to employees	1,500	
Total expenses		4,500
Loss for May		($ 500)

TO THE STUDENT: *Was the entire $4,000 amount received from customers for jobs completed by Kilmer Contractors? If not, how much was received for completed painting jobs? What is the total amount owed but not yet paid by customers?*

REVISED INCOME STATEMENT

Needless to say, Bill Kilmer is less than pleased with the income statement shown above, since it indicates that Kilmer Contractors has experienced a loss of $500 for its operations during May 19X1. Examining this statement, along with the diary-calendar and the bank statement for May, suggests that several modifications of the tentative income statement should be made to depict more accurately the operations of Kilmer Contractors for May 19X1. These modifications, along with explanations of the reasons for making them, are as follows:

RECEIPTS:

1. Decrease receipts from customers by $1,100 (1/3 × $3,300) because this amount represents the portion which Kilmer has not yet earned as of May 31 of the $3,300 total payment made on May 10 by a customer. The customer paid $3,300 for Kilmer to paint three houses. As of May 31, only two of these three houses have been painted. Kilmer "owes" these services to his customer; he has not yet "earned" this $1,100. He has earned only $2,200 for the two houses he painted during May.

2. Increase receipts from customers by $900 because this amount represents money that Kilmer had earned (although not yet received in cash from the customer) on May 19 when he painted a house. He feels certain that he will receive payment from his customer in June.

After these modifications are made, the *revenue* (a term substituted for *receipts* in the income statement because not all items earned had been received in cash) earned from Bill's customers is as follows:

1. May 17—amount received from customer for
   painting house .... $ 700
2. May 19—amount to be received from customer
   for painting house 900
3. May 31—two-thirds of the $3,300 advance
   payment made by the customer on May 10
   for painting 3 houses. Two of the 3 houses
   were painted on May 31 2,200
   Revenue from customers $3,800

Note that the $3,800 in revenue from customers include only amounts that have actually been earned by Kilmer Contractors by painting houses during the month of May. The $700 amount from the house painted on May 17 was received on the day the work was done. The $900 amount from the house painted on May 19 had been earned even though the customer had not yet paid Kilmer since the work had been finished. The $2,200 amount from the house painted on May 31 was two-thirds of the $3,300 advance payment made by a customer on May 10 for painting three houses. It is decided to focus on amounts earned during the month of May 19X1 by Kilmer Contractors in preparing the revised income statement rather than on cash receipts for May, because Kilmer Contractors had been paid before (2/3 of $3,300, or $2,200), at the time of ($700), and after ($900) the time the work was actually done. Revenues, then, are the amounts actually earned whether or not payment is received. Thus, revenues are not necessarily received in cash by a business during the month the work is done.

A similar analysis is made of Kilmer's cash payments.

PAYMENTS:

1. Decrease the amount Bill paid for supplies from $3,000 to $1,000 because the $3,000 payment made on May 5 includes the cost of supplies that have not been used and that are still on hand at May 31. The cost of these unused supplies is estimated to be $2,000.

After this adjustment for the unused supplies, the *expenses* (a term substituted in the statement for *payments* because not all items for which payments were made in cash have been used up during May) were as follows:

1. May 5—one-third of the $3,000 payment is for the
   painting supplies that were actually used during May
   (approximately $2,000 of unused supplies are
   estimated to be on hand at May 31) $1,000
2. May 25—amount paid to employees for all of their
   work done during May 1,500
   Expenses for May $2,500

The total of $2,500 in expenses for May includes only those items that were actually *used* during May (supplies used of $1,000, and $1,500 in salaries earned by employees). The timing of the payment of cash for expenses is not considered to be important for purposes of determining the amount of the *income earned* for the month. (As an aside, it is noted that if an expense has been incurred but not paid—for example, a bill for May expenses paid in cash during June—it should be included in the determination of income for May). The critical factor is when the item is used or consumed (incurred), not the time when the cash is paid out. The revised statement that presents the *revenues earned, expenses incurred*, and resulting *net income* (excess of revenues over expenses) for Kilmer Contractors for the month of May 19X1 is as follows:

Kilmer Contractors
Income Statement
For the Month Ending May 31, 19X1

Revenues from painting		$3,800
Supplies used	$1,000	
Salaries	1,500	
Total **expenses**		2,500
Income for May		$1,300

TENTATIVE STATEMENT of FINANCIAL POSITION

Satisfied that the above "income statement provides an adequate history of the operating results of the company for the month of May 19X1," the focus turns to the current status of Kilmer Contractors. Basic questions to be answered seem to be: (1) what does the company own, and (2) what does it owe?

The analysis of Kilmer Contractors' current position as of May 31, 19X1 proves to be much easier than the analysis of its operations for the month of May 19X1.

OWNED by THE COMPANY:

1. Cash of $2,400, which is the amount shown as of May 31 in both Kilmer Contractors' checkbook and on the bank statement for May (Bill had previously checked all deposits made in May and checks written in May to the bank statement and all of these items had been recorded by the bank during May).

2. The $900 owed to Kilmer Contractors by the customer who had his house painted on May 19.

3. The $2,000 of unused supplies that are still on hand at May 31, 19X1.

OWED by THE COMPANY:

1. The $3,000 balance owed to Mr. and Mrs. Kilmer for the loan that they made to Kilmer Contractors on May 2, 19X1 (The original amount of the loan was $5,000.) A payment of $2,000 was made to the Kilmers by Kilmer Contractors on May 15, reducing the balance owed to them to $3,000.

2. After some thought, it is decided to list the $1,100 advance payment for the house that still has not been painted as an amount owed. On May 10, a customer paid $3,300 to Kilmer for painting three houses at some future date. Kilmer was able to paint two of the houses in May and plans to paint the other house sometime during the summer. Although Kilmer Contractors does not "owe" the $1,100 in the sense that it has to pay the customer $1,100 in cash, it does "owe" a debt to the customer in that it has an obligation to paint the house at a future date and has already received payment in advance for this work.

Using the available information and the above analysis, the following statement of financial position is constructed.

Kilmer Contractors
Statement of Financial Position
May 31, 19X1

Owns:		Owes:	
Cash in bank	$2,400	Advance payment from customer	$1,100
Payment due from customer	900	Loan from Mr. and Mrs. Kilmer	3,000
Supplies on hand	2,000		
	$5,300	Total owed	$4,100

Reviewing the above statement, it appears that since the company owns resources of $5,300 and owes obligations totaling $4,100, Kilmer Contractors is presently "worth" $1,200 ($5,300 less $4,100). Bill feels that this amount seems to be rather low, so it is decided to carefully examine the details of his investment in Kilmer Contractors.

OWNER'S INVESTMENT

After a review of all of the analyses outlined above, the diary-calendar and the bank statement for the month of May, it is concluded that the value or "net worth" of the business, Kilmer Contractors, has been affected by three transactions or events.

1. The original investment of $500 made on May 1 to start the business and open its bank account.
2. The withdrawal of $600 made by Bill on May 12 to pay his summer school tuition.
3. The $1,300 income earned by the business in May (See the income statement for details of the company's income, the difference between its revenues and its expenses).

It was decided that it would be useful to keep separate the original investment from the company's income and the withdrawal made during May.

Using these three transactions, the following statement of Bill's investment in the company is prepared.

Kilmer Contractors
Statement of Owner's Investment
For the Month Ending May 31, 19X1

Original investment		$ 500
Income for May	$1,300	
Less: Withdrawal	(600)	
Income retained in the business		700
"Worth" at May 31		$1,200

It seems logical that Kilmer's original investment should be increased by the company's income for May, since Bill is the sole owner of the business, and decreased by his withdrawal, because he took these funds from the business for his personal rather than business use.

Revised Statement of Financial Position

At this point, it is noted that the investment by Bill Kilmer is equal to the "worth" of the company, as previously determined. It is decided to incorporate this relationship in the statement of financial position, or balance sheet.

Kilmer Contractors
Statement of Financial Position
May 31, 19X1

Owns:		Owes:		
Cash in bank	$2,400	Advance payment from customer	$1,100	
Payment due from customer	900	Loan from Mr. and Mrs. Kilmer	3,000	$4,100
Supplies on hand	2,000	**Owner's investment**		
	$5,300	Original investment	500	
		Income left in the business	700	1,200
		Worth of the business		$5,300

Final Financial Statements

Based on the available information and the analysis reported above, it is decided to submit the following financial reports for Kilmer Contractors to the loan officer.

Kilmer Contractors
Income Statement
For the Month Ending May 31, 19X1

Revenue from painting services		$3,800
Supplies used	$1,000	
Salaries	1,500	
Total **expenses**		2,500
Income for May		$1,300

Kilmer Contractors
Statement of Owner's Investment
For the Month Ending May 31, 19X1

Original investment		$ 500
Income for May	$1,300	
Less: Withdrawal	(600)	
Income retained in the business		700
"Worth" at May 31		$1,200

Kilmer Contractors
Statement of Financial Position
May 31, 19X1

Owns:			Owes:			
Cash in bank		$2,400	Advance payment from customer	....	$1,100	
Payment due from customer	....	900	Loan from Mr. and Mrs. Kilmer	....	3,000	$4,100
Supplies on hand		2,000	**Owner's investment**			
		$5,300	Original investment		500	
			Income retained		700	1,200
						$5,300

Kilmer Contractors
Statement of Cash Receipts and Payments
For the Month Ending May 31, 19X1

Cash received:

From customers		$4,000
From loan		5,000
From owner		500
Total cash received		$9,500

Cash payments:

For supplies		$3,000
To employees		1,500
To repay loan		2,000
To owner		600
Total cash payments		$7,100
Increase in cash		$2,400

TO THE STUDENT: *The exact example used in this chapter is repeated in later chapters where each individual transaction is analyzed in terms of its effect(s) on the financial statements. The identical example also is used and each individual transaction is analyzed, recorded and processed as it would be done in an accounting information system. Needless to say, you will become very familiar with the operations of Kilmer Contractors while learning the preparation of financial statements and the processing of accounting information.*

To the Student Solutions:

Page 2-5   The cash received figure of $9,500 on the financial statement can be traced to the total of the four deposits on the bank statement. These four deposits can be traced to the diary-calendar as follows:

May 1:	$ 500	contributed savings
May 2:	5,000	loan from parents
May 10:	3,300	received payment in advance to paint 3 houses
May 17:	700	received payment for house painted

The cash paid figure of $7,100 on the financial statement can be traced to the total of the four checks on the bank statement. These four checks can be traced to the diary-calendar as follows:

May 5:	$3,000	for supplies
May 15:	2,000	payment on loan
May 25:	1,500	paid employees
May 27:	600	for tuition

Page 2-5   The total amount owed is $3,000, which is the $5,000 loan minus the $2,000 already repaid.

Cash was spent for two painting-related items, $3,000 for supplies and $1,500 to employees, for a total of $4,500.

Page 2-6   No, the entire $4,000 amount received was not from completed painting jobs.

The completed jobs bringing in cash total $1,800. This is $700 for the house painted May 17th and $2,200 for the two houses painted on May 31 (two of the three houses paid for on May 10th).

The $900 amount for the house painted on May 19th has not been received yet and is still owed to Kilmer.

Questions

1. Has Kilmer Contractors received its initial $500 investment in the business back yet? Which statement(s) can be used to help answer this question?

2. How much of the initial loan from Mr. and Mrs. Kilmer has been repaid? How much is still owed? Which statement(s) are useful in answering this question?

3. If Kilmer Contractors goes out of business at this point in time, how much will need to be refunded to customers? Why? On which statement can this information be found?

4. If Kilmer Contractors was to stop operating at this point, paying all debts, selling all remaining supplies for what they cost, collecting all payments due from customers, refunding all money received for jobs not completed, with how much would the company be left?

5. Why do you think that the loan officer initially felt the results of operations for May did not justify Kilmer Contractors' loan request? After seeing the final financial statements, what would you suggest?

Outline

LEARNING OBJECTIVES

Chapter 3 introduces certain basic accounting concepts. Studying this chapter should enable you to:

1. Describe the basic accounting definition and discuss the accounting process of communication.

2. Describe the role of the accountant and explain why this role has increased in significance.

3. Compare and contrast accounting and bookkeeping.

4. Contrast financial accounting with managerial accounting and identify the primary users of each.

5. Describe the objectives of financial reporting.

6. Identify the qualitative characteristics of accounting information.

7. Trace the process of developing generally accepted accounting principles and discuss the major concepts underlying these principles.

8. List and briefly describe certain of the more important influences on accounting principles.

9. Explain the accounting standard-setting process.

10. Describe the extent and nature of opportunities in accounting.

ACCOUNTING: CONCEPTS, STANDARDS, AND PRACTICE

INTRODUCTION

What is accounting? Accounting has been described as "... the art of recording, classifying, and summarizing in a significant manner and in terms of money, transactions and events which are, in part at least, of a financial character, and interpreting the results thereof."[1] This definition emphasizes the professional judgment the accountant applies to a given problem. Another view of the function of accounting, very similar to that reported above, is that "the primary function of accounting is to accumulate and communicate information essential to an understanding of the activities of an enterprise, whether large or small, corporate or non-corporate, profit or non-profit, public or private.[2] The importance of this second definition is the direct relevance of accounting to many enterprises, both private and public, and profit and not-for-profit. For this reason, accounting is often called the "language of business."

Implicit in any definition of accounting is the importance of the accountant's role in the reporting function. In fact, the primary role of the accountant is reporting and communicating information that will aid users in the financial community in making economic decisions. These users of accounting information include current and potential owners, managers, creditors, and others.

It should be noted however, that "financial reporting is not an end in itself but is intended to provide information that is useful in making business and economic decisions."[3] Accounting provides information for business decision-making.

In the past, when businesses were less complex than they are today, there was a very limited number of users of accounting information. For example, at the turn of the century, most businesses in the United States were managed and operated by their owners. Since these owners were intimately involved in the day-to-day operations of their businesses, there was little or no need for accounting reports. The owner or decision-maker already had firsthand knowledge of the information he or she required in order to operate the business effectively. Today, however, the situation is quite different. Many organizations have increased in both size and complexity. In many instances, the ownership and the management of a business have been separated with the firms being managed by professional managers for their absentee owners. These owners often have virtually no involvement in the day-to-day activities of the business. Even professional managers (at all but the most basic levels of authority in the firm) have little *firsthand* involvement in the daily operations of the business. Their decisions are, more often than not, made on the basis of reports and summaries prepared by their subordinates. It should be noted here that these reports and summaries are prepared using accounting estimates. Too often, managers and other users of financial information may overlook this fact.

Although the above discussion might overstate the case just a bit (the corner pizza parlor may still be owner-operated, but it could also be a franchise operation), the basic point is that most decisions are made on the basis of summary-type reports rather than firsthand information.

---

[1] *American Institute of Certified Public Accountants, Accounting Terminology Bulletin No. 1*, "Review and Resume" (New York, NY: AICPA), 9.
[2] *Accounting and Reporting Standards for Corporate Financial Statements* (Columbus, OH: American Accounting Association, 1957), 1.
[3] FASB Statement of Financial Accounting Concepts No. 1, "Objectives of Financial Reporting by Business Enterprises" (Stamford, CT: FASB, 1978), para. 9.

What is the role of accounting and the accountant in this process? One observation that has been made is that the task of the accountant is to observe, interpret, summarize, and communicate information in a form that will enable the user of the data to evaluate, control, plan, and even predict performance. This flow of information from the accountant to the user is depicted in Illustration 1.

It is essential to note the importance of the term "user" in this context. A user could be a manager involved in the evaluation and direction of the continuing operations of the business; a present or a potential stockholder (owner) seeking information for an investment decision; a bank officer in the process of reviewing a loan application; a supplier making a decision with regard to a credit application; a federal, state, or local revenue officer evaluating a tax return: or even a citizen attempting to assess the performance of some governmental unit. In each of the circumstances mentioned above, and in countless other situations as well, user needs are met, at least in part, by a report prepared by an accountant on the basis of accounting information.

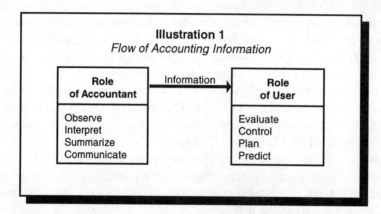

Illustration 1
Flow of Accounting Information

These accounting tasks or functions are described in Illustration 2. First, the accountant observes the business transactions that occur to identity those that have an economic impact on the firm. Second, the impact of these economic events is measured in monetary terms. Third, all of these economic events are summarized so that they can be, lastly, communicated to users through reports.

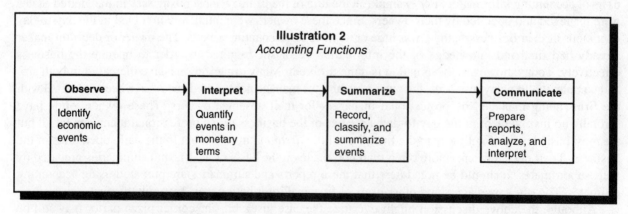

Illustration 2
Accounting Functions

Not to be overlooked is the impact of accounting on our society. The transfer and distribution of the economic resources of society are often related to the actions of the users described above, taken in response to accounting information. Thus, the ability of accounting systems to report information on an accurate and timely basis is crucial. The decisions made by various users based on such accounting information have direct economic consequences for society.

ACCOUNTING vs. BOOKKEEPING

The distinction between accounting and bookkeeping is often misunderstood. Bookkeeping is a clerical skill referring to the actual recording of business transactions. This is only one step in the accounting process. This clerical recordkeeping function may be done manually, but computers are increasingly used to efficiently perform this function. Accounting goes far beyond bookkeeping. The accountant must use professional judgment in the design of the recordkeeping system, the preparation of reports, and in the analysis and communication of financial and quantitative data to users of accounting information. Accounting functions such as budgeting, tax planning, and forecasting go far beyond the recordkeeping function of bookkeeping. The decision-making required of the accounting professional requires a much greater knowledge and comprehension than the limited skills which are needed in bookkeeping.

ACCOUNTING AS A PROCESS OF COMMUNICATION [4]

The previous two sections defined accounting and explained how it differs from bookkeeping. This section discusses the process of communicating this accounting information to users. Accounting may be regarded as a process of communication in a very real sense. Events that affect the operations of an organization occur on a continuing basis. The accountant acts as an observer-reporter, observing events or transactions as they take place, evaluating the significance of these events, then recording, classifying, and summarizing the events in an accounting report. The user receives the report, analyzes its content, and utilizes the information in making economic decisions. Of course, these decisions made by the user cause new events to take place, again setting the chain in process through another cycle.

Two factors of major importance in this communication are shown in Illustration 3. First, there should be mutual understanding and agreement between the accountant preparing the report and the persons using the report on the basis of its preparation and content. The accountant must know the user's needs and perceptions and prepare the report so that what the user understands the report to express will indeed correspond with what the accountant intended to express in the report. Bedford and Baladouni call this fidelity—the relationship between what is understood by the user of accounting statements and what the accountant intended to express in his or her report.

The second factor is that the accountant's report should show a reliable and relevant relationship to the events it attempts to summarize. The report should, to the degree possible and/or practicable, include and describe all the significant events that did, in fact, take place. In the ideal situation, a user would make the same decision based on the analysis of a report that would have been made if firsthand information obtained on a personal basis was used. Bedford and Baladouni refer to this factor as significance—the relationship between the events that take place and the accounting report that attempts to summarize these events.

FINANCIAL ACCOUNTING AND MANAGERIAL ACCOUNTING

Who are the users of accounting information? This section introduces the users of accounting and discusses the types of information they seek. Although there is considerable overlap between the two, accounting may be thought of as consisting of two basic segments, financial accounting and managerial accounting. The basic difference between these two segments of accounting lies in the users they serve. The users of financial information may be divided into *internal* and *external* groups. Financial accounting is primarily concerned with users who are external to the firm and managerial accounting is concerned with internal users.

---

[4] This discussion is based on Norton M. Bedford and Vahe Baladouni, "A Communication Theory Approach to Accountancy," *The Accounting Review* (October 1962), 650-59.

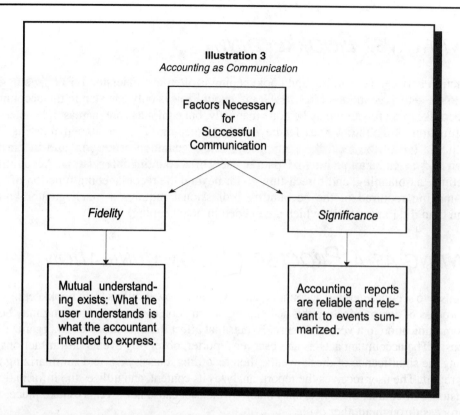

Illustration 3
Accounting as Communication

Factors Necessary for Successful Communication

Fidelity

Mutual understanding exists: What the user understands is what the accountant intended to express.

Significance

Accounting reports are reliable and relevant to events summarized.

External users include owners, lenders, suppliers, potential investors, potential creditors, employees, customers, stockbrokers, financial analysts, taxing authorities, regulatory authorities, trade associations, and teachers. Certain of these external users (e.g., taxing authorities) can specify and obtain both the form and content of the information desired; others lack the authority to prescribe the financial information desired.

Investors and creditors are the most obvious external groups who use financial information and must depend upon financial reports to provide this information. Unlike the Internal Revenue Service (IRS), they cannot simply demand all the information they may wish to have. Their decisions significantly affect the allocation of resources in the economy. In addition, information that meets the needs of investors and creditors is likely to meet the needs of those other external users who rely on financial reporting. Financial accounting attempts to provide external user groups with information concerning the status of the firm and the results of its operations. Accounting information may be used to assist users in answering questions such as:

- Should I purchase this firm?
- If I grant the firm financing, will it be able to repay the loan?
- Has the firm been profitable?
- How do the results of its operations compare with prior years and with other firms?
- Should I purchase stock in this company?
- Is the firm following all government regulations that apply?
- If I enter into a supplier relationship with this company, will it be able to pay me?

The objective of financial accounting is to provide these users with the information they require for making decisions.

Managerial accounting provides the information necessary for internal decision-making to managers within the firm. Internal users such as managers and directors can specify the information they want, can receive additional and more detailed information than is appropriate or necessary for external reports, and can receive information pertaining to planning and controlling operations. This accounting information may be used by different management levels of the firm to decide questions such as:

● Is the firm meeting targeted sales goals?

● Which products are profitable; which are not?

● How will tax law changes affect the firm's net income?

● Can cash dividends be declared to investors this year?

● Which plants operate within their budgets?

● Can the firm afford to meet union demands for wage increases?

● Is the firm able to pay its bills on time?

Managerial accounting, unlike financial accounting, is not constrained by the requirements of the standard-setting bodies discussed later in this chapter.

Although this text discusses both financial accounting and managerial accounting, its primary emphasis is on financial accounting. Again, it is important to note that the two overlap. For example, determining the cost of the products manufactured by a firm may be regarded as a managerial accounting issue; however, it is also a financial accounting issue because the cost of the products manufactured is normally the largest expense on the income statement prepared for financial reporting purposes.

Objectives of Financial Reporting

Financial reporting includes not only the financial statements but also other forms of information such as annual reports filed with the Securities and Exchange Commission (SEC), news releases, and management forecasts.

A *primary objective of financial reporting* is to provide information that is useful to business decision-makers. In order to accomplish this goal, the information communicated must be understood by those with a reasonable understanding of business and economic activities and a willingness to study the information with reasonable diligence.

The users of financial information are concerned not only with past and current performance, but also with the future expectations of a business. Investors are concerned with the amount of money to be received from dividends or selling the stock; creditors are concerned with the amount of money to be received from interest or the maturity value of the debt. Since there is a relationship between a company's cash flows and those to investors and creditors, *a primary focus of financial reporting is on the disclosure of information concerning the earnings of a business,* although information concerning the resources and obligations of an enterprise also is emphasized.

This next section examines the concepts underlying the financial statements. Illustrations 4 and 5 summarize these two groups: (1) those relating to the qualitative characteristics of the information, and (2) those relating to the basic assumptions and principles underlying the financial statements. The accountant's preparation of financial statements in the United States is based upon these generally accepted concepts. It is also important for users to be aware of and understand these basic assumptions and principles so that they can correctly interpret the information found in the financial statements.

Qualitative Characteristics of Accounting Information

What characteristics are desirable in accounting information? In order to be useful, accounting information should possess certain qualitative characteristics. These characteristics increase the value of accounting information to the user. Illustration 4 summarizes these user-oriented information characteristics.

Illustration 4
*Qualitative Characteristics of
Accounting Information*

Benefits and Costs	This pervasive constraint requires that the costs to prepare, communicate, and interpret the information should not exceed the benefits to the users from having the information.
Understandability	Information must be understandable to users with a reasonable comprehension of business activities and who study the information with reasonable diligence. The users should be able to perceive the significance of the information
Decision Usefulness	The information should contribute beneficially to the decision-making process. Decision usefulness may be divided into relevance and reliability.
Relevance	Information is relevant if it makes a difference in a particular decision. Relevant information has predictive value and feedback value. Users need to receive information while it can still be of use in the decision-making process; in other words, it must be received on a timely basis.
Reliability	Information is reliable if it is reasonably free from error and bias and if it represents what was intended to be conveyed.
Comparability	Comparable information allows users to identify and examine similarities and differences between multiple enterprises, or between multiple periods for one enterprise.
Consistency	Information should be consistently prepared from period-to-period so that it is comparable. This means the accounting principles used should remain the same from period-to-period.

Benefits and Costs

In order to justify providing accounting information, the benefits that may be derived from the use of this information must exceed the costs of providing the data. There are several costs of providing information, including: (1) costs of collecting, processing, and disseminating; (2) costs of auditing; (3) costs associated with dangers of litigation and loss of competitive advantage; and (4) costs to the user for analysis and interpretation. The users benefit by having more information on which to base such decisions as investing in or providing credit to particular companies. There are also benefits to the preparers of the information as well as to the users. These benefits include improved access to capital markets and favorable impact on public relations.

Understandability

The information provided by financial reporting should be understandable to those who have a reasonable understanding of business and economic activities and who are willing to study the information with reasonable diligence. Useful information that is difficult to understand should not be excluded. In this context, understandability is the quality that enables users to perceive the significance of information.

Decision Usefulness

Usefulness for decision-making is the most important quality of accounting information. Usefulness provides the benefits from information to offset the costs of providing the information; without usefulness, there are no benefits. Decision usefulness may be separated into the qualities of relevance and reliability, both of which are defined below.

Relevance. In order to be relevant, accounting information must be capable of making a difference in a particular decision by helping users to form predictions concerning the outcome of past, current, or future events (predictive value) or to confirm or correct prior expectations (feedback value). In this context, an "event" is a happening of consequence to an enterprise (for example, the receipt of a sales order or a change in the price of a good which is bought or sold), while an "outcome" is the effect or result of a series of events (for example, the amount of last year's profit or the expected profit for the current year). Relevant information does not necessarily mean that a new decision should be made; the information may support a decision which was made previously.

Timeliness means having information available to decision-makers before the information loses its capacity to influence decisions. Timeliness by itself does not make information relevant. However, information may lose relevance if it is not communicated on a timely basis.

Reliability. *Reliable information is information that is reasonably free from both error and bias and that faithfully represents what it is intended to represent.* To be reliable, accounting information must be verifiable (i.e., it is free from error because an independent party can check it to assure its accuracy), neutral (free from bias—i.e., it does not favor any party at the expense of any other), and possess representational faithfulness (the accounting numbers measure accurately the financial statement numbers—e.g., sales, payables).

The Certified Public Accountant (CPA) is an independent accountant who audits financial statements and attests (or reports) as to whether or not the financial statements "present fairly" the financial position, results of operations and cash flows of an entity. In accounting, verification is a primary concern of auditing and the CPA.

Reliability and relevance often conflict with one another. A gain in relevance from increased timeliness may involve a sacrifice of reliability. The type of information most desired by users of financial accounting information (relevance) is often the most difficult information to obtain in a reliable fashion (for example, only estimates may be available). Trade-offs in the qualitative characteristics of accounting information must be considered by decision-makers. Traditionally, standard setters have favored reliability over relevance in those situations in which the two are in conflict.

Comparability

The significance of information is enhanced greatly when it can be contrasted with similar information concerning other enterprises and with similar information about the same enterprise for some other period or point in time. Information, especially quantitative information, is most useful when it can be compared with such benchmarks. The purpose of these comparisons is to detect and explain similarities and differences.

If all companies used the same accounting methods for reporting financial information, comparability among companies would be easier. But accounting principles allow for different methods to be used. For example, several methods are permitted for determining inventory cost. Disclosure becomes important. Companies must disclose the accounting methods used so that subjective adjustments may be made.

Consistency

The concept of consistency is linked closely to comparability. *Consistency is conformity from one period to another in the use of accounting methods and procedures.*

Accounting principles do not comprise a detailed set of rules and procedures that apply to each and every situation. Rather, they are more in the nature of general guidelines. This is why the accountant may record a particular transaction in alternative ways. Also, different firms may use different accounting methods. Thus, the concept of consistency is essential.

Briefly stated, *the consistency concept requires that once an entity adopts a particular accounting method for its use in recording a certain type of transaction, the enterprise should continue to use that method for all future transactions of the same category.* Note that this concept applies only to the accounting methods used by a particular entity. It does not apply to the methods used by different companies, even though these firms may be engaged in the same line of business or industry.

Consistency, for example, would require that General Motors use the same accounting methods in its reports from one year to the next so that the users of its financial statements are able to make comparisons of the financial position of the company, the results of its operations, and its cash flows between and among years. It would not require, however, that General Motors and Chrysler use the same accounting methods, even though these firms may be similar in many respects. The financial statements of General Motors and Chrysler may or may not be readily comparable with each other, depending upon the accounting methods selected by each of these firms.

Consistency does not mean that a company can never change its accounting methods. A change may occur if a firm can justify that the change makes the financial statements more meaningful or if a firm is required to make a change due to the issuance of a new accounting rule. Such a change must be disclosed in the notes to the financial statements.

BASIC ACCOUNTING ASSUMPTIONS AND PRINCIPLES

The basic assumptions and principles underlying the financial statements are summarized in Illustration 5 and discussed below.

Illustration 5
Assumptions and Principles
Underlying the Financial Statements

Entity Assumption	For accounting purposes, each enterprise is assumed to be, and treated as, an entity separate and distinct from its owners, whether or not this is legally true.
Going-Concern Assumption	It is assumed that each enterprise will continue operating indefinitely.
Stable-Monetary-Unit Assumption	Business transactions and events are recorded in terms of money. Further, it is also assumed that all monetary units are of equal worth; in other words, inflation and deflation are ignored.
Time-Period Assumption	Accounting information is prepared periodically for users so that they may receive it on a timely basis. Even though an indefinite life is assumed for the enterprise, information is presented for shorter time periods, commonly a year, quarter, or month.
Historical-Cost Principle	Assets are recorded and carried in accounting records at their acquisition price or cost. This cost is not adjusted for changes in market value or replacement costs.
Matching Principle	The expenses incurred to generate revenue should be matched with that revenue and recorded in the same period in which the revenue is recorded.
Materiality Principle	The accountant should be concerned with transactions which are of real significance, or material, to the users. If the amount involved is sufficiently large to affect the decision, the amount is material.
Revenue-Recognition Principle	Revenue is recognized (or recorded) when substantially everything has been done that is necessary to earn the revenue.
Full Disclosure	All information needed by users should be presented in an understandable form in the main body of the financial statements or in the related notes.

Entity Assumption

The entity assumption is the basis for the distinction made by the accountant between a business and its ownership. In accounting, an organization, often referred to as an entity, is treated as a unit that is separate and distinct from its owners. The affairs and transactions of the owners of a business are not combined or co-mingled with those of their firms. This is true irrespective of the legal form of organization used by the business.

The entity assumption is a distinction always made in accounting, even though the distinction may not be true in a legal sense for businesses organized as either single proprietorships or partnerships. For example, Kilmer Contractors and Bill Kilmer are treated as separate entities. When Bill Kilmer withdrew $600 from the business to pay for summer school tuition, the transaction was recorded as a withdrawal by the owner. The payment for tuition was not recorded for the business.

Going-Concern Assumption

The going-concern assumption means that it is assumed that an entity will continue its operations for an indefinite future period of time, at least long enough to fulfill its plans and commitments. This assumption is used in accounting unless there is conclusive evidence to the contrary (for example, if a firm is in the process of bankruptcy proceedings).

Stable-Monetary-Unit Assumption

The stable-monetary-unit assumption means that the transactions and events that occur in a business should be recorded in terms of money. As its definition indicates, accounting is "... the art of recording, classifying, and summarizing in a significant manner and *in terms of money....*"[5] In addition, *the stable-monetary-unit assumption assumes that all dollars are of equal worth or value, that is, of the same purchasing power.* Under the stable-monetary-unit assumption, a dollar spent in 1930 is assumed to be equal to a dollar spent in 1975, or to a dollar spent today. Thus, the relevant transactions of an entity are recorded and its accounting reports are prepared on the assumption that a dollar is a stable unit of measure. In other words, any changes that may have occurred in the purchasing power of the dollar due to either inflation or deflation are ignored.

Time-Period Assumption

The most accurate determination of an enterprise's performance would be made at the time in which the business ceases to function. However, investors, creditors, and other interested parties need financial information concerning an enterprise on a much more timely basis. *Therefore, financial statements are prepared for such time intervals as a year or a quarter.* Because of estimates and other factors, the resulting information becomes less reliable as the time period is shortened, although the relevance of the information is increased.

Historical-Cost Principle

The historical-cost principle requires that the original cost (acquisition price) of a resource, and not its current market value or replacement cost, be used as the basis to account for the resources of an entity. This assumption has been justified by accountants on the grounds of its reliability. Its proponents argue that historical cost is a fact, whereas, in many instances, alternative measures such as market values or replacement costs may be somewhat subjective and must be determined each time that the financial statements are prepared. Historical cost also has been justified on the basis of the going-concern concept. An entity is assumed to have an indefinite life, and many of its resources are acquired for use (e.g., property, plant and equipment) rather

---

[5] American Institute of Certified Public Accountants, *Accounting Terminology Bulletin No. 1*, "Review and Resume" (New York, NY: AICPA, 1953), para. 9 (emphasis added).

than for resale. Therefore, there is little need to consider the amount that might be realized if these resources were sold or if the firm was liquidated.

There have been serious objections to the use of historical cost, especially when prices have risen substantially. Under these circumstances, critics believe that the historical cost of an asset has no relation to its "value."

MATERIALITY CONCEPT

Materiality indicates that the amount involved is sufficiently large to affect or make a difference in a decision. The materiality concept indicates that the accountant should be concerned primarily with those transactions that are of real significance or concern to the users of financial information. For example, assume that a company acquires a pencil sharpener at a cost of $10. It is expected that this sharpener will be used by the business over a five-year period before it will be replaced. In theory, the cost of purchasing the pencil sharpener should be spread over all of the years in which it will be used, because it will be of benefit to the company during each of these years. In practice, however, this would be neither realistic nor practical. The benefits that might be obtained by spreading or allocating the cost of the pencil sharpener over the five-year period simply would not be worth the cost that this procedure would involve. This example is a clear-cut case. A precise definition of what is or is not material is often elusive in particular circumstances and can vary from business to business. For example, what might be material to Kilmer Contractors may not be material to Wal-Mart.

A general understanding of the basic concept of materiality may be obtained from the following example. Assume that a transaction occurs. It is recorded in accounting report #1 in a manner that is theoretically correct. In alternative accounting report #2, it is recorded in a way that is expedient (fast and easy), but not necessarily correct in terms of accounting theory. If a user of an accounting report makes the same decision irrespective of whether it is based on accounting report #1 (theoretically correct) or accounting report #2 (expedient, but not necessarily theoretically correct), then the item obviously does not affect the decision at hand and is, therefore, clearly immaterial or insignificant in amount. On the other hand, if the user makes a different decision on the basis of accounting report #1 than might be made using accounting report #2, then the item is considered to be material, because it affects the decision made by the user.

Clearly then, decisions as to whether a particular item is or is not material must be made by the accountant and depend on the exercise of professional judgment. Quantitative factors (the amount) alone are not sufficient to judge the materiality of an item. The nature of the item and the circumstances under which the judgment is to be made must be considered.

MATCHING PRINCIPLE

The *matching principle* is related to the measurement of the earnings or income of an entity. It provides that *expenses that can be associated with revenue should be matched with that revenue when the revenue is realized and recognized during a particular period.* Thus, the matching principle emphasizes a cause-and-effect association in which efforts are matched with accomplishments.

Some costs can be matched directly with revenues. The cost of inventory sold is expensed in the same period in which the sale is made. Other costs cannot be matched directly with revenues. Some costs are matched with the periods in which they provide benefits. For example, the cost of equipment is allocated over the time periods in which the asset is useful to the entity. Still other costs are expensed in the period of acquisition, because they do not provide any future benefits. Examples of such costs are administrative salaries and advertising expense.

REVENUE-RECOGNITION PRINCIPLE

Revenue from sales usually is recognized (recorded) as a component of earnings when it is earned. A revenue is earned when the "... entity has substantially accomplished what it must do to be entitled to the benefits represented by the revenue."[6] Recognition differs from realization. Recognition is the process of formally recording an item in the financial statements; realization is the process of converting goods and services into cash or claims to cash[7] (for example, collecting the cash owed to the business).

Revenue from sales usually is recognized at the time that both an exchange transaction takes place and the earnings process is complete or virtually complete. Recognizing revenue does not depend on the receipt of cash. Revenue from sales usually is recognized at the time of delivery of the product; revenue from services is recognized when the service has been performed. Recognizing revenue at these times is objective and verifiable, because the sales price provides a measure for the amount of revenue realized.

Revenue that is earned by allowing others to use the enterprise's resources is recognized as time passes (examples of such revenue include interest on money lent and rent on buildings leased). The amount of revenue recognized is determined by the amount that is received or is expected to be received.

Cash may be received before production and delivery. In this case, revenue is recognized as the goods are produced and delivered. An example of recognizing revenue in this manner is magazine subscriptions. A publisher may receive payment from subscribers either before or after the subscription period but recognizes revenue only as the magazine is produced and distributed to subscribers.

Full Disclosure Concept

Full disclosure means that all information needed by the users of financial statements should be disclosed in an understandable form. Information should be provided on such items as the following: the method used for costing inventory, the depreciation method used, maturity dates and interest rates on long-term debt, possible future liabilities (e.g., on pending lawsuits), and shares of stock issued. The information may be presented in the main body of the financial statements or in the related notes.

Full disclosure is very important to the efficient operations of the securities market. Efficiency in this context means that security prices react quickly (rise or fall) in response to published financial information.

Developing Generally Accepted Accounting Principles

Generally accepted accounting principles (GAAP) are concerned with the measurement and disclosure of economic activity. GAAP determine the manner in which the accounting process is to be applied in specific situations. *Generally accepted accounting principles have been defined as follows:*

> Generally accepted accounting principles therefore, is a technical term in financial accounting. Generally accepted accounting principles encompass the conventions, rules, and procedures necessary to define accepted accounting practice at a particular time. The standard of "generally accepted accounting principles" includes not only broad guidelines of general application, but also detailed practices and procedures.
>
> Generally accepted accounting principles are conventional—that is, they become generally accepted by agreement (often tacit agreement) rather than by formal derivation from a set of postulates or basic concepts The principles have developed on the basis of experience, reason, custom, usage, and, to a significant extent, practical necessity.[8]

---

[6] *FASB Statement of Financial Accounting Concepts No. 5*, "Recognition and Measurement in Financial Statements of Business Enterprises" (Stamford, CT: FASB, December 1984), para. 83.

[7] *FASB Statement of Financial Accounting Concepts No. 6*, "Elements of Financial Statements" (Stamford, CT: FASB, December 1985), para. 143.

[8] *Ibid.*, para. 95.

Influences on Accounting Principles

Accounting principles derive their authority from their general acceptance and use by the accounting profession and the financial community. For this reason, they may change over time. Some of the more important historical as well as current influences on accounting principles are described in the paragraphs that follow.

American Institute of Certified Public Accountants

The American Institute of Certified Public Accountants (AICPA) is the primary professional association of certified public accountants (CPAs) in the United States today. The AICPA is the accounting profession's equivalent of the American Bar Association (for attorneys) and the American Medical Association (for physicians). The AICPA is responsible for the preparation of the Uniform CPA Examination that is used in all states and that must be completed successfully in order for an individual to become a certified public accountant. For a number of years, this organization has been involved actively in research, which is intended to improve accounting practices and procedures, through its numerous committees and by the publication of *The Journal of Accountancy,* the most widely-read professional publication of the practicing CPA.

Within the last decade, the role of the AICPA has changed. An example of this increased activity is the formation of the Accounting Standards Executive Committee (AcSEC). *AcSEC represents the AICPA in the area of financial accounting and reporting.* It issues Statements of Position (SOPs) in response to the pronouncements of other accounting governing bodies. SOPs have the dual purpose of providing guidance (in accounting and auditing practices) where none previously existed and of influencing the standard-setting process. AcSEC also attempts to bridge the gap between the accounting standard-setting bodies and practicing accountants with the use of issue papers that identify current financial reporting problems, present alternative treatments, and recommend solutions.

The Committee on Accounting Procedure

The Committee on Accounting Procedure (CAP) was formed by the AICPA in 1939 to establish, review, and evaluate accepted accounting procedures. During the period 1939-1959, the CAP issued fifty-one accounting research bulletins dealing with a variety of accounting practices, problems, and issues. The success of this committee was limited somewhat, because it dealt with specific problems as they arose, rather than establishing an over-all framework to deal with these issues, and because the authority of its pronouncements depended solely upon their general acceptance. As the need for additional research into accounting principles intensified, the reasons for the continued existence of the CAP were less evident.

The Accounting Principles Board

In 1959, the AICPA replaced the CAP with the Accounting Principles Board (APB). The APB attempted to establish the basic postulates of accounting as a basis for the formulation of a set of broad accounting principles that would be used to guide the accountant in the specific circumstances of his or her practice. An accounting research division was established simultaneously to assist the board with the research necessary to carry out its assigned tasks.

During its fourteen years of existence, the APB issued a total of thirty-one opinions and four statements. *APB Opinions are authoritative pronouncements that established generally accepted accounting principles; APB Statements (which have all been superseded) were designed to increase the understanding of financial reporting.*

The APB's membership ranged from eighteen to twenty-one. Although all of the members belonged to the AICPA and were CPAs, not all were practicing public accountants; some members were selected from industry, government, and the academic community.

The accounting research division issued fifteen research studies during its term of existence. However, the division did not interact with the APB in selecting the topics to analyze, nor did the APB request the division to examine specific accounting problems. This lack of coordination resulted in the board's issuance of opinions on topics for which little or no prior research had been conducted.

Prior to 1964, the enforcement of APB opinions depended primarily on the prestige and influence of the AICPA and the support of the Securities and Exchange Commission, an independent regulatory agency of the Federal government responsible for administering the Federal laws governing the trading of securities. Then the AICPA *issued Rule 203 of the Rules of Conduct of the Code of Professional Ethics. This rule prohibits a member of the AICPA from expressing an opinion that financial statements have been prepared in accordance with generally accepted accounting principles if there is any material departure from GAAP, unless the member can demonstrate that the financial statements otherwise would be misleading due to unusual circumstances.* In addition, all material departures from these pronouncements must be disclosed and the reasons for such departure must be explained in the financial statements.

The APB was criticized for its structure. In addition, the APB's positions on several controversial topics were perceived to be compromises. In 1971, the AICPA established a study group to examine the organization and operation of the APB and to determine the necessary improvements. Its recommendations were accepted and led to the creation of the Financial Accounting Standards Board.

Financial Accounting Standards Board

The Financial Accounting Standards Board (FASB) came into existence in July of 1973 as the successor to the APB. Unlike its predecessor, *the FASB is an independent board whose membership consists of seven full-time, well-paid, distinguished accountants who are experienced in industry, government, education, and public accounting.* FASB members must sever all ties with former employers or private firms. Like its predecessor, the FASB conducts research in accounting matters using its own full-time technical staff members or commissions outside researchers from the academic and financial communities to work on specific projects of interest to the board.

The FASB's mission is to establish and improve financial reporting for all entities except federal, state, and local governments. Applying these standards should ensure that all businesses present information that is useful to investors and creditors. Capital market efficiency is enhanced by the confidence users have in financial reporting.

The research activities of the FASB serve as the basis for an invitation to comment or a discussion memorandum, which is prepared to outline the key issues involved in a particular accounting problem and to invite public comment. After further consideration, the discussion memorandum or invitation to comment may be modified and an exposure draft may be issued for additional public comment. Depending upon the reaction to the initial exposure draft, the board may issue a new exposure draft for additional comment or, if it is satisfied at this point, may issue its final statement, or may do neither. A 5-to-2 vote of the seven members is required for a statement to be issued. The structure of the FASB and its relationships are depicted in Illustration 6.

The major types of pronouncements which are issued by the FASB are: (1) *statements of financial accounting standards, which define GAAP;* (2) *interpretations of financial accounting standards,* which modify or extend existing standards and which have the same authority as standards; (3) *statements of financial accounting concepts,* which set forth the fundamental objectives and concepts to be used by the FASB in developing financial accounting standards; and (4) *technical bulletins,* which provide guidance on financial accounting and reporting problems. To date, the FASB has issued over two hundred statements, interpretations, and technical bulletins.

Not everyone is satisfied with the FASB's performance. Business groups often complain that the FASB's standards are too difficult and costly to implement and do not provide proportionate benefit to users of financial statements.

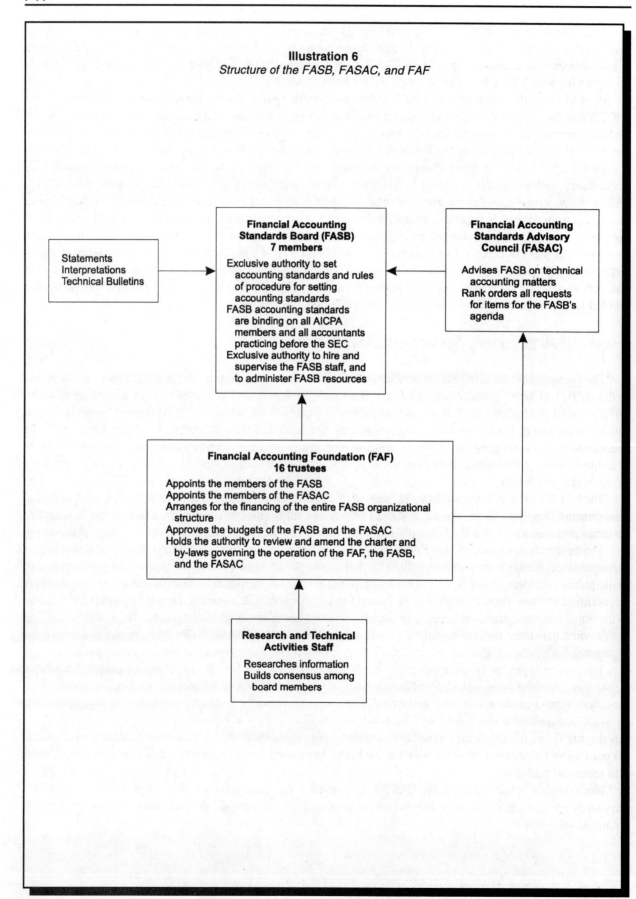

Illustration 6
Structure of the FASB, FASAC, and FAF

Statements
Interpretations
Technical Bulletins

**Financial Accounting
Standards Board (FASB)
7 members**

Exclusive authority to set
  accounting standards and rules
  of procedure for setting
  accounting standards
FASB accounting standards
  are binding on all AICPA
  members and all accountants
  practicing before the SEC
Exclusive authority to hire and
  supervise the FASB staff, and
  to administer FASB resources

**Financial Accounting
Standards Advisory
Council (FASAC)**

Advises FASB on technical
  accounting matters
Rank orders all requests
  for items for the FASB's
  agenda

**Financial Accounting Foundation (FAF)
16 trustees**

Appoints the members of the FASB
Appoints the members of the FASAC
Arranges for the financing of the entire FASB organizational
  structure
Approves the budgets of the FASB and the FASAC
Holds the authority to review and amend the charter and
  by-laws governing the operation of the FAF, the FASB,
  and the FASAC

**Research and Technical
Activities Staff**

Researches information
Builds consensus among
  board members

GOVERNMENTAL ACCOUNTING STANDARDS BOARD

The Governmental Accounting Standards Board (GASB), which was formed in 1984, is an independent organization in the private sector. *The GASB establishes standards for activities and transactions of state and local governmental entities.* The GASB's pronouncements are applicable to governmental entities and activities such as utilities, authorities, hospitals, colleges and universities, and pension plans. If the GASB has not issued a pronouncement applicable to such entities or activities, the FASB's standards should be used.

Like the FASB, the GASB follows due process procedures to provide for broad public participation at all stages of the standard-setting process. The GASB, like the FASB, issues invitations to comment, discussion memorandums, exposure drafts, statements, interpretations, and technical bulletins.

AICPA's ACCOUNTING PRINCIPLE HIERARCHY

Effective June 1993, the AICPA, in its *Statement of Auditing Standards No. 69*, established an accounting principle hierarchy for identifying established principles for nongovernmental entities and state and local entities. This hierarchy is shown in Illustration 7. Certain accounting pronouncements have greater authority because of their position in the hierarchy (the higher in the hierarchy, the greater the authority). For example, AICPA Statements of Position have greater authority than AICPA accounting interpretations.

When accountants or auditors are seeking the answer to whether an accounting practice is acceptable, they should consult the GAAP hierarchy shown in Illustration 7. If the practice is listed in the GAAP hierarchy, it is authoritative (again, the higher the principle, the more authoritative it is). If the practice is not found in the hierarchy, the accountants or auditors must use their own judgment regarding the acceptability of the practice.

SECURITIES AND EXCHANGE COMMISSION

The Securities and Exchange Commission (SEC) was established as an independent governmental regulatory agency with the authority to prescribe accounting practices and standards for the financial reporting of firms that offer securities for sale to the public through national (and interstate) securities exchanges, such as the New York Stock Exchange and the American Stock Exchange. The Securities Act of 1933 and the Securities Exchange Act of 1934 require that these companies file registration statements, periodic reports, and audited annual financial statements with the SEC.

The SEC has worked closely with the accounting profession in establishing and improving accounting practices, particularly in the area of financial reporting. The SEC has stated that the standards issued by the FASB are considered to have authoritative support, and that practices that are contrary to the positions taken by the FASB are considered to be lacking in such support.

INTERNAL REVENUE SERVICE

Although in most cases the Internal Revenue Service (IRS) influences accounting in an indirect rather than a direct manner, the income tax code and regulations do affect accounting procedures and methods. The effects of income taxes on accounting information will be discussed throughout this text.

INSTITUTE OF MANAGEMENT ACCOUNTANTS

The Institute of Management Accountants (IMA) is the professional association of accountants who are employed in industry, and as such, is concerned normally with matters that are primarily related to managerial accounting. Many of these issues also have an effect on financial accounting matters as well. Like the AICPA, the IMA sponsors research in accounting and issues periodic reports to its membership.

Illustration 7
GAAP Hierarchy Summary

	Nongovernmental Entities	*State and Local Governments*
Established Accounting Principles	FASB Statements and Interpretations, APB Opinions, and AICPA Accounting Research Bulletins	GASB Statements and Interpretations, plus AICPA and FASB pronouncements if made applicable to state and local governments by a GASB Statement or Interpretation
	FASB Technical Bulletins, AICPA Industry Audit and Accounting Guides, and AICPA Statements of Position	GASB Technical Bulletins, and the following pronouncements if specifically made applicable to state and local governments by the AICPA: AICPA Industry Audit and Accounting Guides and AICPA Statements of Position
	Consensus positions of the FASB Emerging Issues Task Force and AICPA Practice Bulletins	Consensus positions of the GASB Emerging Issues Task Force and AICPA Practice Bulletins if specifically made applicable to state and local governments by the AICPA
	AICPA accounting interpretations, "Qs and As" published by the FASB staff, as well as industry practices widely recognized and prevalent	"Qs and As" published by the GASB staff, as well as industry practices widely recognized and prevalent
Other Accounting Literature	Other accounting literature, including FASB Concepts Statements; AICPA Issues Papers; International Accounting Standards Committee Statements; GASB Statements, Interpretations, and Technical Bulletins; pronouncements of other professional associations or regulatory agencies; *AICPA Technical Practice Aids*; and accounting textbooks, handbooks, and articles	Other accounting literature, including GASB Concepts Statements; pronouncements in categories *(a)* through *(d)* of the hierarchy for nongovernmental entities when not specifically made applicable to state and local governments; FASB Concepts Statements; AICPA Issues Papers; International Accounting Standards Committee Statements; pronouncements of other professional associations or regulatory agencies; *AICPA Technical Practice Aids*; and accounting textbooks, handbooks, and

Source: AICPA Professional Standards, SAS No. 69, *The Meaning of "Present Fairly in Conformity with Generally Accepted Accounting Principles" in the Independent Auditor's Report* (March 1992), 49.

CONGRESS

Congress also has involved itself directly in the rule-making process. In 1971, the APB adopted a rule concerning the accounting for the investment tax credit. At that time, the SEC stated its support for the APB's position. However, Congress then passed legislation that stated no particular method of accounting for the investment tax credit is required. The APB subsequently rescinded its earlier pronouncement.

In 1994, Congress applied pressure to the FASB to not issue a statement pertaining to the accounting for employee stock options. A Congressional bill was drafted to require the SEC to approve all standards issued by the FASB. Although the bill was not enacted, it was instrumental in forcing the FASB to refrain from requiring the new accounting practice.

The brief descriptions included above are intended to provide a general indication of the major thrust and composition of these organizations. In many cases, there is considerable overlap in the objectives and even the membership of these groups. All of these organizations (with the possible exception of Congress) share the common objective of seeking to improve accounting practice and financial reporting on both a national and multinational basis.

The Accounting Standard-setting Process

A well-accepted view of the accounting standard-setting process asserts that it is essentially a political process involving various user groups, each of which is attempting to advance its own self-interests.[9] User groups often react negatively to those proposed standards that are perceived to be damaging to them and positively to those proposed standards that they perceive to be favorable for them.

User groups are able to politicize the standard-setting process by means of their lobbying efforts with Congress, the SEC, and the President. Since the SEC has both the authority and power to enact accounting standards, the FASB must remain responsive to these user groups or assume the risk of having its standard-setting power usurped. Therefore, accounting standards sometimes lack the theoretical background one might expect as greater emphasis is given to the economic consequences of a proposed standard on various user groups.

Some businesspeople believe that the FASB should not only take accounting theory and the usefulness of accounting information into consideration, but also should support the economic goals of our government. Others believe that if accounting standards are promulgated to achieve macroeconomic objectives, then confidence in these standards would be destroyed.

Most accounting standards have a definite economic impact. For example, the requirement to expense rather than to capitalize research and development costs has been considered to be a threat to technological progress. The requirement to use the method initially required by the FASB for accounting for the exploration and development costs of oil and gas companies was believed to be injurious to these enterprises.

At the time that the FASB issues a discussion memorandum, invitation to comment, or exposure draft, those companies that would be most affected submit their comments. There are always companies that dislike and oppose a proposed standard, and these companies may appeal to the government to become involved. If a standard is adopted that a company does not feel is beneficial, that company may not follow the standard on the basis of immateriality, or the company may alter its behavior in order to circumvent the effect of the standard. In addition, the company may increase its lobbying efforts in an attempt to have the standard modified or repealed.

International Aspects

Accounting principles and practices vary widely across countries. Accounting practices in certain countries (e.g., the United States and Canada) are prescribed by private organizations (e.g., the FASB and the Canadian Institute of Chartered Accountants); accounting practices in other countries (e.g., France) are prescribed by the government.

Some accounting organizations have attempted to standardize practices across national boundaries. For example, the European Economic Community Commission has issued several directives on accounting practices for members of the Common Market.

The International Accounting Standards Committee (IASC), which is a private organization that includes 122 accountancy bodies from 91 countries, has issued numerous International Accounting Standards. Although professional accounting institutes in several countries have conformed their accounting requirements to these International Accounting Standards, the IASC members in many countries (e.g., the AICPA in the United States) have not been able to ensure that the accounting organizations responsible for prescribing accounting practices in those countries (e.g., the FASB in the United States) issue standards that parallel the requirements stated in the International Accounting Standards. Therefore, in the United States, as well as in many other countries, there are differences between the requirements under the International Accounting Standards and domestic generally accepted accounting principles. However, these international standards have gained increasing acceptance in recent years. In July 1995, the Technical Committee of the International Organization of Securities Commissions (IOSCO) gave support to the IASC's plan to develop a comprehensive set of international accounting principles by 1999.

---

[9] Charles Horngren, "The Marketing of Accounting Standards," *Journal of Accountancy* (October, 1973), 61-66.

The financial statements of a foreign subsidiary may be included in the consolidated financial statements of a U.S. company. This foreign subsidiary may have prepared its financial statements in conformity with the requirements of the country in which it is located. Such requirements may or may not have been in agreement with the International Accounting Standards, the European Economic Community Commission, or some other multinational organization. Before the financial statements of this foreign subsidiary are included in the consolidated financial statements of the U.S. company, the foreign statements must be prepared in accordance with the generally accepted accounting principles for the United States.

Although a knowledge of accounting requirements in other countries and in multinational organizations is useful to practicing accountants in the United States, an examination of such requirements is beyond the scope of this text. Specific international aspects of accounting are typically covered in advanced accounting courses.

Opportunities in Accounting

The accounting profession in the United States has achieved a professional status that is comparable to that of both the legal and medical professions. Many opportunities exist for accountants in public, private, and not-for-profit accounting. Illustration 8 summarizes these.

Public Accounting

Certified Public Accountants (CPAs) are accountants who have completed educational requirements specified by the state in which they are licensed and who have successfully completed the uniform CPA examination. Accountants are employed in a wide variety of positions. Any organization, regardless of its purpose, that requires information to be recorded, processed, and communicated usually needs the services of an accountant.

CPAs, in large and small public accounting firms, render a wide variety of services to their clients on a professional basis, much as do attorneys. The services offered by CPA firms include: auditing—the conducting of financial statement audits and rendering of professional opinions as to the fairness of the presentation of the statements; taxes—tax planning and preparation of local, state, and federal tax returns; SEC work—assisting organizations in filings with the Securities and Exchange Commission; and management services—assisting in the design and installation of accounting systems and, in general, services of an advisory nature that do not fall under any one of the other categories mentioned above.

Private Accounting

Private accountants are employed by industry and other organizations. These accountants provide information used to control the operations of the organizations. The accountant fulfilling this role is often given the title of controller. Some of the accounting functions performed by private accountants include cost accounting, budgeting, internal auditing, design of information systems, tax accounting and preparation, and financial reporting and forecasting. In fact, there are far more accountants employed in private accounting than in public accounting.

Managerial accountants may decide to become certified as Certified Management Accountants (CMA). This certification provides evidence of professional competence and requires a college degree, two years of experience and passing of a two day examination.

Certified Internal Auditor (CIA) certification can be earned by accountants who specialize in internal auditing. Internal auditors review and evaluate the organization's system of internal control. They are employees of the organization and, as such, are not "independent" and therefore cannot perform independent audits of the company.

Illustration 8
Opportunities in Accounting

Public Accounting Firms	Private Accounting	Not-for-Profit Accounting
Auditing	Cost Accounting	Governmental Accounting: Federal Agencies: such as FBI, IRS, SEC
Tax Planning and Preparation	Budgeting	State and Local Governmental Units
Management Consulting Services	Internal Auditing	Nonprofit Organizations: Hospitals and Schools
	Financial Reporting and Forecasting	Charities, for example: Red Cross and United Way
	Tax Accounting	
	Information System Design	

Not-for-Profit Accounting

Accountants are also needed in non-profit organizations such as hospitals and schools. Charitable organizations, such as the Red Cross and United Way, also need the services of accountants.

Accountants also find employment in local, state, and federal government, ranging from small local municipal agencies to large federal organizations such as the Internal Revenue Service, Securities and Exchange Commission, and the General Accounting Office. It is interesting to note that special agents of the Federal Bureau of Investigation have most often been trained as either attorneys or accountants. Many accountants employed by the FBI investigate white collar crime. Certified Fraud Examiners (CFE) go beyond the normal role of an auditor and, instead, strive to uncover fraudulent acts or white collar crimes and those who would commit them (fraudsters).

Career Information

At the turn of the present century, there were fewer than 250 certified public accountants in the United States. Today there are more than 400,000 CPAs, and the accounting profession continues to grow at an astonishing rate. An indication that this growth is likely to continue is the increasing demand for accounting graduates reflected in the starting salaries paid to accounting graduates. Along these same lines, it is interesting to note that presidents of large U.S. corporations more often have a background in accounting than in any other single functional area. Clearly, accounting information is vital to success in the business world and those who understand how to use accounting information in business decision-making have an advantage. The increasing demand for accounting professionals creates a bright future for accounting majors. If you are considering a career in accounting, you may wish to contact the following organizations. They will furnish additional information that may be helpful.

- *American Accounting Association*; 5717 Bessie Drive; Sarasota, FL 34233-2399; Telephone (941) 921-7747.

- *American Institute of Certified Public Accountants*; 1211 Avenue of the Americas; New York, NY 10036-8775; Telephone (212) 596-6200.

- *The Institute of Internal Auditors, Inc.*; 249 Maitland Avenue; Altamonte Springs, FL 32701-4201; Telephone (407) 830-7600.

- *Association of Government Accountants*; 2200 Mt. Vernon Avenue; Alexandria, VA 22301; Telephone (800) AGA-7211.

- *American Women's Society of CPAs*; 401 North Michigan Avenue; Chicago, IL 60611; Telephone (312) 644-6610.

- *Institute of Management Accountants*; 10 Paragon Drive; Montvale, NJ 07645-1760; Telephone (201) 573-9000.

- *National Association of Black Accountants, Inc.*; 7429-A Hanover Parkway, Greenbelt, MD 20770; Telephone (301) 474-NABA.

- *American Association of Hispanic CPAs*; 17526 Colima Rd, Suite 270; Rowland Heights, CA 91748; Telephone (818) 965-0643.

- *National Association of Certified Fraud Examiners*; 716 West Avenue; Austin, TX 78701.

- *Information Systems Audit and Control Association; Metropolitan Chapter; G.P.O. Box 1279; New York, NY 10116-1279.*

Accountants and Ethical Issues

Users must rely on the information supplied by accountants. They must have confidence in the reliability and integrity of the accounting information received in order to continue their business and economic decision-making activities. The reliability and integrity of financial statements are dependent on the competence, professional judgment, and ethical behavior of the accountants and auditors involved in their preparation. The accounting profession has a significant ethical responsibility.

Codes of Professional Ethics

Professional ethical behavior is defined as conforming to the accepted principles of moral behavior governing the conduct of a profession. The acceptance of ethical responsibility to the public in providing services is a distinguishing mark of a profession. The American Institute of Certified Public Accountants (for CPAs), The Institute of Management Accountants (for CMAs), and the Institute of Internal Auditors (for CIAs) have all developed and adopted codes of professional ethics to be followed by their members. These codes provide guidelines for accounting professionals in performing their services. It should be noted that ethical conduct is more than just following a list of guidelines; it requires true personal commitment to the ideals of fair and honorable behavior, even if this requires the sacrifice of personal advantage.

Making Moral Choices

Accountants often find they must make moral choices in putting their professional judgment into practice. To make these choices, they need the ability: (1) to recognize ethical dilemmas, and (2) to properly understand and evaluate competing alternatives.

These complex reasoning powers are critical because the majority of ethical dilemmas are not simple. Often the choices are not between an ethical solution and a non-ethical solution, but between two solutions that are either ethical in different aspects or contain varying non-ethical elements. In these situations, the reasoning powers of the accountant are necessary to analyze and evaluate the various alternatives and the consequences of each to the business, the stockholders, the profession, and society.

It should also be remembered that the definition of what is considered ethical can vary among different people, societies, and countries, as well as over time. Also varying experiences, cultural backgrounds, and political beliefs can affect what is thought to be ethical behavior.

Throughout the text, ethical dilemmas will be presented for thought and/or discussion.

Summary

The accounting profession has grown rapidly in recent years both in terms of the number of accountants demanded and employed and in terms of professional stature. Accounting is basically a process of reporting and communicating financial information to a variety of internal and external users. As more and more decisions are based on information obtained from accounting reports, the communication aspect of accounting is of particular significance.

Financial accounting is concerned primarily with providing financial information to users who are external to the firm. Managerial accounting provides necessary information to those individuals responsible for internal decision-making.

Underlying all accounting practices are certain basic accounting concepts. Once accounting principles based on these concepts are accepted and used by the accounting profession, they become authoritative and are referred to as "generally accepted accounting principles." Many groups influence the acceptance of accounting principles.

The acceptance of ethical responsibility to the public is a distinguishing mark of the accounting profession. Users rely on the reliability and integrity of accounting information, which is dependent on the competence, professional judgment and ethical behavior of the accountants.

This chapter has discussed certain of the basic accounting concepts, assumptions, and definitions that will form a framework for the more detailed explanations included in subsequent chapters.

Key Definitions

Accounting—a process of reporting and communicating financial information to a variety of external and internal users.

Accounting Principles Board (APB)—formed in 1959 to replace the Committee on Accounting Procedures (CAP) as the primary agency responsible for establishing, reviewing, and evaluating accounting principles. The APB was replaced in 1973 when criticisms of its structure and positions created the Financial Accounting Standards Board (FASB).

American Institute of Certified Public Accountants (AICPA)—the primary professional association of Certified Public Accountants (CPAs) in the United States. It is involved in research intended to improve accounting practices and procedures.

Benefits and costs—in order to justify providing accounting information, the benefits which may be derived from the use of this information must exceed the costs of providing the data.

Bookkeeping—the actual recording of business transactions. It is a clerical function which may be done manually or electronically with the use of computers.

Committee on Accounting Procedure (CAP)—established in 1939 by the AICPA for the role of establishing, reviewing, and evaluating accepted accounting principles. The CAP's successor in this role was the Accounting Principles Board (APB).

Comparability—the quality of information that enables users to identify similarities in and differences between two sets of economic phenomena.

Consistency concept—this concept requires that once a firm adopts a particular accounting method for its use in recording a certain type of transaction, it should continue to use that method for all future transactions of the same category.

Corporation—an artificial being which has a legal identity that is separate and distinct from its owners or stockholders.

Ethics—the study of moral behavior.

Entity assumption—this assumption is the basis for the distinction which is made between the entity and its owners. The entity is treated as a unit separate and distinct from its ownership and is accounted for as such.

Fidelity of accounting information—the correspondence between the information the accountant wishes to convey and the user's perception of the meaning of the information the accountant reports. The accountant and the user must have a mutual understanding as to certain basic concepts in order for the communication to be valid.

Financial accounting—the segment of accounting primarily concerned with the needs of users who are external to the firm.

Financial reporting—includes not only the financial statements but also such other forms of communicating financial information as annual reports filed with the SEC, news releases, and management forecasts.

Financial Accounting Standards Board (FASB)—an independent board which conducts research and issues opinions as to the correct treatment and presentation of financial information. Its membership includes accountants from industry, government, education, and public accounting. It is the successor to the Accounting Principles Board of the AICPA.

Full-disclosure concept—requires that all information needed by the users of financial statements should be disclosed in an understandable form.

Going-concern assumption—this is the assumption made by the accountant that the business will operate indefinitely unless there is evidence to the contrary.

Governmental Accounting Standards Board (GASB)—establishes standards for activities and transactions of state and local governmental entities.

Historical-cost principle—the assumption that the original acquisition cost of a resource, not its current market value nor replacement cost, is the basis to be used in accounting for the resources of an entity.

Institute of Management Accountants (IMA)—a professional association of industrial accountants who are concerned primarily with managerial accounting.

Internal Revenue Service (IRS)—a government agency which is charged with the collection of taxes. The income tax code and regulations often affect the procedures and methods of accounting.

International Accounting Standards Committee (IASC)—an international accounting organization attempting to harmonize accounting standards across countries.

Managerial accounting—the segment of accounting concerned with the needs of users who are internal to the firm.

Matching principle—requires the accountant to match the expenses incurred during the accounting period with the revenues which were earned during this period.

Materiality principle—this concept indicates that the accountant should be primarily concerned with those transactions which are of real significance to the users of his or her report. No specific value can be assigned to any transaction to determine materiality, but if the information affects a financial statement user's decisions, then it is material. It is the magnitude of an omission or misstatement of accounting information that, in the light of surrounding circumstances, makes it probable that the judgment of a reasonable person relying on the information would have been changed or influenced by the omission or misstatement.

Objective of financial reporting—a primary objective of financial reporting is to "... provide information that is useful to present and potential investors and creditors and other users in making rational investment, credit, and similar decisions. In order to accomplish this goal, it is necessary that the information which is communicated must be understood; it ... should be comprehensible to those who have a reasonable understanding of business and economic activities and are willing to study the information with reasonable diligence."

Partnership—a business owned by two or more persons who share profits or losses according to an agreement and who are personally liable for all of the debts of the business.

Primary focus of financial reporting—the disclosure of information concerning the earnings of a business.

Professional ethical behavior—defined as conforming to the accepted principles of moral behavior governing the conduct of a profession.

Proprietorship—a business owned by one person who is individually liable for all of the debts of the business.

Qualitative characteristics of financial statements—the criteria to be used in the selection and evaluation of accounting and reporting policies.

Relevance—the capacity of information to make a difference in a decision by helping users to form predictions about the outcome of past, present, and future events or to confirm or correct prior expectations.

Reliability—the quality of information that assures that information is reasonably free from error and bias and faithfully represents what it purports to represent.

Revenue recognition principle—revenue is recognized (or recorded) when substantially everything has been done that is necessary to earn the revenue.

Securities and Exchange Commission (SEC)—a government regulatory agency which reviews the financial reporting practices of companies that offer securities for public sale through any national or interstate stock exchange. It works closely with the accounting profession to improve financial accounting practices.

Significance of accounting information—the relationship between the actual transactions of the company and the reports which summarize them. The accounting statements should disclose the events which occurred in a manner such that the user would reach the same decision based on the report that he or she would have made with firsthand information.

Stable-monetary-unit assumption—this is the assumption made by the accountant that all transactions of the business can be recorded in terms of dollars. This concept also assumes that any fluctuations in the purchasing power of the dollar are not significant. For this reason, changes in the purchasing power of the dollar are not recognized in the accounts.

Timeliness—having information available to a decision-maker before it loses its capacity to influence decisions.

Time-period assumption—requires the preparation of financial statements at such intervals as a year or a quarter to meet users' needs on a timely basis.

Understandability—the quality of information that enables users to perceive its significance.

Users of accounting information—those who read and analyze the financial statements in order to use the information contained therein to meet their own needs.

QUESTIONS

1. What is the purpose of accounting?

2. Is accounting useful for both profit and not-for-profit businesses? Explain.

3. Has the need for accounting (and accountants) increased in the United States since the turn of the century? Explain.

4. Who are some of the users of financial statements? Do their needs differ? Why?

5. Explain the similarities and differences between managerial accounting and financial accounting.

6. What is the objective of financial reporting?

7. How do: (a) understandability, (b) decision usefulness, © relevance, and (d) reliability relate to accounting as a process of communication?

8. Why is it important that accounting information be timely?

9. How does comparability enhance accounting information?

10. Why have accountants adopted the consistency concept?

11. How can the accountant determine whether a particular item is material in amount?

12. Why is the entity assumption necessary in accounting?

13. Discuss the relationship between the historical cost concept and the stable-monetary-unit assumption. Are these assumptions realistic?

14. Distinguish between revenue recognition and revenue realization.

15. What is meant by full disclosure?

16. What are the differences between the role of a bookkeeper and an accountant?

17. What does CMA stand for? How do the users of information produced by CMAs differ from the users of information produced by CPAs?

18. Financial statements are prepared in accordance with "generally accepted accounting principles." What are "generally accepted accounting principles" and how are they determined?

19. What is the role of the Financial Accounting Standards Board in accounting?

20. If you were uncertain as to whether a particular procedure was in accordance with "generally accepted accounting principles," what would you do to find out?

21. What is meant by the term "Certified Public Accountant (CPA)"? How does one become a CPA?

FRAUD CASE: The Certified Fraud Examiner and White Collar Crime

A Certified Fraud Examiner (CFE) is a professional who exercises diligence in the performance of his or her duties. He or she must exhibit the highest level of integrity and accept only those assignments that can be completed with reasonable professional competence. A CFE must comply with lawful orders of the courts and testify to matters truthfully and without bias or prejudice.

Unlike a Certified Public Accountant (CPA) in conducting an audit and giving an opinion on the fairness of the financial statements, the CFE cannot give an opinion on the extent or lack of fraud—only the amount of fraud actually found.

Definitions of white collar crime vary considerably. White collar crime is usually committed by persons in managerial or bookkeeping positions that have access to assets—thus the term "white-collar" crime. Usually such criminals have never participated in unlawful activities before and never will again if caught and prosecuted. The white collar fraud perpetrator is more likely to be an ordinary member of the community: intelligent, respected, never suspected of dishonesty, not your typical criminal type. The most frequent comment made regarding convicted fraudsters is "that's the last person I would have suspected."

Because white collar crime is non-violent and is not considered to endanger life, the fines, penalties, and prison sentences have been light. Many convicted embezzlers receive probation. However, some federal, state, and local jurisdictions are becoming more aware of the fraud problem and are marshalling stronger punishment. Lawmakers have recognized that white collar crime is increasing at an alarming rate and harms the economy. Everyone who pays taxes or buys a product bears a portion of the costs of white collar crime—estimated at 2 percent of annual gross sales of U.S. Companies.

Discussion Question:

What characteristics distinguish white collar crime?

FRAUD CASE: WHAT IS FRAUD?

Fraud is an overt act involving misappropriation of assets with an attempt to conceal.

DISCUSSION QUESTIONS:

Jerry Reed steals a box of diamonds from a jewelry store.

1. Has Jerry committed a fraud?
2. Would your answer differ if Jerry worked for the jewelry store?
3. Would your answer differ if Jerry worked for the store and attempted to cover his theft by altering accounting records and supporting documents?

Outline

LEARNING Objectives

Chapter 4 discusses the major financial statements prepared by the accountant. The basic steps in the recording process are traced and explained. Studying this chapter should enable you to:

1. Explain the accounting equation.

2. Analyze the effect of transactions on the balance sheet and income statement accounts.

CHAPTER 4

TRANSACTION ANALYSIS: THE ACCOUNTING PROCESS

INTRODUCTION

Financial statements are the end product of the financial accounting process. The basic objective of the financial statements of a business is to provide the information required by various users for making economic decisions. The financial statements should contribute to providing this information both individually and collectively. The basic set of financial statements included in the accounting reports normally issued to users are the balance sheet, the income statement, the statement of capital, and the statement of cash flows.

THE BALANCE SHEET

The balance sheet, or statement of financial position, is the accounting statement designed to provide information concerning an entity's assets, liabilities, and equity and their relationship among one another at a moment in time. It is not designed to present the current value of a business enterprise but should assist users in assessing this value.

Assets are probable future economic benefits obtained or controlled by a particular entity as a result of past transactions or events. In general, assets are things that are owned by the business and have value. They are the economic resources of the business. An asset is an economic right or a resource that will be of either present or future benefit to the firm. For example, an acre of land purchased by a company is considered to be an asset, because the company can obtain the future economic benefits, can control others' access to these benefits, and has completed the transaction for the purchase of the land. If access to the land cannot be controlled by the company because the city can use it as a right-of-way or if the transaction has not yet occurred, but will in the future, then the land is not considered to be an asset. The assets of a business may take various forms. Examples of assets include: cash, merchandise held for sale to customers, land, buildings, and equipment. In other words, assets are the resources used by the business to continue operations.

At any point in time, the total of the assets of a business are, by definition, equal to the total of the sources of these assets. In other words, every asset has a source; everything comes from somewhere. A business obtains its assets from two basic sources: its owners and its creditors.

Creditors lend resources to the firm. These debts, referred to as liabilities, must be repaid at some specified future date. *Liabilities may be defined as probable future sacrifices of economic benefits arising from present obligations of a particular entity to transfer assets or provide services to other entities in the future as a result of past transactions or events.* Examples of liabilities include payments owed to suppliers of merchandise held for sale, employees, and public utilities.

Owners invest their personal resources in the firm. *Investments by owners are increases in net assets of an enterprise resulting from transfers to it from other entities (including individual people) of something of value in exchange for ownership interests (or equity).* Assets are the most common investments made by owners, but a business may also receive services or payments of its liabilities. The investments of owners in the firm and any profits retained in the business are its equity (or capital). Equity is the residual interest that remains in an entity's assets after deducting its liabilities (i.e., Equity = Assets − Liabilities). In a business enterprise, the equity is the ownership interest. Thus, the sources of a firm's assets are its liabilities and owners' equity.

Balance Sheet Classifications

The various classifications included in the balance sheet are intended to assist the user of the statement in acquiring as much information as possible concerning the assets, liabilities, and owners' equity of the business. The individual elements of the financial statements are the building blocks with which financial statements are constructed—the classes of items that comprise the financial statements. The items included in financial statements represent in words and numbers business resources, claims to those resources, and the effects of transactions and other events and circumstances that result in changes in those resources and claims.

It might appear that if a firm desires to provide the user of its statements with as much information as possible, it can supply him or her with a listing of all transactions that took place during the period so that the user can perform his or her own analysis. However, large firms routinely enter into hundreds of thousands or even millions of transactions during any given period. It is therefore highly unlikely that any user would have either sufficient time, the inclination, or the ability to analyze this type of listing. To simplify the analysis of financial statements, firms group similar items in order to reduce the number of classifications that appear on the balance sheet. For example, a chain store may own many buildings of different sizes, at various locations and serving different functions, but instead of listing these assets separately, all buildings are normally grouped together and presented as a single amount on the balance sheet.

Assets

When assets are acquired by a business, they are initially recorded at the cost of acquisition, or original purchase price. This is true even if the business pays only part of the initial cost in cash at the time of acquisition and owes the remaining balance to the seller of the asset.

Assets vary in such characteristics as their useful life, physical attributes, and frequency of use. Accountants attempt to describe certain characteristics of assets on the balance sheet by the use of general classifications such as current assets; property, plant and equipment; and other assets. Within these broad categories there are also several sub-classifications. The usual ordering of assets on the balance sheet is in terms of liquidity—the order in which the assets are normally converted into cash or used up.

CURRENT ASSETS. Generally, current assets include cash and other assets that are expected to be converted into cash, sold, or used in operations or production during the upcoming accounting period. The accounting period is usually considered to be one year for most businesses. The general subclassifications of current assets normally found in the balance sheet include cash, marketable securities, accounts receivable, inventories, and prepaid expenses. These individual asset categories are briefly described below.

Cash. Cash includes all cash which is immediately available for use in the business including cash on hand, in cash registers, and in checking accounts (demand deposits).

Marketable Securities. Marketable securities are temporary investments in stocks, bonds, and other securities that can be sold readily and that management intends to hold for only a relatively short period of time.

Receivables. The accounts receivable balance represents the amount owed to the business by its customers. If a business has a significant amount of receivables from sources other than its normal trade customers, the receivables from customers are normally classified as trade accounts receivable and the amounts owed by others are classified as other accounts receivable.

A balance sheet may also include notes receivable. Notes receivable are the receivables (from customers or others) for which the business has received written documentation of the debtors' intent to pay.

Inventories. Inventories represent the cost of goods or materials held for sale to customers in the ordinary course of business, in the process of production for such sale, or for use in the production of goods or services to be available for sale at some future date.

Prepaid Expenses. Prepaid expenses represent expenditures that were made in either the current or a prior period and that will provide benefits to the firm at some future time. They result from paying expenses in advance. For example, a fire insurance policy that protects the assets of a firm for a year may be purchased during the current year. Although the policy was paid for and a portion of the protection was used during the current year, the firm benefits from the insurance protection in the upcoming year as well. A portion of the cost of the policy is applicable to the upcoming year and should be considered a prepaid expense.

PROPERTY, PLANT AND EQUIPMENT. Property, plant and equipment assets are those assets acquired for use in the business rather than for resale to customers. They are assets from which the business expects to receive benefits over a number of future accounting periods. Examples of these assets include land, buildings, machinery, and equipment. Since property, plant and equipment are used in the operations of the firm and benefits are derived from their use, the cost of these assets (except for land) is allocated to expense during all those periods that benefit from their use.

OTHER ASSETS. The classification, other assets, includes those assets that are not appropriately classified under either the current or the property, plant and equipment categories described above. This classification may include both tangible and intangible assets. Tangible assets are those that have physical substance, such as land held for investment purposes. Intangibles are assets without physical substance, such as patents, copyrights, and trademarks. Oftentimes these assets are classified as long-term investments or intangible assets rather than all being classified as other assets.

Liabilities

Liabilities are debts. They represent claims of creditors against the assets of a business. Creditors have a prior legal claim over the owners of a business. In the event a business is liquidated, creditors will be paid the amounts owed them before any payments are made to owners. Creditors are very concerned with the ability of a business to repay its debts. In certain instances, creditors may earn interest on the amounts due them. Normally, a liability has a maturity or due date, at which time it must be paid.

Liabilities, like assets, fall into descriptive categories. The two basic classifications usually employed in the balance sheet are current liabilities and long-term liabilities. Both of these general classes may also have sub-classifications.

CURRENT LIABILITIES. Current liabilities include those obligations that are expected to require the use of current assets (usually cash) or the provision of services within one year. Examples of current liabilities include accounts payable, notes payable, taxes payable, and unearned revenues. These are described in the following paragraphs.

Accounts Payable. Accounts payable are claims of vendors who sell goods and services to the company on a credit basis. Accounts payable are usually not evidenced by a formal, written document such as is the case with a note.

Notes Payable. Notes payable normally arise from borrowing or, on occasion, from purchases, and are evidenced by a formal written document. Notes payable may or may not be interest bearing. Notes usually have a fixed or determinable due date.

Taxes Payable. This liability includes any local, state, and federal taxes that are owed by the business at the end of the accounting period but are payable in the next period.

Unearned Revenues. Unearned revenues are amounts received from customers for goods that have not been shipped or services that have not yet been performed. Unearned revenues arise when customers prepay.

LONG-TERM LIABILITIES. Long-term liabilities generally represent claims that will be paid or satisfied in a future accounting period (or periods) beyond one year. Examples of long-term liabilities are bonds payable and mortgages payable.

Owners' Equity

Owners' equity (also referred to as capital for a proprietorship or partnership and stockholders' equity for a corporation) represents the claims of the owners against the net assets of the firm. Owners normally assume risks that are greater than those of creditors, because the return on investment to the owners is usually undefined. In the event of bankruptcy, claims of creditors take priority over those of owners and must be satisfied first. After all creditors have been paid, any assets that remain are then available to the owners of the firm.

Accounting for owners' equity is influenced by the legal status of the company—the form of its organization. The most extensively used legal forms of business in the United States are the sole proprietorship, the partnership, and the corporation. There are certain legal differences associated with these types of organizations; they will be considered in later chapters of this text. Basically, the owners' equity of a business comes from two major sources: direct investments made by the owners and profits retained in the business. Owners' equity accounts will be discussed in detail in later chapters.

Investments by Owners. Investments by owners are increases in the equity of a particular business enterprise resulting from transfers of something of value to the enterprise in exchange for ownership interests (or equity) in it. Investments by owners are most commonly in the form of assets (e.g., cash); investments may also include services performed or the conversion of the enterprise's liabilities.

Profits Retained in the Business. Profits of a business increase the ownership interest (equity) in an enterprise. Losses of a business decrease the ownership interest in an entity.

Distributions to Owners. Distributions to or withdrawals by owners are decreases in the equity of a business enterprise as a result of transferring assets, rendering services, or incurring liabilities by the enterprise to the owners.

Uses and Limitations of the Balance Sheet

Although many accountants and analysts consider the income statement to be the most important of the financial statements, the balance sheet is a very relevant and useful document and considered extremely important by the FASB, especially when used with the cash flow statement. Most of the FASB's recent statements have emphasized the balance sheet. The balance sheet reports the types of assets that are owned by the entity, the various short- and long-term liabilities that are owed, and the owners' equity in the business.

Numerous relationships within the balance sheet and between the balance sheet and the income statement may be observed. A sample of the types of analyses possible is listed below.

- The ability of a company to pay its current debts as they become due depends primarily upon the relationship between its current assets and its current liabilities.
- An indication of the risk that is incurred by the owners in being unable to meet the obligations of the firm may be noted from the firm's debt-to-equity ratio.
- The ability of an enterprise to earn a profit for its owners may be noted by the rate of return on owners' equity.
- The number of times that accounts receivable were converted into cash during the period may be determined by the accounts receivable turnover.

Comparative balance sheets provide even more information, because favorable or unfavorable trends in factors such as those listed above may be observed and noted.

The balance sheet frequently has been criticized for a number of reasons. Because of the historical-cost principle, current values are not reflected in most cases. Investments in debt and equity securities may be shown at current value; however, plant and equipment is presented at its acquisition cost less accumulated depreciation, and inventories are reported at cost (unless lower-of-cost-or-market is used and market value is less than cost). Reporting the current cost of inventories and plant and equipment is not required as a supplemental disclosure.

A further criticism of the balance sheet is that the values of certain significant items are omitted completely because they cannot be easily measured in monetary terms. Examples of omitted items include the quality of the company's management personnel, the location of the enterprise, and the reputation of the firm's products. Some accountants maintain that the balance sheet would be made much more useful by including valuation concepts and additional information not currently reported under the provisions of generally accepted accounting principles.

In spite of the criticisms of its basic nature and content, there is ample evidence that the balance sheet is used frequently by external decision-makers (e.g., investors and creditors) in making investment decisions. Further, it is often maintained that the use of subjective valuations (e.g., current values) instead of using historical cost would result in both the balance sheet and the income statement becoming distorted and less informative. Clearly, the appropriate methods of measuring or valuing the elements of the balance sheet are a highly controversial accounting issue.

THE INCOME STATEMENT

The income statement or statement of earnings provides data concerning the results of operations of the firm during a period of time, usually a year. The results of the operations of a business are determined by its revenues, expenses, gains, losses, and the resulting net income.

Revenues and expenses are defined as follows:

> **Revenues.** *Revenues are inflows or other enhancements of assets of an entity or settlements of its liabilities (or a combination of both) from delivering or producing goods, rendering services, or other activities that constitute the entity's ongoing major or central operations.* For example, a sale of furniture by a furniture manufacturer is considered to be revenue, whereas the sale of one of its short-term investments at a price exceeding its cost is not considered to be revenue.
>
> **Expenses.** *Expenses are outflows or other consumption or using up of assets or incurrences of liabilities (or a combination of both) from delivering or producing goods, rendering services, or carrying out other activities that constitute the entity's ongoing major or central operations.* For example, the cost of the furniture sold by the furniture manufacturer above is considered to be an expense, whereas the sale of one of its short-term investments at a price less than its cost is not considered to be an expense.

Revenues normally result in increased assets (e.g., cash or accounts receivable) from selling merchandise inventory or providing services. If cash is received in advance for providing goods or services, a liability (unearned revenues) is recorded for the amount received. Revenue is then recognized and recorded as the revenue is earned and the liability (unearned revenue) is reduced. Expenses result in outflows of cash or merchandise, using up of assets such as insurance coverage, and incurrences of liabilities such as accounts payable.

> **Gains.** Gains are increases in equity (net assets) from peripheral or incidental transactions of an entity and from all other transactions and other events and circumstances affecting the entity during a period except those that result from revenues or investments by owners. The sale of the short-term investment by the furniture manufacturer at a price exceeding its cost is considered to be a gain.
>
> **Losses.** Losses are decreases in equity (net assets) from peripheral or incidental transactions of an entity and from all other transactions and other events and circumstances affecting the entity during a period except those that result from expenses or distributions to owners. The sale of the short-term investment by the furniture manufacturer at a price less than its cost is considered to be a loss.

The income statement consists of revenues, expenses, gains, and losses to determine net income.

Net Income = Revenues - Expenses + Gains - Losses

The accounting concept of income assumes that various rules and principles are followed. These principles require the accountant to exercise his or her professional judgment in their application since the accounting concept of income measurement stresses the fair determination of income. Note that fair presentation of income does not mean precise presentation. Accounting is an estimating process that requires the accountant to view transactions as objectively as possible in determining both the financial position of a firm and its income for the period.

Since the income statement presents the results of operations for an accounting period, information included in this statement is usually considered to be among the most important data provided by the accountant. This is because profitability is a major concern of those interested in the economic activities of an enterprise.

Classifications that appear in the income statement are intended to be descriptive, functional categories of revenues, expenses, gains, and losses. There are many different formats employed for income statements. Variations among industries are substantial and, to compound this problem, variations among firms in the same industry can also be significant. The classifications used in the income statement will be discussed in detail in later chapters of this text.

The Statement of Stockholders' Equity

The statement of stockholders' equity (sometimes referred to by non-corporate entities as the statement of capital) is designed to reflect an entity's capital transactions during a period, including changes in equity from transactions with owners and the results of operations. Transactions with owners include additional investments as well as dividends distributed to (withdrawals made by) owners. The ending balances of the stockholders' equity accounts determined in this statement appear on the balance sheet.

The Statement of Cash Flows

An entity should report cash flow information concerning its operating, financing, and investing activities in a statement of cash flows. The statement of cash flows explains the causes of changes in cash plus cash equivalents (highly-liquid marketable securities) and provides a summary of the operating, investing and financing activities of an enterprise during a period of time. While the basic purpose of this statement is to provide information concerning the changes in cash plus cash equivalents, the statement is also useful in appraising other factors such as the firm's financing policies, dividend policies, ability to expand productive capacity, and ability to satisfy future debt requirements.

While certain information concerning changes in cash plus cash equivalents can be derived from comparative balance sheets and income statements, neither of these statements provides complete disclosure of the financing and investing activities of an enterprise over a period of time. An income statement discloses the results of operations for a period of time but does not indicate the amount of resources provided by other activities. Further, reported revenues and expenses may not represent increases or decreases in cash during the period. Comparative balance sheets show net changes in assets and equities but do not indicate the specific causes of these changes. Therefore, while partial information concerning changes in cash plus cash equivalents may be obtained from comparative balance sheets and income statements, a complete analysis of the financial activities of a business can be derived only from the statement of cash flows. This statement is discussed in detail in Chapter 15.

The Financial Accounting Process

As discussed previously, an accounting system must be designed to accumulate data concerning economic events, to process these data, and to summarize the data in periodic financial reports. A basic accounting model is used as the basis for the accounting process. This model has its beginnings in the following equation:

Resources = Sources

The concept expressed in this simple equation underlies the recording process used in accounting, and it also serves as the basis for one of the principal financial statements, the balance sheet (or statement of financial position). The balance sheet includes a listing of the assets (A) owned by the firm, the sources of or claims to these assets—the liabilities (L), and owners' equity (OE). The balance sheet discloses the three major categories included in the above equation—assets, liabilities, and owners' equity—as of a particular point in time.

This model is based on the concept that every economic resource of a business can be traced to a source. In other words, everything comes from somewhere. When a business is first organized, only two sources are available from which to obtain assets: resources borrowed from creditors or investments of owners.

Creditors lend resources to the firm, and the business incurs debts for these loans. These debts, referred to as liabilities, are normally repaid at some specific and agreed-upon future date. Owners invest their personal resources in the firm. If the business enterprise is a proprietorship or partnership, these investments from owners are referred to as capital. If the enterprise is a corporation, owners invest through the purchase of stock and the term stockholders' equity is used. These investments and any profits retained in the business are referred to as owners' equity.

The sources of a firm's assets are its liabilities and owners' equity. These liabilities and owners' equity are claims or rights to the assets. At any point in time, the total of the assets of a business are, by definition, equal to the total of the sources of these assets. The basic accounting model may be expressed in equation form as follows:

Assets = Sources of Assets

which can be expanded to:

Assets = Liabilities + Stockholders' Equity
or
A = L + SE

The accounting equation also indicates that the stockholder's equity is equal to the interest of the owners in the net assets (assets - liabilities) of the business. That is, by transposition, the accounting equation may be restated as follows:

A - L = SE

Transaction Analysis

The accounting process involves the identification of economic events affecting the entity and the recording of the relevant financial information. In effect, the recording process in accounting is used to analyze each transaction or event that takes place during the life of a business and to report the effect that each transaction or event has on the financial position, results of operations, and cash flow of the business.

Two types of transactions or events are recognized for financial accounting purposes: (1) exchange transactions between the entity and one or more external parties (e.g., the purchase of an asset); and *(2) other events that are not represented by exchanges but that have economic impact on the entity* (e.g., an assessment of additional taxes by the Internal Revenue Service) *or that involve the internal conversion or use of resources* (e.g., recording an expense for supplies used). The business documents relating to these transactions or events are used as the source of input data in the accounting process. Examples of business documents for external transactions include sales invoices, checks, and purchase orders; internal events are evidenced by such documents as requisitions for the transfer of raw materials to the production process. Once an event or transaction is recorded, the business documents are retained as a means of verifying the accounting records.

The number of transactions that occur in even a small business causes the assets, liabilities, owners' equity, revenues, expenses, gains, and losses to increase and decrease much too frequently to prepare a new set of financial statements each time that a transaction takes place. Consequently, an alternative method of recording information must be used. This recording process, which is basic to every accounting system, is explained in this section of the chapter. The accounting system described is referred to as a *double-entry system* and is applicable to all situations where financial information must be collected and processed.

As described in this chapter, the double-entry accounting system can be maintained by hand in small firms. However, in larger organizations, and even in most small firms today, computerized accounting systems are used. In either circumstance, however, each transaction or event must be recorded in the accounting system, and the basic accounting principles are identical.

In order to illustrate the process of recording transactions and the effect these have on the financial position of a business, we will review the transactions of a small service organization, Kilmer Contractors, during May 19X1, the initial month of its operations (see Chapter 2). As the transactions for Kilmer Contractors are analyzed and recorded, note that the steps shown in Illustration 1 are followed.

Illustration 1
Steps in Analyzing Transactions

Identify Economic Event	Identify an event having an economic effect on the entity.
Measure in Monetary Terms	Determine whether the event can be measured in monetary terms.
Identify Accounts Affected	Identify the accounts affected by the transaction.
Determine if the Accounts Increase or Decrease	Determine if the transaction results in increases or decreases to these accounts.
Record the Transaction	Record the transaction in the accounting records.

First, the transaction is identified as an event having an economic effect on the business. Performing a service in exchange for cash is such an event. Many events affecting the business do not have an economic effect. For example, the hiring of new personnel to replace those retiring does not have an economic effect.

Second, determine whether at this point the economic event can be measured in monetary terms. An investment of cash by the owner in the business can be measured in monetary terms. An example of an economic event that cannot be measured in monetary terms at this point would be the relocation across the street of a prime competitor or the lowering of prices by a competitor. These events will have an economic impact on the business, but at this point in time the impact cannot be measured in monetary terms.

Next, identify the accounts affected by the event (or transaction). Borrowing money by signing a note affects the asset cash and the liability note payable. Fourth, determine whether the transaction causes these accounts to be increased or decreased. Borrowing the money from Mr. and Mrs. Kilmer increased the asset cash and increased the liability note payable. Lastly, record this transaction in the accounting records. These steps are followed in evaluating all transactions of the business entity.

May 1.   Bill Kilmer organized Kilmer Contractors and invested cash of $500 in the business.

This increase in the asset cash is a result of an increase in the investment by the owner, referred to as common stock, and is reflected in the accounting equation as follows:

	Assets	=	Liabilities	+	Stockholders' Equity
	Cash	=			Common Stock
May 1	$500	=			$500

This transaction is an investment of funds in a business by its owner. The asset, cash, was received by the firm and the stockholders' equity was increased. We will assume that Kilmer organized his company as a corporation (to be discussed in detail later in the text) so his investment is recorded as "common stock." Note that the basic accounting equation is in balance.

May 2.   Kilmer Contractors borrowed $5,000 by signing a non-interest bearing note payable to Bill Kilmer's parents.

This increase in both assets (cash) and liabilities (note payable) is reflected in the accounting equation as follows:

	Assets	=	Liabilities	+	Stockholders' Equity
	Cash	=	Note Payable	+	Common Stock
Balance	$ 500	=			$500
May 2	5,000		$5,000		
	$5,500	=	$5,000	+	$500

This transaction is the receipt of an asset, cash, in exchange for a liability, the promise to pay a creditor at some future time. It reflects the promise of the business to repay $5,000 at a future date in order to have cash on hand and available for use at this time. Again, stockholders' equity is not affected; what has occurred is an exchange of a promise to pay the liability, note payable, for the asset cash. The basic accounting equation remains in balance.

May 5.   The company purchased painting supplies, paying the $3,000 purchase price of the supplies in cash.

The increase in supplies and the offsetting decrease in the cash of the business are reflected in the accounting equation as follows:

	Assets			=	Liabilities	+	Stockholders' Equity
	Cash	+	Supplies	=	Note Payable	+	Common Stock
Balance	$5,500			=	$5,000	+	$500
May 5	(3,000)	+	3,000				
	$2,500	+	$3,000	=	$5,000	+	$500

This transaction represents an exchange of one asset for another. Note that only one side of the accounting equation is affected. Both accounts affected are assets. The asset, supplies, was increased while the asset, cash, was decreased. Neither liabilities nor stockholders' equity was affected. The equation is still in balance.

May 10.   Kilmer signed a contract whereby he agreed to paint three houses sometime during the next few weeks. The customer paid the fee of $1,100 per house in advance.

This increase in cash and the corresponding increase in liabilities, unearned fees, are recorded by the business as follows:

	Assets			=	Liabilities			+	Stockholders' Equity
	Cash	+	Supplies	=	Note Payable	+	Unearned Fees	+	Common Stock
Balance	$2,500	+	$3,000	=	$5,000			+	$500
May 10	3,300						$3,300		
	$5,800	+	$3,000	=	$5,000	+	$3,300	+	$500

The company has agreed to paint three houses at a future date and has received its fee now, before it has done the work. The receipt of the $3,300 increases cash and the liability, unearned fees, by the same amount.

Unearned fees is a liability in the sense that it represents an obligation on the part of Kilmer Contractors to perform a service at some future date. It should be noted, however, that if Kilmer does not perform the services as promised, the customer could demand a refund of the cash paid. It could be said that Kilmer Contractors owes the customer either the service or a refund. Again, unearned fees are considered a liability. Stockholders' equity is not affected by this transaction and the accounting equation, $A = L + SE$, remains in balance.

May 15.   Kilmer Contractors repaid $2,000 of the $5,000 it borrowed from Mr. and Mrs. Kilmer.

This decrease of $2,000 in both cash and liabilities affects the accounting equation as follows:

	Assets			=	Liabilities			+	Stockholders' Equity
	Cash	+	Supplies	=	Note Payable	+	Unearned Fees	+	Common Stock
Balance	$5,800	+	$3,000	=	$5,000	+	$3,300	+	$500
May 15	(2,000)				(2,000)				
	$3,800	+	$3,000	=	$3,000	+	$3,300	+	$500

This transaction is a reduction of both liabilities and assets. The business repaid $2,000 of the $5,000 it owed to Mr. and Mrs. Kilmer. Both cash and the note payable decreased by this amount. Stockholders' equity is not affected, and the accounting equation remains in balance. (Recall that it was assumed this was a non-interest bearing note.)

The transactions of Kilmer Contractors for the first fifteen days of May are summarized below in Illustration 2.

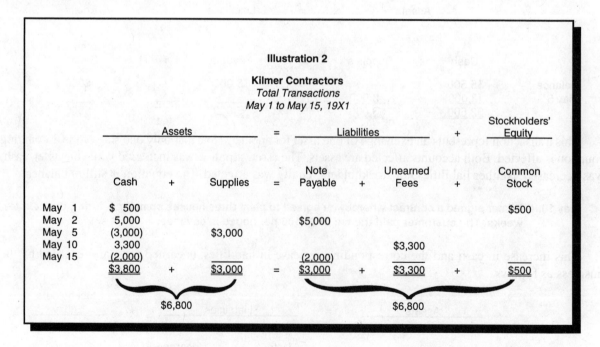

Illustration 2

Kilmer Contractors
Total Transactions
May 1 to May 15, 19X1

	Assets			=	Liabilities			+	Stockholders' Equity
	Cash	+	Supplies	=	Note Payable	+	Unearned Fees	+	Common Stock
May 1	$ 500								$500
May 2	5,000				$5,000				
May 5	(3,000)		$3,000						
May 10	3,300						$3,300		
May 15	(2,000)				(2,000)				
	$3,800	+	$3,000	=	$3,000	+	$3,300	+	$500
	$6,800					$6,800			

At this point in time, we can prepare a balance sheet for Kilmer Contractors. This balance sheet appears below in Illustration 3.

Illustration 3

Kilmer Contractors
Balance Sheet
May 15, 19X1

Assets		Liabilities + Stockholders' Equity	
Cash	$3,800	Note payable	$3,000
Supplies	3,000	Unearned fees	3,300
		Common stock	500
	$6,800		$6,800

The balance sheet for Kilmer Contractors is overly simplified for purposes of illustration. An actual balance sheet includes additional account titles and classifications. These classifications are not arbitrary distinctions made by the accountants who prepare the balance sheet. They represent generally followed classifications that are intended to assist the user of the balance sheet in analyzing and interpreting it for his or her use.

The operations of Kilmer Contractors for the first fifteen days of May, 19X1, have been analyzed. None of the transactions that occurred during this period is relevant to the income statement, because they affected neither the revenues earned nor the expenses incurred by the business. We will now follow the activities for the remainder of May to see how revenue and expense transactions affect both the income statement and the balance sheet.

Before proceeding, certain fundamental relationships should be reexamined. Recall that all assets are obtained initially from two basic sources, creditors and owners. After a firm has been in operation, another source of assets arises: income earned by the firm. Instead of withdrawing the income, the owners may choose to let it remain in the firm; it then becomes an additional source of assets.

Owners may contribute assets either: (1) directly, that is, by the investment of personal resources in the business; or (2) indirectly, by allowing the income earned by the firm to remain with the business and not withdrawing it for their personal use. In other words, just as direct investments made by the owners increase both the resources of the firm and their equity, the income earned by the firm also increases both the assets and the owners' equity of the firm. For the purposes of the illustration in this chapter, revenues will be added to stockholders' equity when they are earned and expenses will be subtracted when they are incurred.[1] The basic accounting equation expressed earlier in the chapter may be expanded and restated for purposes of illustration as follows:

Assets = Liabilities + Investments + Revenues − Expenses − Dividends

$$A = L + I + R - E - D$$

Keep in mind that this restatement is made for purposes of illustration only. It merely emphasizes the fact that one way in which the owners' equity of a business may be increased is by income, that is, revenues less expenses. Nothing else is changed. Now let us return to the Kilmer Contractors example.

---

[1] There are no gains or losses in this example. If there were, gains would be added to and losses subtracted from stockholders' equity.

May 17. Kilmer Contractors painted its first house and billed and collected cash of $700 from the customer.

This transaction was a sale of services for cash. It affects Kilmer Contractors as follows:

	Assets		=	Liabilities		+	Stockholders' Equity	
	Cash	+ Supplies	=	Note Payable	+ Unearned Fees	+	Common Stock	+ Revenue (Expense)
Balance	$3,800	+ $3,000	=	$3,000	+ $3,300	+	$500	
May 17	700							$700
	$4,500	+ $3,000	=	$3,000	+ $3,300	+	$500	+ $700

This transaction reflects the fact that the firm has begun to earn revenue. Cash was received and the stockholders' equity of the business was increased by the amount of the revenue earned, $700. The basic accounting equation is still in balance.

May 19. Kilmer Contractors painted a second house and billed (but did not collect) its fee of $900.

This transaction was a sale of services to a customer on a credit basis. It affects the business as indicated below.

	Assets			=	Liabilities		+	Stockholders' Equity	
	Cash	+ Accounts Receivable	+ Supplies	=	Note Payable	+ Unearned Fees	+	Common Stock	+ Revenue (Expense)
Balance	$4,500 +		+ $3,000	=	$3,000	+ $3,300	+	$500	+ $700
May 19		$900							900
	$4,500 +	$900	+ $3,000	=	$3,000	+ $3,300	+	$500	+ $1,600

Again, this transaction records the revenue earned by the firm by painting a customer's house. Unlike the previous transaction, however, cash was not received. The customer was billed for the service and will pay Kilmer Contractors at some future date. Accounts receivable have increased and stockholders' equity (revenue) has increased by $900, the fee charged for painting the house. This transaction illustrates the very important point that revenue is recorded as it is earned. It is not necessary to wait until cash is received. This concept reflects the accrual basis of accounting, which will be discussed and used throughout the text.

May 25. Kilmer paid his employees salaries of $1,500.

This transaction was the payment of an expense in cash. It affects Kilmer Contractors as follows:

	Assets			=	Liabilities		+	Stockholders' Equity	
	Cash	+ Accounts Receivable	+ Supplies	=	Note Payable	+ Unearned Fees	+	Common Stock	+ Revenue (Expense)
Balance	$4,500 +	$900	+ $3,000	=	$3,000	+ $3,300	+	$500	+ $1,600
May 25	(1,500)								(1,500)
	$3,000 +	$900	+ $3,000	=	$3,000	+ $3,300	+	$500	+ $ 100

Expenses of $1,500 were incurred and paid in cash. This transaction reduces both cash and stockholders' equity. The reduction in stockholders' equity is due to the fact that an expense has been incurred, thereby reducing income. (Remember that revenues less expenses equal income.) The accounting equation is still in balance.

May 27. Kilmer Contractors paid dividends of $600.

This decrease in cash and the corresponding decrease in the stockholders' equity balance are reflected in the accounting equation as follows:

		Assets			=		Liabilities		+		Stockholders' Equity	
	Cash	+	Accounts Receivable	+ Supplies	=	Note Payable	+	Unearned Fees	+	Common Stock	+	Revenue (Expense) - (Dividends)
Balance May 12	$3,000 (600)	+	$900	+ $3,000	=	$3,000	+	$3,300	+	$500	+	$100 - (600)
	$2,400	+	$900	+ $3,000	=	$3,000	+	$3,300	+	$500	+	$100 - ($600)

This transaction represents a withdrawal from the business. Note that since Kilmer Contractors is a corporation, this withdrawal is recorded as a "dividend" to its owner. The accounting equation is still in balance.

May 31. Kilmer Contractors painted two of the three houses contracted for on May 10.

By painting two of the three houses, Kilmer Contractors has partially satisfied the unearned fees liability by performing services and therefore earning income. This transaction is reflected as follows:

		Assets			=		Liabilities		+		Stockholders' Equity	
	Cash	+	Accounts Receivable	+ Supplies	=	Note Payable	+	Unearned Fees	+	Common Stock	+	Revenue (Expense) - (Dividends)
Balance May 31	$2,400	+	$900	+ $3,000	=	$3,000	+	$3,300 (2,200)	+	$500	+	$ 100 2,200 - ($600)
	$2,400		$900	$3,000		$3,000		$1,100		$500		$2,300 - ($600)

On May 10, Kilmer signed a contract to paint three houses and received his fee of $1,100 per house in advance. No revenue was earned at the point the $3,300 in cash were received, because no work had been done at that time. Remember that the revenue-recognition principle requires that revenue is recognized (or recorded) only when substantially everything has been done that is necessary to earn the revenue. Kilmer Contractors has an obligation to paint the three houses at some future date. This liability to perform services was recorded as unearned fees.

Now two of the three houses contracted for have been painted, and that portion of the revenue has been earned. The liability, unearned fees, has been reduced by $2,200 and the revenue for the current period has been increased by the same amount. Again, this transaction emphasizes the point that revenue is recorded as it is earned, not necessarily as cash is received. The accounting equation remains in balance.

May 31. The unused painting supplies on hand at this date had an original cost of $2,000.

The facts of this situation indicate that an expense has been incurred and should be recorded. It affects Kilmer Contractors as indicated below.

		Assets			=		Liabilities		+		Stockholders' Equity	
	Cash	+	Accounts Receivable	+ Supplies	=	Note Payable	+	Unearned Fees	+	Common Stock	+	Revenue (Expense) - (Dividends)
Balance May 31	$2,400	+	$900	+ $3,000 (1,000)	=	$3,000	+	$1,100	+	$500	+	$2,300 (1,000) - ($600)
	$2,400		$900	$2,000		$3,000		$1,100		$500		$1,300 - ($600)

During the month of May, Kilmer Contractors used supplies that had an original cost of $1,000. This amount was determined by subtracting the $2,000 cost of the supplies on hand at May 31 from the $3,000 total cost of supplies available for use (that is, the supplies purchased during the month plus the beginning-of-the-month supplies amount, which in this case is zero). As in the previous May 31 transaction pertaining to painting two of the three houses contracted for, an adjustment is required. The asset, supplies, was decreased by $1,000 (the cost of the supplies used) from $3,000 (the total supplies available for use during the month of May) to $2,000 (the cost of supplies on hand at May 31). This decrease in supplies demonstrates the matching principle. Any expenses incurred in the process of earning revenue (for painting supplies in this example) should be recorded in the same period in which the revenue is recorded. The accounting equation remains in balance.

All of the transactions of Kilmer Contractors for the month of May are summarized in Illustration 4:

Illustration 4

Kilmer Contractors
All Transactions
for the Month of May 19X1

	Assets			=	Liabilities			+	Stockholders' Equity			
	Cash	+ Accounts Receivable	+ Supplies	=	Note Payable	+ Unearned Fees	+	Common Stock	+	Revenue (Expense)	− (Dividends)	
May 1	$ 500							$500				
May 2	5,000				$5,000							
May 5	(3,000)		3,000									
May 10	3,300					$3,300						
May 15	(2,000)											
May 17	700				(2,000)					$ 700		
May 19		$900								900		
May 25	(1,500)									(1,500)		
May 27	(600)										($600)	
May 31						(2,200)				2,200		
May 31			(1,000)							(1,000)		
	$2,400	+ $900	+ $2,000	=	$3,000	+ $1,100	+	$500	+	$1,300	− ($600)	
		$5,300							$5,300			

INCOME STATEMENT

We are now in a position to prepare an income statement for Kilmer Contractors. The income statement for the month of May appears in Illustration 5.

Illustration 5

Kilmer Contractors
Income Statement
For the Month Ending May 31, 19X1

Revenue		$3,800
Less: Expenses:		
Supplies used	$1,000	
Salaries	1,500	
Total expenses		2,500
Income		$1,300

The revenues reported in the income statement include $700 earned by painting the house on May 17, $900 earned on May 19 by painting a second house, and $2,200 earned by painting two of the three houses contracted for on May 10 ($700 + $900 + $2,200 = $3,800). The expenses of $2,500 include the salaries of $1,500 paid to Kilmer Contractors' employees on May 25 and the cost of the painting supplies used during the month of May. The cost of the supplies used was determined by subtracting the $2,000 cost of the supplies on hand at May 31 from the $3,000 cost of the supplies available for use during the month ($3,000 − $2,000 = $1,000). Again, note that revenues are recorded as they are earned and expenses are recorded as they are incurred in generating these revenues, not necessarily as cash is either received or paid. As previously indicated, this practice is referred to as the accrual basis of accounting.

The income for the month is the difference between the total revenues earned ($3,800) and the total of the expenses ($2,500) incurred in order to generate these revenues ($3,800 − $2,500 = $1,300). The basic income statement equation may be written as follows:

Revenues — Expenses = Net Income
or
R — E = NI

At the end of the period, this income is added to the stockholders' equity account.

Statement of Stockholders' Equity

The statement of stockholders' equity reports the details of the changes in the stockholders' equity of the firm over a period of time. The change in stockholders' equity is particularly important, because it represents the net increase or decrease in the stockholders' investment in the firm. This change can be explained by examining investments made by stockholders in common stock, dividends paid to stockholders, and earnings of the business during the period for which the statement of stockholders' equity is prepared. Illustration 6 shows the causes of changes to stockholders' equity.

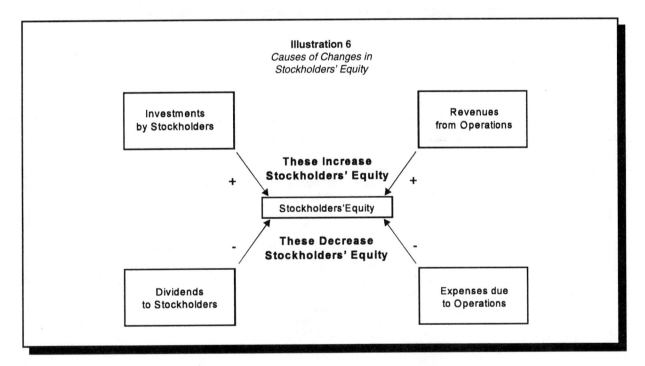

Illustration 6
Causes of Changes in Stockholders' Equity

The balance in stockholders' equity at the end of a period (ESE) is calculated by adding investments (I), adding the net income (NI) and subtracting dividends (D) for the period to the balance in stockholders' equity at the beginning of the period (BSE). This may be expressed in equation form as follows:

Beginning SE + Investments + Net Income - Dividends = Ending SE
or
BSE + I + NI = ESE

Note that the Kilmer Contractors' statement of stockholders' equity, which covers the entire month of May, includes the investment made by Kilmer on May 1, the earnings of the business for the month of May, and the dividend on May 27. The transactions related to earnings appear in summarized form in the income statement. Note the ending amount on the income statement, $1,300, is carried to and appears on the statement of stockholders' equity under the heading Retained Earnings. Also, the dividends of $600 are a negative element in retained earnings. Therefore, the statement of stockholders' equity summarizes all of the transactions that affected stockholders' equity during the month of May. A statement of stockholders' equity for Kilmer Contractors is presented below in Illustration 7.

Illustration 7

Kilmer Contractors
*Statement of Stockholders' Equity
for the Month Ending May 31, 19X1*

	Common Stock	Retained Earnings
Beginning balances	$ 0	$ 0
Investment	500	
Net Income		1,300
Dividends		(600)
Ending balances	$500	$ 700

BALANCE SHEET

The balance sheet for Kilmer Contractors can be taken from the summary of all transactions presented earlier. Note that each side of the equal sign totals $5,300. In other words, the equation balances and, therefore, the balance sheet does also. The balance sheet is presented in Illustration 8.

Illustration 8

Kilmer Contractors
*Balance Sheet
May 31, 19X1*

Assets		Liabilities and Stockholders' Equity		
Cash	$2,400	Note payable	$3,000	
Accounts receivable	900	Unearned fees	1,100	
Supplies	2,000	Total liabilities		$4,100
		Common stock	500	
		Retained earnings	700	1,200
		Total liabilities		
Total assets	$5,300	and stockholders' equity		$5,300

Several items are worth noting. The heading of the balance sheet indicates that it is prepared for only one moment in time by stating the date as May 31, 19X1. This specific date is in contrast to the income statement and statement of stockholders' equity, which indicate in their headings that they are for a period of time, the month ending May 31, 19X1. Next, note that liabilities are totalled before being added to stockholders' equity. Also note that the ending balances from the statement of stockholders' equity are carried to and appear on the balance sheet.

THE STATEMENT OF CASH FLOWS

The statement of cash flows for the month of May for Kilmer Contractors provides a summary of where the company obtained its cash and what it did with its cash. This statement may be prepared by examining the cash account for the changes (increases and decreases) that occurred during May. The statement of cash flows is presented in Illustration 9.

Illustration 9

Kilmer Contractors
Statement of Cash Flows
For the Month Ending May 31, 19X1

Cash flows from operations:		
Receipts from customers[2]		$4,000
Payments to:		
Suppliers	$3,000	
Employees	1,500	4,500
Decrease in cash due to operations		($ 500)
Cash flows from financing activities		
Receipts from:		
Owner's investment	$ 500	
Borrowing	5,000	
Payments for:		
Repaying loan	(2,000)	
Dividends	(600)	
Increase in cash due to financing activities		$2,900
Increase in cash		$2,400

Although the company had a decrease in cash as a result of its operations, it had a net increase in cash because of its financing activities. Note also that the firm began the month with a cash balance of $0. This $0 balance plus the total increase in cash of $2,400 are equal to the cash balance shown on the balance sheet.

The income statement, statement of stockholders' equity, balance sheet, and statement of cash flows presented above were deliberately kept brief and simple for purposes of illustration. They do, however, illustrate the basic principles and procedures followed in the preparation of financial statements. The financial statements were presented here in the order in which they must be prepared. The income statement must be prepared first, because the net income figure is used in preparing the statement of stockholders' equity. The ending balance from the statement of stockholders' equity appears on the balance sheet. Balance sheets for the current and prior periods are used in constructing the statement of cash flows. Illustration 10 shows these relationships among the financial statements. An example of comprehensive financial statements for Wal-Mart is presented as Chapter 1 of this text.

SUMMARY

The basic accounting model is Assets = Liabilities + Stockholders' Equity. The recording process in accounting is used to analyze transactions and events and report their effects on the financial statements. The steps needed in analyzing transactions are (1) identify economic events, (2) measure in monetary terms, (3) identify accounts affected, (4) determine if the accounts increase or decrease, and (5) record the transaction.

The income statement, statement of stockholders' equity, balance sheet, and statement of cash flows are the basic accounting statements that provide data to various external users to be used in making economic

---

[2] This includes the $3,300 received on May 10 plus the $700 received on May 17.

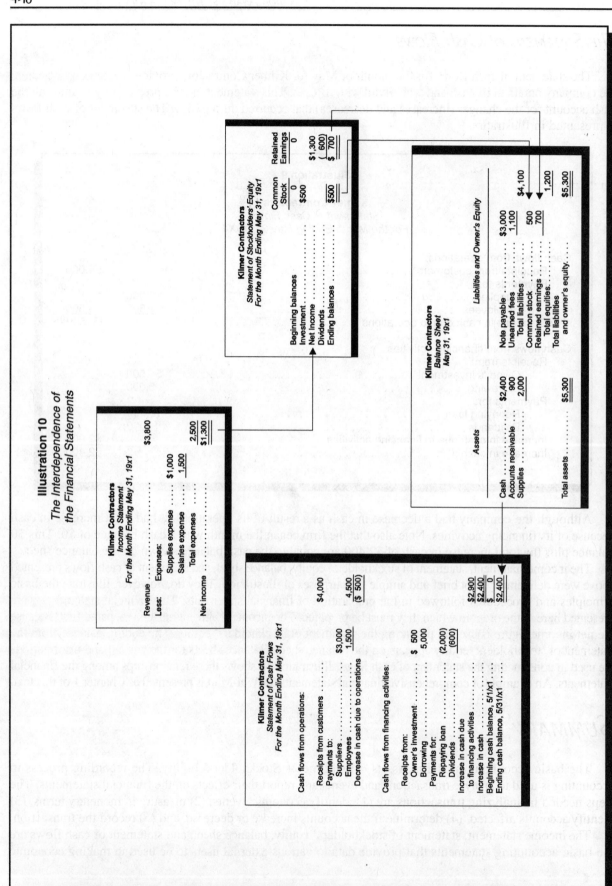

Illustration 10
*The Interdependence of
the Financial Statements*

Kilmer Contractors
*Income Statement
For the Month Ending May 31, 19x1*

Revenue		$3,800
Less: Expenses:		
Supplies expense	$1,000	
Salaries expense	1,500	
Total expenses		2,500
Net income		$1,300

Kilmer Contractors
*Statement of Stockholders' Equity
For the Month Ending May 31, 19x1*

	Common Stock	Retained Earnings
Beginning balances	0	0
Investment	$500	
Net Income		$1,300
Dividends		(600)
Ending balances	$500	$ 700

Kilmer Contractors
*Statement of Cash Flows
For the Month Ending May 31, 19x1*

Cash flows from operations:		
Receipts from customers		$4,000
Payments to:		
Suppliers	$3,000	
Employees	1,500	4,500
Decrease in cash due to operations		($ 500)
Cash flows from financing activities:		
Receipts from:		
Owner's investment	$ 500	
Borrowing	5,000	
Payments for:		
Repaying loan	(2,000)	
Dividends	(600)	
Increase in cash due to financing activities		2,900
Increase in cash		$2,400
Beginning cash balance, 5/1/x1		0
Ending cash balance, 5/31/x1		$2,400

Kilmer Contractors
*Balance Sheet
May 31, 19x1*

Assets		Liabilities and Owner's Equity	
Cash	$2,400	Note payable	$3,000
Accounts receivable	900	Unearned fees	1,100
Supplies	2,000	Total liabilities	$4,100
		Common stock	500
		Retained earnings	700
		Total equities	1,200
Total assets	$5,300	Total liabilities and owner's equity	$5,300

decisions. These and other financial statements are the end products of the accountant's work. Although companies may vary somewhat in the exact detail and format of the data provided, all companies include essentially the same type of information in their financial statements.

The income statement is of particular importance to many users of financial statements because it provides information regarding the results of operations of the firm for a specified period of time, such as a year. Only those transactions involving revenues (earnings from the sale of goods and the rendering of services), gains, expenses (the costs incurred in the process of generating revenues), and losses are reflected on the income statement. Net income is the excess of revenues and gains over expenses and losses for an accounting period.

The statement of stockholders' equity presents a summary of the transactions that affected stockholders' equity in a given time period. Any changes that occurred during that time period in stockholders' equity are reflected and explained in the statement of stockholders' equity.

The balance sheet reflects the financial position of a firm at a particular point in time by providing information regarding the economic resources (assets) of the firm and the sources of these resources (liabilities and stockholders' equity). The format of the balance sheet reflects the basic accounting equation: Assets = Liabilities + Stockholders' Equity. By convention, the assets of the firm are generally presented on the balance sheet in the order of their liquidity. The usual subcategories include current assets; property, plant and equipment; and other assets. Similarly, the liabilities (or debts) of the firm are generally subdivided into current and long-term liabilities. The stockholders' equity section of the balance sheet contains information regarding the direct investment of the owners as well as the income earned by the firm and not paid to the owners in dividends.

The statement of cash flows presents a summary of the increases and decreases in cash due to operating, financing, and investing activities during a given time period. This statement provides information concerning where the company obtained its cash and what it did with its cash.

Key Definitions

Accounting equation—the accounting equation may be expressed as follows: assets = sources of assets or assets = liabilities + stockholders' equity.

Accounting period—usually considered to be one year.

Accounts payable—represents the amounts the company owes to its creditors for purchases of goods or services in the ordinary course of business.

Accounts receivable—represents the amounts owed by customers to the company for goods or services which were sold in the ordinary course of business.

Assets—probable future economic benefits obtained or controlled by a particular entity as a result of past transactions or events.

Balance sheet—The balance sheet or statement of financial position is a financial report which provides information concerning an entity's assets, liabilities, and owners' equity as of a particular point in time.

Cash—any medium of exchange which is readily accepted and used for transactions. Besides currency or demand deposits, cash usually includes certain negotiable instruments, such as customers' checks.

Common stock—the owners' investments in a corporation.

Cash equivalents—time deposits and highly-liquid marketable securities.

Current assets—includes cash and other assets which are expected to be converted into cash, sold, or used in operations or production during the upcoming accounting period.

Current liabilities—includes those obligations for which settlement is expected to require the use of current assets (usually cash) or the provision of services within one year.

Dividends—distributions to owners are decreases in net assets of a particular enterprise resulting from transferring assets, rendering services, or incurring liabilities by the enterprise to owners.

Equity—the residual interest that remains in the assets of an entity after deducting its liabilities (i.e., Equity = Assets - Liabilities).

Expenses—outflows or other consumption or using up of assets or incurrences of liabilities (or a combination of both) from delivering or producing goods, rendering services, or carrying out other activities that constitute the entity's ongoing major or central operations.

4-20

Gains—increases in equity (net assets) from peripheral or incidental transactions of an entity and from all other transactions and other events and circumstances affecting the entity during a period except those that result from revenues or investments by owners.

Income statement—a summary of the operations of a firm. It reports the income (or loss) of the company during a specified period of time.

Intangibles—assets without physical substance, such as patents.

Inventory—includes materials which are used in production, goods which are in the process of production, and finished products held for sale to customers.

Investments by owners—increases in net assets of a particular enterprise resulting from transfers to it from other entities of something of value to obtain or increase ownership interests (or equity) in it. Investments by owners are most commonly in the form of assets, but that which is received may also include services performed or conversion of the enterprise's liabilities.

Liabilities—probable future sacrifices of economic benefits arising from present obligations of a particular entity to transfer assets or provide services to other entities in the future as a result of past transactions or events.

Liquidity—normally refers to the order in which assets would be converted into cash or used up.

Long-term liabilities—generally represent claims which will be paid or satisfied in a future accounting period (or periods) beyond one year.

Losses—decreases in equity (net assets) from peripheral or incidental transactions of an entity and from all other transactions and other events and circumstances affecting the entity during a period except those that result from expenses or distributions to owners.

Marketable securities—temporary investments in stocks, bonds, and other securities which are readily salable and which management intends to sell within a relatively short period of time.

Net income—the excess of revenues and gains earned over expenses and losses incurred for an accounting period.

Notes payable—normally arise from borrowing and are evidenced by a written document or formal promise to pay.

Prepaid expenses—represents expenditures which were made in either the current or a prior period and which will provide benefits to the firm at some future time.

Property, plant and equipment—assets which are acquired for use in the continuing operations of a business over a number of accounting periods rather than for resale to customers.

Retained earnings—earnings retained in the business; i.e., income not distributed as dividends.

Revenues—inflows or other enhancements of assets of an entity or settlements of its liabilities (or a combination of both) from delivering or producing goods, rendering services, or other activities that constitute the entity's ongoing major or central operations.

Statement of cash flows—this statement explains the causes of changes in cash plus cash equivalents and provides a summary of the operating, investing and financing activities of a company during a period of time.

Statement of stockholders' equity—summarizes investments made by the stockholders, additions to stockholders' equity from earnings, and dividends to stockholders during the accounting period.

Stockholders' equity—also referred to as net worth or capital, represents claims against the assets by the owners of the business. The total stockholders' equity represents the amount that the owners have invested in the business including any income that may have been retained in the business since its inception.

Tangible assets—those assets that have physical substance.

Transactions—exchanges or other economic events which occur during the life of a business.

Unearned revenues—amounts collected from customers for goods which have not been shipped or services which have not yet been performed.

Questions

1. What are the main sources of assets for a company? Why does each source provide assets?

2. A = L + SE expresses what accounting concept? Explain the concept.

3. What is a transaction?

4. What is an asset? Distinguish between current and long-term assets.

5. What is a liability? Distinguish between current and long-term liabilities.

6. Explain the difference between liabilities and stockholders' equity.

7. What do the balances in the stockholders' equity accounts represent?

8. What are some advantages of preparing a balance sheet?

9. What periods of time are covered by the income statement, the statement of stockholders' equity, and the balance sheet? How is this recorded in the headings of the statements?

10. What is the relationship between the balance sheet and the income statement at the end of the accounting period?

EXERCISES

11. Using these abbreviations, classify each of the following account titles as to what section of the balance sheet they would appear in.

CA—Current assets   CL—Current liabilities
PE—Property, plant and equipment   LTL—Long-term liabilities
OA—Other assets   SE—Stockholders' equity

CA	Cash		CL	Taxes payable
SE	Common stock		CA	Inventory
CL or LTL	Note payable		CL	Wages payable
CA	Prepaid insurance		CL	Accounts payable
CA	Accounts receivable		CA	Marketable securities
PE	Machinery and equipment		PE	Land
OA	Investments		OA	Goodwill
OA	Patents		CL	Interest payable

12. Given the following information, answer the questions below:

Revenue—19X1	$24,000
Liabilities—December 31, 19X1	25,000
Issuances of common stock—19X1	4,000
Dividends—19X1	12,000
Stockholders' equity—January 1, 19X1	27,000
Stockholders' equity—December 31, 19X1	35,000

(handwritten) c) NI = Rev − Cost − Exp
16,000 = 24,000 − Cost − Exp
8000

a. What are the total assets on December 31, 19X1? A = L + SE = 25,000 + 35,000 = 60,000
b. What is net income for the year? SE = 35,000 − 27,000 ⟹ 8000
c. What is total expense for 19X1? Dividends

(handwritten) 20,000 (stock issue) −4000; 12,000; 20,000; 16,000

13. Fill in the missing figures in the information below:

	19X1	19X2	19X3
Assets—January 1	$100,000	$120,000	(f)
Liabilities—January 1	60,000	(c)	$72,000
Stockholders' equity—January 1	(a)	(d)	75,000
Dividends	20,000	15,000	17,000
Issuances of common stock	18,000	16,000	0
Stockholders' equity—December 31	(b)	(e)	57,000
Income (loss)	20,000	16,000	(g)

(handwritten) (A = L + SE = 72,000 + 75,000 = 147,000)

(handwritten notes at bottom)
a = 40,000 (100,000 − 60,000) b/c A = L + SE   SE = A − L
b = Beg SE = 40,000   BSE + Investments + NI − Dividends = Ending SE
40,000   18,000   20,000   20,000   = Ending SE
58,000

d) Beg SE = 58,000 Div = 15,000   58,000 + 16,000 + 16,000 − 15,000 = 75,000 = e

SEend 57,000 − 18,000
beg 75,000
Div − 17,000
Issue − 0 (1000)

(left margin handwritten) 2/120,000 − 58,000 (A = L + SE) C = 62,000

14. For each transaction listed below, indicate the effect on the total assets, total liabilities, and stockholders' equity of the business. Identify the effect of each transaction by using a (+) for an increase, a (−) for a decrease and a (0) for no effect.

includes revenues expenses

		Assets ⚯	Liabilities +	Stockholders Equity
a.	The owners invested cash in the business to buy common stock	(+)	( )	(+)
b.	Purchased a building for cash	(+)(−)=0	( )	( )
c.	Borrowed cash from the bank	(+)	(+)	( )
d.	Purchased equipment on credit	(+)	(+)	( )
e.	Provided a service and collected cash	(+)	( )	(+) revenue
f.	Paid wages in cash to employees	(−)	( )	(−) expense
g.	Paid a bank loan	(−)	(−)	( )

15. Classify each of the following items as to whether they would be found on the balance sheet (B), income statement (I), or statement of stockholders' equity (S). *RE & dividends*   *Assets, Liab, SE / Revenue, Expenses gains losses*

B	Cash	B	Unearned fees *ie magazine subscriptions*	I	Rental income
I	Revenue	I	Salary expense	B	Accounts receivable
B	Wages payable	I	Insurance expense	B	Bonds payable
S	Dividends	B	Building	B	Prepaid insurance
B	Accounts payable	B	Supplies		
B	Goodwill	I	Rental expense		

liability

anything "prepaid" is an asset

anything "unearned" is a liability

16. Fill in the missing amounts:

Lee Company
Balance Sheet
June 30, 19X1

Assets

Cash	$ 12,000
Marketable securities	31,000
Accounts receivable	7,000
Inventory	44,000
Buildings	193,000
Land	75,000
	(a) 362,000

Liabilities and Stockholders' Equity

Accounts payable	$33,000
Taxes payable	(b)
Bonds payable	76,000
Total liabilities	$120,000
Common stock	100,000
Retained earnings	(c)
	(d) 362,000

120,000
−33,000
−76,000
=11,000

C= 142,000 (362,000 −120,000 −100,000)

(A=C+SE)

Problems

17. The following transactions occurred during the initial month of operations of Kingsbery Automotive Services.

Sept.	3	The owners paid $15,000 cash for the company's common stock.
	9	Auto parts purchased on account, $5,000.
	12	Paid rent for the first month, $2,500.
	18	Repaired cars for a $2,200 fee and billed the customers.
	20	Auto parts used, $1,150.
	26	Collected $850 on customers' accounts.
	29	Paid $1,000 to creditors.

a. Indicate the effects of these transactions on the equation provided below.

		Assets			=	Liabilities	+		Stockholders' Equity	
		Auto		Accounts		Accounts		Common		Revenue
Cash	+	Parts	+	Receivable	=	Payable	+	Stock	+	(Expense)

b. Prepare a balance sheet and an income statement at the end of the month.

18. An auto repair business was started on January 1, 19X1. At the end of 19X1, Jones Auto Repair had the following balances of assets, liabilities, and stockholders' equity:

Accounts payable	$ 5,000
Accounts receivable	20,000
Building	30,000
Common stock	2,000
Cash	10,000
Land	12,000
Note payable	10,000
Prepaid insurance	5,000
Retained earnings	?
Supplies	8,000
Unearned fees	16,000
Wages payable	2,000

Required:

Determine the amount in the retained earnings account at year-end and prepare a balance sheet at December 31, 19X1.

19. Below is a balance sheet for Rich Exterminator Company (REC) at October 31, 19X1.

Rich Exterminator Company
Balance Sheet
October 31, 19X1

Assets

Cash	$7,500
Supplies	2,000
	$9,500

Liabilities and Stockholders' Equity

Note payable	$2,200
Unearned fees	300
Common stock	3,000
Retained earnings	4,000
	$9,500

The unearned fees are the result of receiving in advance a $100 fee for each of three jobs to be performed in the future.

During the month of November, the following transactions occurred.

Nov.	2	REC exterminated a house and billed and collected $100 cash from the customer.
	7	REC exterminated a house and billed but did not collect its fee of $150.
	11	REC paid its employees salaries of $200.
	17	REC exterminated two of the three houses contracted for in October.
	30	The unused supplies on hand at this date had an original cost of $1,500.

Required:

a. Prepare an income statement and a statement of cash flows for Rich Exterminator Company for the month of November.

b. Prepare a balance sheet at November 30, 19X1.

20. Given the following information, prepare an income statement, a statement of stockholders' equity, and a balance sheet for Pate Company on December 31, 19X1.

Prepaid insurance	$ 500
Cash	16,600
Accounts payable	8,800
Unearned revenue	3,840
Utility expense	750
Dividends	3,000
Accounts receivable	8,160
Revenues	25,000
Building	20,000
Supplies expense	2,600
Supplies	140
Wages payable	1,550
Goodwill	2,000
Common stock—January 1, 19X1	2,000
Equipment	7,900
Salary expense	15,000
Rent expense	3,200
Office furniture	4,000
Marketable securities	1,200
Retained earnings—January 1, 19X1	15,860
Bonds payable	20,000
Retained earnings—December 31, 19X1	?
Issuance of common stock	?

21. The following information was taken from the books of the Dawson Company on December 31, 19X1:

Dividends	$ 3,000
Insurance expense	2,400
Cash	28,000
Utilities expense	1,900
Rent expense	10,200
Revenue	60,000
Prepaid rent	18,000
Wages expense	13,400
Supplies expense	1,500

Required:

Prepare an income statement for 19X1.

22. Prepare a balance sheet for the Kang Company as of June 30, 19X1.

Kang Company
Balance Sheet
January 1, 19X1

Assets

Cash	$13,000
Accounts receivable	49,000
Inventory	1,000
	$63,000

Liabilities and Stockholders' Equity

Accounts payable	$20,000
Salaries payable	9,000
Common stock	4,000
Retained earnings	30,000
	$63,000

Transactions which occurred between January 1, 19X1, and June 30, 19X1, were:

a. Accounts receivable of $19,000 was collected in cash.
b. Accounts payable increased by $10,000 due to a purchase of inventory.
c. Salaries payable of $9,000 were paid in cash.

23. Latisha King began operating a tax return preparation service on January 1. During the month of January, the following transactions were completed.

Jan.	2	The owner purchased $10,000 of common stock of the business.
	4	The business acquired $3,000 of supplies on account.
	5	Rent of $500 was paid for an office building.
	11	Prepared tax returns on credit for a $3,000 fee.
	15	Salaries of $1,000 were paid to employees.
	25	Collected $1,500 on customer accounts.
	30	Cash of $1,000 was paid to creditors.
	31	Supplies of $1,000 were used.

Required:

a. Show the effects of these transactions on the equation provided below.

Assets			=	Liabilities	+	Stockholders' Equity	
		Accounts		Accounts		Common	Revenue
Cash +	Supplies +	Receivable	=	Payable +		Stock +	(Expense)

b. Prepare an income statement for the month of January.
c. Prepare a balance sheet as of January 31.

24. The following information was taken from the records of J. S. Wylie and Company as of July 31, 19X1. Prepare the balance sheet at that date.

Wages payable	$ 5,000
Cash	2,345
Land	30,000
Prepaid rent	300
Accounts payable	1,470
Common stock	11,000
Retained earnings	?
Inventory	5,990
Equipment	15,200
Buildings	33,450
Accounts receivable	1,350
Patents (just purchased)	7,000
Mortgage payable (due January 31, 19X9)	40,000
Marketable securities	1,035
Estimated taxes payable	3,000
Unearned revenue	750

25. The statement of financial position of the Zimmerman Co. shows assets of $1,500,000. John Smith advises you that a major accounting firm has reviewed the statements and attested that they were prepared in accordance with generally accepted accounting principles. He tells you that he can buy the total owner's interest in the business for only $1,000,000 and is seriously considering the offer. He says that he would be foolish to pass up the opportunity to buy $1,500,000 of assets for only $1,000,000. Given this limited information, what major pitfalls are apparent in Mr. Smith's thinking?

26. For each of the transactions listed, indicate the effect(s), if any, on the company's year-end: (1) Balance Sheet, (2) Income Statement, and (3) Statement of Cash Flows. Your answers should be as complete and specific as possible.

   a. Owner invests cash in the business.
   b. Company borrows cash, issuing a non-interest bearing note payable.
   c. Company purchases supplies.
   d. Company receives an advance payment from customers for work to be done at a future date.
   e. Company pays a dividend to its stockholders.
   f. Company repays non-interest bearing note payable.

27. For each of the transactions listed, indicate the effect(s), if any, on the company's year-end: (1) Balance Sheet, (2) Income Statement, and (3) Statement of Cash Flows. Your answers should be as complete and specific as possible.

   a. Company performs services and collects cash from its customer.
   b. Company performs services and bills (but does not collect) its fee.
   c. Company pays its employees salaries.
   d. Company performs services for which it had been paid in advance.
   e. Company notes it had used supplies previously purchased.

Refer to the Annual Report in Chapter 1 of the text.

28. What was the income for the most recent year?

29. Did the most recent year's income increase or decrease from the prior year?

30. Were the increases/decreases in income because of a change in revenue, a change in expenses, or both?

31. What was the largest expense in the most recent year?

32. Which expense increased the most during the most recent year? What expense decreased the most?

33. Which current asset is the largest at the end of the most recent year?

34. Comparing the two years presented, what was the change in long-term debt? What factors might have caused these changes?

35. What is the largest asset amount in the balance sheet at the end of the most recent year?

36. Comparing the two years presented, how much did total stockholders' equity increase/decrease?

37. Comparing the two years presented, did cash dividends paid increase or decrease for stockholders?

Ethical Case

Pat is preparing to sit for the CPA examination. As part of the application procedure in her state, signatures of recommendation are required from two CPAs who have known Pat for at least two years.

Pat has asked one of her professors to sign her application. Pat got to know this professor well this past year when she served as an officer in Beta Alpha Psi, the accounting honor society, but she did not know him before this school year began. She has also asked the partner of the local accounting firm with which she interned this past year. The partner rated her performance highly and has asked Pat to consider joining the firm upon graduation. Even though she only worked with the firm one summer, she believes the partner has seen enough of her performance to recommend her.

1. Who is confronted with an ethical issue in this situation?

2. What are the ethical implications and outcomes of this scenario?

3. What alternatives might Pat consider?

FRAUD CASE: Skimming

There are as many forms of employee fraud schemes as the minds of employees lacking honesty and integrity can envision. It is up to the CFE, when fraud is apparent, to uncover these devious schemes.

Skimming involves an employee removing cash before it is recorded in the accounting records. Consider the following actual case:

> The auditors of a Midwestern chain of supermarkets, as a result of applying analytical procedures, concluded that one of the supermarkets in the chain had apparent financial reporting inconsistencies. The analytical procedures indicated that the sales, profit, and inventory figures did not agree and, furthermore, profit levels were below those of the other stores in the chain. Upon closer audit investigation, it was determined that one or more employees were skimming cash at the checkout stands.

A CFE performing an examination to determine the extent of fraud and the identity of the person committing the fraud in a skimming case has a difficult task because there is no documentation supporting the fraud—it is "off-book" fraud in that the fraud takes place before any record of the cash is made.

Usually the only examination approach is to observe employees performing their duties and attempting to identify the dishonest employee(s). Of course, such observations must involve covert (secretive) surveillance to be effective.

Discussion Question:

How would you proceed to determine which employee(s) is stealing or skimming cash from the supermarket?

Outline

Learning Objectives

Chapter 5 traces and explains the basic steps in the recording process. Studying this chapter should enable you to:

1. Explain what an account is and how it is used in the recording process.
2. Discuss the use of debits and credits and how they affect asset, liability, and stockholders' equity accounts.
3. List the basic steps in the recording process.
4. Describe a trial balance and identify the types of errors it will (and will not) detect.
5. Explain the use of adjusting entries.
6. Discuss the purpose and illustrate the process of closing the temporary accounts.
7. Identify when revenues and expenses are recognized in an accrual system of accounting.
8. List the five common types of adjusting entries and give examples of each.

Chapter 5

The Recording Process

Introduction

Because the number of transactions that cause assets, liabilities, equities, revenues, expenses, gains, and losses to increase and decrease occurs much too frequently, even in a small business, to prepare a new set of financial statements each time a transaction takes place, a method of recording and summarizing information must be used. Transaction analysis using the accounting equation, which was demonstrated in the previous chapter, is too cumbersome to use, because most companies have dozens of individual assets, liabilities, revenues, and expenses; the accounting equation would grow to unwieldy proportions. An alternative method of recording information is described in this chapter. This accounting method, referred to as the "double-entry" method, is basic to every accounting system and is applicable to all situations in which financial information is collected and processed. The system may be maintained by hand, just as described in this chapter, but large firms, and even most small firms today, have access to computerized accounting systems to assist in maintaining accounting information. In any situation, however, the basic principles involved are the same.

The Account

For purposes of reporting and facilitating the analysis by users, the transactions of an entity are summarized or grouped in individual accounts. An account is simply a place to group and summarize all of the transactions that affect one particular asset, liability, equity, revenue, expense, gain, or loss item. The accounting system of a firm includes a separate account for each individual asset, liability, revenue, expense, gain, and loss, as well as for common stock and retained earnings.

The increase or decrease in each of these items is recorded in its own account using "debits" and "credits," which are abbreviated as Dr and Cr.[1] At this point, we cannot overemphasize the fact that the words "debit" and "credit" are simply terms used to identify *left and right* sides of an account, respectively, and have absolutely no other meaning in their accounting usage. Accepting this statement as a fact and keeping it in mind will save you untold grief and will greatly enhance your understanding of the recording process. The use of specialized words, or terminology, to indicate left and right by accountants can be compared to the use of "port" and "starboard" by sailors. For purposes of our discussion, a typical account may be illustrated as follows:

(Account Title)	
(Debit side)	(Credit side)

This form of presentation is often referred to as a T-account because of its appearance.

Double-entry Method

Now let's examine again the basic accounting equation introduced in the last chapter:

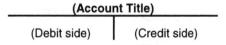

Assets = Liabilities + Stockholders' Equity

---

[1] These terms were derived from the Latin words "debere" and "credere."

Increases in accounts on the left of the equal sign (assets) are recorded in the left column of the T-account and increases in the accounts on the right of the equal sign (liabilities and equity) are recorded in the right column of the T-account. In other words, when assets are increased, they are "debited," which means entered on the left, and when liabilities and equity are increased, they are "credited," which means entered on the right.

Decreases are treated in exactly the opposite manner. Decreases in assets are "credited" or entered in the right column of the T-account, and decreases in liabilities and equity are "debited" or entered in the left column.

The rules of "debit" and "credit" may be summarized as follows, using "+" to indicate increases and "−" to indicate decreases.

Assets		Liabilities		Stockholders' Equity	
Debit	Credit	Debit	Credit	Debit	Credit
(+)	(−)	(−)	(+)	(−)	(+)

It was indicated earlier that the "double-entry" method is used in accounting in order to record transactions. Why is this accounting method called the double-entry method? This method is based on the accounting equation. As you may remember from algebra, for an equation to remain equal, the same operation must be performed on both sides of the equal sign. If assets on the left of the equal sign increase (for example, the cash account is increased), the equation will be out of balance (will not equal) unless liabilities or equity also increases. In other words, a "double-entry" must be made to keep the equation in balance. This method not only tells users what happened to the assets of the business (in this case, cash increased), but also why or where the cash came from (for example, a new loan or additional stock issuances or revenue).

To illustrate, assume that a company issues $500 of common stock. Cash is increased by $500. Since cash is an asset account, the $500 amount is debited to the account. The issuance of the common stock increases stockholders' equity. The $500 increase to the common stock account is credited. Using T-accounts, the transaction is recorded as follows:

Assets		=	Liabilities		+	Stockholders' Equity	
Cash						Common Stock	
500 (+)						500 (+)	

Some transactions affect only one side of the accounting equation. To illustrate, assume $3,000 of supplies are purchased for cash. Supplies, an asset account, is increased, and, therefore, is debited for $3,000. The other account affected is cash, which decreases by $3,000. Cash is, therefore, credited for $3,000. Using T-accounts, this transaction appears as follows.

Assets				=	Liabilities	+	Stockholders' Equity
Cash		Supplies					
	3,000 (−)	3,000 (+)					

Both cash and supplies are asset accounts and are on the left side of the equal sign. One account, supplies, increases by $3,000 and one account, cash, decreases by $3,000. Therefore, total assets remain the same and the accounting equation remains in balance, even though only one side is affected by this transaction.

A simple rule must be kept in mind when using the double-entry method: the total dollar amount of the debits must always equal the total dollar amount of the credits. Otherwise, the accounting equation will not be in balance.

Total Debits = Total Credits

Now let's expand the basic accounting equation to include dividends, revenues, and expenses:

Assets = Liabilities + Common Stock + Revenues - Expenses - Dividends[2]

Revenues, expenses and dividends all affect stockholders' equity. Remember the rules of debits and credits illustrated earlier state that increases to stockholders' equity are entered on the right (credit) side of the T-account. Revenues increase stockholders' equity; therefore, revenues are credited when they increase. Both dividends and expenses are subtracted from, or decrease, stockholders' equity; therefore, dividends and expenses are debited or entered on the left side of the T-account when they are increased.

The rules of debit and credit can be summarized as follows:

To increase an asset, debit the account.
To decrease an asset, credit the account.
To increase a liability or stockholders' equity, credit the account.
To decrease a liability or stockholders' equity, debit the account.
To increase revenue, credit the account.[3]
To decrease revenue, debit the account.
To increase an expense or dividends, debit the account.[4]
To decrease an expense or dividends, credit the account.

The rules of debit and credit can be illustrated in an expanded accounting equation as follows:

Permanent Accounts							Temporary Accounts						
Assets		=	Liabilities		+	Common Stock		+	Revenues		-	Expenses		-	Dividends	
Debit (+)	Credit (−)		Debit (−)	Credit (+)		Debit (−)	Credit (+)		Debit (−)	Credit (+)		Debit (+)	Credit (−)		Debit (+)	Credit (−)

The balance in an account at any point in time is equal to the difference between the total debits and the total credits recorded in that account.

The revenue, expense, and dividends accounts are often referred to as *temporary (or nominal) accounts.* Users of accounting information commonly think of temporary accounts as collecting information only for a certain period of time, for example, expenses for the year or revenue for the year. The income statement accounts are temporary accounts. Each new year starts from zero and summarizes expenses or revenues for the new year separately from those of the prior year.

The asset, liability, and common stock accounts are called *permanent (or real) accounts* because the balances in these accounts at the end of one accounting period appear in the balance sheet and are carried forward to the next period. Permanent accounts do not start over from zero at the beginning of each period. For example, the amounts in checking accounts at the end of the year are carried forward to the new year; likewise, the amount owed on a mortgage payable at the end of the year is carried forward and still owed as mortgage payable in the next year.

In order to further illustrate the use of the double-entry method, assume that a firm obtains a $5,000 cash loan from its bank. This transaction increases the firm's cash, an asset, by $5,000 and also increases its loans payable, a liability, by the same amount. In order to record this transaction, the firm debits (increases) its cash account for $5,000 and, at the same time, credits (increases) its loans payable account for $5,000. This transaction is summarized in the accounts of the firm as follows:

---

[2] A dividend is a distribution of cash (or other assets) to the stockholders of a company. Dividends will be discussed in detail later in the text.
[3] Gains are recorded in the same manner as revenues.
[4] Losses are recorded in the same manner as expenses.

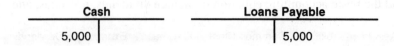

	Cash		Loans Payable	
	5,000			5,000

The total of the debits (in this instance a debit to the cash account of $5,000) is equal to the total of the credits (a credit to the liability account, loans payable, for $5,000). In addition, note that the accounting equation, A = L + SE, remains in balance since both assets and liabilities are increased by $5,000 (stockholders' equity is not affected).

When the firm repays its loan to the bank, the payment of $5,000 decreases the firm's asset, cash, by $5,000 and decreases its liability, loans payable, by $5,000. This transaction is recorded in the accounts by a debit (decrease) to loans payable of $5,000 and a credit (decrease) to cash of $5,000. The effects of the two transactions: (1) borrowing $5,000 from the bank, and (2) repaying the $5,000 to the bank, are recorded in the accounts as follows:

	Cash			Loans Payable		
(1)	5,000	(2)	5,000	(2) 5,000	(1)	5,000

Again the total debits are equal to the total credits and the accounting equation remains in balance.

JOURNAL ENTRIES

A general journal is used to record the transactions of a firm as they occur, i.e., chronologically. It might be compared to the diary of a business. *The journal entry represents the initial input of economic data into the accounting system.* Each entry in the general journal records the debits and credits of a single transaction. The two transactions explained above can be used to illustrate this process.

		Debit	Credit
(1)	Cash	5,000	
	Loans payable		5,000
(2)	Loans payable	5,000	
	Cash		5,000

The format for each journal entry is illustrated above. Write the title of the account to be debited and the amount of the debit on the first line, then indent and write the title of the account to be credited and the amount of the credit on the second line. Debits are always listed before credits. This is simply a matter of convention. Also note that the left column is the debit (Dr) column and the right column is the credit (Cr) column.

Transactions are recorded initially in general journal form and then transferred to the individual T-accounts (as illustrated above). This latter process is referred to as "posting," transferring information from the general journal to the ledger (the book of entry that contains all the individual accounts of the firm). A T-account is just a short-hand way of representing ledger accounts. Again, a separate account exists in the ledger for each and every asset, liability, equity, revenue, expense, gain, and loss. General journal and ledger account pages used in a manual accounting system are described in Illustration 1 and their use will be discussed in more detail later. Note the "T" appearance of the ledgers.

While all transactions can be recorded in a single general journal, most accounting systems include a general journal and several special journals. Each special journal is designed for recording particular types of transactions. We will use only a general journal in our discussion in this chapter. Special journals will be discussed in the appendix to Chapter 6.

Illustration 1
Journalizing and Posting to the Ledgers

Panel A-*Sample Transactions*

May 1. Bill Kilmer organized Kilmer Contractors and issued common stock for $500.
May 5. The company purchased painting supplies, paying the $3,000 purchase price in cash.

Panel B-*Entries in General Journal*

GENERAL JOURNAL

Page 1

DATE			REF.	DEBIT	CREDIT
19 x 1					
May	1	Cash	101	500	
		Common Stock	301		500
		(Issued common stock)			
	5	Supplies	102	3,000	
		Cash	101		3,000
		(Purchased painting supplies)			

Panel C-*Posting to Ledgers*

Cash — Account No. 101

DATE	ITEM	JRNL. REF.	DEBIT	DATE	ITEM	JRNL. REF.	CREDIT
19 x 1							
May 1		J.1	500	May 5		J.1	3,000

Supplies — Account No. 102

DATE	ITEM	JRNL. REF.	DEBIT	DATE	ITEM	JRNL. REF.	CREDIT
19 x 1							
May 5		J.1	3,000				

Common Stock — Account No. 301

DATE	ITEM	JRNL. REF.	DEBIT	DATE	ITEM	JRNL. REF.	CREDIT
				19 x 1			
				May 1		J.1	500

THE ACCOUNTING CYCLE

The steps involved in collecting, processing, and reporting financial information are referred to as the accounting cycle. The key elements of the accounting cycle are as follows:

1. The preparation of general journal entries.
2. Posting these general journal entries to the ledger.

3. The preparation of a trial balance before adjustment.

4. The preparation of adjusting journal entries.

5. Posting these adjusting entries to the ledger.

6. The preparation of the adjusted trial balance.

7. The preparation of closing entries.

8. Posting these closing entries to the ledger.

9. The preparation of the after-closing trial balance.

10. The preparation of the financial statements.

An Illustration

To illustrate the recording process described above, we will again follow the activities of Kilmer Contractors, the small painting contractor described in the previous chapter, through May, the initial month of its operations. Note that as each transaction is analyzed, the same five steps introduced in the previous chapter are followed:

1. The economic event is identified.

2. It is measured in monetary terms, in dollars and cents.

3. The accounts affected are identified.

4. It is determined whether the accounts are increased or decreased and whether the accounts are debited (for an increase to an asset account or a decrease to a liability or stockholders' equity account) or credited (for a decrease to an asset account or an increase to a liability or stockholders' equity account).

5. The transaction is recorded in the accounting records.

General Journal Entries

The transactions that occurred during the month of May 19X1, for Kilmer Contractors, are recorded first in the general journal:

May 1.   Bill Kilmer organized Kilmer Contractors and issued common stock for $500.

This transaction results in an increase in cash from the sale of the company's common stock. The firm's cash account and the common stock account are both increased. It is recorded in the journal as follows:

5/1	Cash	500	
	Common stock		500

This journal entry is then recorded in the ledger as follows (using T-accounts):

Cash		Common Stock	
5/1 500			5/1 500

Note the date of the transaction is recorded as well as the amount. As indicated above, the increase in the asset cash is recorded by a debit to the cash account and the corresponding increase in the common stock is recorded by a credit to the common stock account. This entry illustrates the rules that increases in assets are recorded by debits and increases in equities are recorded by credits. Note that the basic accounting equation,

$A = L + SE$, is in balance and the total debits are equal to the total credits. These rules hold true for each of the transactions of the business as they are recorded.

May 2. Kilmer Contractors borrowed $5,000 by signing a non-interest bearing note payable to Bill Kilmer's parents.

This transaction is the receipt of an asset, cash, in exchange for a liability, the promise to pay a creditor at some future date. It reflects the promise of the business to repay $5,000 at a future date in order to have cash on hand and available for use at this time. It is recorded by the following entry:

5/2	Cash	5,000	
	Note payable		5,000

	Cash			Note Payable	
5/1	500		5/2		5,000
5/2	5,000				

The increase in the asset cash is recorded by a debit to the cash account and the increase in the liability, note payable, is recorded by a credit to the note payable account. This transaction illustrates the rules that increases in assets are recorded by debits and increases in liabilities are recorded by credits.

May 5. The company purchased painting supplies, paying the $3,000 purchase price in cash.

This transaction represents an exchange of one asset for another. The asset supplies is increased while the asset cash is decreased. It is recorded as follows:

5/5	Supplies	3,000	
	Cash		3,000

	Cash					Supplies	
5/1	500	5/5	3,000	5/5	3,000		
5/2	5,000						

The increase in the asset supplies is recorded by a debit to the supplies account while the cash payment is recorded by a credit to the cash account. This entry follows the rules that increases in assets are recorded by debits while decreases in assets are recorded by credits.

May 10. Kilmer Contractors signed a contract whereby the company agreed to paint three houses sometime during the next few weeks. The customer paid Kilmer Contractors the amount of $1,100 per house in advance.

The company has agreed to paint three houses at a future date and has received its fee now, before it has done the work. The receipt of the $3,300 increases cash and the liability, unearned fees, by the same amount. Unearned fees are not a liability in the sense that the company will be required to repay the money. Rather, this account represents an obligation on the part of Kilmer Contractors to provide a service by painting three houses at some future date. This transaction is recorded by the following entry:

5/10	Cash	3,300	
	Unearned fees		3,300

	Cash				Unearned Fees	
5/1	500	5/5	3,000		5/10	3,300
5/2	5,000					
5/10	3,300					

The increase in the asset cash is recorded by a debit to the cash account while the increase in the liability, unearned fees, is recorded by a credit to the unearned fees account. Again, this entry illustrates the rules that increases in assets are recorded by debits and increases in liabilities are recorded by credits.

May 15. Kilmer Contractors repaid $2,000 of the $5,000 it borrowed from Mr. and Mrs. Kilmer.

This transaction is a reduction of both liabilities and assets. The business repaid $2,000 of the $5,000 it owed to the Kilmers. Both cash and the note payable are decreased by this amount. (Recall that it was assumed that this note was not interest bearing.) The following entry is made:

5/15	Note payable	2,000	
	Cash		2,000

	Cash				Note Payable		
5/1	500	5/5	3,000	5/15	2,000	5/2	5,000
5/2	5,000	5/15	2,000				
5/10	3,300						

The repayment of $2,000 to the Kilmers is recorded by a debit to the liability account, note payable, and a credit to the asset account, cash. This entry illustrates the rules that decreases in liabilities are recorded by debits and decreases in assets are recorded by credits.

May 17. Kilmer Contractors painted its first house and billed and collected a fee of $700 from the customer.

This transaction indicates that the firm has begun to earn revenue. It is a sale of services for cash. Cash was received and revenue was increased by the amount earned. It is recorded by the following entry.

5/17	Cash	700	
	Painting fees		700

	Cash				Painting Fee	
5/1	500	5/5	3,000		5/17	700
5/2	5,000	5/15	2,000			
5/10	3,300					
5/17	700					

The sale of services for cash is recorded by a debit to the cash account and a credit to the revenue account, painting fees. This entry illustrates the rules that increases in assets are recorded by debits and increases in revenues are recorded by credits.

May 19. Kilmer Contractors painted a second house and billed (but did not collect) its fee of $900.

Again, this transaction records the revenue earned by the firm in painting a customer's house. Unlike the previous transaction, however, cash was not received. The customer was billed for the service rendered and will pay Kilmer Contractors at some future date. An asset, accounts receivable, has increased and revenue has increased by $900, the fee charged for painting the house. This transaction illustrates the very important principle that revenue is recorded as it is earned, not necessarily as cash is received. This concept reflects the accrual basis of accounting. The transaction is recorded by the following entry:

5/19	Accounts receivable	900	
	Painting fees		900

Accounts Receivable		Painting Fees	
5/19 900		5/17 700	
		5/19 900	

This sale of services to a customer on a credit basis is recorded by a debit to the asset, accounts receivable, and a credit to the revenue account, painting fees. Again, this transaction illustrates the rules that increases in assets are recorded by debits and increases in revenues are recorded by credits.

May 25. Kilmer Contractors paid salaries of $1,500 to its employees.

Expenses of $1,500 were incurred and paid in cash. This transaction reduces the cash balance and increases expenses. This transaction also results in a reduction in stockholders' equity due to the fact that expenses reduce income. The transaction is recorded by the following entry:

5/25	Salaries expense	1,500	
	Cash		1,500

Cash				Salaries Expense	
5/1	500	5/5	3,000	5/25 1,500	
5/2	5,000	5/15	2,000		
5/10	3,300	5/25	1,500		
5/17	700				

The payment of salaries to employees is recorded by a debit to the expense account, salaries expense, and a credit to the asset account, cash. This entry illustrates the rules that increases in expenses are recorded by debits and decreases in assets are recorded by credits.

May 27. Kilmer Contractors paid dividends of $600.

This transaction is a distribution of the earnings of the business. Cash and stockholders' equity are both decreased by $600. It is recorded as follows:

5/27	Dividends	600	
	Cash		600

Cash				Dividends	
5/1	500	5/5	3,000	5/27 600	
5/2	5,000	5/15	2,000		
5/10	3,300	5/25	1,500		
5/27	700	5/27	600		

The $600 distribution of earnings by the business is recorded by a debit to the dividends account and a credit to the cash account. This entry illustrates the rules that decreases in equity accounts are recorded by debits and decreases in asset accounts are recorded by credits.

Posting to the Ledger

The first step in the recording process is to record the transactions in the general journal. The second step in the recording process is to post each of the journal entries to the appropriate ledger accounts. Posting is the process of transferring the individual debits and credits of each entry to the appropriate account or accounts in the ledger. This step enables the accountant to summarize and group the transactions that occurred according to the individual accounts affected. For each transaction, the debit amount in the journal entry is posted by entering it on the debit side of the appropriate ledger account and each credit amount in the entry is posted by entering it on the credit side of the appropriate ledger account. In the previous section, the transactions of Kilmer Contractors were each journalized and then posted to the T-accounts. The general ledger accounts for Kilmer Contractors are shown on the next page.

Now examine the initial May 1 transaction of Kilmer Contractors to illustrate the process of recording and posting in detail. Recall that the initial transaction of Kilmer Contractors was as follows:

May 1.   Bill Kilmer organized Kilmer Contractors and issued common stock for $500.

This transaction is recorded by the following general journal entry:

5/1	Cash	500	
	Common stock		500

It is posted to the ledger as follows:

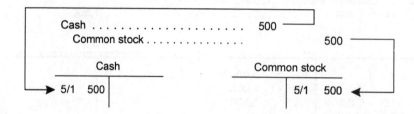

The debit to cash of $500 in the journal entry is posted to the debit side of the cash account in the general ledger and the credit to common stock of $500 is posted to the credit side of the common stock account in the general ledger. The date in the ledger accounts provides a reference back to the original source of the posting, the general journal. The dates of the transactions appear by each amount and are included for reference purposes. Usually, a page reference will also be provided by each entry in the journal and each account in the general ledger in order to facilitate the cross-referencing of transactions. Refer back to Illustration 1 for a detailed example.

Trial Balance

After all of the transactions in the general journal have been posted to the general ledger, the next step in the accounting process is to prepare a trial balance. A trial balance is simply a listing of all of the accounts included in the general ledger along with the balance, debit or credit, of each account.

In preparing the trial balance, first determine the balance in each account, as illustrated below. This balance is the difference between the total debits and the total credits. Next the accounts and their balances are listed in order—assets, liabilities, common stock, dividends, revenues, and expenses. Debits and credits are totalled to prove the accounts are in balance.

Cash			
5/1	500	5/5	3,000
5/2	5,000	5/15	2,000
5/10	3,300	5/25	1,500
5/17	700	5/27	600
Bal.	2,400		

Accounts Receivable			
5/19	900		
Bal.	900		

Supplies			
5/2	3,000		
Bal.	3,000		

Note Payable			
5/15	2,000	5/2	5,000
		Bal.	3,000

Unearned Fees			
		5/10	3,300
		Bal.	3,300

Common Stock			
		5/1	500
		Bal.	500

Dividends			
5/27	600		
Bal.	600		

Painting Fees			
		5/17	700
		5/19	900
		Bal.	1,600

Salaries Expense			
5/25	1,500		
Bal.	1,500		

The purpose of a trial balance is simply to prove that the total of debits equals the total of credits and to "catch" or detect any obvious errors that may have occurred in either the recording or the posting process. You should note, however, that even if the total of the debits in the trial balance is equal to the total of the credits, this proves only that the accounts are "in balance;" it does not indicate that errors have not been made. (For example, a posting could have been made to the wrong account or a transaction may not have been posted at all.)

The trial balance of Kilmer Contractors at May 31, 19X1, before adjustments is presented in Illustration 2.

Illustration 2

Kilmer Contractors
Trial Balance before Adjustment
May 31, 19X1

	Debit	Credit
Cash	$2,400	
Accounts receivable	900	
Supplies	3,000	
Note payable		$3,000
Unearned fees		3,300
Common stock		500
Dividends	600	
Painting fees		1,600
Salaries	1,500	
Total	$8,400	$8,400

Adjusting Entries

As previously indicated, the accrual basis of accounting requires that revenues be recorded as they are earned and expenses be recorded as they are incurred. This procedure is followed whether or not any cash has been received or disbursed. At the end of any period, then, there are usually transactions that are still in the process of completion or that have occurred but have not yet been recorded. These transactions require adjusting entries so that all revenues, expenses, gains, and losses (and related assets and liabilities) are stated properly at the end of the period. In the case of Kilmer Contractors, adjustments are required for: (1) the revenue that was earned by painting two of the three houses contracted for on May 10 and (2) the painting supplies that were used during the month of May. These adjustments, referred to as adjusting entries, are recorded in the accounts by the general journal entries presented below.

May 31. Kilmer Contractors painted two of the three houses contracted for on May 10.

This adjustment records the earning of revenue from painting two of the three houses. The unearned fees have been partially earned. It is recorded by the following journal entry:

| 5/31 | Unearned fees | 2,200 | |
| | Painting fees | | 2,200 |

Unearned Fees					Painting Fees		
5/31	2,200	5/10	3,300			5/17	700
						5/19	900
						5/31	2,200

Recall that on May 10 Kilmer Contractors signed a contract whereby the company agreed to paint three houses at a future date and received its fee of $1,100 per house in advance. No revenue was earned at the point the contract was signed and the cash received, because no work had been done at that time. Kilmer Contractors had an obligation to paint the three houses at a future date. This was a liability to perform services, which was recorded as unearned fees. Now, at the end of May, two of the three houses contracted for have been painted and that portion of the revenue has been earned. The liability, unearned fees, has been reduced by $2,200 and the revenue for May has been increased by $2,200. These facts require that the financial statements be adjusted in order to reflect the current status of the contract. Again, this transaction emphasizes the fact that revenue is recorded as it is earned, not necessarily as cash is received.

The decrease of $2,200 in the liability, unearned fees, is recorded by a debit to the unearned fees account and the increase in the revenue, painting fees, is recorded by a credit to the painting fees account. This adjusting entry illustrates the rules that decreases in liabilities are recorded by debits and increases in revenues are recorded by credits.

May 31. The unused painting supplies on hand at this date had an original cost of $2,000.

The facts of this transaction indicate that an expense has been incurred during the month but has not yet been recorded in the accounts. The following adjusting entry is required at May 31:

| 5/31 | Supplies expense | 1,000 | |
| | Supplies | | 1,000 |

Supplies Expense			Supplies			
5/31	1,000		5/2	3,000	5/31	1,000

During May, Kilmer Contractors used supplies that had an original cost of $1,000. This amount was determined by subtracting the $2,000 cost of the supplies still on hand at May 31 from the $3,000 total cost of supplies that were available for use (that is, the supplies purchased during the month plus the beginning-of-the-month supplies amount, which in this case is zero). As in the previous May 31 transaction, an adjusting entry is required. The asset, supplies, is decreased by $1,000 (the cost of the supplies used), from $3,000 (the total supplies available for use during the month of May) to $2,000 (the cost of supplies still on hand at May 31). This transaction reflects the fact that expenses are recorded when incurred rather than necessarily when cash is disbursed.

The increase in the supplies used is recorded by a debit to the supplies expense account. The decrease in the asset, supplies, is recorded by a credit to the supplies account. This adjusting entry illustrates the rules that increases in expenses are recorded by debits and decreases in assets are recorded by credits.

After these two journal entries have been made, all of the transactions that occurred during the month of May for Kilmer Contractors have been recorded in the accounts.

POSTING THE ADJUSTING ENTRIES

The adjusting entries are then posted to the ledger in the same manner as are the regular journal entries. This has been done below. Again, the dates of the transactions are included for purposes of reference. (Note that the two adjusting entries are dated May 31.)

Cash					Accounts Receivable				Supplies			
5/1	500	5/5	3,000		5/19	900			5/2	3,000	5/31	1,000
5/2	5,000	5/15	2,000									
5/10	3,300	5/25	1,500									
5/17	700	5/27	600									
Bal.	2,400				Bal.	900			Bal.	2,000		

Note Payable					Unearned Fees				Common Stock		
5/15	2,000	5/2	5,000		5/31	2,200	5/10	3,300		5/1	500
		Bal.	3,000				Bal.	1,100		Bal.	500

Dividends				Painting Fees		
5/27	600				5/17	700
					5/19	900
					5/31	2,200
Bal.	600				Bal.	3,800

Salaries Expense			Supplies Expense		
5/25	1,500		5/31	1,000	
Bal.	1,500		Bal.	1,000	

TRIAL BALANCE AFTER ADJUSTMENT

The next step in the recording process is the preparation of a trial balance after adjustment. This trial balance is prepared after the adjusting entries have been made and posted to the general ledger. The trial balance after adjustment for Kilmer Contractors is presented in Illustration 3. Again, the only difference between the trial balance after adjustment and the trial balance before adjustment presented previously is the inclusion of the effect of the adjusting entries that were made.

CLOSING ENTRIES

The purpose of closing entries is to close the temporary accounts (revenues, expenses, gains, losses, and dividends) into the stockholders' equity account retained earnings at the end of the period. This process is facilitated by the introduction of a temporary account created solely for the closing process. This account is

Illustration 3

Kilmer Contractors
Trial Balance after Adjustment
May 31, 19X1

	Debit	Credit
Cash	$2,400	
Accounts receivable	900	
Supplies	2,000	
Note payable		$3,000
Unearned fees		1,100
Common stock		500
Dividends	600	
Painting fees		3,800
Salaries expense	1,500	
Supplies expense	1,000	
Total	$8,400	$8,400

known as the income summary account and is used to collect or summarize all of the revenues, expenses, gains, and losses of the firm in a single account that is then, in turn, closed to the retained earnings account.

The purpose of the closing process is to systematically reduce each of the balances in the temporary accounts to a zero balance at the end of the accounting period. Each temporary income statement account with a debit balance is credited for an amount that results in a zero balance in the account, and the total of these accounts is debited to income summary. Similarly, each of the temporary income statement accounts with a credit balance is debited for an amount that yields a zero balance, and the total of these debits is credited to income summary. The resulting balance in the income summary account is closed to the retained earnings account.

In addition, the dividends account is credited and the retained earnings account is debited for an amount that results in a zero balance in the dividends account. Note that the dividends account is closed directly into the retained earnings account. It does not go through the income summary account. This means that at the beginning of the next period all revenues, expenses, gains, losses and dividends accounts will have zero balances so that these accounts can be used again in order to record the results of operations for the new period.

The closing process is accomplished by the preparation of journal entries known as closing entries. These entries are recorded in the general journal and posted to the ledger in the same manner as all other transactions are processed.

We now illustrate the closing process for Kilmer Contractors. The journal entries required to close out the revenue and expense accounts are made at the end of the month of May, the accounting period used in this illustration. Referring back to the trial balance after adjustment for Kilmer Contractors, the temporary accounts are as follows:

	Balance	
	Debit	Credit
Dividends	$ 600	
Painting fees		$3,800
Salaries expense	1,500	
Supplies expense	1,000	

The entry to close out the revenue account is:

5/31	Painting fees	3,800	
	Income summary		3,800

Painting Fees				
		5/17	700	
		5/19	900	
		5/31	2,200	
5/31	3,800	Bal.	3,800	
			0	

Income Summary	
5/31	3,800

A revenue account has a credit balance. Therefore, the entry that is required in order to close out the balance in a revenue account consists of a debit to the revenue account for the total revenue for the period and a credit to the income summary account for the same amount. This entry closes out (i.e., brings the account balance to zero) the revenue account and transfers the total for the period to the credit side of the income summary account.

In our illustration, the painting fees account is now closed and has a zero balance, and the $3,800 revenue from painting fees has been transferred to the credit side of the income summary account.

The two expense accounts are closed out by the following entry:

5/31	Income summary	2,500	
	Salaries expense		1,500
	Supplies expense		1,000

Salaries Expense			
5/25	1,500		
Bal.	1,500	5/31	1,500
	0		

Supplies Expense			
5/31	1,000		
Bal.	1,000	5/31	1,000
	0		

Income Summary			
5/13	2,500	5/31	3,800

An expense account has a debit balance. Therefore, the entry that is required in order to close out the balance in an expense account credits the expense account for the total expense for the period and debits the income summary account for this amount. This closing entry reduces the expense account balance to zero and transfers the total expenses for the period to the debit side of the income summary account.

Both the salaries expense and the supplies expense accounts are now closed out and the total of these two accounts ($1,500 + $1,000 = $2,500), the total expense for the period, has been transferred to the debit side of the income summary account.

The balance in the income summary account ($3,800 − $2,500 = $1,300) is then transferred to the retained earnings account by the following closing entry:

5/31	Income summary	1,300	
	Retained earnings		1,300

Income Summary			
5/31	2,500	5/31	3,800
5/31	1,300	Bal.	1,300
			0

Retained Earnings	
5/1	0
5/31	1,300

As indicated above, all revenue, expense, gain, and loss accounts are closed to the income summary account. Therefore, the credit side of the income summary account includes the total revenues and gains for the period while the debit side of the account includes the total expenses and losses. The income summary account balance is the income or loss of the business for the period. If the total of the credits (revenues plus gains) in the income summary account exceeds the total of the debits (expenses plus losses), revenues and gains are greater than expenses and losses and the difference is the income for the period. On the other hand, if the total of the credits (revenues plus gains) is less than the total of the debits (expenses plus losses), expenses and losses exceed revenues and gains and the difference is the loss for the period. In either case, the balance in the income summary account after all of the revenue, expense, gain, and loss accounts have been closed is transferred to the retained earnings account.

In the Kilmer Contractors example, the balance in the income summary account, a credit of $1,300 (revenues of $3,800 less expenses of $2,500), is closed and the $1,300 income for the period is transferred to the retained earnings account.

As a final step in the closing process, the balance in any dividends account is closed to retained earnings. In the Kilmer Contractors illustration, this step is to close the balance in the dividends account directly to retained earnings.

5/31	Retained earnings	600	
	Dividends		600

Dividends				Retained Earnings			
5/27	600			5/31	600	5/1	0
Bal.	600	5/31	600			5/31	1,300
	0						

Dividends do not pass through the income summary account since they are not expenses of the period and therefore do not enter into the determination of income. The dividends account has a debit balance. Therefore, the closing entry required to close dividends credits the dividends account and debits the retained earnings account for the dividends during the period.

The closing process (assuming there is income for the period) can be depicted graphically as follows:

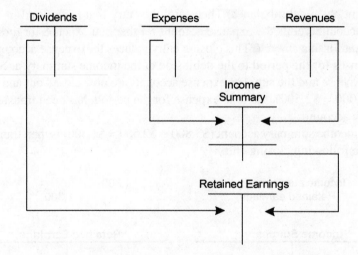

In terms of the specific accounts that were used in the Kilmer Contractors illustration, the closing process is shown below, after all of the closing entries are posted to the accounts.

Closing Entries:

(a) To close revenues to income summary: Painting fees 3,800
                                                  Income summary 3,800

(b) To close expenses to income summary: Income summary 2,500
                                                  Salaries expense 1,500
                                                  Supplies expense 1,000

(c) To close income summary to retained earnings   Income summary 1,300
                                                  Retained earnings 1,300

(d) To close dividends to retained earnings: Retained earnings 600
                                                  Dividends 600

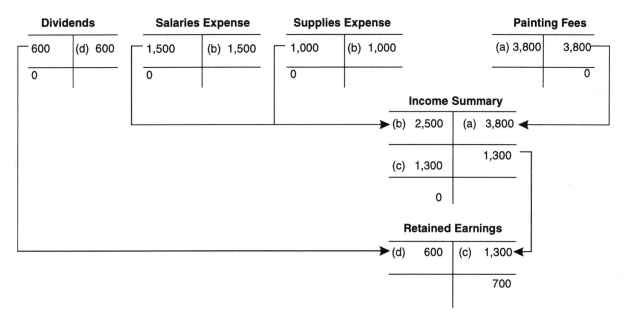

After-Closing Trial Balance

After all of the temporary accounts have been closed, a trial balance, referred to as an after-closing trial balance, may be prepared as a test of the equality of the total debits and credits. The after-closing trial balance of Kilmer Contractors is presented in Illustration 4. Since all of the temporary accounts have been closed, the after-closing trial balance includes only the permanent or balance sheet accounts.

Financial Statements

After all of the adjusting and closing entries have been prepared and the posting process has been completed, the general ledger account balances are up-to-date as of the end of the period. The information regarding the assets, liabilities, common stock, retained earnings, revenues, expenses, gains, and losses included in the general ledger are used as a basis for preparing the financial statements.

The revenues, expenses, gains, and losses for the period are taken from the general ledger and used to prepare the income statement. The trial balance after adjustment and the detailed amounts included in the income summary account may be used as a check on the accuracy of the income statement, because both of these sources include the details of the revenues, expenses, gains, and losses for the period. The statement of stockholders' equity is prepared using the stockholders' equity accounts from the general ledger as a source.

```
                        Illustration 4

                      Kilmer Contractors
                   After-Closing Trial Balance
                          May 31, 19X1

                                          Debit        Credit

    Cash .........................       $2,400
    Accounts receivable ............        900
    Supplies .....................       2,000
    Note payable .................                     $3,000
    Unearned fees ................                      1,100
    Common stock ................                         500
    Retained earnings .............                       700
      Total                            $5,300         $5,300
```

Asset, liability, and stockholders' equity balances as of the end of the period are taken from the after-closing trial balance and used to prepare the balance sheet. The statement of cash flows is prepared by examining the details of the cash account in the general ledger.

The financial statements for Kilmer Contractors for the month of May are shown in Illustrations 5-8.

```
                        Illustration 5

                      Kilmer Contractors
                      Income Statement
                 For the Month Ending May 31, 19X1

    Revenues from painting services ........        $3,800
    Supplies expense ...................   $1,000
    Salaries expense ...................    1,500
        Total expenses ..................            2,500
    Net income for May .................             $1,300
```

In review, several points should be noted for the Kilmer Contractors example. First, the general journal entries were prepared as the transactions occurred. These entries represent a chronological record of the transactions that took place during the month of May. These journal entries were then posted to the ledger accounts. At the end of the month, a trial balance was prepared. The transactions and the status of the company at that point in time were reviewed and any adjustments that were necessary to bring the accounts up-to-date were made.

The next step in the process was the preparation of a trial balance after adjustment. Again, it is important to note that any trial balance proves only the equality of the totals of the debits and the credits; it gives no other assurance as to the absence of errors.

Entries were then prepared to "close-out" all temporary accounts—the revenues, expenses, and dividends for the period. These were the only accounts closed. The permanent accounts—assets, liabilities, common stock and retained earnings—that appear in the balance sheet were not closed. The closing entries summarize the balances of the revenue and expense accounts in an income summary account.[5] The balance in the dividends account was then closed to the retained earnings account. The closing entries were then posted to the ledger, and the after-closing trial balance was prepared. Then the financial statements were prepared.

---

[5] Note that the income summary is, in fact, a duplication of the income statement itself. That is, the credits to the income summary are the revenues for the period and the debits are the expenses for the period. The difference, or balancing figure, is the income (or loss) for the period.

Illustration 6

Kilmer Contractors
Statement of Stockholders' Equity
For the Month Ending May 31, 19X1

	Common Stock	Retained Earnings
Balances, May 1, 19X1	$ 0	$ 0
Issued common stock	500	
Net income		1,300
Dividends		(600)
Balances, May 31, 19X1	$500	$ 700

Illustration 7

Kilmer Contractors
Balance Sheet
May 31, 19X1

Assets		Liabilities and Stockholders' Equity		
Cash	$2,400	Note payable	$3,000	
Accounts receivable	900	Unearned fees	1,100	$4,100
Supplies	2,000	Common stock		500
		Retained earnings		700
Total assets	$5,300	Total liabilities and stockholders' equity . . .		$5,300

Illustration 8

Kilmer Contractors
Statement of Cash Flows
For the Month Ending May 31, 19X1

Cash flows from operations:		
Receipts from customers		$4,000
Payments to:		
Suppliers	$3,000	
Employees	1,500	4,500
Decrease in cash due to operations		($ 500)
Cash flows from financing activities:		
Receipts from:		
Issuance of common stock	$ 500	
Borrowing	5,000	
Payments for:		
Repaying loan	(2,000)	
Dividends	(600)	
Increase in cash due to financing activities		$2,900
Increase in cash		$2,400

COMPARATIVE STATEMENTS

Comparative statements, as opposed to statements of a single period, increase the usefulness of financial statements. *Comparative statements allow the user to learn about the trends affecting the financial position, operating results, and cash flows of an enterprise.* Comparative statements for Wal-Mart are presented in the first chapter of this text.

In addition to comparative financial statements, many companies present a financial review for an extended period of time (e.g., 10 years). *Items that are reported in these financial reviews include revenues, cost of goods sold, interest expense, income taxes, net income, extraordinary items, earnings per share, dividends, current assets, total assets, stockholders' equity, shares of stock outstanding, and average stock prices.* The specific items that are included in the financial review vary from company to company.

DISCLOSURE TECHNIQUES

Footnotes to the financial statements and supporting schedules are used to increase the information that is available in the financial statements. Frequently, the information that is included on the balance sheet is very brief, and more complete explanations are presented in the footnotes and supporting schedules. *Parenthetical notations are used to clarify or cross reference items included on the face of the balance sheet.*

Almost all large companies round the amounts presented in the financial statements to the nearest thousand dollars, or million dollars. Wal-Mart rounded its financial statement amounts to the nearest million dollars.

Although the specific format that is used in the balance sheet varies somewhat among companies, *there are two basic formats that may be used: the report form and the account form.* The report form presents the balance sheet on one page by listing the assets first, followed by the liabilities and the stockholders' equity. The account form differs from the report form in that the balance sheet is presented on two pages; the assets are listed on the left-hand page of the statement and the liabilities and stockholders' equity accounts are listed on the right-hand page. Wal-Mart's balance sheet presented in Chapter 1 is in the report form.

AUDITOR'S REPORT

Since many users rely on the fairness and accuracy of financial statements, independent audits of financial statements by CPAs have evolved and have become common practice. *The certified public accountant audits the accounting records, supporting documents, physical properties, and financial statements to decide whether the financial statements and the accompanying notes have been prepared in accordance with generally accepted accounting principles, and whether they present fairly the financial position, results of operations, and cash flows.* If these conditions are met, the auditor then gives the company an unqualified opinion. If not, then the auditor gives a qualified opinion, an adverse opinion, or a disclaimer of opinion, depending upon his or her findings. These opinions are explained in detail in Chapter 18. For financial reports filed with the Securities and Exchange Commission, an unqualified opinion is required.

SUMMARY

Transactions that affect the financial statements of a firm occur much too frequently to permit a revision of the statements after each transaction takes place. Therefore, firms use various "accounting systems" that record and summarize these transactions. This allows the accountant to use the summarized data provided by the accounting system to prepare financial statements at designated points in time. The most commonly used accounting system, and the one discussed in this chapter, is the "double-entry" system.

The basic element of the double-entry system is the account. An account is simply a place or means of collecting and summarizing all of the transactions that affect a particular asset, liability, or stockholders' equity account. Each account is increased or decreased by use of debits (left-side entries) and credits (right-side entries). A debit entry increases assets and expenses, but decreases liabilities, stockholders' equity, and revenue accounts. Conversely, a credit entry increases liabilities, stockholders' equity, and revenues, but decreases assets and expenses.

The actual recording process involves a number of separate but related steps. The initial step is the preparation of the general journal entries at the time the transactions take place. These general journal entries are then posted to the individual accounts in the ledger. After these two steps are completed, the accountant prepares a trial balance before adjustment. This trial balance is simply a listing of each account and the corresponding debit or credit balance in the account. This listing will detect only the most obvious errors and does not guarantee that other errors have not been made.

The next step in the recording process is the preparation of adjusting entries. These entries are necessary to adjust the accounts so that the final balances will properly reflect the revenues, expenses, gains, and losses of the accounting period. The adjusting entries are then posted to the appropriate ledger accounts and a trial balance after adjustment is prepared.

The next phase in the recording process is the preparation of closing entries. These entries are required to close the temporary accounts (revenues, expenses, gains, losses, and dividends) so that these accounts can be used to accumulate similar data for the next accounting period. To accomplish this, all revenues, expenses, gains, and losses are closed to the income summary account. The income summary account and the dividends account are then closed to the retained earnings account. Once the closing entries are prepared and entered into the general journal, they are then posted to the ledger accounts and an after-closing trial balance is prepared.

The final step is the actual preparation of the financial statements. As indicated in previous chapters, the primary financial statements prepared by the accountant are the income statement, statement of stockholders' equity, balance sheet, and statement of cash flows.

This chapter has introduced and traced the basic recording process used by most accounting systems. The next chapter illustrates and discusses the worksheet, one of the tools employed by accountants in this recording process, and provides more information regarding the nature and function of adjusting entries.

Key Definitions

Account—a place or means of summarizing all of the transactions that affect a particular asset, liability, equity, revenue, expense, gain, or loss item.

Adjusting entries—at the end of an accounting period, adjusting entries record the transactions which are in process or have been completed but not yet recorded. These entries are necessary in order to record revenues when they are earned and expenses when they are incurred, and not necessarily when cash is received or paid. This is in accordance with the accrual concept of accounting.

Closing entries—the purpose of closing entries is to close or transfer the balances in the temporary accounts (revenues, expenses, gains, losses, and dividends) into the retained earnings account.

Credit—the term used to identify the right-hand side of an account. A credit decreases an asset or expense account and increases a liability, equity, or revenue account.

Debit—the term used to describe the left-hand side of an account. By debiting an asset or expense account, the account is increased and by debiting a liability or equity or revenue account, the account is decreased.

Dividends—distributions of cash or other assets to the stockholders (owners) of a corporation.

Double-entry method—this method requires that for every transaction recorded, the total dollar amount of debits must be equal to the total dollar amount of credits.

General journal entry—a means of recording the transactions of a firm chronologically in terms of debits and credits.

General ledger—a compilation of all the accounts of a firm and their balances.

Posting—posting to ledger accounts is the process of transferring the information from the general journal to the individual accounts of the general ledger. This enables the accountant to review and summarize all changes in the accounts.

Trial balance—a listing of all the accounts in the general ledger. If the accounts are "in balance," the total of the accounts with debit balances will equal the total of those with credit balances. The trial balance indicates only that the accounts are in balance. It does not prove that errors have not been made in the recording process.

QUESTIONS

1. What is the purpose of the double-entry system of recording business transactions?

2. Explain the terms "debit" and "credit." What effect does each of these have on asset and liability accounts?

3. What is the general rule of the double-entry system?

4. Describe a general journal entry.

5. What is a T-account?

6. What is "posting?"

7. What is the purpose of a trial balance?

8. What concept of accounting requires adjusting entries? Explain.

9. What type of accounts do closing entries affect? Why are these accounts closed?

EXERCISES

10. The first nine transactions of a newly formed business, Smart Company, appear in the T-accounts below. For each set of debits and credits, explain the nature of the transaction. Each entry is designated by the small letters to the left of the amount.

	Cash					Accounts Receivable		
(a)	10,000	(c)	2,000		(d)	6,000	(g)	2,000
(g)	2,000	(e)	4,000					
(i)	2,500	(f)	1,000					
		(h)	1,500					

	Equipment					Accounts Payable		
(b)	3,000				(f)	1,000	(b)	3,000

	Unearned Fees					Common Stock		
		(i)	2,500				(a)	10,000

	Land					Fees Earned		
(c)	2,000						(d)	6,000

	Wage Expense					Rent Expense		
(e)	4,000				(h)	1,500		

11. Assume that the ledger accounts given in Exercise 10 are for the Smart Company as of December 31, 19X1. Prepare a trial balance for Smart Company as of that date.

12. Prepare the closing entries, the income statement for 19X1 and the balance sheet as of December 31, 19X1, for the Smart Company assuming the data given in 10.

13. Jane Feller opened a driving range and the following transactions took place in July, 19X1:

July 1   The owner purchased $10,000 of the common stock of the business.
     5   Purchased fixed assets for $5,000, made a cash down payment of $2,000, and signed a 60-day note for the balance.
     10   The total revenue for the month was $1,500, $1,200 in cash was collected, and the balance was owed on account by customers.
     15   The total expenses for the month were $1,100, $900 was paid in cash, and the balance was owed on account.
     25   Dividends of $100 were paid.

Required:

Prepare the journal entries to record these transactions and enter the debits and credits in T-accounts.

14. After recording and posting the transactions from 13, prepare a trial balance for Feller Company as of July 31, 19X1.

15. Given the following T-accounts, prepare the closing entries for the White Company for the month of August, 19X0.

	Cash					Accounts Receivable		
B. B.	20,000	1,100	(2)		B.B.	4,000	2,000	(1)
(1)	2,000	5,000	(4)		(6)	7,000		
(3)	35,000	2,800	(5)			9,000		
		14,000	(9)					
		900	(10)					
		500	(11)					
	32,700							

	Supplies					Note Payable		
B.B.	800	1,000	(8)		(5)	2,800	2,800	B.B.
(2)	1,100							
	900							

	Unearned Fees					Common Stock		
(7)	30,000	7,000	B.B.				15,000	B.B.
		35,000	(3)				15,000	
		12,000						

	Dividends				Fees Earned		
(4)	5,000					7,000	(6)
	5,000					30,000	(7)
						37,000	

	Supplies Expense				Salaries	
(8)	1,000			(9)	14,000	
	1,000				14,000	

	Utilities				Property Taxes	
(10)	900			(11)	500	
	900				500	

16. Using the information in Exercise 15, prepare an after-closing trial balance for White Company.

17. From the information given in Exercise 15, prepare a balance sheet, income statement, and statement of stockholders' equity for White Company.

Problems

18. Presented below are the transactions of the Home Finder Realty Company for the month of May, 19X1.

May 1   The owners purchased $20,000 of the common stock of the business.
       3   Purchased office equipment for $1,800 on account.
       5   Purchased a car for $3,000, giving $1,000 in cash and a note payable of $2,000.
     10   Purchased $500 of office supplies on account.
     15   Paid $300 office rent for the month of May.
     16   Paid for office supplies purchased on May 10.
     18   Received a bill for $200 for radio advertising.
     20   Earned and collected $1,500 commission for the sale of a house.
     21   Paid bill for advertising that was received on May 18.
     23   Earned but did not collect an $800 commission.
     25   Paid salaries of $400.
     27   Received payment in full from customer of May 23.
     29   Paid the telephone bill. $50

Required:

Prepare the general journal entries that would be required to record the above transactions.

19. On September 1, 19X1, Mary Walls, a bookkeeper, organized a bookkeeping service business. The following events occurred during September.

Sept. 1   Walls purchased $10,000 of the common stock of the business.
       2   Paid September rent of $250.
       4   Purchased office furniture for $2,000 on account.
       6   Received and paid a bill for $200 for advertising in the local newspaper.
       9   Received cash of $1,400 as payment for services to customers.
     15   Paid the $300 salary of a part-time secretary.
     17   Paid for office furniture purchased on account.
     18   Purchased $150 of office supplies on account.
     20   Received a utilities bill for $75.
     21   Completed $600 of services on credit for customers.
     23   Collected $200 of receivables for credit services provided.
     27   Dividends of $600 were paid.

Required:

a. Prepare the general journal entries to record the above transactions.
b. Post the above journal entries to T-accounts.
c. Prepare a trial balance as of the end of September.
d. Prepare closing entries.

20. The following transactions involving the Mantle Company occurred during the month of July, 19X1:

July 1   Mantle organized the company, purchasing $1,000 of the common stock of the company.
      3   Purchased office supplies paying $100 in cash.
      6   Performed services for his first customer and collected $500 in cash.
      9   Performed services for another customer and agreed to accept his payment of $700 later in the month.
    13   Contracted to perform certain services for a third customer and received the full payment of $1,000 in advance.
    18   Received the payment from the customer for whom services were performed on July 9.
    24   Paid the following operating items:

Salaries for July	$250
Office rent for July and August	300
Other July expense	75

           (Mantle will prepare financial statements at the end of July.)
    31   Noted that exactly one-fourth of the services contracted for on the thirteenth by a customer had been performed. Counted the office supplies on hand and ascertained that supplies with an original cost of $65 were still on hand.

Required:

a. Record the above transactions with general journal entries.
b. Post the journal entries by entering debits and credits in T-accounts.
c. Prepare a trial balance as of July 31, 19X1.
d. Prepare closing entries.

21. Below is the trial balance of the Nittany Lion Company as of October 31, 19X1.

Cash	$10,000	
Accounts receivable	4,000	
Notes receivable	2,500	
Supplies	1,000	
Accounts payable		$ 4,500
Note payable		3,000
Unearned revenue		1,500
Common stock		5,000
Retained earnings		2,500
Dividends	500	
Revenues		3,000
Expenses	1,500	
	$19,500	$19,500

Required:

a. Prepare the entries which are necessary to close the accounts as of October 31, 19X1.
b. Prepare the following statements:

  1. Balance sheet.
  2. Income statement.
  3. Statement of stockholders' equity.

22. Certain data relating to River Corporation are presented below:

Trial balance data as of June 30, 19X1.

Advertising expense	$ 75
Cash	895
Commissions earned	1,900
Commissions receivable	950
Common stock	2,000
Interest earned	5
Land	2,000
Mercantile Company bonds	1,000
Note payable	700
Office rent	80
Retained earnings	1,195
Salaries expense	800

Adjusted trial balance data as of June 30, 19X1.

Accrued interest receivable	5
Accrued interest payable	7
Accrued rent receivable	55
Accrued salaries payable	100
Advertising expense	75
Cash	895
Commissions earned	1,960
Commissions receivable	1,010
Common stock	2,000
Interest earned	10

Interest expense	7
Land	2,000
Mercantile Company bonds	1,000
Note payable	700
Office rent	80
Rent earned	55
Retained earnings	1,195
Salaries expense	900

Required:

Compare the unadjusted and adjusted account balances and prepare the adjusting journal entries made by River Corporation as of June 30, 19X1. Also prepare the closing entries as of June 30, 19X1. (No dividends were paid during the period ending June 30, 19X1.)

23. The following information has been developed by the bookkeeper of the Sneed Company. It relates to the company's operations for 19X1.

	19X0	19X1
Cash receipts:		
From customers	$46,100	
Cash disbursements:		
For expenses	10,600	
Account balances as of December 31:		
Accounts receivable from customers, (all collectible)	$10,400	$9,600
Accrued expenses payable	1,900	1,600

Required:

Prepare the company's income statement for the year ended December 31, 19X1.

24. Following are given the *total debits* and *total credits* for the year (which include beginning-of-the year balances) in selected accounts of the Ace Company, *after the closing entries have been posted to the accounts as of December 31, 19X1.*

	Debits	Credits
Advertising expense	$ 210	$ 210
Salaries expense	700	700
Telephone expense	48	48
Prepaid insurance	90	15
Insurance expense	15	15
Fees earned	1,880	1,880
Dividends	600	600
Income summary	1,880	1,880
Accounts receivable	2,330	2,330
Retained earnings	600	19,257

Required:

Reconstruct the December 31, 19X1, *closing entries* (in general journal form).

25. Given the following data for the Havlicek Company for March, 19X1, prepare the following items:

1. Adjusting entries
2. Closing entries
3. Income statement
4. Statement of stockholders' equity
5. Balance sheet

Havlicek Company
Trial Balance Before Adjustment
March 31, 19X1

	Debit	Credit
Cash	$57,000	
Accounts receivable	4,500	
Supplies	2,000	
Note payable		$ 7,000
Unearned fees		20,000
Common stock		3,000
Retained earnings		30,000
Dividends	2,000	
Earned fees		12,000
Salaries	6,500	
	$72,000	$72,000

Additional data:

1. Supplies on hand at the end of March were $1,500.
2. Unearned fees decreased by $10,000 in March.

26. Presented below are the transactions of the Goodson Realty Company for the month of June, 19X1.

June 2   The owners purchased $15,000 of the common stock of the business.
5   Purchased office furniture for $1,500 cash.
7   Paid $300 in cash for June rent.
9   Office supplies of $200 were purchased on account.
10   Received and paid a bill for $300 for advertising in a local newspaper during June.
13   Paid wages of $200 in cash for the month of June.
15   Received a cash advance of $500 from a customer for services to be rendered during July.
16   Sold a house and collected $800 commission.
17   Sold a house and will collect the $600 commission in July.
21   Dividends of $500 were paid.
23   Received and paid the June telephone bill for $100.
25   Paid for office supplies purchased on June 9.
27   Paid the utilities bill for the month, $35.

Required:

Prepare the general journal entries necessary to record the above transactions.

27. On August 1, 19X1, Bill King began operating a bicycle repair shop. The transactions of the business during the month of August were as follows:

Aug. 2   King began the business by purchasing common stock for $15,000 in cash and then buying repair equipment with a fair value of $2,000 for the shop.
4   Purchased land for $4,000 cash.
7   Purchased a building for $20,000. The terms of the purchase required a cash payment of $5,000 and the issuance of a note payable for $15,000.
11   Purchased supplies on account in the amount of $700.
13   Completed repair work for customers and collected $700 cash.
15   Paid the $400 salary of an employee.
17   Completed repair work of $500 on credit.
19   Paid for supplies purchased on account.
21   Paid dividends of $300.
25   Received $500 cash for repair work previously completed.
27   Paid a $50 utility bill.
30   Made first payment of $1,000 on the note payable.

Required:

    a. Prepare the general journal entries to record each of the above transactions.
    b. Post the above journal entries to T-accounts.
    c. Prepare a trial balance as of the end of August.
    d. Prepare closing entries.

28. The Maryland Wholesale Company has kept no formal books of accounts. The owner has, however, made up a statement of assets and liabilities at the end of each year. For 19X1 and 19X2, a portion of this statement appears as follows, as of December 31:

	19X1	19X2
Cash	$3,000	$ 5,000
Accounts receivable	7,000	5,000
Accounts payable for expenses	8,000	10,000

An analysis of the checkbook for 19X2 shows: (1) deposits of all amounts received from customers totalling $50,000, and (2) cash payments to creditors for expenses amounting to $33,000.

Required:

Prepare the company's income statement for the year ended December 31, 19X2.

29. The following represents the adjusted trial balance for Hunt Company.

Hunt Company
Adjusted Trial Balance
As of December 31, 19x4

Account Title	Debit	Credit
Cash	$ 2,269	
Accounts Receivable	14,482	
Prepaid Rent	2,000	
Equipment	18,000	
Accumulated Depreciation		$12,000
Land	30,000	
Interest Payable		1,200
Notes Payable		10,000
Common Stock		20,000
Retained earnings		18,713
Service Revenue		24,940
Dividends	1,460	
Salary Expense	13,200	
Depreciation Expense	3,000	
Rent Expense	400	
Interest Expense	1,200	
Miscellaneous Expense	842	
Total	$86,853	$86,853

Required:

    a. Provide the closing entries that would be necessary on December 31, 19x4.
    b. Did the company earn a profit or loss during the period? How much?
    c. Prepare a post-closing trial balance.
    d. Explain why the totals on the post-closing trial balance are less than the totals in the adjusted trial balance.

30. Bill and Sue Fullerton are involved in divorce proceedings. When discussing a property settlement, Bill told Sue that he should take over the couple's investment in an apartment complex because she would be unable to absorb the loss that the apartments are generating. Sue was somewhat distrustful and asked Bill to support his contention. Bill produced the following income statement which was supported by a CPA's opinion that the statement was prepared in accordance with generally accepted accounting principles.

Fullerton Apartments
Income Statement
For the Year Ended December 31, 19x3

Rent Revenue		$290,000
Less Expenses:		
Depreciation Expense	$140,000	
interest Expense	100,000	
Maintenance Expense	32,000	
Management Fees	20,000	
Miscellaneous Expense	12,000	($304,000)
Net Loss		$ 14,000

Sue is reluctant to give up the apartments, but feels that she must because her present salary is only $25,000 per year. She says that if she takes the apartments the $14,000 loss would absorb a significant portion of her salary leaving her only $ 11,000 with which to support herself. Sue tells you that while the figures seem to support her husband's arguments, she feels that she is failing to see something.

Required:

Review the facts of this case and provide Sue Fullerton with recommendations.

31. For each of the transactions listed, indicate the effect(s), if any, on the company's year-end: (1) Balance Sheet, (2) Income Statement, and (3) Statement of Cash Flows. Your answers should be as complete and specific as possible.

   a. Owners form a business and purchase its common stock.
   b. Company purchases a truck for cash.
   c. Company performed services and billed (but did not collect) its fee.
   d. Paid employee salaries.
   e. Collected cash from customer for whom services were performed (in "c" above).

Refer to the Annual Report in Chapter 1 of the text.

32. Which account does not appear in the financial statements, but is used in the closing process?

33. Using a T-account, show how retained earnings changed from the previous year to the current year.

34. Using the information from the statement of cash flows, show in T-account form how cash and cash equivalents changed during the most recent year.

35. From the information presented in the income statement, create the Income Summary account and show how it was closed out.

36. Did accrued expenses increase or decrease in the most recent year?

ETHiCAL CASE

Molly is recording journal entries when she comes across a check for $3,500 written to the owner of the company. No documentation is attached so Molly debits owner's withdrawals and credits cash.

1. What is the ethical issue involved?
2. Who is affected by the scenario?
3. What might Molly have done?

FRAUD CASE: Fraud Examination

Fraud examination involves obtaining evidence; taking statements from employees and others; and interrogating the target (the person or persons suspected of committing the fraud). Most frauds are committed by one person acting alone.

Fraud examination also involves writing a report of the findings of the investigation; testifying as to the findings if the case goes to court; and assisting in the detection and prevention of fraud.

Fraud may occur "on book" or "off book" and there are various symptoms that may indicate the possible existence of fraud.

On-book fraud may involve such actions as theft of inventory, cash, or other assets, and an attempt to cover the theft by falsifying accounting records and supporting documents (cook the books). Off-book fraud involves the theft of assets before a record is made of the receipt of those assets. For example, a purchasing agent may strike a deal with a supplier to submit false invoices or inflated invoices with the two crooks splitting the profits from their thefts. Another example is a receiving clerk stealing incoming merchandise before a record is made of the count and compared with the bill of lading (invoice). A shortage is thus reported to the supplier who suffers the loss.

Identifying symptoms of fraud is possible by careful management of a business. Such management requires accounting document examination for any suspicious or irregular items; observation of behavioral characteristics of employees; follow-up on tips and complaints; and other actions.

Management should constantly be on guard for fraud symptoms such as the following:

SUSPICIOUS OR IRREGULAR DOCUMENTS. Those documents that are unusual should be brought to the attention of management for review to determine appropriateness. For example, an unusually large sales return or allowance or several such transactions in a certain store or certain department.

PERFORMANCE OF ANALYTICAL COMPARISONS. The performance of a department or segment of the business should be compared with the expected results to identify unusual fluctuations or events. This is one of the most effective fraud identification techniques. For example, comparing sales and profit in a supermarket chain revealed a fraud at one of the supermarkets in the chain. The fraud was suspected because a particular market's sales and profit was out of line with the other markets. A closer examination detected an employee skimming cash at a checkout stand.

OBSERVATION OF BEHAVIOR CHARACTERISTICS. Any employee behaving in an unusual manner should be watched. There may be a simple explanation for the unusual behavior. On the other hand, the employee may be distraught because of his or her stress due to a fraud coverup over a long period of time. Employees committing fraud usually cannot afford to be sick, take vacations, or be away from work for any reason because their replacement may discover the fraud scheme. Therefore, their behavior may change drastically over time due to stress and management should not let such behavior go uninvestigated.

EMPLOYEE LIFESTYLE SYMPTOMS. An employee who is living beyond his or her means or quits his or her job while enjoying a significant improvement in lifestyle is an employee whose work and records should be carefully examined. As a case in point, a young woman from a very small town in western Nebraska was employed as dormant accounts clerk by Citibank in New York. She worked into a position of responsibility and embezzled $3.3 million from the bank. After terminating her employment, she and her husband built a million dollar mansion in Kansas City and a luxurious cabin on a Missouri lake. When they attempted to join an exclusive Kansas City country club, which required employment references, Citibank management was alerted to her change in lifestyle and began an investigation that uncovered the fraud.

TIPS AND COMPLAINTS FROM EMPLOYEES AND CUSTOMERS. Employee tips and customer complaints are the most important and frequent sources for uncovering fraud schemes. Management should never ignore a customer complaint regarding a billing for an account that has been paid because this may represent "lapping. ' which is a form of fraud involving stealing from one customer to cover shortages in other customers' accounts. Some customer's accounts are always short—not lapped—and, therefore, may be billed erroneously by the company.

Also, all companies should establish a "hot line" for employees to report suspected fraud. An employee reporting a suspected fraud should remain anonymous and be rewarded if fraud is uncovered and a conviction obtained. The Association of CFE maintained a national Hot Line for companies that wish to use the hot line service through the national CFE offices rather than their own offices.

DISCUSSION QUESTIONS:

1. Give some examples of "on-book fraud" and "off-book fraud."
2. Discuss some management action that may result in the detection of fraud (i.e. some fraud symptoms).

ETHICS CASE: BETTY LEE, CPA

Betty Lee, CPA, is the Controller of Pear Corporation, a producer of computer software products. The audit of Pear Corporation is currently under way by a national CPA firm and Betty Lee is being interviewed by one of the independent auditors regarding several important accounting controls. Establishing the controls and making sure they are working is the responsibility of Betty Lee and employees she supervises.

Betty Lee is aware that the controls are weak in some audit-sensitive areas. These weaknesses may result in the financial statements being overstated as to asset values and revenues and understated regarding the company's liabilities and expenses.

During her interview with the independent auditors regarding the controls, several specific questions are asked that relate to the control problems Betty Lee knows are critical and would influence the amount of work the auditors would need to do to determine the appropriateness of the company's financial statements.

DISCUSSION QUESTION:

In responding to the auditor's "specific questions, should Betty Lee give simple "yes" or "no" answers and protect the integrity of the company and save audit cost; or should she, being a CPA, elaborate on the questions put to her and explain fully the control problems that exist within the company?

In your considerations of Betty Lee's best course of action, you should assume that if she adopts a "tell all posture, she will likely cause a significant increase in audit cost and perhaps jeopardize her standing in the company's management structure. What would be the moral and ethical thing for Betty Lee to do?

Outline

LEARNING Objectives

Chapter 6 illustrates how the worksheet is used to facilitate financial statement preparation and discusses in detail the common types of adjusting entries included on the worksheet. Studying this chapter should enable you to:

1. Explain the purpose of the worksheet and how it assists in the preparation of financial statements.

2. Complete a worksheet when given the essential data.

3. Identify when revenues and expenses are recognized in an accrual system of accounting.

4. List the five common types of adjusting entries and give examples of each.

CHAPTER 6

The Worksheet and Adjustments

Introduction

Most businesses prepare annual reports for the use of their owners, creditors, and other interested parties. In addition to these reports, many companies also provide interim reports that cover periods of less than a year, such as a month or a quarter. In order to prepare financial statements at a date other than at the end of the accounting period, a worksheet is often used. The use of a worksheet avoids the necessity of many of the detailed procedures that are normally required in the adjustment and closing process. A worksheet summarizes the trial balance, adjusting entries, and, in effect, closing entries in one simple document. It facilitates the preparation of interim financial statements without recording the adjusting entries in the accounts. A worksheet may also be prepared and used in conjunction with the regular year-end closing process, when the accountant intends to record adjusting and closing entries in the accounts, as a valuable check on the recording process.

An understanding of the worksheet is also important for quite a different reason; it provides an excellent perspective as to the preparation of the income statement, statement of stockholders' equity, and balance sheet. In short, a critical review and understanding of the worksheet will provide you with an excellent overview of the entire reporting process and is particularly useful in developing an understanding of the adjusting and closing process, as well as the preparation of the basic financial statements. The worksheet, then, is a tool that is useful in both a practical and a conceptual sense.

An Illustration of the Preparation of a Worksheet

In order to illustrate the preparation of a worksheet, we will return again to the Kilmer Contractors example used in the previous chapters. Let's begin with the Trial Balance before Adjustment that was prepared in Chapter 5.

Kilmer Contractors
Trial Balance before Adjustment
May 31, 19X1

	Debit	Credit
Cash	$2,400	
Accounts receivable	900	
Supplies	3,000	
Note payable		$3,000
Unearned fees		3,300
Common stock		500
Dividends	600	
Painting fees		1,600
Salaries expense	1,500	
Total	$8,400	$8,400

Note that a trial balance before adjustment as of May 31, 19X1, is entered in the first two columns of the worksheet in Illustration 1. This trial balance before adjustment is the starting point in the preparation of a worksheet. The steps which are involved in the preparation of a worksheet are described below and depicted in Illustrations 1 through 7.

Step 1. As indicated above, the initial step in the preparation of the worksheet is to insert the trial balance before adjustment in the first two columns of the worksheet. This has been done in Illustration 1. Note that the worksheet includes six pairs of columns with each set divided into a debit and credit column. Also note that a line has been inserted for Retained earnings, 5/1/X1 between Common stock and Dividends.

Step 2. This step involves recording the adjusting journal entries in the second set of columns of the worksheet, the adjustment columns. The adjusting entries required for Kilmer Contractors are for: (a) the revenue earned from painting two of the three houses contracted for on May 10, and (b) the painting supplies used during the month of May.

Adjusting entry (a): The company received an advance payment of $3,300 from one of its customers on May 10 for the painting of three houses at some future date. By the end of May, Kilmer Contractors had painted two of the three houses; therefore, two-thirds of the $3,300 has been earned but not recorded in the accounts as earned revenue.

Adjusting entry (b): On May 2, Kilmer Contractors purchased painting supplies at a cost of $3,000. At May 31, the unused painting supplies on hand have an original cost of $2,000 indicating that supplies with a cost of $1,000 (supplies costing $3,000 originally purchased less the supplies still on hand with an original cost of $2,000) have been used during the month of May and should be recorded as supplies expense.

The adjusting entries required are recorded in the second set of columns of Illustration 2. Accounts affected by the adjusting entries but that do not appear in the trial balance before adjustment must be added to the original listing of accounts in the worksheet. For example, in adjustment (b) there is no account for supplies expense in the trial balance before adjustment. Therefore, the account title "supplies expense" is entered on the worksheet below the original trial balance accounts.

For purposes of reference, the debit and the credit amounts of each entry recorded in the adjustments columns have been associated with an identifying letter to the left of each amount. For example, note that the debit to unearned fees and the related credit to painting fees are labeled with the identifying letter (a). This notation indicates that this particular debit and credit go together and represent a single journal entry. Also observe that each adjusting journal entry is explained at the bottom of the worksheet with the same notation used as a reference. The columns are totalled to verify that debits equal credits.

Step 3. The third step in the worksheet process is the preparation of a trial balance after adjustment. The preparation of an adjusted trial balance indicates how the adjusting entries affect the various accounts. The adjusted trial balance is completed by combining the trial balance before adjustment (in the first two columns of the worksheet) with the adjustments made in the second set of columns. These are combined by adding or subtracting across the line. The credit to supplies of $1,000 is subtracted from the supplies balance of $3,000 before adjustment to obtain the balance of $2,000 after adjustment. On the other hand, the credit to painting fees of $2,200 is added to the painting fees balance of $1,600 before adjustment to obtain the balance of $3,800 after adjustment. The rule is that two debits are added, two credits are added, but a debit and a credit are subtracted. The resulting adjusted trial balance appears in the third set of columns of the worksheet in Illustration 3 . Note that the debit and credit columns of the trial balance after adjustment have been totalled in order to check the arithmetic accuracy of this step.

Step 4. The next step involves the transfer of each amount that appears in the adjusted trial balance to the appropriate columns of the income statement, statement of retained earnings, or balance sheet columns of the worksheet. All asset and liability accounts and common stock are transferred to the balance sheet columns. Retained earnings, 5/1/X1 is transferred to the statement of retained earnings columns, the dividends account is transferred to the statement of retained earnings columns, and all revenue and expense accounts are transferred to the income statement columns.

The balances in the cash, accounts receivable, supplies, notes payable, unearned fees, and common stock accounts are transferred directly to the balance sheet columns of the worksheet. The balances in the retained earnings account (which is the beginning retained earnings balance for the period) and the dividends account are transferred to the statement of retained earnings columns. The remaining accounts—painting fees, salaries, and supplies used—are transferred to the income statement columns. The worksheet after the transfer of each

Illustration 1
Kilmer Contractors
Worksheet
For the Month Ending May 31, 19X1

	Trial Balance before Adjustment		Adjustments		Trial Balance after Adjustment		Income Statement		Statement of Retained Earnings		Balance Sheet	
Cash.	2,400											
Accounts receivable.	900											
Supplies.	3,000											
Note payable.		3,000										
Unearned fees.		3,300										
Common stock.		500										
Retained earnings, 5/1/X1		0										
Dividends.	600											
Painting fees.		1,600										
Salaries expense.	1,500											
	8,400	8,400										

Illustration 2
Kilmer Contractors
Worksheet
For the Month Ending May 31, 19X1

	Trial Balance before Adjustment		Adjustments		Trial Balance after Adjustment		Income Statement		Statement of Retained Earnings		Balance Sheet	
Cash	2,400											
Accounts receivable	900											
Supplies	3,000			(b)1,000									
Note payable		3,000											
Unearned fees		3,300	(a)2,200										
Common stock		500											
Retained earnings, 5/1/X1		0											
Dividends	600											
Painting fees		1,600		(a)2,200									
Salaries expense	1,500												
Supplies expense			(b)1,000										
	8,400	8,400	3,200	3,200									

Key to Adjustments:
(a) To record revenue from two of the three houses contracted for on May 10.
(b) To record the cost of the supplies used during the month of May.

Illustration 3
Kilmer Contractors
Worksheet
For the Month Ending May 31, 19X1

	Trial Balance before Adjustment		Adjustments		Trial Balance after Adjustment		Income Statement		Statement of Retained Earnings		Balance Sheet	
Cash	2,400				2,400							
Accounts receivable	900				900							
Supplies	3,000			(b)1,000	2,000							
Note payable		3,000				3,000						
Unearned fees		3,300	(a)2,200			1,100						
Common stock		500				500						
Retained earnings, 5/1/X1		0				0						
Dividends	600				600							
Painting fees		1,600		(a)2,200		3,800						
Salaries expense	1,500				1,500							
Supplies expense			(b)1,000		1,000							
	8,400	8,400	3,200	3,200	8,400	8,400						

Key to Adjustments:
(a) To record revenue from two of the three houses contracted for on May 10.
(b) To record the cost of the supplies used during the month of May.

Illustration 4
Kilmer Contractors
Worksheet
For the Month Ending May 31, 19X1

	Trial Balance before Adjustment		Adjustments		Trial Balance after Adjustment		Income Statement		Statement of Retained Earnings		Balance Sheet	
Cash	2,400				2,400						2,400	
Accounts receivable	900				900						900	
Supplies	3,000			(b)1,000	2,000						2,000	
Note payable		3,000				3,000						3,000
Unearned fees		3,300	(a)2,200			1,100						1,100
Common stock		500				500						500
Retained earnings, 5/1/X1		0				0				0		
Dividends	600				600				600			
Painting fees		1,600		(a)2,200		3,800		3,800				
Salaries expense	1,500				1,500		1,500					
Supplies expense			(b)1,000		1,000		1,000					
	8,400	8,400	3,200	3,200	8,400	8,400						

Key to Adjustments:
(a) To record revenue from two of the three houses contracted for on May 10.
(b) To record the cost of the supplies used during the month of May.

Illustration 5
Kilmer Contractors
Worksheet
For the Month Ending May 31, 19X1

	Trial Balance before Adjustment		Adjustments		Trial Balance after Adjustment		Income Statement		Statement of Retained Earnings		Balance Sheet	
Cash	2,400				2,400						2,400	
Accounts receivable	900				900						900	
Supplies	3,000			(b)1,000	2,000						2,000	
Note payable		3,000				3,000						3,000
Unearned fees		3,300	(a)2,200			1,100						1,100
Common stock		500				500						500
Retained earnings, 5/1/X1		0				0				0		
Dividends	600				600				600			
Painting fees		1,600		(a)2,200		3,800		3,800				
Salaries expense	1,500				1,500		1,500					
Supplies expense			(b)1,000		1,000		1,000					
	8,400	8,400	3,200	3,200	8,400	8,400	2,500	3,800	600			
Net income for May							1,300			1,300		
							3,800	3,800				

Key to Adjustments:
(a) To record revenue from two of the three houses contracted for on May 10.
(b) To record the cost of the supplies used during the month of May.

Illustration 6
Kilmer Contractors
Worksheet
For the Month Ending May 31, 19X1

	Trial Balance before Adjustment		Adjustments		Trial Balance after Adjustment		Income Statement		Statement of Retained Earnings		Balance Sheet	
Cash	2,400				2,400						2,400	
Accounts receivable	900				900						900	
Supplies	3,000			(b)1,000	2,000						2,000	
Note payable		3,000				3,000						3,000
Unearned fees		3,300	(a)2,200			1,100						1,100
Common stock		500				500						500
Retained earnings, 5/1/X1	0				0					0		
Dividends	600				600				600			
Painting fees		1,600		(a)2,200		3,800		3,800				
Salaries expense	1,500				1,500		1,500					
Supplies expense			(b)1,000		1,000		1,000					
	8,400	8,400	3,200	3,200	8,400	8,400	2,500					
Net income for May							1,300			1,300		
							3,800	3,800	600	1,300		
Retained earnings, 5/31/X1									700			700
									1,300	1,300		

Key to Adjustments:
(a) To record revenue from two of the three houses contracted for on May 10.
(b) To record the cost of the supplies used during the month of May.

Illustration 7
Kilmer Contractors
Worksheet
For the Month Ending May 31, 19X1

	Trial Balance before Adjustment		Adjustments		Trial Balance after Adjustment		Income Statement		Statement of Retained Earnings		Balance Sheet	
Cash	2,400				2,400						2,400	
Accounts receivable	900				900						900	
Supplies	3,000			(b)1,000	2,000						2,000	
Note payable		3,000				3,000						3,000
Unearned fees		3,300	(a)2,200			1,100						1,100
Common stock		500				500						500
Retained earnings, 5/1/X1		0				0				0		
Dividends	600				600				600			
Painting fees		1,600		(a)2,200		3,800		3,800				
Salaries expense	1,500				1,500		1,500					
Supplies expense			(b)1,000		1,000		1,000					
	8,400	8,400	3,200	3,200	8,400	8,400	2,500	3,800	600	1,300	3,000	700
Net income for May							1,300			1,300	1,100	
							3,800	3,800			500	
Retained earnings, 5/31/X1									700			700
									1,300	1,300	5,300	5,300

Key to Adjustments:
(a) To record revenue from two of the three houses contracted for on May 10.
(b) To record the cost of the supplies used during the month of May.

of the items included in the adjusted trial balance is shown in Illustration 4. Observe that each account in the adjusted trial balance is transferred to only one of the six remaining columns, as indicated above.

Step 5. The fifth step in the preparation of the worksheet involves the "balancing" of the income statement columns of the worksheet. The income statement columns are totalled. Next an amount that is equal to the difference between the credit (revenue) column and the debit (expense) column ($3,800 - $2,500 = $1,300) is entered in both the debit column of the income statement set of columns (as a balancing figure) and the credit column of the statement of retained earnings set of columns. This amount is the net income for the period. The purpose of entering net income as a credit in the retained earnings set of columns is that the excess of the revenues over the related expenses for the period is income and results in an increase in stockholders' equity. An increase in stockholders' equity is recorded by a credit. If the balance in the debit (expense) column exceeds the balance in the credit (revenue) column of the income statement set of columns, the difference between the two totals represents a net loss for the period; this amount is entered as a credit in the income statement set of columns as the balancing figure and in the debit column of the statement of retained earnings set of columns as a reduction of the stockholders' equity.

It is also important to note that the income statement set of columns of the worksheet corresponds to: (1) the income summary account used in the closing process, (2) the summary journal entry that may be used in order to close out revenues and expenses for the period, and (3) the income statement for the period. Step 5 of the worksheet process is presented in Illustration 5.

Step 6. This step involves the determination of the ending balance in the retained earnings account for the period by adjusting the retained earnings balance for the income (or loss) of the business and for any dividends declared. This ending balance in the retained earnings account is entered in both the credit column of the balance sheet set of columns and the debit column of the statement of retained earnings set of columns (as a balancing figure). The statement of retained earnings set of columns corresponds to the retained earnings column in the statement of stockholders' equity. Illustration 6 presents this step.

Step 7. The final step in the process of preparing a worksheet is the balancing of the final two columns, the balance sheet, as a test of the arithmetic accuracy of the process. These two columns correspond to the balance sheet of the firm. The step is shown in Illustration 7.

As previously indicated, the completed worksheet is a one page summary of the adjusting and closing procedures. A critical review of Illustration 7 will provide you with an excellent overview of this process. Observe that preparing the financial statements from the completed worksheet is an easier process because all of the necessary information has already been sorted into the appropriate worksheet columns.

When the worksheet is used at the end of the period, it permits the financial statements to be prepared before adjusting and closing entries are recorded in the accounts. At year-end, after the statements are prepared, the adjusting entries indicated on the worksheet and the normal closing entries must still be entered into the journal and then posted to the ledger. When a worksheet is used in the preparation of financial statements at the end of the period, the steps involved in the accounting process described in Chapter 5 are modified as follows:

1. The preparation of general journal entries.
2. Posting these journal entries to the ledger.
3. The preparation of a trial balance before adjustment.
4. The preparation of the worksheet.
5. The preparation of the financial statements.
6. The preparation of the adjusting entries in the journal and posting them to the ledger.
7. The preparation of the closing entries in the journal and posting them to the ledger.
8. The preparation of the after-closing trial balance.

In addition to the end-of-period financial statements, many companies prepare interim financial statements that cover shorter periods of time, such as a month or a quarter. The worksheet is a valuable aid to the accountant in preparing these interim statements since the adjustments made on the worksheet need not be journalized and posted to the accounts. This makes the worksheet especially useful in preparing interim financial statements.

If a worksheet is used, the journalizing and posting of the adjustments will usually be done only at the end of the accounting period.

Adjusting Entries

As previously indicated, the accrual basis of accounting requires that all revenues be recorded as they are earned and that expenses be recorded as they are incurred. That is, there is a proper matching of revenues and expenses only if the income statement for the period includes all of the revenues and expenses applicable to the accounting period without regard to the timing of either the receipt or the disbursement of cash. At the end of any accounting period, then, there will usually be certain transactions that are still in the process of completion or that have occurred but that have not been recorded in the accounts. These transactions require adjusting entries to record revenues and expenses and to allocate them to the proper period or periods. All adjusting entries, then, will involve either an expense or a revenue.

In the case of Kilmer Contractors, adjustments are required to record the revenue earned by painting two of the three houses for which payment had been received in advance and to record the cost of the painting supplies used during the month of May. In general, the types of transactions that require end-of-period adjusting entries fall into the following groups:

1. Allocation of prepaid expenses to the proper periods.

2. Recognition of unrecorded (accrued) expenses.

3. Allocation of a portion of the recorded cost of property, plant and equipment to the accounting periods that benefit from their use (depreciation).

4. Allocation of unearned revenue to the proper periods.

5. Recognition of unrecorded (accrued) revenues.

Illustration 8 summarizes these adjusting journal entries.

Illustration 8
Classification of Adjusting Entries

Entries to Adjust Expenses:

- Prepaid Expenses
  Purpose: Allocate prepaid assets to expense as they are used.
  Example: Time passing on a multi-year insurance policy.

- Accrued Expenses
  Purpose: Record expenses incurred, but not yet recorded.
  Example: Wages owed to employees, but not yet paid.

- Depreciation Expense
  Purpose: Spread asset cost over periods that benefit.
  Example: A year's depreciation for a delivery vehicle.

Entries to Adjust Revenues:

- Unearned Revenues
  Purpose: Record the earning of a portion of unearned revenues.
  Example: Completed the house painting job that had been paid for in advance.

- Accrued Revenues
  Purpose: Record revenues earned, but not yet recorded.
  Example: Interest earned, but not yet received on a Certificate of Deposit.

In order to illustrate the different types of adjusting entries, the trial balance before adjustment of Brown Company as of December 31, 19X1, will be used. This trial balance appears in Illustration 9.

Illustration 9
Brown Company
Trial Balance before Adjustment
December 31, 19X1

	Debit	Credit
Cash	$ 2,760	
Accounts receivable	4,000	
Supplies	3,000	
Office furniture	3,600	
Accumulated depreciation—Office furniture		$ 360
Accounts payable		2,000
Unearned rent		3,000
Common stock		1,600
Retained earnings, 1/1/X1		3,400
Dividends	1,000	
Service revenues		20,000
Rent expense	9,000	
Salaries expense	6,000	
Other expense	1,000	
	$30,360	$30,360

Prepaid Expenses

Certain goods and services, such as insurance, rent, and supplies, are purchased prior to their use by the business. If these goods have been used or the services have expired during the accounting period, these costs should be classified as expenses. However, the portion of the goods that are unused or the services that have not expired should be included in the balance sheet and classified as an asset. These assets are referred to as prepaid expenses.[1] A prepaid expense will be reclassified as an expense in a subsequent accounting period (or periods) as it is used or as it expires. Adjusting entries are necessary in order to allocate the cost of each item between the asset account and the expense account.

To illustrate, assume that Brown Company purchases supplies at a cost of $3,000 on June 30 This transaction is recorded by the following journal entry:

Supplies	3,000	
Cash		3,000

This entry indicates that an asset has been acquired by the company. Supplies are carried in the accounts as an asset until they are used, at which time they become an expense and are reclassified as such. Note that the trial balance before adjustment reflects the $3,000 balance in the supplies account as an asset.

At the end of December, the supplies still on hand have a cost of $2,000. Subtracting the cost of the supplies on hand at December 31 ($2,000) from the cost of the supplies that were available for use during the year ($3,000 of supplies purchased on June 30) indicates that it is necessary to record the difference of $1,000, the cost of the supplies used during the year, as an expense. This is accomplished by means of the following entry:

Supplies expense	1,000	
Supplies		1,000

---

[1] The term "mixed account" is sometimes applied to these accounts that, at the end of the period and before adjustments, consist of both asset and expense elements.

In some instances, companies purchase supplies or prepay expenses that will be entirely used or consumed during the period and prior to the preparation of the financial statements. In these instances, the amounts paid may be recorded directly to expense when the purchase is made, simply as a matter of convenience. For example, assume that Brown Company pays the monthly rent of $750 on its office space in advance on the first day of each month. This outlay can be recorded on December 1 as follows:

Prepaid rent	750	
Cash		750

If the transaction is recorded in this manner, the following adjusting entry is required at the end of December in order to reclassify the outlay as an expense:

Rent expense	750	
Prepaid rent		750

Alternatively, it might be expedient to record the expenditure as an expense on December 1, because the benefit from the rent payment is received during the month:

Rent expense	750	
Cash		750

If Brown Company records the transaction in this manner, an adjusting entry is not required at the end of the month, since the expense has been fully incurred and the "prepayment" has been fully used by December 31.

Accrued Expenses

At the end of an accounting period there are usually expenses that have been incurred but that have not been paid because payment is not yet due. Many expenses, such as wages and salaries or interest on loans, may be incurred during a period but not recorded in the accounts, because they do not have to be paid as of the end of the period. These expenses are referred to as accrued expenses.[2] Adjusting entries are necessary at the end of an accounting period in order to record all accrued expenses.

For example, assume that Brown Company places a newspaper advertisement that appears during the month of December, but is not billed the $75 for the ad until some time in January. Since Brown Company does not owe any money for the advertisement during December, this amount does not appear on the trial balance before adjustment. Therefore, the following adjusting entry is required at the end of December:

Advertising expense	75	
Accounts payable		75

This adjusting entry records the expense incurred during December but not owed as of December 31 and the corresponding liability.

When the bill is received in January and is paid, the payment is recorded by the following journal entry:

Accounts payable	75	
Cash		75

This entry records the fact that the liability has been satisfied (and assets reduced) by the cash payment. The timing of the recognition of the expense is not determined by the date of the payment; the expense was recorded during the previous month when it was incurred.

---

[2] It may be helpful to think of "accrued expense" as expenses that have "built up" but no cash has yet changed hands.

DEPRECIATION EXPENSE

Businesses normally acquire assets that are used in operations over a number of years. Buildings and equipment are examples of this type of asset.

For example, assume that Brown Company acquires office furniture on January 1, 19X0, and expects to use this furniture for ten years. Assuming that the cost of this furniture is $3,600, the purchase is recorded as follows:

Office furniture	3,600	
Cash		3,600

The office furniture is an asset of the business and is recorded as such. Its cost should be spread over the periods that benefit from its use, in this case, ten years, so that each year bears part of the expense of buying the furniture. The process of allocating the cost of an asset to expense over its useful life is referred to as depreciation. *Depreciation is the systematic allocation of the cost of an asset to the periods that benefit from its use.* Since the cost of the furniture is $3,600 and the expected useful life of this asset is ten years, depreciation in the amount of $360 ($3,600 ÷ 10) is recorded annually. Assuming that Brown Company makes yearly entries to record the depreciation, the adjusting entry made on December 31, 19X0 (and every December for 10 years) in order to record depreciation expense is as follows:

Depreciation expense	360	
Accumulated depreciation		360

The debit to depreciation expense records the portion of the asset's cost that is allocated to expense for the year. The credit is to accumulated depreciation, a contra account that appears as an offset to or deduction from the related asset account in the balance sheet. As the title accumulated depreciation implies, the depreciation taken over the useful life of the asset is accumulated in this account. Usually, a reduction in an asset account is recorded with a credit made directly to the account; however, a contra account is used for property, plant and equipment in order to provide additional information concerning the asset—that is, both the original cost and the depreciation expense that has been taken to date may be reported in the balance sheet. The asset and the related accumulated depreciation account appear in the balance sheet as follows at the end of 19X1 after the adjusting entry for depreciation for $360 for 19X1 has been recorded:

Office furniture	$3,600	
Less: Accumulated depreciation	720	$2,880

A more complete discussion of the procedures involved in determining depreciation expense is presented in a later chapter.

UNEARNED REVENUES

Revenue that is collected before a business actually performs a service or delivers merchandise to a customer is referred to as unearned revenue. Since cash is received prior to the performance of the service or delivery of the goods, the amount received represents a liability to the firm. Unearned revenues are not a liability in the sense that the company will be required to repay the money. Rather, they represent an obligation of the company to perform a service or deliver goods at some future date (i.e., revenues that have been received but not earned). Examples of unearned revenues include rent collected in advance and subscription fees received prior to delivery of a magazine or newspaper.

To illustrate, assume that Brown Company subleases a portion of its office space to Smith for a rental of $3,000 per year. Terms of the lease agreement specify that Smith will pay the yearly rental in advance on July 1. The entry to record the receipt of the $3,000 advance payment on July 1, 19X1 is as follows:

Cash   3,000
    Unearned rent   3,000

Note that the trial balance before adjustment includes the $3,000 balance in the unearned rent account. Since no service is performed at the time the cash is received, the entire amount is initially recorded in a liability account, unearned rent. Since rent is earned over the twelve-month period that Brown Company provides office space to Smith, exactly one-half of the service is rendered during the period July 1 to December 31, 19X1. Accordingly, $1,500 (½ x $3,000) of the rent have been earned and the rental revenue is recorded by the following adjusting entry on December 31:

Unearned rent   1,500
    Rental revenue   1,500

The liability account, unearned rent, has been reduced by $1,500 and revenue for the period has been increased by this amount. The remaining balance in the unearned rent account represents an obligation to provide office space to Smith during the first six months of 19X2. This adjusting entry made on December 31 emphasizes the fact that revenue is recorded as it is earned, not necessarily as cash is received.

Accrued Revenues

Accrued revenues are revenues that have been earned but not recorded in the accounts during an accounting period because payment is not yet due. As such, accrued revenues are the opposite, so to speak, of unearned revenues.[3] Therefore, adjusting entries are necessary in order to record any revenue that has been earned but not recorded in the accounts as of the end of the accounting period.

To illustrate, assume that Brown Company enters into an agreement with the Fooler Brush Company on December 1, 19X1. Brown Company agrees to display a line of brushes at its offices in return for a commission of 10 percent on any sales made by Fooler if the initial contact with the customer is made by Brown Company. The commissions are payable on a quarterly basis. Assume that Brown Company earns commissions of $100 during the month of December. The following adjusting journal entry is made on December 31:

Commissions receivable   100
    Commissions earned   100

This entry increases the assets (commissions receivable) of Brown Company by the $100 due from Fooler Brush Company and records the revenue that has been earned to-date by providing the agreed-upon service.

When payment is received from the Fooler Brush Company, the following journal entry is made:

Cash   100
    Commissions receivable   100

It is important to note that this second entry simply records the fact that one asset, cash, is received in exchange for another, commissions receivable; revenues are not affected. The revenues are recorded at the time the service is performed, which is when they are earned by Brown Company.

Accrual Basis of Accounting

When a company records revenues as they are earned and records expenses as they are incurred, the company is using the accrual basis of accounting. Under the accrual basis, revenues are recorded as they are

---

[3] Again, it may be helpful to think of "accrued revenues" as those revenues that have "built up" but no cash has yet changed hands.

earned and expenses recorded as they are incurred without regard to the timing of either the receipt or disbursement of cash. Thus, the purpose of end-of-period adjusting entries is to update the accounting records of a business so that they are on the accrual basis. A comprehensive illustration of adjusting entries is presented in Appendix A.

Preparation of the Worksheet

In order to illustrate the different types of adjustments that typically are made in the preparation of a worksheet, we will prepare the worksheet for Brown Company at December 31, 19X1. The trial balance before adjustment as of December 31, 19X1 (see Illustration 9), appears in the first two columns of the worksheet in Illustration 10.

The procedures to follow in preparing the worksheet for Brown Company include the following:

1. The adjusting entries discussed in the prior section are entered in the adjustments columns.
2. Each amount in the trial balance is combined with the adjustment to that account, if any, and is entered in the trial balance after adjustment columns.
3. Each amount in the trial balance after adjustment columns is transferred to either the income statement columns, the statement of retained earnings columns, or the balance sheet columns. The revenue and expense accounts are extended to the income statement columns; the retained earnings and dividends accounts are extended to the statement of retained earnings columns; and the asset and liability accounts and the common stock account are extended to the balance sheet columns.
4. The income statement columns are totalled, and the difference between the debit and credit totals is entered as a balancing figure in the income statement debit column and in the credit column of the statement of retained earnings columns. This difference is equal to the net income for the year.
5. The statement of retained earnings columns are totalled, and the difference between the debit and credit totals is entered as a balancing figure in the statement of retained earnings debit column and in the credit column of the balance sheet columns. This difference is equal to the retained earnings at the end of the year.
6. The balance sheet columns are totalled as a test of the arithmetic accuracy of the process. If the debit and credit balance sheet columns are not equal, the worksheet is prepared inaccurately.

At this point, the completed worksheet can be used in preparing the formal financial statements for Brown Company. All necessary information is included in the income statement, statement of retained earnings, and the balance sheet columns of the worksheet.

After the preparation of the financial statements, all adjustments appearing in the adjustments columns of the worksheet are entered in the journal and then are posted to the ledger accounts. Then, the entries to close the revenue and expense accounts are journalized and posted to the ledger.

Summary

The worksheet is a tool that can be used by the accountant to facilitate the adjusting and closing procedures and to simplify the preparation of financial statements. The worksheet, in essence, summarizes the trial balance, adjusting entries, and closing entries in one document. Although the worksheet is particularly useful in the preparation of interim financial statements, since adjusting entries are usually not entered in the records at such times, it may also be used in conjunction with the regular closing process to prepare year-end statements.

Illustration 10
Brown Company
Worksheet
For the Year Ending December 31, 19X1

	Trial Balance before Adjustment Dr	Cr	Adjustments Dr	Cr	Trial Balance after Adjustment Dr	Cr	Income Statement Dr	Cr	Statement of Retained earnings Dr	Cr	Balance Sheet Dr	Cr
Cash	2,760				2,760						2,760	
Accounts receivable	4,000				4,000						4,000	
Supplies	3,000			(a)1,000	2,000						2,000	
Office furniture	3,600				3,600						3,600	
Accumulated depreciation—Office furniture		360		(c)360		720						720
Accounts payable		2,000		(b)75		2,075						2,075
Unearned rent		3,000	(d)1,500			1,500						1,500
Common stock		1,600				1,600						1,600
Retained earnings, 1/1/X1		3,400				3,400				3,400		
Dividends	1,000				1,000				1,000			
Service revenues		20,000				20,000		20,000				
Rent expense	9,000				9,000		9,000					
Salaries expense	6,000				6,000		6,000					
Other expense	1,000				1,000		1,000					
Supplies expense			(a)1,000		1,000		1,000					
Advertising expense			(b)75		75		75					
Depreciation expense			(c)360		360		360					
Rental revenue				(d)1,500		1,500		1,500				
Commissions earned				(e)100		100		100				
Commissions receivable			(e)100		100						100	
	30,360	30,360	3,035	3,035	30,895	30,895	17,435	21,600	1,000			
Net income							4,165			4,165		
							21,600	21,600	6,565	7,565	12,460	6,565
Retained earnings, 12/31/X1									6,565			
									7,565	7,565	12,460	12,460

Key to Adjustments:
(a) To adjust for supplies used.
(b) To adjust for accrued advertising expense.
(c) To adjust for depreciation on office furniture.
(d) To adjust for portion earned of rent collected in advance.
(e) To adjust for accrued commissions earned.

The general format of the worksheet includes a listing of all general ledger accounts and six pairs of columns. The initial step in the preparation of the worksheet is to insert the trial balance before adjustment in the first two columns. Any necessary adjustments are then entered in the adjustment columns (columns three and four). Adjusting entries are usually required under the accrual system of accounting to ensure that there is a proper matching of revenues and expenses for the period, without regard to the timing of either the receipt or disbursement of cash. Such entries generally fall into the following groups: (1) allocation of prepaid expenses, (2) recognition of unrecorded (accrued) expenses, (3) recognition of depreciation, (4) allocation of unearned revenue, and (5) recognition of unrecorded (accrued) revenue. Adjusting entries are generally coded in some manner, and a key to the adjustments is included as a footnote to the worksheet.

The next step is to combine each amount in the trial balance before adjustment to the adjustment to that account, if any, and to enter the resulting amount in the trial balance after adjustment columns (columns 5 and 6). Each amount in the trial balance after adjustment columns is then transferred to either the income statement columns (columns 7 and 8), the statement of retained earnings columns (columns 9 and 10), or the balance sheet columns (columns 11 and 12). Specifically, the revenue and expense accounts are extended to the income statement columns, the retained earnings and dividends accounts are extended to the statement of retained earnings columns, and the asset and liability accounts are extended to the balance sheet columns.

The income statement columns are then "balanced" by entering a debit in the amount of net income for the period or a credit in the amount of net loss for the period. At the same time, a credit in the amount of net income or a debit in the amount of net loss is entered in the appropriate statement of retained earnings column.

The statement of retained earnings columns are similarly "balanced" by entering an amount equal to the difference between the debit and credit totals in the statement of retained earnings debit column and in the balance sheet credit column. This difference represents the retained earnings at the end of the period.

As a final step in the worksheet preparation, the balance sheet columns are totalled as a test of the arithmetic accuracy of the process. At this point, all necessary information for preparing the formal financial statements is included in the income statement columns, the statement of retained earnings columns, and the balance sheet columns. If the worksheet is being used as part of a year-end closing, the adjusting entries included on the worksheet, as well as the normal closing entries, are entered in the general journal and posted to the ledger.

KEY DEFINITIONS

Accrual basis of accounting—the process of recording revenues in the period in which they are earned and recording expenses in the period in which they are incurred, regardless of whether cash is received or paid.

Accrued expenses—expenses, such as wages and salaries or interest on loans, that have been incurred during a period but not yet recorded in the accounts because they do not have to be paid as of the end of the period.

Accrued revenues—revenues that have been earned but not yet recorded in the accounts during the accounting period because payment is not yet due.

Accumulated depreciation—a contra account that appears as an offset or deduction from the related asset account in the balance sheet. The depreciation taken over the useful life of the asset is accumulated in this account.

Adjusted trial balance—prepared by combining the trial balance before adjustment with the related adjusting entries.

Adjusting entries—at the end of any accounting period there are usually certain transactions that are still in the process of completion or that have occurred but that have not yet been recorded in the accounts. These transactions require adjusting entries in order to record revenues and expenses and to allocate them to the proper period.

Closing entries—entries that are prepared in order to close out or transfer the balances in temporary accounts to the retained earnings account.

Contra account—an account that is offset against or deducted from another account in the financial statements.

Depreciation—the systematic allocation of the cost of an asset to the periods that benefit from its use.

Interim financial statements—these are financial statements that cover periods of less than a year such as a month or a quarter.

Prepaid expenses—certain goods and services, such as insurance, rent, and supplies, are often paid for prior to their use by the business. The portion of the goods that have not been used up or the services that have not expired should be included in the balance sheet and classified as an asset.

Unearned revenues—revenues that are collected before a business actually performs a service or delivers goods to a customer.

Worksheet—summarizes the trial balance, adjusting entries, and closing entries in one document. It also permits the preparation of interim financial statements without recording the adjusting entries in the accounts. The worksheet may also be prepared and used in conjunction with the regular year-end closing process. Even if the accountant intends to record the adjusting and closing entries in the accounts, such as would be the case at year-end, the worksheet may still be used as a valuable check on the recording process.

Questions

1.   What is the purpose of the worksheet?

2.   How is the adjusted trial balance prepared?

3.   Which accounts are closed at the end of the period?

4.   Explain how the net income for the period is calculated and presented on the worksheet.

5.   How are the adjusting entries for the period included in the worksheet?

6.   Explain the relationship of the worksheet to the financial statements.

7.   Are prepaid expenses reclassified as expenses in future periods? Why?

8.   How is revenue, which is collected before a business actually performs a service, classified in the financial statements?

9.   Explain the accrual basis of accounting. How does it differ from the cash basis?

10.   What check may be used in order to determine if the worksheet was prepared accurately?

Exercises

11.   Gardner Company leases a building to a client at a rental of $2,400 per year on June 1, 19X1. Give the required December 31, 19X1, adjusting entry on the books of Gardner Company under each of the following assumptions.

   a.   The rent is paid in advance on June 1, 19X1, and is recorded by crediting unearned rent.
   b.   The rent is paid in advance on June 1, 19X1, and is recorded by crediting rental income.
   c.   The rent for the period of June 1, 19X1, to May 31, 19X2, is to be paid on May 30, 19X2.

12.   Prepare the adjusting entries required at December 31, 19X1, in each of the following cases:

   a.   Herman Company was assessed property taxes of $350 for 19X1. The taxes were due April 15, 19X2.
   b.   Norton Company's payroll was $6,000 per month and wages were paid on the 15th of the following month. The company closes its books on December 31.
   c.   Frazier Company has $3,000 of savings bonds. Interest receivable on these bonds was $180 at December 31.
   d.   Foreman Company owns a building costing $30,000. $1,000 of the cost is to be allocated to expense in 19X1.

13.   The income statement for 19X2 for the Lang Company reflected wage expense of $80,000. The year-end balances in the wages payable account were $10,000 at December 31, 19X1, and $12,000 at December 31, 19X2. Determine the amount of cash paid for salaries during 19X2.

14.   Henderson Incorporated purchased $7,800 of office supplies on August 1. On December 31, it was determined that 35 percent of these supplies had been used. Prepare the journal entries for the initial purchase and the later

adjustment. Prepare one set of entries assuming supplies are initially recorded as an asset and another assuming they are recorded as an expense.

15. The Kupshak Company is adjusting its accounts as of December 31. Make the adjusting entries for the following accounts:

   a. Depreciation on equipment is $2,000 for the year.
   b. Two years' rent was paid on January 1. The amount paid ($36,000) was debited to prepaid rent.
   c. Unpaid salaries as of December 31 were $9,000.
   d. Interest not yet received on an investment was $1,700.
   e. Unearned revenues were reduced by $4,500.

Problems

16. The following information for adjustments was available at December 31, the end of the accounting period. Prepare the necessary adjusting entry for each item of information.

   a. Annual office rent of $1,200 was paid on July 1, when the lease was signed. This amount was recorded as prepaid rent.
   b. The office supplies account had a $100 balance at the beginning of the year and $600 of office supplies were purchased during the year. An inventory of unused supplies at the end of the year indicated that $150 of supplies were still on hand.
   c. Wages earned by employees during December but not yet paid amounted to $700 on December 31.
   d. The company subleased part of its office space at a rental of $50 per month. The tenant occupied the space on September 1 and paid six months rent in advance. This amount paid was credited to the unearned rent account.
   e. Equipment was purchased on January 1 for $5,000. The useful life was estimated to be ten years with no salvage value.
   f. Services provided for clients which were not chargeable until January amounted to $800. No entries had yet been made to record these earned revenues.

17. From the information given below concerning the College Inn Ski Resort, prepare the adjusting entries required at December 31, 19X1.

   a. Accrued property taxes at December 31, 19X1, were $500.
   b. Accrued wages payable at December 31, 19X1, were $2,400
   c. Interest receivable on United States government bonds owned at December 31, 19X1, was $75.
   d. A tractor had been obtained on October 31 from Equipment Rentals, Inc, at a daily rate of $4. No rental payment had yet been made. Continued use of the tractor was expected through the month of January.
   e. A portion of the land owned by the resort had been leased to a riding stable at a yearly rental of $3,600. One year's rent was collected in advance at the date of the lease (November 1) and credited to unearned rental revenue.
   f. Another portion of the land owned had also been rented on October 1 to a service station operator at an annual rate of $1,200 No rent had as yet been collected from this tenant.
   g. On December 31, the College Inn Ski Resort signed an agreement to lease a truck from Gray Drive Ur-Self Company for the next calendar year at a rate of 10 cents for each mile of use. The resort estimates that they will drive this truck for about 1,000 miles per month.
   h. On September 1, the company purchased a three year fire insurance policy for $360. At the time the policy was acquired, the company debited insurance expense and credited cash.

18.   Below is given the September 30, trial balance *before* adjustment of the Cavilier Company.

Cavilier Company
Trial Balance
September 30, 19X1

Cash	$ 2,700	
Supplies	1,250	
Prepaid rent	1,800	
Land	10,000	
Accounts payable		$ 3,500
Fees received in advance		2,500
Common stock		3,000
Retained earnings		4,250
Dividends	500	
Commissions earned		5,800
Fees earned		2,200
Wages and salaries expense ..	4,000	
Utilities expense	550	
Miscellaneous expense	450	
	$21,250	$21,250

Other data:

1.   Supplies on hand at the end of September totalled $750.
2.   In accordance with the terms of the lease, the annual rental of $1,800 was paid in advance on April 1, 19X1.
3.   Wages and salaries earned by employees but unpaid at September 30, 19X1, amounted to $450.
4.   Of the balance in the fees received in advance account, $1,500 had not been earned as of September 30, 19X1.
5.   On September 1, 19X1, the company rented certain equipment to the Alpha Fraternity under the following terms: $50 per month payable on the first day of each month following the start of the rental arrangement.

Required:

Prepare all journal entries necessary to: (1) adjust the accounts, and (2) close the books as of September 30, 19X1.

19.   As chief accountant for Ford Company, it is your job to prepare end-of-period financial statements for the firm. You had an assistant prepare the following unadjusted trial balance from the books of the company.

Ford Company
Trial Balance
December 31, 19X1

Cash	$ 1,100	
Accounts receivable	800	
Prepaid insurance	900	
Office furniture	4,000	
Accumulated depreciation—		
office furniture		$ 400
Land	8,000	
Accounts payable		900
Unearned revenues		1,500
Note payable		2,500
Common stock		3,000
Retained earnings		6,600
Dividends	400	
Service revenues		4,100
Rent expense	600	
Salaries expense	1,000	
Supplies expense	2,000	
Other expenses	200	
	$19,000	$19,000

The following information was also gathered from the books of the Ford Company:

1. The company paid $900 for a three-year insurance policy on June 30, 19X1.
2. The office furniture was purchased January 1, 19X0, and is expected to have a ten-year life and no salvage value. Depreciation for 19X1 has not been recorded.
3. The unearned revenues account was created when Ford Company was paid $1,500 for services to be rendered. One-third of these services were rendered on December 1, 19X1.
4. Interest of $20 has accrued on the note payable at December 31.
5. Ford Company paid $600 on August 1 as annual rent for its warehouse. This amount was debited to rent expense.
6. $100 of salaries have been earned by employees but not yet paid or recorded on the books.
7. Supplies on hand at December 31 had a cost of $500.

Required:

a. Prepare a worksheet for Ford Company at December 31, 19X1.
b. Prepare the company's balance sheet, income statement, and statement of stockholders' equity.

20. Given below is a trial balance before adjustment for Unseld Company.

Unseld Company
Trial Balance Before Adjustment
December 31, 19X3

Cash	$ 2,500	
Accounts receivable	1,600	
Notes receivable	2,100	
Office furniture	3,000	
Accumulated depreciation—		
office furniture		$ 300
Accounts payable		1,800
Unearned fees		425
Common stock		2,000
Retained earnings		3,900
Dividends	360	
Service fees		2,050
Rent income		350
Supplies expense	800	
Insurance expense	115	
Wage expense	350	
	$10,825	$10,825

On December 31, the accountant for Unseld Company found several items which he thought needed adjustment in the preparation of the worksheet. Below are listed these items which may or may not need adjustment.

1. The office furniture which was purchased on January 1, 19X1, is being depreciated over a twenty-year life with no salvage value.
2. Wages for the last week of the year amounted to $50 which would not be paid until January 6, 19X4.
3. Unearned fees worth $200 will be earned as of December 31, and the rest will be earned in January.
4. Insurance of $100 was unexpired as of December 31.
5. Supplies worth $500 were on hand at the end of the year.
6. Accrued interest on notes receivable amounts to 6 percent of the ending notes receivable balance.
7. Rental income earned but not yet received included $200 for the month of November and $100 for December.

Required:

Prepare a worksheet as of December 31 19X3 for Unseld Company using 14-column worksheet paper.

21. Given below is a trial balance before adjustment for Holmes Company.

Holmes Company
Trial Balance Before Adjustment
December 31, 19X1

Cash	$1,100	
Accounts receivable	800	
Notes receivable	1,500	
Office furniture	2,000	
Accumulated depreciation—		
office furniture		$ 400
Accounts payable		1,250
Unearned fees		500
Common stock		3,000
Retained earnings		1,350
Dividends	400	
Service fees		2,000
Rent income		300
Supplies expense	1,500	
Insurance expense	900	
Wage expense	600	
	$8,800	$8,800

After preparing the worksheet, the accountant for Holmes Company produces the following balance sheet for the year.

Holmes Company
Balance Sheet
As of December 31, 19X1

Assets		
Cash		$1,100
Accounts receivable		800
Interest receivable		20
Supplies		250
Prepaid insurance		600
Notes receivable		1,500
Office furniture	$2,000	
Less: Accumulated depreciation	600	1,400
Total assets		$5,670
Liabilities and Stockholders' Equity		
Accounts payable		$1,250
Unearned fees		300
Unearned rent		100
Total liabilities		$1,650
Common stock		3,000
Retained earnings		1,020
Total liabilities and stockholders' equity ...		$5,670

Required:

Reproduce the worksheet generated by the accountant for Holmes Company.

22. The trial balance of the Aggie Company as of September 30, 19X1, was as follows:

Aggie Company
Trial Balance
September 30, 19X1

Cash	$ 6,000	
Supplies	500	
Prepaid rent	900	
Land	8,500	
Accounts payable		$ 4,000
Unearned revenues		1,050
Common stock		6,000
Retained earnings		4,000
Dividends	1,000	
Commissions earned		10,100
Salaries expense	7,500	
Miscellaneous expense	750	
	$25,150	$25,150

Other financial data:

1. The cost of supplies on hand at the end of September was $100.
2. In accordance with the terms of its lease, the company paid its annual rent of $900 on September 1.
3. Salaries earned by employees but not paid as of September 30, 19X1, totalled $500.
4. Of the balance in the unearned revenues account, $450 had not been earned as of September 30, 19X1.
5. Included in the miscellaneous expense account was the cost of a fire insurance policy purchased on August 31, 19X1 at a cost of $180. The Policy expires on August 31, 19X3.

Required:

Prepare adjusting journal entries for the above data. Prepare closing entries.

23. Complete the following worksheet and prepare a balance sheet, an income statement, and a statement of stockholders' equity as of December 31, 19X1, for the Grow-It Company (see next page).

24. From the following independent transactions select those which would require a December 31 adjusting entry. Provide the appropriate adjusting entry for the transactions that you selected.

1. Purchased delivery equipment which cost $84,000 on January 1. The equipment was expected to have a four year useful life and a salvage value of $4,000.
2. Provided services on account. The clients were sent bills amounting to $12,400 on September 1.
3. Received $24,000 on August 1 for consulting services to be provided to the client over two years.
4. Paid salary expenses amounting to $6,200 on April 15. The payment covered work which had been performed during the first two weeks of April.
5. Purchased land to be used for a future plant site. The property was purchased on July I and cost $48,000.
6. Purchased supplies on account which cost $480 on April 1. Supplies on hand as of December 31 amounted to $124.

25. Based on the following adjusting entries, provide the journal entry of the original transaction with which each adjusting entry is associated.

a.	Prepaid Insurance	XXX	
	Insurance Expense		XXX
b.	Unearned Fees	XXX	
	Repair Fees		XXX
c.	Rent Expense	XXX	
	Prepaid Rent		XXX
d.	Supplies Expense	XXX	
	Supplies		XXX
e.	Subscription Revenue	XXX	
	Unearned Subscriptions.		XXX

Grow-It Company
Worksheet
For the Year Ending December 31, 19X1

	Trial Balance before Adjustments		Adjustments		Trial Balance after Adjustments		Income Statement		Statement of Retained Earnings		Balance Sheet	
Cash	5,170				5,170						5,170	
Accounts receivable	1,300				1,300						1,300	
Supplies	2,675			400	2,275						2,275	
Office furniture	12,000				12,000						12,000	
Accumulated depreciation—Office furniture		400		100		500						500
Accounts payable		900		1,000		1,900						1,900
Common stock		10,000				10,000						10,000
Retained earnings		7,845				7,845				7,845		
Revenues		7,000				7,000		7,000				
Rent expense	1,000				1,000		1,000					
Salaries expense	4,000				4,000		4,000					
Depreciation expense			100		100		100					
Supplies expense			400		400		400					
Advertising expense			1,000		1,000		1,000					
	26,145	26,145	1,500	1,500	27,245	27,245	6,500	7,000				500
												1,900
												10,000
Net income							(e)	(f)	(h) / (b) / (c)	(e) / (d) / (c)	(a)	(b) / (a)
							7,000	7,000				

26. On August 31, 19x6 the Argo Company purchased an insurance policy that offered the company protection over a two year period beginning on the date of purchase. The adjustments columns on Argo's December 31, 19x6 work sheet contained a debit to a prepaid insurance account and a credit to an insurance expense account in the amount of $5,280.

    Required:

    a. Determine the amount that Argo paid for the original policy.
    b. Provide the general journal entry that Argo used to record the purchase of the policy on August 31, 19x6.
    c. Provide an alternate entry that could have been used to record the purchase of the policy on August 31, 19x6.
    d. Provide the adjusting entry that would be required on December 31, 19x6. assuming that Argo had originally recorded the transaction in accordance with the alternate method that you developed in requirement "c" of this problem.

27. The Southern Corporation began the 19x6 accounting period with a $6,800 credit balance in the accrued salaries payable account. The 19x6 earnings statement indicated that salaries expense for the 19x6 accounting period amounted to $93,269. The ending balance in the accrued salaries payable account was $8,300.

    Required:

    Assuming that all of the transactions associated with the salaries expense are described above, compute the amount of cash that was disbursed during 19x6 for the payment of salaries.

28. The president of the Bush Company is perplexed. The company had $20,000 in cash at the beginning of 19x2. The 19x2 earnings statement indicated that the company had net earnings for the year which amounted to $40,000. However, the company's controller informed management that the company would have difficulty paying a $15,000 obligation which was due on January 15, 19x3 The controller had prepared the following list of accounts that had changed during the period, which he said could explain why the company was experiencing a cash shortage.

Account Title	Beginning Balance	Ending Balance
Unearned Fees	$45,000	$15,000
Accrued Salaries Payable	8,000	2,000
Accounts Receivable	4,000	12,000
Accrued Rent Receivable able	0	10,000

    A note was attached to the list which indicated that any other changes in the accounts were so small that they were considered to be irrelevant. On the day that the controller was scheduled to meet with the president to explain the cause of the cash shortage, he was involved in an automobile accident and was unable to attend the meeting.

    Required:

    Assume that you are the assistant controller of the company and that you were required to substitute for the controller in the scheduled meeting with the president. The president asks you to explain how the company can start the year with $20,000, earn $40,000 and still have trouble paying a $15,000 debt.

29. Account balances are likely to appear in more than one of the columns of a work sheet. Listed below are several account titles and a partial work sheet. For each account title place a check mark (✔) in the columns where the account balance would be likely to appear. The first account has been completed for your convenience.

Account Title	Trial Balance		Earnings Statement		Balance Sheet	
	Debit	Credit	Debit	Credit	Debit	Credit
Cash	✔				✔	
Accounts Receivable						
Prepaid Insurance						
Equipment						
Accumulated Depreciation						
Land						
Accounts Payable						
Unearned Revenue						
Common Stock						
Retained Earnings						
Service Revenue						
Insurance Expense						
Salary Expense						
Depreciation Expense						
Utility Expense						
Advertising Expense						
Net Income						

30. For each of the transactions listed, indicate the effect(s), if any, on the company's year-end: (1) Balance Sheet, (2) Income Statement, and (3) Statement of Cash Flows. Your answers should be as complete and specific as possible.

   a. Paid two months rent (May and June) in advance on May 1.
   b. Received a bill for an advertisement which had appeared in the daily newspaper last week.
   c. Recorded depreciation on the company's delivery truck.
   d. Received advance payment from a customer for work to be done next month.
   e. Recognized May rent expense with an adjusting entry.

Refer to the Annual Report in Chapter 1 of the text:

31. Did accrued expenses and liabilities increase or decrease in the most recent year?

FRAUD CASE: FRAUD EXAMINATION

As indicated in an earlier case, the CFE in conducting a fraud examination must gather evidence, take statements from company employees (called interviewing), interrogate the target (the suspect), and report the findings of the examination in written form. The CFE may also be called to testify in court regarding his or her investigation and findings.

Most CFEs, when engaged to investigate a potential or known fraud use the hypothesis approach (or case approach) in determining the existence and/or extent of fraud.

The case approach involves putting oneself in the shoes, so to speak, of the alleged fraudster and asking the question "If I were going to steal from the company and cover-up my theft, what would be the best way for me to accomplish this objective?" Once the CFE arrives at a hypothesis (best guess) as to the methods the fraudster may have used to embezzle company funds and cover his or her tracks, the CFE will attempt to prove or disprove the hypothesis. If proved, the fraudster is trapped. If the hypothesis is invalid, the CFE starts over with another assumption.

To summarize, a case fraud plan, as discussed, involves a "hypothesis," thinking like the target, and attempting to gather facts through interview and interrogation and the creation of documentation (a paper trail) to prove or disprove the hypothesis.

DISCUSSION CASE:

Assume the following facts:

1. CPAs auditing a consolidated farmers cooperative contact you (a CFE) regarding a potential fraud at one of the grain operations in Arkansas. The Arkansas operation is managed by a family (father, mother, and son) with absentee ownership.

2. The CPAs, by applying analytical procedures, have discovered an unusually large number of sales of farm goods out of season. Also, a number of these sales have been returned for refunds or allowances.

3. There are missing purchase orders. Inventory counts cannot be reconciled with purchases and sales.

4. The CPAs have learned, from discussions with employees, that the wife recently purchased a $120,000 pleasure boat for use on the Arkansas lakes. When asked about the boat, the wife explained that she purchased the boat with money she inherited through a relative's will.

DISCUSSION QUESTIONS:

Referring to the DISCUSSION CASE above, answer the following questions using the case approach.

1. Assume you are the CFE contacted by the CPAs auditing the consolidated farmers cooperative. They have asked you to investigate the peculiar items 1-4 in the case discussed above and determine if fraud has been committed and, if so, the extent of the fraud. You may assume the family members managing the cooperative have access to all the records of the business operation and all the assets of the cooperative. Each of them also exercises authority over the other employees of the Arkansas cooperation. Construct your hypothesis (use the case approach).

2. Would your hypothesis change if you knew that the wife's $120,000 pleasure boat was not purchased with money received from an inheritance? Assume a search of court records provided evidence that no money had been willed to her in the last five years.

FRAUD CASE: EDP AND FRAUD

Whether an accounting information system employs manual or electronic data processing (EDP) does not change the requirement of management to maintain good internal controls throughout the business' operations. The establishment of controls, the review of transactions, and the search for fraud, however, are complicated somewhat when EDP is used.

In an EDP operation, one or a few people have access to accounting records and company assets and hard copy back-up exists for only a short time or not at all. Furthermore, an EDP system provides far less opportunity for checks and balances than does a manual accounting system. The lack of paper back-up and checks and balances is almost completely eliminated in an "on-line, real-time" EDP operation where there is constant access to the computer from several terminal stations.

In any good control structure, the idea is to consider the errors and fraud that could occur and then design controls and procedures to either prevent occurrences or detect them when they do occur. Although good controls decrease the probability of computer fraud occurring, frauds do occur and audit procedures should be in place.

Discussion Question:

Consider an on-line, real-time EDP system. The system is very user friendly and the company has installed 1,500 computer real time input devices located throughout the country used by its stores and sales persons. The computer processing starts at the point of sale and records the sale, creates a receivable, makes an entry to cash, inventory (if applicable), and all other related accounts. Paper trails of changes to these accounts do not exist or exist for only a short period of time.

What management control policies and procedures do you think would likely be effective in preventing errors and fraud in the on-line, real-time EDP system described?

Appendix A
Comprehensive Illustration

Accruals

Accruals happen when revenues are earned or expenses are incurred from day-to-day activities but cash has not yet changed hands. Usually entries are made when the payment occurs but if an accounting period ends before the payment occurs, an adjusting entry must be made to accrue the revenue or expense.

Revenue Example

Company A loans $10,000 to Company B on July 1, 19X1, due on June 30, 19X5. The note bears interest at 12 percent per year. Interest is payable annually on June 30. The entry required on A's books to accrue the interest due at December 31, 19X1, is as follows:

```
Accrued interest receivable ..............................      600
     Interest revenue ($10,000 x 12% x ½) ..................              600
To record the accrual of interest revenue
for six months in 19X1
```

The *accrual of revenue* results in an asset account (accrued interest receivable) that will be eliminated when the cash is received.

The entry required on A's books to record the cash receipt of the interest at June 30, 19X2, is:

```
Cash ($10,000 x 12%) ...................................    1,200
     Accrued interest receivable ..........................              600
     Interest revenue ($10,000 x 12% x ½) .................              600
To record the accrual of interest revenue for six months in
19X2 and record the receipt of the annual interest payment.
```

This entry is a *compound entry* since two different transactions are recorded simultaneously (the accrual of the interest revenue earned in 19X2 and the receipt of $1,200 representing the cash payment for the interest earned in 19X1 and 19X2).

As an alternative to the June 30, 19X2 entry above, the following two entries can be made:

```
Accrued Interest receivable ..............................      600
     Interest revenue ($10,000 x 12% x ½) .................              600
To record the accrual of interest revenue for
six months in 19X2

Cash ................................................    1,200
     Accrued interest receivable ..........................            1,200
To record the receipt of annual interest due from
Company B.
```

Expense Example

Company A pays its employees every two weeks. December 31, 19X1, falls in the middle of a two-week pay period. The checks will be written on January 7, 19X2, for $50,000. The entry needed to accrue the salary expense at December 31, 19X1, is:

```
Salary expense ......................................     25,000
     Salaries payable ................................                25,000
To accrue salaries at December 31, 19X1
($50,000 x ½ = $25,000).
```

The *accrual of expense* results in a liability account (salaries payable) that will be eliminated when the cash is paid.

The entry needed to record the payment of salaries at January 7, 19X2, is:

```
Salary expense ......................................     25,000
Salaries payable ....................................     25,000
     Cash ...........................................                50,000
To record salary expense for January 1, 19X2, to
January 7, 19X2, and record the payment of salaries.
```

This entry is a compound entry since two different transactions are recorded simultaneously (the recording of the salary expense for 19X2 and the payment of $50,000 representing the cash payment of salaries for both 19X1 and 19X2).

As an alternative to the January 7, 19X2 entry above, the following two entries can be made:

```
Salary expense ......................................     25,000
     Salaries payable ................................                25,000
To accrue salary expense at January 7, 19X2.


Salaries payable ....................................     50,000
     Cash ...........................................                50,000
To record the payment of accrued salaries payable at
January 7, 19X2.
```

Deferrals

Deferrals occur when cash is received (for revenues) or cash is paid (for expenses) before the proper period for revenue recognition or expense matching occurs. An entry is made when the cash changes hands but if the revenue has not been earned or the expense benefit has not been received, the revenue or expense must be deferred on the balance sheet. When the revenue is earned or expense benefit received, the amount deferred is "released" from the balance sheet by making a second accounting entry.

Revenue Example

Company A loans Company B $10,000 and insists on the prepayment of one year's interest at 12 percent. The loan is made on July 1, 19X1, and is due on June 30, 19X5. The entry Company A makes to record the receipt of unearned interest revenue at July 1, 19X1, is:

```
Cash ...............................................     1,200
     Unearned interest revenue .......................                1,200
To record prepayment of one year's interest on loan
($10,000 x 12% = $1,200).
```

The *deferral of revenue* results in a liability account (unearned interest revenue) when the cash is received. This account will be eliminated as the revenue is earned and recognized in the income statement.

The entry Company A makes to record interest earned at December 31 19X1, is:

```
Unearned interest revenue . . . . . . . . . . . . . . . . . . . . . . . . . . . . . .    600
     Interest revenue  . . . . . . . . . . . . . . . . . . . . . . . . . . . . . . . .            600
To record the portion of unearned interest earned
in 19X1 ($1,200 x 6/12 = $600).
```

The entry Company A makes to record interest earned at June 30, 19X2, is:

```
Unearned interest revenue  . . . . . . . . . . . . . . . . . . . . . . . . . . .    600
     Interest revenue . . . . . . . . . . . . . . . . . . . . . . . . . . . . . . . . .            600
To record the portion of unearned interest earned in 19X2
($1,200 x 6/12 = $600).
```

Expense Example

Company A borrows $50,000 from Bank B on June 30, 19X1, due June 30, 19X5. Interest is payable annually at June 30 at the rate of 12 percent per year. The bank requires that the interest be prepaid in advance each year. The entry Company A makes to record the prepayment of interest on June 30, 19X1, is:

```
Prepaid interest . . . . . . . . . . . . . . . . . . . . . . . . . . . . . . . . . . . .    6,000
     Cash . . . . . . . . . . . . . . . . . . . . . . . . . . . . . . . . . . . . . . . . . . .          6,000
To record prepaid interest ($50,000 x 12% = $6,000)
```

The *deferral of expense* results in an asset account (prepaid interest) when the cash is paid. This account will be eliminated as the expense benefit occurs and the expense is "matched" to revenue in the income statement.

The entry Company A makes to record interest expense at December 31, 19X1, is:

```
Interest expense . . . . . . . . . . . . . . . . . . . . . . . . . . . . . . . . . . . .    3,000
     Prepaid interest . . . . . . . . . . . . . . . . . . . . . . . . . . . . . . . . . .          3,000
To record interest expense for 19X1
($6,000 x 6/12 = $3,000).
```

The entry Company A makes to record interest expense at June 30, 19X2, is:

```
Interest expense . . . . . . . . . . . . . . . . . . . . . . . . . . . . . . . . . . . .    3,000
     Prepaid interest . . . . . . . . . . . . . . . . . . . . . . . . . . . . . . . . . .          3,000
To record interest expense for six months ended
June 30, 19X2 ($6,000 x 6/12 = $3,000).
```

Recording Deferrals

With deferrals, the accounting entries may be handled in one of two ways:

1. Record the cash payment or receipt with an offsetting entry to a *balance sheet deferral account* (as in the examples above). Then, when the revenue is earned or the expense benefit occurs, make entries to transfer the deferred item from the balance sheet to the income statement.

2. Record the initial cash payment or receipt with an offsetting entry to the *income statement* (i.e., recognize all of the revenue or expense immediately). Then, at the end of the accounting period, make an entry to "back out" the unearned revenue or prepaid expense via an adjustment that transfers the unearned or prepaid amount from the income statement to the balance sheet.

Appendix B
A Model of a Financial Accounting System

Introduction

A primary function of accounting is to accumulate the information required by decision-makers and to communicate these data to them. The accounting system used for communicating information consists of business documents (such as invoices or checks) and records the procedures used in recording transactions and preparing reports. A financial accounting system must communicate data to users in such a way that the operating performance and current financial position of a company are reported in a manner that is both meaningful and useful. All pertinent information required for decision-making and planning and control purposes must be made available to the user on a timely basis. There are also certain other basic housekeeping functions that the system should accomplish. For example, detailed information must be made available in order to identify the specific accounts receivable balance of each customer, detailed information regarding payroll and deductions is required in order to pay employees and satisfy government regulations, and inventory balances must be available on a current basis for purposes of inventory planning and control. The accounting system of an organization should be designed to handle all of the many facets of accounting, and the system must operate in a manner that is efficient, effective, accurate, and timely.

Model of a Financial Accounting System

A model of a basic financial accounting system is presented in tabular form in Illustration 11 and in the form of a diagram in Illustration 12 below. The financial accounting system shown in these illustrations indicates the procedures followed during the accounting cycle and provides a comprehensive picture or overview of the information flows that are required in a typical organization. Note that the model depicted in Illustration 11 is a summarization of the recording process steps that were discussed in this chapter. Illustration 12 diagrams the same general data flows in a financial accounting system. Certain features, which will be discussed in this appendix, have been added to the system to provide for a more efficient means of processing the accounting data.

The basic components of the system are as follows:

1. A chart of accounts.
2. A coding system.
3. A general journal.
4. A general ledger.
5. Subsidiary ledgers.
6. Special journals.
7. Internal control.
8. An audit trail.

These components of the financial accounting system are discussed in the following paragraphs.

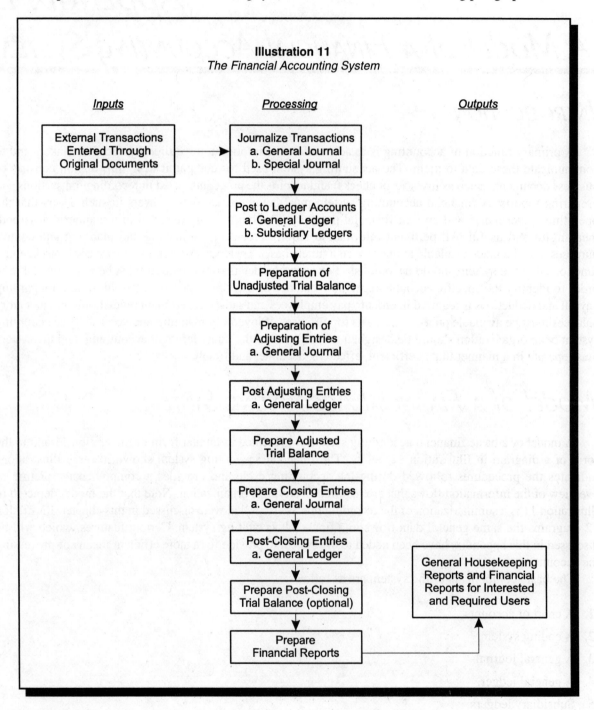

Illustration 11
The Financial Accounting System

The Chart of Accounts

A chart of accounts is a listing of all of the accounts that an organization may use in its accounting system. The scope of the chart of accounts and the ability to adapt new account titles to the existing listing are very important factors to be considered in the process of designing and installing an accounting system. The design of the chart of accounts affects the manner in which accounting information is accumulated, summarized, and used by the organization.

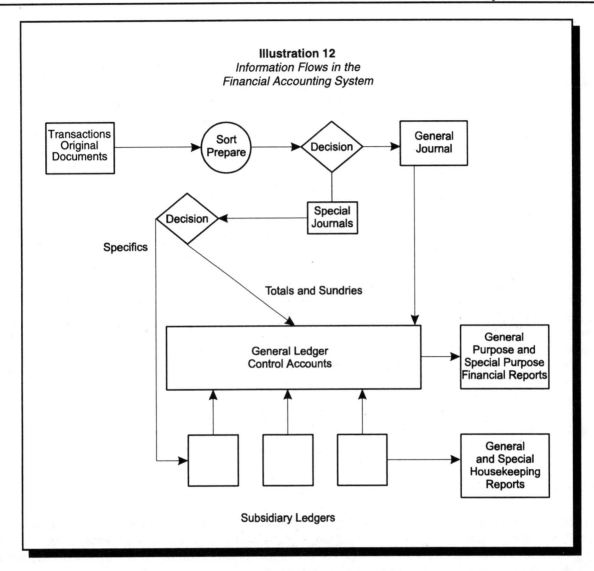

Illustration 12
Information Flows in the
Financial Accounting System

At a minimum, the chart of accounts should include all of the accounts that appear on the balance sheet, income statement, and statement of stockholder' equity. In most cases, however, limiting the chart to only these accounts is inadequate, because management often requires information that is more detailed than that which is included in the basic financial statements. This detailed information is required in order to manage the day-to-day operations of the business. Also, external users such as governmental agencies frequently require information, often in detailed and specified formats, not included in the financial statements. In addition to the basic functional classifications, management normally requires:

1. Accounting information that is based on cost behavior patterns for purposes of planning and control.

2. Accounting information that is based on areas of responsibility for purposes of performance measurement and control. For example, information regarding divisions or geographical regions may be used in order to measure the performance of these segments.

Many of the accounts used by the organization are utilized for multiple purposes in the management and operations of the business. For example, production cost data are required in the process of inventory valuation, but it is also necessary for evaluating the performance of the specific departments involved in the production process.

Coding the Chart of Accounts

In order to facilitate the use of data and to provide a unique identity for each account, the chart of accounts is normally coded numerically. A normal pattern of arrangement and coding of the chart of accounts is in the order of the financial statements and the accounts included in these statements. A simplified example of the broad categories of accounts that might be included in a typical chart of accounts is presented below:

1000—1999	Asset accounts
2000—2999	Liability accounts
3000—3999	Stockholders' equity accounts
4000—4999	Revenue accounts
5000—5999	Manufacturing cost accounts
6000—6999	Distribution expense accounts
7000—7999	Administrative expense accounts
8000—8999	Other income accounts
9000—9999	Other expense accounts

To illustrate the usefulness of coding and the means of identifying specific items using numerical codes, a code for asset accounts will be expanded and explained. The first digit in the code may be used to identify the general account classification. Any search of the accounts is then limited to one thousand possible accounts in that category. The second digit could be used to identify an asset's location; that is, for example, whether the asset is located at the home office or at a division. The third digit could be used to identify the classification of the asset; that is, whether the asset is a current asset, a plant and equipment asset, an intangible asset, etc. The fourth digit might be used to identify the specific asset itself.

In a large organization the coding structure may be very complex. In order to deal with the complexity of the coding structure, a code dictionary, identifying the specific accounts and their codes, is often employed. In situations where automated equipment with sensing or scanning capability is used, numerical characters are usually considered necessary for reasons of both economy and efficiency.

The General Journal and General Ledger

Until this point, the mechanics of recording and handling transactions described in this text have been limited to the general journal and the general ledger. As previously indicated, each transaction is recorded in the general journal chronologically, and then the debits and credits from the general journal are posted individually to the appropriate accounts in the general ledger.

In the accounting procedures illustrated to this point, the general journal was used as the book of original entry while the general ledger served as the book of final entry. Financial statements were usually prepared from an adjusted trial balance or worksheet. The mechanics of this system make it almost impossible for all but the smallest business to operate effectively or, at least, efficiently. This type of system is simply unable to process large volumes of transactions on a timely basis, primarily because no effective division of labor is possible since each and every journal entry must be written out on an individual basis.

In addition, this system might not provide the detailed information necessary to operate the business efficiently. For example, the system previously described did not always identify the specific individual who purchased goods on account. Likewise, it did not provide information as to the identity of individual creditors. Division of labor and necessary detail may be accomplished in this basic system by the use of special journals and subsidiary ledgers in addition to the general journal and general ledger.

Subsidiary Ledgers

Subsidiary ledgers are supplemental detailed records that provide underlying support for the amounts recorded in the corresponding control accounts included in the general ledger. Subsidiary ledgers are necessary to permit the classification of a large group of accounts under a single control account in the general ledger. The subsidiary ledgers found in most systems include: accounts receivable, accounts payable, inventories, employee pay records, property records, and the stockholders' register. If no recording errors are made, the total of the balances in a subsidiary ledger should be equal to the total in the corresponding control account.

An example of a subsidiary ledger is the accounts receivable subsidiary ledger. An individual record must be maintained on a current basis for every customer for purposes of control, billing, and for handling any inquiries. The use of individual customer records eliminates the problem of including large numbers of detailed accounts receivable accounts in the general ledger.

There are many other advantages to the use of subsidiary ledgers other than the accumulation of necessary detail. Subsidiary ledgers permit a division of duties among employees by allowing a number of different individuals to assist in the preparation of the records. In addition, personnel with less experience may be used to post to subsidiary ledgers. Also, an error in a trial balance may be localized in a subsidiary ledger, thus reducing the effort necessary to locate the error.

Special Journals

One means of reducing the amount of individual recording and posting is to separate the transactions into groups that have common elements and to provide special journals for recording the transactions in each group. A decision is then made as to whether the transaction falls into a class that should be entered in a special journal or is an infrequently occurring transaction that should be entered directly in the general journal. A special journal is useful in those instances where there is a large volume of transactions that result in debits and credits to the same accounts. For such transactions, the recording process is facilitated by entering the amounts in the columns of a special journal and posting the totals periodically to the general ledger. The types of transactions that normally occur with sufficient frequency to justify the use of special journals include receipts of cash, disbursements of cash, sales of merchandise on credit, and purchases of merchandise on account. Transactions not recorded in any of the special journals are recorded in the general journal. That is, every transaction must be recorded in some type of journal, and the effects of all transactions are still posted, either individually or by cumulative totals, to the ledger.

The accounts receivable example that was employed to illustrate the use of subsidiary ledgers is also applicable to special journals. When goods are sold on account, the sale should be recorded at that time. The relevant aspects of credit sales from a data gathering standpoint include: identity of the customer; amount of the sale; nature of any credit terms;[4] date of the sale; and, for any future inquiries, the invoice number. These are repetitive data that are accumulated for each and every sale.

Special journals permit a division of labor, allow the use of less experienced personnel, employ preprinted account columns or summaries that reduce the incidence of error, and allow special transactions of like kind to be easily analyzed because the original data are accumulated by category rather than on an individual basis.

An Example—Special Journals and Subsidiary Ledgers

The credit sales and cash collections for the Yello Brewery for January illustrate the interrelationships of special journals, subsidiary ledgers, and the general ledger.

Jan.	2	Sold 200 cases at $4 per case to Harry the Hat's Bar & Grill (on account) — Invoice #101.
	5	Sold fifty cases at $4 per case to Big Brother's Place (on account) — Invoice #102.
	7	Received a check from Harry the Hat's Bar & Grill for $800.
	11	Sold 200 cases at $4 per case to Harry the Hat's Bar & Grill (on account) — Invoice #103.
	13	Sold ten cases at $4.50 per case to the Bachelors Club (on account) — Invoice #104.
	15	Sold twenty cases at $4.10 per case to Dink's Place (on account) — Invoice #105.
	25	Received a check from Big Brother's Place for $200.
	31	Received a check from the Bachelor's Club for $45.
	31	Received a dividend check of $50 on a stock investment.

---

[4] Credit terms include the time allowed for payment and any discounts allowed. Payment required within thirty days would be shown by the notation n/30 indicating that the full amount is due in thirty days.

SALES JOURNAL. The transactions for the Yello Brewery are journalized and posted in the special journals, subsidiary ledgers, and general ledger in Illustration 13. Note that each individual credit sale is recorded in the sales journal. Any merchandise sold for cash is recorded directly in the cash receipts journal. The amount of each credit sale is posted daily to the individual customer account in the accounts receivable subsidiary ledger. This procedure assures that each customer's account will be kept up-to-date for purposes of responding to inquiries from customers and for making decisions regarding future extensions of credit to individual customers. The check mark (✓) in the sales journal indicates that the posting to the subsidiary ledger has been made. At the end of the month, the total of the sales journal column ($1,927) is debited to accounts receivable control and credited to sales revenue in the general ledger.

CASH RECEIPTS JOURNAL. Similarly, a cash receipts journal is used to record all transactions involving the receipt of cash. The cash receipts journal must include several columns for recording transactions since the source of the receipts may differ. For example, note that the cash receipts journal in Illustration 13 includes credit columns for collections on accounts receivable, sales of merchandise for cash, and all other (sundry) transactions. A receipt of cash is recorded by entering the amount received in the debit column for cash and in the appropriate column to record the credit.

As in the case of the sales journal, the individual credits in the accounts receivable credit column are posted daily to the customer accounts in the accounts receivable subsidiary ledger. The check mark (✓) in the cash receipts journal indicates that the posting has been made to the subsidiary ledger.

Cash sales of merchandise in the business are typically recorded in total at the end of the day by means of an entry in the cash receipts journal. This entry is recorded in the cash debit column and the sales credit column of the journal. Cash received from sources other than collections of receivables or cash sales are recorded in the sundry credit column.

At the end of the month, the column totals in the cash receipts journal are posted to the appropriate general ledger accounts. Prior to this posting, it is necessary to prove that the total of the debit columns is equal to the total of the credit columns. After the totals in the cash receipts journal have been checked, the total in the cash column is posted as a debit to the cash account and the total of the accounts receivable column is posted as a credit to the accounts receivable control account. Similarly, the total of the credits in the column for cash sales is posted to the sales account in the general ledger. The individual items in the sundry account column are posted separately to the appropriate general ledger accounts.

CASH DISBURSEMENTS JOURNAL. A cash disbursements journal (see Illustration 14) may be used to record all expenditures of cash made by the business. A journal of this type may include individual credit columns for cash and purchase discounts and a sundry or other credit column. The totals of the credits to cash and to purchase discounts are posted directly to these accounts on a monthly basis while the amounts included in the other credit column are posted to the individual accounts at any time that it is convenient to do so. Debit columns are normally included for accounts frequently affected by cash disbursements, such as purchases and accounts payable. The totals of these account columns are posted directly to the purchases and accounts payable control accounts on a monthly basis. The individual debits in the accounts payable debit column are posted daily to the accounts payable subsidiary ledger. Debits to accounts other than purchases and accounts payable may be recorded in a sundry or other debit column; these entries are posted to the appropriate general ledger accounts as it is convenient to do so.

The mechanics of the cash disbursements journal are almost identical to those of the cash receipts journal. Like any other special journal, the cash disbursements journal should be designed in a manner that meets the specific requirements of its user. It should include debit and credit columns for the accounts most often affected by the payment of cash. The columns suggested above are typical of those included in the cash disbursements journals of many businesses, but others may be required in particular circumstances.

PAYROLL JOURNAL. A payroll journal is a specialized form of a cash disbursements journal. As its name implies, it is used exclusively to record the payment of salaries and wages to employees. A payroll journal normally includes debit columns for gross salaries and wages and payroll tax expense and credit columns for cash, federal income taxes withheld, state income taxes withheld, social security taxes withheld (employees' share), other deductions such as union dues and employee health care, the employer's share of social security

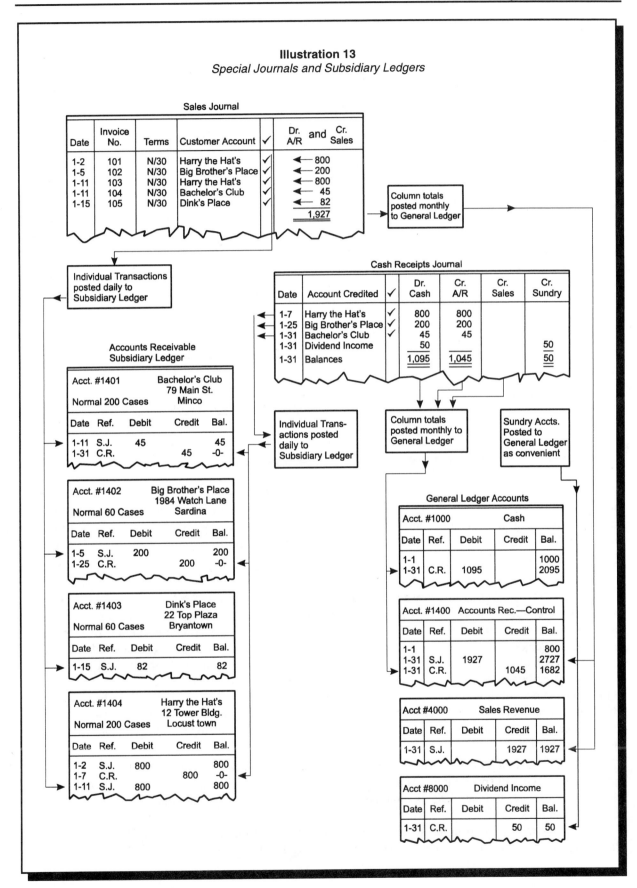

Illustration 13
Special Journals and Subsidiary Ledgers

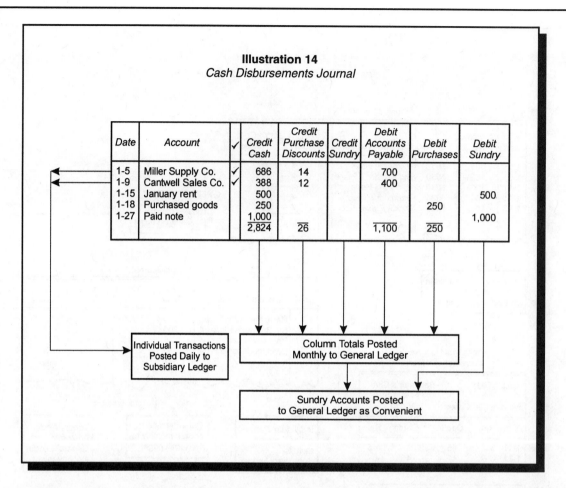

Illustration 14
Cash Disbursements Journal

Date	Account	✓	Credit Cash	Credit Purchase Discounts	Credit Sundry	Debit Accounts Payable	Debit Purchases	Debit Sundry
1-5	Miller Supply Co.	✓	686	14		700		
1-9	Cantwell Sales Co.	✓	388	12		400		
1-15	January rent		500					500
1-18	Purchased goods		250				250	
1-27	Paid note		1,000					1,000
			2,824	26		1,100	250	

Individual Transactions Posted Daily to Subsidiary Ledger

Column Totals Posted Monthly to General Ledger

Sundry Accounts Posted to General Ledger as Convenient

taxes and federal and state unemployment taxes. Summary entries are made to record gross salaries and wages, total payroll tax expense, payment of the salaries and wages, and the incurring of the liabilities related to the payroll. Information for individual employees is posted to the separate payroll records maintained for each employee. These records are, in effect, subsidiary records for payroll from which various reports and tax returns are prepared and filed.

Purchases Journal. A purchases journal (see Illustration 15) is very similar to a sales journal. Credit purchases are entered in the journal, with a notation made of such information as the date of purchase, the name of the vendor, date of the invoice, terms of the purchase, and the purchase amount. As individual purchases are made, they are recorded in the accounts payable subsidiary ledger, which includes a separate account for each of the suppliers of the business. Periodically, the total amount of the purchases is posted as a debit to the purchases account and a credit to the accounts payable control account. At this time, the balance in the control account should be equal to the total of the balances in the accounts payable subsidiary ledger. The information included in the accounts payable subsidiary ledger is used for making decisions regarding future purchases from particular suppliers, for checking prices, and for testing the accuracy of billings made by suppliers.

Form of Special Journals. There is no specified format for special journals nor is there any limit as to the number of types of special journals and subsidiary ledgers that are necessary. As mentioned previously, special journals and subsidiary ledgers should be designed so as to meet the individual needs of the particular company that uses them.

The check marks found in the special journals are made for purposes of control. The bookkeeper will check the transactions as he or she posts them to the appropriate ledger accounts.

Illustration 15
Purchases Journal

Date	Invoice Date	Account	✓	Amount
1/3	1/2	Miller Supply Co.	✓	700
1/7	1/6	Cantwell Sales Co.	✓	400
1/15	1/15	Harwell Co.	✓	600
1/20	1/17	Walter & Son	✓	300
1/27	1/26	Burton Inc.	✓	900
				2,900

General Ledger

Purchases

1/31 2,900

Accounts Payable

1/31 2,900

Accounts Payable Subsidiary Ledger

Miller Supply Co.

1/3   700

Cantwell Sales Co.

1/7   400

Harwell Co.

1/15   600

Walter & Son

1/20   300

Burton Inc.

1/27   900

PROVING THE CONTROL ACCOUNTS

After all posting is completed for a period, the general ledger control accounts should be checked (often referred to as proved) against the balances in the corresponding subsidiary ledger accounts. This proof is usually made by preparing a schedule of the individual balances in the subsidiary ledger. The total of the individual balances must be equal to the balance in the corresponding control account; otherwise, an error has occurred in the accounting process.

INTERNAL ACCOUNTING CONTROL

Certain accounting controls are necessary within a business to safeguard the assets from waste, fraud, and inefficiency and to ensure the accuracy and reliability of the accounting data. Ideally, the system of internal control should provide assurance regarding the dependability of the accounting data relied upon in making business decisions. Generally, these accounting controls include a specified system of authorization and approval of transactions, separation of the record keeping and reporting functions from the duties concerned with asset custody and operations, physical control over assets, and internal auditing.

A subdivision of responsibility in a financial accounting system is necessary to provide adequate checks on the work of company personnel. When one transaction is handled from beginning to end by a single individual and that person makes an error, the mistake is probably carried through in the mechanics of recording the transaction and is very difficult to locate. On the other hand, if different aspects of a transaction are processed by different people, each acting on an independent basis, an error is much more readily identifiable. Many of the errors that affect the accounts never occur, because the mistake may be identified and corrected on a timely basis.

A division of responsibility among employees is also necessary for control purposes. In a properly designed accounting system that has adequate division of duties, fraud and embezzlement are very difficult and require the collusion of two or more people. However, even in a properly designed system, the possibility of errors and embezzlement cannot be completely eliminated.

The division of duties should be logically based on the desired purposes of the system. For example, the person who maintains the subsidiary ledger of accounts receivable should not have access to cash. This prevents him or her from being able to manipulate the accounts receivable and retain the cash. Likewise, a single individual should not be given the responsibility of both approving purchases and then signing the checks that are used to pay for them. Payments made to nonexistent companies for fictitious purchases are difficult to prevent if one person is able to approve both the purchase and the payment.

The goals of an effective system of accounting controls and the elements of such a system can be summarized as follows:

Goals:
1. Safeguard assets.
2. Ensure an efficient accounting system with reliable financial statements.

Subgoals:
1. Ensure that transactions are carried out according to management's policies.
2. Ensure that transactions are recorded as needed so that:
   a. Financial statements are prepared according to GAAP.
   b. Specific employees are held accountable for assets.
3. Ensure that only authorized individuals have access to assets.
4. Ensure accounting records agree with actual existing assets under company's control.

Emphasis on Transactions:
1. Ensure that transactions are properly authorized.
2. Ensure that transactions are properly executed.
3. Ensure that transactions are properly recorded.
4. Ensure that employees are accountable for assets acquired in transactions.

General Principles:
1. Competent and responsible employees.
2. Separation of duties.
3. Rotation of duties.
4. Rules for control of assets.
5. Well-designed source documents.
6. Internal auditing.

A system of internal control is frequently justified because it assists the business in the detection of errors and the prevention of embezzlement. Another major benefit of a system of internal control is that it provides an atmosphere and system that are deterrents to inefficient utilization of the company's resources, fraudulent conversion of assets, and inefficient and inaccurate handling of the company's accounts. Independent auditors also rely upon the system of internal controls in determining the extent and nature of their audit work. Many firms have internal audit departments. The internal auditors are normally involved in evaluating and maximizing the effectiveness of the internal control system.

Ethical Issues in Accounting

Unfortunately, there are always inherent limitations in any system of internal control. One source of these limitations is human abilities, carelessness, fatigue, errors in judgment, misunderstanding of instructions, etc. Another source relates to the integrity of managers. Internal controls are only as effective as the integrity and competence of the individuals who develop, administer, and monitor these controls. Integrity must be based upon appropriate ethical values and it must be initiated by the senior management of a company and permeate the entire organization.

Serious questions have been raised concerning the activities and accountability of publicly-owned corporations as a result of unexpected failures and disclosures of questionable and illegal activities by management. Many believe that the emphasis on short-term results in our society—particularly as evidenced by the focus on reported income—is one of the greatest threats to ethical behavior in business. In a recent annual report of a large corporation, the chief executive officer wrote that "as long as investors—including supposedly sophisticated institutions—place fancy valuations on reported 'earnings' that march steadily upward, you can be sure that some managers and promoters will exploit GAAP (generally accepted accounting principles) to produce such numbers, no matter what the truth may be."

Deceptive financial reporting clearly decreases the value of financial reports to decision-makers. Such deception may be a result of either fraud or questionable, but not explicitly illegal, activities. Fraud represents an intentional manipulation of the financial data for the benefit of the perpetrator. Most fraudulent reporting practices cause an overstatement of assets and/or understatement of liabilities with a resulting positive effect on current income. Examples of fraudulent practices include recording transactions without substance (e.g., creating fictitious sales), failing to disclose information (e.g., concealing a significant decline in value of certain assets), or falsifying records or documents (e.g., changing invoice amounts to understate the amount of recorded expense).

A more frequent problem of deceptive reporting involves legal but unethical or questionable practices. Unfortunately, no precise definition has been developed to adequately differentiate between acceptable and unacceptable practices. Some of the practices that have been cited as questionable include:

1. Choosing the most liberal accounting method allowable under generally accepted accounting principles.

2. Changing accounting methods to increase reported income.

3. Timing the amounts of expenses or significant write-downs of assets (e.g., writing down assets in the fourth quarter or postponing write-downs until later periods.)

4. Changing judgments or estimates to manipulate reported income.

The primary cost of deceptive financial reporting is the suboptimal decisions made by those who rely upon such information. Financial resources of the economy are not allocated effectively to the most deserving entities. Investors and lending institutions suffer losses as reported results depart from economic reality and disclosures of these abuses undermine both the integrity and the reliability of the entire corporate financial reporting process. Clearly, the ethical environment in business is critical to the well-being of our society.

There are a number of outside factors that encourage fraudulent and questionable financial reporting practices. However, it is clear that there are also internal (within the organization) factors that influence the likelihood of such practices. Commonly, organizations evaluate and reward managerial performance on the basis of short-term results (e.g., income, sales). As salaries, bonuses, and even holding one's job are tied to short-term results, managers are often motivated to respond with fraudulent or questionable financial reporting practices. Moreover, lack of clear communication within the organization also contributes to questionable practices. In many instances, the managers involved in questionable behavior either did not know what they were doing was wrong or inappropriately assumed that they were acting in the best interests of the organization.

In order to overcome the problems of conflicting incentives and misinformation, top management of a company must provide ethical guidance by clearly written regulations. They must supply leadership and act as role models to communicate the message that the regulations are important. A National Commission on Fraudulent Reporting (1987) recommended that companies develop and implement codes of conduct. A documented code of conduct provides all employees with a common foundation in implementing the firm's ethical policies. To be effective, a code of conduct must be supported by top management, monitored continuously, and vigorously enforced. The internal audit function should incorporate reviews to assure compliance with the corporate goals and to provide for corrective action for any deviations from the code.

The Audit Trail

An audit trail is the traceability factor that is built into an accounting system. It permits a person, normally an independent certified public accountant (referred to as an auditor), to follow the processing of a specific transaction from the beginning of the system to the final output of the system. This procedure should also be reversible; that is, the final output of the system should be traceable back to the original source documentation that represents the transactions that cause the final output. An audit trail provides a path that can be followed in order to verify the accuracy with which transactions are handled as well as their legitimacy. The audit trail relies on a good system of internal control and documentation of transactions.

A flowchart of the purchase, receipt, payment, and use of office supplies for the Brown Grass Seed Company is presented in Illustration 16. This flowchart describes both the internal control and audit trail for these types of transactions. Note that only three sets of forms are used: a purchase requisition (the invoice prepared by purchasing, which is the first of a series of invoices in this case), the bill of lading, and the invoice received from the vendor. Multiple copies of these documents are used by the business for internal control purposes. The entire transaction may be traced from the financial statements to any point in the accounting system.

Automated Accounting Systems

The introduction of a computer system into the accounting function does not alter the data flow, but instead parallels the manual processing system. The computer system simply performs many functions that are performed by people in a manual system. Any automated system affects the form of transaction documentation and other factors such as:

1. Methods of establishing source documents.
2. Methods of transmitting data.
3. Techniques of data preparation.
4. Amount of data handled.
5. Speed and accuracy.
6. Processing of the data.
7. Methods of data storage.
8. Methods of information retrieval.
9. Number of accounting reports used.
10. Types of controls necessary for adequate internal control.

The objective of any accounting information system (whether manual or automated) is to produce the financial information required by internal and external users. The basic components of any computer system are the "hardware" and appropriate "software."

Computer Hardware

Computer hardware is the equipment used to process the accounting information. Hardware can range from the very sophisticated and expensive system that possesses tremendous computing capability to the relatively simple and inexpensive system such as a personal computer that costs less than $2,000. In general, the equipment can be classified into three categories: mainframe computers, minicomputers, and microcomputers.

Mainframe computers are large-scale systems that are used when a large volume of data needs to be processed rapidly. Minicomputers are much cheaper and less powerful. Minicomputers provide the computing capacity required by many small to medium size companies that need the capability to process many transactions but do not necessarily need the power and efficiency of a mainframe computer.

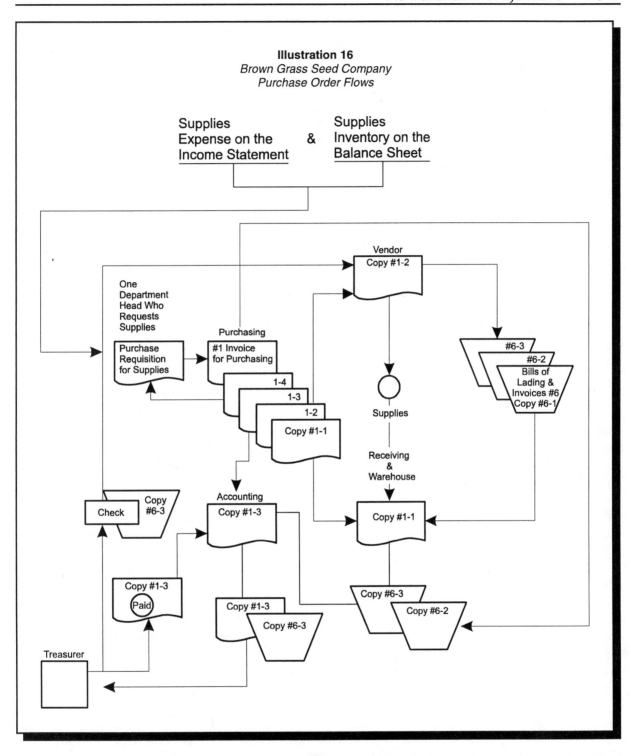

Illustration 16
Brown Grass Seed Company
Purchase Order Flows

A microcomputer is a system that is smaller than a minicomputer and can be used by a small business that does not have a large number of transactions to process. In many business firms, microcomputers are widely used in conjunction with mainframe or minicomputer systems. Selected data can be transferred between mainframe computers and microcomputers. Some tasks are better suited for microcomputer applications, such as spreadsheet analysis or word processing applications.

Computer Software

Computer software consists of the instructions that are developed to make the hardware perform the functions that are necessary to process transactions. The software controls the computer activities by instructing the hardware, in a step-by-step program, to perform a specific function. For example, in a payroll program (software), all the deductions from each person's paycheck (such as taxes and other payroll deductions) have to be programmed and "read" into or made available to the computer. When each employee's hours and pay rate are entered, the program calculates payroll deductions and, with the proper hardware, prints the employees' checks. When a program is written to handle a specific application such as payroll or order handling or inventory, the programs for that application are usually called a software package. Software packages are available from most computer vendors to perform the usual accounting functions. In addition, a company can have a program "tailored" or written to its specifications when it has unique processing and/or control requirements.

Summary

A financial accounting system must communicate economic information efficiently, effectively, accurately, and on a timely basis. Basic components of the system include: (1) a chart of accounts, (2) a coding system, (3) a general journal, (4) a general ledger, (5) special journals, (6) subsidiary ledgers, (7) a system of internal control, and (8) an audit trail.

A chart of accounts is a listing of all the accounts that may be used by a company. The basic design of the chart of accounts determines how accounting information is accumulated, summarized, and used. A coding system is necessary for the chart of accounts to provide a unique identity for each account included. Special journals are used for recording transactions that occur frequently. A general journal is used to record those transactions that occur on an infrequent basis. A general ledger contains the control accounts for the system. Subsidiary ledgers are supplemental detailed records that provide underlying support for the control accounts included in the general ledger. An effective system of internal control serves as a deterrent to the inefficient utilization of a company's resources; it discourages the fraudulent conversion of assets and the inefficient and inaccurate handling of a company's accounts. An audit trail is necessary to allow traceability of transactions after the fact.

The use of automated equipment in the financial accounting system does not alter the data flows in the system per se; but the equipment may cause significant changes in: (1) the source documents, (2) methods of transmitting data, (3) techniques of data preparation, (4) amount of data handled, (5) speed and accuracy, (6) processing of data, (7) methods of data storage, (8) methods of information retrieval, (9) the number of accounting reports used, and (10) the types of controls necessary for adequate internal control.

Key Definitions

Audit trail—the traceable sequence of steps through which a transaction is processed from the beginning of the accounting system to the final output. The procedures and documentation should be clear so as to provide traceability from the output back to the original documents.

Cash disbursements journal—a special journal that may be used to record all expenditures of cash made by the business.

Cash receipts journal—a special journal that may be used to record all transactions involving the receipt of cash.

Chart of accounts—the list of all accounts that a company uses in conducting its business. It includes all accounts used in the preparation of the balance sheet, income statement, and statement of stockholders' equity, and in addition, all accounts that management needs for planning and control purposes. The design of the chart of accounts determines how the information is gathered, summarized, and used in the accounting system.

Coding—the process of assigning a system of numbers to the various accounts included in the chart of accounts.

Coding dictionary—identifies an account with its coding number to simplify use of the coding system and the accounts.

Control account—a general ledger account that is supported by detailed information included in subsidiary accounts.

Internal control—comprises the plan of organization and all of the coordinate methods and measures adopted within a business to safeguard its assets, check the accuracy and reliability of its accounting data, promote operational efficiency, and encourage adherence to prescribed managerial policies.

Payroll journal—a specialized form of a cash disbursements journal used exclusively to record the payment of salaries and wages to employees.

Purchases journal—a special journal that may be used to record credit purchases.

Sales journal—a special journal that may be used to record credit sales.

Special journals—designed to record large volumes of transactions that occur on a frequent basis. Special journals are often used for accounts receivable, accounts payable, and cash receipts and disbursements.

Subsidiary ledgers—a supplementary record that provides underlying support for control accounts that are included in the general ledger. A subsidiary ledger includes more detail than the related general ledger account, and the total of all subsidiary accounts equals the balance of the applicable control account.

Outline

LEARNING OBJECTIVES

Chapter 7 introduces the financial statement of corporations and discusses the differences between and among sole proprietorships, partnerships, and corporations. Studying this chapter should enable you to:

1. Compare and contrast the three basic types of business organizations: sole proprietorships, partnerships, and corporations.

2. Explain how corporate financial statements differ from those of a proprietorship and a partnership.

3. Explain how corporate equity accounts are affected by earnings and the investments of and distributions made to stockholders.

4. Discuss the corporate statement of stockholders' equity.

5. Discuss the classifications used in corporate financial statements.

6. Describe and apply the concept of ratio analysis of financial statements.

7. Understand the criticisms of financial statements.

8. Identify and discuss interrelationships among the financial statements.

CHAPTER 7

UNDERSTANDING CORPORATE FINANCIAL STATEMENTS

INTRODUCTION

In Chapter 2, you were introduced to Kilmer Contractors, a small contracting company owned by Bill Kilmer. The financial statements of Kilmer Contractors—the income statement, the statement of financial position (or balance sheet), the statement of cash receipts and payments (or statement of cash flows) and the statement of stockholders' equity—were constructed from the available information pertaining to the company's activities in its initial month of operations. In this chapter, you will learn about the financial statements of a much larger business, which has many owners rather than just a single owner, and is much more complex. But first, it may be useful to have some information about the different types of organizations that engage in business activities.

TYPES OF BUSINESS ORGANIZATIONS

There are three basic types of business organizations, each of which have certain advantages and disadvantages when compared to the others. These three basic types of business organizations are sole proprietorships, partnerships, and corporations.

SOLE PROPRIETORSHIPS. A sole proprietorship is a business that has a single owner. A sole proprietorship is relatively easy to start and put into operation. Additionally, the owner has total control over all of the activities of the business; there are no other owners to consult with or persuade with regard to decisions pertaining to the business and its operations. Many small businesses are organized as sole proprietorships. Examples include plumbers and veterinarians.

PARTNERSHIPS. A partnership is a business that has two or more owners. Having more than a single owner allows a business to combine the economic resources and skills of more than one individual; however, because there are two or more owners (partners) no single or individual owner (partner) has total control over the business and its operations. A partnership agreement is needed to formalize a number of issues, such as the duties of each partner and the division of profits among the partners. Partnerships may be small businesses (e.g., two doctors) or large ones (e.g., large law or public accounting firms).

CORPORATIONS. A corporation is a business that has a number of owners, with ownership interest evidenced by shares of stock. Unlike a sole proprietorship or partnership, the ownership of a corporation whose stock is traded on an organized stock exchange can change on a daily basis. Large corporations may have thousands of stockholders (owners). You can buy or sell stock in a corporation by simply placing an order with a broker or other financial institution. With thousands of owners and even more potential owners, it is much easier for a corporation than either a sole proprietorship or partnership to raise money for its operations.

Corporations are legal entities separate and apart from their owners. Unlike sole proprietorships and partnerships, corporations pay income taxes; the owners of the other two types of business organizations, sole proprietorships and partnerships, report the profits of their businesses on their individual or personal tax returns.

The financial statements you will study in this chapter are those of Wal-Mart Stores, Inc., a large corporation with over 2 billion shares of stock outstanding. The annual report of Wal-Mart is included as Chapter 1 of this text. Comparison will be made between Wal-Mart's financial statements and those of Kilmer Contractors.

As you would expect, Wal-Mart's financial statements are much more complicated than those of Kilmer Contractors. Of course, you are not expected to understand all of the elements included in these statements even after studying this chapter. The purpose of this chapter is to provide you with a broad overview of a corporation's financial statements. You will understand financial statements much more thoroughly as you proceed through this book.

Background of Wal-Mart

Sam M. Walton's Ben Franklin Variety Store, the predecessor to Wal-Mart, began operations in 1945 in Newport, Arkansas. The first Wal-Mart Discount City opened in 1962. Today, Wal-Mart is America's largest retailer in terms of total revenue. In addition to the over nineteen hundred Wal-Mart stores (discount department stores), Wal-Mart has over four hundred Sam's Clubs (warehouse membership clubs), and over three hundred Wal-Mart Supercenters (combination full-time supermarket and discount department stores). Wal-Mart also is the largest discount retailer in Canada. In addition, Wal-Mart has operations in Mexico, Puerto Rico, Brazil, Argentina, China, and Indonesia.

The majority of Wal-Mart's sales are those of nationally-advertised merchandise. Wal-Mart also sells a number of store brands such as Sam's American Choice and other merchandise under licensed brands such as Kathie Lee.

The Income Statement

The income statement is the financial statement that provides data concerning the results of operations of a company for a specified period of time. Income is determined by the firm's revenues, expenses, gains, and losses. Revenues and expenses result from the firm's primary operations (e.g., a furniture company selling furniture and incurring expenses in this activity); gains and losses result from peripheral operations or events such as a gain on the sale of an operating asset that is no longer needed or a loss due to a fire.

The income for Kilmer Contractors is the difference between its revenues and expenses (the firm has no gains or losses). The income statement of Kilmer Contractors for the month of May is presented below in Illustration 1.

Illustration 1
Kilmer Contractors
Income Statement
For the Month Ending May 31, 19X1

Revenues from painting		$3,800
Supplies used	$1,000	
Salaries	1,500	
Total expenses		2,500
Income for May		$1,300

Revenues normally result in increased assets such as cash or accounts receivable (promises to pay cash to the company). Recall that revenues for Kilmer Contractors included $700 cash received from a customer for painting a house and $900 to be received from another customer for painting a house (an account receivable). If cash is received in advance for providing goods or services, this is not revenue—a liability (unearned revenues) is assumed and recorded for the amount of cash received. Revenue is recorded as it is earned—when the goods or services are provided. The liability is thereby reduced as the revenue is earned. Kilmer Contractors received a payment of $3,300 in advance to paint three houses. This liability was reduced and revenue was recorded for $2,200 (two-thirds of $3,300) when Kilmer painted two of the three houses. The revenue of $3,800 included on Kilmer Contractors' income statement consists of the $700 plus the $900 plus the $2,200.

Expenses result from outflows of cash or merchandise, the use of assets such as supplies and insurance coverage, and the incurrence of liabilities for services provided to the firm (e.g., electricity). The expenses of $2,500 included on Kilmer Contractors' income statement consist of $1,000 of supplies used and $1,500 in payments to employees for salaries.

The income statements for Wal-Mart are presented in Illustration 2. These are comparative statements; income statements are shown for three years, not just the most recent year. The title "statement of income" is a commonly-used alternative title to "income statement." Note that the dollar amounts in the income statements (except for the bottom figure for net income per share) are stated in millions of dollars; therefore, Wal-Mart's net sales for 1997 are over $104 billion, not $104 thousand.

Wal-Mart's revenues consist mainly of net sales to customers. The cost of sales is the cost of the merchandise sold to Wal-Mart customers. If Wal-Mart bought an item for $21 and sold it for $26, the company would earn a gross profit of $5 on the sale—the difference between the selling price and the cost of the item sold. The total gross profit must be large enough to cover the firm's other expenses in order for income to be earned. Comparing the gross profit or gross profit percentage (gross profit divided by net sales) of the current year with those of past years is an indication on the effectiveness of the company in its purchasing and selling activities. Wal-Mart's income before income taxes is $4,850 million in 1997. After taxes, income is reduced to $3,056 million. Recall that, unlike a sole proprietorship or partnership, a corporation must pay income taxes on the income it earns.

Wal-Mart's income statement is much more complicated than that of Kilmer Contractors. Wal-Mart sells many thousands of items of merchandise; Kilmer Contractors does not sell any merchandise, but earns its revenue by providing a service (painting). Included in Wal-Mart's operating, selling and general administrative expenses are hundreds of expense categories (e.g., salaries, advertising, accounting, shipping, and electricity); Kilmer Contractors has only two expenses—supplies used and salaries of employees.

Wal-Mart reports a net income per share figure, which is computed by dividing net income by the average number of shares of stock outstanding (owned by stockholders) for the year.

The accounting concept of income assumes that various rules and principles are followed. These principles require the accountant to exercise his or her professional judgment in their application since the accounting concept of income measurement stresses the fair determination of income. Note that fair presentation of income does not mean precise presentation. Accounting is an estimating process that requires the accountant to view transactions as objectively as possible in determining both the financial position of a firm and its income for the period.

Since the income statement presents the results of operations for an accounting period such as a month (Kilmer Contractors) or a year (Wal-Mart), information included in this statement is usually considered to be among the most important data provided by the company. This is because profitability is a major concern of those interested in the economic activities of a business. For those who invest in a company's stock, decisions to buy and sell securities are based on their assessment or analysis as to whether the company will be more or less successful in future years. Investors attempt to ascertain whether a company's stock price is likely to increase or decrease in future periods. Creditors, those who loan money to a company, make lending decisions based on their analysis as to whether the company will be able to repay its loans. The company's profitability is a key consideration in these decisions.

Classifications that appear in the income statement are intended to be descriptive, functional categories of revenues, expenses, gains, and losses. There are many different formats employed for income statements. Variations among industries are substantial and, to compound this problem, variations among firms in the same industry can also be significant.

Illustration 2

CONSOLIDATED STATEMENTS OF INCOME

(Amounts in millions except per share data)

Fiscal years ended January 31,	1997	1996	1995
Revenues:			
Net sales	$ 104,859	$ 93,627	$ 82,494
Other income-net	1,287	1,122	918
	106,146	94,749	83,412
Costs and Expenses:			
Cost of sales	83,663	74,564	65,586
Operating, selling and general and administrative expenses	16,788	14,951	12,858
Interest Costs:			
Debt	629	692	520
Capital leases	216	196	186
	101,296	90,403	79,150
Income Before Income Taxes	4,850	4,346	4,262
Provision for Income Taxes			
Current	1,974	1,530	1,572
Deferred	(180)	76	9
	1,794	1,606	1,581
Net Income	$ 3,056	$ 2,740	$ 2,681
Net Income Per Share	$ 1.33	$ 1.19	$ 1.17

See accompanying notes.

The Statement of Stockholders' Equity

The statement of stockholders' equity for Kilmer Contractors is presented in Illustration 3. The owners' investment in a corporation is evidenced by shares of stock. Bill Kilmer invested $500 in the business and was issued shares of common stock. The net change in stockholders' equity due to income and due to withdrawals, which are called "dividends" for a corporation, is represented by an account called "retained earnings." There may be other accounts also included as part of the statement of stockholders' equity for a corporation, but an explanation of these accounts is beyond the scope of our discussion at this time. We will consider these other accounts in detail later in this text.

Illustration 3
Kilmer Contractors
Statement of Stockholders' Equity

	Common Stock	Retained Earnings
Beginning balance	$ 0	$ 0
Issued stock	500	
Net income		1,300
Dividends		(600)
Ending balance	$500	$ 700

In a statement of stockholders' equity (or statement of shareholders' equity) for a corporation, elements of stockholders' equity are shown across the top of the statements to form columns; the changes in these elements during each year are listed down the left side of the statement. Wal-Mart's statement of shareholders' equity is presented in Illustration 4. As in the case of Wal-Mart's income statement, these are comparative statements for three years. All amounts included in this statement, except for amounts per share of stock, are stated in millions.

On January 31, 1994 Wal-Mart had 2,299 million shares of its stock outstanding. Due to purchases of Wal-Mart stock by the company in each year (for reasons to be discussed later in this book), there were only 2,285 million shares of stock outstanding on January 31, 1997.

Look at the retained earnings column. The amount of retained earnings on January 31, 1994 is $9,987 million. The net income for the year ended January 31, 1995 is $2,681 million. You can also find this number at the bottom of the 1995 column on Wal-Mart's income statement in Illustration 2. The net income for the year is added to retained earnings. The cash dividends of $391 million are subtracted from retained earnings. These dividends are not an expense that is reported in the income statement, but instead are considered to be a distribution of earnings. After deducting $64 million (to be discussed later in the text), the ending retained earnings balance on January 31, 1995 is $12,213 million. Similarly, net income is added and dividends are subtracted in computing the retained earnings amounts for 1996 and 1997.

The relationship between income and dividends can be seen in the retained earnings column of Wal-Mart's statement of shareholders' equity. Some companies believe their shareholders wish to receive high dividends and attempt to please them. Other companies distribute little or no dividends but instead use the money for growth purposes, which hopefully will provide a return to shareholders by increasing the value of its shares of stock. Wal-Mart's cash dividends per share increased from $.17 to $.20 to $.21 (look down the left side of the statement in Illustration 4). Cash dividends as a percentage of net income increased from 14.6% ($391/$2,681) in 1995 to 16.7% ($458/$2,740) in 1996, but then fell to 15.7% ($481/$3,056) in 1997. Consequently, the one cent per share increase (from $.20 to $.21) in cash dividends from 1996 to 1997 is offset by the 10.3% increase in income (from $2,740 million to $3,056 million).

Illustration 4

CONSOLIDATED STATEMENTS OF SHAREHOLDERS' EQUITY

(Amounts in millions except per share data)	Number of shares	Common stock	Capital in excess of par value	Retained earnings	Foreign currency translation adjustment	Total
Balance - January 31, 1994	2,299	$ 230	$ 536	$ 9,987	$ —	$ 10,753
Net income				2,681		2,681
Cash dividends ($.17 per share)				(391)		(391)
Purchase of Company stock	(3)		(4)	(64)		(68)
Foreign currency translation adjustment					(256)	(256)
Other	1		7			7
Balance - January 31, 1995	2,297	230	539	12,213	(256)	12,726
Net income				2,740		2,740
Cash dividends ($.20 per share)				(458)		(458)
Purchase of Company stock	(5)		(4)	(101)		(105)
Foreign currency translation adjustment					(156)	(156)
Other	1	(1)	10			9
Balance - January 31, 1996	2,293	229	545	14,394	(412)	14,756
Net income				3,056		3,056
Cash dividends ($.21 per share)				(481)		(481)
Purchase of Company stock	(8)		(7)	(201)		(208)
Foreign currency translation adjustment					12	12
Other	(1)		9			8
Balance - January 31, 1997	2,285	$ 228	$ 547	$ 16,768	$ (400)	$ 17,143

See accompanying notes.

THE BALANCE SHEET

The balance sheet, or statement of financial position, is the accounting statement designed to provide information concerning an entity's assets, liabilities, and equity and their relationship among one another at a point in time. It is not designed to present the current value of a business enterprise, but the information provided in the balance sheet should assist users in assessing this value.

The basic accounting equation is depicted by the balance sheet. This equation is as follows:

Assets = Liabilities + Stockholders' Equity

The balance sheet for Kilmer Contractors is presented in Illustration 5.

Illustration 5
Kilmer Contractors
Balance Sheet
May 31, 19X1

Assets		Liabilities	
Cash	$2,400	Advance payment from customers	$1,100
Accounts receivable	900	Note payable	3,000
Supplies on hand	2,000	Total liabilities	$4,100
Total assets	$5,300	Stockholders' equity	
		Common stock	500
		Retained earnings	700
		Total liabilities and	
		stockholders' equity	$5,300

Assets are probable future economic benefits obtained or controlled by a particular entity as a result of past transactions or events. In general, assets are things that are owned by the business and have value. They are the economic resources of the business. An asset is an economic right or a resource that will be of either present or future benefit to the firm. For example, an acre of land purchased by a company is considered to be an asset because the company can obtain future economic benefits from the ownership of the land, can control others' access to these benefits, and has completed the transaction for the purchase of the land. If access to the land cannot be controlled by the company, for example, because the city can use it as a right-of-way or if the transaction has not yet occurred, but will take place in the future, then the land is not considered to be an asset. The assets of a business may take various forms. Examples of assets include: cash, merchandise held for sale to customers, land, buildings, and equipment. In other words, assets are the resources used by a business to continue its operations.

What are the assets of Kilmer Contractors? The assets are cash, accounts receivable, and supplies on hand. At any point in time, the total of the assets of a business are, by definition, equal to the total of the sources of these assets, liabilities and equity. In other words, every asset has a source; everything comes from somewhere. A business obtains its assets from two basic sources: its owners and its creditors.

Creditors lend resources to the firm. These debts, referred to as liabilities, must be repaid at some specified date. Liabilities may be defined as probable future sacrifices of economic benefits arising from present obligations of a particular entity to transfer assets or provide services to other entities in the future as a result of past transactions or events. Examples of liabilities include payments owed to suppliers of merchandise held for sale, to employees, and to public utilities.

What are the liabilities of Kilmer Contractors? The liabilities are an advance payment received from a customer (the company has to provide—i.e., is liable for providing—a service to this customer at a future time) and a loan from Mr. and Mrs. Kilmer (which will be repaid in cash).

Owners invest their personal resources in the firm. Investments by owners are increases in the net assets of an enterprise resulting from transfers to the company from other entities (including individual people) of something of value in exchange for ownership interests (or equity). Assets are by far the most common investments made by owners, but a business may also receive services or payments of its liabilities. Kilmer invested $500 of his own personal cash in his business receiving shares of common stock. The investments of owners in the firm and any profits retained in the business are its equity (or capital). Kilmer Contractors earned $1,300 in income and paid dividends of $600. Therefore, the company retained profits of $700 in the business. Equity is the residual interest that remains in an entity's assets after deducting its liabilities (i.e., Equity is equal to Assets minus Liabilities). In a business enterprise, the equity is the ownership interest. Thus, the sources of a firm's assets are its liabilities and owners' equity.

The balance sheet for Wal-Mart is presented in Illustration 6. This balance sheet has many more accounts than does the balance sheet of Kilmer Contractors; therefore, it must be structured in a manner to enhance its understandability to the users of the financial statements.

The various classifications included in the balance sheet are intended to assist the users of the statement in acquiring as much information as possible concerning the assets, liabilities, and owners' equity of the business. The individual elements of the financial statements are the building blocks with which financial statements are constructed—the classes of items that comprise the financial statements. The items included in financial statements represent in words and numbers business resources, claims to those resources, and the effects of transactions and other events and circumstances that result in changes in these resources and claims.

It might appear that if a firm desires to provide the users of its statements with as much information as possible, it can supply them with a listing of all transactions which took place during the period so that the users can perform their own analysis. However, large firms routinely enter into hundreds of thousands or even millions of transactions during any given period. It is therefore highly unlikely that any user would have either sufficient time, the inclination, or the ability to analyze this type of listing. To simplify the analysis of financial statements, firms group similar items in order to reduce the number of classifications which appear on the balance sheet. For example, a chain store may own many buildings of different sizes, at various locations and serving different functions, but rather than listing these assets separately, all buildings are normally grouped together and presented as a single amount on the balance sheet.

ASSETS

When assets are acquired by a business, they are initially recorded at the cost of their acquisition, or original purchase price. This is true even if the business pays only a part of the initial cost in cash at the time of acquisition and owes the remaining balance (a liability that will be paid to the seller of the asset).

Assets vary in such characteristics as their useful life, physical attributes, and frequency of use. Accountants attempt to describe certain characteristics of assets on the balance sheet by the use of general classifications such as current assets; property, plant and equipment; and other assets. Within these broad categories there are also several sub-classifications. The usual ordering of assets on the balance sheet is in terms of their liquidity—the order in which the assets are normally converted into cash or used up in the operations of the business.

CURRENT ASSETS. Generally, current assets include cash and other assets that are expected to be converted into cash, sold, or used in operations or production during the next year. All of Kilmer Contractors' assets are current assets. For most companies, the year encompasses several operating cycles. For Kilmer Contractors, the operating cycle is the amount of time required to provide the service (e.g., painting a house) plus the amount of time required to collect any account receivables from its customers. For the customer who paid in advance, the operating cycle is the time required to provide the service. For Wal-Mart, the operating cycle is the amount of time needed to buy the inventory, sell the item to a Wal-Mart customer, and collect the cash. For a manufacturing company, the operating cycle is the amount of time required to produce the product, sell it, and collect the cash.

Illustration 6

CONSOLIDATED BALANCE SHEETS

(Amounts in millions)

January 31,	1997	1996
Assets		
Current Assets:		
Cash and cash equivalents	$ 883	$ 83
Receivables	845	853
Inventories		
At replacement cost	16,193	16,300
Less LIFO reserve	296	311
Inventories at LIFO cost	15,897	15,989
Prepaid expenses and other	368	406
Total Current Assets	17,993	17,331
Property, Plant and Equipment, at Cost:		
Land	3,689	3,559
Building and improvements	12,724	11,290
Fixtures and equipment	6,390	5,665
Transportation equipment	379	336
	23,182	20,850
Less accumulated depreciation	4,849	3,752
Net property, plant and equipment	18,333	17,098
Property under capital lease	2,782	2,476
Less accumulated amortization	791	680
Net property under capital leases	1,991	1,796
Other Assets and Deferred Charges	1,287	1,316
Total Assets	$ 39,604	$ 37,541
Liabilities and Shareholders' Equity		
Current Liabilities:		
Commercial paper	$ –	$ 2,458
Accounts payable	7,628	6,442
Accrued liabilities	2,413	2,091
Accrued income taxes	298	123
Long-term debt due within one year	523	271
Obligations under capital leases due within one year	95	69
Total Current Liabilities	10,957	11,454
Long-Term Debt	7,709	8,508
Long-Term Obligations Under Capital Leases	2,307	2,092
Deferred Income Taxes and Other	463	400
Minority Interest	1,025	331
Shareholders' Equity		
Preferred stock ($.10 par value; 100 shares authorized, none issued)		
Common stock ($.10 par value; 5,500 shares authorized, 2,285		
and 2,293 issued and outstanding in 1997 and 1996, respectively)	228	229
Capital in excess of par value	547	545
Retained earnings	16,768	14,394
Foreign currency translation adjustment	(400)	(412)
Total Shareholders' Equity	17,143	14,756
Total Liabilities and Shareholders' Equity	$ 39,604	$ 37,541

See accompanying notes.

The general subclassifications of current assets normally found in the balance sheet include cash, marketable securities, accounts receivable, inventories, and prepaid expenses. These individual asset categories are briefly described below:

CASH. Cash includes all cash that is immediately available for use in the business, including cash on hand, in cash registers, and in checking accounts (demand deposits).

MARKETABLE SECURITIES. Marketable securities are temporary investments in stocks, bonds, and other securities that can be sold readily and that management intends to hold for only a relatively short period of time. If these investments have a maturity (i.e., they become due or will be converted into cash) of three months or less, they are considered to be cash equivalents. Note in Illustration 6 that the first item under current assets for Wal-Mart is cash and cash equivalents. Wal-Mart does not hold any items classified as short-term marketable securities.

RECEIVABLES. The accounts receivable balance represents the amount owed to the business by its customers. If a business has a significant amount of receivables from sources other than its normal trade customers, the receivables from customers are normally classified as trade accounts receivable and the amounts owed by others are classified as other receivables. A balance sheet may also include notes receivable, which are receivables (from customers or others) for which a business has received written documentation of the debtors' intent to pay.

INVENTORIES. Inventories represent the cost of goods or materials held for sale to customers in the ordinary course of business, in the process of production for such sale, or for use in the production of goods or services to be available for sale at some future date.

PREPAID EXPENSES. Prepaid expenses represent expenditures that were made by the company in either the current or a prior period and that will provide benefits to the firm at some future time. Prepaid expenses result from paying expenses in advance. For example, a fire insurance policy that protects the assets of a firm for a year may be purchased during the current year. Although the policy was paid for and a portion of the protection was used during the current year, the firm benefits from the insurance protection in the upcoming year as well. A portion of the cost of the policy is applicable to the coming year and should be considered a prepaid expense.

All of Kilmer Contractors' assets (cash, accounts receivable and supplies) are current assets. Wal-Mart has current assets of $17,993 million in 1997. These current assets consist of cash and cash equivalents, receivables, inventories, and prepaid expenses. Inventories constituted 88 percent ($15,897/$17,993) of Wal-Mart's current assets.

PROPERTY, PLANT AND EQUIPMENT. Property, plant and equipment are those assets acquired for use in the business rather than for resale to customers. They are assets from which the business expects to receive benefits over a number of future accounting periods. Examples of these assets include land, buildings, machinery, and equipment. Since property, plant and equipment are used in the operations of the firm and benefits are derived from their use, the cost of these assets (except for land) is allocated to depreciation expense during all periods that benefit from their use.

Wal-Mart has land, buildings and improvements, fixtures and equipment, and transportation equipment classified as property, plant and equipment. The accumulated depreciation account balance is equal to the total amount of depreciation expense that has been allocated to these assets owned as of January 31, 1997. Depreciation expense is recorded over the useful lives of these assets.

OTHER ASSETS. The classification, other assets, includes those assets that are not appropriately classified under either the current or the property, plant and equipment categories described above. This classification may include both tangible and intangible assets. Tangible assets are those assets that have physical substance, such as land held for investment purposes. Intangibles are assets without physical substance, such as patents, copyrights, and trademarks. The cost of intangible assets is allocated to expense over their useful lives by a process called amortization. Long-term investments include purchases of stock of another company. Such stock may be acquired to exercise influence or control over the operations of the other company. Some companies classify long-term investments under a title of the same name and intangible assets separately under its own title, rather than listing these assets under the "other assets" heading.

Liabilities

Liabilities are debts. They represent the claims of creditors against the assets of a business. Creditors have a prior legal claim over the owners of a business. In the event a business is liquidated, creditors will be paid the amounts owed them before any payments are made to the owners of the business. Creditors are very concerned with the ability of a business to repay its debts. In certain instances, creditors may earn interest on the amounts due them. Normally, a liability has a maturity or due date, at which time it must be paid.

Liabilities, like assets, fall into descriptive categories. The two basic classifications usually employed in the balance sheet are current liabilities and long-term liabilities. Each of these general classes may also have sub-classifications.

CURRENT LIABILITIES. Current liabilities include those obligations that are expected to require the use of current assets (usually cash) or the provision of services within one year. Examples of current liabilities include accounts payable, notes payable, taxes payable, and unearned revenues. These are described in the following paragraphs.

ACCOUNTS PAYABLE. Accounts payable are the claims of vendors who sell goods and services to the company on a credit basis. Accounts payable are usually not evidenced by a formal, written document such as is the case with a note. Wal-Mart's accounts payable on January 31, 1997 totaled $7,628 million.

NOTES PAYABLE. Notes payable normally arise from borrowing or, on occasion, from purchases of assets and are evidenced by a formal written document. Notes payable may or may not be interest bearing. Notes usually have a fixed or determinable due date. Kilmer Contractors has a note payable of $3,000 to Mr. and Mrs. Kilmer on May 31, 19X1.

TAXES PAYABLE. This liability includes any local, state, and federal taxes owed by the business at the end of the accounting period but payable in the next period. Wal-Mart has accrued income taxes payable of $298 million on January 31, 1997.

UNEARNED REVENUES. Unearned revenues are amounts received from customers for goods that have not been shipped or services that have not yet been performed. Unearned revenues arise when customers make prepayments for goods and services. Kilmer Contractors has unearned revenue of $1,100 on May 31, 19X1.

LONG-TERM LIABILITIES. Long-term liabilities generally represent claims that will be paid or satisfied in a future accounting period (or periods) beyond one year. Examples of long-term liabilities are bonds payable, mortgages payable, long-term notes payable, and obligations under certain types of lease contracts, called "capital leases," that give the company the right to use specified properties in exchange for future cash payments. Wal-Mart reports long-term debt as a total on the balance sheet ($7,709 million at January 31, 1997), with the details being reported in a note to the financial statements. Wal-Mart also reports long-term obligations under capital leases of $2,307 million on January 31, 1997.

Long-term liabilities are reclassified and reported as current liabilities when they become due within one year. For example, a note payable classified as a long-term liability in 19X1 because it is due in 19X3 is reclassified to a current liability at the end of 19X2. The last two current liabilities on Wal-Mart's balance sheet are long-term debt due within one year and obligations under capital leases due within one year.

Owners' Equity

Owners' equity (also referred to as capital for a proprietorship or partnership and stockholders' equity for a corporation) represents the claims of the owners against the net assets of the firm. Owners normally assume risks that are greater than those of creditors, because the return on investment to the owners is usually uncertain or undefined. In the event of bankruptcy, claims of creditors take priority over those of owners and must be satisfied first. After all creditors have been paid, any assets that remain are then available for distribution to the owners of the firm.

Accounting for owners' equity is influenced by the legal status of the company—the form of its organization. The most extensively used legal forms of business in the United States are the sole proprietorship, the partnership, and the corporation. There are certain legal differences associated with these types of organizations; these will be considered in later chapters of this text. Basically, the owners' equity of a business comes from two major sources: direct investments made by the owners from their personal resources and profits retained in the business. Owners' equity accounts will be discussed in detail in later chapters.

INVESTMENTS by OWNERS. Investments by owners are increases in the equity of a particular business enterprise resulting from transfers of something of value to the enterprise in exchange for ownership interests (or equity) in the business. Investments by owners are most commonly made in the form of assets (e.g., cash); investments may also include services performed or the conversion of the enterprise's liabilities.

As was explained when the statement of stockholders' equity was discussed, Bill Kilmer's investment in the common stock of the company was $500. In contrast, approximately 250,000 shareholders who have invested in Wal-Mart are represented by common stock and capital in excess of par value. These terms will be explained later in this book. The stockholders' investment in Wal-Mart on January 31, 1997 is $228 million for common stock and $547 million for capital in excess of par value. Basically, this indicates that the stockholders contributed $775 million to the company in exchange for their ownership interests.

The retained earnings account for a corporation reports the profits retained in the business over its lifetime. Retained earnings are increased (decreased) by profits (losses) and decreased by dividends. Kilmer Contractors has $1,300 of income for May 19X1.The profits retained in the business are $700, income of $1,300 less the $600 dividends. The retained earnings balance for Wal-Mart is $16,768 million on January 31, 1997.

USING THE BALANCE SHEET

Numerous relationships within the balance sheet and between the balance sheet and the income statement may be observed. A sample of some of the types of analyses possible is listed below:

- The ability of a company to pay its current debts as they become due depends primarily upon the relationship between its current assets and its current liabilities.

- An indication of the risk that is incurred by the owners in being unable to meet the obligations of the firm may be noted from the firm's debt-to-equity ratio.

- The ability of an enterprise to earn a profit for its owners may be noted by the rate of return on owners' equity.

The ability of a company to pay its current debts as they become due is called "liquidity." An indication of liquidity is a company's working capital, the difference between its current assets and current liabilities.

Working Capital = Current Assets - Current Liabilities

Excessive working capital may indicate that the firm is not investing sufficiently in productive assets such as new equipment; too little working capital may indicate that the firm may not be able to pay its bills as these obligations become due.

Assuming that the loan from Mr. and Mrs. Kilmer is due within one year (the note payable in Illustration 5), the working capital for Kilmer Contractors on May 31, 19X1 is determined as follows:

$$\$5,300 - \$4,100 = \$1,200$$

Working capital for Wal-Mart (see Illustration 6) for 1996 and 1997 is as follows:

1996 $17,331 million - $11,454 million = $5,877 million

1997 $17,993 million - $10,957 million = $7,036 million

Wal-Mart's working capital increased from 1996 to 1997.

A related measure of liquidity, the current ratio, is used to compare a company's liquidity over time, one company's liquidity with the liquidity of another company (even if the companies are not the same size), and a company's liquidity with an industry average. The current ratio is computed as follows:

$$\text{Current Ratio} = \frac{\text{Current Assets}}{\text{Current Liabilities}}$$

Companies in different industries have different typical current ratios. Therefore, whether a current ratio is good or bad depends on the type of business.

Kilmer Contractors current ratio is computed as follows:

$$\text{Current Ratio} = \frac{\$5,300}{\$4,100} = 1.29$$

Wal-Mart's current ratio for 1996 and 1997 is as follows:

1996 $$\text{Current Ratio} = \frac{\$17,331 \text{ million}}{\$11,454 \text{ million}} = 1.51$$

1997 $$\text{Current Ratio} = \frac{\$17,993 \text{ million}}{\$10,957 \text{ million}} = 1.64$$

The current ratio for Wal-Mart increased from 1996 to 1997.

A word of caution regarding Wal-Mart's current ratio. Inventories are a large part of Wal-Mart's current assets. Receivables are more liquid than inventories, because inventories must be sold to obtain receivables or cash. The composition of the current assets held by a company is important. Another ratio, the acid-test ratio, measures liquidity by comparing cash, short-term securities and receivables to current liabilities. This ratio is much smaller for Wal-Mart than its current ratio.

Wal-Mart's acid test ratio for 1996 and 1997 is as follows:

1996 $$\text{Acid-Test Ratio} = \frac{\$936 \text{ million}}{\$11,454 \text{ million}} = .08$$

1997 $$\text{Acid-Test Ratio} = \frac{\$1,728 \text{ million}}{\$10,957 \text{ million}} = .16$$

Although the acid-test ratio for Wal-Mart increased (doubled) from 1996 to 1997, it is low because almost 90% of Wal-Mart's current assets are inventories, which are excluded in calculating the acid-test ratio. A low acid-test ratio is not unusual for retailers such as Wal-Mart.

An indication of the risk incurred by the owners in being able to meet the firm's obligations is the debt-to-equity ratio:

$$\text{Debt-to-Equity Ratio} = \frac{\text{Total Liabilities}}{\text{Stockholders' Equity}}$$

The debt-to-equity ratio is a measure of a company's solvency, its ability to meet its obligations in the long term. Debt must be repaid. If a company has too much debt, it may not be able to make interest payments and repay the face amount of the debt as it becomes due. On the other hand, too little debt may indicate a company is not taking advantage of profitable opportunities in which the income to be earned from borrowing exceeds the interest cost of the debt.

The debt-to-equity ratio for Kilmer Contractors is computed as follows:

$$\text{Debt-to-Equity Ratio} = \frac{\$4,100}{\$1,200} = 3.42$$

The debt-to-equity ratio for Wal-Mart for 1996 and 1997 is as follows:

$$1996 \qquad \text{Debt-to-Equity Ratio} = \frac{\$22,785 \text{ million}}{\$14,756 \text{ million}} = 1.54$$

$$1997 \qquad \text{Debt-to-Equity Ratio} = \frac{\$22,461 \text{ million}}{\$17,143 \text{ million}} = 1.31$$

Wal-Mart's debt-to-equity ratio has decreased from 1996 to 1997 primarily due to the increase in stockholders' equity from retained earnings.

A related solvency measure is the debt-to-total assets ratio, which measures the percentage of assets financed by creditors.

$$\text{Debt-to-Total Assets Ratio} = \frac{\text{Total Liabilities}}{\text{Total Assets}}$$

The debt-to-total assets ratio for Kilmer Contractors is as follows:

$$\text{Debt-to-Total Assets} = \frac{\$4,100}{\$5,300} = 0.77$$

From the debt-to-equity ratio and the debt-to-total assets ratio, Kilmer Contractors has almost all of its assets financed by debt. However, $1,100 of the $4,100 in debt can be repaid by painting houses (the advance payment it received from a customer) rather than by paying cash.

The debt-to-total assets ratio for 1996 and 1997 for Wal-Mart is as follows:

$$1996 \qquad \text{Debt-to-Total Assets} = \frac{\$22,785 \text{ million}}{\$37,541 \text{ million}} = 0.61$$

$$1997 \qquad \text{Debt-to-Total Assets} = \frac{\$22,461 \text{ million}}{\$39,604 \text{ million}} = 0.57$$

Wal-Mart's debt-to-total assets ratio has declined from 1996 to 1997. In 1996, $.61 out of every dollar was provided by creditors; in 1997, $.57 out of every dollar was provided by creditors. These ratios are discussed more fully later in this book.

The ability of an entity to earn a profit for its owners is measured by the rate of return on owners' equity. This rate of return is defined as follows:

$$\text{Rate of Return on Owners' Equity} = \frac{\text{Net Income}}{\text{Average Owners' Equity}}$$

For Kilmer Contractors, the rate of return on owners' equity is computed as follows:

$$\text{Rate of Return on Owners' Equity} = \frac{\$1,300}{(\$0 + \$1,200)/2} = 2.17$$

The company earned $2.17 for each dollar invested in the business.

For Wal-Mart, the rate of return on owners' equity for 1996 and 1997 is as follows (amounts are taken from Illustration 4):

$$1996 \quad \text{Rate of Return on Owners' Equity} = \frac{\$2,740 \text{ million}}{(\$12,726 \text{ million} + \$14,756 \text{ million})/2} = 0.20$$

$$1997 \quad \text{Rate of Return on Owners' Equity} = \frac{\$3,056 \text{ million}}{(\$14,756 \text{ million} + \$17,143 \text{ million})/2} = 0.19$$

The rate of return on owners' equity has declined slightly in 1997.

All of these ratios must be used very carefully. Note that the ratios for Kilmer Contractors and Wal-Mart cannot be meaningfully compared. These are two very different companies. Kilmer Contractors is a small company that is just beginning its operations. Wal-Mart is a multimillion dollar, multinational corporation that has been in business for many years. Kilmer Contractors provides a service; Wal-Mart sells numerous products. Kilmer Contractors should be compared to other small contractors. Wal-Mart should be compared to other large retailers such as K-Mart and Target.

Criticisms of the Balance Sheet

The balance sheet has been criticized for a number of reasons. Most assets are reported on the balance sheet at their original costs. On Wal-Mart's balance sheet, only cash equivalents are reported at year-end market value. Inventories and property, plant and equipment are reported at their cost. While some accountants and financial analysts favor using current values rather than costs, others maintain that such reporting would result in the financial statements becoming distorted and less informative.

A further criticism of the balance sheet is that the values of certain significant items are omitted completely because they cannot be easily measured in monetary terms. Examples of omitted items include the quality of the company's management personnel, the location of the enterprise, and the reputation of the firm's products. Some accountants maintain that the balance sheet would be made much more useful by including valuation concepts and additional information not currently reported under the provisions of generally accepted accounting principles.

The Statement of Cash Flows

A company reports information pertaining to its cash receipts and cash payments in a statement of cash flows. This statement explains the causes of changes in cash plus cash equivalents (highly-liquid marketable securities) and provides a summary of the operating, investing and financing activities of an enterprise during a period of time. Operating activities pertain to the firm's income-producing activities such as buying and selling inventories, providing services, and incurring expenses for salaries and advertising. An income statement reports revenues as they are earned and expenses as they are incurred, regardless of when cash is received and paid. On the other hand, cash flows from operating activities report revenues when cash is received and expenses when cash is paid. Investing activities are concerned with the purchase and sale of such noncurrent assets used in the business as plant and equipment. Financing activities pertain to issuing stocks or short-term or long-term debt, repaying debt, and paying dividends.

The statement of cash flows is useful in appraising factors such as the firm's financing policies, dividend policies, ability to expand productive capacity, and ability to satisfy future debt requirements. Numerous questions can be answered using the statement of cash flows, for example:

- How much cash did the company generate from its operations?
- What is(are) the main source(s) of the company's cash?
- Does the company rely too little or too heavily on nonoperating sources of cash?
- How much cash has been expended on increasing the productive capacity of the company?
- How much debt has the company incurred or repaid?

While certain information concerning changes in cash plus cash equivalents can be obtained from an analysis of comparative balance sheets and income statements, neither of these statements provides complete disclosure of the financing and investing activities of an enterprise over a period of time. An income statement discloses the results of operations for a period of time but does not indicate the amount of resources provided by other activities. Further, as we have seen in the case of Kilmer Contractors, reported revenues and expenses may not represent actual increases or decreases in cash during the period. Comparative balance sheets show net changes in assets and equities but do not indicate the specific causes of these changes. Therefore, while some information concerning changes in cash plus cash equivalents may be obtained from comparative balance sheets and income statements, a complete analysis of the financial activities of a business can be derived only from the statement of cash flows.

The statement of cash flows for Kilmer Contractors is presented in Illustration 7. This statement is a rearrangement of the statement of cash receipts and payments presented in Chapter 2 for Kilmer Contractors. The company did not generate a positive cash flow from its operations. Cash increased mainly because of the loan from Bill Kilmer's parents. This scenario cannot continue for long if Kilmer Contractors is to remain in business.

Illustration 7
Kilmer Contractors
Statement of Cash Flows
For the Month Ending May 31, 19X1

Cash flows from operating activities	
Cash received from customers	$4,000
Cash paid for supplies	(3,000)
Cash paid to employees	(1,500)
Net cash flow from operating activities	($ 500)
Cash flows from financing activities	
Cash received from loan	$5,000
Repayment of loan	(2,000)
Issuance of common stock	500
Payment of dividends	(600)
Net cash flow from financing activities	$2,900
Increase in cash	$2,400

The statement of cash flows for Wal-Mart is presented in Illustration 8. The company generated cash from operations in all three years presented. Payments for property, plant and equipment are the primary reason for the outflow of cash in each year for investing activities. Although cash increased by over $900 million from financing activities in 1995 and 1996, the net cash outflow from financing activities was over $3 billion in 1997. The cash inflow from operating activities in 1997 exceeds the cash outflows from investing and financing activities by $800 million.

Illustration 8

CONSOLIDATED STATEMENTS OF CASH FLOWS

(Amounts in millions)

Fiscal years ended January 31,	1997	1996	1995
Cash flows from operating activities			
Net income	**$ 3,056**	$ 2,740	$ 2,681
Adjustments to reconcile net income to net cash provided by operating activities:			
Depreciation and amortization	**1,463**	1,304	1,070
Increase in accounts receivable	**(58)**	(61)	(84)
Decrease/(increase) in inventories	**99**	(1,850)	(3,053)
Increase in accounts payable	**1,208**	448	1,914
Increase in accrued liabilities	**430**	29	496
Deferred income taxes	**(180)**	76	9
Other	**(88)**	(303)	(127)
Net cash provided by operating activities	**5,930**	2,383	2,906
Cash flows from investing activities			
Payments for property, plant and equipment	**(2,643)**	(3,566)	(3,734)
Proceeds from sale of photo finishing plants	**464**		
Acquisition of assets from Woolworth Canada, Inc.			(352)
Sale/leaseback arrangements			502
Other investing activities	**111**	234	(208)
Net cash used in investing activities	**(2,068)**	(3,332)	(3,792)
Cash flows from financing activities			
(Decrease)/increase in commercial paper	**(2,458)**	660	220
Proceeds from issuance of long-term debt		1,004	1,250
Net proceeds from formation of real estate investment trust (REIT)	**632**		
Purchase of Company stock	**(208)**	(105)	(68)
Dividends paid	**(481)**	(458)	(391)
Payment of long-term debt	**(541)**	(126)	(37)
Payment of capital lease obligations	**(74)**	(81)	(70)
Other financing activities	**68**	93	7
Net cash (used in)/provided by financing activities	**(3,062)**	987	911
Net increase in cash and cash equivalents	**800**	38	25
Cash and cash equivalents at beginning of year	**83**	45	20
Cash and cash equivalents at end of year	**$ 883**	$ 83	$ 45
Supplemental disclosure of cash flow information			
Income tax paid	**$ 1,791**	$ 1,785	$ 1,390
Interest paid	**851**	866	658
Capital lease obligations incurred	**326**	365	193

See accompanying notes.

Interrelationship among the Financial Statements

There are numerous relationships among the financial statements. Some of these relationships are as follows:

1. The income reported on the income statement is an increase to retained earnings in the statement of stockholders' equity. Kilmer Contractors' income of $1,300 in Illustration 1 is added to the beginning retained earnings balance of $0 in Illustration 3; Wal-Mart's 1997 income of $3,056 million in Illustration 2 is added to the beginning 1997 retained earnings balance in Illustration 4.

2. The ending balance of retained earnings in the statement of stockholders' equity is reported on the balance sheet. Kilmer Contractors' retained earnings of $700 at May 31 in Illustration 3 is reported on the balance sheet in Illustration 5; Wal-Mart's 1997 retained earnings of $16,768 million in Illustration 4 is reported on the 1997 balance sheet in Illustration 6. In addition to retained earnings, the 1997 ending balances in Wal-Mart's statement of stockholders' equity for common stock, capital in excess of par value, and foreign currency translation adjustment are reported on its 1997 balance sheet. Likewise, the ending balance in Kilmer Contractors' statement of stockholders' equity for common stock of $500 is reported on the May 31, 19X1 balance sheet.

3. The ending balance of cash in the statement of cash flows is reported on the balance sheet. The ending balance of cash for Kilmer Contractors (which, in this case, is equal to the increase in cash, because May is the initial month of the company's operations) in the statement of cash flows in Illustration 7 is reported on the balance sheet in Illustration 5; Wal-Mart's ending cash balance of $883 million in 1997 in the statement of cash flows in Illustration 8 is reported on the 1997 balance sheet in Illustration 6.

4. When Kilmer Contractors computes cash flows from operating activities in the statement of cash flows, it directly compares cash receipts to cash payments. On the other hand, Wal-Mart computes cash flows from operating activities by starting with its net income (from Illustration 2) and then making numerous adjustments to obtain net cash flow from operating activities (Illustration 8).

Questions

1. What are the three basic types of business organizations?

2. If you started your own business, which form of organization would you choose? Why?

3. How does the income statement of Kilmer Contractors differ from Wal-Mart's?

4. What information is included in the statement of stockholders' equity?

5. How does Kilmer Contractors' balance sheet differ from Wal-Mart's?

6. Define assets.

7. Where does a business obtain its assets?

8. How are assets recorded in the financial statements?

9. What are current assets?

10. Define liabilities.

11. Define current liabilities.

12. Define working capital.

13. Why would the user of the financial statements be interested in the amount of a business's working capital?

14. Define the current ratio.

15. Define the acid-test ratio.

16. Why would the user of financial statements be interested in a business's current and acid-test ratios?

17. Why would Kilmer Contractors' acid-test ratio differ from Wal-Mart's?

18. What information is provided by the debt-to-equity ratio? The debt-to-total assets ratio?

19. What does the rate of return on stockholders' equity tell the reader of the financial statements?

20. What are some limitations of a balance sheet?

21. What information is provided in the statement of cash flows?

Exercises

Below are the condensed financial statements of the Carol Company. You are to use this information in answering Exercises 22 through 30.

Carol Company
Balance Sheet
December 31

	19X1	19X2
Cash	$ 50	$ 60
Marketable securities	20	50
Receivables	100	90
Inventories	150	160
Prepaid expenses	20	30
Property, plant and equipment	500	560
Other assets	60	50
	$900	$1,000
Accounts payable	$ 80	$ 45
Notes payable	50	30
Taxes payable	30	40
Unearned revenues	10	15
Long-term liabilities	280	230
Common stock	250	400
Retained earnings	200	240
	$900	$1,000

[handwritten annotations: 340 and 390 (current assets); 170 and 130 (current liab)]

Carol Company
Income Statement
For the years ending December 31

	19X1	19X2
Sales	$890	$1,180
Cost of goods sold	450	620
Gross profit	440	560
Operating expenses	300	400
Operating income	140	160
Taxes	30	40
Net income	$110	$ 120

Carol Company
Statement of Stockholders' Equity
For the years ending December 31

	19X1		19X2	
	Capital Stock	Retained Earnings	Capital Stock	Retained Earnings
Beginning balances	$250	$150	$250	$200
Sale of capital stock			150	
Net income		110		120
Dividends		(60)		(80)
Ending balances	$250	$200	$400	$240

22. What is the working capital at December 31, 19X2?

23. What is the company's current ratio at December 31, 19X2?

24. What is the company's acid-test ratio at December 31, 19X2?

25. How has the company's liquidity changed since the prior year? Is this change favorable? Provide support for your answer using the information included in the financial statements.

26. Calculate the company's debt-to-equity ratio at December 31, 19X2.

27. Calculate the company's debt-to-total assets ratio at December 31, 19X2.

28. Are creditors in a better (or worse) position at December 31, 19X2 than a year earlier? Support your answer using the information included in the financial statements.

29. Calculate the company's rate of return on total assets for 19X2. How does this compare to the return for the previous year?

30. In general, how would you assess Carol Company at the end of 19X2 compared to the previous year from the perspective of: (a) its creditors; and (b) its owners? Provide support for your answer using the information included in the financial statements.

Outline

LEARNING OBJECTIVES

Chapter 8 discusses the accounting for a company that sells a product and the alternative methods of accounting for inventory. Studying this chapter should enable you to:

1. Illustrate the accounting for a retailing firm.

2. Discuss the components of inventory cost, including purchase discounts, freight-in, returns, and allowances.

3. Distinguish between periodic and perpetual inventory methods.

4. Distinguish between product and period costs.

5. Discuss the objective of inventory accounting.

6. Identify the primary cost basis used in accounting for inventories and describe the elements of this cost.

7. Discuss inventory cost flow methods and the basic assumption each makes.

8. Explain the concept of lower of cost or market as it relates to inventories.

9. Apply the retail and gross profit methods of estimating inventory costs.

MERCHANDISING TRANSACTIONS AND INVENTORIES

INTRODUCTION

The preceding chapters have illustrated the basic steps of the complete accounting cycle for Kilmer Contractors, a firm rendering personal services. The income of a service business is equal to the excess of its revenues (i.e., its fees, commissions, etc.) earned for the services it provides over the expenses incurred by the company in rendering these services. Service companies, such as travel agencies, hotels and airlines, are responsible for a significant dollar volume of business in our economy. However, the majority of businesses in the United States are engaged in selling products. Businesses that earn revenues by selling products may be either merchandising firms or manufacturing companies. Merchandising companies, both wholesalers and retailers, acquire merchandise in ready-to-sell condition, whereas manufacturing companies acquire input materials and produce a product for sale. In contrast to a service type business, the net income of a merchandising or manufacturing company results when the revenues earned from selling products exceed the total of the cost of goods sold and the operating expenses.

A differentiation can be made between product costs and period costs. A product cost is a cost that can be directly identified with the purchase or manufacture of goods available for sale. A period cost is recognized on the income statement as an expense of the period in which it occurred.

While many of the accounting concepts discussed previously are also applicable to product oriented companies, there are certain additional techniques required to account for the purchase and sale of products.

ACCOUNTING FOR MERCHANDISING OPERATIONS

PERIODIC AND PERPETUAL INVENTORIES

The cost of merchandise sold during the period is included in the income statement as an expense referred to as the cost of goods sold. The merchandise available for sale but not sold during the period is referred to as inventory on hand at the end of the year. The cost of this inventory is included in the balance sheet as an asset.

There are two general recordkeeping methods used in accounting for inventories: the periodic and the perpetual inventory methods. The basic differences between these two methods are in the determination of the inventory quantities and the timing of the recording of the cost of goods sold for the period.

Under the periodic method, the cost of goods sold is determined at the end of the period by making a physical count of the goods on hand and subtracting the cost of the goods still on hand from the total cost of goods available for sale. Using the periodic method, inventory is debited when goods are acquired.[1] The inventory account is adjusted at the end of the period when a physical count of the goods on hand is made. This method of accounting for inventory quantities is relatively simple and accurate as of the end of the period. However, the periodic method does not provide the up-to-date inventory quantities summary that is often essential for effective managerial control over inventories.

---

[1] Some accountants prefer to use a separate purchases account to accumulate the cost of inventory purchased. If used, this account is closed out at the end of the period when the ending inventory and cost of goods sold are determined. The use of the purchases account is illustrated in an example later in this chapter.

The perpetual inventory method provides a continuous summary of the quantities on hand by recording all receipts and withdrawals of each inventory item as these occur. Individual records are maintained for each type of inventory item. These records may be maintained in terms of quantities only or in both quantities and dollars. If the record is in terms of quantities only, the accounting entries used under the perpetual system are generally identical to those that are employed under the periodic method. With a perpetual system on a quantity basis, a "running count" of each class or category of inventory item may be maintained, either manually or by the use of electronic data processing equipment, in order to provide information with regard to the quantity of a particular inventory item on hand at any particular point in time. On the other hand, if the perpetual records are maintained in terms of both quantities and dollars, ledger accounts for each type of inventory are debited for increases (e.g., purchases) and credited for withdrawals (e.g., sales). Under this procedure, *the valuation of both inventory and the cost of goods sold to date are available immediately from the accounting records on a current basis.*

When either type of perpetual inventory system is used, a physical count of the goods on hand should be made at least once during each period in order to verify the accuracy of the inventory records. Some companies use various statistical sampling techniques that often make a complete physical count unnecessary.

The perpetual inventory method is most appropriate for a business that has only a limited number of sales of relatively high unit-cost items each day. Examples include retailers of automobiles, jewelry, and expensive furniture. In such a case, it is not difficult to determine the cost of each item sold and to record the specific cost of goods sold expense at the time of the sales transaction. However, in a business with a high volume of sales and/or a variety of merchandise items, it may not be practical to record the cost of each item sold at the time the sale is made. For example, a grocery store can keep continuous track of the units sold of its thousands of items by use of the sensing glass at the checkout stands; however, the store would have a difficult time trying to keep continuous track of the dollar amount of the units sold. Instead, the periodic method can be used by taking a physical count of goods on hand at the end of the period to determine the cost of goods sold.

If perpetual records are kept for both quantities and dollars, variations between the book records and the actual quantities determined by a physical count should be recognized. To correct the inventory records, the inventory account is debited or credited for any difference, with the offsetting debit or credit made to an inventory adjustment or to a gain or loss account. If an inventory adjustment account is used, the balance usually is closed out to cost of goods sold at the end of the period.

The basic difference between the perpetual and periodic methods is illustrated by the following example:

1. Purchased ten cases of beer @ $8 per case (assume that the firm had no inventory at the beginning of the period).

	Perpetual			*Periodic*	
Inventory	80		Inventory	80	
Cash		80	Cash		80

2. Sold seven cases of beer of $12 per case.

	Perpetual			*Periodic*	
Cash	84		Cash	84	
Sales		84	Sales		84
Cost of goods sold	56				
Inventory		56			

3. Ending inventory is two cases of beer by physical count. The ending inventory is 2 cases @ $8 per case, or $16.

Perpetual			Periodic		
Loss	8		Cost of goods sold	64	
Inventory		8	Inventory		64

An analysis of the entries presented above indicates that, using the perpetual system, the cost of goods sold is $56 and a loss of $8 is shown for the missing case of beer.

10	cases purchased	$80
7	cases sold	56
		$24
	ending inventory 2 cases	16
	1 case missing	$ 8

Using the periodic method, the $8 cost of the missing case is included in the cost of goods sold, because the cost of goods sold under this method is determined by subtracting the $16 cost of ending inventory from goods available for sale of $80 and assuming that the difference represents inventory that was sold. This is a disadvantage of the periodic method, because the cost of sales under this method includes not only the cost of the goods actually sold, but also the cost of any merchandise lost or stolen as well. More effective control over inventories may be established by using the perpetual method, either on a dollar or a quantity basis.

To illustrate the application of accounting for merchandising operations, assume that Kilmer Contractors decides to expand its operations by selling carpet to its customers in addition to its painting activities. Recall that its balance sheet at May 31, 19X1, is as follows:

Kilmer Contractors
Balance Sheet
May 31, 19X1

Assets		Liabilities and Stockholders' Equity		
Cash	$2,400	Note payable	$3,000	
Accounts receivable	900	Unearned fees	1,100	$4,100
Supplies	2,000	Common stock		500
Total assets	$5,300	Retained earnings		700
		Total liabilities and		
		stockholders' equity		$5,300

Cost of Merchandise Purchased

Using either the periodic or the perpetual method, the cost of items purchased for sale is debited to the inventory account. To illustrate, assume that on June 1, Kilmer Contractors purchases 1,000 square yards of carpet, paying $5 per yard in cash. The journal entry to record the purchase of this carpet is as follows:

Inventory	5,000	
Cash		5,000

This transaction represents an exchange of one asset for another (i.e., cash for inventory). The debit to the inventory account records the acquisition of the carpet, and the credit to cash indicates the cash expenditure. Because the carpet has not been sold, its cost is considered an asset and not reclassified as an expense until the period in which the carpet is sold.

Sales of Merchandise

When a business sells merchandise to its customers, it either receives immediate payment in cash from its customer or acquires a receivable that will be collected in cash at a future date. In this illustration, assume that during the month of June, Kilmer sold 800 square yards of this carpet at a selling price of $9 per yard. These sales are recorded as follows, assuming that they are made for cash:

Cash	7,200	
Sales		7,200

This transaction is a sale of a product for cash. The debit to the cash account records the increase in cash, and the credit to sales records the total amount of revenue generated from the sale of the carpet. If a sale is made on a credit basis, the entry is a debit to accounts receivable and a credit to sales.

Under the periodic method, no other entry is made at the time of sale. But if a perpetual method is used, the cost of goods sold needs to be recorded also. With a cost of $5 per yard, the cost of goods sold for the 800 square yards of carpet is $4,000.

Cost of goods sold	4,000	
Inventory		4,000

Determination of Income

To continue our illustration, assume that the only expense (other than the cost of the carpet itself) incurred by Kilmer Contractors during the month of June is the payment of salaries to the crew hired to install carpet. This outlay of $1,500 is recorded as follows:

Salaries expense	1,500	
Cash		1,500

This journal entry reflects the fact that period expenses of $1,500 are incurred and paid in cash. This cost is a period cost, because it cannot be associated with the purchase or manufacture of a product and because the benefits are obtained by the firm from this outlay (that is, installation of the carpet sold) during the current accounting period.

The next step in the recording process is to post the journal entries to the appropriate ledger accounts in order to summarize the transactions that have occurred. This process is identical to that described in Chapter 5 and is not repeated here.

After the posting process is completed, the trial balance if the periodic method is used appears as follows:

Kilmer Contractors
Trial Balance before Adjustment
June 30, 19X1

Cash	$ 3,100	
Accounts receivable	900	
Inventory	5,000	
Supplies	2,000	
Note payable		$ 3,000
Unearned fees		1,100
Common stock		500
Retained earnings		700
Sales		7,200
Salaries expense	1,500	
	$12,500	$12,500

At the end of the accounting period, the balance accumulated in the inventory account represents the total cost of the beginning inventory ($0) plus the merchandise purchased during the period. An adjusting journal entry is now required to determine the cost of goods sold for the month. Note that the balance in the inventory account is $5,000, representing the cost of the 1,000 square yards of carpet purchased during the month of June. It is necessary to allocate this balance to record the cost of the carpet still on hand as of June 30 and the cost of the carpet sold during the month of June. The cost of the items still on hand at the end of the period represents an asset, inventory. The cost of the items sold during the period is an expense called cost of goods sold. The adjusting entry necessary to record the cost of the 800 square yards of carpet sold during June and the cost of the 200 square yards of carpet still on hand at June 30, 19X1, is as follows:

Cost of goods sold	4,000	
Inventory		4,000

The debit to cost of goods sold records the cost of the carpet sold during June (800 yards × $5), which leaves in inventory the cost of the carpet still on hand at June 30 (200 yards × $5). The balance in the inventory account at June 30 is also the inventory at the beginning of the next period. Thus, the cost of goods available for sale during the next accounting period will include the beginning inventory plus any purchases made during July. Note that cost of goods available for sale is divided into two components at the end of the period—the cost of goods sold and the inventory on hand. This is done by means of an adjusting entry that is then posted to the ledger accounts.

If the perpetual method is used, the trial balance before adjustment on June 30, 19X1 includes the inventory account for $1,000 and the cost of goods sold for $4,000. No adjusting entry must be made at the end of the period for Kilmer Contractors.

Whether the periodic or perpetual method is used, the next step in the recording process is the preparation of a trial balance after adjustment. This trial balance is presented below:

Kilmer Contractors
Trial Balance after Adjustment
June 30, 19X1

Cash	$ 3,100	
Accounts receivable	900	
Supplies	2,000	
Inventory	1,000	
Note payable		$ 3,000
Unearned fees		1,100
Common stock		500
Retained earnings		700
Sales		7,200
Salaries expense	1,500	
Cost of goods sold	4,000	
	$12,500	$12,500

This trial balance is identical whether the periodic or perpetual method is used.

The next step in the recording process is to prepare closing entries. The journal entries required to close out the revenue and expense accounts of Kilmer Contractors are as follows:

Sales	7,200	
Income summary		7,200
Income summary	5,500	
Salaries expense		1,500
Cost of goods sold		4,000

The balance in the income summary account is then transferred to the retained earnings account by the following entry:

Income summary	1,700	
Retained earnings		1,700

The closing entries are then posted to the general ledger. You should note that the closing entries for a retailing concern are almost identical to those for a service organization.

After the closing entries have been made and posted to the ledger, the financial statements are then prepared as follows:

Kilmer Contractors
Income Statement
For the Month Ending June 30, 19X1

Sales		$7,200
Less: Cost of goods sold:		
Beginning inventory	$ 0	
Purchases	5,000	
Goods available for sale	$5,000	
Ending inventory	1,000	
Cost of goods sold		4,000
Gross profit		$3,200
Salaries expense		1,500
Income		$1,700

Kilmer Contractors
Statement of Stockholders' Equity
For the Month Ending June 30, 19X1

	Common Stock	Retained Earnings
Beginning balances at June 1, 19X1	$ 500	$ 700
Add: Income for the month of June		1,700
Ending balances at June 30, 19X1	$ 500	$2,400

Kilmer Contractors
Balance Sheet
June 30, 19X1

Assets		Liabilities and Stockholders' Equity	
Cash	$3,100	Note payable	$3,000
Accounts receivable	900	Unearned fees	1,100
Supplies	2,000	Common stock	500
Inventory	1,000	Retained earnings	2,400
	$7,000		$7,000

Kilmer Contractors
Statement of Cash Flows
For the Month Ending June 30, 19X1

Cash flows from operations:		
Cash receipts:		
From customers		$7,200
Cash payments:		
To suppliers	$5,000	
To employees	1,500	
		6,500
Increase in cash		$ 700

Note that the difference between the balance sheet for a service business and that of a retailing firm is that the latter includes inventory as an asset. The primary difference between the financial statements of the two types of organizations is in the income statement. The income statement for a service business (see Chapter 5) usually includes a revenue account for each major source of revenue followed by a grouping of expenses which are deducted, in total, from the total revenues for the period in order to determine income. The income statement for a retailing firm includes two major segments or sections. The revenue from the sale of goods is shown first. The determination of the cost of the goods sold is then made and is deducted from sales in order to disclose the gross profit from sales for the period (sales less cost of goods sold). The other expenses are then subtracted from the gross profit figure in order to determine the income for the period.

Objective of Inventory Accounting

The objective of inventory accounting is two-fold. First, it is concerned with valuation of the asset inventory. Valuation of the asset account is important, because the funds invested by a firm in its inventories are usually quite significant; the inventory of a business is often the largest of its current assets. Second, and at least of equal importance, is the proper determination of gross profit of the business for the period by matching the appropriate costs (the cost of the inventory sold) against the related revenue (the revenue earned from the sale of the inventory). In other words, the matching process requires that costs be assigned: (1) to those goods that are sold during the period, and (2) to those goods that are still on hand and available for sale at the end of a period. It should be noted that this is really a single process; the procedures employed in the valuation of inventories also simultaneously determine the cost of goods sold.

In order to illustrate this general process, consider the following activities of Art's Wholesalers for the month of June:

1. Purchased one hundred cases of Coca-Cola at a cost of $4 per case.
2. Sold eighty cases of Coca-Cola at a price of $6 per case.
3. Selling expenses for June totalled $35.
4. On June 1, Art had ten cases of Coke, which had cost him $4 per case, on hand. At June 30, Art's inventory consisted of thirty cases of Coke.

Art's income statement for the month of June is as follows:

Art's Wholesalers
Income Statement
For the Month of June

Sales (80 cases $6)		$480
Less: Cost of goods sold:		
Beginning Inventory,		
June 1 (10 cases @ $4)	$ 40	
Add: Purchases (100 cases @ $4)	400	
Goods available for sale	$440	
Deduct: Ending inventory,		
June 30 (30 cases @ $4)	120	
Cost of goods sold		320
Gross profit from sales		$160
Selling expenses		35
Income		$125

Several points should be noted from the analysis of the above income statement. The total inventory of Coke available for sale, identified in the income statement as the *goods available for sale*, is accumulated by combining the cost of goods on hand at the start of the period (*beginning inventory*) with the cost of Coke purchased during the period (*purchases*).

Goods available for sale are then divided into two components: (1) the cost of Coke still on hand and available for sale at the close of the period (*ending inventory*), and (2) the cost of Coke sold during the period (*cost of goods sold*). *Cost of goods sold* is subtracted from the sales revenue for the period (*sales*) in order to determine *gross profit from sales*. Note that the *gross profit from sales* is determined and presented before the other expenses incurred during the period are considered. The next step in the preparation of the income statement is the deduction of these expenses, in this example *selling expenses*, in order to arrive at the income for the period.

The example used above is uncomplicated for purposes of illustration. All Coke is assumed to have been acquired at a single price and no discounts, returns, or losses are encountered. Our purpose has been to illustrate the general concepts of inventory accounting. We now consider some of the detailed procedures that are normally involved in this process.

INVENTORY COSTS

Inventory values should reflect all costs that are required in order to obtain merchandise (by a retailer or wholesaler) in the desired condition and location. If any costs of obtaining inventory (in addition to the purchase price) are not included as a part of the cost of the asset and instead are considered to be an expense of the period, inventory values on the balance sheet are understated and expenses on the income statement are overstated. When these goods are sold in a later period, expenses on the income statement of that period will be understated.

All indirect costs incurred by the business in obtaining and placing the goods in a marketable condition should be included as a part of inventory cost if it is possible and practical to identify these costs with inventory purchases. Examples of these costs include such items as sales taxes, duties, freight-in, storage costs and insurance. In most cases, the cost of allocating these costs to each of hundreds or thousands of inventory items is greater than the benefit derived and, consequently, these costs are simply charged to expense as incurred. The cost of merchandise is reduced by any discounts, returns, and allowances.

PURCHASE DISCOUNTS

Sellers of goods frequently offer discounts to their customers to recognize quantity purchases and to encourage prompt payment for goods sold on account. Quantity discounts, often referred to as trade discounts, usually represent an adjustment of a catalog or list price to arrive at the selling price of merchandise to a particular customer. For this reason, trade discounts are not usually reflected in the accounts. For example, assume that a distributor offers Coke at a list price of $5 per case and allows Art's Wholesalers a trade discount of 20 percent. From an accounting viewpoint, Art determines the cost to be employed in his accounts as follows:

List price per case	$5
Less: Trade discount (20% of $5)	1
Cost per case	$4

Art uses the $4 figure as his cost; the $5 list price and the $1 discount do not appear anywhere in the accounts.

Discounts that are offered to encourage the prompt payment of purchases made on a credit basis are another matter. These discounts may be reflected in the accounts. Such discounts, often referred to as purchase discounts, are usually stated in terms such as 2/10; n/30. This notation means that a 2 percent discount is offered to the customer if his or her account is settled within ten days of the date of sale; the full amount is due at the end of the thirty-day period. Two methods may be used in accounting for these discounts, the *net* method and the *gross* method. In order to illustrate these two methods, we return to the transactions of Art's Wholesalers for the month of June and record the purchase of the one hundred cases of Coke at $4 per case in Art's books and in the distributor's accounts using both the net and gross methods. We assume that the terms offered are 2/10; n/30. In this example, we will also illustrate the use of a separate purchases account. See Illustration 1.

The seller of merchandise normally records the sale at the gross amount. One reason for this procedure lies in the fact that the seller has no control over whether or not the purchaser will make payment during or after the discount period. If payment is made by the purchaser during the discount period, the difference between the cash payment and the amount of the receivable (which was set up for the gross amount of the sale) is recorded by the seller as a *sales discount*. If payment is made after the expiration of the discount period, the purchaser is required to pay the gross amount in full. If this is the case, the seller debits cash and credits accounts receivable for the amount of cash received. See Illustration 1.

Illustration 1
Discounts

Transaction	Coca-Cola Distributor	Art's Net Method	Art's Gross Method
Sale of 100 cases of Coca-Cola; terms: 2/10; n/30.	Accounts receivable........ 400 Sales................ 400	Purchases............. 392 Accounts payable........ 392	Purchases............. 400 Accounts payable........ 400
Payment made *during* the discount period.	Cash............... 392 Sales discounts......... 8 Accounts receivable....... 400	Accounts payable......... 392 Cash.............. 392	Accounts payable........ 400 Cash.............. 392 Purchase discount....... 8
Payment *after* the discount period.	Cash............... 400 Accounts receivable....... 400	Accounts payable......... 392 Discount lost........... 8 Cash.............. 400	Accounts payable........ 400 Cash.............. 400

In the purchaser's accounts, the sales price less the purchase discount is recorded at the time of the purchase if the net method is used. If payment for the goods is made during the discount period, the purchaser debits accounts payable and credits cash for the amount paid. On the other hand, if payment is made after the discount period has passed, the purchaser is required to pay the full or gross price. Since the payable is originally recorded at the net amount, the entry for the payment requires a debit to accounts payable for the net amount and a credit to cash for the amount paid (gross price); the difference between the gross and the net price is debited to a *discounts lost* account. Discounts lost are considered to be expenses of the period and are included as such in the income statement.

Under the gross method of recording purchases, the initial entry for the buyer is to debit purchases and credit accounts payable for the full (gross) price. If payment is made during the discount period, the entry consists of a debit to accounts payable for the original amount recorded as a liability (gross price), a credit to cash for the amount actually paid (net price), and a credit for the difference to a *purchase discounts* account. Purchase discounts are reported as a deduction from the purchases made during the period. If the payment is made after the discount period has expired, the entry consists of a debit to accounts payable and a credit to cash for the full or gross price.

Note that the difference between the two methods lies in the information provided by each. The net method provides information as to the discounts that were lost but gives no data as to those that were taken. The gross method indicates the amount of discounts taken but gives no information as to the discounts lost. Because of the significance[2] of discounts lost to the business, the authors feel that information regarding the discounts not taken is critical and for this reason believe that the net method should be used by purchasers. We feel that any discounts lost are, in fact, interest costs and should be disclosed as such and not included as a part of the cost of inventories.

Freight-in, Returns, and Allowances

The purchase of merchandise often involves payment of shipping costs necessary to bring the goods to the purchaser's place of business. The cost of the merchandise logically includes these transportation costs. Goods may be shipped F.O.B. shipping point or F.O.B. destination. The initials F.O.B. stand for free on board. F.O.B. shipping point means that the seller pays the costs to the shipping point only; the buyer pays the cost of transit from the shipping point to the destination. Alternatively, F.O.B. destination terms require the seller to pay all shipping costs (e.g., by railroad or truck) or deliver the product to the buyer personally.

The shipping terms determine whether the buyer or the seller owns the goods at the end of the accounting period. If goods are shipped F.O.B. shipping point at the end of the year but have not reached the buyer at that time, the goods still are the property of the buyer (legal title passes from the seller to the buyer). The buyer should record a purchase; the seller should record a sale. On the other hand, if goods are shipped F.O.B. destination, the goods remain the property of the seller until they reach the buyer. The buyer does not record the purchase this year; the seller does not record the sale.

Sometimes, purchasers of goods find it necessary to return goods to their suppliers because the goods are damaged or unacceptable. These are considered to be purchase returns by the buyer and sales returns by the seller. A separate purchases returns account is used by the buyer rather than reducing purchases directly. Similarly, a separate sales returns account is used by the seller rather than reducing sales directly. In other instances, such goods are retained by the purchaser and the supplier allows an adjustment of the purchase price, known as an allowance. The buyer uses a separate purchase allowance account rather than reducing purchases directly. Likewise, the seller uses a separate sales allowance account rather than reducing sales directly.

---

[2] Failure to take a discount when the terms are 2/10; n/30 represents an interest cost In excess of 36 percent per annum. Not paying an account with the 2 percent discount gives a business an extra twenty days to pay. There are over 18 twenty-day periods in a year. At 2 percent for each twenty-day period, the interest rate exceeds 36 percent.

To illustrate freight-in, returns, and allowances, assume the following facts:

1. Art orders fifty cases of Coke, fifty cases of Pepsi, and fifty cases of Dr. Pepper, all at a price of $4 per case. The terms were F.O.B. shipping point, 2/10; n/30, and Art uses the net method for recording purchases. Art pays the freight of $10.

2. Art's distributor ships him fifty cases of Pepsi, and, by mistake, one hundred cases of Coke instead of fifty and fifty cases of Orange Crush instead of the Dr. Pepper.

3. Art returns fifty cases of the Coke, agrees to keep the Orange Crush in lieu of the Dr. Pepper since the distributor gives him a $5 allowance, and pays the balance in full within the discount period.

The entries to record these transactions are as follows:

Art				*Distributor*		
Purchases	784			Accounts receivable	800	
Freight-in	10			Sales		800
Accounts payable		784				
Cash		10				
				Cash	583	
				Sales returns	200	
Accounts payable	784			Sales allowance	5	
Purchase returns		196		Sales discount	12	
Purchase allowance		5		Accounts receivable		800
Cash		583				

Art debits purchases and credits accounts payable for the net amount of the purchase ($800 less 2% of $800, or a net amount of $784). Even though Art received one hundred cases of Coke rather than fifty, he records the purchase for all two hundred cases of soft drinks. He debits freight-in and credits cash for the $10 freight charge that he pays in cash, since according to the terms of the purchase (F.O.B. shipping point) this is his responsibility. The seller, using the gross method, simply debits accounts receivable and credits sales for the full price of the sale (200 cases @ $4).

At the time payment is made, Art debits accounts payable for the amount of the liability originally recorded (net price). He credits purchase returns for the net cost of the fifty cases of Coke that he returned to the seller (50 cases @ $4 or $200, less 2% of $200, or a net of $196) and credits purchase allowances for the $5 adjustment made to Art for keeping the Orange Crush, rather than the Dr. Pepper that he ordered. The credit to cash is for the net cash paid ($784 less the $196 return, less the $5 allowance, or a net amount of $583).

When the seller receives Art's payment, he debits cash for the $583 received, debits sales returns for $200 (the 50 cases of Coke returned @ $4), debits sales allowance for the $5 adjustment, and debits sales discounts for $12 (150 cases @ $4 or $600 multiplied by 2%). The distributor credits accounts receivable for the amount he originally recorded, the gross amount of $800.

The partial income statement presented in Illustration 2 is an example of how these items can be disclosed in an income statement. The numbers are assumed for the example. They are not related to the numbers in the discussion above.

Note that the account purchase discounts does not appear in the income statement because we assumed that Art is using the net method of recording purchases. If the gross method is used, purchases are included at their gross rather than net amount and purchase discounts appear along with purchase returns and purchase allowances as a deduction in arriving at the net purchases for the period. Discounts lost do not appear in the income statement when using the gross method.

Illustration 2
Art's Wholesalers
Partial Income Statement
For the Year Ending December 31, 19X1

Sales				$102,800
Less:	Sales returns		$ 500	
	Sales allowances		300	
	Sales discounts		2,000	2,800
Net sales				$100,000
Cost of goods sold:				
Beginning inventory			$10,000	
Purchases		$70,000		
Less:	Purchase returns	$1,000		
	Purchase allowances	100	1,100	
			$68,900	
Add:	Freight-In		600	
Net purchases			69,500	
Goods available for sale			$79,500	
Ending Inventory			15,500	
Cost of goods sold				64,000
Gross profit on sales				$ 36,000
Discounts lost		$ 100		
All other expenses		20,000		20,100
Income				$ 15,900

INCOME STATEMENT ANALYSIS

Gross profit is the difference between net sales and cost of goods sold. For Art's wholesalers in Illustration 2, gross profit for 19X1 is computed as follows:

Net sales	$100,000
Cost of goods sold	64,000
Gross profit	$ 36,000

Gross profit has to be large enough to cover the firm's operating expenses and still result in income for the period. In the case of Art's Wholesalers, the gross profit of $36,000 is large enough to cover discounts lost and all other expenses and leave an income amount of $15,900.

Wal-Mart's gross profit for 1997 is computed as follows (numbers are in millions):

Net sales	$104,859
Cost of goods sold	83,663
Gross profit	$ 21,196

Coca-Cola's gross profit for 1996 is computed as follows (numbers are in millions):

Net sales	$ 18,546
Cost of goods sold	6,738
Gross profit	$11,808

Gross profit numbers should not be examined in isolation. Wal-Mart's gross profit in 1997 should be compared with its gross profits in prior years and with those of other firms in the industry. A similar statement can be made in regards to Coca-Cola's gross profit in 1996.

If gross profit is divided by net sales, the gross profit rate is obtained. The gross profit rates for Art's Wholesalers for 19X1, Wal-Mart for 1997, and Coca-Cola for 1996 are as follows (dollars are in millions for Wal-Mart and Coca-Cola):

	Art's Wholesalers	Wal-Mart	Coca-Cola
Gross profit	$ 36,000	$ 21,196	$11,808
Net sales	$100,000	$104,859	$18,546
Gross profit rate	36%	20%	64%

The gross profit rate for each should be compared with the gross profit rates in prior years and with those of other firms in its industry. Changes in gross profit rates and differences among companies in the same industry are due to many causes. For example, Wal-Mart had a slight decrease in its gross profit rate in 1997 due in part to markdowns resulting from a reduction in the assortment of selected categories of merchandise. Coca-Cola had an increase in its gross profit rate in 1996 due to a shift from bottling and canning operations to its higher-margin concentrate business and to changes in product mix.

Operating income is computed by subtracting cost of goods sold and selling and administrative expenses from net sales. The ratio of operating income to net sales is a measure of operating efficiency. The ratios for Wal-Mart for 1995 and Coca-Cola for 1996 are as follows (dollars are in millions):

	Wal-Mart	Coca-Cola
Operating income	$ 4,408	$ 3,915
Net sales	$104,859	$18,546
Ratio	4%	21%

Wal-Mart's ratio of operating income to sales in 1997 was about the same as that for 1996. Coca-Cola's ratio decreased from 1995 to 1996 due to disposing of some foreign bottling and canning operations and to several nonrecurring charges.

INVENTORY TURNOVER

The amount of inventory a company has on hand is an important consideration. While inventory is considered an asset, companies are searching for ways to reduce the inventories they hold. For example, Wal-Mart reduced its inventories by $1 billion in 1997 and plans on an additional reduction of $500 million in 1998. Lower inventories allow Wal-Mart to devote less retail space to storing goods and more to selling them. In addition, smaller inventory levels free up capital for more productive purposes.[3] Too much inventory means higher than necessary storage costs, obsolescence costs, and interest costs; too little inventory means possible lost sales due to stockouts.

The inventory turnover ratio is calculated by dividing cost of goods sold by average inventory. The ratios for Wal-Mart for 1997 and Coca-Cola for 1996 are as follows (dollars are in millions):

	Wal-Mart	Coca-Cola
Cost of goods sold	$83,663	$6,738
Average inventory	$15,943	$1,035
Inventory turnover	5.2	6.5

As stated before, the inventory turnover ratio for each should be compared with the inventory turnover ratios in prior years and with those of other firms in its industry.

---

[3] "Why Wall Street's Buying Wal-Mart Again," *Fortune* (February 16, 1998), 92-94.

INVENTORY ERRORS

Inventory errors may occur due to counting or costing errors or due to errors in determining which party (buyer or seller) has legal title to goods shipped. Such errors affect both the balance sheet and the income statement.

Assume that a company reports the information for 19X1 and 19X2 presented in Illustration 3 (see columns labeled As Reported). Now assume that $30 of inventory purchased on terms F.O.B. destination was included in the 19X1 year-end inventory balance although it did not arrive until the third day of the following year. The ending inventory for 19X1 is overstated by $30, the cost of goods sold is understated by $30, and gross profit and income are overstated by $30. Subsequently, the beginning inventory for 19X2 is overstated by $30, cost of goods available is overstated by $30, cost of goods sold is overstated by $30, and gross profit and income are understated by $30.

Illustration 3
Effect of Inventory Error

	As Reported 19X2	Corrected 19X2	As Reported 19X1	Corrected 19X1
Net sales	$4,800	$4,800	$4,000	$4,000
Cost of goods sold:				
Beginning inventory	$ 700	$ 670	$ 800	$ 800
Purchases, net	2,100	2,100	2,200	2,200
Cost of goods available	$2,800	$2,770	$3,000	$3,000
Ending inventory	900	900	700	670
Cost of goods sold	$1,900	$1,870	$2,300	$2,330
Gross profit	$2,900	$2,930	$1,700	$1,670

The error in determining the ending inventory for 19X1 has opposite effects in the two years. Cost of goods sold is understated and gross profit is overstated in 19X1; cost of goods sold is overstated and gross profit is understated in 19X2. The total gross profit over the two years is correct, but the gross profit in each of the two years is incorrect. Ratios in which inventories or gross profit are used are also incorrect for each of the two years. For example, these ratios include the gross profit rate, operating income to sales, the inventory turnover, and the current ratio.

INVENTORY COST FLOW METHODS

Once the quantity of goods on hand at the end of the period and the quantity of goods sold during the period are determined, the next step is to decide how costs should be allocated between cost of goods sold and ending inventory. If all purchases of inventory are made at the same unit price, this allocation does not create any problems. However, if the inventory items are acquired at different unit costs, it is necessary to determine which costs should be assigned to each inventory item. One method of determining the cost of the inventory on hand is to maintain records of the exact cost of each item sold during the period and each item on hand at the end of the period. In businesses that sell high unit-cost items such as automobiles or jewelry, this *specific identification* method is useful. The exact item sold, along with its unit cost, can be easily identified. But in many cases, this specific identification procedure requires excessive record-keeping costs, while in other instances it is impossible to do so. In addition to practical considerations, specific identification also presents a potential problem, because this method allows for the potential manipulation of reported income. When identical units are acquired or produced at different unit costs, management may manipulate cost of goods sold and net income by selecting either a higher- or lower-priced item at the time a good is sold. Consequently, some systematic method for assigning costs to inventory is usually necessary both for practical reasons and for obtaining a more objective inventory valuation and income determination.

The cost flow methods are based on assumptions that are made regarding the assumed flow of inventory costs. Cost flow refers to both the inflow of costs when goods are purchased or manufactured and the outflow of costs when the goods are sold. The cost flow assumptions are systematic procedures that determine the order in which unit costs are assigned to cost of goods sold and inventory. Using alternative cost flow assumptions has generated considerable controversy regarding inventory accounting, because the use of different methods may result in substantial variations in net income and inventory valuations in the financial statements.

There are a number of cost flow methods that are acceptable for financial accounting purposes. Each of the acceptable cost flow methods is based on the cost principle; they differ only in terms of the costs that are assigned to cost of goods sold and those that are assigned to inventory.

There are three commonly used methods in costing inventories (excluding the specific identification method discussed above) and, therefore, determining cost of goods sold for the period: *the average-cost method; the first-in first-out (FIFO) method; and the last-in, first-out (LIFO) method. These methods employ assumptions regarding the flow of inventory costs, not the actual physical flow of goods.* Accordingly, the order in which costs are assigned to cost of goods sold does not have to be consistent with the physical order in which the goods are sold. The application of these methods results in a different amount of ending inventory and cost of goods sold for each period because they are based upon different arbitrary assumptions as to the flow of costs of merchandise through the business. The major objective in selecting a cost-flow method should be to choose the one that most clearly reflects periodic income under the circumstances.

The following data relating to a special brand of foreign beer, again taken from the inventory records of Art's Wholesalers, will be used to illustrate these methods:

January 1:	Beginning inventory (100 cases @ $2)	$200
February 7:	Purchase (150 cases @ $3)	450
March 25:	Purchase (200 cases @ $4)	800
October 6:	Purchase (150 cases @ $5)	750
November 10:	Purchase (100 cases @ $6)	600

The goods available for sale during the year were 700 cases at a total cost of $2,800. Art's records indicate that 500 cases were sold during the year. The accounting problem is in assigning or allocating the $2,800 cost of goods available for sale between the ending inventory and the cost of goods sold. The valuation of the ending inventory (and therefore, the determination of the cost of goods sold) under each of the alternative methods of inventory valuation using the periodic method is illustrated in the paragraphs that follow.

Average-Cost Method

Using the periodic system, the average-cost method (often called the weighted-average cost method) assigns costs to inventory and to cost of goods sold based on the weighted-average cost of all the items that were available for sale during the period. A weighted-average unit cost is computed at the end of the period by dividing the total cost of the beginning inventory plus the purchases by the total number of units included in the inventory. The weighted-average cost is multiplied by the number of units sold to derive the cost of goods sold and is also applied to the units on hand to determine the valuation of the ending inventory. A feature of the average-cost method is the assignment of cost on an equal unit basis to both the ending inventory and cost of goods sold.

In the example stated above, the average cost is calculated as follows:

January 1:	Inventory (100 cases @ $2)	$ 200
February 7:	Purchase (150 cases @ $3)	450
March 25:	Purchase (200 cases @ $4)	800
October 6:	Purchase (150 cases @ $5)	750
November 10:	Purchase (100 cases @ $6)	600
	Total 700 cases	$2,800

The total cost of the goods available for sale ($2,800) is divided by the number of cases (700) and the result of $4 is the average cost of the inventory. This average-cost figure is used both in valuing the ending inventory (200 × $4 = $800) and in determining the cost of goods sold for the period (500 × $4 = $2,000).

First-in, First-Out (FIFO) Method

The FIFO method assumes that the costs of the first items acquired or produced are the costs of the first items used or sold. In many cases, the assumption is also consistent with the actual flow of goods. FIFO inventories are priced by using the actual invoice costs or production costs for the latest purchased or produced quantities that are still on hand.

The major advantage of FIFO is that it assigns the most recent costs to inventories included on the balance sheet, because the ending inventory is composed of the most recent purchases. FIFO is a good method to use when the inventory turnover is rapid or when the composition of the inventory changes frequently, because the costs associated with the oldest inventory are transferred to cost of goods sold first.

The primary disadvantage of the FIFO method is that it fails to match the most recent costs with current revenues. If prices are rising, matching the oldest unit costs with current revenues may result in an overstatement of income in terms of current dollars.

The FIFO inventory and the related cost of goods sold for Art's Wholesalers is calculated as follows:

FIFO Cost of Goods Sold
The First 500 Units

January 1:	Inventory (100 cases @ $2)	$ 200
February 7:	Purchase (150 cases @ $3)	450
March 25:	Purchase (200 cases @ $4)	800
October 6:	Purchase (50 cases @ $5)	250
	FIFO cost of goods sold	$1,700

FIFO Ending Inventory
The Last 200 Units

October 6:	Purchase (100 cases @ $5)	$ 500
November 10:	Purchase (100 cases @ $6)	600
	FIFO cost of ending inventory	$1,100

Last-In, First-Out (LIFO) Method

The last-in, first-out (LIFO) method assumes that the costs of the last items acquired or produced are the costs of the first items used or sold. A principal advantage of the LIFO method is that it matches current costs more nearly with current revenues. Another advantage of LIFO is the fact that in periods of price increases, income computed using LIFO is less than the amount that would result from using FIFO or the average-cost method; therefore, it reduces federal income taxes. The disadvantage is that reported income is reduced as well as taxable income. Unlike many other instances where alternative accounting procedures exist. Federal income tax laws require the use of the LIFO inventory method for financial reporting purposes whenever it is used for income tax purposes. Another disadvantage is that LIFO gives a "noncurrent" value to inventories in the balance sheet.

The cost of the LIFO inventory and the related cost of goods sold for Art's Wholesalers is calculated as follows:

LIFO Ending Inventory
The First 200 Units

January 1:	Inventory (100 cases @ $2)	$	200
February 7:	Purchase (100 cases @ $3)		300
	LIFO cost of ending inventory	$	500

LIFO Cost of Goods Sold
The Last 500 Units

February 7:	Purchase (50 cases @ $3)	$	150
March 25:	Purchase (200 cases @ $4)		800
October 6:	Purchase (150 cases @ $5)		750
November 10:	Purchase (100 cases @ $6)		600
	LIFO cost of ending inventory	$2,300	

Conceptually, the LIFO inventory method may be described as a series of cost layers. Under the periodic basis, an increase in inventory quantities during a period results in an ending inventory that consists of the beginning inventory layer plus a purchase layer that is added at the cost of the earliest acquisitions made during the period. If inventory quantities decrease during any period, the cost of the most recently added layers and some or all of the beginning inventory layer are allocated to the cost of goods sold. Once all or part of a layer is removed from the inventory and added to the cost of goods sold, the cost of that layer is never restored to the inventory. If the inventory quantity increases in the next period, a new layer is added at the earliest cost at which the purchases are made during that period.

Differences in Methods

The effect of the differences in the three methods that we described above is illustrated by the following summary:

	Average	*FIFO*	*LIFO*
Sales (500 cases @ $10)	$5,000	$5,000	$5,000
Less: Cost of goods sold:			
Beginning inventory			
(100 cases)	$ 200	$ 200	$ 200
Purchases			
(600 cases)	2,600	2,600	2,600
Goods available for sale			
(700 cases)	$2,800	$2,800	$2,800
Ending inventory			
(200 cases)	800	1,100	500
Cost of goods sold			
(500 cases)	$2,000	$1,700	$2,300
Gross profit on sales	$3,000	$3,300	$2,700

The total cost of goods available for sale ($2,800) was allocated either to cost of goods sold or ending inventory in every case. The sales, beginning inventory, and purchases included in the example are identical irrespective of the inventory method chosen. An inventory method is used only to cost the ending inventory and to determine the cost of goods sold. It does not necessarily reflect the actual physical flow of goods. That is, a bakery may use the LIFO method for accounting purposes although obviously the physical flow is FIFO—who wants a ten-year-old cake!

The alternative choices of inventory valuation methods may have a substantial impact on both the financial statements and income taxes. Therefore, management must consider the effects on the reported data and on cash flows in selecting or changing an inventory method. Although a firm may select any one of several acceptable methods, the consistency principle requires that a firm use the same method over time.

Many businesses use different inventory valuation methods for various components of their inventories. The inventory methods a company uses must be disclosed in the financial statements.

Lifo Reserve

Many companies that use LIFO report a LIFO reserve on their balance sheets (either directly or, more commonly, by means of a footnote). The LIFO reserve is the difference between the inventory reported at LIFO and what it would have been if FIFO or replacement cost had been used. For example, inventories (in millions of dollars) for 1996 and 1997 for Wal-Mart are reported as follows:

	1997	1996
Inventories		
At replacement cost	$16,193	$16,300
Less LIFO reserve	296	311
Inventories at LIFO cost	$15,897	$15,989

Wal-Mart's current assets for 1997 are reported at $17,993 million. The company's current liabilities are $10,957 million. If replacement cost had been used, Wal-Mart's 1997 inventory would have been $296 million higher and its current assets would have been $18,289 million. The current ratios with LIFO being used and if replacement cost had been used are as follows (dollars are in millions):

	LIFO	Replacement Cost
Current assets	$17,993	$18,289
Current liabilities	$10,957	$10,957
Current ratio	1.64	1.67

While the difference is not large in this case, it can be for other companies.

The LIFO reserve can also be used to compute what income would have been if FIFO or replacement cost had been used. The LIFO reserve for Wal-Mart increased by $15 million. Consequently, cost of goods sold for 1997 would have been $15 million higher and income would have been $15 million lower if FIFO or replacement cost had been used instead of LIFO.

Lower-of-cost-or-market

As previously indicated, the primary basis for accounting for inventories is cost. Therefore, if the value of the item increases or decreases prior to its sale, no record of this fact is normally entered in the records. However, an exception to this rule may occur when the market price, which is defined as the current replacement cost of the goods, is less than their historical cost. In this case, the inventory may be carried at its replacement cost. In other words, inventories may be carried at the lower of their cost or their market value. If the market price for a firm's inventory falls below its original cost, an entry is made recognizing the difference between cost and market as a loss and reducing the carrying value of the inventory to market. The reduced figure becomes the new "cost" of the inventory for accounting purposes. However, if the market price exceeds the original cost, no entry is made in the accounts. The recognition of losses but not gains prior to sale is based on the principle of conservatism—losses can be anticipated, but not gains.

By using the lower-of-cost-or-market method, the entity recognizes the loss in the value of the inventory in the period in which the loss occurs. Subsequently, the "normal" gross profit is recognized in the subsequent period in which the item is sold.

To illustrate the lower-of-cost-or-market method, assume the same facts as presented previously—that a firm had 700 cases of beer available for sale and that this beer had been purchased at an average price of $4 per case. Sales for the period were 500 cases at a selling price of $10 per case. If the business uses the average-cost inventory method, the gross profit on sales is calculated as follows:

Sales (500 cases @ $10)	$5,000
Less: Cost of goods sold:	
Beginning Inventory (100 cases)	$ 200
Purchases (600 cases)	2,600
Goods available for sale (700 cases)	$2,800
Ending inventory (200 cases)	800
Cost of goods sold	$2,000
Gross profit on sales	$3,000

If the replacement cost of the ending inventory declines to $750 as of the end of the period, the ending inventory may be written down from its original cost of $800 to its current replacement cost of $750 by the following entry:

Loss on inventory decline	50	
Inventory		50

The effect of the write-down of inventory, by recognizing the reduction in the replacement cost of the inventory below its original cost, is to reduce income for the period by $50. In the next period, the beginning inventory is carried at a "cost" of $750 and this amount will be used in determining the cost of goods sold.

The lower-of-cost-or-market method may be applied: (1) to each individual type of inventory item, (2) to major classes of inventory, or (3) to the inventory as a whole. Although the application of lower-of-cost-or-market valuation is optional, once the method is adopted it should be followed consistently from year-to-year.

The lower-of-cost-or-market rule may be viewed as an extension of the convention of conservatism. Although this rule yields a conservative balance sheet and income statement in the period of the write-down, it provides a *greater net income in subsequent periods* than would be determined using the cost basis. Consequently, this procedure has been criticized for allowing the manipulation of income, because an excessive write-down in one period can result in excessive income in a subsequent period.

The procedure has also been criticized because of its *apparent inconsistency in the treatment of anticipated losses and anticipated gains.* Market decreases are recognized in the period in which the decrease in utility occurs, but market increases are not recognized until the period in which the goods are sold. The only logical explanation for this discrepancy is that the conservatism convention is more important than treating market decreases and increases alike.

Gross Profit Method

In many instances, such as in the case of the preparation of interim (e.g., quarterly) financial statements, it may be desirable to estimate the amount of the ending inventory rather than take a physical inventory. One method that is often used in estimating inventories is the gross profit method. *The primary uses of the gross profit method include: (1) to estimate inventories for interim statement purposes, (2) to test the reasonableness of inventory values determined by physical count or perpetual inventory records, and (3) to estimate the value of inventory destroyed or lost by a casualty or other causes.* The gross profit method is not a generally acceptable method that is appropriate for annual financial reporting purposes, because it is an estimating procedure rather than a costing method; however, it is generally acceptable for quarterly financial statements.

The gross profit method assumes that the relationship among sales, cost of goods sold, and gross profit remains relatively constant from one accounting period to the next. This relationship is normally based upon actual amounts from the preceding year, adjusted for any changes that occurred in the current year.

To illustrate, consider the following example for Art's Wholesalers for the month of January, 19X1.

Sales	$10,500
Sales returns	500
Purchases	5,500
Purchase returns	100
Purchase allowances	50
Freight	150
Inventory, January 1, 19X1	15,500

Information from the 19X0 income statement for Art's Wholesalers was as follows:

Sales	$100,000	100%
Cost of goods sold	64,000	64%
Gross profit on sales	$ 36,000	36%

The gross profit percentage of 36% (gross profit of $36,000 divided by net sales of $100,000) is used to estimate the cost of the ending inventory on hand at January 31, 19X1, as follows:

1. Determine the cost of goods available for sale to date, using the ledger accounts.

2. Estimate the cost of goods sold by multiplying the net sales by the estimated costs of goods sold percentage (100% minus the estimated gross profit rate).

3. Subtract the estimated cost of goods sold from the cost of goods available for sale to determine the estimated inventory on hand.

The calculation of the estimated inventory at January 31, 19X1, for Art's Wholesalers is as follows:

Beginning inventory			$15,500
Purchases		$ 5,500	
Less: Purchase returns	$100		
Purchase allowances	50	150	
Net purchases		$ 5,350	
Freight-in		150	5,500
Goods available for sale			$21,000
Less: Estimated cost of goods sold			
Sales		$10,500	
Less: Sales returns		500	
Net sales		$10,000	
Multiply by the cost of goods sold percentage (100% – 36%)		x 64%	
Estimated cost of goods sold			6,400
Estimated cost of January 31, 19X1, inventory			$14,600

Retail Inventory Method

The retail inventory method is commonly used by retail businesses to simplify their accounting for inventories. An advantage of the use of this method is that the physical inventory is computed on the basis of selling prices, which are readily available. The physical inventory at selling prices is then converted to its estimated cost by applying the average ratio of costs to selling prices of goods that were on hand during the period. It is an averaging method that assumes that the cost of merchandise on hand at any time bears the same relationship to total retail prices as the total cost of all goods handled during the period bears to original selling prices. As goods are purchased, information regarding the goods is accumulated on both a cost and a selling price basis. Sales are subtracted from goods available for sale at retail selling prices to obtain the estimated ending inventory at retail prices. Then, this amount is multiplied by the average ratio of cost to selling prices to give an estimate of ending inventory at cost.

The principal advantages of the retail inventory method are: (1) it provides a clerically feasible means of determining inventories on hand; (2) it provides a measure of control over inventories and a means of computing the cost of merchandise sold at any time, even though the store handles a large number of items and has a very high volume of sales transactions; (3) it simplifies the taking and pricing of physical inventories; (4) it provides information for a monthly determination of gross profit for each department and store; and (5) it helps control inventory by disclosing shortages that may indicate either thefts or sales made at unauthorized prices.

The determination of the estimated cost of inventory using the retail method is illustrated with the following example:

Sales	$16,000
Purchases at cost	10,000
Purchases at retail	18,000
Freight	500
Beginning inventory at cost	1,500
Beginning inventory at retail	2,000

The calculation of the ending inventory using the retail method is as follows:

	Cost	Selling Price
Beginning inventory	$ 1,500	$ 2,000
Add: Purchases	10,000	18,000
Freight	500	
	$12,000	$20,000
Deduct: Sales		16,000
Ending inventory (at retail)		$ 4,000

Cost percentage:

Ending inventory (at cost): $4,000 x 60% = $2,400

SUMMARY

This chapter has discussed certain of the operational differences in companies, with special emphasis placed on the differences in retailing and service organizations.

For accounting purposes, inventories include all goods that are held for sale to customers, those in the process of being produced for sale, and those to be used in the production of goods for sale. The objective of inventory accounting is to provide a proper valuation of inventory, both for balance sheet reporting purposes and for the proper determination of income.

Inventories are normally accounted for at historical cost, with any savings due to trade and purchase discounts and expenses due to freight charges considered in the determination of historical cost. In addition, inventory costs must be adjusted for any returns or allowances on inventory items. When the market price falls below cost, inventories may be written down to their current replacement cost using the lower-of-cost-or-market concept.

The periodic and perpetual inventory methods are the two general methods of determining inventory amounts. The perpetual method requires recording the cost of goods sold as inventory items are sold. The periodic method involves making a physical count of goods on hand and subtracting this amount from the total goods available for sale to determine the cost of goods sold. Each inventory system can be maintained on either a dollar or unit basis or both.

Two basic general classifications of cost used for purposes of income determination are product costs and period costs. A product cost is a cost that can be directly identified with the purchase or manufacture of goods that are available for sale. A period cost, which is usually associated with the passage of time, is recognized on the income statement as an expense of the period in which it is incurred.

Where inventory items are purchased at different prices, certain assumptions regarding cost flows must be made to allocate costs between cost of goods sold and ending inventory. The average-cost method assumes that all units are carried at the same cost. The first-in, first-out (FIFO) method assumes that the costs of the first items acquired or produced are the costs of the first items used or sold. The last-in, first-out (LIFO) method assumes that the costs of the last items acquired or produced are the costs of the first items used or sold. The FIFO method results in balance sheet valuations that reflect current cost more appropriately than LIFO, but the LIFO method results in a better matching of current costs with current revenues.

For a variety of reasons, firms may wish to estimate ending inventory amounts instead of taking an actual physical count. Two methods for such estimation are the retail method and the gross profit method. Neither of these should be considered costing methods; they are basically methods of estimating cost.

Key Definitions

Average-cost inventory method—a method based on the theory that one unit cannot be distinguished from another. The average cost is computed by dividing the total cost of the beginning inventory plus purchases by the total number of units.

Beginning inventory—includes the goods on hand and available for sale at the beginning of the period.

Cost of goods sold—the cost of the inventory sold during the period. Beginning inventory plus purchases minus the ending inventory equals the cost of goods sold.

Cost of inventory—the price of the inventory itself plus all direct and indirect outlays incurred in order to bring it to the firm's location in the desired form.

Cost percentage—the percentage obtained from the ratio of the goods available for sale at cost to the goods available for sale at selling price. This percentage is used in the retail method in order to calculate the estimated cost of the ending inventory.

Discounts lost—an account used under the net method of recording purchases to record the amount of the discounts not taken.

Ending inventory—goods still on hand and available for sale at the end of the period.

F.O.B.—means "free on board."

F.O.B. destination—requires the seller to pay all shipping costs.

F.O.B. shipping point—means that the seller pays the costs to the shipping point only. The buyer pays the cost of transit from the shipping point to the destination.

First-in, first-out (FIFO)—an inventory method that assumes that the costs of the first items acquired or produced are the costs of the first items used or sold.

Freight-in—the shipping costs incurred for goods purchased.

Goods available for sale—includes the beginning inventory plus the net purchases for the period.

Gross method—a method of recording purchases (sales) whereby purchases (sales) are recorded at the gross price.

Gross profit from sales—the difference between the revenue from sales and the cost of the goods sold.

Gross profit method—this is a method that estimates the cost of the ending inventory by assuming that the relationship among sales, cost of goods sold, and gross profit remains constant.

Gross profit rate—the gross profit (sales minus cost of goods sold) divided by sales.

Inventories—includes those assets acquired and/or produced for sale in the continuing operations of a business.

Inventory turnover ratio—cost of goods sold divided by average inventory.

Last-in, first-out (LIFO)—an inventory method that assumes that the costs of the last items acquired or produced are the costs of the first items used or sold.

Lower-of-cost-or-market—a method of pricing inventory whereby the original cost or the market value, whichever is lower, is used to value inventory for financial statement purposes.

Net method—a method of recording purchases whereby purchases are recorded at the net price—that is, the gross price less the purchase discount.

Period cost—a cost that cannot be directly identified with the production of a specific product or products. It is usually more closely associated with the passage of time.

Periodic method—under the periodic method, the cost of goods sold is determined at the end of the period by making a physical count of the goods on hand and subtracting the cost of the goods still on hand from the total cost of goods available for sale. This inventory system may also be maintained on a quantity basis.

Perpetual method—under the perpetual method, an entry recording the cost of goods sold is usually made at the time a sale is made. This inventory system may also be maintained on a quantity basis.

Product cost—a cost that is directly associated with the production or purchase of goods that arc available for sale.

Purchases—includes all inventory acquired by purchase during the period.

Purchase allowances—adjustments of the purchase price by the seller.

Purchase discounts—discounts offered to encourage the prompt payment of purchases made on account. Purchase discounts are reflected in the accounts under the gross method to record purchases.

Purchase returns—the account used by the buyer to record the cost of goods returned to the seller.

Retail method—this is an inventory estimation method that assumes that the cost of merchandise on hand at any time bears the same relationship to total retail prices as the total cost of all goods handled during the period bears to the original selling prices.

Sales allowances—adjustments of the purchase price by the seller.

Sales discounts—discounts offered by the seller to the purchaser to encourage the prompt payment of purchases made on account.

Sales returns—the account used by the seller to record the goods returned by the buyer.

Trade discount—a quantity discount that represents an adjustment of a catalog or list price. It is made in order to arrive at the selling price to a particular customer. Trade discounts are not reflected in the accounts.

QUESTIONS

1. What are the major differences between the income statements of a service organization and that of a retailer?

2. Why do businesses offer discounts and how do they affect the financial statements?

3. Explain how the gross price method and the net price method each provide an evaluation of management. Which method is preferred?

4. Explain F.O.B. shipping point and F.O.B. destination. What effect do these have on the valuation of inventory?

5. What are two methods of accounting for inventory? Describe these methods.

6. How is the cost of goods sold figure arrived at under the periodic inventory method?

7. How does the perpetual inventory method act as a control?

8. Why should a company have accounting control over its inventory?

9. What are "goods available for sale"?

10. Explain the term "cost" with respect to accounting for inventories.

11. Briefly discuss three inventory cost flow methods.

12. Give examples of some kinds of inventories in which average cost, FIFO, and LIFO would actually match the flow of goods.

13. What problems of valuation occur with FIFO? With LIFO?

14. What is the primary advantage of LIFO?

15. Explain the exception to the general cost rule for inventories.

16. What are some reasons why a company would want to estimate its inventory?

17. What is the basic assumption of the retail method of estimating inventory? What are some advantages of this method?

18. What is the gross profit method? When is it especially useful?

EXERCISES

19. Using the following information, calculate the total sales for the period.

Purchases of inventory during the period	$ 50,200
Beginning inventory	10,350
Wage expense	9,300
Rent expense	1,500
Interest expense	700
Ending inventory	9,350
Net income	12,000

20. The following information was taken from the records of Norris Company. Using this information, calculate the amount of the beginning inventory.

Sales	$510,000
Ending inventory	84,000
Purchases of inventory	300,000
Net income	162,000
Other expenses	108,000

21. Fill in the blanks:

Beginning inventory	$ 20,000
Purchases of inventory during the period	(a)
Ending inventory	22,000
Cost of goods sold	54,000
Expenses	(d)
Net income	(c)
Beginning retained earnings	200,000
Dividends	8,000
Ending retained earnings	230,000
Gross margin	(b)
Net sales	108,000

22. Determine and fill in the missing amounts in the following situations. Each column of figures is a separate situation.

	A	B	C	D
Sales	$100,000	$100,000	$200,000	?
Beginning inventory	10,000	?	30,000	$15,000
Purchases of inventory during the period	?	70,000	100,000	75,000
Ending inventory	20,000	10,000	?	10,000
Cost of goods sold	50,000	?	110,000	?
Gross profit	?	25,000	?	40,000
Expenses	?	?	60,000	25,000
Net income	20,000	10,000	?	?

23. Record the following events under both a perpetual and a periodic inventory system.

a. Purchased fifteen dozen apples @ $2 per dozen (assume that the firm had a beginning inventory of three dozen apples which were purchased at $2 per dozen).

b. Sold fourteen dozen apples @ $3 per dozen.

c. Counted the remaining apples and discovered that three dozen were on hand.

24. Scott ordered fifty cases of Swan soap, ninety cases of Sweet Breath mouthwash, seventy cases of Brush-It toothpaste, and forty cases of Talc deodorant. Each case cost $15 regardless of the item. Carbo Distributor, the seller, extended credit terms of 2/10; n/30; however, Scott must pay the freight of $50. Carbo made an error in shipping the merchandise. Instead of the Swan soap, they shipped Rose soap. Scott agreed to keep this soap in return for a $20 allowance. Scott also returned thirty cases of Sweet Breath. Scott uses the net method for recording the purchases, and pays the balance within the discount period.

Required:

1. Make the journal entries for Scott.
2. Make the journal entries for Carbo.

25. Determine the missing figures in each of the following independent cases.

	Sales	Beginning Inventory	Ending Inventory	Gross Profit	Expenses	Net Income	Purchases of Inventory	Cost of Goods Sold
1.	$1,000	$300	a	b	$100	c	$500	$600
2.	a	100	$200	$400	b	$200	700	c
3.	800	a	150	100	100	b	400	c

26. Grasso, Inc. began its operations on January 1, 19X1. It purchased goods for resale during the month as follows:

January 3	3 units @ $3
January 11	2 units @ $4
January 20	3 units @ $5
January 30	2 units @ $6

Sales for the month totaled 6 units. The selling price per unit was $10. A count of the units as of January 31, 19X1, shows four (4) units on hand.

Required:

The inventory at January 31, 19X1 would be carried at the following amounts (for each method listed below):

FIFO . . . .   _____
LIFO . . . .   _____
Weighted Average . . . .   _____

All computations should be shown.

27. On December 31, 19X1, the end of its first year of operations, the management of the Busby Company is trying to decide whether to use the FIFO or LIFO method of measuring inventory. Inventory prices have been increasing steadily since the company began its operations.

Required:

1. Which method would produce the higher cost of goods sold?
2. Which method would produce the higher net income for 19X1?
3. Which method would produce the higher cost of goods available for sale for 19X1?
4. Would your answers to questions 1 through 3 above change if the inventory prices have been decreasing steadily since the company began its operations?

28. The following information was available from the records of a merchandising company at the end of an accounting period.

	At Cost	At Retail
Beginning inventory	$10,000	$ 20,000
Purchases of inventory	69,000	100,000
Freight-in	1,000	(n/a)
Sales	(n/a)	90,000

Required:

Estimate the cost of the ending merchandise inventory using the retail inventory method.

29. Bando Company determines its ending inventory by taking a physical inventory at the end of each accounting period. On June 15, the merchandise inventory was completely destroyed by a fire. In the past, the normal gross profit rate was 20 percent. The following data were salvaged from the accounting records:

Inventory, January 1	$ 20,000
Purchases, January 1 to June 15	90,000
Sales, January 1 to June 15	100,000

Required:

Estimate the cost of the merchandise destroyed by the fire.

30. For the month of March, Lynn Distributors had the following transactions:

Sales	$ 50,000
Sales returns	6,000
Purchases of inventory	24,000
Returns of purchases to suppliers	900
Purchase allowances by suppliers	200
Freight	575

Inventory at the beginning of March was $32,700. This amount, as well as the gross profit percentage of 34 percent, was obtained from the February financial statements.

Required:

Use the gross profit method to estimate the ending inventory for March.

Problems

31. The following transactions took place during October, 19X1. Prepare the journal entries to record these transactions.

Oct.	1	Purchased merchandise from supplier A on account, $5,000.
	2	Merchandise was sold on account to R. P. Jones for $1,000.
	3	A $1,500 credit sale was made to J. R. Lowry.
	6	Purchased merchandise from supplier B on account, $3,000.
	9	Received payment from R. P. Jones.
	15	Sales on account of $2,000 and $2,500 were made to K. L. Putnam and A. R. Hardy, respectively.
	17	Paid supplier A in full.
	18	Received payment from J. R. Lowry.
	23	Sold merchandise on account to M. S. Fletcher for $2,500.
	24	Received payment of half of K. L. Putnam's account.
	25	Paid supplier B half of the amount owed to him.
	26	Received full payment from A. R. Hardy.
	30	Received balance of payment from K. L. Putnam.
	31	Paid supplier B the balance of the account.

32. A trial balance of the Sport Shop at the end of the first year of its operations is:

Sport Shop
Trial Balance
December 31, 19X1

Cash	$ 7,000	
Accounts receivable	9,000	
Supplies	3,000	
Inventories	15,000	
Accounts payable		$ 1,000
Notes payable		4,000
Common stock		10,000
Retained earnings		5,000
Sales		20,000
Wage expense	4,000	
Other expense	2,000	
	$40,000	$40,000

There was no beginning inventory. Purchases of inventories during 19X1 totaled $15,000. The inventory on hand at December 31, 19X1 was determined to be $3,000.

Required:

Prepare the income statement for the year ended December 31, 19X1.

33. Paul Peach opened a small office supply store on January 1, 19X1. The following trial balance was taken from the ledger at the end of the first year of operation.

Peach Office Supply
Trial Balance
December 31, 19X1

Cash	$ 3,500	
Accounts receivable	13,500	
Inventory	40,000	
Prepaid insurance	1,000	
Equipment	20,000	
Accounts payable		$ 5,000
Unearned revenue		15,000
Common stock		13,000
Sales		75,000
Wage expense	10,000	
Rent expense	12,000	
Other expense	8,000	
	$108,000	$108,000

There was no beginning inventory. Purchases of inventory during 19X1 totaled $40,000. A physical count taken on December 31, 19X1, showed merchandise on hand in the amount of $7,000. Other information available on December 31 included the following:

a. The equipment was purchased on January 1, 19X1, and had an estimated useful life of 10 years and no salvage value.
b. The amount of insurance that expired during the year was $400.
c. Certain customers paid in advance for regular deliveries of supplies. The amounts collected were credited to Unearned Revenue. As of December 31, $5,000 of the supplies purchased had been delivered.
d. Accrued wages payable amounted to $500.

Required:

1. Prepare the necessary adjusting journal entries at December 31, 19X1.
2. Prepare the entries required to close the books.
3. Prepare an income statement for the year ended December 31, 19X1.

34. The following transactions took place between Flintstone's Friendly Fish Market and Barney's Beanery during June of 19X1.

   June 1   Barney buys the following items from Flintstone:

   > 10 cases of Charlie the Tuna Fish @ $10 per case
   > 1 Fishing submarine @ $2,000,000

   > Terms of the sale are 2/10; n/30. The purchase was made on account.
   9   Barney notifies Flintstone that the shipment included eight cases as ordered, one case of horse meat, and one case of caviar. The submarine was O.K. Barney proposes that he keep the caviar and deduct 50¢ from the net amount which would otherwise be due. He plans to return the horse meat. Flintstone agrees and Barney mails him a check for the net amount after making the agreed-on deductions.
   15   Barney pays for the submarine.

Required:

1. Record the above transactions on Flintstone's books assuming that he records sales using the gross method.
2. Record the above transactions on Barney's books assuming he uses:
   a. The net method of recording purchases.
   b. The gross method of recording purchases.

35. Peterson Company sells a single product. The company began 19X1 with twenty units of the product on hand with a cost of $4 each. During 19X1 Peterson made the following purchases:

February 3, 19X1	10 units @ $5
April 16, 19X1	25 units @ $6
October 6, 19X1	10 units @ $7
December 7, 19X1	10 units @ $8

During the year, fifty units of the product were sold. The periodic inventory method is used.

Required:

Compute the ending inventory balance and the cost of goods sold under each of the following methods:

1. FIFO.
2. LIFO.
3. Weighted Average.

36. Dente Company began business on January 1, 19X1. Purchases of merchandise for resale during 19X1 were as follows:

January 1	300 units	@ $3.00	$ 900.00
February 7	600 units	@ $3.50	2,100.00
March 25	400 units	@ $3.00	1,200.00
October 6	800 units	@ $2.50	2,000.00
November 10	300 units	@ $2.50	750.00
November 16	300 units	@ $2.25	675.00
	2,700 units		$7,625.00

A total of 2,200 units were sold during 19X1.

Required:

1. Compute the ending inventory at December 31, 19X1, under each of the following methods: (1) FIFO; (2) LIFO; (3) Average.

2. Considering the information given above and your computations for Dente Company, answer the following:

   a. Would the net income for 19X1 have been greater if the company had used (a) FIFO or (b) LIFO in computing its inventory?
   b. Assume that the market cost of the merchandise sold by Dente Company was $2.15 per unit at December 31, 19X1. Assuming the FIFO method of inventory valuation, what would the total carrying value of the inventory be if the lower of cost or market method is used?
   c. Give the journal entry necessary to reduce the inventory to market in (b) above.

37. On February 1, 19X1, the Sporting Goods Department of the Most Store had an inventory of $11,000 at retail selling price; the cost of this merchandise was $8,000. During the three months ended April 30, purchases of $18,000 were made for that department and were marked to sell for $25,000. Freight-in on this merchandise was $1,000. Sales for the period amounted to $25,000. Sales returns and allowances were $900. The physical inventory at retail amounted to $2,500.

Required:

Estimate the cost of theft or shrinkage.

38. The McDermott Company had a fire on June 30, 19X2, which completely destroyed its inventory. No physical inventory count had been taken since December 31, 19X1. The company's books showed the following balances at the date of the fire:

Sales		$180,000
Sales returns and allowances	$ 1,400	
Inventory, December 31, 19X1	40,000	
Purchases	130,000	
Purchases returns and allowances		2,000
Transportation-in	1,600	
Selling expenses	50,000	
Administrative expenses	30,000	

Assume that the company's records show that in prior years it made a gross profit of approximately 25 percent of net sales, and there is no indication that this percentage cannot be considered to have continued during the first six months of this year.

Required:

Determine the cost of inventory destroyed by fire on June 30, 19X2.

39. A condensed income statement for the year ended December 31, 19X1 for Murcer Products shows the following:

Sales	$80,000
Cost of goods sold	50,000
Gross profit on sales	$30,000
Expenses	20,000
Net income	$10,000

An investigation of the records discloses the following errors in summarizing transactions for 19X1.

a. Ending inventory was overstated by $3,100.
b. Accrued expenses of $400 and prepaid expenses of $900 were not given accounting recognition at the end of 19X1.
c. Sales of $250 were not recorded although the goods were shipped and excluded from the inventory.

d. Purchases of $3,000 were made at the end of 19X1 but were not recorded although the goods were received and included in the ending inventory.

Required:

1. Prepare a corrected income statement for 19X1.
2. Prepare the entries necessary to correct the accounts in 19X1, assuming the books have not been closed.

40. The Yost Company began business on January 1, 19X1. Its reported net losses for the calendar years 19X1 and 19X2 were as follows:

19X1	$95,000 loss
19X2	$40,000 loss

Selected information from its accounting records is presented below:

Purchases of Goods for Resale

Date	Units		Price
February 1, 19X1	10,000	@	$10
May 1, 19X1	10,000	@	12
September 1, 19X1	10,000	@	15
December 1, 19X1	10,000	@	18
January 1, 19X2	10,000	@	20
March 1, 19X2	10,000	@	24
June 1, 19X2	10,000	@	25
November 1, 19X2	10,000	@	26

Sales

19X1	25,000 units
19X2	40,000 units

Other data:

The company uses the last-in, first-out (LIFO) method of inventory valuation.

Required:

1. Using the company's present inventory method (LIFO) compute:
   a. Ending inventory for the calendar years 19X1 and 19X2.
   b. Cost of goods sold for the calendar years 19X1 and 19X2.
2. Determine what the net income or net loss for each year would have been if the company had used the first-in, first-out (FIFO) method of inventory valuation.

41. Purchases and sales for the Yastrzemski Company are as follows:

Date		Event	Units	Unit Cost	Total Value
June	1	Balance	300	$1.00	$300.00
	8	Sale	150		
			150		
	15	Purchase	330	2.00	660.00
			480		
	23	Sale	300		
			180		
	29	Purchase	400	2.10	840.00
	30	Balance	580		

Required: (Assume a periodic inventory.)

1. What is ending inventory under FIFO?
2. Determine ending inventory under LIFO.
3. Under FIFO, what is the cost of goods that were sold on June 23?
4. Using the average price, what is ending inventory?
5. Determine gross profit on sales of $4,000 for June, assuming the average, FIFO, and LIFO methods of inventory accounting.

42. **CASE. Stephens Company.**

Part A:

John Stephens is concerned about the level of inventory losses that his company is incurring. Mr. Stephens believes as much as $50,000 per year may be lost as a result of damaged or stolen merchandise. However, he is unable to verify this figure because his company employes a periodic inventory system. The company's income statement for 19x5 was as follows:

Sales		$800,000
Beginning inventory	$155,000	
Plus purchases	495,000	
Goods available for sale	$650,000	
Less ending inventory	120,000	
Cost of goods sold		530,000
Gross margin		$270,000
Operation expenses		120,000
Net income		$150,000

Mary Rester is Stephens Company's accountant. She advised Mr. Stephens that he would be able to identify his inventory losses if he would replace his periodic inventory systems with a perpetual system. Mr. Stephens told Ms. Rester that while he was interested in identifying inventory losses for internal management purposes, he had no desire to show such losses on his income statement. He explained that his business partner would be quite upset if his $50,000 inventory loss estimate were correct, thereby causing earnings to decline by a third (i.e., from $150,000 to $100.000).

Required:

Respond to Mr. Stephens comments. Also, prepare a revised income statement for 19x5 assuming that a perpetual system is used. Assume that Mr. Stephens' estimate of a $50,000 inventory loss is accurate for 19x5.

Part B.

Stephens Company can purchase a security system that is expected to reduce inventory losses by $30,000. The system has a list price of $25,000 and will be shipped under terms FOB shipping point, freight collect. Freight costs are expected to be $3,000. The initial installation costs are expected to amount to $4,000.

Required.

Determine the full cost of the security system. Would you recommend the purchase of the security system?

43. Wilson Company began its operations on May 1, 19x1. It purchased goods for resale during the month as follows:

May 4	3 units @ $3
12	2 units @ $4
20	3 units @ $5
28	2 units @ $6

A physical count of the inventory on hand as of May 31, 19x1 revealed 4 units.

Required:

a. At what amounts would the inventory at May 31, 19xI be carried for each method listed below. (Assume a periodic system.)
   1. FIFO
   2. LIFO
   3. Weighted Average
b. Which method would result in the largest amount of net income for the month of May?

44. On January 1, 19x3 Gindler's Boutique had a beginning inventory cost of $1 10,000 which could be sold for $180,000. During the first quarter Gindler purchased inventory of $38,000 which had a retail value of $50,000. In addition, Gindler paid $1,500 for transportation-in. Sales for the first quarter amounted to $90,000.

Required:

a. Determine the ending inventory at retail and at cost.
b. Which number will appear on Gindler's balance sheet?

45. For each of the transactions listed, indicate the effect(s), if any, on the company's year-end: (1) Balance Sheet, (2) Income Statement, and (3) Statement of Cash Flows. Your answers should be as complete and specific as possible.

a. Purchased inventory for resale to customers agreeing to pay the supplier at a later date.
b. Sold inventory to customers who agree to pay at a later date.
c. Purchased inventory for resale to customers paying cash to the supplier.
d. Sold inventory to customers for cash.
e. Collected cash from customers who had previously purchased inventory on a credit basis (see "b" above).

46. For each of the transactions listed, indicate the effect(s), if any, on the company's year-end: (1) Balance Sheet, (2) Income Statement, and (3) Statement of Cash Flows. Your answers should be as complete and specific as possible.

a. At the end of a period, the current replacement cost of inventory was less than its original cost.
b. At the end of a period, it was determined that some of the company's inventory was missing, due to employee theft.
c. Inventory is destroyed in an accidental fire at the company's warehouse.

Refer to the Annual Report in Chapter 1 of the text.

47. What inventory methods are used?

48. Comparing the two years presented, was there an increase or decrease in inventories?

49. Using the beginning and ending inventory figures for the most recent year, calculate the average inventory for this year.

50. During the most recent year, what were net sales?

51. Did gross profit increase or decrease in the most recent year?

52. What caused the increase or decrease in gross profit during the most recent year?

53. During the most recent year, what percentage gross profit was earned in relation to sales?

Outline

LEARNING Objectives

Chapter 9 discusses the accounting procedures used for recording and allocating the cost of plant and equipment, the disposition of plant and equipment, and the accounting for intangible assets and natural resources. Studying this chapter should enable you to:

1. Identify the purpose of, and information included on, a fixed asset ledger card.

2. Recognize the three basic factors that must be considered in recording periodic depreciation.

3. Discuss and apply the depreciation methods discussed in the chapter.

4. Differentiate between capital expenditures and revenue expenditures.

5. Record the disposition of plant and equipment.

6. Discuss the nature of intangible assets and the computation of amortization.

7. Explain the concept of depletion of natural resources.

CHAPTER 9

LONG-TERM ASSETS

INTRODUCTION

The term property, plant and equipment (also called fixed assets) refers to long-lived tangible assets that are used in the continuing operations of a business over a number of years. They are assets acquired for *use* in the firm's operations as contrasted to those assets purchased for *sale* to the customers of a business. Examples of property, plant and equipment include land, buildings, equipment, furniture, and fixtures. Property, plant and equipment may be regarded as a "bundle" of services that are used over the life of the asset in the process of generating revenue. In accordance with the matching principle, as these services expire through use in generating revenue, a portion of the cost of the asset is allocated to expense. The costs that are to be allocated to expense in future periods may be considered deferred costs and are shown as assets on the balance sheet. The process of periodically allocating the cost of property, plant and equipment to expense is referred to as *depreciation*.

In this chapter we will discuss the accounting procedures used to record the acquisition and use of long-lived assets, including tangibles and material resources, and those procedures used to determine depreciation expense for the period.

CONTROL OVER PROPERTY, PLANT AND EQUIPMENT

A fixed asset ledger card should be prepared and maintained for each individual property, plant and equipment asset purchased. This card should include all of the pertinent information relating to the asset and its use. These data enable the management of the firm to establish and maintain control over each individual asset (for example, by providing the basis for taking a physical inventory of all property, plant and equipment assets owned by the firm). It also assists in accounting for all transactions relating to plant assets. For example, the fixed asset ledger card provides the information required in order to calculate the periodic depreciation expense for the asset and the data required to adjust the accounts as assets are sold or retired.

Using a ledger card for an automobile as an illustration, the following information is ordinarily provided:

Asset Ledger Account

Description	Cost	Depreciation	Other Information
Name of asset	Date acquired	Estimated life	Repairs:
Account number	Invoice cost	Estimated salvage	Date
Asset number	Other costs	value	Amount
Manufacturer's serial		Depreciation to date	Actual life
number			Date on disposal:
Horsepower			Date
Insurance carried			Sales price
Property tax valuation			(if any)
			Gain or loss
			To whom sold

Property, plant and equipment may be classified into two categories for accounting purposes: land and depreciable assets. Since the assumption is made that land is not used up over time, the cost of land is not subject to depreciation. All other items of property, plant and equipment are assumed to have a limited useful life and, therefore, the cost of these items is allocated to expense through periodic depreciation charges.

Accounting for Property, Plant and Equipment

All costs incurred in acquiring an asset and preparing the asset for productive use are capitalized as the cost of the asset by debiting them to the asset account. The costs include the net invoice price, transportation costs, and installation costs. All costs that are incurred before the asset becomes productive, such as demolition of old buildings on a building site or repairs to used equipment acquired for production, is considered to be a cost of the acquired asset. A proper determination of the total cost of a plant asset is important because the cost of an asset (less any salvage value, i.e., the amount the firm can recover when the firm has finished using the asset) becomes an expense that should be charged against the income of the business during the periods the asset is used by the firm.[1] This process of allocating the cost of an asset to expense is known as depreciation.

Plant assets are normally acquired either by cash purchase or by incurring a liability (or by a combination of a cash down payment and incurring a liability for future payments). If a liability is incurred, the interest cost associated with the liability is recorded as interest expense and not as a cost of the asset acquired. Plant assets may be acquired in exchange for other assets owned by the firm. The procedures used in accounting for assets acquired by exchange are discussed in Appendix B to this chapter.

In certain cases, more than a single asset may be acquired for a lump sum purchase price. Because the assets acquired may have different useful lives (or, in the case of land, an unlimited life), it is necessary to allocate the total purchase price among the assets acquired. Normally, this allocation is based upon the relative appraisal values of the assets involved. For example, assume that a company acquires land, building, and equipment for a total cost of $200,000. Assume that the company making the acquisition determines the following appraisal values for the individual items:

Land	$ 75,000
Building	150,000
Equipment	25,000
Total appraised value	$250,000

The apportionment of the $200,000 purchase price is made on the basis of the relative values of the assets and is as follows:

Asset	Appraisal Value	Fraction of Total Appraisal Value			Allocation of Cost
Land	$ 75,000	$ 75,000 ÷ $250,000	=	.3	$ 60,000
Building	150,000	$150,000 ÷ $250,000	=	.6	120,000
Equipment	25,000	$ 25,000 ÷ $250,000	=	.1	20,000
	$250,000				$200,000

The cost of an asset includes all expenditures that are necessary to acquire the asset and place it in use. For example, a company buys a delivery truck with a list price of $10,000. The company receives a 10 percent reduction in price from the dealer and also a 2 percent cash discount. The company pays a 5 percent sales tax

---

[1] The cost of land, which is not used up in the generation of revenue, is not allocated to expense. Instead, the original cost of the asset is maintained in the accounts until the asset is disposed of.

and, in addition, purchases a stereo for the truck paying $300 including installation. The cost of the new truck is computed as follows:

List price	$10,000
Less: 10% reduction	1,000
	$ 9,000
Less: 2% cash discount	180
	$ 8,820
Sales taxes	441
Stereo	300
Cost of the truck	$ 9,561

The $9,561 cost is the balance in the asset account and is the basis for computing depreciation. To charge the sales tax and the stereo to the expenses in the year the truck is acquired overstates expenses for that period and understates expenses for the following periods.

Land. The cost of land includes the purchase price, commissions, any taxes due, and other similar costs. Any costs incurred to grade, level, and demolish old buildings are added to the cost of the land, but any proceeds from the sale of scrap reduces the cost. Land is not subject to depreciation because of its unlimited life and its cost is retained in the land account until the land is sold. On the other hand, land improvements, which include fencing and parking lots, have limited lives and are subject to depreciation.

Buildings. The cost of constructing a building includes excavations, building materials, labor, and all other costs necessary to place the building in use. Costs such as interest on borrowed construction funds and real estate taxes incurred during the construction are also part of the total building cost.

Machinery and Equipment. In addition to the normal costs of acquiring machinery and equipment, such costs as supports, wiring, inspection, and testing are charged to the machinery and equipment account.

Depreciation

As previously indicated, the process of charging the cost of a property, plant and equipment asset to expense over its useful life is referred to as depreciation. *Depreciation is defined more formally as the systematic and rational allocation of the cost of an asset, less its salvage value (if any), over the periods in which benefits are received from the use of the asset.* Note that this definition indicates only that the allocation of cost should be systematic and rational. A basic problem with this approach is that there is no precise definition of "systematic and rational." The criterion of rationality normally is related to the expected benefits (decline in service potential) of an asset. In this context, depreciation is a process of allocating the cost of an asset, and not a process of asset valuation. Therefore, the accounting definition of depreciation does not consider either a change in market value or a physical change in an asset.

Depreciation accounting is a method of allocation by which an attempt is made to match the cost of an asset against the revenue that has been generated or produced from using the asset. In this cost-allocation approach, the depreciation expense for a particular period represents an estimate of the portion of the asset's cost that is used up or that otherwise expires during that period.

The basic nature of and the problems involved in depreciation accounting may be illustrated by the use of a simple example. Assume that you decide to purchase a Chevrolet for use as a taxi cab. The cost of the auto is $18,000. You feel that you will be able to earn approximately $24,000 each year in fares, and the estimated operating costs (gas, oil, repairs, insurance, etc.) will be approximately $7,000 per year. You further estimate that the auto will last for four years at which time it will probably have to be replaced. At the end of the four-year period you estimate that your used Chevrolet may be sold for about $2,000. What are your earnings over the four years if your estimates prove to be accurate? Total income for the four-year period might be calculated as follows:

Your Taxi Company
Income Statement
For Four Years

Revenues ($24,000 per year for 4 years)		$96,000
Operating costs ($7,000 per year for 4 years)	$28,000	
Cost of the taxi ($18,000 cost less $2,000 received from its sale at the end of the four-year period)	16,000	
Total costs		44,000
Net income		$52,000

Assume now that you wish to prepare separate income statements for each of the four years. You can do the following:

Your Taxi Company
Income Statements

	For the Year				
	1	*2*	*3*	*4*	*Total*
Revenues	$24,000	$24,000	$24,000	$24,000	$96,000
Operating costs	7,000	7,000	7,000	7,000	28,000
Cost of the taxi	18,000	0	0	(2,000)*	16,000
	$25,000	$ 7,000	$ 7,000	$ 5,000	$44,000
Net income (loss)	($ 1,000)	$ 17,000	$ 17,000	$19,000	$52,000

*The negative two thousand dollars shown as "cost of the taxi" represents the proceeds received from its sale at the end of the fourth year (i.e., its salvage value).

But do these statements really reflect the actual facts of the situation? Is it reasonable to report that your income increases significantly during year two, remains constant during the third year and then increases slightly in year four? Of course not. The total for the four years seems to be reasonable, but the problem lies in attempting to measure the income for *each* individual year. This difficulty arises because you purchased the car and paid for it at the beginning of year one, used it for four years and sold it at the end of the fourth year. In order to measure the income for each year properly, it is necessary to allocate, in a rational and systematic manner, the net cost of owning the auto (i.e., the purchase price of the car less its estimated salvage value) over the periods that benefit from its use.

From a theoretical viewpoint, depreciation expense for a particular period represents an estimate of the portion of the asset's cost that is used up or that otherwise expires during that period. A precise determination of the depreciation expense related to an individual asset for any given year is difficult, because it is almost impossible to accurately predict the exact useful life of an asset. The life of an asset, and therefore its depreciation, is affected by a combination of factors such as the passage of time, normal wear and tear, physical deterioration, and obsolescence. Even though the various techniques that can be employed in determining the depreciation may appear to be precise (and from a mathematical viewpoint they are), it should be noted that because of the estimating of useful life, salvage value, etc., depreciation is always an estimate or approximation. However, periodic measurement of that portion of the asset's cost that has been used up or has expired during a period is a necessary element in determining the income of the firm for that period. Depreciation accounting is a method of allocation by which an attempt is made to "match" the cost of an asset against the revenue that has been generated or produced from using the asset.

Elements Affecting the Determination of Periodic Depreciation

The depreciation process represents the allocation of the costs (less any estimated residual or salvage value) of property, plant, and equipment over the expected useful life of the asset. As discussed previously, the cost of a long-lived asset includes all of the expenditures associated with its acquisition and preparation for use. The additional factors that must be considered in the estimate of periodic depreciation for an asset include:

1. Estimated useful life
2. Estimated salvage (residual) value
3. Methods of allocation.

Useful Life

The useful life of an asset is that period of time during which it is of economic use to the business. The estimation of the useful life of an asset should consider such factors as economic analysis, engineering studies, previous experience with similar assets, and any other available information concerning the characteristics of the asset. However, regardless of the quantity of information available, the determination of the useful life of an asset is a judgment process that requires the prediction of future events.

The period of economic usefulness of an asset to a business is a function of both physical and functional factors. Physical factors include normal wear, deterioration and decay, and damage or destruction. These physical factors limit the economic useful life of an asset by rendering the asset incapable of effectively performing its intended function. Thus, the physical factors limit the maximum potential economic life of the asset.

Functional factors may also cause the useful life of an asset to be less than its physical life. The primary functional factors that may limit the service life of an asset are obsolescence and inadequacy. Obsolescence is caused by changes in technology or changes in demand for the output product or services. These factors cause the asset to be inefficient or uneconomical before the end of its physical life. Inadequacy may result from changes in the size or volume of activity. These factors cause an asset to be economically incapable of handling or processing the required output. In a high technology, growth-oriented economy such as that of the United States, functional factors generally impact significantly upon the determination of the useful life of an asset.

Salvage Value

Salvage value is the estimated realizable value of an asset at the end of its expected life. Depending upon the expectations regarding the disposition of an asset, this amount may be based on such factors as scrap value, secondhand market value, or anticipated trade-in value. The depreciation base used for an asset normally is equal to the difference between the acquisition cost of the asset and its salvage value. This depreciation base is the amount of the asset's cost that is allocated to expense over the expected useful life of the asset.

The relationship between salvage value and the cost of an asset varies considerably. In some cases, particularly when the estimated useful life of an asset is significantly less than its physical life, salvage value may be substantial. On the other hand, in certain instances, the estimated residual value of an asset may be so small that the salvage value is assumed to be zero in computing the depreciation base. The validity of the periodic depreciation expense is dependent upon a reasonably accurate estimate of both the salvage value of an asset and its useful life.

Depreciation Methods

Theoretically, the selection of a depreciation method should be based on the expectations regarding the pattern of decline in the service potential of the asset under consideration. Because both the nature and the characteristics of various assets may vary significantly, alternative depreciation patterns may be justified. Accordingly, there are a number of acceptable depreciation methods that mathematically approximate the possible pattern of use expected from an asset. However, in practice, the criteria for selecting a particular depreciation method are often not determinable. It has been suggested by some that depreciation accounting is used by management as a factor in implementing its financial policy. That is, management may select the method(s) that contribute to the desired financial results that it hopes to achieve over time. The consistency principle does require that once a method has been adopted for a particular type of asset, the firm must continue to use that method over time. Because of the number of alternative methods available, the depreciation expense for each period may vary significantly depending upon the method selected. Each of the methods, however, results in the identical total depreciation expense over the useful life of the asset(s).

In recording the periodic depreciation for property, plant and equipment, three basic factors must be considered:

1. The cost of the asset—the invoice cost plus all costs necessary to place it in use.

2. The estimated useful life of the asset.

3. The estimated salvage or scrap value of the asset—the amount that will be recovered when the asset is retired.

This section of the chapter discusses five depreciation methods that are used in accounting for property, plant and equipment of businesses: the straight-line method, the units-of-activity method, the declining-balance method, the sum-of-the-years'-digits method, and the accelerated cost recovery system. Each of these methods results in identical total depreciation over the life of a fixed asset—an amount equal to the original cost of the asset or, when appropriate, the original cost less its estimated salvage value. The methods differ, however, in the amount of cost allocated to expense during each year of the life of the asset. To illustrate these techniques, the following data will be used:

Type of asset	Chevrolet
Date acquired	January 1, 19X1
Cost (Including delivery, sales tax, etc.)	$18,000
Estimated useful life	4 years
Estimated useful life in miles driven	100,000
Estimated salvage value	$2,000

Straight-Line Depreciation. One of the simplest and most commonly-used methods of computing depreciation is the straight-line method. This method considers the passage of time to be the most important single factor for or limitation on the useful life of an asset. It assumes that other factors such as wear and tear and obsolescence are somewhat proportional to the elapsed time; this may or may not be the case in fact. The straight-line method allocates the cost of an asset, less its salvage value, to expense equally over its useful life. A formula that may be employed in calculating depreciation using the straight-line method is as follows:

$$\frac{\left(\begin{array}{c} \text{Cost of} \\ \text{the Asset} \end{array} - \begin{array}{c} \text{Estimated} \\ \text{Salvage} \\ \text{Value} \end{array} \right)}{\text{Estimated Useful Life}} = \text{Depreciation for the period}$$

Substituting the illustrative data presented above in the formula, we obtain the following calculation of depreciation for 19X1:

$$\frac{(\$18,000 - \$2,000)}{4 \text{ years}} = \$4,000 \text{ per year}$$

Since the straight-line method of depreciation allocates an identical dollar amount of depreciation expense to each period, depreciation for the years 19X2, 19X3, and 19X4 (the remaining useful life of the automobile) would also be $4,000 each year.

UNITS-OF-ACTIVITY METHOD OF DEPRECIATION. The units-of-activity or units-of-production method can be used for assets that have useful lives related to use rather than time. For example, the useful life of an automobile can be measured in terms of miles driven; the useful life of factory machinery can be measured in terms of units produced.

A formula that may be used to compute depreciation expense with the units-of-activity method is as follows:

$$\frac{\left(\begin{array}{c} \text{Cost of} \\ \text{the Asset} \end{array} - \begin{array}{c} \text{Estimated} \\ \text{Salvage} \\ \text{Value} \end{array}\right)}{\text{Estimated Useful Life in Units}} \times \text{Units in Current Period} = \text{Depreciation for the period}$$

Using the illustrative data and assuming that the Chevrolet was driven 30,000 miles in 19X1, depreciation for 19X1 is computed as follows:

$$\frac{(\$18,000 - \$2,000)}{100,000 \text{ miles}} \times 30,000 \text{ miles} = \$4,800$$

ACCELERATED METHODS OF DEPRECIATION. Business persons recognize that the benefits obtained from the use of a plant asset frequently may not be uniform over its useful life. Both the revenue-producing ability of an asset and its value may decline at a faster rate during the early years of its life. Also the costs of repairing and maintaining the asset may increase during the later years of its life. In general, accelerated methods of calculating depreciation allow the recording of larger amounts of depreciation in the early periods of an asset's life rather than in later years. Furthermore, one accelerated depreciation method, Modified Accelerated Cost Recovery System (MACRS) is permitted for income tax purposes and may benefit the taxpayer by postponing or deferring the payment of taxes to a later year. The increased depreciation charges (which do not require the outlay of cash, since the cash expenditure was made at the time the asset was acquired) reduce taxable income and therefore reduce the amount of income tax currently payable. By postponing or deferring the payment of income taxes from an earlier to a later year of an asset's life, the business has obtained, in effect, an interest-free loan from the taxing authority.[2] Although a business may use different methods of computing depreciation for accounting and tax purposes, firms often wish to simplify their recordkeeping by using the same method for both purposes. For this reason, many businesses adopt MACRS.

Three commonly-used methods of accelerated depreciation will be illustrated: the double-declining-balance method, the sum-of-the-years' digits method, and MACRS.

THE DOUBLE-DECLINING-BALANCE METHOD. The procedures used in applying the double-declining-balance method arbitrarily double the depreciation rate that would be used in calculating depreciation under the straight-line method.[3] This increased rate is then applied to the book value (i.e., the cost of the asset less the total depreciation taken to-date) of the assets. The formula used in calculating double-declining-balance depreciation is as follows:

$$(2 \times \text{Straight-line rate}) \times (\text{Cost} - \text{Depreciation taken in prior periods})$$
$$= \text{Depreciation for a period}$$

Salvage value is ignored in the computation of depreciation under the double-declining-balance method until the depreciation expense taken reduces the book value of the asset to an amount equal to its salvage value. At that point, depreciation is no longer taken.

---

[2] See Chapter 16 for a detailed discussion of income tax allocation.
[3] The straight-line rate may be calculated by dividing the useful life of the asset (in years) into 100 percent. For the example used, the straight-line rate is 100 percent divided by 4, or 25 percent.

Using the same data as in the previous example, the calculation of double-declining-balance depreciation may be illustrated as follows:

$$(2 \times 25\%) \times (\$18{,}000 - \$0) = \$9{,}000 \text{ depreciation for 19X1}$$

The straight-line rate is 25 percent; since the asset has a useful life of four years, one-fourth (or 25%) of the cost is expensed each year using the straight-line method. The doubled rate ($2 \times 25\%$) is applied to the full cost of $18,000 since the salvage value is ignored in the initial years of the asset's life and there is no depreciation from prior years.

The depreciation charge for 19X2 is calculated as follows:

$$(2 \times 25\%) \times (\$18{,}000 - \$9{,}000) = \$4{,}500 \text{ depreciation for 19X2}$$

The only change from the previous year is that $9,000, the depreciation taken in 19X1, is substituted for $0 in the first calculation.

Depreciation for 19X3 is:

$$(2 \times 25\%) \times (\$18{,}000 - \$13{,}500) = \$2{,}250 \text{ depreciation for 19X3}$$

Again, the only change in the formula is in the depreciation taken in prior years. The $13,500 amount used in the computation of depreciation for 19X3 is the 19X1 depreciation of $9,000 plus the 19X2 depreciation of $4,500.

The formula is not used to calculate the depreciation expense for 19X4, since its use would reduce the asset's book value below its salvage value. Depreciation for 19X4 is computed as follows:

Cost of the asset		$18,000
Less: Depreciation taken in prior years:		
19X1	$9,000	
19X2	4,500	
19X3	2,250	15,750
Net book value of the asset at January 1, 19X4		$ 2,250
Less: Estimated salvage value		2,000
Depreciation for 19X4		$ 250

The Sum-of-the-Years'-Digits Method. The use of the sum-of-the-years'-digits method also produces greater charges for depreciation in the early years of an asset's useful life. The life-years of an asset are totalled[4] and utilized as the denominator of a fraction that uses the number of years of life remaining from the beginning of the year (i.e., the years in reverse order) as the numerator. This fraction is then applied to the cost of the asset less its estimated salvage value in order to compute the depreciation for the period.

Again, using the same data as in the previous illustrations, the depreciation expense for each of the four years, 19X1 through 19X4, using the sum-of-the-years'-digits method, is calculated as follows:

Sum-of-the-years'-digits:

$$1 + 2 + 3 + 4 = 10$$

Depreciation for each period:

19X1: $4/10 \times (\$18{,}000 - \$2{,}000) = \$6{,}400$
19X2: $3/10 \times (\$18{,}000 - \$2{,}000) = \$4{,}800$
19X3: $2/10 \times (\$18{,}000 - \$2{,}000) = \$3{,}200$
19X4: $1/10 \times (\$18{,}000 - \$2{,}000) = \$1{,}600$

---

[4] The sum of the numbers from one to the estimated life of an asset in years is computed. For example, the life-years of an asset with a three-year estimated life is $1 + 2 + 3 = 6$. [Sum of arithmetic progression of n consecutive numbers $= n \frac{(n+1)}{2}$]

MACRS and ACRS. Effective January 1, 1981, the Accelerated Cost Recovery System (ACRS) was implemented, introducing significant changes in the manner in which depreciation expense is computed for federal income tax purposes. The Tax Reform Act of 1986 made some additional changes and adopted the Modified Accelerated Cost Recovery System (MACRS). While the straight-line, sum-of-the-years' digits, and double-declining balance methods may still be used for financial accounting and reporting purposes, MACRS methods are the only accelerated methods that may be used for federal income tax purposes.[5] Essentially, MACRS places all depreciable assets into six classes of depreciable personal property or into one of two classes of real property, summarized on the below.

MACRS Property Classifications

MACRS Classes and Methods	Special Rules
Three-year, 200% declining balance	Includes some race horses and road tractors. Excludes cars and light trucks.
Five-year, 200% declining balance	Includes cars and lights trucks, heavy general purpose trucks, typewriters, computers, and copiers.
Seven-year, 200% declining balance	Includes office furniture and fixtures, single-purpose agricultural and horticultural structures placed in service before 1989. Includes property never assigned a class life.
Ten-year, 200% declining balance	Includes water transportation equipment, fruit or nut-bearing trees or vines, and single purpose agricultural and horticultural structures placed in service after 1988.
Fifteen-year, 150% declining balance	Includes telephone distribution plants.
Twenty-year, 150% declining balance	Includes farm buildings. Excludes real property with ADR midpoint of twenty-five years or more.
27.5-year, straight-line	Residential rental property.
39-year, straight-line	Nonresidential real property.

Although the property classes described are identified by years, the concept of useful life for the calculation of depreciation expense has been discontinued under the MACRS rules. Rather, depreciation expense for the three-, five-, seven-, and ten-year classes is calculated using double-declining-balance depreciation. Depreciation on assets in the fifteen- and twenty-year classes is computed using the 150 percent declining-balance method. A switch to a straight-line approach is permitted in the year that the depreciation

---

[5] MACRS is used for tangible assets placed in service after 1986. For tangible assets acquired prior to 1981, the depreciation methods that are permissible for tax purposes are: straight-line, double-declining balance, and sum-of-the-years'-digits.

expense using the straight-line method exceeds MACRS depreciation. The straight-line method must be used for all real estate. Under MACRS rules, a taxpayer may elect to use the straight-line method of depreciation rather than MACRS. Also, the taxpayer electing MACRS must use the half-year convention that requires that the taxpayer take one-half year's depreciation expense in the year an asset is acquired and disposed of, regardless of the actual dates. Salvage value may be ignored in calculating depreciation under MACRS.

Using the same data as in the previous examples, the depreciation expense using MACRS for an asset in the five-year class is calculated as follows:

Year					Annual Depreciation Expense	Year-End Accumulated Depreciation
19X1	(2 x 20%)	×	($18,000 – 0) x ½	=	$3,600	$3,600
19X2	(2 x 20%)	×	($18,000 – $3,600)	=	5,760	9,360
19X3	(2 x 20%)	×	($18,000 – $9,360)	=	3,456	12,816
19X4	(2 x 20%)	×	($18,000 – $12,816)	=	2,074	14,890
19X5	(2 x 20%)	×	($18,000 – $14,890)	=	1,244	16,134
19X6	$18,000	–	$16,134	=	1,866	18,000

Note that only one-half year's depreciation is taken in 19X1, the year of acquisition, because of the half-year convention. The remaining undepreciated cost is charged to depreciation in 19X6, also because of the half-year convention.

As is now apparent, except for MACRS (which ignores salvage value), the *total* amount of depreciation taken for a fixed asset over its useful life will be identical regardless of the method used, although the timing and pattern of the depreciation charges vary widely according to the particular method chosen. The effects of the various methods on the example data are illustrated below:

Year	Straight-Line	Double-Declining Balance	Sum-of-the-Years'-Digits	MACRS
19X1	$ 4,000	$ 9,000	$ 6,400	$ 3,600
19X2	4,000	4,500	4,800	5,760
19X3	4,000	2,250	3,200	3,456
19X4	4,000	250	1,600	2,074
19X5	0	0	0	1,244
19X6	0	0	0	1,866
Total	$16,000	$16,000	$16,000	$18,000

bc don't include $2000 salvage value in MACRS

The differences in the depreciation expense depending on the method chosen are illustrated graphically on the following page.

Because depreciation expense is an important factor that enters into the determination of the income of a firm for a period, the reported income varies according to the depreciation method selected. *The consistency principle requires that once a method has been adopted for a particular type of asset, the firm must continue to use that method consistently over time.*

RECORDING PROPERTY, PLANT AND EQUIPMENT

Using the Chevrolet as an example, the accounting procedures for recording the acquisition and use of plant assets will be illustrated.

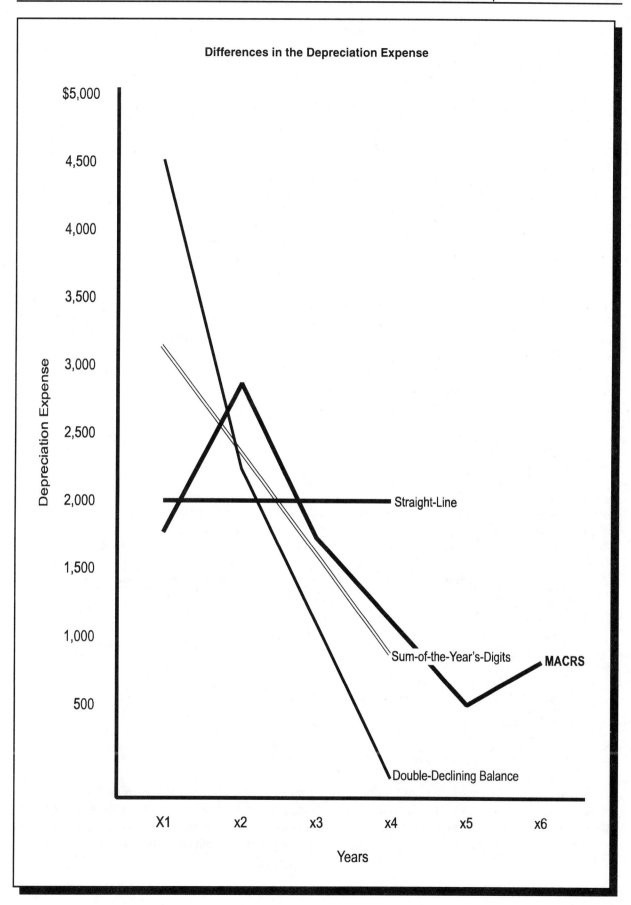

Differences in the Depreciation Expense

On January 1, 19X1, the acquisition of the automobile is recorded as follows:

Automobile	18,000	
Cash		18,000

The debit to the asset account is for the total cost of the Chevrolet including delivery charges, sales tax, etc. In this instance, the car was paid for in cash. Had a liability been incurred, it would have been recorded by a credit. The procedures required when an old asset is traded in on a new asset are discussed in Appendix B to this chapter.

At the end of 19X1, it is necessary to record depreciation on the asset in order to charge to expense the portion of the asset's cost that has been "used up" during the period. For purposes of illustration, we will assume that the straight-line method of depreciation is used. On December 31, 19X1, depreciation is recorded by the following entry:

Depreciation expense	4,000	
Accumulated depreciation		4,000

The debit to depreciation expense records the portion of the asset's cost charged as an expense of the period. The credit to the accumulated depreciation account adds the current period's depreciation to that which was taken in prior years (in this case zero since this is the initial year of the asset's useful life); the total of this account indicates the total amount of depreciation taken to-date at any given point in time. The depreciation expense of $4,000 appears in the income statement along with the other expenses of the period and is deducted from revenue in the determination of income. Accumulated depreciation appears as an offset (called a contra account) against the related asset account in the balance sheet as follows:

Current assets		$10,000
Automobile	$18,000	
Less: Accumulated depreciation	4,000	14,000
Total assets		$24,000

Since the straight-line method of depreciation is used, the entries required in order to record depreciation expense for the years 19X2, 19X3, and 19X4 will be the same as the one which is made on December 31, 19X1, shown above. The automobile and accumulated depreciation accounts appears as follows:

Automobile		Accumulated Depreciation	
(a) 18,000		(b)	4,000
		(c)	4,000
		(d)	4,000
		(e)	4,000
		(f)	16,000

Key:
(a) Cost of the automobile on January 1, 19X1.
(b) Depreciation for 19X1.
(c) Depreciation for 19X2.
(d) Depreciation for 19X3.
(e) Depreciation for 19X4.
(f) Balance In the account at December 31, 19X4.

Occasionally, plant assets are used for periods of time beyond their originally estimated lives. Since the purpose or objective of depreciation accounting is to allocate the cost of a plant asset to expense over its useful life, no additional depreciation should be recorded for an asset that has already been fully depreciated. The cost of the asset, along with the associated accumulated depreciation should remain in the accounts until the asset is disposed of.

INTEREST COSTS

Frequently, firms borrow substantial sums for the purpose of constructing or acquiring property, plant, and equipment. A basic accounting issue that exists with regard to the interest costs relating to these borrowings is whether the interest should be considered an expense of the period or included (capitalized) as a part of the cost of the asset acquired or constructed. The charging of interest to expense has been defended on the grounds that interest represents the cost of financing and is not a cost that should be associated with a specific asset. Capitalizing interest costs, on the other hand, has been justified on the basis that an asset should be charged with all of the costs necessary to place it in its intended use. It may be argued that the interest incurred is as much a cost of acquiring an asset as is the cost of any other resources used or expended.

In 1979, the proper accounting for interest costs became a resolved issue when the FASB issued its *Statement No. 34*, "Capitalization of Interest Costs," that *requires* capitalizing interest as a part of the cost of acquiring *certain* assets. In this pronouncement, the FASB concluded:

> On the premise that the historical cost of acquiring an asset should include all costs necessarily incurred to bring It to the condition and location necessary for its intended use, ... in principle, the cost incurred in financing expenditures for an asset during a required construction or development period is itself a part of the asset's historical acquisition cost.

The assets that qualify for interest capitalization generally are those assets that require a period of time to place them in their intended use. Interest *should be capitalized* for those assets that are: (1) constructed by a company for its own use (e.g., a manufacturing facility), (2) constructed for a company by another entity and for which progress payments are made, and (3) constructed as discrete projects (e.g., shipping or real estate developments) intended for sale or lease. Interest should not be capitalized as a part of the cost of inventories that are routinely manufactured or otherwise produced in large quantities on a repetitive basis even if these inventories require lengthy maturation periods, such as is the case with whiskey or tobacco. Interest cost eligible for capitalization is limited to amounts incurred on borrowings and other obligations. *The amount of interest to be capitalized during the construction period is that portion of the incurred interest charges that theoretically could have been avoided by either not borrowing additional funds for the asset or by using the amounts expended on the asset for the retirement of existing debt.*

DISCLOSURE IN THE FINANCIAL STATEMENTS

Plant assets are carried in the balance sheet at their acquisition cost, less any accumulated depreciation. The depreciation on long-term assets is included in the income statement as an expense and is deducted in determining income from operations. Gains or losses on the disposal of long-term assets appear on the income statement.

Because the amount of periodic depreciation depends on the method or methods of depreciation in use, it is necessary that information on the depreciation method(s) be disclosed in the financial statements. Such information is necessary for a meaningful comparison of the depreciation charges of different companies or for prediction of future depreciation charges of a company. Consequently, the Accounting Principles Board in Opinion No. 12 indicated that the following disclosures should be made in the financial statements or accompanying notes:

1. Depreciation expense for the period.
2. Balances of major classes of depreciable assets, by nature or function, at the balance sheet date.
3. Accumulated depreciation, either by major classes of depreciable assets or in total, at the balance sheet date.
4. A general description of the method or methods used in computing depreciation with respect to major classes of depreciable assets.[6]

---

[6] *Opinions of the Accounting Principles Board No. 12*, "Omnibus Opinion-1967" (New York: AICPA, 1867), para 5.

Costs Incurred after Acquisition

It is often necessary to make additional expenditures relating to plant assets subsequent to the date of acquisition. These expenditures occur for various reasons, from routine maintenance and repairs to major additions and improvements.

The major accounting issue relating to these expenditures is determining whether they should be charged to expense in the period in which they are incurred or capitalized as an asset. The general rule for handling these costs is that *those expenditures that increase future economic benefits should be capitalized (i.e., be recorded as capital expenditures), whereas those expenditures that simply maintain the existing economic benefits should be expensed (i.e., recorded as revenue expenditures).* An increase in future economic benefits may occur if the expenditure extends the economic life of the asset, increases its productivity, or increases the quality or reduces the cost of the items produced by the asset.

It is important to classify an expenditure properly as either an asset or an expense. If the cost of an asset is classified incorrectly as an expense, then the net income for the current period is understated and the net income of the future periods, in which the benefits of the expenditures are received, will be overstated due to an understatement of depreciation expense.

Since capital expenditures increase the future economic benefits of an asset, the costs incurred are recorded in an asset account. On the other hand, revenue expenditures benefit only the current operations, and these costs are recorded by debits to expense accounts.

Capital expenditures for existing assets are often classified as additions or improvements. An addition represents an increase in the physical substance of an asset, such as a new wing on a building. Improvements (or replacements) involve the substitution of new parts on an existing asset. Examples of improvements include the installation of elevators in a building or an air conditioner in a delivery truck. If the addition or improvement has the same economic life as the existing asset, the cost is capitalized directly to the asset account. When the expenditure extends the economic life of the asset, the depreciable life of the asset is extended accordingly. If the item has a different economic life than the existing asset, the cost is capitalized in a separate asset account and expensed over the period of expected benefit.

Revenue expenditures are routine and recurring expenditures incurred to maintain an asset in operating condition and do not increase the economic benefits associated with the asset. Examples of typical revenue expenditures are routine maintenance (e.g., oil change and lubrication) and ordinary repairs (e.g., replacing a worn tire).

Theoretically, if an expenditure increases the economic benefits originally expected from an asset, then the cost should be capitalized. In practice, however, it is often difficult to make a distinction between a capital expenditure and a revenue expenditure. In many companies, arbitrary policies are established for defining capital and revenue expenditures. For example, an expenditure might be capitalized only if it: (1) clearly increases the economic benefits associated with an existing asset, and (2) exceeds a minimum cost (such as $1,000). The use of a minimum cost for capitalization eliminates the need to recompute depreciation schedules for minor improvements or additions.

To illustrate the accounting for a capital expenditure, assume that in January, 19X5, a company spends $3,000 to recondition an existing delivery truck. The truck had been acquired on January 1, 19X1, for $16,000, and at that time, had an estimated useful life of five years and a salvage value of $1,000. The truck is being depreciated using the straight-line method. Therefore, as of December 31, 19X4, the balance in accumulated depreciation is $12,000 [($15,000 ÷ 5) x 4]. The company estimates that the reconditioning process significantly improves the gas mileage of the truck and extends the useful life to a total of seven years (with no change in salvage value). The journal entry to record the improvement is:

Delivery truck	3,000	
Cash		3,000

The new balance in the asset account is $19,000 (the original cost plus the improvement). The remaining book value of $7,000 ($19,000 - $12,000) less the estimated salvage value of $1,000 is divided equally over the three remaining years of the estimated life. Thus, the depreciation expense for 19X5, 19X6, and 19X7 is recorded as follows:

Depreciation expense	2,000	
Accumulated depreciation		2,000

Disposal of Plant and Equipment

At some point in time, the cost of continuing to use a particular asset exceeds the benefits derived from its use and it is to the advantage of the firm to dispose of it. Upon disposal of an asset, the cost of the asset must be removed from the asset account and the accumulated depreciation at the date of disposal must be removed from the accumulated depreciation account.

For example, assume that after using the Chevrolet for four years, it is sold for $2,000, its book value at that time. (Recall that the auto had an original cost of $18,000, an estimated life of four years, and an anticipated salvage value of $2,000.) The entry to record the sale of the Chevrolet is as follows:

Cash	2,000	
Accumulated depreciation	16,000	
Automobile		18,000

The debit to cash records the amount of cash received while the debit to accumulated depreciation and the credit to automobile remove the automobile and its related accumulated depreciation account from the books of the company. In this example, the estimates of useful life and salvage value were precise. This occurs only infrequently in actual practice.

At the time of the disposal of an asset, if the book value of the asset (cost less accumulated depreciation) is not equal to the amount received from the sale, the difference is a gain or loss on disposal. If the selling price exceeds the book value, there is a gain; if the selling price is less than the book value, there is a loss. Such gains and losses are included in the income statement.

For example, if the same Chevrolet is sold at the end of the fourth year for $2,200, the entry to record this transaction is as follows:

Cash	2,200	
Accumulated depreciation	16,000	
Automobile		18,000
Gain on disposal		200

The only difference between this entry and the preceding entry is that the amount of cash received is $2,200 rather than $2,000. This amount of $2,200 exceeds the book value of the asset (original cost of $18,000 less accumulated depreciation of $16,000, or $2,000); therefore, a gain ($2,200 - $2,000, or $200) is realized. On the other hand, if the car is sold for $350, a loss is incurred. The entry for the loss situation is as follows:

Cash	350	
Accumulated depreciation	16,000	
Loss on disposal	1,650	
Automobile		18,000

Again, the only difference between this entry and the two preceding entries is the amount of cash received, $350. Since the cash received is less than the book value of the automobile ($18,000 less $16,000, or $2,000) a loss equal to the difference ($2,000 less $350, or $1,650) occurs and is recorded in the accounts.

The calculation of the gain or loss on the disposal of the automobile in all three cases mentioned above may be summarized as follows:

		A	B	C
Selling price		$2,000	$2,200	$ 350
Cost of automobile	$18,000			
Accumulated depreciation	(16,000)			
Book value		(2,000)	(2,000)	(2,000)
Gain (loss) on the sale of the automobile		$ 0	$ 200	($1,650)

In some instances, an asset may be discarded prior to the end of its useful life. For example, assume that the automobile is involved in an accident at the end of its third year of use and is damaged to the extent that repairs are not considered to be feasible. The entry to record the loss from the accident is as follows:

Loss on disposal	6,000	
Accumulated depreciation	12,000	
Automobile		18,000

If the automobile is insured and $2,500 are received from an insurance policy on the automobile, the entry is as follows:

Cash	2,500	
Accumulated depreciation	12,000	
Loss on disposal	3,500	
Automobile		18,000

In any case, cash is debited for the amount received (if any), accumulated depreciation is debited for the depreciation taken to the date of disposal, and the asset is credited for its original cost in order to remove these accounts from the books. A loss or gain is recorded for the difference between the book value of the asset and the cash received (if any).

In each of the illustrations included above, it was assumed that the disposal of the asset took place at the end of the period. If the disposal is made during the period, the only difference is that an entry is required to record the depreciation for the period from the end of the preceding year up to the date of the disposal. The entry to record the disposal itself is exactly the same as those illustrated above.

Analyzing Plant and Equipment

Companies do not report the exact lives of their plant assets, but instead, sometimes state a range of years over which depreciation is being charged. For example, McDonald's reports that the estimated useful lives of its buildings are up to 40 years and its equipment are from three to twelve years. On the other hand, neither Coca-Cola nor PepsiCo state any range of estimated useful lives. In some cases, companies reconsider the useful lives of their assets. For example, Waste Management, Inc. recently took a $3.54 billion writedown to reflect overly aggressive accounting practices. Included in this writedown were reductions in the scrap value of dumpsters and reductions in the estimated useful lives of trash trucks and other equipment. By depreciating their trucks and equipment over fewer years, Waste Management's depreciation expense will increase by $165 million in 1998.[7]

The average useful life of plant assets can be estimated by dividing the average cost of plant and equipment by depreciation expense. The calculations for Coca-Cola and PepsiCo for 1996 are as follows:

---

[7] "Waste Management, Inc. Takes Charges of $3.54 Billion, Restates Past Results" Wall Street Journal (February 25, 1998): A4.

$$\text{Average useful life} = \frac{\text{Average Cost of Plant Assets}}{\text{Depreciation Expense}}$$

Coca-Cola
(in millions) : $\dfrac{(\$6,657 + \$5,581)/2}{\$442} = 13.8 \text{ years}$

PepsiCo
(in millions) : $\dfrac{(\$16,751 + \$17,840)/2}{\$1,418} = 12.2 \text{ years}$

Another useful piece of information is the average age of plant assets. Older assets are less efficient and require more maintenance. The calculations for Coca-Cola and PepsiCo for 1996 are as follows:

$$\text{Average age of Plant Assets} = \frac{\text{Accumulated Depreciation}}{\text{Depreciation Expense}}$$

Coca-Cola
(in millions) : $\dfrac{\$2,031}{\$442} = 4.6 \text{ years}$

PepsiCo
(in millions) : $\dfrac{\$7,649}{\$1,418} = 5.4 \text{ years}$

The asset turnover ratio indicates the sales generated by each dollar of assets. Higher asset turnover ratios indicate higher levels of efficiency. The calculations for Coca-Cola and PepsiCo for 1996 are as follows:

$$\text{Asset Turnover Ratio} = \frac{\text{Net Sales}}{\text{Average Total Assets}}$$

Coca-Cola
(in millions) : $\dfrac{\$18,546}{(\$15,041 + \$16,161)/2} = 1.19 \text{ times}$

PepsiCo
(in millions) : $\dfrac{\$31,645}{(\$24,512 + \$25,432)/2} = 1.27 \text{ times}$

Natural Resources

In addition to property, plant, and equipment, a firm may own assets in the form of natural resources. These resources include such items as oil deposits, tracts of timber, and coal deposits. Like other long-term assets of a firm, the basis for accounting for these resources is primarily cost. As these resources are converted into salable inventory by drilling, cutting, and mining operations, the cost of these operations along with the original cost of the resources themselves are transferred to inventory.

The process of writing off or amortizing the cost of these natural resources is generally referred to as depletion. Since the natural resource provides a salable product, the depletion charges are included in inventory costs as production occurs and cost of goods sold as the natural resource is sold. The primary difference between depreciation and depletion is that depreciation represents the allocation of the cost of a productive asset in relation to the decline in service potential, while depletion represents the allocation of cost of a natural resource in relation to the quantitative physical exhaustion of the resource.

Depletion

The depletion base of any natural resource (or wasting asset) is the total cost of acquiring and developing the property less the estimated residual value of the land after the natural resource has been economically exhausted. The total cost of the natural resource may be classified into three categories: (1) acquisition cost of the property, (2) exploration costs, and (3) development costs.

Generally, depletion for the period is determined on the basis of the relationship between actual production for the period and total estimated production during the economic life of the resource. To apply this approach, the quantity of economically recoverable units of the natural resource must be estimated. Then the total cost of the natural resource less any estimated residual value is divided by the estimated number of recoverable units to obtain a cost per unit of output. This cost per unit is multiplied by the number of units extracted during the period to determine the depletion charge.

To illustrate this process, consider the following example:

1. An oil field is acquired at a cost of $1,000,000. Geological surveys indicate that a total of approximately 400,000 barrels of oil will ultimately be taken from the field.

2. The estimated residual value of the field after the oil has been extracted is approximately $200,000 (net of restoration costs).

3. During the first year of operations, the drilling costs total $125,000. The cost of drilling is assumed to be entirely applicable to the oil taken during the year. A total of 25,000 barrels of oil are extracted and sold at a price of $10 per barrel.

These transactions are recorded as follows:

Acquisition of the Field

Oil field	1,000,000	
Cash		1,000,000

Drilling During the First Year

Inventory of oil	125,000	
Cash		125,000
Inventory of oil	50,000	
Accumulated depletion—oil field		50,000

The depletion of $50,000 is calculated as follows:

Cost of the field	$1,000,000
Estimated residual value of the field	200,000
Cost of the 400,000 barrels of oil	$ 800,000
Divide by 400,000 in order to obtain the *cost per barrel*	$ 2
$2 x 25,000 barrels extracted	$ 50,000

The drilling cost per barrel, which is assigned to the inventory of oil, is equal to drilling costs of $125,000 divided by the 25,000 barrels extracted, or $5 per barrel. The total cost per barrel is the depletion per barrel of $2 plus the drilling cost of $5 per barrel, or $7.

Sale of the 25,000 Barrels of Oil

Cash	250,000
Sales	250,000
Cost of goods sold	175,000
Inventory of oil	175,000

The sales of $250,000 are equal to 25,000 barrels multiplied by the selling price of $10 per barrel. The cost of goods sold of $175,000 is equal to the 25,000 barrels multiplied by $7 per barrel.

Frequently, additional development costs may be incurred after the production begins or estimates of recoverable units are revised based on production data. In either case, a revision in the unit depletion charge is necessary. In the revision process, a new rate is determined by dividing the unamortized total cost (cost less accumulated depletion) less the estimated residual value by the estimate of the remaining recoverable units.

The procedures described above are known as cost depletion and are required for accounting and financial reporting purposes. For income tax purposes, independent producers use either depletion based on cost or percentage depletion. Further, if cost depletion is used for tax purposes, the amount of periodic tax depletion need not be equal to the cost depletion determined for financial reporting purposes. It is often advantageous from a tax standpoint to use the percentage depletion method. In many cases it allows the taxpayer to deduct more than the cost of the property over its useful life. The percentage depletion method allows the firm to deduct from revenues a given percentage of gross income depletion without regard to the number of units produced or the cost of the property. In this method, the amount of depletion for tax purposes may exceed the total cost of the natural resource. Percentage depletion is not acceptable for financial accounting purposes.

Accounting for Oil and Gas Producers

Normally the exploration costs of oil and gas companies are substantial. There have been two methods used by oil and gas companies to account for costs incurred in the exploration, development, and production of crude oil and natural gas—the successful efforts method and the full cost method. The larger oil and gas companies have tended to use the successful efforts method; the smaller companies have tended to use the full cost method.

Under the successful efforts method, only the costs of successful drilling efforts are capitalized and subsequently charged against the revenue of the producing wells. Costs in connection with nonproducing wells are written off as expenses in the period incurred. Under the full cost method, the costs of both successful and unsuccessful drilling efforts are capitalized and amortized against subsequent petroleum production in the same relatively large cost center (e.g., a country or a continent).

There was considerable pressure on the accounting profession to eliminate the alternatives available for accounting for exploratory costs in the oil and gas industry. In December, 1977, the FASB issued *Statement No. 19*, "Financial Accounting and Reporting by Oil and Gas Producers," which essentially required the adoption of a form of the successful efforts method by all oil and gas producers. However, in *Accounting Series Release No. 253* issued in August, 1978, the SEC rejected the FASB's attempt to eliminate use of the full cost method, asserting that both cost-based methods were so inadequate that it did not matter which method was employed. Subsequently, the SEC issued requirements for the supplemental disclosure of information relating to proved oil and gas reserves.

In 1982, the FASB issued *Statement No. 69*, "Disclosures about Oil and Gas Producing Activities," which superseded the disclosure requirements of all previous FASB statements concerned with oil and gas producing activities. In applying *Statement No. 69*, companies are required to disclose information about quantities of reserves, capitalized costs, costs incurred, and a standardized measure of discounted cash flows related to proved reserves. Accounting requirements for financial statement presentation of exploration and development costs are not affected by this pronouncement.

Intangible Assets

From a legal viewpoint, an intangible asset normally is defined as an asset without physical substance, the value of which resides in the rights that its possession confers upon its owner. This definition alone is insufficient to describe the distinguishing characteristics of intangibles for accounting purposes. For example, certain items that lack physical substance, such as accounts receivable and prepaid rent, are classified as current assets. Similarly, certain noncurrent assets, such as long-term investments, that lack physical substance are not classified as intangible assets. Thus, the absence of physical existence alone does not indicate that an item should be classified as and accounted for as an intangible asset.

Several characteristics are attributed to intangible assets. Probably the most important of these characteristics is the high degree of uncertainty regarding the future benefits that may be expected to be derived from the asset and the difficulty of associating these benefits with either specific revenues or periods. An additional factor distinguishing intangibles from the many other assets that also lack physical substance is that intangible assets are expected to benefit the firm beyond the current operating cycle of the business, even though intangibles have indeterminate life spans.

Rather than attempting to define the characteristics of intangible assets succinctly, many accountants rely on tradition to classify assets as intangible rather than tangible. *Those assets that typically are classified as intangibles include copyrights, patents, trademarks, trade names, organization costs, franchises, and goodwill.* In certain types of businesses, the value of intangible assets may be greater than the value of the tangible assets.

A copyright gives the owner the exclusive right to reproduce or sell an artistic or published work. A copyright, which is granted by the federal government, extends for fifty years plus the life of the creator.

A patent, which is granted by the United States Patent Office, is an exclusive right to sell, manufacture, or control an invention for a period of 17 years. The cost includes the acquisition cost plus any costs to successfully defend the patent from infringement.

A trademark or trade name is a symbol, name, or phrase that provides identification for a product or service. Registration of the trademark or trade name provides legal protection for twenty years plus an indefinite number of renewal periods.

Organization costs include costs such as legal fees and registration fees incurred to start a company. These costs are amortized over a number of years.

A franchise is a contractual agreement under which one party (the franchisor) grants another party (the franchisee) the right to sell certain products or provide certain services. The franchisee records any intangible assets for the costs incurred to acquire the franchise.

Individual intangible assets differ in many respects. These assets may be subdivided on the basis of the following characteristics:

1. *Identifiability*—separately identifiable or lacking specific identification.

2. *Manner of acquisition*—acquired singly, in groups, or in business combinations, or developed internally.

3. *Expected period of benefit*—limited by law or contract, related to human or economic factors, of indefinite or indeterminate duration.

4. *Separability from an entire enterprise*—rights transferable without title, salable, or inseparable from the enterprise or a substantial part of it.

A firm may obtain an intangible asset by purchase or by development within the firm. The objectives of accounting for intangible assets are similar to those for long-lived tangible assets. The cost of the asset is recorded upon acquisition and this cost is allocated to expense over the useful life of the intangible. The cost of an intangible asset includes all expenditures incurred in the acquisition of the rights or privileges. The cost of an intangible asset acquired by purchase can usually be measured with little difficulty. The cost of internally developed intangibles is often more difficult to determine. For example, it may be quite difficult to estimate how much of the total research and development cost for a particular period should be allocated to the development of a single patent. For this reason the cost of internally developed patents includes only legal fees. Any other costs incurred in developing the patent are charged to expense as they are incurred. This treatment is consistent with the handling of research and development costs in general.

AMORTIZATION

The costs of intangible assets are written off to expense over their estimated useful lives in a manner similar to the depreciation of tangible fixed assets. This process is referred to as amortization. Amortization is recorded by a debit to amortization expense and a credit to the intangible asset account. Like tangible fixed assets, the cost of intangibles should be amortized over their estimated useful lives. However, according to *Accounting Principles Board Opinion No. 17*, the period of amortization should not exceed a maximum of forty years or the asset's legal life, whichever is shorter. The board also concluded that the straight-line method of amortization should be used unless the firm shows evidence that some other systematic method is more appropriate in the circumstances.

To illustrate the accounting for intangible assets, assume that Landry Company purchased a patent from Allen Company for $10,000 on January 1, 19X1. The purchase is recorded as follows:

Patents	10,000	
Cash		10,000

If the remaining useful or economic life of the patent is ten years, the adjusting entry required to record the amortization of the patent at the end of each year of its useful life is as follows:

Amortization expense	1,000	
Patents		1,000

Note that the amortization is credited directly to the asset account rather than to an accumulated amortization account as in the case of tangible fixed assets. There appears to be no logical reason for this procedure other than tradition.

Goodwill

Certain intangibles, such as patents, copyrights, and franchises may be identified with a specific right or privilege. The costs of these intangibles when purchased can be measured and amortized or allocated to expense over their useful lives. Other intangibles, however, cannot be specifically identified. This type of intangible is usually referred to as goodwill. The intangible asset goodwill represents the sum of all the special advantages that are not identifiable and that relate to the business as a whole. It encompasses such items as a favorable location, good customer relations, and superior ability of management. The existence of such factors enables the firm to earn an above normal rate of return.

Unlike tangible assets or identifiable intangible assets, goodwill cannot be sold or acquired separately from the business as a whole. Because of the uncertainty involved in estimating the goodwill of a business enterprise, goodwill is recorded only when a business is acquired by purchase. In a purchase transaction, goodwill may be measured as the excess of the purchase price of an entity over the sum of the fair values of all its identifiable assets less its liabilities. The source of this excess is the ability or potential of the firm to earn an above average rate of return.

To illustrate, assume that Richard Smith purchases the Campus Book Store on January 1, 19X1, for $100,000 cash. Further, assume that the identifiable assets are determined to have a total fair value of $90,000 at the date of purchase (consisting of inventory, $10,000; equipment, $20,000; building, $40,000; and land, $20,000). The liabilities assumed by the purchaser are accounts payable of $20,000. The $30,000 excess of the purchase price over the value of all the identifiable assets less the liabilities represents the value of the goodwill. The purchase is recorded as follows:

Inventory	10,000	
Equipment	20,000	
Building	40,000	
Land	20,000	
Goodwill	30,000	
Accounts payable		20,000
Cash		100,000

Once goodwill is recorded in a purchase transaction, it is amortized like all other intangible assets—the recorded cost is allocated to expense over its estimated life with a maximum of forty years.

RESEARCH AND DEVELOPMENT

Many businesses engage in research and development (R&D) activities in order to develop new products or processes or to improve present products. A problem in accounting for R&D expenditures lies in determining the amount and timing of the future benefits associated with such activities. Prior to 1974, there was considerable diversity in the procedures used in accounting for R&D costs. In 1974, however, the FASB issued its *Statement No. 2,* which simplifies the accounting for R&D expenditures by requiring that most research and development costs should be charged to expense as they are incurred. This treatment eliminates the need to assess the uncertain future benefits associated with R&D costs and to measure the cause and effect relationship of these costs for accounting purposes.

FASB Statement No. 2 states that R&D costs include the costs of materials, personnel, purchased intangibles, contract services, and a reasonable allocation of indirect costs that are specifically related to R&D activities and have no alternative future uses. Disclosure should be made in the financial statements of the total R&D costs charged to expense for each period for which an income statement is presented.

Disclosure of Intangibles

Intangible assets normally are reported separately in the balance sheet. The financial statements should disclose the method of amortization, the period of amortization, and the amount of amortization expense for the latest period. The example shown below provides a typical disclosure regarding intangible assets.

Disclosure of Intangible Assets

	19X2	19X1
Goodwill and other intangibles:		
Goodwill	$4,618	$4,675
Patents	1,248	1,248
Organization costs	206	206
Other	290	382
Goodwill and other intangibles—net	$6,362	$6,511

Goodwill and Other Intangibles:
Goodwill represents the excess of cost over the amount ascribed to the net assets of ongoing businesses purchased. Goodwill arising from acquisitions prior to November 1, 1970, is not being amortized. Capitalized organization costs and goodwill acquired after November 1, 1970, are being amortized on a straight-line basis over a forty-year period.
The cost of internally developed patents is charged to income as incurred. Purchased patents are amortized over their estimated economic lives.

Summary

A firm's resources that are used in the continuing operations of a business over a number of years are referred to as plant and equipment or fixed assets or plant assets. Control over these assets is usually achieved by the use of ledger cards that include all data related to the assets. This card reflects the cost of the item, which includes all expenditures necessary to place the asset in use as well as the actual invoice price.

Since plant assets benefit a firm over an extended period of time, the cost of the assets (except for land) must be allocated in some manner through the process of depreciation to the periods that benefit from their use. In the case of most plant assets, the depreciation process results in either a uniform charge for each year (under the straight-line depreciation method) or larger charges in the early years of operation (under the accelerated depreciation methods). In either case, the consistency principle requires that the same method of depreciation be used in all periods. Property, plant and equipment are presented on the balance sheet at their acquisition cost along with a deduction for accumulated depreciation.

Costs incurred for existing assets subsequent to acquisition are classified as either capital expenditures or revenue expenditures. Capital expenditures increase the economic benefits of the existing asset; therefore, the cost is debited to an asset account. Revenue expenditures are routine expenditures incurred to maintain an asset in operating condition, and such costs are debited to expense.

Eventually, the economic usefulness of an item of property, plant and equipment expires and the asset must be sold, scrapped, retired, or traded-in on a new asset. When an asset is disposed of, the cost of the asset is removed from the asset account and the accumulated depreciation balance is eliminated. When a plant asset is sold, there is a gain or loss equal to the difference between the asset's book value (cost less accumulated depreciation) and its sales price.

Identifiable intangible assets, which generally involve property rights rather than physical property, are amortized over their estimated useful lives in a similar manner to depreciation. Goodwill differs from tangible assets and identifiable intangible assets in that it cannot be sold or acquired separately from the business. Therefore, due to the uncertainty of measuring goodwill, it is recorded and amortized only when one firm purchases another and the cost is greater than the fair market value of the firm's assets minus liabilities. A similar uncertainty exists in matching expenses incurred by research and development efforts with possible future revenues resulting from these efforts. Therefore, R&D expenditures are considered expenses of the period in which they are incurred.

Allocation of the cost of natural resources is referred to as depletion. For financial accounting purposes, depletion must be calculated on a cost basis over the estimated units to be produced. However, for tax purposes, firms may take the higher of cost depletion or a specified percentage of gross income (referred to as percentage depletion).

Key Definitions

Accelerated methods of depreciation—depreciation techniques that assume the rate of depreciation decreases with the passage of time.

Accumulated depreciation—a contra account that appears as an offset or deduction from the related asset account in the balance sheet. The depreciation taken over the useful life of the asset is accumulated in this account.

Book value of a plant asset—the cost of a plant asset less accumulated depreciation. The book value of a plant asset is the remaining undepreciated cost.

Capital expenditures—expenditures that extend the useful life or quality of services provided by plant assets.

Contra account—an account that is offset against or deducted from another account in the financial statements.

Declining balance method—an accelerated method of depreciation that assumes the rate of depreciation to be some multiple of the rate that would have been used in the case of the straight-line method.

Depletion—the process of writing-off or amortizing the cost of natural resources over the periods that benefit from their use.

Depreciation—the systematic allocation of the cost of a fixed asset, less the salvage value (if any), over its estimated useful life.

Fixed asset ledger card—prepared for each individual fixed asset purchased. It includes all of the important information relating to the asset and its use.

Goodwill—may be measured as the excess of the purchase price of an entity over the sum of the fair values of all its identifiable assets less its liabilities.

Intangible asset—one that does not have physical substance, usually a property right.

Modified Accelerated Cost Recovery System (MACRS)—MACRS is an accelerated method of depreciation permitted for federal income tax purposes and may also be used for financial accounting purposes

Property, plant and equipment—a firm's resources that are used in the continuing operations of a business over a number of years.

Revenue expenditures—expenditures for ordinary maintenance, repairs, and other items necessary for the operation and use of plant and equipment.

Salvage value—a plant asset's residual amount that a firm expects to recover at the end of the useful life of the asset.

Straight-line depreciation—this method of depreciation assumes that factors such as wear and tear and obsolescence are somewhat uniform over time. The method allocates the cost of a plant asset, less its salvage value, to expense equally over its useful life.

Sum-of-the-years'-digits method—this is an accelerated method of depreciation where the life years of an asset are totalled and utilized as the denominator of a fraction that uses the number of years of life remaining from the beginning of the year as the numerator.

Units-of-activity method—a method of depreciation that assumes that depreciation should be measured in terms of use rather than time.

QUESTIONS

1. Which expenditures are included in the total cost of a fixed asset?

2. What is the purpose of depreciation accounting?

3. What factors should be considered when determining periodic depreciation?

4. Explain the equations used in calculating straight-line, double-declining balance, and sum-of-the-years'-digits depreciation.

5. Four basic depreciation methods are straight-line, sum-of-the-years'-digits, double-declining balance and MACRS. In what ways are the four depreciation methods similar? In what ways are they different?

6. What is the purpose of the accumulated depreciation account?

7. What does the balance in the accumulated depreciation account indicate at any given point in time?

8. What is the difference between a capital expenditure and a revenue expenditure?

9. Why is periodic depreciation not recorded for land?

10. What factors must be known to compute depreciation on a plant asset?

11. How is accumulated depreciation reported in the balance sheet?

12. When a plant asset is disposed of for cash, how is the gain or loss on the sale determined?

13. If an old asset is traded in on a dissimilar new asset, how should the cost basis of the new asset be measured?

14. Explain the rules for recognizing gains or losses on the exchange of similar productive assets.

15. Over what period should the cost of an intangible asset be amortized?

16. When should goodwill be recorded in the accounts?

17. Discuss the appropriate accounting treatment of research and development costs.

18. List some possible causes of goodwill.

19. What is the basis for accounting for natural resources? Is this basis the same as that for other long-term assets?

20. What is depletion? Is it similar to depreciation, and if so, in what way?

21. What is the difference in the accounting for intangible assets and the accounting for tangible assets?

EXERCISES

22. A machine was purchased for an invoice price of $10,000, F.O.B. destination. The freight charges were $200. Costs of installation amounted to $500. At what cost should the machine be recorded?

23. Determine which of the following accounts would be increased by each of the transactions below.

A. Buildings
B. Accumulated Depreciation
C. Land
D. Patents
E. Depreciation Expense

F. Machinery
G. Insurance Expense
H. Freight Expense
I. General Repairs
J. Legal Fees

A,C Purchased land and unusable building.
C Paid legal fees for above purchase.
A Constructed new building on site.
F Purchased machinery for building.
H Paid freight on machinery.
F Paid cost of installing machinery.
I Paid minor repairs on building.
E, D Recorded depreciation of equipment.
G Paid insurance for year on building.
D Obtained patent from U.S. Patent Office.

24. A machine was installed at a total cost of $8,000, assumed to have an estimated useful life of five years and a salvage value of $2,000. Calculate the initial year's depreciation assuming: (a) the straight-line method is used, (b) the sum-of-the-years'-digits method is used, (c) the double-declining balance method is used, and (d) MACRS depreciation is used.

25. In each of the following cases, make the journal entry for the initial year of depreciation, assuming the straight-line method is used by Pat Kelly. (Round to the nearest dollar.)

a. Original cost, $9,000; salvage value, $500; useful life, 4 years; purchased on April 1.
b. Original cost, $25,000; salvage value, $5,000; useful life, 5 years; purchased on October 1.
c. Original cost, $16,000; salvage value, $0; useful life, 8 years; purchased on December 1.
d. Original cost, $5,000; salvage value, $1,000; useful life, 2 years; purchased on July 31.
e. Original cost, $30,000; salvage value, $2,000; useful life, 7 years; purchased on May 31.

26. Smith Company paid $100,000 to acquire land, building, and equipment. At the time of acquisition, appraisal values for the individual assets were determined as: land, $30,000; building, $60,000; and equipment, $30,000. What cost should be allocated to the land, building, and equipment, respectively?

27. Which of the following items are capital expenditures and which are revenue expenditures?

a. Cost of a major overhaul of a machine. *CE*
b. Routine maintenance of a delivery truck. *RE*
c. Replacement of an oil furnace with a gas furnace. *CE*
d. Replacement of stairs with an escalator. *CE*
e. Annual repainting of the administrative offices. *RE*
f. Lubricating, inspecting, and cleaning factory machinery. *RE*
g. Addition to a new wing on the factory building. *CE*

28. A company had a plant asset with an original cost of $15,000 and accumulated depreciation to date of $12,000. Give the journal entry to record the disposition of the asset under the following circumstances:

a. Sold the asset for $5,000.
b. Sold the asset for $2,000.
c. The asset was destroyed by fire; insurance proceeds of $1,500 were received.
d. Abandoned the asset.

29. The Bratton Company purchased a patent for $56,000 on January 1, 19X1. Additional legal costs of $4,000 were incurred in obtaining the patent. The patent was estimated to have a useful life of 10 years. (Its legal life is 17 years.) What will be the patent amortization expense for 19X1?

30. From the following information make the necessary journal entries for the trade-in of an asset by the Singleton Company. Assume that the old and new assets were dissimilar.

List-price of new machine	$20,795
Original cost of old machine	18,560
Accumulated depreciation on old machine at trade-in date	10,560
Trade-in allowance	2,000
Fair market value of old machine at trade-in date	1,000
Cash difference paid	18,795

31. Al Bumbry bought Billy's Grocery on March 27 for $250,000 cash. On the date of purchase, the following fair values were determined: inventory, $50,000; equipment, $18,000; building, $68,000; land, $45,000; and accounts payable, $7,000. Make the entry required on the date of purchase.

32. For each of the following items owned by Mark Belanger, determine what the gain or loss will be upon the disposition of the asset and make the necessary journal entries.

   a. Original outlay, $7,900; sales price, $1,750; accumulated depreciation, $6,450.
   b. Original outlay, $13,050; sales price, $5,110; accumulated depreciation, $10,250.
   c. Original outlay, $21,400; sales price, $9,790; accumulated depreciation, $8,330.
   d. Original outlay, $91,625; sales price, $40,000; accumulated depreciation, $40,580.
   e. Original outlay, $47,985; sales price, $25,470; accumulated depreciation, $29,645.

Problems

33. For each of the depreciation methods listed, complete the following schedule of depreciation over the first two years of the life of a delivery truck costing $8,800 and having a salvage value of $800. The truck has an estimated life of 5 years.

Method	Year	Depreciation Expense	Accumulated Depreciation	Book Value
Straight-line	1	$_____	$_____	$_____
Straight-line	2	_____	_____	_____
Sum-of-the-years'-digits	1	_____	_____	_____
Sum-of-the-years'-digits	2	_____	_____	_____
Double-declining balance	1	_____	_____	_____
Double-declining balance	2	_____	_____	_____
MACRS	1	_____	_____	_____
MACRS	2	_____	_____	_____

34. Snowden Manufacturing Company decided to construct a new plant in 19X1 rather than continue to rent its present plant. On January 1, 19X1, the company purchased 10 acres of land with two old buildings standing on it. The old buildings were demolished and construction of the new plant was begun. The company set up a Land and Buildings account to which all expenditures relating to the new plant were charged.

The balance in the Land and Buildings account after completion of the plant was $740,450. Entries in the account during the construction period were:

a.	Cost of land and old buildings (old buildings appraised at $17,000)	$137,000
b.	Legal fees involved in securing title to property	250
c.	Cost of demolishing old buildings	9,500
d.	Surveying costs	1,200
e.	Price paid for construction of new building	425,000
f.	Salary paid to Jim Seales, engineer, supervisor of construction of new plant	12,500
g.	Fencing of plant property	3,000
h.	Machinery for new plant	113,000
i.	Installation costs of new machinery	9,500
j.	Landscaping of grounds	6,250
k.	Office equipment	12,000
l.	Payment to architect for designing plans and for services during construction	13,000
m.	Paneling and finishing work done on executive offices	2,250
	Total Debits	$744,450
n.	Proceeds from sale of scrap from old buildings	4,000
	Total Credit	$ 4,000
	Balance	$740,450

Required:

Reclassify the items presently in the Land and Buildings account to the proper general ledger accounts.

35. Blintz, Inc. has followed the practice of depreciating its building on a straight-line basis. The building has an estimated useful life of 20 years and a salvage value of $20,000. The company's depreciation expense for 19X3 was $20,000 on the building. The building was purchased on January 1, 19X1.

Required:

1. The original cost of the building.
2. Depreciation expense for 19X2 assuming:
  a. The company has used the double-declining balance method.
  b. The company has used the sum-of-the-years'-digits method.

36. On October 30, 19X1, Thomas Brothers, Inc. purchased a used machine for $7,800 from a company in a neighboring state. The machine could not be shipped until November 15, so Thomas Brothers were forced to pay $150 storage costs and $35 insurance fees. After the asset was received and $250 shipping costs had been paid, it was overhauled and installed at a cost of $320, including parts costing $130. On December 21, additional repair work was performed at a cost of $180 in order to put the asset in working condition. At what value should this machine be recorded on the balance sheet on December 31?

37. For each of the depreciation methods listed, complete the following schedule of depreciation over the first two years of the life of a building costing $57,500. The building is expected to have a salvage value of $7,500 at the end of five years.

Method	Year	Depreciation Expense	Accumulated Depreciation	Book Value
Straight-line	1	$_____	$_____	$_____
Straight-line	2	_____	_____	_____
Sum-of-the-years'-digits	1	_____	_____	_____
Sum-of-the-years'-digits	2	_____	_____	_____
Double-declining balance	1	_____	_____	_____
Double-declining balance	2	_____	_____	_____
MACRS	1	_____	_____	_____
MACRS	2	_____	_____	_____

38. Marshall Furniture Manufacturers purchased a new lathe on January 1, 19X1, for $1,600. It has an estimated salvage value of $100 and an estimated useful life of 3 years. The company uses the sum-of-the-years'-digits depreciation method and maintains records on a calendar year basis. Prepare the journal entries to record the disposal of the lathe under each of the following independent conditions:

   a. Sold for $725 cash on October 1, 19X2.
   b. Destroyed by flood on July 1, 19X3. Insurance proceeds were $200.
   c. Traded in on purchase of new lathe on January 1, 19X2. List price of new lathe was $2,000, market value of old lathe was $1,200, and $700 cash was paid on the transaction.

39. On January 1, 19X1, the Confused Company purchased a new truck for $5,600 paying cash. On May 1, 19X2, the Company purchased a new truck which had a list price of $6,200. They were given a trade-in allowance of $2,000 for the old truck, the balance being paid in cash. On December 1, 19X2, the second truck was completely destroyed by fire. Confused received $3,200 from their insurance company as full settlement for the loss. Truck operating expense for 19X2 totaled $2,200.

   You are called in by the company's accountant who states that in preparing the December 31, 19X2, trial balance he noted that the truck account had a balance of $8,800 although the company does not own any trucks. He also tells you that he failed to record depreciation on either truck during 19X2, although the company's accounting manual requires straight-line depreciation, two-year life, and $800 salvage value for all automotive equipment.

   You obtain a copy of the company's ledger account "Trucks," which shows the following:

	Trucks	
5,600		2,000
6,200		3,200
2,200		
8,800		

Required:

1. Prepare all journal entries regarding the trucks as they should have been made originally.
2. Prepare an entry to correct the accounts as of December 31, 19X2. You may assume that the books have not yet been closed for 19X2.

40. During an audit of Lee May Company for the year ended December 31, 19X2, you find the following account:

		Machinery		
(a)	42,000	(b)		7,273
(c)	200	(d)		6,545
		(e)		5,600

Key:
(a) Cost of machinery purchased on January 1, 19X0.
(b) Credit to record the depreciation expense for 19X0. (Debit was to Depreciation Expense.)
(c) Cost of minor repairs which will not lengthen the life of the machine.
(d) Credit to record depreciation expense for 19X1. (Debit was to Depreciation Expense.)
(e) Credit to record sale of machinery on March 31, 19X2. The machinery had an estimated life of ten years with a salvage value of $2,000. The company uses the sum-of-the-years'-digits method of recording depreciation.

Required:

Give all of the adjusting and correcting entries (or entry) required.

41. A truck was purchased on October 1, 19X1, at a cost of $29,400. The expected life of this truck was four years with an expected salvage value of $600. The company used the straight-line depreciation method and the accounting records are maintained on a calendar year basis.

Required:

Prepare journal entries to record the disposal of the truck on *May 1, 19X3* under *each* of the following *separate* conditions:

a. Sold for $18,000 cash.
b. Completely destroyed by fire, and the insurance company paid $6,000 as full settlement of the loss.
c. Traded in on the purchase of another truck which had a cash price of $34,000; trade-in allowance granted on the old truck was $20,000 and the balance was paid in cash.

42. Kelly Company acquired a mine for $2,500,000. It was estimated that the land would have a value of $400,000 after completion of the mining operations, and that 1,000,000 tons of ore could be extracted from the mine. During the first year of operations, 100,000 tons of ore were extracted and additional production costs of $200,000 were incurred.

Required:

Prepare the journal entries to record the acquisition of the property and the cost of production for the year.

43. Winston Corporation purchased a building and the land on which it was located. The purchase price of the two assets was $200,000 and $80,000, respectively. As part of the agreed-upon purchase price, Winston assumed an existing mortgage on the building of $65,000. Sales taxes of 5 percent of the selling price were paid on both purchases.. Attorneys' fees and legal documents cost $14,000 and were apportioned to the assets on the basis of the purchase price. A small building on the lot was demolished for $12,000 with the scrap sold for $3,500. The major building was renovated at a cost of $32,000 and the lawns were landscaped and shrubbery planted for $8,400.

Required:

a. Prepare a schedule showing the cost of the building and the cost of the land.
b. Prepare one or more journal entries to account for all of the events surrounding the purchase of the building and land.

44. Stephens Company paid $10,000 in cash and signed a mortgage note for $250,000 for the total purchase of a group of assets consisting of building, equipment and land. An independent appraisal indicated that the assets were worth the following:

Asset	Appraised Value
Building	$100,000
Equipment	185,000
Land	40,000
	$325,000

Required.

Determine how much should be allocated to the purchase price of each asset and make a journal entry to account for the purchase.

45. Handy, Inc. manufactures sporting goods. The following information applies to a machine purchased on April 1, 19x1:

Purchase Price	$24,000
Delivery Cost	$ 200
Installation Charge	$ 1,000
Estimated Life	16 years
Estimated Units	27,000
Salvage Estimate	$ 3,600

During 19x1 the machine produced 3,000 units and during 19x2 produced 4,000 units.

Required:

Prepare journal entries to account for the depreciation expense for 19x1 and 19x2 under the following methods:

a. straight-line
b. sum-of-the-years'-digits
c. double-declining balance

46. On May 1, 19x1 Harper Oil Company purchased an oil well with estimated reserves of 1,000,000 barrels of oil for $5,000,000. The following transactions pertain to the purchase:

a. Acquisition of the oil well.
b. During 19x1, 15,000 barrels of oil were extracted.
c. During 19x2, 35,000 barrels of oil were extracted.
d. At the beginning of 19x3, a revision in the estimate indicated that only 850,000 barrels remained. During the year 18,000 barrels were extracted (carry computations to three decimals).

Required:

Prepare general journal entries for the above transactions.

47. For each of the transactions listed, indicate the effect(s), if any, on the company's year-end: (1) Balance Sheet, (2) Income Statement, and (3) Statement of Cash Flows. Your answers should be as complete and specific as possible.

a. Purchased land, building, and equipment for $1 million.
b. Recorded depreciation on equipment.
c. Paid for routine maintenance on equipment.
d. Paid for reconditioning equipment, extending the useful life of the equipment by several years.

48. For each of the transactions listed, indicate the effect(s), if any, on the company's year-end: (1) Balance Sheet, (2) Income Statement, and (3) Statement of Cash Flows. Your answers should be as complete and specific as possible.

a. Over a two-year period, the company constructed a building for its own use.
b. Produced whiskey for resale. The production process required two years.

49. For each of the transactions listed, indicate the effect(s), if any, on the company's year-end: (1) Balance Sheet, (2) Income Statement, and (3) Statement of Cash Flows. Your answers should be as complete and specific as possible.

a. Sold a delivery truck for its book value.
b. Sold a delivery truck at a price exceeding its book value.
c. Sold a delivery truck at a price less than its book value.

50. For each of the transactions listed, indicate the effect(s), if any, on the company's year-end: (1) Balance Sheet, (2) Income Statement, and (3) Statement of Cash Flows. Your answers should be as complete and specific as possible.

a. Acquired an oil field, paying cash.
b. Paid drilling costs in cash.
c. Recorded depletion.
d. Sold half of the oil produced for cash.

51. For each of the transactions listed, indicate the effect(s), if any, on the company's year-end: (1) Balance Sheet, (2) Income Statement, and (3) Statement of Cash Flows. Your answers should be as complete and specific as possible.

   a. Purchased the copyright for a book, paying cash.
   b. Recorded amortization on the copyright.
   c. Purchased a business. The purchase price, paid in cash, exceeded the net value (assets minus liabilities) acquired.

Refer to the Annual Report in Chapter 1 of the text.

52. Comparing the two years, what are the changes in gross and net property, plant and equipment?

53. What caused the difference in the change in net property, plant and equipment and in the change in gross property, plant and equipment mentioned above?

54. What assets are included in property, plant and equipment?

55. Which of these assets is the largest?

56. What is the amount of the depreciation expense in the most recent year?

57. What is the balance in the accumulated depreciation account at the end of the most recent year?

58. Does the difference in the amount of accumulated depreciation from the previous year to the current year equal the amount of depreciation expense in the current year? Why not?

59. What is the amount of the intangible assets at the end of the most recent year?

60. What assets are included in intangible assets?

Appendix A
Assets Acquired During the Period

In the example in the chapter, the automobile was acquired at the beginning of the period. In practice, assets are acquired throughout the accounting period and this requires that depreciation be recorded for a part of a period in the year of acquisition. For example, assume that an automobile is purchased on June 1, 19X1. This acquisition is recorded as follows:

Automobile 18,000
    Cash 18,000

At the end of 19X1, it is necessary to record depreciation on the asset for the seven-month period that it was used during the year (June 1, 19X1 to December 31, 19X1). Again, we will assume the same facts as before ($18,000 cost, 4-year life, $2,000 salvage value) and that the straight-line method of depreciation is used. The calculation is as follows:

$$\frac{(\$18,000 - \$2,000)}{4 \text{ years}} = \$4,000 \text{ per year}$$

$$\frac{\$4,000}{12 \text{ months}} = \$ \ 333.33 \text{ per month}$$

Depreciation for the period June 1, 19X1 to December 31, 19X1, is 7 months x $333.33 per month for a total of $2,333 (rounded). At December 31, 19X1, depreciation for the period is recorded by the following entry:

Depreciation expense 2,333
    Accumulated depreciation 2,333

Depreciation expense for the years 19X2, 19X3, and 19X4 each covers a full year. The entry to record depreciation in each year is as follows:

Depreciation expense 4,000
    Accumulated depreciation 4,000

In 19X5, depreciation is recorded for the final five months of the life of the asset (5 months x $333.33 per month, or $1,667) by the following entry:

Depreciation expense 1,667
    Accumulated depreciation 1,667

The automobile and accumulated depreciation accounts appear as follows:

Automobile		Accumulated Depreciation	
(a) 18,000		(b)	2,333
		(c)	4,000
		(d)	4,000
		(e)	4,000
		(f)	1,667
		(g)	16,000

Key:
(a) Cost of the automobile on June 1, 19X1.
(b) Depreciation for 19X1 (7 months).
(c) Depreciation for 19X2 (12 months).
(d) Depreciation for 19X3 (12 months).
(e) Depreciation for 19X4 (12 months).
(f) Depreciation for 19X5 (5 months).
(g) Balance in the account at May 31, 19X5.

In the above example, depreciation is calculated from the exact date of acquisition until the end of the useful life of the asset. In practice, as a matter of convenience, a business may establish a procedure whereby it will always take six months' depreciation in the year an asset is acquired and six months' depreciation in the year it is disposed of, irrespective of the exact dates of acquisition or disposal. Alternatively, a firm might take a full year's depreciation in the year of acquisition and no depreciation in the year of disposal, or vice-versa. The use of procedures such as these does not change the format of the entries illustrated and is generally acceptable as long as there is no significant distortion of depreciation expense or income.

Appendix B
Trade-Ins

In acquiring assets, a firm may trade in an old asset in purchasing a new asset. In these cases, a trade-in allowance is given on the old asset and the balance of the purchase price is paid in cash or by a combination of cash and debt. The accounting procedures used in recording a trade-in depend on whether the assets exchanged are *similar* (an automobile traded in on another automobile) or *dissimilar* (an automobile traded in on a printing press). When an item of property, plant and equipment is acquired by trading in a *dissimilar* asset, the transaction is accounted for using the fair market values of the assets involved. Thus, the cost of the acquired asset is the fair market value of the assets given up (old asset and cash) or the fair market value of the asset acquired, if its fair value is more clearly determinable. Any difference between the fair value and the book value of the old asset should be recognized as a gain or a loss on the disposition of the old asset. Caution must be used in determining and recording the fair values of the assets involved, as the quoted list prices of new assets and trade-in allowances are often not accurate indicators of actual market values. Dealers often establish list prices that are in excess of the actual cash price to allow them to offer inflated trade-in allowances to their customers.

When *similar* assets are exchanged, a loss may be recognized based upon the fair market value of the asset traded in, but not a gain. If the terms of the exchange of similar assets indicate that there is a gain, this "gain" is not recognized. Rather, the new asset is recorded at an amount equal to the total of the book value of the old asset traded in and the cash paid. The logic supporting the nonrecognition of gains is that the income of a firm should not be increased by the act of substituting a new productive asset for an old one. The "gain" is recognized in future years because the recorded cost of the new asset is less than if the gain is recognized in the current period. Consequently, depreciation expense will be less in future years (and income greater) because of the reduced recorded cost of the new asset.

Assume that a company trades in its Chevrolet on a new automobile on January 1, 19X5. The following data are used in the example:

List price of the new asset	$20,000
Cost of the Chevrolet (at January 1, 19X1)	18,000
Accumulated depreciation on the Chevrolet	
(at December 31, 19X4)	16,000
Trade-in allowance	1,000
Fair market value of the Chevrolet	
(at January 1, 19X5)	400
Cash difference paid	19,000

The entry to record the acquisition of the new automobile is as follows:

Automobile (new)	19,400	
Accumulated depreciation	16,000	
Loss on disposal	1,600	
Automobile (old)		18,000
Cash		19,000

The debit to the new automobile records the $19,400 "cost" of the new automobile as the $19,000 cash paid plus the $400 fair market value of the Chevrolet traded in. The debit to accumulated depreciation of $16,000 and the credit to automobile (old) of $18,000 remove the original cost of the Chevrolet and its related accumulated depreciation from the accounts. The debit to loss of $1,600 records the loss on the disposal of the Chevrolet and is calculated as follows:

Original cost of the Chevrolet	$18,000
Less: Accumulated depreciation	
as the date of trade-in	16,000
Book value of the Chevrolet	
at the date of trade-in	$ 2,000
Less: Fair market value of the Chevrolet	
at the date of the trade-in	400
Loss	$ 1,600

The credit to cash of $19,000 records the cash outlay made in order to acquire the new asset.

If, in the above example, the fair market value of the old car is not available, but it is known that the new automobile can be acquired for a cash price of $19,600, this value is used in recording the acquisition of the new automobile. In this situation, the apparent value of the old automobile is $600 (the $19,600 cash price—the $19,000 cash paid) even though the trade-in allowance is stated at $1,000. Thus, the loss on this exchange is $1,400, the difference between the actual or apparent trade-in value ($600) and the book value ($2,000) of the old asset. The entry required to record this transaction is as follows:

Automobile (new)	19,600	
Accumulated depreciation	16,000	
Loss on disposal	1,400	
Automobile		18,000
Cash		19,000

In the above example, there is a loss on the trade, so the entries are the same whether the assets are similar (as is the case in the example) or dissimilar. We now modify the example as follows:

Trade-in allowance	$3,000
Fair market value of the Chevrolet	
(at January 1, 19X5)	3,000
Cash difference paid	17,000

These facts indicate a gain on the disposal of the Chevrolet, calculated as follows:

Fair market value of the Chevrolet		
at the date of the trade-in		$3,000
Original cost of the Chevrolet	$18,000	
Less: Accumulated depreciation		
as of the date of trade-in	16,000	
Book value of the Chevrolet		
at the date of the trade-in		2,000
Gain		$1,000

If the assets are dissimilar, the entry to record the acquisition of the new asset is as follows:

New asset	20,000	
Accumulated depreciation	16,000	
Automobile		18,000
Cash		17,000
Gain on disposal		1,000

The debit of $20,000 to the new asset is equal to the fair market value of the asset traded in ($3,000) plus the cash paid ($17,000). If the assets are assumed to be similar, the entry required to record the trade is as follows:

New asset	19,000	
Accumulated depreciation	16,000	
Automobile		18,000
Cash		17,000

Note that the debit of $19,000 to the new asset is the total of the cash paid and the book value of the asset traded in ($17,000 + $2,000).

In the preceding examples, the trade-in takes place at the beginning of the period. If a trade-in is made during the period, depreciation is recognized on the old asset for the period up to the time of the trade-in, and the entry to record the exchange recognizes the book value of the old asset as of the date of exchange.

For federal income tax purposes, a gain or loss is never recognized on the exchange of similar productive assets. Rather, the cost of the new asset is considered to be the book value (cost less accumulated depreciation) of the old asset plus the additional cash paid (or cash and debt incurred) in the exchange.

Outline

LEARNING Objectives

Chapter 10 discusses the accounting procedures used to record and control cash and the procedures used for recording receivables and payables. Studying this chapter should enable you to:

1. Describe the basic procedures for controlling cash receipts and disbursements.

2. Discuss the steps involved in preparing a bank reconciliation statement.

3. Describe the procedures used to control and account for imprest funds.

4. Illustrate the use of control and subsidiary accounts for recording receivables.

5. Discuss the purposes and mechanics of estimating bad debt expense.

6. Make the entries necessary to record the issuance and payment of a note and the related interest on the books of both the borrower and the lender.

7. Describe the process of discounting a note and the effect it has on a firm's accounts.

8. Calculate and prepare the entry to record the payroll taxes levied on an employer.

Chapter 10
Cash, Receivables, and Current Liabilities

Introduction

Cash includes currency, coins, checks, money orders, and monies on deposit with banks. On the balance sheet, cash is classified as a current asset. The total of all cash on hand and cash on deposit in multiple bank accounts is shown as a single amount in the balance sheet.

Almost every transaction of any business organization will eventually result in either the receipt or disbursement of cash. The accounting procedures that enable a business to establish effective control over its cash transactions are among the most important, if not *the* most important, controls necessary for the operation of a business. While it is certainly true that cash is no more important than any of the other individual assets of the business, cash is more susceptible to misappropriation or theft because it can easily be concealed and because it is not readily identifiable. It is essential, therefore, that the company institute procedures or controls throughout every phase of its operations in order to safeguard cash from the time of its receipt until the time it is deposited in the company's bank account.

A good system of internal control over cash transactions should provide adequate procedures for protecting both cash receipts and cash disbursements. Such procedures should include the following elements:

1. Responsibilities for handling cash receipts, making cash payments, and recording cash transactions should be clearly defined.

2. Employees who handle cash transactions should not maintain the accounting records for cash.

3. All cash receipts should be deposited daily in a bank account and all significant cash payments should be made by check.

4. The validity and amount of cash payments should be verified, and different employees should be responsible for approving the disbursement and for signing the check.

The application of these procedures in developing an adequate system of internal control over cash transactions varies from company to company depending upon such factors as the size of the company, the number of its employees, and its sources of cash. The following discussion illustrates typical procedures that may be used effectively in the control of cash receipts and cash disbursements.

Cash Receipts

The effective control of cash transactions begins at the moment cash is received by the business. Among the basic principles to be followed in controlling cash receipts are the following:

1. A complete record of all cash receipts should be prepared as soon as cash is received. This involves the listing of all cash items received by mail and the use of devices such as cash registers to record "over-the-counter" sales. The immediate recording of each cash transaction is important because the likelihood of misappropriations of cash receipts occurring is usually greatest before a record of the receipt has been prepared. Once the receipt of cash has been properly recorded, misappropriation or theft is much more difficult to accomplish and conceal.

2. Each day's cash receipts should be deposited intact into the company's bank account as soon as possible. Disbursements should never be made directly from cash receipts; each and every cash item received should be promptly deposited in the bank. All major disbursements should be made by check, while outlays of smaller amounts may be made from controlled petty cash funds (described in a later section of this chapter). Adherence to these procedures will provide the firm with a valuable test of the accuracy of its cash records since every major cash transaction will be recorded twice: by the firm in its accounting records and by the bank. The periodic comparison or reconciliation of the accounting records of the business with those maintained by an independent, external source (the bank) is an important control feature in itself and will be discussed in detail in a later section of this chapter.

3. The employees charged with the responsibility of handling cash receipts should not be involved in making cash disbursements. This is a normal procedure employed by most firms of any size. Insofar as possible, the internal functions of receiving and disbursing cash should be kept separate in order to prevent the possible misappropriation or theft of cash. The employees handling cash receipts should not have access to the other accounting records of the firm for the same reasons.

OVER THE COUNTER SALES

The cash proceeds at the time a sale is made should be recorded by means of a cash register. In larger firms, it may be preferable to have all sales recorded by a cashier at a centrally-located cash register. One employee may "make the sale" and prepare a prenumbered sales slip that is given to the cashier who then records the sale on the cash register and accepts the customer's payment. Involving two (or more) employees in each sales transaction, rather than permitting a single employee to handle a transaction in its entirety, increases the control over cash. The use of a cash register provides certain other benefits. Customers will observe that their purchases are recorded at the proper amount (another form of control). You may recall making a purchase where your money was refunded "if a star appears on your receipt" or where your drink was free if the waiter failed to give you a receipt. These are simple, yet effective examples of control procedures that are intended to encourage customers to note whether the sale has been properly recorded at the correct amount. The cash register may also be used as a means of classifying the sources of receipts, such as sales by departments.

At the end of each day, or more often if necessary (for example, at the end of each cashier's shift), the cash in the register should be counted and recorded on a cash register summary or other report by an employee who does not have access to the sales slips. A second employee should total the sales slips and reconcile the total of the sales slips to the cash register total. As previously indicated, all cash received should be deposited intact into the bank and the receipts should be recorded in the accounting records.

In certain circumstances, it may not be feasible to use prenumbered sales slips. If this is the case and a cash register is used, the above procedures should still be followed to the extent applicable. The major difference is that the cash in the register is reconciled to the totals contained in the register rather than to totals obtained from sales slips.

RECEIPTS FROM CHARGE SALES

Remittances from customers for sales made on account may be received either by mail or by payment in person. In either case, procedures should be employed so that the receipt and the recording of the cash are performed by different employees whenever it is possible and practical to do so. If this separation of duties can be effectively maintained, the misappropriation of cash would require the collusion of two or more employees, thus diminishing the likelihood of the occurrence of any irregularity.

The employee who opens the mail should immediately prepare a listing of all cash items received. This listing, along with a summary of over-the-counter receipts described previously, may be used to record each day's receipts in the cash receipts summary. Mail remittances are then combined with over-the-counter receipts, and the daily bank deposit is prepared and made. The amount deposited is equal to the total cash receipts for the day. The employee making the bank deposit should obtain a duplicate deposit slip or other receipt from the bank for subsequent comparison to the cash receipts book.

The advantages of the procedures described above are many. The most important of these benefits may be summarized as follows:

1. The possibility of irregularities with respect to cash transactions are reduced, since any misappropriation will generally require the collusion of two or more employees.

2. The prompt deposit of each day's receipts intact (along with the disbursement procedures described in a later section of this chapter) provides the basis for an independent, external check on the internal records of the firm by reconciliation with bank statements.

3. Frequent deposits of receipts minimize the idle cash and thereby reduce interest or other carrying charges that might otherwise be incurred by the business.

It is obvious that the owners and management of any organization are naturally concerned with establishing effective controls that will prevent irregularities, but it may not be as apparent that every employee of the business also has a definite interest in these safeguards. If, for example, cash is misappropriated in an instance where the control procedures are ineffective or not in existence, any employee who might possibly be involved will be under suspicion. Although it may not be possible to identify the guilty person, no employee will be able to prove his or her innocence. Employee morale and efficiency will be adversely affected. An effective system of internal control avoids this situation; responsibilities are well-defined, definite, and fixed. Internal control is often an excellent preventive measure, as it often removes the temptation that might cause an otherwise good employee to succumb.

Cash Over and Short

Regardless of the care exercised in handling cash transactions, employees may make errors that cause cash overages or shortages. These differences are normally detected when the cash on hand is counted and reconciled to the beginning cash balance plus any inflows of cash less any cash outlays.

Assume, for example, that total "over the counter" cash sales for the day are shown as $1,500 on the cash register while cash on hand, after deducting the $100 beginning balance, is counted and found to be $1,505. The following journal entry is made to record the cash sales for the day:

Cash	1,505	
Sales		1,500
Cash over and short		5

The cash over and short account is credited for any cash overages and debited for any cash shortages. At the end of the accounting period, the net balance in the cash over and short account is treated as miscellaneous revenues if there is a net credit balance or as a miscellaneous expense if there is a net debit balance.

Cash Disbursements

As previously indicated, one of the basic rules of effective internal control over cash transactions is that each day's receipts should be deposited intact into the bank and that all disbursements should be made by check. The functions of handling cash receipts and cash disbursements should be separated or divided among employees to the greatest extent practical. Other procedures that may be used to establish effective control over cash disbursements include the following:

1. All checks should be prenumbered consecutively and should be controlled and accounted for on a regular basis. Checks that are voided or spoiled should be retained and mutilated to prevent any possible unauthorized use.

2. Each disbursement should be supported or evidenced by an invoice and/or voucher that has been properly approved.

3. Invoices and vouchers should be indelibly marked as "paid" or otherwise cancelled in order to prevent duplicate payments.

4. The bank statement and returned checks should be routed to the employee charged with the preparation of the bank reconciliation statement (described below). This employee should be someone other than the person who is responsible for making cash disbursements.

The Bank Reconciliation Statement

As indicated earlier, if all receipts are deposited intact into the bank and all major disbursements are made by check, each cash transaction is recorded twice: by the business in its accounting records and by the bank in its records. It might seem logical, then, that at any given time the cash balance obtained from the accounting records of the firm is equal to the balance in the business's checking account at the bank; however, this is very seldom the case. Comparison of the balance shown in the firm's records with the balance shown at the same date by the bank statement usually reveals a difference in the two amounts. One reason for the difference could be erroneous entries made either by the firm or by the bank. A more frequent cause for the difference is attributable to differences in the timing of the recording of the transactions by the firm and the bank. If all transactions are recorded simultaneously by the business and by the bank, no differences result (except in the case of errors), but this is almost never the case. For example, the firm may write a check and immediately deduct the amount of the expenditure from the cash balance in its checkbook. The bank does not deduct this same disbursement from the firm's account until the check is presented to the bank for payment, perhaps several days later. Until the disbursement is deducted by the bank, the balance in the firm's account at the bank exceeds the firm's cash balance in its checkbook by the amount of the check. Similarly, the bank may levy a service charge against the firm's bank account from time to time. The business is usually unaware of the amount of this charge until it receives its monthly statement from the bank. Until the bank statement is received and the service charge is deducted, the balance in the firm's records exceeds the bank statement balance by the amount of the service charge.

The above examples are but two of the many items that may cause a difference between the bank statement balance and the cash balance as shown in the accounting records of the business. Other items which are often reflected in the bank statement before being recorded by the depositor include:

1. N.S.F. checks—checks that were received from the depositor's customers and deposited in the bank, but for which the bank on which the check was written refuses payment (usually because of insufficient funds in the customer's account).

2. Deductions for printing of checks, safe deposit box rentals, etc.

3. Collections by the bank in acting as a collecting agent for the depositor.

A bank reconciliation is prepared to identify and account for all items that cause a difference between the cash balance as shown on the bank statement and the balance as it appears in the firm's accounting records. One often-used format for this statement is that both the book and bank balances are adjusted to the actual amount of cash available to the business. This amount, which appears on the balance sheet, is often referred to as the "adjusted cash balance" or "true cash." A typical bank reconciliation statement is presented in Illustration 1.

The initial step in preparing a bank reconciliation statement is to examine the bank statement and any debit and credit memoranda accompanying it. A debit memorandum is a deduction made by the bank from a depositor's account due to a transaction other than the normal payment of a check by the bank. Likewise, a credit memorandum is an addition to the depositor's account due to a transaction other than a normal deposit. These memoranda should be compared with the firm's accounting records in order to determine whether or not they have been previously (and properly) recorded by the business. If these transactions have not been recorded, they must be included as additions or deductions in the bank reconciliation statement and then recorded at a subsequent time. Examples of three types of memoranda that are included in Illustration 1 are as follows:

1. The $1,000 addition to the book balance represents the proceeds from a note collected by the bank for Carol's Bakery and added to Carol's bank account.

2. The bank charge of $5 for the month of June was deducted from Carol's account by the bank.

3. The N.S.F. (Not Sufficient Funds) check of $40 represents a check received from a customer and deposited by Carol. The check was returned unpaid by the customer's bank.

Illustration 1
Carol's Bakery
Bank Reconciliation Statement
June 30, 19X1

Balance per the bank statement, June 30, 19X1		$4,590
Add: Deposit in transit		500
Bank error, check drawn by Carol's Tavern		
charged to the account of Carol's Bakery		10
Less: Outstanding checks:		
Number 95 – $50		
Number 101 – 15		
Number 106 – 30		
Number 110 – 5		(100)
"True" cash balance, June 30, 19X1		$5,000
Balance per the books, June 30, 19X1		$4,000
Add: Note collected by the bank		1,000
Error made by the accountant in recording		
a receipt of payment on account		45
Less: Bank charges		(5)
N.S.F. check		(40)
"True" cash balance, June 30, 19X1		$5,000

The second step in preparing the reconciliation is to arrange the paid checks returned with the bank statement in numerical sequence. The checks returned by the bank are then compared with the checks issued as listed in the business checkbook or cash disbursements journal. Distinctive *tick marks* or symbols (such as a ✓) may be used in the checkbook in order to indicate those checks which have been returned by the bank. The amount of each check should be compared to the amount listed in the checkbook during this process. The outstanding checks are those that have been issued but not yet returned by the bank (because the recipients have not cashed the checks).

Checks that were outstanding at the beginning of the month and that cleared the bank during the month may be traced to the bank reconciliation statement prepared at the end of the previous month. Any checks that were outstanding at the beginning of the month and that did not clear the bank are still included as outstanding in the current month's reconciliation. In the example, the $100 total of outstanding checks included in the bank reconciliation statement is determined by comparing the cancelled checks returned with the bank statement with the checkbook and the listing of outstanding checks included in the previous month's bank reconciliation.

In our example, examination of the cancelled checks returned with the bank statement discloses the fact that the bank had deducted a check written by Carrol's Tavern in the amount of $10 from the Carol's Bakery account. This item is shown as an addition to the balance per bank in the reconciliation and should be called to the attention of the bank for correction.

The next step in the reconciliation process is to ascertain whether or not there are any deposits in transit. A deposit in transit is a receipt that has been included in the cash balance per books and deposited in the bank (for example, in a night depository or by mail) but that has not yet been processed by the bank and credited to the depositor's account. In the illustration, the total receipts of $500 for June 30th were deposited in the bank's night depository on that date; however, the bank did not credit the firm's account until the next day, July 1st. The $500 amount is shown as a deposit in transit in the June 30, 19X1, bank reconciliation statement.

An excellent test of the accuracy of the firm's cash receipts records is to reconcile the total receipts for the month (or other period) to the total deposits credited to the bank account in the bank statement. In order to perform this test, the following information is required:

1. The total deposits included in the bank statement for the month of June [including a deposit in transit at the beginning of the month (May 31, 19X1) of $700] $15,000

2. The total cash receipts shown in the firm's accounting records for the month of June (including the receipts of June 30th of $500) 14,755

The receipts, as per the books for the month of June, are reconciled with the deposits as per the June 30, 19X1, bank statement as follows:

Deposits per bank statement		$15,000
Less: Deposit In transit at the end of the prior month		700
		$14,300
Add: Deposit in transit at the end of the current month		500
Cash receipts should be per the books		$14,800

There is a $45 difference between the total cash receipts shown in the accounting records for the month of June ($14,755) and the cash receipts that should be shown per the books ($14,800). A closer examination reveals that the receipt of a payment on account of $572 was erroneously recorded as $527 by the firm, a difference of $45.

In many instances, deposits in transit, outstanding checks, service charges, and errors are the only reconciling items between the book and the bank balances. Omissions from, or errors in, the accounting records of the firm should be corrected immediately. If errors made by the bank are discovered in the reconciliation process (such as a check charged to the wrong account), they should be called to the attention of the bank for immediate correction.

In the example, several adjusting or correcting entries are required. These are as follows:

Note Collected by the Bank

Cash	1,000	
Notes receivable		1,000

Error

Cash	45	
Accounts receivable		45

Bank Service Charges

Service charge expense   5
    Cash   5

N.S.F. Check

Accounts receivable   40
    Cash   40

The effect of these four entries is to adjust the balance per books as of June 30, 19X1, to the "true cash" balance as of that date. This adjustment procedure may be illustrated as follows:

Cash	
4,000	
1,000	5
45	40
5,000	

It should be noted that only those items that are adjustments of the "balance per books" in the bank reconciliation statement require adjusting or correcting entries, because these items either have not been previously recorded on the books of the firm (in the example, the note collected by the bank, the bank charge, and the check returned N.S.F.) or have been recorded erroneously (in the example, the $572 receipt recorded by the firm as $527[1]). Items that are included as adjustments of the "balance per the bank statement" do not require adjustment in the firm's books since these items are either transactions that have been already recorded by the firm but not by the bank (in the example, the deposit in transit and the outstanding checks) or errors that were made by the bank (in the example, the check of Carrol's Tavern that was erroneously charged to the account of Carol's Bakery).

The bank reconciliation procedure may be summarized as follows:

Balance per the bank statement—adjust for:
1. Transactions recorded by the firm but not by the bank (deposits in transit, outstanding checks, etc.).
2. Errors made by the bank.

Balance per the books—adjust for:
1. Transactions recorded by the bank but not by the firm (collections made for the firm by the bank, service charges, N.S.F. checks, etc.).
2. Errors made by the firm.

Petty Cash Funds

A basic principle of control over cash is that all cash disbursements should be made by check. This is not practicable, however, in instances where small expenditures are required for items such as postage, freight, carfare, employees' "supper money," etc. In circumstances such as these, it is usually more convenient and cost effective to make payments in currency and/or coin. This can be accomplished and effective control over cash still maintained by the use of an imprest fund called petty cash.

A petty cash fund is established by drawing a check on the regular checking account, cashing it, and placing the proceeds in a fund. The amount of the fund depends upon the extent to which petty cash will be used and how often it will be reimbursed. As a practical matter, it should be large enough to cover petty cash disbursements for a reasonable period of time—for example, a week. A single employee should be placed in charge of the fund and made responsible for its operation.

---

[1] Transposition errors (e.g., $572 – $527) are always divisible by nine. This fact may be helpful in locating differences, errors, etc.

A major difference between making disbursements from a petty cash fund and from a regular checking account is that disbursements from petty cash funds are recorded in the accounting records not as they are made, but when the fund is reimbursed. At the time each expenditure is made from the fund, a petty cash voucher, such as the one illustrated below, is prepared. If an invoice or other receipt is available in support of the disbursement, it should be attached to the voucher. In any event, the person receiving the cash should always be required to sign the petty cash voucher as evidence of his or her receipt of the disbursement. If this procedure is followed, at any given time the total of the cash on hand in the petty cash fund plus the unreimbursed receipts should be equal to the original amount of the fund.

The fund is reimbursed on a periodic basis or whenever necessary. In order to obtain reimbursement for the fund, the employee acting as petty cashier brings the paid petty cash vouchers to the person who is authorized to write checks on the firm's bank account and exchanges them for a check equal to the total of the vouchers. At this point, the petty cash vouchers are separated and summarized according to the appropriate expense category for recording in the firm's accounting records. Before the check is issued, the vouchers are reviewed in order to ascertain that all the expenditures made were for valid business purposes. After the petty cash vouchers are approved and the fund replenished, the vouchers and the underlying support either should be marked as *paid* or should be mutilated in order to prevent their reuse, either intentionally or unintentionally.

Petty Cash Voucher #53

TO _Vince Brenner_ DATE ___May 1___ 19x1

EXPLANATION   ACCOUNT   AMOUNT
Postage   _119_   _$5.00_

APPROVED   RECEIVED
BY ___PD___   PAYMENT ___V. B.___

To illustrate the operation of a petty cash fund, assume that Barney Company establishes a $100 petty cash fund on January 1, 19X1, by cashing a check in the amount of $100 and placing the proceeds in the fund. The entry to record this transaction is as follows:

```
January 1:     Petty cash ..........................    100
                  Cash .............................            100
```

Assume further that during the month of January, disbursements from the fund (supported by vouchers) total $85. In order to replenish the fund on January 31, the employee responsible for the fund exchanges the vouchers for a check drawn on the regular cash account for $85. This check is cashed and the $85 proceeds are used to restore the fund to its original cash balance of $100. This transaction is recorded by the following entry:

```
January 31:    Various expenses ......................    85
                  Cash ..............................            85
```

Note that no entry is made to the *petty cash* account after the fund is established (unless the firm wishes to increase or decrease the fund balance).

Effective control over petty cash operations is accomplished in two ways: (1) at any time the cash on hand in the fund plus the unreimbursed petty cash vouchers must be equal to the fund balance, and (2) the expense vouchers must be examined and approved upon reimbursement by a person other than the employee who made the disbursement. If considered necessary or desirable, surprise counts of the petty cash fund may be made in order to ensure that the fund is operating according to its intended purposes.

Receivables and Payables

The extension of credit is a significant factor in the operation of many businesses. Most businesses are both grantors of credit (creating receivables) and receivers of credit (creating payables). Receivables are assets representing the claims that a business has against others. While receivables may be generated by various types of transactions, the most common source of receivables is the sale of merchandise or services on a credit basis. Normally, these assets are realized or converted into cash by the business. Payables are obligations that arise from past transactions and that are to be discharged at a future date by payment of cash, transfer of other assets, or performance of a service. Typically, claims against a firm originate from transactions such as purchases of merchandise or services on credit, purchases of equipment on credit, and loans from banks. In an economic system such as ours, which is based so extensively on credit, almost all business concerns incur liabilities. The procedures that are necessary to establish effective control over receivables and payables, and the accounting practices and procedures that are employed with regard to these assets and liabilities are discussed in the following sections of this chapter.

Classification of Receivables and Payables

Receivables are classified according to the timing of their expected realization—i.e., as current assets if realization is anticipated within the longer of the operating cycle of the firm or a year, or as noncurrent assets if collection is expected subsequent to the current period. The operating cycle of a business is the average period of time that elapses between the purchase of an inventory item and the conversion of the inventory item into cash. This cycle includes the initial purchase of the inventory, the sale of the item on credit, and the collection of the receivable. Receivables are also classified according to their form. Notes receivable are claims supported by "formal" or written promises to pay. These may or may not be negotiable instruments, depending on such factors as the terms, form, and content of the note. An example of a note receivable is the written promise by a borrower to repay a loan with interest at a stated date. Accounts receivable, on the other hand, are not supported by "formal" or written promises to pay. An example of an account receivable is the claim of a business against a customer who makes a purchase on account.

Creditors of a business have claims against the assets of the firm. Depending upon the nature of the particular liability, a claim may either be against specific assets or against assets in general. In any case, claims of creditors have a priority over the claims of owners. In the event of the liquidation of a business, all debts must be satisfied before any payments are made to owners.

Amounts shown in the balance sheet as liabilities may be classified as either current or noncurrent liabilities. A proper distinction between current and noncurrent liabilities is essential because comparison of current assets with current liabilities is an important means of evaluating the short-run liquidity or debt-paying ability of the firm.

Current liabilities are those debts or obligations that either must be paid in cash or settled by providing goods or services within the operating cycle of the firm or one year, whichever is longer. The most common current liabilities include accounts payable, notes payable, and accrued liabilities.

Control over Receivables

At the time an over-the-counter sale is made, whether it is a cash sale or a charge sale, it should be recorded by means of a cash register. The controls described in this chapter apply to both charge or credit sales as well as to cash sales. If a sale is made on account, a prenumbered sales ticket should be prepared and signed by the customer making the purchase. At a minimum, this charge ticket should include the following information:

1. The date.
2. The customer's name and account number.
3. A description of the item(s) purchased by the customer.
4. The total amount of the sale.
5. The customer's signature.

Effective control procedures require that the sales slip be prepared in triplicate: one copy is given to the customer, a second copy is placed in the cash register, and a third copy is retained by the salesperson. An invoice dispenser that automatically retains a copy in a locked container is an ideal control device for this purpose. At the end of each day, or more often if necessary, the charge slips accumulated in the register are used in the reconciliation of the cash register receipts.

The charge slips serve as the basis for recording credit purchases in customers' accounts. A control account, trade accounts receivable, is used to record the total charge sales and the total payments received from customers. Individual ledger accounts, referred to as subsidiary accounts, are maintained for each customer. The amount of each charge sale is recorded individually in the particular customer's account, and the total sales are recorded in the control account. Bills are prepared from the individual customers' ledger accounts and mailed out periodically, usually on a monthly basis. As payments are received from customers, the remittances are recorded individually in the customer's account and in total in the control account. Cash receipts, received either by mail or "over-the-counter," are controlled according to the procedures outlined earlier in this chapter. At any point in time, the balance in the control account should be equal[2] to the total of the balances in the individual customers' accounts. Therefore, a periodic reconciliation should be made of the control and the subsidiary accounts.

Accounts Receivable

The most common type of receivable is the account receivable that arises from the sale of goods or services on a credit basis in the normal operations of the business. *A determination must be made of both the timing of the recognition of the asset and of the measurement of the value of the asset. The timing factor is intertwined with the recognition of revenue—the point at which a sale is made or a service has been performed.* The measurement factor depends on the due date of the receivable, the terms of payment, and the probability of collection.

As credit sales are made, entries are recorded in both the control and the subsidiary accounts. For purposes of illustration, assume that a department store makes the following sales during the month of June:

To Larry Killough	$ 100
To Gene Seago	150
To Pat Kemp	200
To all other charge customers	10,000
	$10,450

These sales are recorded in the control account, trade accounts receivable. At the same time, these sales are recorded in the individual customers' accounts, so that at all times the balance in the control account (accounts receivable) is equal to the total of all the balances in the subsidiary accounts (individual customers' accounts). Using T-accounts, this process is illustrated as follows:

---

[2] If a special journal is used, they may be equal only at the end of the period.

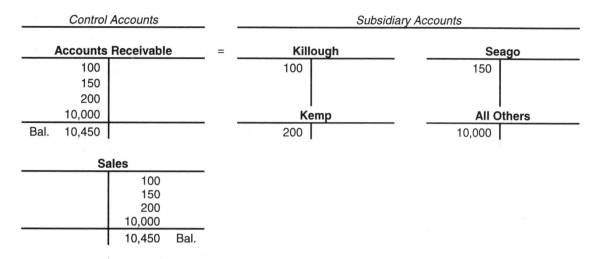

Control Accounts				Subsidiary Accounts			

Accounts Receivable = **Killough** **Seago**

Accounts Receivable			Killough		Seago	
100			100		150	
150						
200			**Kemp**		**All Others**	
10,000			200		10,000	
Bal. 10,450						

Sales	
	100
	150
	200
	10,000
	10,450 Bal.

Now assume that the collections received from customers are as follows:

From Killough	$ 100
From Seago	100
From other customers	8,000
	$8,200

These collections are recorded in the control account. At the same time, the collections are recorded in the subsidiary accounts, thereby maintaining a balance with the control account. This procedure is illustrated as follows:

Control Accounts				Subsidiary Accounts			

Accounts Receivable		Killough		Seago	
Bal. 10,450	100	100	100	150	100
	100				
	8,000				
2,250		0		50	

Kemp		All Others	
200		10,000	8,000
		2,000	

Uncollectible Receivables

One of the costs of making sales on a credit basis results from the fact that some of the customers who make purchases on account may never pay the amounts owed to the firm. This is to be expected and should be considered a normal cost of doing business. If a firm is able to identify the particular customers who will ultimately fail to pay their accounts, it will not sell to them on a credit basis. Unfortunately, although credit investigations of varying degrees of effectiveness are made by firms, some bad debts still result. In fact, if a firm has no bad debts whatsoever, this might be an indication that its credit department is performing unsatisfactorily. If credit standards are set so high as to eliminate all those potential customers whose credit ratings are judged to be marginal, the revenue lost from refusing credit to these customers would no doubt exceed the potential losses, thus decreasing the firm's net income. From a theoretical viewpoint, the firm should grant credit to its customers up to that point where the marginal revenue from the granting of credit sales is equal to the marginal expense, including the cost of bad debts. This goal is impossible to attain in actual practice, but a firm's credit policy should attempt to approximate this objective to the extent possible or practical.

The experience of Sears Credit (the financing division of Sears Roebuck & Co.) Illustrates the pitfalls of selling to customers on account. Soon after Jane Thompson took charge of Sears Credit in 1993, she doubled the number of new credit card issuances to over six million a year. Unfortunately, an increasing number of Sears' customers chose personal bankruptcy over paying their bills. Steve Kernkraut, a Bear Stearns analyst and former president of J.C. Penny Credit Services, observed that "...Sears was being very generous when everyone else was tightening credit standards."[3]

Uncollectible receivables are generally referred to as bad debts. *A bad debt represents a loss of the revenue that was recognized at the time the receivable originated. Therefore, the accounting for bad debts requires a decrease in accounts receivable and a related decrease in income for the period.*

Bad debt expense is a normal business expense that should be expected by those firms selling goods or services on a credit basis. The proper determination of income for a period requires that the revenue earned during that period be matched with the expenses incurred in generating that revenue. For firms that make sales or render services on a credit basis, this requires that bad debt expense be matched against revenue in the period in which the revenue is earned. Most accountants agree that this is the period in which the sale is originally made, and not the period in which a particular account is determined to be uncollectible. For example, assume that a credit sale made during the month of June is determined to be uncollectible during July, due to the bankruptcy of the customer. This would represent an expense of the month of June (when the sale was made and the revenue recognized) not the month of July (when the account was found to be uncollectible).

The basic accounting problem in recording bad debts is determining the timing for recording the decrease in income and the related reduction in receivables. Two procedures for the recognition of bad debts are as follows:

1. Record bad debts in the period that a specific receivable has been identified as uncollectible—referred to as the direct write-off method. The direct write-off method is not acceptable unless the amount of bad debts either is not material or cannot be reasonably estimated.

2. Record an estimate of the expected uncollectible accounts on the basis of either sales or outstanding receivables at the end of the period in which the sales on account were made—referred to as the allowance method.

In both methods, the entry to record bad debts is a debit to bad debt expense and a reduction in the receivables. The direct write-off method records the reduction in the receivables with a credit directly to accounts receivable, whereas the allowance method records the decrease in receivables through an increase in a contra account to the receivables, allowance for bad debts.

To illustrate the use of the direct write-off method, assume that a company, which has a balance of $13,000 in accounts receivable, believes that the Woods Corporation is not going to pay its $500 account because Woods is bankrupt. The journal entry to record the bad debt is as follows:

Bad debt expense	500	
Accounts receivable		500

The basic problem with this approach is that the bad debt expense, in all probability, is not matched with the revenue from the sale. Most of the time, a company does not recognize an account receivable as a bad debt in the same period in which the receivable originated. Therefore, if a sale is made in one period and the customer's account is deemed to be worthless in a subsequent period, there is an improper matching of revenue and expense. Further, this approach does not result in stating receivables at their estimated realizable value on the balance sheet.

In the allowance method, bad debt expense must be estimated, because the particular accounts that ultimately will prove to be uncollectible are unknown. Proper determination of income requires that bad debt expense be matched against revenue in the period in which the revenue is earned, when the sale originally is made, not when a particular account is determined to be uncollectible. Similarly, the establishment of an allowance account that is contra to accounts receivable achieves an estimate of the net realizable value of the

---

[3] "Sears' Big Turnaround Runs Into Big Trouble," *Fortune* (February 16, 1998): 34.

accounts receivable at the end of a period. Even though estimates of future events are required in the application of the allowance method, it is argued that it is preferable to approximate the bad debts relating to the current period using the allowance method rather than to ignore the reality of future bad debts as is done with the direct write-off approach.

There are two commonly-used approaches for the estimation of bad debts: (1) a percentage of either total sales or credit sales, and (2) a percentage of accounts receivable at the end of the period. In either approach, when the estimate has been made at the end of the period, the entry to record the bad debt is a debit to bad debt expense and a credit to allowance for bad debts. *The allowance account is reported on the balance sheet as a direct deduction from accounts receivable.*

Bad Debts as a Percentage of Sales

The estimate of bad debts in the percentage of sales approach is normally based on an analysis of the firm's past relationship between credit sales and bad debts. The percentage relationship may be adjusted for current circumstances such as changes in credit policies or economic conditions. The analysis may be on the basis of total sales if there is a stable relationship between credit sales and total sales. It should be noted that the approach used is an income statement approach. The primary consideration is to estimate correctly the bad debt expense for the period.

Assume, for purposes of illustration, that the credit experience of a small firm has been as follows:

Year	Credit Sales	Losses From Bad Debts
19X1	$120,000	$2,300
19X2	130,000	2,650
19X3	150,000	3,050
	$400,000	$8,000

For 19X4, it might be reasonable for the firm to estimate that its losses from uncollectible accounts will be similar to its experience in prior years. A percentage that can be used in estimating bad debts is $8,000 divided by $400,000, or 2 percent of credit sales. In practice, this percentage would be adjusted for any expected changes in general economic conditions, credit policies, etc.

Returning to the example used earlier in the chapter in the section entitled Accounts Receivable, recall that credit sales for the period were $10,450. Using the percentage of sales method, the estimated bad debts from these sales are calculated by multiplying $10,450 by 2 percent, or $209. This estimated bad debt expense is recorded in the accounts by the following journal entry:

Bad debt expense	209	
Allowance for bad debts		209

Note that the credit portion of this entry is to an allowance for bad debts account and not to accounts receivable. While the firm's best estimate of its bad debt expense, based on its past experience, indicates that approximately $209 of the receivables arising from sales made during the month of June will not be collectible, it is unable to identify at this time the particular individual(s) whose account(s) may ultimately prove to be uncollectible. A direct credit to accounts receivable is inappropriate, because such a procedure eliminates the equality of the control and the subsidiary accounts. The effect of the journal entry to record bad debt expense on the control and subsidiary accounts is as follows:

	Control Accounts				Subsidiary Accounts		

Accounts Receivable

Debit	Credit
10,450	8,200
2,250	

Killough

Debit	Credit
100	100
0	

Seago

Debit	Credit
150	100
50	

Allowance for Bad Debts

Debit	Credit
	209

Kemp

Debit	Credit
200	

All Others

Debit	Credit
10,000	8,000
2,000	

Bad Debt Expense

Debit	Credit
209	

The allowance for bad debts account has a credit balance after this end-of-period entry. At this point, neither the control account for Accounts Receivable nor the subsidiary accounts are affected. The credit balance for Allowance for Bad Debts is deducted on the balance sheet from the asset account, accounts receivable, to produce the net value for the receivables.

In the percentage of sales approach, the entry to record bad debt expense at the end of the period is unaffected by any balance existing in the allowance account. The logic for this approach is that the purpose of the entry is to obtain a proper matching between sales and bad debt expense.

When uncollectible accounts are written off in the subsequent year, the allowance account is debited, accounts receivable is credited, and the individual accounts in the subsidiary ledger are credited. It is unlikely that the total of the amounts written off is equal to the estimated amount. Any remaining balance (either debit or credit) in the allowance account at the end of the period, but before the current period's adjusting entry is made, represents an underestimate or overestimate of previous periods (assuming that no account originating in the current year is written off in the current year). Recognition of the estimation error is not necessary, unless the amount involved is material.

Bad Debts as a Percentage of Receivables

An alternative to the percentage of sales approach is to base the estimate of uncollectible accounts on the past relationship between receivables and bad debts (again adjusted for any changes in current circumstances). This relationship can be based on either total receivables or on receivables segregated by various age categories. In most circumstances, the use of such aging schedules provides a better predicter of future uncollectible accounts. Under this balance sheet approach, the emphasis is on the measurement of economic resources rather than income determination.

The objective of estimating bad debts on the basis of outstanding receivables is to provide a good estimate of the appropriate balance in the allowance account and, therefore, a reasonably accurate measure of the net realizable value of the accounts receivable in the balance sheet. Consequently, when the estimate of uncollectible accounts is determined at the end of the period, the entry is made to bring the allowance account to the estimated balance. That is, any balance remaining in the allowance account at year-end is taken into account in preparing the journal entry. Another way of viewing this process is that by considering the balance in the allowance account in determining the year-end entry, this approach corrects automatically for any underestimation or overestimation of bad debts made in previous periods.

The most commonly-used method of estimating the uncollectible receivables is to analyze the accounts receivable balance at the end of the period using an aging process to make a judgment as to which accounts are likely to prove to be uncollectible. *Aging involves the classifying or grouping of accounts according to the period of time that the accounts have been outstanding.* The basic assumption is that, all other factors being equal, the collectibility of receivables decreases as the account remains outstanding. An example of an aging schedule is as follows:

		Number of Days Outstanding			
Account	Balance	0-30	31-60	61-90	91 and Older
Killough	$ 0	$ 0	$ 0	$ 0	$ 0
Seago	50	50	0	0	0
Kemp	200	200	0	0	0
All others	2,000	1,350	400	50	200
	$2,250	$1,600	$400	$50	$200

Based on the experience of the firm, different percentages may be applied to the different classifications of accounts to estimate the amount of uncollectible receivables. For example, the following calculations might be appropriate:

Number of Days Outstanding	Amount	Percentage	Estimated to be Uncollectible
0-30	$1,600	1%	$ 16
31-60	400	10	40
61-90	50	50	25
91 and older	200	75	150
	$2,250		$231

The percentage used would be determined by the credit experience of the firm, adjusted as considered necessary for such factors as changes in economic conditions, credit policies, etc. The older accounts, as well as those that are known to be in financial difficulty, should be reviewed on an individual basis as an additional test of the amount estimated to be uncollectible.

Assume that, after this review, the firm decides that the calculation of the amount estimated to be uncollectible using the analysis of receivables by age is appropriate. The balance in the allowance for bad debts account is increased to $231, the amount estimated to be uncollectible at the end of June. Since this approach is based on the question of how large of an allowance account is needed to reduce the net receivables balance to the amount expected to be collected, it is necessary to consider any balance in the allowance account before making the adjusting entry. The allowance account has a debit or credit balance at the end of the period, prior to the adjustment, if the receivables actually determined to be uncollectible during the period are not equal to the balance in the allowance account at the beginning of the period. The procedure for writing-off an uncollectible receivable is discussed in the next section. Assuming that the allowance for bad debts account has a debit balance of $20 prior to this determination, the following journal entry is required:

Bad debt expense	251	
Allowance for bad debts		251

After this entry has been posted to the allowance account, the balance in the account is $231.

Allowance for Bad Debts

20	251
	231

Note that when bad debts are based on an analysis of accounts receivable, the total amount that is estimated to be uncollectible is determined and then compared to the existing balance in the allowance for bad debts account. The journal entry required adjusts the allowance for bad debts account to the appropriate amount.

A difference between the percentage of sales approach and the percentage of receivables approach lies in the handling of any overestimation or underestimation of the previous period (which is evidenced by a credit or debit balance in the allowance account). In the percentage of sales method, any balance in the allowance account is ignored in determining the year-end entry to bad debts expense. This method theoretically provides the appropriate matching of the bad debt expense with the revenues of the period. In the percentage of receivables method, any balance in the allowance account is considered in determining the year-end entry to bad debts expense. This method theoretically provides the appropriate measure of the net realizable value of the receivables. In practice, if the estimation procedures are reasonably accurate, there should not be a significant difference between the two approaches.

BALANCE SHEET PRESENTATION

In the balance sheet, the allowance for bad debts appears as an offset to, or deduction from, accounts receivable. For example, the receivables of the firm may be shown as follows:

Accounts receivable	$2,250
Less: Allowance for bad debts	231
	$2,019

WRITING Off AN UNCOLLECTIBLE ACCOUNT

When a particular account balance is determined to be uncollectible, an entry is made in the accounts to recognize this fact. Returning to the example used earlier in the chapter, assume that the $50 balance owed by Seago proves to be uncollectible. The following entry is required:

Allowance for bad debts	50	
Accounts receivable		50

After this entry has been posted to the accounts, the control[4] account appears as follows:

Accounts Receivable		Allowance for Bad Debts	
2,250	50	50	231
2,200			181

In the balance sheet, the receivables appear as follows:

Accounts receivable	$2,200	
Less: Allowance for bad debts	181	$2,019

It is important to note that the entry for the write-off of the uncollectible receivable affects neither expense nor total assets. The net receivable balance (accounts receivable less the allowance for bad debts) remains the same since both accounts receivable and the allowance for bad debts are reduced by the same amount. The expense related to bad debts is recorded when the estimated bad debts are recorded (i.e., when the provision for bad debts is made). The entry to record bad debts expense is normally made during the year-end adjustment process.

Even though a company writes off an account as uncollectible, it will still attempt to collect the balance due. In some instances, it may continue its own efforts to collect the account; in others, it may turn the account over to a collection agency. In any event, if the collection efforts prove to be successful, the company will receive cash. Two entries are required in order to record this receipt. The first entry reinstates the balance written off by reversing the original entry made at the time of the write-off. The second entry records the collection of the account balance.

---

[4] The effect on the subsidiary accounts is to reduce the balance in Seago's account from $50 to zero, thereby maintaining the equality between the control and the subsidiary accounts.

To illustrate the recovery of an account that had previously been written off, we return to the example used above. Assume now that Seago's $50 balance written off as uncollectible is subsequently collected. The collection is recorded by the following entries:

Accounts receivable	50	
Allowance for bad debts		50
Cash	50	
Accounts receivable		50

Again, note that the first entry simply reverses the previous write-off. The second entry records the collection of the balance.

Accounts Receivable Turnover

A measure of liquidity for a company's accounts receivable is its *accounts receivables turnover*. This ratio depicts the number of times that receivables are collected during the period. The formula for the accounts receivable turnover is as follows:

$$\text{Accounts Receivable Turnover} = \frac{\text{Net Credit Sales}}{\text{Average Accounts Receivable}}$$

The turnover in the current period should be compared with the company's turnover in prior periods and with those of other companies in the industry. If the turnover is too slow, the company's accounts receivable may not be liquid enough. The credit department, in an effort to boost sales, may be extending credit too liberally. Conversely, the turnover ratio can be too fast, indicating that credit policies are too tight and that sales are being missed.

The accounts receivable turnovers for Coca-Cola and PepsiCo for 1996 are as follows (dollars are in millions):

Accounts.Receivable Turnover

Coca-Cola: $\dfrac{\$18,546}{(\$1,695 + \$1,641)/2} = 11.1$

PepsiCo: $\dfrac{\$31,645}{(\$2,407 + \$2,516)/2} = 12.9$

Using the accounts receivable turnover, the *average collection period* can be calculated. The average collection period can be compared to the firm's credit term period to ascertain if customers are paying their accounts within the period allowed for payment. The average collection period is computed as follows:

$$\text{Average Collection Period} = \frac{365 \text{ days}}{\text{Accounts Receivable Turnover}}$$

The average collection period for Coca-Cola and PepsiCo for 1996 are as follows:

Average Collection Period

Coca-Cola: $\dfrac{365 \text{ days}}{11.1} = 32.9$ days

PepsiCo: $\dfrac{365 \text{ days}}{12.9} = 28.3$ days

Credit Card Sales

Most retailers and service businesses accept credit cards such as VISA, MasterCard, American Express, and Discover Card. Businesses accept these cards for three reasons: (1) to accelerate cash collections, (2) to eliminate bad debts, and (3) to remain competitive. The credit card issuer investigates the customer's creditworthiness, maintains account records, and collects payments. The business sends a copy of the invoice to the issuer for payment of the bill, less a collection fee of about 5 percent. Some credit card issuers even allow a business to deposit the invoice in the business's bank account in the same way checks are deposited.

To illustrate, assume that a business sells $600 of merchandise to customers using VISA cards. The journal entries to record the sale, the collection of the amount due, and the credit card issuer's 4 percent service fee is as follows:

Accounts receivable—VISA	600	
Sales		600
Cash	576	
Service fee expense	24	
Accounts receivable—VISA		600

Current Liabilities

Liabilities are probable future sacrifices of economic benefits that arise from present obligations to transfer cash or other assets or to provide services to other entities in the future, due to past transactions or events. In an economic system such as ours, which is based so extensively on credit, almost all business concerns incur liabilities.

Creditors of an enterprise have claims against the assets of the firm. Depending upon the nature of the particular liability, a claim may be either against specific assets or against assets in general. In any case, the claims of creditors have priority over the claims of owners. Thus, in the event of the liquidation of a business, all debts must be satisfied before any payments are made to the owners.

Amounts that are shown in the balance sheet as liabilities are classified as either current or noncurrent liabilities. A proper distinction between current and noncurrent liabilities is essential, because comparison of current assets with current liabilities is an important means of evaluating the short-run liquidity or debt-paying ability of the firm. A firm has a liquidity problem if it does not have sufficient liquid assets to pay its current liabilities.

Two ratios widely used to determine a company's liquidity are the current ratio and the acid-test (quick) ratio.

$$\text{Current Ratio} = \frac{\text{Current Assets}}{\text{Current Liabilities}}$$

$$\text{Acid-test Ratio} = \frac{\text{Cash} + \text{Short-term Investments} + \text{Net Receivables}}{\text{Current Liabilities}}$$

The current ratios for Coca-Cola and PepsiCo for 1996 are as follows (dollars are in millions):

$$\text{Coca-Cola:} \quad \frac{\$5,910}{\$7,406} = 0.80$$

$$\text{PepsiCo:} \quad \frac{\$5,139}{\$5,139} = 1.00$$

The acid-test ratios for Coca-Cola and PepsiCo for 1996 are as follows (dollars are in millions):

$$\text{Coca-Cola:} \quad \frac{\$1,433 + \$225 + \$1,641}{\$7,406} = 0.45$$

$$\text{PepsiCo:} \quad \frac{\$447 + \$339 + \$2,516}{\$5,139} = 0.64$$

The current ratios and acid-test ratios of companies vary widely depending on management policies and the type of industry. Some companies may have high current ratios and acid-test ratios and be considered to have no liquidity problems, whereas other companies have low ratios and still do not have liquidity problems.

The difference between the values for the current ratio and acid-test ratio can be quite dramatic for some companies. For example, the current ratio and acid-test ratio for Wal-Mart for 1997 are as follows (dollars are in millions):

$$\text{Current Ratio} = \frac{\$17,993}{\$10,957} = 1.64$$

$$\text{Acid-test Ratio} = \frac{\$883 + \$845}{\$10,957} = 0.16$$

According to the Management Discussion and Analysis section of its 1997 annual report, the management of Wal-Mart believes that the company is in a strong liquidity position.

Current liabilities are debts or obligations that are reasonably expected to require the use of existing current assets (e.g., cash), the creation of current liabilities, or the provision of goods and services within the company's operating cycle or one year, whichever is longer. Current liabilities include obligations that arose during the operating cycle (e.g., payables incurred in the purchase of inventory), money received in advance for the provision of future services (e.g., rent collected in advance), payables accruing during the operating cycle but not due to be paid as of the date of the balance sheet (e.g., accrued wages), other liabilities that will be paid within the upcoming operating cycle (e.g., payments on serial bonds), and contingent liabilities that must be accrued (e.g., warranty obligations).

Accounts payable arise from the purchase of inventory and services in the normal course of business. If discounts are allowed by a company's supplier, the accounts payable may be recorded at either gross amounts (so as to record purchase discounts if payments are made within the specified period) or net amounts (so as to record purchase discounts lost if payments are not made within the specified period).

Accounts payable normally are classified in the balance sheet in terms of their origin. The major source of accounts payable is debts to trade creditors for goods or services that are purchased on a credit basis. An account payable usually does not involve the payment of interest; in addition, the debtor does not sign a formal written promise to pay.

Entries for accounts payable are recorded in both the control account and the subsidiary accounts in a manner similar to the procedures used to record accounts receivable. As payables are incurred, credit entries are recorded in both the control and the individual subsidiary accounts. As the balances are paid, debit entries are recorded in both the control and subsidiary accounts.

Unearned revenues arise from a company receiving payment in advance for services to be rendered in the sfuture. The liability is satisfied by providing the services. For example, a magazine publisher may receive payment in advance for a one-year subscription to the magazine. Revenue is earned and the liability is reduced as an issue of the magazine is published and mailed to the subscriber.

Some costs are incurred due to the passage of time. The liability must be recorded even though payment is not due as of the date of the balance sheet. For example, if wages are paid every Friday, but the accounting period ends on a Thursday, four days' wages must be accrued and recorded as an expense and a liability.

Some long-term liabilities have payments due on a periodic basis. Any payments due in the upcoming year or operating cycle, whichever is longer, should be reclassified as current. For example, if a company has a note payable for $9,000 on December 31, 19X1 with payments of $3,000 due on January 1, 19X2, 19X3, and 19X4, then the $3,000 due on January 1, 19X2 should be reclassified from long-term debt to short-term debt and be reported under current liabilities as the current portion of long-term debt.

Contingent liabilities involve a condition that has an outcome that may or may not occur. If the contingent liability is probable and can be reasonably estimated, it should be accrued. For example, if a company provides a warranty with its products, an estimation of the repair costs is made and the warranty expense and estimated liability are recorded. If the sale of the product is made in 19X1, then the warranty cost due to the sale should be recorded in 19X1 to match the cost with the revenue. Some contingent liabilities either are not probable or cannot be reasonably estimated (e.g., a lawsuit). These contingent liabilities should be disclosed in the footnotes to the financial statements, but not on the balance sheet (nor should an expense be recorded in the income statement).

Conceptually, current liabilities may be classified into three basic groups: (l) liabilities that are both easily identifiable and definitely determinable in amount, (2) liabilities that are identifiable but have amounts that are dependent upon operating results, and (3) liabilities that are identifiable but are not definitely determinable in amount. The third type requires an estimation of the amount of the liability. The common current liabilities that are classified into the three types are as follows:

1. Definite amounts:

    a. Accounts payable.
    b. Short-term notes payable.
    c. Dividends payable.
    d. Advances from officers, employees, or stockholders.
    e. Accrued liabilities.
    f. Compensated absences (e.g., vacation pay and sick pay).

2. Amounts dependent upon operations:

    a. Income taxes (subject to verification by the Internal Revenue Service).
    b. Payroll taxes.
    c. Bonus payments.

3. Amounts to be estimated:

    a. Property taxes.
    b. Warranty obligations.
    c. Premiums and coupons.
    d. Refundable deposits made by customers.

Current liabilities include all of those obligations that are due on demand by the company that granted the credit or the bank that loaned the money or will be due on demand within one year or the company's operating cycle, whichever is longer. Classification as current liabilities is required even though liquidation may not be expected within that period. Further, long-term obligations may be classified as current liabilities if they are or will be callable by the creditor, because either: (a) the debtor's violation of a provision of the debt agreement at the balance sheet date causes the obligation to be callable, (for example, the company's current liabilities exceed its current assets) or (b) the violation will make the debt callable if not cured within a specified grace period. These obligations are classified as current liabilities unless: (a) the creditor waives or loses the right to demand repayment for more than one year or beyond the company's operating cycle, whichever is longer, or (b) the obligation will not become callable, because the violation will probably be cured during the grace period.

Theoretically, liabilities should be accounted for at the present value of the future outlays required to satisfy the obligations. However, in practice, most current liabilities are reported at their maturity amount. This practice is considered to be justified on the basis of materiality, because the difference between the present value and maturity value is minimal due to the limited time period involved (usually less than one year).

Notes Receivable and Payable

As previously indicated, notes receivable are claims that, unlike accounts receivable, are supported by formal or written promises to pay. A typical note is shown below.

The note shown above is an interest-bearing note. Don Sutton (the maker of the note) agrees to pay Willie Davis (the payee) $1,000 (the principal amount of the note) plus interest at 18 percent on July 1, 19X1 (the maturity date). The 18 percent annual interest is the charge that Sutton pays for the use of Davis' funds. Interest, which is an expense for Sutton and income for Davis, is calculated by the following formula:

$$\text{Principal} \times \text{Rate} \times \text{Time} = \text{Interest}$$
$$\$1,000 \times .18 \times 2/12 = \$30$$

The maturity value of this note is $1,030 (the principal amount of $1,000 plus interest at $30); this is the amount that Sutton must pay Davis on July 1, 19X1, when the note becomes due and payable (matures).

The interest rate stated in a note is usually expressed in terms of an annual or yearly rate. Since the note used in the illustration is for a duration of two months, time is expressed as a fraction of a year, 2/12. In some instances, time may be stated in days. If this is the case, this textbook considers a year to have 360 days in order to simplify the computation of interest. For example, if the note in the illustration is for a period of sixty days, the calculation of interest is as follows:

$$\$1,000 \times .18 \times 60/360 = \$30$$

To illustrate the accounting for notes receivable, the entries necessary to record the transactions regarding the Sutton-Davis note will be presented in the sections that follow.

Issuance of the Note

On May 1, 19X1, when Sutton borrows the $1,000 from Davis, the following entry is made on Davis' books to record the loan:

Notes receivable	1,000	
Cash		1,000

This entry indicates that Davis has exchanged one asset (cash of $1,000) for another asset of equal value (a note receivable of $1,000).[5]

The following entry is made by Sutton:

Cash	1,000	
Notes payable		1000

This entry indicates that Sutton has incurred a liability (a note payable of $1,000) in order to obtain an asset (cash of $1,000).

Accrual of Interest

Interest is the cost of borrowing to the maker of the note or, from the payee's (lender's) viewpoint, the income that is earned. In the example, Davis' earnings during the month of May are calculated as follows:

$$\$1,000 \times .18 \times 1/12 = \$15$$

If Davis wishes to accrue the interest earned during the month of May (i.e., record it in his books), the following entry is necessary:

Interest receivable	15	
Interest revenue		15

This entry recognizes that Davis' assets have increased by $15 because of the interest earned during the month of May. This entry is necessary only if Davis prepares financial statements as of the end of May.

If Sutton wishes to record the interest expense incurred during May, the following entry is required:

Interest expense	15	
Interest payable		15

This entry recognizes that Sutton has incurred an expense of $15 for the use of the money borrowed from Davis for the month of May. Again, an entry is necessary only if financial statements are prepared as of the end of May.

Payment of the Note

On July 1, 19X1, the maturity date, the note becomes due and payable. As previously indicated, the interest for the two-month period is:

$$\$1,000 \times .18 \times 2/12 = \$30$$

---

[5] In some instances, a note may be taken in settlement of an open account receivable (dr. notes receivable, cr. accounts receivable) or at the time of sale (dr. notes receivable, cr. sales). Except for the initial entry, these circumstances do not change the accounting or recording considerations illustrated and discussed.

The maturity value, (i.e., the total amount that Sutton has to pay to Davis), is $1,000 plus $30 or $1,030. Since we are assuming that Davis previously recorded or accrued the $15 of interest earned during the month of May, the entry required on Davis' books in order to record the receipt of the $1,030 from Sutton at the maturity date of the note is as follows:

Cash	1,030	
Notes receivable		1,000
Interest receivable		15
Interest revenue		15

Analyzing this entry, the debit to cash of $1,030 records the total proceeds of the note (i.e., its maturity value). This maturity value includes both the principal amount and the total interest earned by Davis during the two-month period that he held the note. The credit to notes receivable removes the note balance from Davis' books because it has been paid at maturity. The credit of $15 to interest receivable eliminates the receivable that had been set up at the end of May when Davis accrued the interest earned for that month. The $15 credit to interest revenue is made in order to record the interest revenue on the note for the month of June.

The entry that is required on Sutton's books to record the payment by Sutton to Davis is:

Notes payable	1,000	
Interest payable	15	
Interest expense	15	
Cash		1,030

The debit to notes payable of $1,000 removes the note balance from Sutton's books because it has been paid at maturity. The debit to interest payable of $15 eliminates the payable that had been recorded at the end of May when Sutton accrued the interest expense for the month. The $15 debit to interest expense is made to record the interest expense for June. The credit to cash of $1,030 records the payment of the maturity value of the note (i.e., principal and interest) by Sutton.

Dishonored Note

If Sutton does not pay the note at maturity, the note is said to be dishonored. Davis will continue his efforts to collect the amount due him and Sutton will still be liable for his obligation. In the event that the note is not paid at maturity, Davis makes an entry to remove the note from the notes receivable account as follows:

Receivable from dishonored note	1,030	
Notes receivable		1,000
Interest receivable		15
Interest revenue		15

This entry removes the note from the notes receivable account and places it in a separate receivable classification—receivable from dishonored notes. If Sutton subsequently pays the note, Davis records the receipt by debiting cash and crediting receivable from dishonored note. If Davis is unable to collect the $1,030 from Sutton, he eventually writes-off the receivable as an uncollectible account against the allowance for bad debts account.

Notes Issued at a Discount

In some circumstances, the interest on notes is deducted in advance (i.e., at the time the note is issued). The difference between the amount due at maturity and the amount loaned is classified as unearned interest at the date of issuance on the books of the lender. As the note matures, this unearned interest is earned and is reclassified as interest income. For example, assume that on November 1, 19X1, Wynn Company borrows $1,000 from Osteen Company on a three-month note with an 18 percent rate of interest. The entry made on November 1, 19X1, by Osteen Company to record the loan of $955 [$1,000 - ($1,000 × .18 × 3/12)] is as follows:

Notes receivable	1,000	
Unearned interest		45
Cash		955

Wynn Company records the transaction with the following entry:

Cash	955	
Discount on notes payable	45	
Notes payable		1,000

Since interest accrues over time, the $45 amount shown as a discount on notes payable at the date the note is issued is not interest expense at that point in time. The actual net liability to Osteen at the date of the loan is equal to the amount of cash received, or $955. Therefore, a balance sheet prepared at the time of the loan includes discount on notes payable as a contra-liability deducted from notes payable as follows:

Notes payable	$1,000
Less: Discount on notes payable	(45)
	$ 955

At December 31, the following adjusting entry is necessary in order for Osteen to record the interest earned of $30 ($1,000 × .18 × 2/12) for the months of November and December:

Unearned interest	30	
Interest revenue		30

Wynn Company records its interest expense for the two-month period with the following adjusting entry:

Interest expense	30	
Discount on notes payable		30

At December 31, Wynn Company's liability appears in its balance sheet as follows:

Notes payable	$1,000
Less: Discount on notes payable	(15)
	$ 985

Note that the original amount of $45 in the discount on notes payable has been reduced by $30 (interest expense for the months of November and December) to $15 (which represents the amount to be charged to interest expense in January).

When the note matures and is paid, the entry to record the receipt is as follows:

Cash	1,000	
Unearned interest	15	
Notes receivable		1,000
Interest revenue		15

The total interest income earned on the note and recorded in the accounts is $45 ($30 in 19X1 and $15 in 19X2). Although a rate of 18 percent is used in determining the original discount on the note, the effective interest rate is actually 18.8 percent, because the borrower paid $45 for the use of $955 (not $1,000) for a period of three months.

Wynn Company makes the following entry to record its payment:

Notes payable	1,000	
Interest expense	15	
Cash		1,000
Discount on notes payable		15

This entry records the payment of the note at maturity by Wynn and the interest expense for the month of January.

STATEMENT PRESENTATION of RECEIVABLES

Receivables are classified first according to their form: notes receivable and accounts receivable. Those expected to be converted into cash within a year or the current operating cycle, whichever is longer, are classified as current assets while those that will be realized in subsequent periods are included in a noncurrent category. Any interest receivable from interest-bearing notes is classified according to the timing of its expected collection. The income from interest appears on the income statement, usually as an addition to income from operations, as follows:

Davis Company
Income Statement
For the Year Ended December 31, 19X1

Sales	$100,000
Cost of sales	60,000
Gross profit on sales	$ 40,000
Expenses	25,000
Income from operations	$ 15,000
Other income:	
Interest income	100
Net income	$ 15,100

If there are receivables from sources other than normal operations, such as from officers, employees, affiliated companies, etc., these would be shown as separate items rather than included as a part of regular accounts or notes receivable in the balance sheet.

According to *FASB Statement No. 105*, "Disclosure of Information about Financial Instruments with Off-Balance-Sheet Risk and Financial Instruments with Concentrations of Credit Risk," disclosures pertaining to significant concentrations of credit risk for a company's accounts receivable are required. Such concentrations of credit risk may exist if a number of the company's customers are engaged in similar activities, are located in the same geographical area, or have similar economic characteristics. Such a circumstance may cause the company's ability to pay its debts to be affected similarly by changes in economic or other conditions (e.g., government regulations).

SUMMARY

The proper recording and controlling of cash receipts and disbursements is a concern common to all firms. Certain basic control procedures must be followed to eliminate the probability that cash will be lost or misappropriated. Control procedures applicable to the receipt of cash include preparing a complete record immediately upon the receipt of cash, depositing the cash intact in the company's bank on a daily basis, and involving more than one employee in the handling and recording of cash transactions. In addition, employees involved in handling cash receipts should not also be authorized to make cash disbursements. Cash disbursement control measures include using pre-numbered checks to make payments for all items not paid for from petty cash, supporting each disbursement with an invoice or voucher, and having an employee that does not make cash disbursements reconcile the bank statement at frequent intervals.

Receivables are assets representing the claims that a business has against others. The two principal forms of receivables are accounts receivable and notes receivable. Accounts receivable generally arise from a company's normal course of trade or business and are normally not supported by formal written promises to pay. Notes receivable, on the other hand, are claims that are supported by formal written promises to pay.

Liabilities are claims against the business by its creditors. As such, they represent obligations that must be discharged at some future date. Current liabilities are those obligations that must be discharged within the operating cycle of the firm or one year, whichever is longer. The two major types of current liabilities are accounts payable that arise from transactions with trade creditors and short-term notes payable. A note payable is supported by a written promise to pay and requires the accrual and payment of interest.

Accounting for receivables requires the use of both a control account and individual subsidiary accounts. At the end of a period, the total of the subsidiary balances should equal the balance in the control account. In addition, bad debt expense must be estimated for each period to match this cost of selling on a credit basis with the appropriate revenues. Two common methods of estimating the bad debt expense are: (1) the use of a percentage based on the firm's past credit sales, and (2) the analysis of the receivables balance at the end of the period. An allowance for bad debts account is used to record and report the resulting offset to accounts receivable.

Accounting procedures for notes receivable include recording the initial issuance of the note at either face or discounted value, accruing the interest income earned on the note, and recording the collection of the principal and interest.

Receivables are classified on the balance sheet as accounts receivable or notes receivable and according to their status as current or noncurrent assets. Current receivables are those that are expected to be converted into cash within a year or the operating cycle, whichever is longer.

Key Definitions

Accounts receivable—receivables not supported by formal or written promises to pay.

Aging of accounts receivable—the process of classifying accounts according to the period of time that the accounts have been outstanding.

Allowance for bad debts—a contra account that reflects the portion of the accounts receivable that are expected to be uncollectible.

Bad debt expense—the expense that occurs from customers' failure to pay debts to the firm.

Balance per bank statement—this balance is the amount in the cash account of the business according to the bank's records.

Balance per books—this amount is the balance in the cash account according to the firm's records.

Bank reconciliation—an analysis made to identify and account for all items that cause differences between the cash balance as shown on the bank statement and the cash balance as it appears in the firm's accounting records.

Cash—consists of currency, coins, checks, money orders, and monies on deposit with banks.

Cash disbursement—a cash outlay made by the firm.

Cash over and short—an account that is credited for any cash overages and debited for any cash shortages. The net balance in this account at the end of a period is treated as miscellaneous revenue or expense.

Cash receipt—an inflow of cash into the firm.

Cash transaction—an accounting transaction that involves either a cash receipt or a cash disbursement.

Charge sales—sales in which the firm provides a customer with goods or services in exchange for the customer's promise to pay at a later date.

Contra account—an account that is offset against or deducted from another account in the financial statements.

Control account—used to record the total charge sales and the total payments received from customers.

Credit memorandum—this memorandum is an addition made by the bank to a depositor's account. The addition arises from a transaction other than a normal deposit.

Current liability—current debts must be paid within the operating cycle of the firm or one year, whichever is longer.

Debit memorandum—this memorandum is a deduction made by the bank from a depositor's account. The deduction arises from a transaction other than the normal payment of a check by the bank.

Deposit in transit—this deposit is a receipt that has been included in the cash balance per books and deposited in the bank, but not yet processed by the bank and credited to the depositor's account.

Discounted note—on discounted notes payable, the interest is deducted from the maturity value of the note at the time the note is issued.

Dishonored notes receivable—notes that are not paid at their maturity.

Interest expense—the cost to the borrower of borrowing funds (principal × rate × time).

Interest receivable—interest earned but not yet received.

Interest revenue—the revenue to the lender from the lending of funds (principal × rate × time).

Liability—an obligation that arises from a past transaction and that is to be discharged at a future date by the transfer of assets or the performance of services.

Maker—the borrower of funds on a note receivable.

Maturity date—the date a note becomes due and payable.

Maturity value—the value of a note at its maturity (i.e., principal plus interest).

Note payable—represents a written promise to pay a definite amount of money on demand or at some specified future date to the holder of the note.

Note receivable—a receivable supported by a formal or written promise to pay.

Outstanding check—this is a check that has been issued by the business but not yet presented to the bank for payment.

Over-the-counter sales—these sales are consummated by the immediate payment of cash for the goods or services purchased.

Payee—the lender of funds on a note receivable.

Petty cash fund—a fund established to make cash disbursements for small expenditures.

Petty cash voucher—this voucher is an authorization to disburse cash from the petty cash fund and is usually retained as a receipt for the expenditure.

Principal—the face amount of a note receivable.

Rate—the percentage, usually expressed as an annual rate, used to calculate interest.

Receivable—an asset representing the claim that a firm has against others.

Receivable from dishonored note—this receivable is equal to the maturity value of a note arising from the failure of the maker to pay it at maturity.

Time—the period, usually expressed in years or a fraction thereof, used to calculate interest.

True cash—the amount of cash that is actually available to the entity. One format for the bank reconciliation statement adjusts both the book and bank balances to true cash.

QUESTIONS

1. Why is control over cash transactions considered to be more important than control over the other assets of a business?

2. List a few basic principles in connection with cash control. You may wish to organize your discussion along the line of the normal cash flow.

3. What are the principal advantages of maintaining a separation of duties involving cash transactions?

4. In order to establish control over the cash receipts from over the counter sales, a small firm installs a cash register with each sales clerk responsible for ringing up his or her own sales. Discuss.

5. List some procedures other than separation of duties which may be employed in order to establish effective control over cash disbursements.

6. What is the purpose of a bank reconciliation statement?

7. What are the necessary adjustments in the bank reconciliation statement to the balance per the bank statement? To the balance per the books?

8. The petty cash account has a debit balance of $300. At the end of the accounting period there is $35 in the petty cash fund along with petty cash vouchers totaling $265. Should the fund be replenished as of the last day of the period? Discuss.

9. What are some of the steps necessary to achieve effective control over cash disbursements?

10. Compare and contrast accounts receivable and notes receivable.

11. Distinguish between current and long-term liabilities.

12. Why is control over receivables important? How can control be achieved?

13. Explain how the control account, accounts receivable, is related to the individual subsidiary ledger accounts. What could make the two be out of balance?

14. Theoretically, when should a firm cease to grant credit to its customers?

15. Another method for handling bad debt expense—called the direct write-off method—is to wait until the account is known to be uncollectible. The journal entry then is a debit to bad debt expense and a credit to accounts receivable. Compare and contrast this with the allowance method. Which method is theoretically correct? Why?

16. What accounting principle does the allowance method rest upon?

17. What are the two methods for estimating bad debts?

18. Could an allowance method be used with notes receivable? Would it be feasible?

19. What is the entry to increase Allowance for Bad Debts? To decrease it?

20. Suppose an account is written off as uncollectible, but later the customer remits payment. What would the entry be?

21. Calculate the interest on a $10,000, 6-month note, with interest at 6 percent.

22. What adjusting entries may be required with regard to notes receivable at the end of the period?

23. Smith Co. borrowed $5,000 from the bank and signed a 60-day, 6 percent note dated June 1. (1) What is the face amount of the note? (2) What is the amount of interest on the note? (3) What is the maturity value of the note?

24. What is the nature of the notes receivable discounted account?

25. Why is an entry on the books of the payee necessary whether or not a discounted note is paid by the maker at maturity?

26. Explain how the proceeds from the discounting of a note receivable are calculated.

EXERCISES

27. State whether the following bank reconciliation items would need an adjusting or correcting entry on the depositor's books:

    a. Checks totaling $1,850 were issued by the depositor but not paid by the bank.
    b. A $1,000 note was collected for the depositor by the bank and was deposited in his account. Notice was sent to the depositor with the bank statement.

c. The last day's receipts ($1,750) for the month were not recorded as a deposit by the bank until the following month.

d. The depositor issued a check for $180 but entered it in his records as $810.

e. The bank paid a check for $150 but entered it as $510 on their records.

f. The bank charged a bad check that it received in a deposit back against the depositor's account. Notice to the depositor was made by the bank with the bank statement.

g. The bank charged $21 for service charges and notified the depositor with the bank statement.

h. The bank had erroneously charged a check, drawn by another depositor with a similar name, to the depositor's account.

28. Prepare the journal entries that are necessary to adjust the cash account on the depositor's books, based on the information included in Exercise 27 above.

29. The following information is taken from the books and records of the Terp Company.

Balance per the cash account (before adjustment)	$2,860
Outstanding checks	820
Deposit in transit	208
Bank service charges	18
Cash on hand-unrecorded on the books and	
not yet deposited in the bank	180
Balance per the bank statement unavailable	unavailable

Required:

Prepare a bank reconciliation showing the "true" cash balance.

30. Prepare, in general journal form, the entries that Terp Company should make to adjust its cash balance as a result of the bank reconciliation in Exercise 29 above.

31. Test the accuracy of Willard Company's cash receipts records for August given the following information:

Total cash receipts as shown in the firm's records were $14,910.
Payment of $1,110 was received on August 31 but the deposit was not yet recorded by the bank.
Total deposits included in the August bank statement were $14,700.
Deposit in transit at end of July was $900.

32. The Gibbons Company reconciles its one bank account on a monthly basis. The company follows the procedure of reconciling the balance as reported on the bank statement and the balance per books to a corrected balance. The corrected balance appears on the balance sheet.

    The facts stated in items 1 through 10 below are involved in a reconciliation for the month of December. Decide which of the five answer choices best indicates how each fact should be handled in the December 31 bank reconciliation.

Answer choices for items 1 through 9:

(1) An addition to the balance per books.
(2) A deduction from the balance per books.
(3) An addition to the balance per bank.
(4) A deduction from the balance per bank.
(5) Should not appear in the reconciliation.

    1. A deposit of $ 100 made on December 31 did not appear in the December bank statement . . . . ( )

    2. A deposit of $ 130 made on November 30 was recorded by the bank on December 1 . . . . ( )

3. Three checks totalling $180 drawn in December did not clear the bank .... ( )

4. A check from customer Kay for $75 was returned by the bank marked N.S.F .... ( )

5. The bank statement was accompanied by a credit memo dated December 30 for the proceeds of a note ($198) which Gibbons Company had left with the bank for collection .... ( )

6. Gibbons Company discovered that a December check recorded in the check register as $150 was actually drawn for $105. This check was cleared by the bank in December .... ( )

7. Two checks totalling $120 drawn in November had cleared the bank in December .... ( )

8. Accompanying the December bank statement was a cancelled check for $60 of Gibson Company .... ( )

9. The bookkeeper of Gibbons Company had recorded a $90 check received from customer Fay on December 29 as $190 .... ( )

10. Which of the facts disclosed in items 1 through 9 above require adjusting entries on the books of the Gibbons Company? .... ( )

(1) 1, 3, 8   *(2)* 6, 8, 9

(3) 1, 2, 3, 7   *(4)* 4, 5, 6, 9

(5) Some other group

33. Show in general journal form all entries that should be made to reflect the operation of the Eljon Corporation's petty cash fund.

May 10   The company established a petty cash fund of $225.
12   Paid miscellaneous office expenses amounting to $52.
14   Paid $15 to messengers for cab fares.
19   Paid telephone bill of $63.
25   Paid $21 in postage.
30   The petty cash fund was reimbursed for the first time.
31   Eljon Corporation increased its petty cash fund to $300.

34. By reviewing their past credit experience, Brown Company estimated that its losses from uncollectible accounts would be three percent of credit sales for 19X1. Sales for 19X1 amounted to $360,000, of which $100,000 were in cash. Make the entry recording bad debt expense for the year in the books of the Brown Company.

35. Based on an aging of receivables, Blue Company estimated doubtful accounts to be a total of $5,000. Give the adjusting entry for bad debts under each of the following independent situations:

a. The Allowance for Bad Debts has a zero balance.
b. The Allowance for Bad Debts has a debit balance of $400.
c. The Allowance for Bad Debts has a credit balance of $700.

36. On February 1, 19X1, Alex Grammas borrowed $700 from Vic Wertz and signed a note in evidence of the loan. Grammas agreed to pay Wertz $700 plus 10 percent interest on August 31, 19X1. Wertz's accounting period ends June 30. Make all entries related to the note on the books of Wertz (assume Grammas does not default on payment).

37. Determine the maturity value of the following notes receivable held by Staubach Company.

a. $1,000 principal, 4 percent interest, matures in 6 months.
b. $ 800 principal, 7 percent interest, matures in 60 days.
c. $ 600 principal, 3 percent interest, matures in 100 days.
d. $ 500 principal, 5 percent interest, matures in 1 month.
e. $ 900 principal, 6 percent interest, matures in 3 months.
f. $ 200 principal, 7 percent interest, matures in 30 days.
g. $ 400 principal, 4 percent interest, matures in 10 days.

38. Prepare the necessary journal entries in Henderson's books for the following events.

    a. On March 1, Sam Donaldson agreed to pay David Henderson $2,000 plus 7 percent interest on August 1.
    b. Henderson accrued interest earned on June 30 for the months of March, April, May, and June.
    c. Donaldson did not pay the note at maturity.

39. Prepare the necessary journal entries in Martin's books for the following events.

    a. Mike Mason purchased merchandise on credit from Martin's Retail Outlet for $150.
    b. Mason's account proves to be uncollectible. (Assume an allowance for bad debts account already exists.)
    c. Mason's account was subsequently collected.

40. Determine the interest on each of the following notes:

	Face Amount	Interest Rate	Days to Maturity
a.	$1,000	6%	60
b.	$5,000	8%	90
c.	$4,000	4%	180
d.	$2,500	5%	36

41. On December 1, King, Inc. issued a 90-day, 6 percent note for $3,000 to Miller Co. to replace an account payable. Give the journal entries necessary to record the following on the books of King, Inc.

    a. Issuance of the note by King, Inc.
    b. Adjusting entry on December 31.
    c. Payment of the note at maturity.

Problems

42. Red, Inc.'s bank statement for the month ending June 30 shows a balance of $231. The cash account as of the close of business on June 30 indicates a credit balance or overdraft of $123. In reconciling the balances, the auditor discovers the following:

    Receipts on June 30 of $1,860 were not deposited until July 1.
    Checks outstanding on June 30 were $2,215.
    The bank has charged the depositor $10 for service charges.
    A check payable to S. S. Dohr for $56 was entered in Red's cash payments journal in error as $65.

Required:

Prepare a bank reconciliation.

43. The following refers to Ginger's Floral Shop:

    a. Prepare a bank reconciliation showing the "true" cash balance for July 31, given the following information:
        1. Balance per bank statement at July 31, $4,610.
        2. Balance per books at July 31, $3,900.
        3. Deposits in transit not recorded by banks, $445.
        4. Bank error, check drawn by the Ginger Bread Shop debited to account of Ginger's Floral Shop, $20.
        5. Note collected by bank, $1,025.
        6. Debit memorandum for bank charges, $10.
        7. N.S.F. check returned by bank, $35.
        8. Accountants credited cash account for $175 rather than the correct figure of $100 in recording check #55.
        9. Outstanding checks of $120 on July 31.
    b. Prepare the adjusting or correcting entries required.

44. The Medich Company's petty cash fund for the first month of operations was as follows:

a. $1,000 was placed in the fund on April 1.

b. Petty cash record for April:

	April 1-15	April 16-30
Postage	$ 50	$ 60
Supplies	400	600
Miscellaneous expenses	90	70
Total	$540	$730

c. On April 16 the fund was replenished.

d. On April 30 the fund was replenished and decreased by $100.

Required:

Prepare all entries.

45. Prepare a bank reconciliation for the May Company for September 30, 19X1.

a. Book cash balance on September 30 was $230.80.

b. On August 31 outstanding checks totaled $1,394.80. By September 30, only two of these checks had not cleared. Because of the amount of time it had been outstanding, one of the checks for $100 had a stop payment put on it. The other outstanding check was for $57.10.

c. Checks drawn and still outstanding in September amount to $1,733.48 (assume this figure is correct).

d. A check was written for $472, but was recorded as $652. It is among the outstanding checks at the end of September.

e. The September service charge of $6.80 has not been recorded by the company.

f. Receipts of $236.30 were deposited by mail on September 30.

g. The bank statement showed the collection of a note by the bank in the amount of $406.

h. Included in the checks accompanying the September bank statement was a check drawn by Moy Company but charged to May Company for $ 114.32.

46. The Patrick Company had poor internal control over its cash transactions. Information about its cash position at November 30, 19X1 was as follows:

The cash books showed a balance of $18,901.62, which included undeposited receipts. A credit of $100 on the bank's records did not appear on the books of the company. The balance per bank statement was $15,550. Outstanding checks were: No. 62 for $116.25, No. 183 for $150, No. 284 for $253.25, No. 8621 for $190.71, No. 8623 for $206.80, and No. 8632 for $145.28.

The cashier embezzled all undeposited receipts in excess of $3,794.41 and prepared the following reconciliation:

Balance, per books, November 30, 19X1		$18,901.62
Add: Outstanding checks:		
8621	$190.71	
8623	206.80	
8632	145.28	442.79
		$19,344.41
Less: Undeposited receipts		3,794.41
Balance per bank, November 30, 19X1		$15,550.00
Deduct: Unrecorded credit		100.00
True cash, November 30, 19X1		$15,450.00

Required:

1. Prepare a supporting schedule showing how much the cashier embezzled.
2. How did he attempt to conceal his theft?
3. Taking only the information given, name two specific features of internal control which were apparently missing.

(AICPA adapted)

47. When aging their accounts receivable, the Wingfoot Company drew up the following schedule:

Accounts Receivable Balance	Number of Days Outstanding			
	0-30	*31-60*	*61-90*	*91 and older*
$5,250	$3,450	$900	$650	$250
	Estimated % Uncollectible			
	1%	5%	15%	50%

Required:

Prepare a table calculating the estimated bad debt expense for the period and make the appropriate journal entry on the books of the Wingfoot Company, assuming that there is a credit balance of $100 in the Allowance for Bad Debts before adjustment.

48. During 19X1, Squeeze, Inc. had $800,000 of sales on credit. Also, during 19X1 the company wrote off $14,000 of accounts receivable as definitely uncollectible and collected $700 from individuals whose accounts had been written off during previous years. The company estimates its bad debts each year to be 2% of credit sales. On January 1, 19X1, the accounts receivable balance was $60,000. Collections on account for 19X1 totaled $775,000 and customers returned goods for credit in the amount of $20,000. The company offers no cash discounts. On December 31, 19X1, after all adjustments and accruals, accounts receivable net of the allowance for uncollectible accounts amounted to $45,400.

Required:

1. Prepare journal entries for all transactions during 19X1 involving accounts receivable and the related allowance account.
2. The balance in the allowance account at:

   a. January 1, 19X1.
   b. December 31, 19X1 (after all adjustments).

49. Charlie Tuna, owner of Tuna's Fish Wholesalers, has instructed his accountant, Jack D. Ripper, to make sure the Allowance for Bad Debts account is at least 10 percent of total accounts receivable at the end of each calendar year. The January 1, 19X1, balance in Allowance for Bad Debts is $10,000. During 19X1, the following transactions took place:

Jan. 13   Notice was received that I. M. Acrook, who owed the company $4,000, was in bankruptcy and no payment could be expected.

May 13   Wheel & Deal, Inc. paid $14,000 applicable to its account which totaled $20,000. Its treasurer was last seen boarding a steamer for South America (with all the company's funds), so no other payments would be forthcoming.

July 10   Received a check for $2,000 from A. Lincoln whose account had been written off as uncollectible in 19X0.

Oct. 13   H. E. Asucker, a customer, notified Charlie that his partner had absconded with all the company funds. Asucker stated that their business had folded and he was unable to pay Charlie the $8,000 he owed him.

Dec. 31   The balance of accounts receivable, as of the close of today's business, was $200,000.

Required:

Prepare general journal entries to record the above transactions.

50. Determine whether the following items included in a bank reconciliation will require adjusting or correcting entries on the *depositor's* books and record the necessary adjusting entries in general journal format.

   a. The depositor recorded $517 of receipts on March 31, 19x3 which were deposited in the night depository of the bank.
   b. The bank collected a $785 note for the depositor which was listed on the bank statement.
   c. Two checks for a total of $75 were returned to the bank because of insufficient funds and were noted on the bank statement.
   d. Five checks totaling $240 written during the month of March were not included with the March bank statement.
   e. Service charges for the month of March of $10 were noted on the bank statement.
   f. A $48 check written to Jim's Repair Shop, a creditor, was recorded in the cash disbursements journal as $84.
   g. In error the bank charged a check in the amount of $150 from another customer with a similar name to the depositor's account and included the check in the depositor's statement.
   h. A check written for $340 and recorded in that amount in the cash disbursements journal was deducted as $430 from the depositor's account.
   i. A check from a customer received and deposited for $128 was recorded in the cash receipts journal as $182.

51. The following data applies to Beta Enterprises for June, 19x6.

   1. Balance per the books at June 30; $4,721.
   2. Balance per the bank at June 30; $4,964.
   3. Deposits in transit not recorded by the bank; $720.
   4. Bank error, check written by Better Enterprises was drawn on Beta Enterprises; $125.
   5. The following checks written and recorded by Beta were not included in the bank statement.

1072	$ 27
1091	1,020
1099	60

   6. Note collected by the bank; $400.
   7. Service charge for collection of note; $5.
   8. Accountant recorded a check written for S850 as S580 in the cash disbursements journal to pay a creditor.
   9. Bank service charge in addition to the collection fee; $25.
   10. NSF checks returned by the bank; $ 119.

Required:

   a. Prepare a bank reconciliation showing the "true cash" balance for Beta Enterprises for June, 19x6.
   b. Prepare the necessary adjusting entries in general journal format.

52. The following data pertain to the petty cash fund of Scharff Gallaries.

   1. The petty cash fund was created on an imprest basis at $250 on May 1.
   2. On June 15, a physical count revealed: $49.30 in currency and coins; vouchers authorizing meal allowance totaling $48.75; vouchers authorizing purchase of postage stamps, $36; vouchers for payment of delivery charges, $98.15; and vouchers for payment of taxi fares, $15.80.

Required:

   a. Record the journal entry necessary to create the fund.
   b. Record the journal entry necessary to replenish the fund on June 15. Use the cash short and over account for any overage or shortage.

53. On January 1, 19x1 Delta Company's allowance for doubtful accounts contained a $300 credit balance. During the year Delta sold $50,000 in merchandise, $20,000 of which were cash sales; wrote off uncollectible accounts of $390 and collected a previously written-off account of $60. On December 31, 19x1 Delta had a $25,000 debit balance in accounts receivable.

Required:

   a. Prepare the adjusting entry for bad debt expense assuming that Delta uses 3 percent of accounts receivable to estimate bad debts.
   b. Prepare the adjusting entry for bad debt expense assuming that Delta uses 2 percent of credit sales to estimate bad debts.

54. According to the balance sheet of Standards Corporation dated December 31, 19x8 the company had accounts receivable and allowance for doubtful accounts which amounted to $200,000 and $10,000 respectively. During 19x9, Standards generated revenues on credit sales of $1,100,000 and wroteoff accounts receivable in the amount of $12,000. The balance in the receivables account as of December 31, 19x9 amounted to $230,000. A review of the Corporation's accounting records indicated that bad debts expense normally approaches I percent of credit sales or 5 percent of the ending receivables balance.

Required:

   a. Provide the general journal entry that would have been necessary to record the $12,000 write-off of receivables during 19x9.
   b. Compute the amount of bad debts expense for 19x9 assuming that Standards Corporation utilizes the percent of sales method.
   c. Compute the amount of bad debts expense for 19x9 assuming that Standards Corporation utilized the percent of receivables method.

55. **Southern Company.** Southern Company's sales have remained relatively stable over the last four years. Sales are made on cash basis and on store credit to selected customers. The terms of credit sales are n/30. Southern estimates its bad debt expense as 3/4 percent of credit sales. This percentage is the average rate reported in Southern's industry. Credit sales for the past five years, as well as year-end balances for allowance for doubtful accounts and for accounts receivable, are given below:

Year	Credit Sales	Allowance for Doubtful Accounts	Accounts Receivable
19x2	$595,000	$ 1,580	$28,000
19x3	598,000	3,765	22,700
19x4	621,000	6,573	18,850
19x5	589,000	9,431	17,940
19x6	613,000	12,559	18,170

Shelly Jacobus, the president of Southern, is concerned about the growing balance in the Allowance for Doubtful Accounts. She feels that most of her credit customers pay their bills and that the net account receivables, reported on the company's financial statements, may be undervalued. Ms. Jacobus has asked you to analyze the company's method of accounting for uncollectible receivables and to recommend possible changes.

Required:

   1. Determine the changes in the allowance for doubtful accounts for 19x3 through 19x6. That is, determine the addition to the allowance for doubtful accounts (in accruing bad debt expense) and the accounts written *Off.*
   2. Advise Ms. Jacobus as to the reasonableness of the 3/4 percent of credit sales estimate of bad debt expense.

3. Prepare an analysis proposing estimation of bad debt expense: (a) as a percentage of credit, sales, and (b) with the percentage of accounts receivable method. The analysis should show the effect on the allowance for doubtful accounts for the four years being analyzed.

4. Which method developed in (3) above would you recommend to Ms. Jacobus? State your reasons for your choice.

56. For each of the transactions listed, indicate the effect(s), if any, on the company's year-end: (1) Balance Sheet, (2) Income Statement, and (3) Statement of Cash Flows. Your answers should be as complete and specific as possible.

   a. Sold goods to customers on account.
   b. Estimated and recorded bad debt expense for the period.
   c. Wrote off a specific account as uncollectible.
   d. Received payment from a customer whose account had previously been written off as uncollectible.

57. For each of the transactions listed, indicate the effect(s), if any, on the company's year-end: (1) Balance Sheet, (2) Income Statement, and (3) Statement of Cash Flows. Your answers should be as complete and specific as possible.

   a. Borrowed cash, issuing an interest-bearing note payable.
   b. Recognized interest owed but unpaid at the end of the accounting period.
   c. Paid the note in full, principal and interest.

58. For each of the transactions listed, indicate the effect(s), if any, on the company's year-end: (1) Balance Sheet, (2) Income Statement, and (3) Statement of Cash Flows. Your answers should be as complete and specific as possible.

   a. Established a petty cash fund.
   b. Paid an expense from the fund.
   c. Reimbursed the fund.

Refer to the Annual Report in Chapter 1 of the text.

59. Did the cash balance increase or decrease in the most recent year?

60. Where does the company receive most of its cash from?

61. What are the major cash outflows of the company?

62. What were the total collections from receivables during the most recent year, assuming that all sales were made on account?

63. Comparing the two most recent years presented, what was the increase in current liabilities?

64. By how much did the allowance for bad debts change?

65. What is included in short-term borrowings in the current year?

FRAUD CASE: Employee Swapping Checks

Most employee fraud occurs in the cash account, accounts receivable, or inventory. Fraud schemes come in a wide variety, but some are more common than others. One common and simple scheme involves an employee swapping checks for cash.

This fraud scheme is possible only when controls over the receipt and deposit of cash are lax. If an employee is responsible for his or her own working cash fund, this fraud scheme will work. Consider the following actual fraud involving check swapping for cash:

A clerk in a county treasurer's office allegedly "borrowed" $7,800 from county cash fund deposits by placing twenty personal checks in the deposits which represented various county cash transactions at decentralized locations. She placed her own personal checks in each deposit as a method of keeping track of the amount of money which had been "borrowed. " Of course, she had to delay the processing of her personal checks because the funds in her checking account were insufficient to cover the twenty checks. Most of the county cash deposits, covered by the clerk's personal checks, were delayed for up to six months.

DISCUSSION QUESTIONS:

1. What procedures would you suggest to detect the clerk's "swapping checks for cash" scheme?

2. What suggestions would you make to the county officials to prevent such occurrences in the future?

FRAUD CASE: Lapping

A fraud that is sometimes encountered in accounts receivable is lapping. Lapping involves misappropriating the receipts from customers and covering the shortages in customers' accounts with receipts from subsequent customer payments. Thus, the shortage is not eliminated but transferred to other accounts. For example, an employee may misappropriate $100 of the receipt from Customer A. Then, when Customer B pays, $100 of Customer B's payment is credited to Customer A's account. When Customer C pays, $100 of Customer C's payment is credited to Customer B's account, etc.

Lapping schemes are almost never just for a single amount, the amount lapped continues to grow and more and more account payments are needed to lap the shorted accounts.

Although lapping is difficult to accomplish unless there is collusion between the bookkeeper and a person that has access to cash (or the same person performs both functions), management should recognize that lapping may occur. However, if the accounts receivable for all customers are examined as of the same date, there is a good chance that lapping will be discovered if it exists. If lapping is suspected, the examination should be on a surprise basis to prevent substitution of cash from other sources (lapped) for the missing amounts.

DISCUSSION QUESTIONS:

Assume there are three major accounts receivable in question at AB Best Company:

Customer A's account shows a Dr. of $50,000 and a Cr. of $50,000 representing payment.

Customer B's account shows a Dr. of $ 75,000 and a Cr. of $30,000, representing a payment on account.

Customer C's account shown a Dr. of $30,000 and no payment to date.

Management and auditor investigations indicate that Customer A's $50,000 account payment was misappropriated; $75,000 was misappropriated from Customer's B's account payment; and $30,000 was misappropriated from Customer C's account payment.

1. How much was embezzled from these three customers? What type fraud was perpetrated?

2. What happened to the $155,000 of misappropriated funds?

FRAUD CASE: Kiting

Kiting involves drawing a check on one bank and depositing this check in another bank to cover a cash shortage in the second bank. However, neither the check written on the first bank account nor the cash deposit to the second bank account is recorded in the accounting records. Consequently, until the check clears the paying bank, it appears that the cash balance in the bank that was short has been increased without any change in the company's accounting records. The cash is double-counted by both banks. Banks have a daily report that reveals kiting, but banks do not generally report the matter until the customer accounts approach zero.

To illustrate kiting, assume that $50,000 has been misappropriated from Bank S Account, and thus a reconciliation of this account will show a $50,000 difference between the adjusted bank balance and the adjusted book balance. An embezzler might try to cover this shortage by writing a $50,000 check on another one of the client's bank accounts, depositing the amount in Bank S, and not recording the cash receipt or cash payment in the accounting records. Until the check clears the paying bank, the balance in Bank S will increase by $50,000 with no apparent change in cash balances per books or in the balance for the Paying bank. Kiting can cover up the fraud for a short period of time.

One way to detect kiting is to examine the bank statements of all the company's banks shortly after the date of financial statements or the period of a fraud examination, to determine if there are any interbank check transfers not reflected in the company's accounting records.

DISCUSSION QUESTION:

Assume the following information regarding Bogus Company:

The company has three large checking accounts at three local banks to provide funds for working capital. Edward Bogus, the founder of the company and major stockholder, signs all company checks in excess of $1,000.

Edward Bogus is heavily in debt. Furthermore, the stock of Bogus Company has declined considerably in value. Edward and the management team were able to negotiate a sizable bank loan (payable on demand) to shore-up the company.

Mr. Adams, CPA, controller of the company, has strong suspicions that someone, very possibly Edward, is embezzling from the company. Adams receives a phone call from one of the company's banks indicating that it has just processed a check, payable to one of the other company's banks, for a very sizable amount.

What action would you take to determine if embezzlement is in fact occurring at the Bogus Company?

Appendix A
Discounting Notes Receivable

Introduction

Notes receivable are sometimes sold by the payee to a third party in order to obtain funds prior to the maturity date of a note. The process of selling a note in this manner is referred to as discounting a note. The payee endorses the note, delivers it to the purchaser (usually a bank) and receives his or her funds. The payee discounting the note is usually contingently liable on the note (i.e., he or she must pay the note at the maturity if the maker fails to do so).

The calculation of the discount charged by the purchaser is somewhat similar to the calculation of interest:

$$\frac{\text{Maturity}}{\text{Value}} \times \frac{\text{Discount}}{\text{Period}} \times \frac{\text{Discount}}{\text{Rate}} = \text{Discount}$$

As previously indicated, the maturity value is the total amount, both principal and interest, due at the maturity of a note. The discount period is the period of time from the date a note is discounted to the maturity date of the note. The discount rate is the rate charged by the purchaser to discount a note. The amount received by the payee, referred to as the proceeds of the note, is calculated as follows:

$$\text{Maturity Value} - \text{Discount} = \text{Proceeds}$$

To illustrate the procedures involved in discounting a note, assume that *before* recording the interest earned for the month of May, Davis sells (or discounts) the Sutton note on May 31 and is charged a discount rate of 20 percent. The calculation of the amount of the discount and the net proceeds to Davis from the note is as follows:

$1,000 × .18 × 2/12	= $30	(interest)
$1,000 + $30	= $1,030	(maturity value)
$1,030 × .20 × 1/12	= $17.17	(discount)
$1,030 − $17.17	= $1,012.83	(proceeds)

The discounting of the note is recorded in the accounts by Davis as follows:

Cash	1,012.83	
Interest expense	2.17	
Interest revenue		15.00
Notes receivable discounted		1,000.00

The debit of $1,012.83 to cash records the proceeds received from the sale of the note. The charge to interest expense of $2.17 is calculated as follows:

Principal		$1,000.00
Interest earning during May		15.00
Book value of the note at the date of sale		$1,015.00
Principal	$1,000.00	
Total interest for the note to maturity	30.00	
Maturity value of the note	$1,030.00	
Discount	17.17	
Net proceeds		1,012.83
Interest expense		$ 2.17

As the above calculation indicates, interest expense represents the difference between the cash proceeds and the total of: (1) the face or principal amount of the note, and (2) the interest earned up to the date the note was discounted.[6] The credit to interest revenue records the interest that has been earned for the time Davis has held the note (the month of May). It should be noted that the credit in the entry is to notes receivable *discounted*, rather than to notes receivable. The credit to notes receivable discounted indicates that Davis is contingently liable for the note (i.e., in the event that Sutton fails to pay the note at maturity, Davis must pay it). On Davis' balance sheet the notes receivable appear as follows:

Cash		$10,000
Notes receivable	$1,000	
Less: Notes receivable discounted	1,000	0
Other assets		50,000
Total assets		$60,000

Offsetting the notes receivable discounted account against the notes receivable account discloses the contingent liability of Davis with regard to the Sutton note. An alternative to this presentation is to disclose the contingent liability by means of a footnote to the balance sheet. Such a footnote might be worded as follows: "Davis is contingently liable for notes receivable discounted in the amount of $1,000."

If Sutton pays the note at its maturity, Davis would be notified of this payment and the following entry would be made on Davis' books:

Notes receivable discounted	1,000	
Notes receivable		1,000

By removing both the notes receivable discounted and the notes receivable balances from the accounts, the effect of this entry is to recognize the fact that the contingent liability for the note no longer exists.

If Sutton fails to pay the note at maturity, Davis' *contingent* liability becomes a *real* liability that he must now pay. Davis would recognize this fact by the same entry as that made above:

Notes receivable discounted	1,000	
Notes receivable		1,000

It should be noted that both the contingent liability and the notes receivable balance are removed from the books at the maturity date of the note whether or not it is paid by the maker. If it is paid, that is all that is required—no further action on the part of Davis is necessary. If it is not paid, Davis must pay the full amount due (principal plus interest, or full maturity value) to the holder of the note. This payment would be recorded as follows:

Receivable from dishonored note	1,030	
Cash		1,030

Davis would then attempt to recover the $1,030 from Sutton.

---

[6] Had the discount rate been 10 percent, the entry would have been as follows:

Cash	1,021.42	
Notes receivable discounted		1,000.00
Interest revenue		21.42

In this instance, the credit of $21.42 to interest revenue represents the excess of the proceeds over the principal amount of the note including the interest of $15.00 earned in May.

Appendix B
Payroll Accounting

Introduction

An employer incurs certain liabilities to the federal and state governments for taxes related to its payroll—both for the taxes levied on the business itself and for taxes withheld from the earnings of its employees. The employer may also deduct from employees' salaries and wages amounts withheld for such items as union dues, insurance premiums, pension plans, and investment plans.

An employer incurs a number of liabilities relating to state and federal payroll taxes. These include the following taxes:

1. Federal old-age, survivors, disability, and hospital insurance (Social Security).
2. Federal unemployment insurance.
3. State unemployment insurance.
4. Income taxes withheld.

Social Security Taxes. The Federal Insurance Contributions Act (FICA) imposes equal taxes on both employers and employees. This act provides for old age, disability, hospitalization, and survivors' benefits for qualified employees and members of their families. The tax rate is applied to the employee's gross wages up to a designated maximum. Both the rate and the maximum earnings to which the tax is applied have been increased frequently over the years. The rate for 1998 for Social Security is 6.2 percent of the initial $68,400 of the salary or wage paid to each employee. The rate for 1998 for Medicare is 1.45 percent of all salaries and wages paid to the employees. The employee's share of this tax is withheld from the wage payment, and employers periodically remit the amounts withheld together with the amounts matched by the employer.

Federal Unemployment Tax. The Federal Unemployment Tax Act (FUTA) provides for a system of unemployment insurance with joint participation of the federal and state governments. Employers are also required to pay state and federal unemployment taxes for their employees. No tax is levied on the employee. Under current provisions, the federal rate is currently 6.2 percent of the initial $7,000 in salary or wage paid to each employee during the year. However, the employer is allowed a 5.4 percent credit against the federal unemployment tax for paying on time and for state unemployment tax payments, bringing the rate down to 0.8 percent.

State Unemployment Tax. The provisions of the unemployment programs of the various states differ in certain respects. All states levy a payroll tax on employers and a few states levy a tax on employees as well. The basic rate in most states is 2.7 percent of the first $9,000 in salary or wage paid to each employee.

Income Tax Withholding. Employers of one or more persons are required to withhold income taxes from their employees and remit these withholdings to the federal government. A number of states and cities also levy income taxes that are required to be withheld by the employer from the earnings of the employees. The amounts to be withheld by the employer may be computed by formulas provided by law or from tax withholding tables made available by the government. The federal income tax withheld and the FICA taxes (both employer's and employee's shares) are remitted to the federal government at regular intervals.

Recording the Payroll. To illustrate the accounting for wages and salaries and the related taxes, assume that the gross salaries of a small business total $10,000 for the month of January. Assume that the FICA rate is 6.2 percent for the employer and employee, and that the state unemployment tax is 2.7 percent of gross salaries. The rate for Medicare is 1.45 percent. The federal unemployment tax (net of the credit for state unemployment taxes) is .8 percent, and federal income taxes withheld for the month total $710. The employer's taxes are computed as follows:

FICA (.062 x $10,000)	$ 620
Medicare (.0145 x $10,000)	145
State unemployment (.027 x $10,000)	270
FUTA (.008 x $10,000)	80
Total employer's taxes	$ 1,115

The cash paid to employees is:

Salaries earned		$10,000
Withholding:		
FICA	$ 620	
Medicare	145	
Income taxes	710	1,475
Net amount paid to employees		$ 8,525

The journal entries to record the payroll and the employer's payroll taxes are as follows:

Salaries expense	10,000	
FICA taxes payable		620
Medicare payable		145
Income taxes withheld		710
Cash		8,525
Payroll tax expense	$ 1,115	
FICA taxes payable		$ 620
Medicare payable		145
State unemployment taxes payable		270
Federal unemployment taxes payable		80

The liabilities recorded in the above entries are eliminated when the employer remits the taxes to the appropriate governmental units.

Outline

LEARNING Objectives

Chapter 11 presents information relating to the determination and presentation of bonds payable and investments in corporate securities and the use of consolidated financial statements. Studying this chapter should enable you to:

1. Describe the various classes of bonds.

2. Explain the concepts of bond discount and bond premium and how they are handled for accounting purposes.

3. Record the early retirement of bonds, including either a gain or loss if applicable.

4. Identify the elements of cost of stocks and bonds purchased as investments.

5. Discuss the methods of accounting for long-term and temporary investments subsequent to acquisition.

6. Describe the criterion used to determine when to prepare consolidated financial statements.

7. Illustrate the procedures and necessary worksheet adjustments for preparing consolidated financial statements.

8. Differentiate between the purchase and pooling of interests methods in accounting for business combinations.

CHAPTER 11

LONG-TERM LIABILITIES AND INVESTMENTS

INTRODUCTION

*L*ong-term debt includes all obligations that exist because of a past transaction or event and that are not *expected to be repaid within a year of the balance sheet date or during the current operating cycle of the business, whichever is longer.* These long-term obligations may vary considerably with regard to the nature of the debt and the conditions and covenants attached to it. Examples of long-term debt include bonds payable, mortgage notes, long-term notes, lease obligations, pension obligations, and deferred income tax liabilities. This chapter focuses on those forms of long-term debt that are issued under formal agreements or contracts, such as bonds.

When a corporation desires to raise additional capital for long-term purposes, it has several alternatives. It may borrow funds by issuing bonds, or it may obtain funds by issuing additional shares of common stock to shareholders. Each source of funds has its particular advantages and disadvantages to the issuing corporation. A bondholder is a creditor of a corporation while a stockholder is an owner. As creditors, bondholders normally do not participate in the management of the firm. Therefore, by issuing bonds, a corporation does not spread or dilute control of management over a larger number of owners. Interest expense is deductible for federal income tax purposes while dividends are not a tax deduction. Earnings per share may be higher on issuing bonds rather than shares of common stock because the number of shares of common stock, the denominator in the calculation of earnings per share, is lower.

The interest expense on a bond is a fixed obligation to the borrower. If the interest is not paid on the dates specified by the contract, legal action may be brought by the bondholders. Dividends on stock, on the other hand, are declared at the discretion of the board of directors of the issuing corporation.

Bond Obligations

Bonds are issued as a means of borrowing money for long-term purposes. The desired funds are obtained by issuing a number of bonds with a certain denomination (usually $1,000). A bond indenture is a legal document that summarizes the terms of the bond issue (face value, stated interest rate), the rights of the bondholders, and the obligations of the issuing company. Normally, a corporation sells all of its bonds to an investment firm, referred to as an underwriter. The underwriter then resells the bonds to investors. For accounting purposes, only the amount received from the underwriter is relevant to the issuing firm. Individual bonds are sold to investors with a promise to pay a definite sum of money to the holder at a fixed future date and periodic interest payments at a stated rate throughout the life of the liability. Since bonds usually do not name individual lenders, they may be bought and sold by investors until their maturity.

When funds are borrowed by issuing bonds, interest payments and the repayment of the principal of the debt to bondholders are obligations that are fixed in amount and must be paid at specified dates regardless of the amount of income earned by the firm. If the expected rate of earnings on invested funds exceeds the interest rate on the bonds, it is usually to the owners' advantage for the firm to issue bonds. This is called "trading on the equity" and increases the firm's asset base. On the other hand, if the expected rate of earnings is less than the interest rate, it is not to the advantage of the owners to borrow funds. The interest rate leverage does not exist, and the firm's asset base declines from indebtedness, as interest payments must be made when due regardless of whether or not sufficient income is earned. If interest payments are not made, the bondholders may bring action in order to foreclose against the assets of the corporation in the settlement of their claims.

Bondholders are creditors and their claims for interest and the repayment of principal have priority over the claims of owners.

Bond interest payments are a deductible expense in the computation of taxable income, while dividends paid to owners are not deductible for tax purposes. Because of the magnitude of corporate income taxes, the effect of taxes is often an important factor in determining the source to be used by the business to obtain its long-term funds.

Approval of the board of directors and stockholders of the corporation is normally required prior to issuance of bonds. In addition, the firm issuing bonds selects a trustee to represent the bondholders. The trustee acts to protect the bondholders' interests, and takes legal action if the pledged responsibilities of the corporation are not satisfied.

Classes of Bonds

Bonds may be either secured by specific assets or unsecured. Unsecured bonds are referred to as debenture bonds. Debenture bonds have as "security" the general credit standing of the issuing corporation. Therefore, debenture bonds are usually issued successfully only by companies with a favorable financial position.

A secured bond gives the bondholder a prior claim against specific assets in the event that the issuing corporation is unable to make the required interest or principal payments as they become due. Secured bonds differ as to the type of assets pledged. Real estate mortgage bonds are secured by a mortgage on specific land or buildings. Equipment trust bonds are secured by mortgages on tangible personal property such as equipment. Collateral trust bonds are secured by stocks and bonds of other companies owned by the corporation issuing the bonds.

A bond issue that matures on a single date is referred to as a term bond. Bonds that mature on several different dates and are retired in installments over a period of time are called serial bonds. Bonds that may be retired before maturity at the option of the issuing corporation are referred to as callable bonds. Bonds that may be exchanged for a specified amount of stock at the option of the bondholder are termed convertible bonds.

Bonds may also differ as to the method of interest payment. Registered bonds require that the bondholders' names be registered with the issuing corporation. The corporation issuing bonds is required to maintain a record of the current owners; periodic interest payments are mailed directly to the registered owners. Other bonds, called coupon bonds, have interest coupons attached that call for the payment of the required amount of interest on specified dates. A bond coupon is similar to a note payable to the holder at the date specified on the coupon. At each interest date, the appropriate coupon may be detached by the bondholder and presented at a bank for payment.

Despite the wide variety of bonds offered, it should be noted that the value of bonds to the investor depends to a significant degree on the financial condition and long-term earning prospects of the issuing corporation. While the various optional provisions that may be included in a bond issue may affect the issue price of the bonds, it is difficult for a company in poor financial condition to issue bonds regardless of the provisions.

Issuance of Bonds

When a corporation issues bonds, it is obligated to pay the principal or face amount of the bonds at a specified maturity date and to make periodic interest payments as well. The interest rate specified on the bonds is referred to as the coupon rate. The interest rate that investors are willing to accept on a bond at the time of its issue depends upon factors such as the market evaluation of the quality of the bond issue as evidenced by the financial strength of the business, the firm's earnings prospects and the particular provisions of the bond issue. This rate is referred to as the market or effective interest rate.

The price of a bond is a function of the relationship between its coupon rate (the amount specified on the bond indenture) and the prevailing market interest rate for bonds of similar investment quality. *The bond will sell at an amount more or less than the principal amount so as to provide the effective yield demanded by the investors at the time that the bond is issued.* The coupon rate may not be exactly the same as the market (effective) rate, because the bond contract must be finalized some time prior to the actual sale of the bonds. Interest rates, and therefore bond prices, change on a daily basis, not only because of the particular company's financial condition and outlook, but also because of overall economic conditions and business events. By allowing the price of the bond to vary from the face amount in this manner, the bond may be issued without amending the coupon rate specified in the bond contract.

If the effective interest rate exceeds the coupon rate, the issue price of the bonds will fall below the face amount of the bonds. When the issue price is less than face value, the difference is referred to as a discount. For example, if a company offers bonds with an interest rate of 7 percent when the market rate is 8 percent for similar bonds, the selling price of the bonds will be less than their face value. Since annual interest payments on each $1,000 of bonds will be $70 (.07 × $1,000), the issue price of the bonds will fall to the point where the interest received will yield an effective rate of 8 percent. Similarly, if the coupon rate exceeds the market interest rate for comparable bonds at the time of the issue, the price of the bonds will exceed the face amount. That is, the bonds will be issued at a premium. The bonds will sell at their face amount only when the coupon rate is exactly equal to the market rate.

Interest and Present Value Concepts

Timing of the cash flows is important because of the following principle: *an amount of cash to be received in the future is not equivalent to the same amount of cash held at the present time.* This statement is true because money has a time value—it can be invested to earn a return (i.e., interest or dividends). For this reason, in both borrowing and investing decisions, consideration must be given to the time values of the various cash inflows and outflows.

In order to understand the implications of such decisions, the accountant must be able to determine the *present value* of future cash flows. Although there are a number of important applications of present value concepts in the financial accounting area, this discussion is limited to the application of these concepts to long-term liabilities.

Interest

Interest represents the amount received by the lender and paid by the borrower for the use of money for a given period of time. Thus, upon payment of a debt, interest is the excess of the cash paid over the amount originally borrowed (referred to as the *principal*). Interest is normally stated as a rate for a one-year period.

Simple interest is the amount of interest that is computed on the principal *only* for a given period of time. Simple interest is computed as follows:

$$\text{Interest} = \text{Principal} \times \text{Rate} \times \text{Time}$$
$$\text{Interest} = P \times I \times T \qquad (1)$$

To illustrate, interest on $1,000 for six months at an annual interest rate of 10 percent is:

$$\$50 = \$1,000 \times .10 \times 6/12$$

Compound interest is interest that is computed for a period of time both on the principal and on the interest that has been earned but not paid. That is, interest is compounded when the interest earned in each period is added to the principal amount and both principal and interest earn interest in all subsequent periods. To illustrate, assume that $1.000 is deposited in a bank that pays interest at 10 percent annually. If the interest is withdrawn each year (simple interest), the depositor collects $100 in interest each year (or $300 in interest over a three-year period):

$$\text{Interest per year} \quad = \$1,000 \quad \times \text{ .10} \times 1 \ = \$100$$
$$\text{Total interest for 3 years} \quad = \$100 \ \times \ 3 \ = \quad \$300$$

However, if the interest at the end of each period is added to the principal sum (compound interest), the amount earned over the three-year period is computed as follows:

Original investment $1,000

Balance at the
end of the year: 1. $1,000 + (.10 × $1,000 × 1) 1,100
                 2. $1,100 + (.10 × $1,100 × 1) 1,210
                 3. $1,210 + (.10 × $1,210 × 1) 1,331

Compound interest for the three-year period is $331 ($1,331 − $1,000), the difference between the balance at the end of the three-year period and the original investment. This amount exceeds simple interest because interest is earned each year both on the principal and on the interest earned in previous years.

Since compounding occurs when interest is earned on previously accumulated interest, a formula can be developed for computing the compound amount at which the principal sum will increase over a given time period. To develop this formula, consider the compound interest on one dollar invested at an interest rate of 10 percent. The amount accumulated at the end of the first year is $[1 + (1 \times I)]$ or $(1 + I)$. If this amount is allowed to accumulate and earn interest for the second year, the amount accumulated is $(1 + I)(1 + I)$ which is equal to $(1 + I).^2$ Similarly, the amount at the end of T periods is $(1 + 1)^T$. Consequently, the amount (A) to which a principal amount (P) will accumulate over a time period (T) at an interest rate (I) is expressed as:

$$A = P(1 + I)^T \tag{2}$$

For example, if $1,000 is invested for three years at 10 percent interest per year, the amount accumulated at the end of three years is computed as follows:

$$A = \$1,000 \ (1 + .10)^3$$
$$A = \$1,000 \ (1.331)$$
$$A = \$1,331$$

This computation of the sum for a single principal amount and the compound interest at a specified future time may be illustrated as follows:

$$1,000 \xrightarrow{\hspace{4cm}} \$1,331$$

```
0              1              2              3
              Time (years)
```

Present Values of a Future Sum

The present value of a given amount at a specified future time is the sum that has to be invested at the present time in order to equal that future value at a given rate of compound interest. For example, $1,000 invested at 10 percent compound interest accumulate to a total of $1,331 in three years. Therefore, $1,000 are the *present value* of $1,331 three years from the present time (given a 10% rate of interest). That is, if you can earn 10 percent on a bank deposit, you are indifferent between receiving $1,000 now (which can be deposited to accumulate to $1,331 in 3 years) or $1,331 three years from now, all other factors being equal.

The value of a future amount (A) is determined by computing the amount that a principal sum (P) will accumulate to over a specified period of time. Consequently, by dividing equation (2) by $(1 + I)^T$, we obtain the formula for computing the present value of a future amount:

$$P = \frac{A}{(1 + I)^T} \tag{3}$$

For example, the present value of $1,331 three years from now is computed as follows:

$$P = \frac{(\$1,331}{(1 + .10)^3}$$
$$P = \$1,000$$

Because of the number and variety of decisions based on the present value of future cash flows, tables have been developed from the formula to give the present value of $1 for various interest rates and for various periods of time. These values may be multiplied by any future amount to determine its present value. The factors for the present value of $1 are listed in Table I.

To illustrate the use of this table, let us compute the present value of $1,331 to be received three years from now at a compound interest rate of 10 percent. The value from the table for three years at 10 percent is .7513. This is the present value of $1. Accordingly, the present value of $1,331 is computed as $1,331 x .7513 = $999.80 (this amount is not exactly equal to $1,000 because of rounding in the present value factor included in the table). The computation of the present value of a simple payment due in the future may be illustrated as follows:

```
$1,000 ◄─────────────────────── $1,331

   0         1         2         3
              Time (years)
```

Compound Interest and Present Value of a Series of Equal Payments

Business decisions involving a series of cash flows to be paid or received periodically are more common than decisions involving the accumulation of a single principal sum. It is possible to determine the present value of a series of payments (or receipts) by computing the present value of each payment or receipt and adding these values to obtain the present value for the entire series. However, if all the payments are equal, formulas or tables may be used to compute the present value of a series of payments. Such a series of equal periodic payments is normally referred to as an *annuity*. If the payments are made at the end of each period, the annuity is referred to as an *ordinary annuity*.

The accumulated amount (future value) of an ordinary annuity is the sum of the periodic payments and the compound interest on these payments. For example, the future value of an annuity of $1,000 per year (at the end of each year) for three years at 10 percent interest can be determined as follows:

The initial payment accumulates at 10% for 2 years to	$1,210
The second payment accumulates at 10% for 1 year to	1,100
The third payment is due at the end of the third year	1,000
Amount of an ordinary annuity of $1,000 for 3 years at 10%	$3,310

The computation of the future value of a series of payments may be expressed as follows:

```
$1,000 ─────────────────────────► $1,210
              $1,000 ─────────────► 1,100
                        $1,000─► 1,000
 ─────────────────────────────────────
   0         1         2         3   $3,310
              Time (years)
```

TABLE I

Present Value of $1.00

Periods (n)	1%	1½%	2%	2½%	3%	3½%	4%	4½%	5%	6%	7%	8%	10%
1	0.9901	0.9852	0.9804	0.9756	0.9709	0.9662	0.9615	0.9569	0.9524	0.9434	0.9346	0.9259	0.9091
2	0.9803	0.9707	0.9612	0.9518	0.9426	0.9335	0.9246	0.9157	0.9070	0.8900	0.8734	0.8573	0.8264
3	0.9706	0.9563	0.9423	0.9286	0.9151	0.9019	0.8890	0.8763	0.8638	0.8396	0.8163	0.7938	0.7513
4	0.9610	0.9422	0.9238	0.9060	0.8885	0.8714	0.8548	0.8386	0.8227	0.7921	0.7629	0.7350	0.6830
5	0.9515	0.9283	0.9057	0.8839	0.8626	0.8420	0.8219	0.8025	0.7835	0.7473	0.7130	0.6806	0.6209
6	0.9420	0.9145	0.8880	0.8623	0.8375	0.8135	0.7903	0.7679	0.7462	0.7050	0.6663	0.6302	0.5645
7	0.9327	0.9010	0.8706	0.8413	0.8131	0.7860	0.7599	0.7348	0.7107	0.6651	0.6227	0.5835	0.5132
8	0.9235	0.8877	0.8535	0.8207	0.7894	0.7594	0.7307	0.7032	0.6768	0.6274	0.5820	0.5403	0.4665
9	0.9143	0.8746	0.8368	0.8007	0.7664	0.7337	0.7026	0.6729	0.6446	0.5919	0.5439	0.5002	0.4241
10	0.9053	0.8617	0.8203	0.7812	0.7441	0.7089	0.6756	0.6439	0.6139	0.5584	0.5083	0.4632	0.3855
11	0.8963	0.8489	0.8043	0.7621	0.7224	0.6849	0.6496	0.6162	0.5847	0.5268	0.4751	0.4289	0.3505
12	0.8874	0.8364	0.7885	0.7436	0.7014	0.6618	0.6246	0.5897	0.5568	0.4970	0.4440	0.3971	0.3186
13	0.8787	0.8240	0.7730	0.7254	0.6810	0.6394	0.6006	0.5643	0.5303	0.4688	0.4150	0.3677	0.2897
14	0.8700	0.8118	0.7579	0.7077	0.6611	0.6178	0.5775	0.5400	0.5051	0.4423	0.3878	0.3405	0.2633
15	0.8613	0.7999	0.7430	0.6905	0.6419	0.5969	0.5553	0.5167	0.4810	0.4173	0.3624	0.3153	0.2394
16	0.8528	0.7880	0.7284	0.6736	0.6232	0.5767	0.5339	0.4945	0.4581	0.3936	0.3387	0.2919	0.2176
17	0.8444	0.7764	0.7142	0.6572	0.6050	0.5572	0.5134	0.4732	0.4363	0.3714	0.3166	0.2703	0.1978
18	0.8360	0.7649	0.7002	0.6412	0.5874	0.5384	0.4936	0.4528	0.4155	0.3503	0.2959	0.2502	0.1799
19	0.8277	0.7536	0.6864	0.6255	0.5703	0.5202	0.4746	0.4333	0.3957	0.3305	0.2765	0.2317	0.1635
20	0.8195	0.7425	0.6730	0.6103	0.5537	0.5026	0.4564	0.4146	0.3769	0.3118	0.2584	0.2145	0.1486
21	0.8114	0.7315	0.6598	0.5954	0.5375	0.4856	0.4388	0.3968	0.3589	0.2942	0.2415	0.1987	0.1351
22	0.8034	0.7207	0.6468	0.5809	0.5219	0.4692	0.4220	0.3797	0.3418	0.2775	0.2257	0.1839	0.1228
23	0.7954	0.7100	0.6342	0.5667	0.5067	0.4533	0.4057	0.3634	0.3256	0.2618	0.2109	0.1703	0.1117
24	0.7876	0.6995	0.6217	0.5529	0.4919	0.4380	0.3901	0.3477	0.3101	0.2470	0.1971	0.1577	0.1015
25	0.7798	0.6892	0.6095	0.5394	0.4776	0.4231	0.3751	0.3327	0.2953	0.2330	0.1842	0.1460	0.0923
26	0.7720	0.6790	0.5976	0.5262	0.4637	0.4088	0.3607	0.3184	0.2812	0.2198	0.1722	0.1352	0.0839
27	0.7644	0.6690	0.5859	0.5134	0.4502	0.3950	0.3468	0.3047	0.2678	0.2074	0.1609	0.1252	0.0763
28	0.7568	0.6591	0.5744	0.5009	0.4371	0.3817	0.3335	0.2916	0.2551	0.1956	0.1504	0.1159	0.0693
29	0.7493	0.6494	0.5631	0.4887	0.4243	0.3687	0.3207	0.2790	0.2429	0.1846	0.1406	0.1073	0.0630
30	0.7419	0.6398	0.5521	0.4767	0.4120	0.3563	0.3083	0.2670	0.2314	0.1741	0.1314	0.0994	0.0573
40	0.6717	0.5513	0.4529	0.3724	0.3066	0.2526	0.2083	0.1719	0.1420	0.0972	0.0668	0.0460	0.0221
50	0.6080	0.4750	0.3715	0.2909	0.2281	0.1791	0.1407	0.1107	0.0872	0.0543	0.0339	0.0213	0.0085

TABLE I Continued
Present Value of $1.00

12%	14%	15%	16%	18%	20%	22%	24%	25%	26%	28%	30%	40%	50%
0.893	0.877	0.870	0.862	0.847	0.833	0.820	0.806	0.800	0.794	0.781	0.769	0.714	0.667
0.797	0.769	0.756	0.743	0.718	0.694	0.672	0.650	0.640	0.630	0.610	0.592	0.510	0.444
0.712	0.675	0.658	0.641	0.609	0.579	0.551	0.524	0.512	0.500	0.477	0.455	0.364	0.296
0.636	0.592	0.572	0.552	0.516	0.482	0.451	0.423	0.410	0.397	0.373	0.350	0.260	0.198
0.567	0.519	0.497	0.476	0.437	0.402	0.370	0.341	0.328	0.315	0.291	0.269	0.186	0.132
0.507	0.456	0.432	0.410	0.370	0.335	0.303	0.275	0.262	0.250	0.227	0.207	0.133	0.088
0.452	0.400	0.376	0.354	0.314	0.279	0.249	0.222	0.210	0.198	0.178	0.159	0.095	0.059
0.404	0.351	0.327	0.305	0.266	0.233	0.204	0.179	0.168	0.157	0.139	0.123	0.068	0.039
0.361	0.308	0.284	0.263	0.225	0.194	0.167	0.144	0.134	0.125	0.108	0.094	0.048	0.026
0.322	0.270	0.247	0.227	0.191	0.162	0.137	0.116	0.107	0.099	0.085	0.073	0.035	0.017
0.287	0.237	0.215	0.195	0.162	0.135	0.112	0.094	0.086	0.079	0.066	0.056	0.025	0.012
0.257	0.208	0.187	0.168	0.137	0.112	0.092	0.076	0.069	0.062	0.052	0.043	0.018	0.008
0.229	0.182	0.163	0.145	0.116	0.093	0.075	0.061	0.055	0.050	0.040	0.033	0.013	0.005
0.205	0.160	0.141	0.125	0.099	0.078	0.062	0.049	0.044	0.039	0.032	0.025	0.009	0.003
0.183	0.140	0.123	0.108	0.084	0.065	0.051	0.040	0.035	0.031	0.025	0.020	0.006	0.002
0.163	0.123	0.107	0.093	0.071	0.054	0.042	0.032	0.028	0.025	0.019	0.015	0.005	0.002
0.146	0.108	0.093	0.080	0.060	0.045	0.034	0.026	0.023	0.020	0.015	0.012	0.003	0.001
0.130	0.095	0.081	0.069	0.051	0.038	0.028	0.021	0.018	0.016	0.012	0.009	0.002	0.001
0.116	0.083	0.070	0.060	0.043	0.031	0.023	0.017	0.014	0.012	0.009	0.007	0.002	
0.104	0.073	0.061	0.051	0.037	0.026	0.019	0.014	0.012	0.010	0.007	0.005	0.001	
0.093	0.064	0.053	0.044	0.031	0.022	0.015	0.011	0.009	0.008	0.006	0.004	0.001	
0.083	0.056	0.046	0.038	0.026	0.018	0.013	0.009	0.007	0.006	0.004	0.003	0.001	
0.074	0.049	0.040	0.033	0.022	0.015	0.010	0.007	0.006	0.005	0.003	0.002		
0.066	0.043	0.035	0.028	0.019	0.013	0.008	0.006	0.005	0.004	0.003	0.001		
0.059	0.038	0.030	0.024	0.016	0.010	0.007	0.005	0.004	0.003	0.002			
0.053	0.033	0.026	0.021	0.014	0.009	0.006	0.004	0.003	0.002	0.002	0.001		
0.047	0.029	0.023	0.018	0.011	0.007	0.005	0.003	0.002	0.002	0.001	0.001		
0.042	0.026	0.020	0.016	0.010	0.006	0.004	0.002	0.002	0.002	0.001	0.001		
0.037	0.022	0.017	0.014	0.008	0.005	0.003	0.002	0.001	0.001	0.001	0.001		
0.033	0.020	0.015	0.012	0.007	0.004	0.003			0.001				
0.011	0.005	0.004	0.003	0.001	0.001								
0.003	0.001	0.001	0.001										

The present value of an ordinary annuity is the amount that, if invested at the present time at a compound rate of interest, provides for a series of equal withdrawals at the end of a certain number of periods. The present value of an ordinary annuity may be computed as the present values of each of the individual payments. For example, the present value of an ordinary annuity of $1,000 per year for three years at 10 percent can be computed as follows (see Table I):

Present value of $1,000 in 1 year	.9091	×	$1,000	=	$ 909.10
Present value of $1,000 in 2 years	.8264	×	$1,000	=	826.40
Present value of $1,000 in 3 years	.7513	×	$1,000	=	751.30
Present value of an annuity of $1,000 for 3 periods at 10%					$2,486.80

This computation indicates that if $2,486.80 are invested at an interest rate of 10 percent, it will be possible to withdraw $1,000 at the end of each year for three years.

The formula for the present value of an ordinary annuity of $R per period for T periods at I rate of interest may be stated as follows:

$$P = R \left[\frac{1 - \dfrac{1}{(1 + I)^T}}{I} \right]$$

Table II gives the present value of an ordinary annuity of $1 per period for various periods at varying rates of interest. By multiplying the appropriate value from the table by the dollar amount of the periodic payment, the present value of the payments may be calculated. For example, the present value of three annual cash payments of $1,000 made at the end of the next three years at a 10 percent interest rate is computed as follows:

$$\$1,000 \times 2.4869 = \$2,486.90^{[1]}$$

This amount may be interpreted as the present cash payment that is exactly equivalent to the three future installments of $1,000 if money earns 10 percent compounded annually. The computation of the present value of a series of future payments may be illustrated as follows:

$
\begin{array}{l}
\$\ 909.10 \leftarrow \$1,000 \\
\ \ \ \ 826.40 \leftarrow \text{———————} \$1,000 \\
\ \ \ \ \underline{751.30} \leftarrow \text{————————————} \$1,000 \\
\$2,486.80
\end{array}
$

```
0            1            2            3
        Time (years)
```

---

[1] Difference of $.10 due to rounding in tables.

TABLE II
Present Value of Annuity of $1.00 per Period

Periods (n)	1%	1½%	2%	2½%	3%	3½%	4%	4½%	5%	6%	7%
1	0.9901	0.9852	0.9804	0.9756	0.9709	0.9662	0.9615	0.9569	0.9524	0.9434	0.9346
2	1.9704	1.9559	1.9416	1.9274	1.9135	1.8997	1.8861	1.8727	1.8594	1.8334	1.8080
3	2.9410	2.9122	2.8839	2.8560	2.8286	2.8016	2.7751	2.7490	2.7232	2.6730	2.6243
4	3.9020	3.8544	3.8077	3.7620	3.7171	3.6731	3.6299	3.5875	3.5460	3.4651	3.3872
5	4.8534	4.7826	4.7135	4.6458	4.5797	4.5151	4.4518	4.3900	4.3295	4.2124	4.1002
6	5.7955	5.6972	5.6014	5.5081	5.4172	5.3286	5.2421	5.1579	5.0757	4.9173	4.7665
7	6.7282	6.5982	6.4720	6.3494	6.2303	6.1145	6.0021	5.8927	5.7864	5.5824	5.3893
8	7.6517	7.4859	7.3255	7.1701	7.0197	6.8740	6.7327	6.5959	6.4632	6.2098	5.9713
9	8.5660	8.3605	8.1622	7.9709	7.7861	7.6077	7.4353	7.2688	7.1078	6.8017	6.5152
10	9.4713	9.2222	8.9826	8.7521	8.5302	8.3166	8.1109	7.9127	7.7217	7.3601	7.0236
11	10.3676	10.0711	9.7868	9.5142	9.2526	9.0016	8.7605	8.5289	8.3064	7.8869	7.4987
12	11.2551	10.9075	10.5753	10.2578	9.9540	9.6633	9.3851	9.1186	8.8633	8.3838	7.9427
13	12.1337	11.7315	11.3484	10.9832	10.6350	10.3027	9.9856	9.6829	9.3936	8.8527	8.3577
14	13.0037	12.5434	12.1062	11.6909	11.2961	10.9205	10.5631	10.2228	9.8986	9.2950	8.7455
15	13.8651	13.3432	12.8493	12.3814	11.9379	11.5174	11.1184	10.7395	10.3797	9.7122	9.1079
16	14.7179	14.1313	13.5777	13.0550	12.5611	12.0941	11.6523	11.2340	10.8378	10.1059	9.4466
17	15.5623	14.9076	14.2919	13.7122	13.1661	12.6513	12.1657	11.7072	11.2741	10.4773	9.7632
18	16.3983	15.6726	14.9920	14.3534	13.7535	13.1897	12.6593	12.1600	11.6896	10.8276	10.0591
19	17.2260	16.4262	15.6785	14.9789	14.3238	13.7098	13.1339	12.5933	12.0853	11.1581	10.3356
20	18.0456	17.1686	16.3514	15.5892	14.8775	14.2124	13.5903	13.0079	12.4622	11.4699	10.5940
21	18.8570	17.9001	17.0112	16.1845	15.4150	14.6980	14.0292	13.4047	12.8212	11.7640	10.8355
22	19.6604	18.6208	17.6580	16.7654	15.9369	15.1671	14.4511	13.7844	13.1630	12.0416	11.0612
23	20.4558	19.3309	18.2922	17.3321	16.4436	15.6204	14.8568	14.1478	13.4886	12.3034	11.2722
24	21.2434	20.0304	18.9139	17.8850	16.9355	16.0584	15.2470	14.4955	13.7986	12.5504	11.4693
25	22.0232	20.7196	19.5235	18.4244	17.4131	16.4815	15.6221	14.8282	14.0939	12.7834	11.6536
26	22.7952	21.3986	20.1210	18.9506	17.8768	16.8904	15.9828	15.1466	14.3752	13.0032	11.8258
27	23.5596	22.0676	20.7069	19.4640	18.3270	17.2854	16.3296	15.4513	14.6430	13.2105	11.9867
28	24.3164	22.7267	21.2813	19.9649	18.7641	17.6670	16.6631	15.7429	14.8981	13.4062	12.1371
29	25.0658	23.3761	21.8444	20.4535	19.1885	18.0358	18.9837	16.0219	15.1411	13.5907	12.2777
30	25.8077	24.0158	22.3965	20.9303	19.6004	18.3920	17.2920	16.2889	15.3725	13.7648	12.4090
40	32.8347	29.9158	27.3555	25.1028	23.1148	21.3551	19.7928	18.4016	17.1591	15.0463	13.3317
50	39.1961	34.9997	31.4236	28.3623	25.7298	23.4556	21.4822	19.7620	18.2559	15.7619	13.8007

TABLE II Continued

Present Value of Annuity of $1.00 per Period

50%	40%	30%	28%	26%	25%	24%	22%	20%	18%	16%	15%	14%	12%	10%	8%
0.667	0.714	0.769	0.781	0.794	0.800	0.806	0.820	0.833	0.847	0.862	0.870	0.877	0.893	0.9091	0.9259
1.111	1.224	1.361	1.392	1.424	1.440	1.457	1.492	1.528	1.566	1.605	1.626	1.647	1.690	1.7355	1.7833
1.407	1.589	1.816	1.868	1.923	1.952	1.981	2.042	2.106	2.174	2.246	2.283	2.322	2.402	2.4869	2.5771
1.605	1.849	2.166	2.241	2.320	2.362	2.404	2.494	2.589	2.690	2.798	2.855	2.914	3.037	3.1699	3.3121
1.737	2.035	2.436	2.532	2.635	2.689	2.745	2.864	2.991	3.127	3.274	3.352	3.433	3.605	3.7908	3.9927
1.824	2.168	2.643	2.759	2.885	2.951	3.020	3.167	3.326	3.498	3.685	3.784	3.889	4.111	4.3553	4.6229
1.883	2.263	2.802	2.937	3.083	3.161	3.242	3.416	3.605	3.812	4.039	4.160	4.288	4.564	4.8684	5.2064
1.922	2.331	2.925	3.076	3.241	3.329	3.421	3.619	3.837	4.078	4.344	4.487	4.639	4.968	5.3349	5.7466
1.948	2.379	3.019	3.184	3.366	3.463	3.566	3.786	4.031	4.303	4.607	4.772	4.946	5.328	5.7590	6.2469
1.965	2.414	3.092	3.269	3.465	3.571	3.682	3.923	4.192	4.494	4.833	5.019	5.216	5.650	6.1446	6.7101
1.977	2.438	3.147	3.335	3.544	3.656	3.776	4.035	4.327	4.656	5.029	5.234	5.453	5.988	6.4951	7.1390
1.985	2.456	3.190	3.387	3.606	3.725	3.851	4.127	4.439	4.793	5.197	5.421	5.660	6.194	6.8137	7.5361
1.990	2.468	3.223	3.427	3.656	3.780	3.912	4.203	4.533	4.910	5.342	5.583	5.842	6.424	7.1034	7.9038
1.993	2.477	3.249	3.459	3.695	3.824	3.962	4.265	4.611	5.008	5.468	5.724	6.002	6.628	7.3667	8.2442
1.995	2.484	3.268	3.483	3.726	3.859	4.001	4.315	4.675	5.092	5.575	5.847	6.142	6.811	7.6061	8.5595
1.997	2.489	3.283	3.503	3.751	3.887	4.033	4.357	4.730	5.162	5.669	5.954	6.265	6.974	7.8237	8.8514
1.998	2.492	3.295	3.518	3.771	3.910	4.059	4.391	4.775	5.222	5.749	6.047	6.373	7.120	8.0216	9.1216
1.999	2.494	3.304	3.529	3.786	3.928	4.080	4.419	4.812	5.273	5.818	6.128	6.467	7.250	8.2014	9.3719
1.999	2.496	3.311	3.539	3.799	3.942	4.097	4.442	4.844	5.316	5.877	6.198	6.550	7.366	8.3649	9.6036
1.999	2.497	3.316	3.546	3.808	3.954	4.110	4.460	4.870	5.353	5.929	6.259	6.623	7.469	8.5136	9.8181
2.000	2.498	3.320	3.551	3.816	3.963	4.121	4.476	4.891	5.384	5.973	6.312	6.687	7.562	8.6487	10.0168
2.000	2.498	3.323	3.556	3.822	3.970	4.130	4.488	4.909	5.410	6.011	6.359	6.743	7.645	8.7715	10.2007
2.000	2.499	3.325	3.559	3.827	3.976	4.137	4.499	4.925	5.432	6.044	6.399	6.792	7.718	8.8832	10.3711
2.000	2.499	3.327	3.562	3.831	3.981	4.143	4.507	4.937	5.451	6.073	6.434	6.835	7.784	8.9847	10.5288
2.000	2.499	3.329	3.564	3.834	3.985	4.147	4.514	4.948	5.467	6.097	6.464	6.873	7.843	9.0770	10.6748
2.000	2.500	3.330	3.566	3.837	3.988	4.151	4.520	4.956	5.480	6.118	6.491	6.906	7.896	9.1609	10.8100
2.000	2.500	3.331	3.567	3.839	3.990	4.154	4.524	4.964	5.492	6.136	6.514	6.935	7.943	9.2372	10.9352
2.000	2.500	3.331	3.568	3.840	3.992	4.157	4.528	4.970	5.502	6.152	6.534	6.961	7.984	9.3066	11.0511
2.000	2.500	3.332	3.569	3.841	3.994	4.159	4.531	4.975	5.510	6.166	6.551	6.983	8.022	9.3696	11.1584
2.000	2.500	3.332	3.569	3.842	3.995	4.160	4.534	4.979	5.517	6.177	6.566	7.003	8.055	9.4269	11.2578
2.000	2.500	3.333	3.571	3.846	3.999	4.166	4.544	4.997	5.548	6.234	6.642	7.105	8.244	9.7791	11.9246
2.000	2.500	3.333	3.571	3.846	4.000	4.167	4.545	4.999	5.554	6.246	6.661	7.133	8.304	9.9148	12.2335

Application of Present Value Concepts to Bonds Payable

A bond is a contract between an issuing company and the purchasers of the bond. There are two types of payments that a company has to make to bondholders. One payment is a lump-sum payment made at the end of the life of the bond, which is the return of the *face value* or *maturity value* of the bond. The other payment is for interest, which is made at specific intervals in fixed amounts over the life of the bond. Interest is usually paid semiannually by the issuing company. Bond contracts state the *coupon* or *nominal rate* of interest on an annual basis.

To calculate the selling price of a bond (the amount the firm receives upon issuance of the bond), consider a company that sells a $1,000 face-value bond with a nominal rate of interest of 8 percent. The bond will mature in five years and the interest is payable June 30 and December 31 of each year. The company makes two promises to the purchasers of the bond:

> Promise 1: To pay $1,000 at the end of five years.
> Promise 2: To pay $40 semiannually for five years.

The price that any investor pays for a bond depends upon the *effective rate*[2] of interest on the date that the investor decides to buy the bond. The effective rate is dependent upon many factors such as the prime interest rate in money markets, the risks involved in buying the bond of that specific company, and the bond provisions that may make it more attractive for investment purposes. In general, the effective rate is determined by supply and demand in the bond market.

There are three possible general cases that illustrate the potential selling price of the bond. These three cases are dependent upon the earnings expectations of buyers of bonds in the market place. In the prior example, where the nominal rate is 8 percent, the three possible cases are:

1. The effective (market) rate of interest is equal to 8 percent.

2. The effective (market) rate of interest is below 8 percent.

3. The effective (market) rate of interest is greater than 8 percent.

If the market is demanding an 8 percent return on bonds of like kind, and the company enters the market with an 8 percent coupon rate on its bond, the bond sells at its face value of $1,000. The buyer is demanding 8 percent and the seller is paying 8 percent; therefore, the bond sells at *par*.

If the market is demanding a return that is less than 8 percent and the company enters the market with an 8 percent coupon rate on its bond, the company is paying a greater return than is demanded in the market. Therefore, the bond sells for a price in excess of $1,000. This excess is referred to as a *premium*. The investors buy the bond at a price greater than $1,000 because the coupon rate exceeds the rate demanded by the market.

If the market is demanding a return that is greater than 8 percent and the company enters the market with an 8 percent coupon rate on its bond, the company is paying less than the return demanded by the market. Therefore, the bond sells for less than $1,000. The difference between $1,000 and the selling price is a *discount* on the bond.

To calculate the selling price of the bond, assume that the market rate of interest is either 8 percent, 6 percent, or 10 percent. Note that the bond contract provides for a lump-sum payment at maturity and semiannual interest payments over the life of the bond. Thus, in order to find the current value, or selling price, of the bond, it is necessary to determine the present value of the lump-sum payment at maturity and the present value of the periodic interest payments (an ordinary annuity). Illustration 1 presents the calculations necessary to determine the selling price of the $1,000 bond at the three market rates of interest assumed above.

---

[2] The effective rate is also referred to as the market rate or the yield.

```
                                    Illustration 1
                                Selling Price of a Bond with
                           8 Percent Coupon Rate, Five-Year Life,
                                 and Semiannual Payments

                                                    Present Value Factors for
                                                    Ten Periods at Market Rate
                                                      Semiannual Interest

                                              Table 1      Table 2           Totals
   8 percent coupon, 8 percent
   market, bond sells at par:
      Promise #1 = $1,000 – lump sum . . . . . . . . . . . . .   .6756                    =   $  675.60
      Promise #2 = $    40 – annuity . . . . . . . . . . . . . . .           8.1109       =      324.44
                             Selling price (rounded)                         =   $1,000.00
   8 percent coupon, 6 percent
   market, bond sells at premium:
      Promise #1 = $1,000 – lump sum . . . . . . . . . . . . .   .7441                    =   $  744.10
      Promise #2 = $    40 – annuity . . . . . . . . . . . . . . .           8.5302       =      341.21
                             Selling price (rounded)                         =   $1,085.31
   8 percent coupon, 10 percent
   market, bond sells at discount:
      Promise #1 = $1,000 – lump sum . . . . . . . . . . . . .   .6139                    =   $  613.90
      Promise #2 = $    40 – annuity . . . . . . . . . . . . . . .           7.7217       =      308.87
                             Selling price (rounded)                         =   $  922.77
```

Even though the selling price of the bond will vary according to the three different market rate assumptions, it is important to remember that the bond is a fixed contract that will pay a return of $40 to the bondholder semiannually and $1,000 at its maturity date. These amounts are paid regardless of the initial selling price of the bond.

ACCOUNTING FOR PREMIUM OR DISCOUNT ON BONDS—THE INTEREST METHOD

The following example is used to illustrate the accounting treatment of a bond issue sold at a premium or discount using the interest method, which is the only method considered generally accepted when amounts are material. Assume that on July 1, 19X1, a company sells a $1,000,000 bond issue with a nominal interest rate of 8 percent and a maturity date of July 1, 19X6. Interest will be paid on June 30 and December 31. The company's fiscal year ends on December 31.

The calculations necessary in order to compute the initial selling price of the bond are the same as the calculations in Illustration 1, except that the entire issue, $1,000,000, is under consideration. If the market rate of interest demanded is 8 percent, the bonds sell for $1,000,000. If the market rate of interest is 6 percent, the bonds sell at a premium. The selling price is ($1,000,000 × .7441) + ($40,000 × 8.5302) = $1,085,308. If the market rate of interest demanded is 10 percent, the bonds sell at a discount. The selling price is ($1,000,000 × .6139) + ($40,000 × 7.7217) = $922,768.

The face value of the bonds is paid to bondholders at the maturity date regardless of the original price of the bonds. The premium or discount on a bond is paid or received, respectively, to adjust the interest that will be paid on the bond to the return on the investment demanded by the market (market rate of interest) given the type of bond and the risk involved as perceived by investors.

The interest method of amortization[3] uses a constant rate of interest, the effective (market) rate, on the bond liability over the life of the bond. The interest expense for each period is computed by multiplying the effective interest rate by the beginning liability for that period.

Bonds Sold at a Premium

If the market rate of interest in the prior example is 6 percent, the bonds sell at a premium of $85,308 ($1,085,308 – $1,000,000). The interest method yields a different interest expense for each interest period. To determine the interest expense, the carrying value of the liability (face value plus unamortized premium or minus unamortized discount) is multiplied by the semiannual effective rate of interest. Thus, the interest expense is a constant percentage (equal to the effective semiannual interest rate on the issuance of the bonds) of 6 percent per year or 3 percent on the outstanding liability at the beginning of each semiannual interest period (see Illustration 2). The following journal entries are made in 19X1 under the interest method:

July 1, 19X1	Cash	$1,085,308.00	
	Bond premium		$ 85,308.00
	Bonds payable		1,000,000.00
December 31, 19X1	Interest expense	32,559.24	
	Bond premium	7,440.76	
	Cash		40,000.00

(Interest expense = $1,085,308.00 × .03 = $32,559.24)
(Bond premium = $40,000.00 – $32,559.24 = $7,440.76)

Illustration 2
*Interest Expense and
Premium Amortization Schedule*

	Debit to Interest Expense*	Debit to Bond Premium	Credit to Cash	Bond Premium Balance	Total Liability
July 1, 19x1	0	0	0	$85,308.00	$1,085 308.00
December 31, 19x1	$32,559.24	$ 7,440.76	$ 40,000	77,867.24	1,077,867.24
July 1, 19x2	32,336.02	7,663.98	40,000	70,203.26	1,070,203.26
December 31, 19x2	32,106.10	7,893.90	40,000	62,309.36	1,062,309.36
July 1, 19x3	31,869.28	8,130.72	40,000	54,178.64	1,054,178.64
December 31, 19x3	31,625.36	8,374.64	40,000	45,804.00	1,045,804.00
July 1, 19x4	31,374.12	8,625.88	40,000	37,178.12	1,037,178.12
December 31, 19x4	31,115.34	8,884.66	40,000	28,293.46	1,028,293.46
July 1, 19x5	30,848.80	9,151.20	40,000	19,142.26	1,019,142.26
December 31, 19x5	30,574.27	9,425.73	40,000	9,716.53	1,009,716.53
July 1, 19x6	30,291.47*	9,716.53	40,000	0	1,000,000.00
		$85,308.00	$400,000		

*To determine interest expense, the total liability at the beginning of the period was multiplied by the semiannual market interest rate of 3 percent. Any rounding errors are included in the July 1, 19x6, debit to interest expense.

---

[3] APB Opinion No. 21 (New York: AICPA, 1972).

At the end of 19X1, the balance sheet presentation of the liability includes both the bonds payable and bond premium accounts. As indicated in Illustration 2 below, the bond premium account balance is the original bond premium of $85,308.00 less the $7,440.76 of premium amortized during the first six months.

Bonds payable	$1,000,000	
Add: Bond premium	77,867	
Total bonds payable		$1,077,867

When bonds are issued at a premium, use of the interest method causes the interest expense to decrease over the life of the bond, because both the premium account and the carrying value of the liability decrease over the life of the bonds. The bond premium amortization increases because the cash payment to bondholders remains constant and the interest expense decreases each period. The total interest expense and premium amortization schedule is given in Illustration 2.

Bonds Sold at a Discount

If the market rate of interest demanded by investors is 10 percent, the bonds in the prior example sell at a discount because the face rate of interest is 8 percent. The discount is the difference between the maturity value of $1,000,000 and the selling price of $922,768, or $77,232.

The concepts underlying the *interest* method for bond discount are the same as those discussed in the prior section on bonds sold at a premium (see Illustration 3). The journal entries for 19X1 for bonds sold at a discount are:

July 1, 19X1	Cash	$922,768.00	
	Bond discount	$ 77,232.00	
	Bonds payable		$1,000,000.00
December 31, 19X1	Interest expense	46,138.40	
	Bond discount		6,138.40
	Cash		40,000.00

(Interest expense = $922,768 × .05 = $46,138.40)
(Bond discount = $46,138.40 − $40,000.00 = $6,138.40)

At the end of 19X1, the balance sheet presentation of the liability includes both the bonds payable and the bond discount account. As indicated in Illustration 3 below, the bond discount account is the original bond discount of $77,232.00 less the $6,138.40 of discount amortized during the first six months.

Bonds payable	$1,000,000	
Less: Bond discount	71,094	
Total bonds payable		$928,906

In the case of bonds sold at a discount, using the interest method causes interest expense to increase over the life of the bond, because discount decreases and the carrying value of the bonds increases. The total interest expense and discount amortization schedule is given in Illustration 3.

Convertible Bonds

In certain circumstances, a company may issue bonds that are convertible at a specific rate into the common stock of the corporation at the option of the bondholder. This provision may be attached to a bond in order to enhance the marketability of the bond issue. Usually, these convertible bonds may be sold at a higher price and lower yield rate than nonconvertible bonds. The bondholder initially has the rights of a creditor, but later may convert the bonds to stock and become a stockholder and share in the earnings of the business.

Illustration 3
Interest Expense and
Discount Amortization Schedule

	Debit to Interest Expense*	Credit to Bond Discount	Credit to Cash	Discount	Total Liability
July 1, 19x1	0	0	0	$77,232.00	$ 922,768.00
December 31, 19x1	$46,138.40	$ 6,138.40	$ 40,000	71,093.60	928,906.40·
July 1, 19x2	46,445.32	6,445.32	40,000	64,648.28	935,351.72
December 31, 19x2	46,767.59	6,767.59	40,000	57,880.69	942,119.31
July 1, 19x3	47,105.97	7,105.97	40,000	50,774.72	949,225.28
December 31, 19x3	47,461.26	7,461.26	40,000	43,313.46	956,686.54
July 1, 19x4	47,834.33	7,834.33	40,000	35,479.13	964,520.87
December 31, 19x4	48,226.04	8,226.04	40,000	27,253.09	972,746.91
July 1, 19x5	48,637.35	8,637.35	40,000	18,615.74	981,384.26
December 31, 19x5	49,069.21	9,069.21	40,000	9,546.53	990,453.47
July 1, 19x6	49,522.53*	9,546.53	40,000	0	1,000,000.00
		$77,232.00	$400,000		

*To determine interest expense, the total liability at the beginning of the period was multiplied by the semiannual market interest rate—in this case, 5 percent. Any rounding errors are included in the July 1, 19x6, debit to interest expense.

The primary accounting problem associated with the issuance of convertible debt is the valuation of the liability at the date of issuance. There are two treatments that have been proposed for this valuation issue: (1) a portion of the proceeds from the sale of the debt occurs because of the conversion privilege, and that amount should be credited to paid-in capital; or (2) convertible debt should be treated solely as debt with none of the proceeds allocated to paid-in capital, because of the inseparability of the debt and the conversion option and the consequent lack of an objective value for the conversion option.

The Accounting Principles Board took the latter view in the issuance of *APB Opinion No. 14*, "Accounting for Convertible Debt and Debt Issued With Stock Purchase Warrants." This pronouncement provided that no portion of the proceeds should be accounted for as attributable to the conversion feature. Any premium or discount on issuance should be amortized over the period from issuance until the maturity date, because it is impossible to predict when (and if) such bonds will be converted.

The entries to record the issuance of convertible bonds are similar to those discussed previously. At the date of the conversion, the carrying value of the bond (face value plus any premium or less any discount) is normally transferred to the stockholder equity accounts associated with the new shares of stock issued in the conversion. To illustrate, assume that a corporation had issued a $1,000, ten year convertible bond for $1,100 on January 1, 19X1. The bond is convertible into twenty shares of $10 par value common stock at the option of the holder. Further assume that the holder converts the bond into common stock on December 31, 19X5. At the time of the conversion, there is an unamortized premium of $50. The entry to record the conversion is as follows:

Bonds payable	1,000	
Bond premium	50	
Common stock		200
Additional paid-in capital		850

The value for common stock is equal to the number of shares (20) multiplied by the $10 par value.

Retirement of Bonds

Bonds may be retired by the issuing corporation at maturity or before the maturity date either by redeeming callable bonds or by purchasing bonds in the open market. If bonds are retired at maturity, any premium or discount has been completely amortized and the entry to record the retirement of the bonds is a debit to bonds payable and a credit to cash for an amount equal to the face or maturity value of the bonds.

Callable bonds may be redeemed at the option of the issuing corporation within a specified period and at a stated price referred to as the call price. The call price is usually an amount in excess of face value, with the excess referred to as a call premium. In the absence of a call provision, the issuing corporation may retire its bonds by purchasing them in the open market at the prevailing market price. Bonds may be retired early because the company has the cash to do so and wants to eliminate the periodic interest payments that must be made or bond prices may have fallen due to rising interest rates and the company can retire the bonds at a favorable price.

If bonds are purchased by the issuing corporation at a price less than their book or carrying value (i.e., face value less any unamortized discount or plus any unamortized premium), the corporation realizes a gain on the retirement of the bonds. Similarly, if the purchase price is greater than the carrying value, a loss is incurred on the retirement of the debt.[4]

To illustrate a redemption prior to maturity, assume that the Carpenter Co. has a $50,000 bond issue outstanding with $2,000 of unamortized premium. Further assume that the corporation has the option of calling the bonds at 105 (i.e., 105% of the face value) and that the company exercises its call provision. The entry to record the redemption of the bonds for $52,500 ($50,000 × 1.05) is as follows:

Bonds payable	50,000	
Bond premium	2,000	
Loss on redemption	500	
Cash		52,500

If the bonds do not include a call provision, the corporation may purchase the bonds in the open market. For example, assume that instead of calling the bonds Carpenter Co. in the above example purchases one-fifth of the $50,000 face value of $10,000 bonds outstanding for $9,800. The carrying value of the bonds purchased is $10,400 (face value of $10,000 plus one-fifth of the $2,000 unamortized premium), while the purchase price is $9,800. Therefore, the company realizes a $600 gain on the retirement. The entry to record the retirement of the bonds is as follows:

Bonds payable	10,000	
Bond premium	400	
Gain on retirement		600
Cash		9,800

Bond Sinking Fund

In order to offer additional security to the investors, a provision may be included in the bond indenture that requires the issuing corporation to set aside funds for repayment of the bond at maturity by periodic accumulations over the life of the issue. These funds may be accumulated by periodically depositing cash in a bond sinking fund. The cash deposited in the fund is usually invested in income-producing assets. Therefore, the total deposits made by the issuing corporation over the life of the bond issue are normally less than the total maturity value of the bonds. At maturity, the securities in the fund are sold and the proceeds are used to retire the bonds.

---

[4] According to *FASB Statement No. 4*, "Reporting Gains and Losses From Extinguishment of Debt" (1975), gains or losses from retirement of bonds should be aggregated and, if material in amount, classified in the income statement as an extraordinary item (net of the related income tax effect).

Cash and securities included in a sinking fund are not available for the retirement of current liabilities; they are normally shown as a single total and included under the caption of investments. Similarly, earnings on the sinking fund assets are shown as a separate item in the income statement.

Restriction on Dividends

Another means of increasing the security of the bondholder is a provision whereby dividend payments by the issuing company will be restricted during the life of the bond issue. The actual restriction on dividends may vary. For example, a restriction may limit the payment of dividends during a given year to the excess of net income over the sinking fund requirements for the period. There are various methods for disclosing this restriction in the financial statements. Such a restriction is usually shown by a footnote or parenthetically in the balance sheet. Alternatively, the restriction could be indicated by appropriating retained earnings each year. To illustrate, assume that the sinking fund requirement for the year is $20,000 and that net income is $35,000. If dividends are limited to the excess of net income over the sinking fund requirement, an appropriation of retained earnings, which would be reported in the equity section of the balance sheet, may be made with the following entry:

Retained earnings	20,000	
Appropriation for bonded debt		20,000

Balance Sheet Presentation

The presentation of long-term liabilities in the balance sheet should disclose all information relevant to the debt including the maturity dates, interest rates, and conversion privileges. In addition, if a liability is secured by specific assets, or restricts the payment of dividends, such information should also be disclosed in the financial statements. To illustrate, the long-term liabilities section of the balance sheet might appear as follows:

Long-term liabilities		
Twenty-five year, 18 percent mortgage bonds due on December 31, 19X9	$100,000	
Less: Unamortized discount	4,000	$ 96,000
Twenty year, 18 percent debenture bonds, convertible into fifteen shares of common stock, due on December 31, 19X4	$ 50,000	
Add: Unamortized premium	1,000	51,000
Total long-term liabilities		$147,000

Long-term Notes Payable

Long-term notes payable are a common component of a company's long-term debt. For example, all of Coca-Cola's long-term debt in 1996 consists of notes payable, almost all of PepsiCo's long-term debt in 1996 consists of notes payable, and about 84 percent of Wal-Mart's long-term debt in 1996 consists of notes payable. The interest rate on long-term notes may be fixed or may be variable (floating) depending on specified market rates.

Each payment on a long-term note is allocated between interest and principal. To illustrate, assume a company issues a five-year, 8% note payable for $1,000,000 with payments to be made quarterly. The payments due each quarter are computed as follows:

Payments × Present Value of an Annuity at 2% for 20 periods = $1,000,000
Payments × 16.3514 = $1,000,000
Payments = $1,000,000/16.3514
Payments = $61,156.84

The interest rate for each quarter is 2 percent. There are 20 quarters in five years.

A schedule for allocating the payments between interest and principal reduction can be constructed. The first year for such a schedule is presented below. Interest expense is always 2 percent of the beginning unpaid principal balance.

Period	Payment	Interest Expense	Reduction of Principal	Principal Balance of Note Payable
Issue Date				$1,000,000.00
1	$61,156.84	$20,000.00	$41,156.84	958,843.20
2	61,156.84	19,176.86	41,979.98	916,863.22
3	61,156.84	18,337.26	42,819.58	874,043.64
4	61,156.84	17,480.87	43,675.97	830,367.67

The journal entries to record the issuance of the note and the first payment are as follows:

Issue date	Cash	1,000,000.00	
	Notes payable		1,000,000.00
End of first	Interest expense	20,000.00	
quarter	Notes payable	41,156.84	
	Cash		61,156.84

LONG-RUN SOLVENCY

Solvency ratios measure a company's ability to meet its debts over a number of years. One ratio that is used to measure a company's solvency is *debt (short-term debt plus long-term debt) to total assets.* This ratio measures the percentage of total assets financed by external borrowing. Another ratio used is the *times interest earned ratio*, which indicates a company's ability to meet its interest payments. The ratio is computed by dividing income before income taxes and interest expense by interest expense.

The debt to total assets ratio and the times interest earned ratio for Coca-Cola and PepsiCo for 1996 are computed as follows (dollars are in millions):

$$\text{Debt to Total Assets Ratio} = \frac{\text{Short-term Debt} + \text{Long-term Debt}}{\text{Total Assets}}$$

$$\text{Coca-Cola:} \quad \frac{\$3,397 + \$1,116}{\$16,161} = 27.9\%$$

$$\text{PepsiCo:} \quad \frac{\$26 + \$8,439}{\$24,512} = 34.5\%$$

$$\text{Times Interest Earned Ratio} = \frac{\text{Income before Income Taxes and Interest Expense}}{\text{Interest Expense}}$$

$$\text{Coca-Cola:} \quad \frac{\$3,492 + \$1,104 + \$286}{\$286} = 17.1 \text{ times}$$

$$\text{PepsiCo:} \quad \frac{\$1,149 + \$898 + \$600}{\$600} = 4.41 \text{ times}$$

These ratios indicate that Coca-Cola is in a better solvency position than PepsiCo. The ratios should be compared with the industry average also.

Investments in Debt and Equity Securities

For financial reporting purposes, the investments of a firm in both debt or equity securities of other entities are classified as either short-term investments (also referred to as temporary investments) or long-term investments. The distinction between the short-term and long-term classifications is based both upon the intent of management in making the investment and the nature of the investment.

Short-term investments normally represent the conversion of otherwise idle cash balances (such as those that result from seasonal excesses of cash) to productive use (earning interest or dividends) on a short-term basis. To be classified as a short-term investment, a security must meet two basic criteria. First, the security must be readily salable and the volume of trading of the security should be such that the sale does not affect the market price materially. Second, there should be an intention on the part of the firm to sell the securities if the need for cash arises within the current operating cycle or one year, whichever is longer.

Mark-to-market refers to the practice of adjusting assets and liabilities to the value at which the item would be sold in an "arms length" transaction. Those who support market value argue that the use of historical cost fails to reflect changes in value in the period in which these changes occur. Those who support historical cost argue that market values cannot be easily verifiable and therefore are subject to manipulation by management.

Proponents of a change to using market values, whether higher or lower than historical cost, are concerned that the use of historical cost allows companies to sell securities that have risen in value so as to report gains on the income statement and to delay the recognition of losses on many of their investment securities (e.g., all investments in bonds). Opponents claim that the needed market values may be difficult and costly to obtain and that changing market values may introduce too much volatility in the income statement as unrealized gains and losses are recognized.

Richard Breeden, head of the Securities and Exchange Commission, campaigned vigorously for the use of market values rather than historical cost for investment securities. In testimony before the Committee on Banking, Housing and Urban Affairs of the United States Senate in 1990, Breeden argued that the use of historical cost for valuing investment securities may have been a significant contributor to the collapse of the savings and loan industry. Using market values may have alerted regulators to the liquidity problems far earlier and may have resulted in closings while the losses of these financial institutions were still manageable.

Alan Greenspan, Chairman of the Federal Reserve Board, does not agree. He believes that when banks have to mark their financial instruments to market, the result is increased volatility in reported earnings. To avoid this occurrence, banks invest more heavily in short-term bonds, whose market values are less susceptible to large swings than long-term bonds, and avoid municipal bonds, which are often relatively risky, not actively traded, and therefore more likely to have wide swings in value.

After Breeden's testimony, a meeting was held involving representatives of the SEC, the FASB, and the AICPA. The SEC wanted a resolution to this problem by the end of 1991.

Although the SEC has jurisdiction over accounting and financial reporting for those companies that issue securities through national and interstate securities exchanges, it has for the most part ceded this authority to the accounting profession. The FASB has been prodded and circumvented by the SEC in the past. Consequently, the FASB may have felt pressure to meet the expectations of the SEC in its proposal for instituting market value accounting for investment securities.

FASB Statement No. 115

In May 1993, the FASB issued _Statement No. 115_, "Accounting for Certain Investments in Debt and Equity Securities," that requires the use of fair (market) value for investments in debt and equity securities, except for investments in debt securities that are to be held until maturity. Under _FASB No. 115_, investments in debt and equity securities are classified into three categories and accounted for as follows:

1. Debt securities that the entity has the positive intent and ability to hold to maturity are classified as held-to-maturity and reported at amortized cost.

2. Debt and equity securities that are held for current resale are classified as trading securities and reported at fair value, with unrealized gains and losses included in earnings.

3. Debt and equity securities not classified as either held-to-maturity or trading securities are classified as available-for-sale and reported at fair value, with unrealized gains and losses excluded from earnings and reported as a separate component of shareholders' equity.

Held-to-Maturity

Investments in debt securities classified as held-to-maturity are accounted for in a similar manner to the present value concepts applied to bonds payable. The investment remains at historical cost, adjusted for the amortization of any premium or discount.

If a debt security is held-to-maturity, the face value will be realized. Any interim unrealized gains or losses will reverse. Amortized cost is relevant only if the security is actually held-to-maturity. At acquisition, the company must establish the intent and ability to hold the security to maturity, regardless of changes in such factors as market interest rates and general liquidity needs.

Trading Securities

Securities that are held for current resale are classified as trading securities. Such securities are held for short periods of time for the purpose of generating profits on short-term differences in price. Unrealized holding gains and losses for trading securities are included in income. Dividend and interest income are also included in income.

Assume that Elizabeth Company acquires 100 shares of Avon stock for $60 per share and classifies it as a trading security. If the end-of-year price is $58 per share, the company has a $200 unrealized loss (100 × $2). If the end-of-year price is $63 per share, the company has a $300 unrealized gain (100 × $3). The unrealized loss or gain is reported in the income statement. The journal entry for the case in which the market value increases by $300 is as follows:

Investment in stock—trading security	300	
Unrealized gain on trading securities		300

If the stock is sold during the following year for $67 per share, a realized gain of $400 is recognized. The journal entry to record the sale is as follows:

Cash	6,700	
Investment in stock—trading security		6,300
Gain on sale of trading securities		400

The stock was originally purchased for $6,000 and was subsequently sold for $6,700. The $700 gain was recognized in the two years as follows:

Unrealized gain (first year)	$ 300
Realized gain (second year)	400

Available-for-Sale Securities

Unrealized gains and losses for available-for-sale securities are not reported in the income statement. Instead, they are reported as a separate component of stockholders' equity. The reason for this approach is to reduce the volatility in reported earnings.

Using the same example as above, assume this time that the 100 shares of stock at $60 per share are classified as available for sale. If the market value increases by $300 by the end of the year, the credit is to a separate stockholders' equity account rather than to income. If the stock is sold during the following year for $67 per share, a realized gain of $700 is recognized. The journal entry to record the increase in the market value of the stock is as follows:

Investment in stock—available-for-sale	300	
Unrealized gain on		
available-for-sale securities*		300
*Reported as a separate		
stockholders' equity account		

The journal entry to record the sale is as follows:

Cash	6,700	
Unrealized gain on available-for-sale		
securities	300	
Investment in stock—available-for-sale		6,300
Gain on sale of available-for-sale		
securities		700

The stockholders' equity account, unrealized gain on available-for-sale securities, is reduced by $300, and the $700 realized gain is reported in the income statement.

Available-for-sale securities are classified as current or noncurrent according to the usual criteria. The accounting for these equity securities is not affected by the classification; however, the accounting for these debt securities is affected by the classification (any premium or discount must be amortized if the securities are classified as noncurrent).

INVESTMENTS IN STOCK

Investments in stock are the temporary or long-term conversion of cash into productive use by the purchase of securities. Such investments are found among the assets of almost all businesses. In general, investments are classified as either temporary or long-term depending on the nature of the security and the intention of the investor firm.

It should be noted that when stock is purchased as an investment, the seller of the stock receives the money paid. Most investment transactions in stock are between two individual investors, one who already owns the stock and then sells it to the new investor who purchases it. The corporation whose stock is traded in the transaction becomes involved directly only if the shares exchanged are a part of a new issue of securities it sold to raise funds.

CONTROL OVER INVESTMENTS

The effective control over marketable securities includes the physical safeguarding of the certificates. This usually means that the securities should be kept in a safe if they are retained by the firm, and access to the certificates controlled. In many instances, the firm leaves its investments in the custody of its broker. The authority to purchase and sell is usually vested in the board of directors of the firm or in a specifically designated investments committee. In either case, requiring written authorization in order to either acquire or dispose of investments is another important control feature. Finally, the accounting records themselves are important in establishing control over investments. The periodic reconciliation of the accounting records to the securities on hand or in the custody of the broker and the reconciliation of the recorded income to the income that should have been earned (as determined by calculation and reference to sources such as *Standard & Poor's Dividend Record*) help to provide effective control over investments.

LONG-TERM INVESTMENTS IN STOCK

Investments in stocks that are not held as temporary investments are classified as long-term assets. While companies make investments in the securities of other corporations (investee companies) for a variety of reasons, *the primary purpose is normally to increase the income of the investor company (the company making the investment).* This effect on income may be either direct, through the income generated by the investments (in the form of dividends or interest) and appreciation in the market value of the securities, or indirect, by creating positive operational relationships with other businesses. The indirect effect on the income of the investor company results from obtaining a degree of influence or control over the management of another company, such as a major supplier, a customer, or a competitor. Establishing this type of relationship through the ownership of common stock often improves the operational efficiency or financial strength of the investor company. Such investments are recorded at their cost as of the date of acquisition. This cost includes the purchase price of the shares plus all brokerage fees, transfer costs, and excise taxes paid by the purchaser.

The method of accounting for long-term investments in stock subsequent to acquisition may be determined by *FASB Statement No. 115* and management intent on the classification of the stock investment, as previously discussed. However, the percentage of the investee corporation's outstanding common stock held by the investor has an influence on the appropriate accounting standards. When the investor holds 20 percent to 50 percent or more of the common stock of another corporation and has significant influence or control over the operating policies of the investee, *FASB Statement No. 115* accounting does not apply.

When the investor company owns an amount of voting stock that allows significant influence over the management of the investee, the equity method is used to reflect the changes in the underlying net assets of the investee company. Such influence usually results when the investor holds 20 percent to 50 percent of the investee's outstanding common stock.

When a company acquires more than 50 percent of the common stock of a corporation (referred to as a controlling interest), consolidated statements that reflect the investor and investee as a single economic entity are prepared. If financial statements for the parent company only are prepared, the investment must be accounted for in the investor corporation's books. Either the "cost method" or the "equity method" may be used for this purpose.

The cost method is based on the fact that the two corporations are separate legal entities. Therefore, the carrying value of the investment included in the accounts of the investor remains at the original cost. Any changes that may have occurred in the underlying net assets of the investee corporation as a result of its operations are ignored under this method. The equity method, on the other hand, is intended to reflect the economic relationship that exists between the two companies. This method recognizes that an investment in stock that allows the investor company to exercise significant control or influence over the operations of the investee company should be accounted for in such a way that changes in the underlying net assets of the investee company are reflected in the accounts of the investor company. When a parent and its majority-owned subsidiary are consolidated (as required by *FASB Statement No. 94*), the investment account on the parent's books, maintained by either the cost or equity method, must be eliminated. Accordingly, the accounting method used in the bookkeeping process is not reflected in the consolidated financial statements.

While an investment of less than 50 percent of the voting stock does not represent legal control, it is possible for such an investment to provide "significant influence." Ability to exercise such influence may be evidenced by such factors as representation on the board of directors, participation in policy-making processes, material intercompany transactions, interchange of managerial personnel, and technological dependency. Another important consideration in the determination of significant influence is the percentage ownership felt by the investor relative to the ownership percentage of any other investors with substantial ownership interest.

The choice between the cost and equity methods was, for all practical purposes, optional prior to the issuance of *Opinion No. 18* of the Accounting Principles Board in 1971. However, the board stated in this opinion that the equity method should be used if the investment in stock enables the investor company to exercise significant influence over the operating and financial policies of an investee. The board assumed that, in the absence of evidence to the contrary, ownership of 20 percent or more of the voting stock of an investee represented evidence of the ability of the investor company to exercise significant influence over the activities of the investee firm.

Market Value Method. Under the market value method previously described, the investment account is carried at the market value of the investment. Any increases or decreases in the net assets of the investee company resulting from earnings or losses do not affect the investor company's investment account. Dividends received by the investor company are recorded as dividend income.

Equity Method. Under the equity method, the investment is initially recorded at its original cost. After acquisition, the investment account is adjusted for any increases or decreases that have occurred in the investee company's net assets since the stock was acquired. Net income of the investee results in an increase in its net assets. Therefore, the investor company increases the carrying value of its investment and recognizes investment income to the extent of its share (determined by the percentage of the investee's stock owned by the investor company) of the net income of the investee. For example, assume that an investor firm owns 20 percent of the outstanding voting stock of an investee. If the investee reports earnings of $50,000, the investor increases the carrying value of its investment by $10,000 and simultaneously recognizes investment income of $10,000. Similarly, a net loss incurred by the investee company results in a reduction of the investment account and the recognition of a loss on investments by the investor firm. Since dividends also reduce the net assets of the investee, any dividend distributions made to the investor are recorded by a decrease in the investment account balance. The effect of the equity method is to value the investment at the original cost plus the investor's share of the undistributed retained earnings (net income less dividends) of the investee company since the acquisition of the stock.

To illustrate the difference between the market value and the equity methods, assume that Ann Company purchases 1,000 of the 5,000 outstanding shares of Bud Company stock on January 1, 19X1, at a cost of $10 per share. During 19X1, Bud Company reports net income of $20,000 and pays dividends of $10,000, and during 19X2 Bud Company reports a net loss of $5,000 and pays no dividends. The market value of the stock, classified as available for sale if the market value method is used, is $10.50 at the end of 19X1 and $10.10 at the end of 19X2. The journal entries of Ann Company under both the market value and the equity methods are shown in Illustration 4.

These entries have the following effect on the financial statements of Ann Company as of the end of 19X2.

	Market Value Method	Equity Method
Investment in Bud Company—		
December 31, 19X2	$10,100	$11,000
Income statement:		
19X1	2,000	4,000
19X2	0	(1,000)

Under the market value method, Ann Company reports its investment in Bud Company at December 31, 19X2, at its market value on that date of $10,100. Under the equity method, the investment is carried at $11,000. The $1,000 increase in the investment account under the equity method reflects Ann Company's share (20%) of the $5,000 increase in the net assets of Bud Company since the time the Bud Company stock was acquired by Ann.

Under the market value method, the investor recognizes income only to the extent of assets received from the investee (i.e., dividends). The equity method, on the other hand, recognizes income to the extent of the investor's share of the net income of the investee company, whether or not dividends are received. No unrealized gain or loss for changes in market value is recognized under the equity method.

11-24

Illustration 4
Market Value and Equity Methods

Event	Market Value Method	Equity Method
January 1, 19X1 Acquisition of 1,000 shares of the common stock of Bud Company	Investment in Bud Company .... 10,000 Cash 10,000	Investment in Bud Company .... 10,000 Cash 10,000
December 31, 19X1 Net income of $20,000 reported by Bud Company	**No Entry**	Investment in Bud Company .... 4,000 Investment income .... 4,000 To record Ann Company's $4,000 share (20% × $20,000) of Bud Company's net income
Ann Company received dividends of $2,000 (20% of $10,000 dividend paid by Bud Company)	Cash .... 2,000 Dividend income 2,000	Cash .... 2,000 Investment in Bud Company 2,000
Market value $10.50 per share	Investment in Bud Company .... 500 Unrealized gain on available-for-sale securities 500	**No Entry**
December 31, 19X2 Net loss of $5,000 reported by Bud Company	**No Entry**	Investment loss .... 1,000 Investment in Bud Company .... 1,000 To record Ann Company's $1,000 share (20% × $5,000) of Bud Company's $5,000 net loss
Market value $10.10 per share	Unrealized gain on available-for-sale securities .... 400 Investment in Bud Company 400	**No Entry**

Consolidated Financial Statements

In many instances, investments in stock are made to secure ownership of a controlling interest in the voting stock of another company. A firm owning a majority of the voting stock of another company (more than 50% of the outstanding voting stock) is referred to as a *parent company*, and the company whose stock is owned is called the *subsidiary company*. A parent company and its related subsidiary companies are usually referred to as *affiliated companies*. Since a parent and its subsidiary(ies) are separate legal entities, separate financial statements are prepared for the stockholders and creditors of each subsidiary company. However, *FASB Statement No. 94* requires that the financial statements of a parent company, which are to be submitted to its shareholders, be consolidated with all its subsidiary companies. The only exceptions to this rule are where *ownership of a subsidiary is temporary or control does not rest with the parent company.*

Ownership of a subsidiary is considered temporary, for example, if an investor has a trading investment in the stock of a company and usually owns 40-45 percent of the voting stock at any given balance sheet date. By chance, at a particular balance sheet date, the investor owns 51 percent of the stock for a temporary period (say, 2 weeks) and then its investment drops back to 40 percent. In this unusual case, consolidation is not appropriate.

An example of a situation in which control of a subsidiary does not rest with the parent is when the subsidiary is in bankruptcy and control of its assets and operations are in the hands of the bankruptcy court.[5]

Consolidated statements provide the stockholders and creditors of the parent company with an overall view of the combined financial position and operating activities of the parent company and its subsidiaries. There are a variety of economic, legal, and tax advantages that encourage large organizations to operate through a group of affiliated corporations, rather than a single legal entity. From a legal standpoint, a subsidiary company is a separate entity. Accordingly, the subsidiary maintains its own accounting records and prepares separate financial statements. However, since the parent owns a majority of the voting stock of its subsidiary, the parent and subsidiary companies are a business entity under common control. Therefore, individual financial statements of the parent and subsidiary do not provide a comprehensive view of the financial position of the affiliated companies as a single economic unit. Consolidated financial statements, which ignore the legal distinction between the parent and its subsidiary, serve this purpose by reflecting the financial position and results of operations of the affiliated companies as a single economic entity. Consolidated financial statements are discussed in detail in the Appendix to this chapter.

Summary

To raise additional funds for long-term purposes, a firm may borrow by issuing bonds. Bonds require the firm to pay a definite amount (the face value) at a specified date (the maturity date) and may be traded by the investors until that date. In addition, the firm agrees to make periodic interest payments at a stated rate throughout the life of the liability. Bonds may be secured either by specific assets or, in the case of debenture bonds, by only the general credit rating of the issuing corporation.

The selling price received by the issuing corporation may vary from face value. If the selling price of the bond is less than the face value, the bond is selling at a discount; if the selling price is greater than face value, the bond is selling at a premium. This discount or premium is amortized over the life of the bond and results in either an increase or a decrease in the interest expense incurred on the bond issue.

Bonds may be retired prior to maturity, either by redeeming callable bonds or by purchasing bonds on the open market. In either case, it may be necessary for the firm to recognize either a gain or loss on the early retirement of the debt, depending on the purchase price. A firm may be required to provide investors with a degree of security, either by periodically setting aside funds in a sinking fund or by making an appropriation of retained earnings.

Companies often make temporary investments in marketable securities to obtain productive use of seasonal excesses of cash. Temporary investments are considered current assets and include both stocks and bonds that

---

[5] FAS No. 94, para. 13.

are readily salable. Because of this liquidity, careful control should be exercised over the investment documents. Market (fair) value is used in accounting for debt and equity securities, except for investments in debt securities that are to be held until maturity.

If the investor company may exercise significant influence over the investee company (e.g., as evidenced by an ownership of 20 percent to 50 percent of its voting stock) subsequent increases and decreases in the net assets of the investee must be reflected in the carrying value of the investment on the investor's books. This is accomplished by the use of the equity method.

If two firms are associated in such a manner that one owns a controlling interest in the other, the firms are referred to as affiliated companies. Since these firms remain separate legal entities, separate financial statements are prepared for each company. However, if the subsidiary company is under the continuing control of the parent company, consolidated financial statements must be prepared.

Key Definitions

Amortization of premium or discount—the process of allocating a portion of the discount or premium on bonds payable to interest expense.

Bond—an issuance of debt used as a means of borrowing money for long-term purposes.

Bond discount—the amount by which the face value of a bond payable exceeds the issue price. A discount occurs when the coupon rate on the bonds is less than the market interest rate at the time the bonds are issued.

Bond premium—the amount by which the issue price of a bond payable exceeds the face value. A premium occurs when the coupon rate of interest on a bond is higher than the market interest rate at the time of issuance.

Bond sinking fund—accumulated by the issuing corporation specifically for the payment of bonds at maturity. A sinking fund may be created voluntarily or required by provisions of the bond issue.

Callable bonds—may be purchased at the option of the issuing corporation within a specified period at a specified price

Consolidated statements—consolidated financial statements present the combined assets. equities, and results of operations of affiliated corporations.

Convertible bonds—may be exchanged for a specified amount of common stock at the option of the bondholder.

Coupon bonds—interest coupons attached that call for the payment of a specified amount of interest on the interest dates.

Coupon rate—the interest rate specified on the bond. Periodic interest payments equal the coupon interest rate multiplied by the face amount of the bond.

Debenture bonds—not secured by any specific assets of the corporation. Their security is dependent upon the general credit standing of the issuing corporation.

Equity method—used for an investment in the stock of another company in which the investment account is adjusted for changes in the net assets of the investee, and income is recognized by the investor company as the investee earns profits or incurs losses.

Long-term investment in stock—this involves the acquisition of stock of other corporations as long-term, income-producing investments. Such purchases are often made for the purpose of obtaining a controlling interest in a company or for some other continuing business advantage.

Market value method—used for an investment in the stock of another company in which the investment account is carried at market value and income is recognized when dividends are received.

Maturity value—constitutes the amount that the holder of a note is entitled to receive at the due date. This amount includes the principal plus any accrued interest.

Parent company—a firm owning a majority of the voting stock of another company.

Registered bonds—have the name of the owner registered with the issuing corporation. Periodic interest payments are mailed directly to the registered owner.

Retirement of bonds—the process of redeeming bonds or purchasing bonds in the open market.

Secured bond—secured by prior claim against specific assets of the business in the event that the issuing corporation is unable to make the required interest or principal payments .

Serial bonds—bonds that mature on several different dates.

Subsidiary company—a firm that has a majority of its voting stock owned by a parent company.

Temporary investments—a security that is readily salable, and the volume of trading of the security should be such that the sale does not materially affect the market price. In addition, there should be an intention on the part of the investor firm to sell the security in the short run as the need for cash arises.

Term bonds—a bond issue that matures on a single date.

QUESTIONS

1. Define each of the following terms related to the issue of bonds: (a) debenture, (b) secured, (c) callable, (d) convertible, (e) serial bonds.

2. How are interest payments made to the holders of (a) coupon bonds, and (b) registered bonds?

3. How can bonds be sold when the market interest rate for comparable bonds is higher than the stated contract rate on the bond certificate?

4. How does a discount on the issuance of bonds affect the total cost of borrowing to the issuing corporation?

5. What is the effect of a premium on the interest expense of the company issuing bonds? Explain.

6. What is the effect of a discount on the interest expense of the company issuing bonds? Explain.

7. Determine the amount that $1,000 will accumulate to in three years at an 8 percent annual interest rate.

8. Determine the present value of $1,000 due in five years at each of the following interest rates:

    a.   6 percent
    b.   8 percent
    c.   10 percent

9. An investor wishes to have $5,000 available at the end of five years. State the amount of money that must be invested at the present time if the interest rate is:

    a.   6 percent
    b.   8 percent
    c.   12 percent

10. Determine the present value of an ordinary annuity for a period of five years with annual payments of $2,000, assuming that the interest rate is:

    a.   7 percent
    b.   10 percent
    c.   12 percent

11. What is the maximum amount you would be willing to pay at the present time in order to receive 10 annual payments of $1,000 beginning one year from now? The current interest rate is 10 percent.

12. Hays Company leases a building at an annual rental of $2,000 paid at the end of each year. The company has been given the alternative of paying the remaining 10 years of the lease in advance on January 1, 19X0. Assuming an interest rate of 8 percent, what is the maximum amount that should be paid now for the advance rent?

13. Determine the selling price of the bonds in each of the following situations (assume that the bonds are dated and sold on the same date):

    a.   A 10-year, $1,000 face value bond with annual interest of 9 percent (payable annually) sold to yield 8 percent effective interest.
    b.   A 10-year, $1,000 face value bond with annual interest of 9 percent (payable annually) sold to yield 10 percent effective interest.
    c.   A 10 year, $1,000 face value bond with annual interest of 9 percent (payable annually) sold to yield 9 percent effective interest.

14. Give the journal entries required for the amortization of (a) Discount on Bonds Payable and (b) Premium on Bonds Payable.

15. How should Discount on Bonds Payable and Premium on Bonds Payable be classified and presented on the balance sheet?

16. Differentiate between long-term (permanent) and short-term (temporary) investments in stocks.

17. Explain the essential characteristics of the market value method.

18. Explain the essential characteristics of the equity method.

19. Under what circumstances would each of the following methods of accounting for long-term investment in stocks be used: (a) market value method? (b) equity method?

20. Define: (a) parent company, (b) subsidiary company, and (c) affiliated companies.

21. Describe the essential condition for the preparation of consolidated financial statements.

EXERCISES

22. Stengel Company has authorization to issue $200,000 of 10-year, 7 percent bonds on January 1, 19X1, with semiannual interest payments on June 30 and December 31. Stengel Company issues $100,000 of the bonds on January I at face value. Another $100,000 of bonds are issued on August 1, 19X1, at face value plus accrued interest. Assume Stengel Company's accounting period ends March 31.

Required:

Give the firm's journal entries with respect to the bonds for 19X1.

23. Nancy Company issued $10,000 of bonds payable on January 1, 19X1 with an 8 percent coupon interest rate, payable annually on December 31. The bonds mature in 5 years and were sold at a 10 percent effective interest rate.

   a. Determine the selling price of the bonds.
   b. Prepare a schedule showing the amount of discount to be amortized each year for the life of the bonds, assuming the interest method of amortization.
   c. Give the journal entry to record the interest payment on December 31, 19X1.

24. Joyce Company issued $10,000 of bonds payable on January 1, 19X1, with an 8 percent coupon interest rate payable annually on December 31. The bonds mature in five years and were sold at a 7 percent effective interest rate.

Required:

   1. Determine the selling price of the bonds.
   2. Prepare a schedule showing the premium to be amortized each year for the life of the bonds, assuming the interest method of amortization.
   3. Give the journal entry to record the interest payment on December 31, 19X1.

25. Terry Tractors, Inc., has outstanding a $100,000, 10-year bond issue which was sold on January 1, 19X0, at a price of $110,000. The following liability, shown below, appeared on the balance sheet on December 31, 19X4.

Bonds payable	$100,000	
Premium	5,000	$105,000

Make the entry necessary to record the retirement of the bonds in each of the following two situations:

a. The firm calls the bonds at 106 on January 1, 19X5.
b. Terry Tractors, Inc., purchases half of the outstanding bonds in the open market for $51,000 on January 1, 19X5.

Problems

26. Boyer, Inc., issued 100, $1,000, 20-year convertible bonds at a price of $1,020 each on January 1, 19X1. Each of the bonds is convertible into 20 shares of $20 par value common stock. On December 31, 19X7, 50 of these bonds were converted into common stock. Make the journal entry necessary to record the conversion on the books of Boyer, Inc.

27. The transactions of Cammie Company relating to marketable securities during 19X1 are listed below.

Jan.	10	Purchased 500 shares of Smith Corporation common stock at a price of $42 per share.
Feb.	5	Purchased 100 shares of Dade Corporation common stock at a price of $75 per share.
Mar.	1	Received a cash dividend of $2 per share on Smith Corporation common stock.
Apr.	16	Purchased 200 shares of Consolidated Company common stock at $150 per share.
June	1	Received a cash dividend of $3 per share on Dade Corporation common stock.
Aug.	20	Sold 70 shares of Dade Corporation stock at $80 per share.
Sept.	1	Received a $2 per share dividend on Consolidated Company common stock.

Required:

1. Prepare the journal entries necessary to record the above transactions.
2. Assuming the fair values of the stocks are as follows, prepare the journal entries necessary to record the changes in market value according to *FASB Statement No. 115* assuming the investments are classified as: (a) trading securities, or (b) available for sale securities:

Smith	$ 45
Dade	82
Consolidated	160

3. Assuming the rest of the shares are sold for the following prices in 19X2, prepare the journal entries necessary to record the sales assuming the investments are classified as: (a) trading securities, or (b) available for sale securities:

Smith	$ 47
Dade	83
Consolidated	156

28. On January 1, 19X1, Lang Company acquired 25 percent of the outstanding shares of stock of Brenner Company at a cost of $250,000. On that date, Brenner Company had common stock of $750,000 and retained earnings of $250,000. Brenner Company reported net income of $100,000 during 19X1 and paid a cash dividend of $20,000. The market value of the stock at the end of 19x1 was $261,000. Make the necessary journal entries on Lang's books during 19X1 using:

a. the market value method, assuming the investment is classified as available for sale securities.
b. the equity method.

29. Dean Co. issued $100,000 of 6 percent, 20-year debenture bonds on January 1, 19X1. Interest is payable semiannually on June 30 and December 31. The following information is given on the bonds at December 31, 19X1:

Carrying value of bonds	$103,800
Interest expense for the year	5,800

    a. Were the bonds issued at a premium or discount?
    b. What was the amount of premium or discount on the issuance of the bonds?
    c. How much of the discount or premium was amortized during the year?

30. On the first day of its fiscal year, Stevens Company sold $2,000,000 of ten-year, 9 percent bonds at an effective interest rate of 8 percent.

    a. Make the journal entry to record

        1. the sale of bonds
        2. the first semiannual interest payment (by effective interest amortization method)
        3. the second semiannual interest payment

    b. At the end of the first year, how will the bonds be presented in the financial statements?

31. The Weston Corporation is experiencing financial difficulty. The company is faced with an anticipated net loss for the 19X6 accounting period. The president, Carl Young, is very concerned that dissatisfied stockholders will elect a different set of directors who would in turn seek changes in corporate management. He opened his strategy meeting with corporate officers by telling them that they had a choice to make. They could look for ways to report a profit or they could look for new jobs. After a few moments of tense silence, the company's treasurer, Linda Thomas, said that she had an idea. She noted that the company had made a sizeable investment in bonds back when interest rates were high. As interest rates had fallen, the value of the bonds had risen. She suggested that the company sell the bonds which would trigger the recognition of a gain significant enough to turn the anticipated loss into a respectable picture of profitability. She provided the following data regarding the bonds.

    The company had purchased bonds with a face value of fifty million dollars at a price of 94. The bonds had a twenty year term from the date of purchase. They had been held for five years. The current market price of the bonds is 102. Ms. Thomas indicated that proceeds from the sale of the bonds would have to be reinvested at today's lower rates of return.

Required.

    a. Determine the amount of gain that Weston will recognize if management sells the bond investment. Provide the entry to record the retirement of the bond investment.
    b. How would the gain be reported in the income statement? Would stockholders be likely to believe that similar gains will recur in the future?
    c. How would the sale affect the future earnings of the company?

32. For each of the transactions listed, indicate the effect(s), if any, on the company's year-end: (1) Balance Sheet, (2) Income Statement, and (3) Statement of Cash Flows. Your answers should be as complete and specific as possible.

    a. Sold a bond. The selling price was equal to maturity value.
    b. Paid interest on the bond sold (in "a" above).
    c. Sold a bond. The selling price was less than maturity value.
    d. Paid interest on the bond sold (in "c" above).
    e. Sold a bond. The selling price exceed maturity value.
    f. Paid interest on the bond sold (in "e" above).

33. For each of the transactions listed, indicate the effect(s), if any, on the company's year-end: (1) Balance Sheet, (2) Income Statement, and (3) Statement of Cash Flows. Your answers should be as complete and specific as possible.

    a. Purchased debt securities for cash with the intent of holding them to maturity. The purchase price was less than maturity value.
    b. Received annual interest payment on securities purchased (in "a" above).

34. For each of the transactions listed, indicate the effect(s), if any, on the company's year-end: (1) Balance Sheet, (2) Income Statement, and (3) Statement of Cash Flows. Your answers should be as complete and specific as possible.

    a. Purchased equity securities for cash with the intent to hold them for current resale.
    b. At year-end, the market value of the securities exceeded their cost.
    c. At year-end, the market value of the securities were less than their cost.

35. For each of the transactions listed, indicate the effect(s), if any, on the company's year-end: (1) Balance Sheet, (2) Income Statement, and (3) Statement of Cash Flows. Your answers should be as complete and specific as possible.

    a. Purchased debt securities not classified as either held-to-maturity or trading securities for cash.
    b. At year-end, the market value of the securities exceeded their cost.
    c. At year-end, the market value of the securities were less than their cost.

36. For each of the transactions listed, indicate the effect(s), if any, on the company's year-end: (1) Balance Sheet, (2) Income Statement, and (3) Statement of Cash Flows. Your answers should be as complete and specific as possible.

    a. Acquired 20 percent of the stock of A company. This investment will be accounted for using the market value method.
    b. A company reports net income for the year.
    c. At year-end, the market value of A company stock is in excess of the purchase price.
    d. A company pays a dividend.
    e. A company reports a net loss for the year.
    f. At year-end, the market value of A company stock is less than the original purchase price.

37. For each of the transactions listed, indicate the effect(s), if any, on the company's year-end: (1) Balance Sheet, (2) Income Statement, and (3) Statement of Cash Flows. Your answers should be as complete and specific as possible.

    a. Acquired 20 percent of the stock of A company. This investment will be accounted for using the equity method.
    b. A company reports net income for the year.
    c. At year-end, the equity value of A company stock is in excess of the purchase price.
    d. A company pays a dividend.
    e. A company reports a net loss for the year.
    f. At year-end, the equity value of A company stock is less than the original purchase price.

Refer to the Annual Report in Chapter 1 of the text.

38. Does the company have any long-term bond (or long-term debt) outstanding?

39. How much is interest expense in the current year?

40. In the last three years, has more money been received from issuing long-term debt or been paid to retire long-term debt?

41. What are the total liabilities due in more than one year at the end of the most recent year?

42. Are current liabilities greater than long-term liabilities at the end of the most recent year?

43. Is total debt greater or less than stockholders' equity?

FRAUD CASE: Fraud Examination Methodologies

One of the most often used fraud examination methods, other than analytical review, is the net worth method. Net worth analysis is used when unusual displays of wealth or other events, such as an extravagant lifestyle, bring into question unexplained significant increases in an employee's or member of management's financial resources.

Net worth change can be estimated using either an "asset approach" or an "expenditures approach." The net worth method is used by the Internal Revenue Service in its investigations of potential income tax evasion and is sanctioned by the courts.

The "asset approach" should be used when the suspected fraudster has allegedly used illegal funds to accumulate assets—such as automobiles, investments, cash accounts, expensive homes, etc. The "expenditures approach" is used when the fraudster has allegedly spent large sums of illegal funds on goods and services—such as entertainment, travel, clothing, and other items that would not cause an increase in measurable net worth.

The asset approach utilizes the accounting equation as its starting point.

The formula is:

ASSETS — LIABILITIES = NET WORTH [EQUITY]

NET WORTH — PRIOR YEAR'S NET WORTH = NET WORTH INCREASE

NET WORTH INCREASE + LIVING EXPENSES = ANNUAL INCOME

ANNUAL INCOME = MAXIMUM EXPENDITURES

MAXIMUM EXPENDITURES — FUNDS FROM KNOWN SOURCES [BORROWING] = FUNDS FROM UNKNOWN SOURCES [ILLEGAL FUNDS]

The Expenditures Method requires establishing the target's known expenditures for the relevant year and estimating the unknown expenditures. Many fraudsters spend the fruits of their crime; they do not hoard their money. Expenditures include the use of funds for such purposes as travel and entertainment, payments of home and auto loans, purchase of major assets, bank deposits—any outflow of funds for any purpose is an expenditure. The problem is to identify all legal expenditures and the remaining expenditures must be from illegal funds, if they exceed current spendable income.

The formula is:

EXPENDITURES [FUNDS APPLIED]

— KNOWN SOURCES OF FUNDS

= FUNDS FROM UNKNOWN [ILLEGAL] SOURCES

If fraud exists, you may assume, as in most cases, the money taken was not reported for federal income tax purposes as required by law. The IRS is likely to take action to recover back taxes, interest, fines, and penalties on the money fraudulently acquired and the IRS takes priority over all other parties in recovery. In other words, if the fraudster hasn't spent all the funds, after the IRS is finished there may be little or nothing left for the lawyers and the damaged parties, the company and its owners.

DISCUSSION QUESTIONS:

1. Explain the difference between the "asset method" and "expenditures method" and usefulness in fraud detection.

2. Using the following information, determine the estimated extent of fraud [funds from unknown sources]:

LSH CONTRACTING, 19xx

	$20,000,000	Assets
	15,000,000	Liabilities
		Prior year's net
worth	8,000,000	
		Living expenses
[estimated]	287,000	
		Funds from
known sources	1,000,000	[bank loan]

3. Discuss what action or actions may be taken against LSH for the fraud (recover the funds, criminal punishment etc.), if in fact a fraud has been committed?

FRAUD CASE: NET WORTH ESTIMATION— Expenditures Approach

As indicated in a previous case, an often used fraud examination method is the net worth analysis using the expenditures approach. The expenditures approach is used when the suspected fraudster has allegedly spent large sums of illegal funds on goods and services, such as entertainment, travel, clothing, and other items that would not cause an increase in measurable net worth (assets).

The expenditures method requires establishing the target's actual and estimated expenditures for the relevant year(s) and comparing those expenditures with legal earnings for the year(s) in question. If expenditures greatly exceed legal earnings plus other sources of income, fraud is indicated.

The expenditures method uses the formula:

EXPENDITURES [FUNDS APPLIED]
— ALL KNOWN SOURCES OF FUNDS
= FUNDS FROM UNKNOWN [ILLEGAL] SOURCES

Application of the expenditures method requires the CFE to identify (or estimate) all funds applied (or spent) by the target during a given period. This includes such items as the purchase of residence, payment of mortgage(s), increases in investments, credit card purchases, increase in cash balances, purchases of automobiles, living expenses, and medical and dental costs.

All sources of funds provided by the target during a given period also must be identified (or estimated). Typical sources of funds include salary, bonus, gifts, borrowings, interest and investment income, cash, and gambling winnings less losses.

Most of the information needed is readily available from business and banking records.

DISCUSSION QUESTIONS:

1. Use the following information, obtained from business and banking records and estimated about Mr. Yeary, an employee of LSH Corporation, and the formula given for the expenditures method, to establish whether or not Mr. Yeary has been spending funds from unknown (or illegal) sources:

Mr. Yeary's funds applied during the year:

Increase in cash	$ 60,000
Purchase of residence (down payment)	80,000
Living expenses(actual and estimated)	72,000
Entertainment expenses	40,000
Total	$252,000

Mr. Yeary's Sources of funds during the year:

Salary	$102,000
Sale of old resident-net of tax	23,000
Interest income	6,000
Borrowing	40,000
Cash in bank	6,320
Total	$177,320

2. Do you think a case can be made for fraud? If so, how?

Appendix
Consolidated Financial Statements

Consolidated Balance Sheet at Date of Acquisition

In preparing a consolidated balance sheet, the accounts included in the individual parent and subsidiary company records are combined. In the process of this combination, however, certain adjustments must be made to avoid duplication or double-counting in determining the balances to be used. For example, the investment account of the parent company reflects its equity in the net assets of the subsidiary. Including both the parent company's investment account and the net assets of the subsidiary in a consolidated statement results in double-counting the net assets of the subsidiary. Therefore, the parent's investment account is not included in the consolidated statements. Since the stockholder's equity of the subsidiary is represented by the investment account, it is also excluded from the consolidated financial statement. The investment of the parent company is referred to as the reciprocal of the stockholders' equity of the subsidiary. Therefore, these accounts and any other reciprocal accounts that may exist as a result of transactions between the parent and its subsidiaries must be eliminated in combining the accounts of the parent and subsidiary companies.

Separate financial records are not maintained for the consolidated entity. The amounts reported in consolidated financial statements are determined using a worksheet and combining the amounts of like items from the financial statements of the affiliated companies. Entries included on the consolidation worksheet are made for the sole purpose of preparing consolidated financial statements. Consequently, consolidating adjustments and eliminations are not posted to the books of either the parent or its subsidiary.

Preparation of consolidated balance sheets under varying circumstances is illustrated by the following examples. First, let us consider the process of consolidating two balance sheets at the time a parent company initially acquires the stock of a subsidiary company.

Complete Ownership Acquired at Book Value

Assume that the parent company, P, acquires 100 percent of the common stock of a subsidiary company, S, at a price of $20,000 on December 31, 19X1. The money was paid directly to the stockholders of S Company. Before the acquisition, S Company had several stockholders. After the acquisition, S Company has only one stockholder—P Company. Separate balance sheets of P Company and S Company immediately following the acquisition are presented in Illustration 5.

P Company pays an amount equal to the stockholders' equity (common stock and retained earnings) of the subsidiary for 100 percent ownership of S. This indicates that the acquisition is made at the book value of the subsidiary's net assets (i.e., its assets less liabilities). Since no transactions have occurred between the companies, the only adjustment required is to eliminate the investment account of the parent against the stockholders' equity accounts of the subsidiary, as shown in Illustration 6.

As previously indicated, the elimination entry is made on a worksheet that is used in order to facilitate the preparation of the consolidated balance sheet. No entries are made in the accounting records of either the parent or the subsidiary.

Illustration 5
P Company and S Company
Balance Sheets
At December 31, 19X1

	P Company	S Company
Cash	$ 10,000	$ 5,000
Accounts receivable	10,000	5,000
Fixed assets	60,000	20,000
Investment in S Company	20,000	0
Total assets	$100,000	$30,000
Accounts payable	$ 10,000	$10,000
Common stock	60,000	15,000
Retained earnings	30,000	5,000
Total liabilities and equities	$100,000	$30,000

Illustration 6
P Company and S Company
Consolidated Worksheet
At December 31, 19X1

	P Company	S Company	Eliminations Dr.	Eliminations Cr.	Consolidation
Cash	$ 10,000	$ 5,000			$ 15,000
Accounts receivable	10,000	5,000			15,000
Fixed assets	60,000	20,000			80,000
Investment in S Company	20,000			$20,000[a]	
Total assets	$100,000	$30,000			$110,000
Accounts payable	$ 10,000	$10,000			$ 20,000
Common stock	60,000	15,000	$15,000[a]		60,000
Retained earnings	30,000	5,000	5,000[a]		30,000
Total liabilities and equities	$100,000	$30,000			$110,000

[a] Elimination of the investment account against book value of the subsidiary's stock.

COMPLETE OWNERSHIP ACQUIRED AT MORE THAN NET ASSET VALUE

In most cases, when the parent acquires stock in a subsidiary, the cost of the investment differs from the recorded value of the net assets of the subsidiary. From a consolidated standpoint, the purchase of subsidiary stock may be regarded as similar to the purchase of the subsidiary's net assets. Consequently, the subsidiary's net assets are recorded at an amount equal to the price paid by the parent for its 100 percent interest in the subsidiary. To adjust the carrying values of the subsidiary's net assets to reflect the price paid by the parent for the stock, information concerning the fair values of the subsidiary's net assets at the time of acquisition must be obtained.

The amount paid by the parent company for the subsidiary's stock may differ from the net asset value of the subsidiary for two primary reasons. First, the subsidiary's net assets may have a fair market value that differs from their recorded book value, because the accounting methods used for recording assets and liabilities are normally not intended to reflect the fair value of the net assets of the firm. Thus, if the parent company pays an amount in excess of book value, this excess may exist because the net assets of the subsidiary are undervalued (that is, the book value of the net assets determined on the basis of proper accounting methods is less than their fair market value). Also, the excess may be due to the existence of unrecorded intangible assets of the subsidiary or from anticipated advantages that are expected because of the affiliation. If the assets of the subsidiary are undervalued, any specific tangible or intangible assets with fair market values in excess of recorded book values are restated at fair market value in the consolidation worksheet. Thus, identifiable assets are reported in the consolidated balance sheet at an amount equal to their fair market values at the date of acquisition. If the cost of the subsidiary stock still exceeds the amount assigned to the net assets of the subsidiary in the consolidation worksheet, this excess is assigned to an intangible asset, goodwill or "excess of cost over book value." Therefore, the total excess of the cost of the subsidiary's stock over the book value of the subsidiary's net assets is included among consolidated net assets—either as increases (decreases) in the value of specific assets (liabilities) or alternatively as goodwill. Again, it is important to note that these adjustments are made only in the consolidation worksheet.

To illustrate, assume the same facts as in the previous illustration except that P Company acquires all of the stock of S Company at a cost of $25,000. Thus, the cost of the investment ($25,000) exceeds the stockholders' equity of the subsidiary ($20,000) by $5,000. The management of P Company believes that the fair values of specific assets of S Company are greater than their recorded book value or that there are advantages of affiliation, such as future earnings prospects, that justify payment of $5,000 in excess of book value for S Company's net assets. In this illustration, assume that the excess of cost over book value exists because the fair market value of S Company's land exceeds its recorded book value by $5,000. Therefore, this excess is assigned to land (which is summarized in fixed assets in this example) in the consolidation worksheet. The consolidation worksheet is as shown in Illustration 7. The eliminating entries on the consolidation worksheet are:

(a)	Fixed assets—S Company	5,000	
	Investment in S Company		5,000
(b)	Common stock—S Company	15,000	
	Retained earnings—S Company	5,000	
	Investment in S Company		20,000

Illustration 7
P Company and S Company
Consolidation Worksheet
At December 31, 19X1

	P Company	S Company	Eliminations Dr.	Eliminations Cr.	Consolidation
Cash	$ 5,000	$ 5,000			$ 10,000
Accounts receivable	10,000	5,000			15,000
Fixed assets	60,000	20,000	$ 5,000[a]		85,000
Investment in S Company	25,000			$ 5,000[a] $20,000[b]	
Total assets	$100,000	$30,000			$110,000
Accounts payable	$ 10,000	$10,000			$ 20,000
Common stock	60,000	15,000	$15,000[b]		60,000
Retained earnings	30,000	5,000	5,000[b]		30,000
Total liabilities and equities	$100,000	$30,000			$110,000

[a] Adjustment for undervaluation of subsidiary's assets.
[b] Elimination of the investment account against the book value of the subsidiary's stock.

Again, it is important to note that these entries do not appear in the accounts of either P Company or S Company. These are worksheet entries that are used to facilitate the consolidation of the financial reports of the parent and subsidiary company.

If the excess cannot be assigned to any specific assets (that is, the recorded book values of the subsidiary's net assets are equal to their fair values at acquisition), the $5,000 excess is reported in the consolidated balance sheet as goodwill or "excess of cost over book value." This is a new account that is introduced in the consolidated worksheet—it does not appear in the accounts of either P Company or S Company.

Complete Ownership Acquired for Less Than Net Asset Value

If the cost of the stock acquired by the parent company is less than book value, a similar problem exists. When specific overvalued assets can be identified, the excess is reflected on the balance sheet by reducing the value of specific assets of the subsidiary. Thus, subsidiary assets would be reported at their fair values in the consolidated balance sheet. When specific assets that are overvalued cannot be identified, the excess is used to reduce noncurrent assets. If the allocation reduces the noncurrent assets to zero, the remainder of the excess is credited to an account referred to as "excess of book value of subsidiary interest over cost." This account is shown as a reduction of assets on the consolidated balance sheet. For example, assume P Company purchased 100 percent of the stock of S Company at a price of $18,000 on December 31, 19X1. At that date, the stockholders' equity of S Company was $20,000, consisting of $15,000 of common stock and $5,000 of retained earnings. Eliminating entries on the consolidation worksheet are as follows:

(a)	Investment in S Company	2,000	
	Specific assets of S Company		2,000
(b)	Common stock—S Company	15,000	
	Retained earnings—S Company	5,000	
	Investment in S Company		20,000

Less Than Complete Ownership

A parent company may obtain control of a subsidiary by acquiring less than 100 percent of the common stock of the subsidiary. When a parent owns less than 100 percent of the stock, the remainder of the stock held by stockholders outside the affiliated companies is classified as a *minority interest* in the consolidated balance sheet. The existence of a minority interest does not affect the amounts at which the assets and liabilities of the affiliated companies appear on the consolidated balance sheet. However, only a portion of the equity in the net assets of the subsidiary company is owned by the parent since a portion of the owners' equity is held by minority stockholders. Equity held by minority stockholders, or minority interest, may be considered a part of the stockholders' equity of the consolidated entity.

To illustrate, assume that P Company acquires only 90 percent of the common stock of the subsidiary at a cost of $18,000. The remaining 10 percent of the subsidiary's stock represents the minority interest in S Company. The only change required in the elimination entries is that only 90 percent of the common stock and retained earnings of S Company is eliminated. The remaining 10 percent of S Company stockholders' equity represents the minority interest in the subsidiary and is classified as such in the consolidated balance sheet. The consolidated worksheet used to prepare the consolidated balance sheet is shown in Illustration 8.

The initial consolidation entry (a) eliminates 90 percent of the common stock and retained earnings of S Company against the investment account of the parent. The remaining 10 percent of the stockholders' equity of S Company is then reclassified as a minority interest in entry (b).

Illustration 8
P Company and S Company
Consolidation Worksheet
At December 31, 19X1

	P Company	S Company	Eliminations Dr.	Eliminations Cr.	Consolidation
Cash	$ 12,000	$ 5,000			$ 17,000
Accounts receivable	10,000	5,000			15,000
Fixed assets	60,000	20,000			80,000
Investment in					
S Company	18,000			$18,000[a]	
Total assets	$100,000	$30,000			$112,000
Accounts payable	$ 10,000	$10,000			$ 20,000
Common stock	60,000	15,000	$ 1,500[b]		60,000
			$13,500[a]		
Retained earnings	30,000	5,000	500[b]		30,000
			4,500[a]		
Minority interest	0	0		2,000[b]	2,000
Total liabilities					
and equities	$100,000	$30,000			$112,000

[a] Elimination of investment against 90 percent of the subsidiary's stockholders' equity.
[b] Adjustment to reclassify 10 percent of the subsidiary's stockholders' equity as minority interest.

It should be noted that, in this example, the parent company pays an amount equal to book value for its interest in the subsidiary. Therefore, the investment account is exactly equal to 90 percent of the stockholders' equity of S Company at acquisition (i.e., $18,000 equals 90 percent of $20,000). The existence of a minority interest, however, does not affect the procedures required when the investment is acquired at either more or less than book value. Any difference between the cost of the investment and the amount representing the parent company's interest in the stockholders' equity of the subsidiary increases consolidated net assets if cost exceeds book value and reduces consolidated net assets if cost is less than book value.

CONSOLIDATED BALANCE SHEET AFTER THE DATE OF ACQUISITION

Net assets of a subsidiary change subsequent to the date of affiliation as a result of the difference between the net income earned and the dividends paid by the subsidiary since the date the parent acquired its interest in the subsidiary. If the parent company carries its investment using the equity method, the parent's share of such changes in the net assets of a subsidiary is reflected in the investment account. This occurs because the parent company increases the investment account and records investment income for its share of subsidiary earnings and reduces the investment account for any dividends that it receives from the subsidiary. Similarly, a loss incurred by the subsidiary is recorded by the parent as a decrease in the investment account and a corresponding decrease in the parent company's earnings. At any time subsequent to the date of affiliation, the change in the parent's investment account for each year must be equal to the parent company's share (that is, the parent company's percentage ownership of the voting stock of its subsidiary) of the change in the retained earnings of the subsidiary company. The eliminations required in order to prepare a consolidated balance sheet are basically the same as those required at the date of acquisition except that the amount eliminated from the investment account of the parent and the stockholders' equity of the subsidiary change each year. Since the two entries made in the elimination of the parent's investment account against the stockholders' equity of the subsidiary change by the same amount, the original difference between the cost of the investment and the book value of the subsidiary is the same for each period.

To illustrate the procedures required for the preparation of a worksheet for a consolidated balance sheet, assume that P Company purchases 90 percent of the outstanding stock of S Company on December 31, 19X1, at a price of $21,000. At that time, S Company has common stock of $15,000 and retained earnings of $5,000. The book value of the net assets purchased was 90% × $20,000, or $18,000. Therefore, the cost of the investment exceeds the book value of the subsidiary's stock by $3,000. This excess of cost over book value is attributed to the excess of the market value of land owned by the subsidiary over the book value of the land. Further, assume that the subsidiary company has net income of $20,000 and pays dividends totaling $10,000 during 19X2. The effect of these transactions is to increase the retained earnings of the subsidiary by $10,000, from $5,000 to $15,000 (retained earnings on December 31, 19X1, of $5,000 plus 19X2 net income of $20,000 minus 19X2 dividends of $10,000). Similarly, net income and dividends paid by the subsidiary cause a net increase of $9,000 in the parent company's investment account (90% of $20,000 net income minus 90% of the $10,000 dividends). The remaining 10 percent of the increase in the subsidiary's retained earnings represents an increase in the equity of the minority stockholders and is classified as such. The worksheet (see Illustration 9) for consolidation illustrates the procedures required in preparing a consolidated balance sheet (see Illustration 10) one year after the date of acquisition of the subsidiary.

Illustration 9
P Company and S Company
Consolidation Worksheet
At December 31, 19X2

	P Company	S Company	Eliminations Dr.	Eliminations Cr.	Consolidation
Cash	$ 10,000	$ 7,000			$ 17,000
Accounts receivable	10,000	6,000			16,000
Fixed assets	70,000	20,000	$ 3,000[a]		93,000
Investment in S Company	30,000			$ 3,000[a] $27,000[b]	
Total assets	$120,000	$33,000			$126,000
Accounts payable	$ 15,000	$ 3,000			$ 18,000
Common stock	60,000	15,000	$ 1,500[c] $13,500[b]		60,000
Retained earnings	45,000	15,000	1,500[c] 13,500[b]		45,000
Minority interest	0	0		3,000[c]	3,000
Total liabilities and equities	$120,000	$33,000			$126,000

[a] Adjustment for undervaluation of subsidiary's assets.
[b] Elimination of investment against 90 percent of the subsidiary's stockholders' equity.
[c] Adjustment to reclassify 10 percent of the subsidiary's stockholders' equity as minority interest.

OTHER RECIPROCAL ACCOUNTS

In preparing a consolidated balance sheet, the investment account of the parent company must be eliminated against the stockholders' equity accounts of its subsidiary. If any transactions occur between the parent and subsidiary companies, there might be additional reciprocal accounts that must also be eliminated in the consolidation worksheet in order to avoid the double-counting of assets and liabilities.

Illustration 10
P Company and S Company
Consolidated Balance Sheet
at December 31, 19X2

Current assets:
Cash	$17,000	
Accounts receivable	16,000	
Total current assets		$ 33,000
Fixed assets		93,000
Total assets		$126,000

Liabilities:
Accounts payable		$ 18,000
Minority interest in S Company		3,000

Stockholders' equity:
Common stock	$60,000	
Retained earnings	45,000	105,000
Total liabilities and equities		$126,000

One of the most common of these additional reciprocal accounts involves intercompany receivables and payables. If one affiliated company borrows from another, the debtor firm incurs a liability (payable) equal to an asset (receivable) of the creditor company. From a consolidated standpoint, the payable does not represent an amount owed to an entity outside the affiliated group, nor does the related asset represent a receivable from an outside group. Therefore, in the consolidation worksheet, both the reciprocal asset and liability are eliminated.

To illustrate this point, assume that the parent company owes the subsidiary company $5,000 as of December 31, 19X2. The following entry is made on the consolidation worksheet in order to eliminate the reciprocal accounts:

Accounts payable—P Company	5,000	
Accounts receivable—S Company		5,000

Pooling of Interests

In the above discussion of consolidated statements, it is assumed that the parent company purchases the stock of the subsidiary with cash or other assets. The consolidated statements are prepared on the premise that the purchase of stock represents a purchase of the underlying net assets of the subsidiary. Therefore, in the consolidated statements, the cost of the acquisition is allocated to the individual assets and liabilities of the subsidiary with any excess reported as "excess of cost over book value."

A subsidiary may also be acquired by the exchange of the parent's stock for the stock of the subsidiary. Under certain circumstances, this combination may be accounted for as a *pooling of interests*. Because the stockholders of the subsidiary become stockholders of the parent company, one group has not acquired the interests of the other. Rather, both have "pooled" their interests in a combined entity. A pooling of interests unites the ownership interests of two or more firms by the exchange of stock. A purchase transaction is not recognized because the combination is accomplished without disbursing the assets of either company. A key feature of a pooling is that the former ownership interests continue and the basis of accounting remains the same.

Since no purchase is recognized and basically the same ownership interests continue, there is no justification for revaluing assets in a pooling of interests. All assets and liabilities of the companies are carried forward to the consolidated statements at their recorded book values. The parent company records the acquisition by debiting the investment account for the net amount of S Company's net assets. Since assets and liabilities are combined at their recorded amounts, there is no excess of cost over book value to be accounted for in the consolidated statements. In addition, retained earnings of the subsidiary at acquisition may be combined with the parent's retained earnings in determining consolidated retained earnings.

To illustrate, assume that P Company issues 1,000 shares of its $50 par value common stock in exchange for all of the common stock of S Company. Assume that S Company has 6,000 shares of $10 par value common stock outstanding and retained earnings of $40,000. The parent company records the issuance of its stock and the acquisition of the stock of S Company as follows:

Investment in S Company	100,000	
Common stock		50,000
Additional paid-in capital		10,000
Retained earnings		40,000

This entry records the investment at the net asset amount of S Company (common stock of $60,000 plus retained earnings of $40,000), credits the common stock account for the par value of the shares issued (1,000 × $50), credits additional paid-in capital for the difference in the par value of the shares issued by P ($50,000) and the par value of S's stock ($60,000) and credits retained earnings for the amount of S's retained earnings.

Under the pooling of interests method, the fair values of the subsidiary's net assets are not considered to be relevant for purposes of consolidation. Therefore, the entry required on the worksheet eliminates the investment account of the parent company against the common stock and retained earnings of the subsidiary. The consolidation worksheet at the date of acquisition is shown in Illustration 11. If the par value of the stock issued exceeds the par value of the shares acquired, the difference may be charged or debited to additional paid-in capital. If additional paid-in capital is insufficient to absorb the difference, the remainder may be charged against retained earnings.

Illustration 11
P Company and S Company
Consolidation Worksheet
At December 31, 19X1

	P Company	S Company	Eliminations Dr.	Eliminations Cr.	Consolidation
Other assets	$250,000	$120,000			$370,000
Investment in S Company	100,000	0		$100,000[a]	0
Total	$350,000	$120,000			$370,000
Liabilities	$ 30,000	$ 20,000			$ 50,000
Common stock:					
P Company ($50 par value)	150,000	0			150,000
S Company ($10 par value)	0	60,000	$60,000[a]		0
Additional paid-in capital	60,000	0			60,000
Retained earnings	110,000	40,000	40,000[a]		110,000
Total	$350,000	$120,000			$370,000

[a] Elimination of investment account against an equal amount of the stockholders' equity.

Prior to 1970, accountants often considered the purchase and pooling of interests methods to be acceptable alternatives for accounting for any given business combination. The pooling of interests method was popular because in circumstances where the fair value of the subsidiary's net assets exceeds the recorded book value, the pooling treatment results in higher future net income and earnings per share to be reported than does the purchase method. In addition, pooling normally causes higher retained earnings than the purchase method. The Accounting Principles Board, however, attempted to resolve this problem by issuing *Opinion No. 16*. With respect to the purchase versus pooling issue, the board concluded that "... the purchase method and the pooling of interests method are both acceptable in accounting for business combinations, although not as alternatives in accounting for the same business combinations." The board specified the conditions under which each of the two methods is applicable to a business combination.[6]

Usefulness of Consolidated Statements

In a situation where one corporation owns a majority of the voting stock of one or more other corporations, financial statements prepared for the separate legal corporate entities may not provide the most useful information to management, stockholders, and potential investors of the parent company. Instead, these users are interested in the financial position and results of operations of the combined entity (i.e., the parent company and all other companies under the control of the parent).

On the other hand, minority stockholders of a subsidiary company ordinarily have little use for consolidated financial statements. Since minority stockholders are primarily concerned with their ownership in the subsidiary company, separate financial statements of the subsidiary are usually more useful to them. Similarly, creditors of either the parent or a subsidiary are primarily concerned with their individual legal claims. Therefore, separate financial statements based on the individual entities concerned are of primary interest to these creditors.

Consolidated Income Statement

A consolidated income statement is prepared by combining the revenues and expenses of the parent and subsidiary companies. If the parent company owns 100 percent of the subsidiary's stock and there have been no transactions between the parent and its subsidiary, consolidation is simply a combination of revenues and expenses resulting from the parent and subsidiary companies' operations. The only adjustment necessary is that which is required in order to eliminate the investment income of the parent company (the parent company's share of the subsidiary's net income). This amount must be eliminated in order to avoid duplication or double-counting of earnings in the consolidated income statement.

As in the case of the consolidated balance sheet, elimination of reciprocal accounts may be necessary in order to avoid duplication or double-counting of revenues and expenses resulting from transactions that have occurred between the parent and its subsidiary. For example, interest expense of one company and interest income of the other resulting from an intercompany loan are eliminated, because they do not change the net assets of the total entity from a consolidated viewpoint.

Minority Interest

If the parent owns less than 100 percent of the subsidiary's stock, an additional adjustment is required in the consolidated worksheet in order to allocate the net income of the subsidiary between the parent company and the minority stockholders of the subsidiary. This division of the consolidated income is based on the percentage of the subsidiary's stock owned by the parent company and by the minority stockholders.

To illustrate the consolidation procedure for the income statement, again assume that P Company purchases 90 percent of the common stock of S Company on December 31, 19X1. The 19X2 income statement for P Company is presented in Illustration 12. Also, assume that the parent rents a building to its subsidiary at a rental of $5,000 per year. The procedures necessary in order to prepare a consolidated income statement are illustrated in the consolidation worksheet in Illustration 13. It should be noted that the worksheet has a self-balancing format. That is, the net income figures have been included along with the expenses so that the revenues are equal to income plus expenses.

---

[6] Discussion of the specific criteria for purchase vs. pooling is beyond the scope of this text.

Illustration 12
P Company and S Company
Income Statements
For the Year Ended December 31, 19X2

	P Company	S Company
Revenues:		
Sales	$195,000	$100,000
Rent revenue	5,000	0
Investment income	18,000	0
Total revenues	$218,000	$100,000
Expenses:		
Cost of goods sold	$150,000	$ 70,000
Other expenses	20,000	10,000
Total expenses	$170,000	$ 80,000
Net income	$ 48,000	$ 20,000

Illustration 13
P Company and S Company
Consolidation Worksheet
at December 31, 19X2

	P Company	S Company	Eliminations Dr.	Eliminations Cr.	Consolidation
Sales	$195,000	$100,000			$295,000
Rent revenue	5,000	0	5,000[a]		
Investment income	18,000	0	18,000[b]		
Total revenues	$218,000	$100,000			$295,000
Cost of goods sold	$150,000	$ 70,000			$220,000
Other expenses	20,000	10,000		$ 5,000[a]	25,000
Net income:					
P Company	48,000				48,000
S Company		20,000		$ 2,000[c]	
				18,000[b]	
Minority Interest in net income			2,000[c]		2,000
Total expenses and net income	$218,000	$100,000			$295,000

[a] Elimination of intercompany rent revenue and rent expense.
[b] Elimination of investment income against 90 percent of subsidiary net income.
[c] Adjustment to reclassify 10 percent of the subsidiary's net income as minority interest.

Elimination (a) removes the duplication or double-counting effect of the intercompany building rental. This entry has no effect on consolidated net income since it simply offsets rent revenue of P Company against an equal amount of rent expense of S Company. Elimination (b) cancels the investment income which P Company records as its share of the net income of S Company under the equity method. This entry corrects the double-counting of S Company's net income. Elimination (c) allocates 10 percent of S Company's net income to the minority stockholders of the subsidiary company.

The amounts in the consolidation column of the worksheet are used in order to prepare the consolidated income statement in Illustration 14. Notice that the minority interest in net income is treated as a reduction of net income of the consolidated entity to arrive at consolidated net income.

Illustration 14
P Company and Subsidiary
Consolidated Income Statement
for the Year 19X2

Sales	$295,000
Cost of goods sold	220,000
Gross profit	$ 75,000
Other expenses	25,000
Combined income	$ 50,000
Less minority interest in net income	2,000
Consolidated net income	$ 48,000

Profit on Intercompany Sales

An additional problem occurs if the assets transferred in intercompany sales are sold at a price that differs from the cost to the selling affiliate. If these assets are not resold by the end of the period, the gain or loss on the sale between the affiliates must be eliminated in the consolidation process. To illustrate this point, assume that the following transactions take place between a parent company (P) and its subsidiary (S):

1. P purchases two ten-speed bicycles for $100.

2. P sells the two bicycles to S for $120 on account.

3. S sells one of the bicycles to an outsider for $80 in cash.

These entries are recorded on the books of P Company and S Company as follows:

	P Company Books				S Company Books		
1.	Inventory	100			No entry		
	Cash		100				
2.	Accounts receivable	120			Inventories	120	
	Sales		120		Accounts payable		120
	Cost of goods sold	100					
	Inventories		100				
3.	No entry				Cash	80	
					Sales		80
					Cost of goods sold	60	
					Inventories		60

As a result of these transactions, there is a receivable of $120 from S Company on P Company's books and a payable of $120 to P Company on S Company's books. Also, P Company's books show sales of $120 (to S) and a related cost of goods sold of $100, while S Company's books show the cost of the bicycle sold to the outsider as $60. The unsold bicycle is carried in S Company's inventory at a cost of $60.

The problem, in terms of preparing consolidated financial statements, is that the intercompany receivables and payables and the effects of the intercompany sales must be eliminated. Also, the cost of the bicycle remaining in S Company's inventory must be reduced from $60 to $50 (the cost to P) and the $10 profit on the "sale" of this bicycle by P Company to S Company must be eliminated from the net income of P Company. The worksheet entries required to accomplish these objectives are as follows:

Accounts payable	120	
Accounts receivable		120
Sales	120	
Cost of goods sold		120
Cost of goods sold	10	
Inventories		10

The first entry eliminates the intercompany receivables and payables. The second entry eliminates the intercompany sale and the related cost of goods sold. At this point, the sales for the consolidated company is the $80 from the sale by S Company and cost of goods sold is $40 ($100 from P Company's sale to S Company plus $60 from S Company's sale less $120 from the second entry above). The final entry corrects the cost of goods sold (and therefore net income) by eliminating the intercompany profit in the ending inventory. It increases the cost of goods sold from $40 to $50 (the cost of one bicycle to P Company) and decreases the cost of the bicycle on hand from $60 to $50.

EXERCISES

1. On December 31, 19X1, P Company acquired a controlling interest in S Company. The balance sheets prior to acquisition were as follows:

	P Company	S Company
Current assets	$100,000	$ 50,000
Fixed assets (net)	300,000	70,000
	$400,000	$120,000
Liabilities	$ 40,000	$ 20,000
Common stock	300,000	80,000
Retained earnings	60,000	20,000
	$400,000	$120,000

Prepare a consolidation worksheet at the date of acquisition assuming that P Company paid $100,000 cash for all the outstanding common stock of S Company.

2. Prepare a consolidation worksheet at the date of acquisition assuming that P Company (of Exercise 1) paid $90,000 cash for 90 percent of the outstanding common stock of S Company.

3. On December 31, 19Xl, the account balances of a parent and its subsidiary included the following amounts:

	Parent	Subsidiary
Notes receivable	$ 10,000	$ 20,000
Notes payable	30,000	15,000
Sales	500,000	100,000
Purchases	300,000	70,000

All of the subsidiary sales were made to the parent company. All of the goods purchased from the subsidiary were sold by the parent company during the year. The parent company owed the subsidiary $10,000 as of December 31, 19Xl.

   a.   What amounts of notes receivable and notes payable should be reported on the consolidated balance sheet?

   b.   What amount of sales and purchases should be reported on the consolidated income statement?

4.   Walton, Inc. is a 100 percent owned subsidiary of Portland Company. The following transactions occurred in 19X1.

   a.   Portland Company purchased two basketballs for $10.

   b.   Portland Company sold the two basketballs to Walton, Inc. for $12 on account.

   c.   Walton, Inc. sold one of the basketballs to an outsider for $8.

Required:

   1.   Prepare journal entries on the books of Portland Company and Walton, Inc., to reflect the above information.

   2.   Prepare the necessary elimination entries for consolidation.

5.   Prepare the following worksheet entries which would appear on the consolidation worksheet of the Samson and Goliath Company as of December 31, 19X1.
Do not prepare a consolidation worksheet.

   a.   The Samson Company had purchased 90 percent of the common stock of the Goliath Company, for $38,000, on January 1, 19X1, when the stockholders' equity portion of Goliath Company's balance sheet appeared as follows:

Capital stock	$30,000
Retained earnings	10,000
	$40,000

      The management of the Samson Company believes that the fair value of specific assets of Goliath Company is greater than their recorded assets.

   b.   During the year, Samson sold Goliath two chariots (the company's stock-in-trade) on account for a total of $2,000. Prior to this sale, Samson had purchased the chariots for $800 each. Neither of these chariots were sold by Goliath during the remainder of the year.

   c.   Goliath rented a building to Samson during the year at a rental of $300 per month.

6.   Below are the income statements for Dodger and Red Companies. Red owns 100 percent of Dodger.

	Red Company	Dodger Company
Sales	$56,000	$25,000
Investment income	6,000	0
	$62,000	$25,000
Cost of goods sold	$29,000	$18,000
Operating expenses	6,000	1,000
	$35,000	$19,000
Net income	$27,000	$ 6,000

During 19X1, Red Company sold $15,000 of its goods to Dodger Company at a mark-up of 30 percent (cost to Red Company being $15,000). At the end of the year, Dodger Company still had $3,900 (cost plus mark-up) in its ending inventory.

Required:

Prepare the worksheet to develop a consolidated income statement on December 31, 19X1.

Outline

LEARNING Objectives

Chapter 12 discusses the issues related to the formation and accounting for sole proprietorships, partnerships and corporations. The focus is on the corporation, the dominant form of business organization in terms of both total assets and dollar value of output of goods and services. The chapter considers issues relating to the formation of a corporation, the issuance of capital stock, and the retained earnings and dividends of a corporation. Studying this chapter should enable you to:

1. Discuss the advantages and disadvantages of the sole proprietorship, partnership, and corporate forms of business organization.

2. Explain how equity accounts are affected by investments, distributions, and earnings.

3. Identify the purpose of the partnership agreement and the information it normally includes.

4. Summarize the significant characteristics of proprietorships, partnerships, and corporations.

5. Discuss the steps required to form a corporation and the accounting treatment of any related expenditures incurred in so doing.

6. Distinguish between capital stock authorized, issued, and outstanding.

7. Recognize the accounting entries required to record the declaration and payment of both cash and stock dividends.

8. Discuss the purpose of and accounting procedures for treasury stock.

CHAPTER 12

Types of Business Organizations

Introduction

There are three basic types of business organizations: (1) the sole proprietorship, (2) the partnership, and (3) the corporation. This chapter considers the accounting for both unincorporated business organizations—sole proprietorships and partnerships—and corporations.

The Sole Proprietorship

The simplest form of business organization is the sole proprietorship, a business owned by a single individual. In terms of the absolute number of business firms, the sole proprietorship greatly outnumbers all other forms of business organizations in the United States. Because of their size, however, corporations account for the greatest dollar amount of both assets and sales. Sole proprietorships are the dominant form of business organization among smaller firms, particularly among businesses engaged in retail trade and in the rendering of services.

One of the principal advantages of the sole proprietorship is the ease of establishing this type of business. Other than local and possibly state licensing requirements, an owner need only have the necessary capital and begin operations in order to establish his or her firm. Legal contracts are not necessary and the proprietor is not required to comply with provisions of certain regulations or laws that apply to corporations. A proprietor owns, controls, and usually manages the firm's assets and receives the profits (or losses) from its operations. All earnings of the business are taxable to the owner whether he or she withdraws them from the firm or not. A sole proprietorship is not considered to be a separate entity for income tax purposes.

Usually, the primary disadvantage of a sole proprietorship as a form of business organization is its unlimited liability feature. If the assets of the business are insufficient to meet its obligations, a sole proprietor is required to satisfy business creditors from his or her own personal resources. Other principal disadvantages of the sole proprietorship form of business organization include limitations on the availability of funds to the business and difficulties involved in the transferability of ownership. Funds or resources available to a sole proprietorship are limited to the personal assets of the owner and what he or she is able to borrow. Ownership may be transferred only by selling the entire business or by changing to another form of business organization.

Accounting for a Proprietorship

It is primarily in the accounting for owner's equity that the accounts of an unincorporated business differ significantly from those of a corporation. The owner's equity accounts of a sole proprietorship normally include only a capital account and a withdrawals account.

The capital account reflects the proprietor's equity in the assets of the business as of a specific point in time. Capital is credited for the investments made by the owner in the business and for the earnings of the period, and it is debited for a net loss during the period.

A separate withdrawals or drawing account, which is debited for the withdrawals of cash or other business assets made by the owner or for any payments made from business funds in order to satisfy personal debts of the owner, may be maintained. The balance in the withdrawals account is closed or transferred to the capital account during the preparation of the closing entries made at the end of the period. As an alternative, the withdrawals account may be omitted with all changes in the owner's equity recorded directly in the capital account. Either procedure accomplishes the same end result.

The Partnership

A somewhat more complicated form of business organization is the partnership. A major difference between the sole proprietorship and the partnership is that the partnership has more than a single owner. The partnership form of business organization is often used as a means of combining the resources and special skills or talents of two or more persons. In addition, state laws sometimes prevent the incorporation of certain businesses that provide professional services such as certified public accounting firms or associations of physicians. Although only two persons are required to form a partnership, there is no limit as to the number of partners. For example, in some CPA firms there are more than 800 partners.

The Uniform Partnership Act defines a partnership as "an association of two or more persons to carry on, as co-owners, a business for profit." Even though two or more persons may, in fact, operate a business as a partnership without a formal agreement, it is important that a written contract, known as the articles of co-partnership, be drawn up in order to clearly delineate the rights and duties of all partners and thereby avoid possible misunderstandings and disagreements. The partnership agreement serves as the basis for the formation and operation of the partnership. At a minimum, the partnership contract should usually include the following points:

1. Names of all partners.
2. Rights and duties of each partner.
3. Name of the partnership.
4. Nature and location of the business.
5. Effective date and the duration of the agreement.
6. Capital contribution of each partner.
7. Procedures for dividing profits and losses.
8. Any rights or limitations on withdrawals of partners.
9. Accounting period to be used.
10. Provisions for dissolution.
11. Procedures for arbitrating disputes.

Characteristics of a Partnership

The significant characteristics of the partnership form of organization are summarized briefly in the following paragraphs.

Ease of Formation. Partnerships may be formed with little difficulty. As is the case with a sole proprietorship, there are few legal formalities or regulations (aside from local and possibly state licensing requirements) to be complied with.

Mutual Agency. Normally, all partners act as agents of the partnership and as such have the power to enter into contracts in the ordinary course of business. These contracts bind the remaining partners. The concept of mutual agency provides an important reason for the careful selection of partners.

Unlimited Liability. Usually, each partner may be held personally liable to partnership creditors for all the debts of the partnership in the event that the partnership assets are insufficient to meet its obligations. If one partner is unable to meet his or her obligations under the partnership agreement, the remaining partners are liable for these debts.

If a new partner is admitted to a partnership, the partnership agreement should indicate whether he or she assumes a liability for debts incurred prior to his or her admission into the partnership. When a partner withdraws from a partnership, he or she is not liable for partnership debts incurred *after* his or her withdrawal if proper notice has been given to the public, for example, by a legal notice in a newspaper. He or she is, however, liable for all debts incurred prior to his or her withdrawal unless he or she is released from these obligations by the creditors of the partnership.

Since any partner may bind the entire partnership when making contracts in the normal scope of business, a lack of good judgment on the part of a single partner could jeopardize both partnership assets and the personal resources of the individual partners. The mutual agency and unlimited liability features may discourage certain individuals with substantial personal resources from entering into a partnership agreement.

Limited Life. Since a partnership is based on a contract, a partnership is legally ended by the withdrawal, death, incapacity, or bankruptcy of any of its partners. Addition of a new partner also terminates the old partnership. Although the entry of a new partner or the exit of an old partner legally dissolves the partnership, the business may be continued without interruption by the formation of a new partnership. This is done on a continual basis by firms of attorneys, doctors, and CPAs.

Co-Ownership By Partners. Partners are the co-owners of both the assets and the earnings of a partnership. The assets invested by each partner in the partnership are owned by all of the partners collectively. The income or loss of a partnership is divided among the partners according to the terms specified in the partnership agreement. If the partnership agreement specifies a method of dividing profits among the partners but is silent as to the division of losses, then losses are shared in the same manner as profits. If the manner of dividing profits or losses is not specified in the partnership agreement, then the partners share profits and losses equally.

Evaluation of the Partnership Form of Organization

The primary disadvantages of organizing a business as a partnership include the unlimited liability of the owners, the mutual agency of all partners, and the limited life of the partnership. However, a partnership has certain advantages over both the sole proprietorship and the incorporated forms of business organization. In comparison to a sole proprietorship, a partnership has the advantage of being able to combine the individual skills or talents of partners and of pooling the capital of several individuals, both of which may be required to carry on a successful business. A partnership is much easier to form than a corporation and is subject to much less governmental regulation. In addition, a partnership may provide certain tax advantages. Like the sole proprietorship, the partnership itself is not subject to taxes. Individual partners are, however, required to pay income taxes on their share of the income of the partnership, whether or not these earnings are withdrawn from the business.

Accounting for a Partnership

The accounting for a partnership is very similar to that of a proprietorship except with regard to specific transactions involving the accounting for owners' equity. Since a partnership is owned by two or more persons, a separate capital account must be maintained for each owner and a separate withdrawals account may also be used for each partner. Further, the net income or loss for a period must be divided among the partners as specified by the terms of the partnership agreement. Additional accounting problems unique to partnerships may occur with the formation of a partnership, admission of a partner, withdrawal or death of a partner, and liquidation of a partnership.

The Corporation

A corporation is an artificial "legal" person that is both separate and distinct from its owners and, as such, is permitted to engage in any acts that can be performed by a natural person. It may hold property, enter into contracts, and engage in other activities not prohibited by law. The classic definition of a corporation was given by Chief Justice Marshall in 1819 as "... an artificial being, invisible, intangible, and existing only in contemplation of the law."

Although there are fewer businesses organized as corporations than as either sole proprietorships or partnerships, corporations are by far the dominant form of business organization in terms of both total assets and dollar value of output of goods and services. Because of the dominance of the corporate form of business organization and the widespread ownership interests in corporations, accounting for corporations is a very important topic.

Characteristics of the Corporation

Because it is a separate legal entity, a corporation has several characteristics that differentiate it from both partnerships and sole proprietorships. The most important of these characteristics are described in the following paragraphs.

Separate Legal Existence

A corporation, unlike both a sole proprietorship and a partnership, is a legal entity that is separate and distinct from its owners. Accordingly, a corporate entity may acquire and dispose of property, enter into contracts, and incur liabilities as an individual entity separate from its owners.

Transferable Units of Ownership

Ownership of a corporation is usually evidenced by shares of capital stock. These shares permit the subdivision of ownership into numerous units that may be readily transferred from one person to another without disrupting business operations and without prior approval of the other owners.

Continuity of Life

Status as a separate legal entity provides the corporation with a continuity of life. Unlike a partnership, the life or existence of a corporation is not affected by factors such as the death, incapacity, or withdrawal of an individual owner. A corporation may have a perpetual life or, in some instances, its existence may be limited by the terms specified in its charter.

Limited Liability of Owners

As a separate legal entity, a corporation is legally liable for any debts that it incurs. Usually, the creditors of a corporation may not look to the personal property of the corporate stockholders for payment of any debts that are incurred by the corporation. Thus, the maximum loss that may be incurred by an individual stockholder is normally limited to the amount of his or her investment in the capital stock he or she owns. This limited liability feature is a primary advantage of the corporate form of business organization from the viewpoint of the owners. In addition, the absence of stockholder liability and the transferability of ownership usually increase the ability of a corporate entity to raise substantial capital by means of individual investments made by many owners. On the other hand, the limited liability feature may limit the ability of a corporation to obtain funds from creditors in those instances where solvency of the corporate entity may be questionable.

Separation of Ownership and Management

Although a corporation is owned by the individuals who hold its shares of capital stock, their control over the general management of the business is generally limited to their right to elect a board of directors. The board of directors, as representatives of individual owners or stockholders of the corporation, establishes corporate policies and appoints corporate officers who are responsible for the day-to-day management of the business and its operations. Officers of a corporation usually include a president, one or more vice presidents responsible for various functions within the business, a treasurer, a secretary, and a controller. The controller is the officer responsible for the accounting function of the business. A summary organization chart indicating the normal structure of a corporation is presented in Illustration 1.

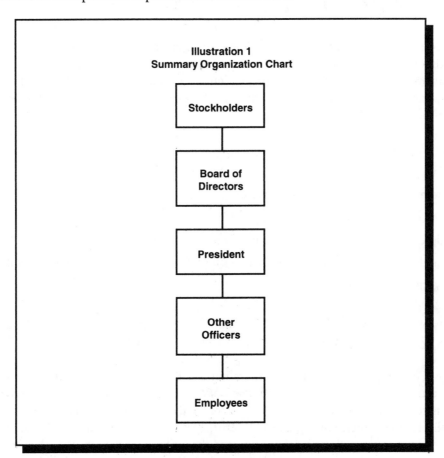

CORPORATE TAXATION

As a separate legal entity, corporations are required to file and pay local, state, and federal income taxes on corporate earnings. In addition, when corporate earnings are distributed to shareholders as dividends, these distributions are included in the taxable income of individuals receiving the dividend. Consequently, "double taxation" occurs because earnings of a corporation are taxed twice—initially as corporate income and subsequently as dividend income when distributed to stockholders.

Certain businesses may elect to operate as corporations without filing and paying corporate income taxes. In order to qualify for such an election, a corporation must meet certain requirements—for example, it must have only a single class of stock and thirty-five or fewer stockholders. If this election is made, corporate income is taxed directly to the shareholders as it is earned by the corporation, just as would be the case if the business were organized as a partnership.

GOVERNMENT REGULATION

Corporations are subject to numerous state and federal regulations and restrictions that are not imposed on either partnerships or sole proprietorships. This occurs primarily because corporations are separate legal entities and shareholders normally have limited liability for actions of the corporation. As an example, corporations that sell stock on a national stock exchange must comply with the mandates of the Securities and Exchange Commission.

Forming a Corporation

A business corporation may be created by obtaining a charter from the state in which the business is to be incorporated. Although requirements for establishing a corporation vary, most states require a minimum of three natural persons to act as incorporators. An application for a corporate charter is usually made by filing articles of incorporation with the appropriate state official. Some of the more important information usually included in the articles of incorporation are:

1. Name of the corporation.
2. Location of its principal offices.
3. Nature of the business to be conducted by the corporation.
4. Identity and addresses of incorporators.
5. A detailed description of the capital stock authorized to be issued.
6. Identity of, and the amounts paid by, the original subscribers for the corporation's capital stock.
7. Names of the initial directors.

If the articles of incorporation are approved, the state issues a corporate charter that includes the general corporation laws of the state as well as any specific provisions of the articles of incorporation. The state usually charges a fee or organization tax for the privilege of incorporation.

Upon approval of the corporate charter, a corporation is authorized to begin its operations. Incorporators are required to hold a meeting in order to elect a board of directors and to adopt a set of bylaws that provide detailed operating regulations for the corporation. Directors of the corporation then elect appropriate corporate officers and authorize the issuance of capital stock certificates to the original stockholders.

Various expenditures such as those for state taxes and charter fees, legal costs, and other organization costs are necessary in order to establish a corporation. These costs are normally accumulated in an intangible asset account referred to as organization costs. Since organization costs are expenditures that are necessary in order to provide for the creation and continued existence of a business, benefits obtained from these costs extend over the entire life of a corporation. Therefore, from a theoretical viewpoint, organization costs should be amortized over the life of the business. However, except when otherwise specified in the corporate charter, the life of a corporation is considered to be indefinite. Consequently, two different methods have evolved for accounting for organization costs. One is to simply charge organization costs to expense in the period incurred. The other alternative is to amortize these costs over a selected reasonable, but somewhat arbitrary, period of time, usually a period not exceeding five years. Although this alternative is certainly not justified in theory, it is usually acceptable in practice since organization costs are normally immaterial in amount and since this procedure is acceptable for income tax purposes.

Capital of a Corporation

Owners' equity of a corporation is commonly referred to as stockholders' equity and is accounted for in separate classifications according to the source of capital. Two primary sources of equity capital are: (1) contributed capital—amounts invested directly by shareholders, and (2) earned capital—amounts provided by profitable operations and retained in the business. A third major source of corporate capital, amounts obtained from creditors through borrowing, is discussed in Chapter 11.

Corporate capital provided by operations of the corporation is referred to as retained earnings. At the end of each period, any income or loss from operations of the corporation is transferred from the income summary account to retained earnings. The dividends account, which is used to record the dividends declared during the period, is also closed out to retained earnings during the closing process. Therefore, the balance in retained earnings at any point in time is equal to the total accumulated earnings of the business (net of any losses) less the total distributions paid to the stockholders in the form of dividends since the corporation's inception. If losses and dividends paid to stockholders exceed the cumulative earnings of the corporation, the resulting debit balance in retained earnings is referred to as a deficit. This deficit is deducted from contributed capital in order to determine total stockholders' equity of the corporation.

Nature of Capital Stock

The investments made by stockholders in a corporation are represented by shares of ownership referred to as capital stock. Ownership of corporate stock is evidenced by a stock certificate. This certificate usually includes such information as the name of the corporation, rights of the shareholders, and the number of shares owned by each individual shareholder.

The corporate charter indicates the maximum number of shares of stock authorized for issuance by the corporation. The number of *authorized* shares may be recorded by a memorandum notation and be reported parenthetically in the capital stock account. The number of shares *issued* refers to the total number of shares that have been issued to stockholders since the formation of the corporation. Under certain circumstances, a corporation may reacquire shares that were originally issued to its stockholders. The remaining shares held by stockholders are referred to as *outstanding* shares. A current listing of the stockholders who own outstanding shares is maintained by the corporation's registrar or by the firm itself in a stockholders' ledger.

A corporation with many shares of stock being held by investors and traded on a national stock exchange such as the New York Stock Exchange is called a publicly-held corporation. On the other hand, a corporation with few shares of stock being held by investors and no shares traded on a national stock exchange is called a privately-held (or closely-held) corporation.

A corporation with a large number of outstanding shares that are traded regularly on an organized stock exchange must assign the function of transferring stocks and maintaining stock records to a stock transfer agent and a registrar. Banks or trust companies usually fulfill these functions for corporations. When a stockholder wishes to sell his or her stock, he or she endorses the stock certificate and forwards it to the transfer agent. The transfer agent cancels the certificate and prepares a new certificate that he or she sends to the registrar. The registrar records the stock transfer and issues a new stock certificate to the purchaser(s). Independent records maintained by the independent transfer agent and registrar provide additional controls that are intended to decrease the possibility of error or fraud in a corporation's ownership records.

Rights of Stockholders

Many corporations issue only a single class of stock. In this instance, each shareholder possesses identical ownership rights and privileges. For an individual stockholder, these rights are proportionate to the number of shares of stock owned. Among these basic rights are:

1. The right to vote in stockholders' meetings. This includes the right to vote for directors and on decisions requiring stockholder approval as specified by the terms of the corporate charter. A stockholder has one vote for each share of stock that he or she owns. For example, if a stockholder owns 1,000 shares of stock, he or she is entitled to 1,000 votes. If a shareowner does not wish to attend a stockholders' meeting, he or she may assign his or her votes to a specified representative through a proxy statement.

2. The right to share in corporate earnings through dividends declared by the board of directors.

3. The right to maintain a proportionate interest in the ownership of the corporation whenever any additional shares of stock are issued by the corporation. This right, referred to as the preemptive right, provides that each stockholder may purchase a percentage of the number of new shares to be issued so that his or her ownership percentage remains equal to his or her ownership percentage in the number of shares outstanding prior to the new issuance. To illustrate, assume that Aaron owns 100 (10%) of the 1,000 outstanding shares of stock of Matthews Co. If Matthews Co. decides to issue an additional one hundred shares of stock, Aaron has a right to purchase 10 percent (100 ÷ 1,000), or ten of the new shares issued. Therefore, Aaron will be permitted to maintain his 10 percent interest (110 ÷ 1,100) in the corporation. Thus, by exercising his or her preemptive right, a stockholder is able to maintain his or her relative interest or ownership in the corporation. However, a shareholder is not required to exercise his or her preemptive right; he or she may elect to do so at his or her option.

4. The right to a proportionate share in assets upon the liquidation of the corporation. Shareholders, however, are entitled to only those assets that remain after all corporate creditors have been paid in full.

When a corporation issues only a single class of stock, its shares are referred to as common stock and the four basic rights described above apply to all shares issued and outstanding. In certain circumstances, a corporation may issue additional types of capital stock in order to satisfy management objectives and to appeal to investors who may have various investment objectives. These additional classes of stock usually grant certain preferential rights to the holders of these shares. Accordingly, such shares are usually referred to as preferred stock. Ordinarily, preferred stockholders have either no voting rights or only limited voting rights under certain conditions specified by the corporate charter. Preferred stock usually has one or more of the following preferences or privileges:

1. *Dividend Preference.* Stock that is preferred as to dividends entitles its owner to receive a stated dividend *before* any distributions are made to owners of common stock. Dividends on preferred stock are normally limited to a fixed amount per share. However, this dividend preference does not assure the stockholder that he or she will receive a dividend. Thus, if the board of directors of a corporation chooses not to declare a dividend, neither common nor preferred shareholders will receive any distribution from the corporation.

As an example, assume that a corporation has outstanding 40,000 shares of $20 par, 7 percent preferred stock and 60,000 shares of $5 par common stock. If the board of directors does not declare a dividend, the preferred and common shareholders do not receive any distributions. If the board of directors declares a $60,000 dividend, the preferred stockholders receive $56,000 (40,000 shares multiplied by $20 per share multiplied by .07) and the common stockholders receive the remaining $4,000.

2. *Cumulative Preference.* Cumulative preferred stock provides that if all or part of the required dividend on preferred stock is not paid during a given year, the unpaid dividend accumulates and carries forward to succeeding years. The accumulated amount of unpaid dividends as well as current dividends must be paid before any dividends can be paid on common stock. To illustrate, assume that a corporation has 10,000 shares of cumulative preferred stock outstanding and a $5 stated dividend per share was not paid in the preceding year. In the current year, no dividends may be paid on the common stock until preferred dividends of $50,000 ($5 x 10,000) from the preceding year and the dividend of $50,000 for the current year are paid. Unpaid dividends on cumulative preferred stock are referred to as dividends in arrears. Dividends in arrears are not considered to be a liability of the corporation until they are declared by the board of directors. However, because this information is important to the users of financial statements, any dividends in arrears on preferred stock should be disclosed, usually by means of a footnote to the balance sheet.

Preferred stock not having cumulative rights is referred to as noncumulative. Dividends omitted in any one year on noncumulative preferred stock do not carry forward. Therefore, dividends may be paid on common stock if preferred stock dividends are paid for the current year. Since a dividend preference is usually one of the most important rights or features of preferred stock, noncumulative preferred stock is normally not considered to be a very desirable investment under most circumstances. Consequently, most preferred stock issues provide for cumulative dividends.

3. *Participating Preference.* Preferred stock is usually entitled to receive a dividend of a specified amount each year. Preferred stock is nonparticipating when preferred stockholders receive only this amount regardless of the dividends paid to common stockholders. In some cases, however, certain types of preferred stock also provide for the possibility of dividends in excess of the normal amount. This preferred stock, referred to as participating, has the right to participate with common stockholders in dividends in excess of a specified amount paid to common shareholders. The preferred stock contract must indicate the extent to which preferred shares will participate with common shares. Fully participating preferred stock is entitled to dividends at an amount equal to the following: the preferred stockholders receive dividends up to their regular rate and the common stockholders receive a like rate; then any excess dividends declared are divided proportionately between the preferred and common stockholders. The proportionate rate may be based on the par value of the stock. If the common stock does not have a par value, then its stated value may be used. If the common stock has neither a par nor a stated value, then the board of directors is required to assign a value to the common stock for purposes of computing dividend distributions. Partially participating preferred stock is entitled to participate with common stock, but it is limited to a maximum rate or amount. Issues of preferred stock normally do not include participation rights.

To illustrate, assume that a corporation has outstanding 50,000 shares of $25 par, 8 percent fully participating preferred stock and 80,000 shares of $10 par common stock. If the board of directors declares a $369,000 dividend, the distribution between the preferred and common stockholders is as follows:

a. The preferred stockholders initially are allocated $100,000 according to the following computation:

$$50,000 \times \$25 \times .08 = \$100,000$$

b. The common stockholders initially are allocated dividends based on a like rate. Therefore, the following computation is used:

$$80,000 \times \$10 \times .08 = \$ 64,000$$

c. The remaining $205,000 (the declared dividend of $369,000 less the amount already allocated, $164,000) is divided in proportion to the relative par values. The computation for the preferred stockholders is as follows:

$$\frac{50,000 \times \$25}{(50,000 \times \$25) + (80,000 \times \$10)} \times \$205,000 = \$125,000$$

The common stockholders are allocated the remaining $80,000 ($205,000 less $125,000).

d. The total distribution is as follows:

Preferred—$225,000
Common—$144,000

Using the same example, we now assume that the preferred stock is partially participating up to a maximum of 2 percent above its stipulated 8 percent rate. In this case, the remaining $205,000 are allocated as follows:

Preferred—50,000 × $25 × .02 = $25,000
Common—$205,000 - $25,000 = $180,000

4. *Liquidation Preference.* Preferred stock is normally preferred as to assets upon liquidation of the corporation. That is, owners of such preferred stock are entitled to receive the stated liquidation value for their shares before any payments may be made to common stockholders.

5. *Convertible Preferred Stock.* Preferred stock is convertible when it includes a privilege that allows stockholders to exchange their preferred shares for a specified number of common shares of the corporation at the shareholders' option. A conversion privilege allows the owner of preferred stock the option of obtaining common stock on which there is no dividend limitation in exchange for his or her preferred stock.

6. *Callable Preferred Stock.* Preferred stock contracts frequently allow corporations to repurchase outstanding shares from preferred stockholders at a fixed price in excess of the issue price of the stock. When a corporation has this option, the preferred stock is referred to as callable.

Stock Issuance Costs

Typically, there are various costs incurred by a corporation in the issuance of capital stock. These costs include administrative and printing costs involved in preparing and issuing the certificates, legal fees, advertising costs, and underwriters' fees.

There are two methods generally used in accounting for these issue costs. *One method is to treat these costs as a reduction of the amounts received from the sale of the securities.* Under this method, any costs incidental to the sale are considered to be a reduction of additional paid-in capital. *An alternative method is to view issue costs as an intangible asset, usually referred to as organization costs, which yields a benefit to the corporation over an indefinite future period.* These organization costs are either charged to expense as incurred or charged to expense over an arbitrary period of time, usually not to exceed five years.

Par Value and No-par Value

The par value of a share of capital stock is an arbitrary value established by the corporate charter. It is usually printed on the stock certificate and may be any amount decided upon by the corporation. The par value specified has no relationship whatsoever to the actual market value of the stock. Market value, which is the price at which a share of stock can be bought or sold, is dependent upon factors such as expected earnings and dividends, financial condition of the corporation, and general economic conditions. It is not unusual for a stock with a par value of $5 per share to be traded at a market value of $50, $100, or more.

The primary significance of par value is that it is used in many states in order to establish the corporation's "legal capital." The concept of legal capital is used by state laws to protect corporate creditors from possible dishonest actions of stockholders or corporate directors. In the absence of such a provision, corporate assets could be distributed to stockholders prior to the final liquidation of a corporation. Since stockholders have no liability for corporate debts, creditors would be unable to obtain satisfaction of their claims. Therefore, the concept of legal capital limits the assets that may be distributed to stockholders prior to the liquidation of the corporation and the settlement of its debts. Consequently, dividends cannot be declared by a corporation if such payments would decrease the owners' equity to an amount below the specified minimum legal capital—that is, the par value of the outstanding shares or, in some instances, par value plus a certain additional amount. Most state laws also provide that if the amount invested by individual stockholders is less than the established par value of the stock purchased, the stockholders may be held liable to the corporation's creditors for any difference between the amount paid and par value in the event the corporation is unable to meet its debts.

Laws requiring that stock have a par value were originally intended to protect the creditors of a corporation by restricting the distribution of a portion of corporate capital; however, the existence of a par value for capital stock has also caused certain problems. In some instances, investors have confused an arbitrary par value with the actual value of the ownership interest in the corporation. Also, if the market value of the stock falls below the par value established by the corporate charter, a potential liability to the investor may prevent the sale of additional[1] shares of stock by the corporation unless or until the corporate charter is amended to change the par value of the stock. Consequently, some states have enacted legislation permitting the issuance of stock without par value, referred to as no-par stock. In these states, the legal capital of the corporation may be the total amount paid for the shares by the stockholders, or a stated value per share may be established by the board of directors.

Occasionally, a corporation may desire to make certain changes in the structure of its contributed capital. Such action requires approval of the corporation's board of directors and also must conform with applicable state laws. Changes in the capital structure of a corporation typically involve either a change in the par or stated value of a class of stock or the replacement of par value stock with no-par stock. The new capital structure is recorded by debiting the existing contributed capital accounts and crediting the appropriate new capital accounts.

Issuance of Par Value Stock

The primary significance of par value from an accounting viewpoint is that the capital stock account is credited with the par value of shares issued regardless of the amount received when the stock is sold. For example, if 1,000 shares of $10 par value common stock are sold at par value for cash, the entry is as follows:

Cash	10,000	
Common stock		10,000

When stock is sold for more than its par value, the amount received in excess of the par value is recorded as "additional paid-in capital." To illustrate, assume that 1,000 shares of $10 par value common stock are sold for $12 per share. The entry to record the issuance is as follows:

Cash	12,000	
Common stock		10,000
Additional paid-in capital		2,000

The additional paid-in capital account is added to the capital stock account in reporting the total contributed (invested) capital of the corporation. Contributed capital of the corporation in the above example is shown in the stockholders' equity section of the balance sheet as shown below:

Stockholders' Equity:
Common stock, $10 par value,	
5,000 shares authorized,	
1,000 shares issued and outstanding	$10,000
Additional paid-in capital on common stock	2,000
Total contributed capital	$12,000

If capital stock is issued for an amount less than its par value, the difference is charged or debited to a "discount on capital stock" account. This account would be shown as a deduction from the capital stock account in the balance sheet. Since selling stock at a discount is illegal in most states and usually represents a contingent liability to the creditors of the corporation in the remaining states, it is seldom encountered in practice. The par value of stock is normally set at an amount that is less than its anticipated selling price, thus avoiding this problem.

Issuance of Stock for Noncash Assets

Sometimes a corporation may issue shares of its capital stock in exchange for assets such as land, buildings, or equipment. In such a case, the transaction may be recorded at the market value of the shares issued or at the market value of the assets acquired, whichever is a better indicator of market value. The

---

[1] This liability applies only to the original Issue of stock, not to stock purchased and then resold by investors.

purpose of this approach is to record the transaction either at the amount of cash that could have been received from the sale of the stock or the amount that would have been paid for the property or services in a cash transaction. If the issuance of stock for noncash assets or services represents an arm's-length transaction, these fair values should be approximately equal. Therefore, if the value of only one of the items in the exchange is known or determinable, it is used as the basis for valuing the exchange. The market value of stock may be determined by reference to recent cash purchases and sales of the same class of stock by investors; many shares of a large, publicly-held corporation are traded daily through stock exchanges. Alternatively, if the market value of the shares issued cannot be determined, recent cash sales of similar assets or an independent appraisal of the asset may be used in order to record the transaction. Usually, the board of directors is given the responsibility by law for establishing a proper valuation for the issuance of stock for assets other than cash.

To illustrate, assume that a corporation acquires land in exchange for 500 shares of its $10 par value common stock. If the stock is traded on an established stock exchange and the current market price is $20, the transaction is recorded as follows:

Land	10,000	
Common stock		5,000
Additional paid-in capital		5,000

If there is no established market for the stock, the market value of the asset acquired may be used in recording the exchange. For example, if similar acreage has recently sold for $11,000, the entry to record the transaction is:

Land	11,000	
Common stock		5,000
Additional paid-in capital		6,000

ISSUANCE of NO-PAR STOCK

At one time, all states required that stocks have a specified par value. However, to eliminate problems such as the liability for issuance of stock at a discount and potential confusion over the meaning of par value, many states now permit the issuance of stock without par value.

The accounting entries that are necessary in order to record the issuance of no-par capital stock depend upon the specific laws of the state in which the shares are sold. Some states require that the entire issue price of no-par stock be regarded as legal capital. In these states, the capital account is credited for the entire amount received when the stock is issued. To illustrate, assume that a corporation issues 1,000 shares of its no-par common stock for $12 per share. This transaction is recorded as follows:

Cash	12,000	
Common stock		12,000

Other states allow the corporation to specify a stated value for no-par shares. When a stated value has been established, that amount is credited to capital stock and any excess is credited to additional paid-in capital in excess of stated value. For example, assume that the board of directors establishes a stated value of $10 per share for its stock. Issuance of 1,000 shares at a price of $12 is recorded as follows:

Cash	12,000	
Common stock		10,000
Additional paid-in capital		2,000

The additional paid-in capital account is reported as a part of contributed capital in the stockholders' equity section of the balance sheet.

Stockholders' Equity in the Balance Sheet

The stockholders' equity section of the balance sheet should report adequate information concerning each class of corporate stock outstanding. The balance sheet presentation, classification, and footnote disclosure associated with stockholders' equity should report, at a minimum, the following information:

1. The par or stated value of each class of stock.

2. The rights and priorities of the various classes of stock.

3. The number of shares authorized, issued, and outstanding for each class of stock.

4. The terms and provisions of convertible securities, of stock options, and other arrangements involving the future issuance of stock.

5. The additional paid-in capital associated with each class of stock.

The method of disclosure of capital stock and the amount of detail vary considerably among companies. Presentation of stockholders' equity in the balance sheet might appear as follows:

Stockholders' Equity:

6% preferred stock, $100 par value, 10,000 shares authorized, 6,000 shares issued and outstanding		$ 600,000
Common stock, $10 par value, 100,000 shares authorized, 50,000 shares issued and outstanding		500,000
Additional paid-in capital:		
Common stock	$140,000	
Preferred stock	60,000	200,000
Total contributed capital		$1,300,000
Retained earnings		450,000
Total stockholders' equity		$1,750,000

The stockholders' equity section of a corporation is divided into two major segments, contributed capital and retained earnings. Retained earnings represent accumulated earnings retained in the business. The retained earnings account is increased by the net income of the business and reduced by net losses and distributions to shareholders in the form of dividends. In the end-of-period closing entries, revenue, expense, gain, and loss accounts are closed to the income summary account. When revenues and gains exceed expenses and losses, the credit balance that remains in the income summary account is equal to the firm's net income for the period. Conversely, a debit balance in the income summary account indicates a net loss for the accounting period. The balance in the income summary account is closed to retained earnings. Similarly, the debit balance in the dividends account is transferred or closed out as a reduction in retained earnings.

Dividends

Dividends are distributions made by a corporation to its shareholders. Such distributions are paid in proportion to the number of shares owned by each stockholder. Dividends may be in the form of cash, other assets, or shares of the corporation's own stock. Unless otherwise specified, a dividend represents a distribution of cash. Payment of dividends is provided by action of the board of directors. The board has complete control of the type, amount, and timing of any and all dividend payments. However, once dividends are declared, they become a legal liability of the corporation to its stockholders.

In most cases, dividends represent a distribution of accumulated corporate earnings. It is ordinarily illegal to declare dividends in excess of the balance in the retained earnings account. In other words, an ordinary dividend usually may not be paid from any amounts that were invested by stockholders. The existence of a credit balance in the retained earnings account, however, does not necessarily indicate that there is cash available for the payment of dividends. Retained earnings is unrelated to the balance in the cash account, because funds obtained from the accumulated income of the business may have been used to increase noncash assets or to decrease liabilities. Thus, a corporation with a large retained earnings balance may be unable to distribute cash dividends to its stockholders. On the other hand, a corporation with a substantial amount of cash may decide to pay little or no dividends to its stockholders so that the cash may be retained and used for other corporate objectives.

Because dividends are important to investors and therefore have an effect on the market price of the stock, most corporations attempt to adhere to a well-formulated or established dividend policy. Although the percentage of earnings paid out in dividends varies widely according to the objectives of the firm, most corporations usually attempt to maintain a stable or increasing record of dividend payments.

While ordinary dividends are usually limited to the amount of retained earnings, a corporation may pay a liquidating dividend in order to return to the stockholders a portion of their original investment. Such a dividend is normally paid in conjunction with a permanent reduction in the size of a business or, alternatively, upon liquidation of a firm. Accordingly, such distributions are recorded by reducing capital stock and additional paid-in capital accounts.

Important Dates Related to Dividends

There are three important dates related to dividends:

1. Date of declaration.
2. Date of record.
3. Date of payment.

On the date of declaration, the board of directors of a corporation formally establishes a liability of a specified amount to its stockholders. The dividend and related liability, dividends payable, are recorded at that time. If financial statements are prepared after dividends are declared but before they are paid, dividends payable are classified as a current liability in the balance sheet. Following the declaration date, the corporation prepares a list of the stockholders as of the date of record—these are the stockholders who are entitled to receive the dividends. No entry is required by the corporation on the record date.

A period of time is usually necessary between the record date and the date of payment to allow the corporation sufficient time to identify those stockholders who will receive dividends and to process the dividend checks. An entry is made on the date of payment to record the distribution of cash and to remove the liability for dividends payable.

Cash Dividends

Dividends are usually paid in cash. Such dividends result in a reduction of both the cash and retained earnings of a corporation. Dividends on common stock are usually stated as a specific amount per share, while preferred stock dividends may be stated at either a specific dollar amount or a percentage of the par value per share. For example, a dividend on $100 par value preferred stock might be specified as either $5 or as 5 percent of par value. In either case, dividends paid to each stockholder are in proportion to the number of shares owned.

To illustrate, assume that the Jet Co. has 10,000 shares of common stock and 5,000 shares of 6 percent, $100 par value preferred stock outstanding. Further assume that on December 15 the company declares the preferred dividend and a $5 per share dividend on common stock. The $30,000 preferred dividend (.06 × $100 × 5,000 shares) and the $50,000 common dividend ($5 × 10,000 shares) are payable on January 15 to stockholders of record on December 20. The entries required to record the declaration of the dividend on December 15 and its payment on January 15 are as follows:

Dec. 15	Preferred dividends	30,000	
	Common dividends	50,000	
	Dividends payable		80,000
20	No entry		
Jan. 15	Dividends payable	80,000	
	Cash		80,000

The dividend accounts are closed to retained earnings during the normal year-end closing process. Assuming that the accounting period for the Jet Co. ends on December 31, the following entry is made on that date:

Dec. 31	Retained earnings	80,000	
	Preferred dividends		30,000
	Common dividends		50,000

In some instances, the corporation may debit retained earnings directly, rather than a dividend account. In these instances, a closing entry is not required.

The *dividend payout ratio* is calculated by dividing cash dividends to common stockholders by net income. Some companies, particularly high-technology firms, pay low dividends and instead reinvest their earnings; other companies pay a large percentage of their earnings in dividends. The dividend payout ratios for Wal-Mart in 1997 and Coca-Cola in 1996 are presented below (dollars are in millions):

$$\text{Dividend Payout Ratio} = \frac{\text{Cash Dividends to Common Stockholders}}{\text{Net Income}}$$

$$\text{Wal-Mart:} \quad \frac{\$481}{\$3,056} = 15.7\%$$

$$\text{Coca-Cola:} \quad \frac{\$1,247}{\$3,492} = 35.7\%$$

While Wal-Mart plans to increase its dividends, Coca-Cola intends to gradually reduce its dividend payout ratio in the future to allow for more cash to be invested in the business.

Stock Dividends

A distribution made to stockholders in the form of additional shares of a company's own stock is referred to as a stock dividend. Usually, such a distribution consists of additional common stock given to common stockholders. A stock dividend results in a proportionate increase in the number of shares owned by each stockholder. For example, a 10 percent stock dividend entitles a stockholder to receive one additional share of stock for each ten shares of stock he or she owns.

Since a stock dividend is paid on a pro rata basis, each stockholder retains the identical percentage interest in the firm after the dividend as he or she owned prior to the distribution. For example, assume that a stockholder owns 100 of 1,000 outstanding shares of a corporation. Thus, the stockholder owns 10 percent (100 ÷ 1,000) of the corporation's outstanding stock. Further assume that the corporation declares a 5 percent stock dividend. The stockholder receives five (.05 × 100) of the fifty (.05 × 1,000) additional shares of stock issued. Consequently, the stockholder's percentage interest in the corporation remains at 10 percent (105 ÷ 1,050) after the stock dividend. A stockholder benefits from a stock dividend if there is less than a proportionate decrease in the market price of the stock associated with the distribution, because the market value of the total shares owned by the stockholder increases.

Unlike a cash dividend, a stock dividend does not result in a decrease in either the corporation's assets or its total stockholders' equity. If a stock dividend has no effect on either the assets or the equity of the corporation, or in the relative ownership interests of the shareholders, why do corporations distribute such dividends? A primary purpose of issuing stock dividends is to enable the corporation to give its stockholders some evidence of increased retained earnings without actually distributing cash. Thus, although a stock dividend does not affect corporate assets or increase the individual stockholder's relative interest in the corporation, it is perceived to be a distribution of earnings by many shareholders.

Another reason for distributing a stock dividend is to reduce the selling price of the corporation's stock. Because a stock dividend of a sizable amount increases the number of shares outstanding with no change in corporate assets, the market price of the stock normally decreases. A corporation may desire to reduce the market price of its stock so that it will be more readily marketable among investors.

Since a stock dividend increases the number of shares outstanding, many states require an associated increase in the legal capital of the corporation. Therefore, even though such a dividend has no effect on total stockholders' equity, an entry is required in order to transfer a portion of retained earnings to contributed capital. This is referred to as "capitalizing" a part of retained earnings. Consequently, the retained earnings "capitalized" is no longer available for distribution to stockholders in the form of cash dividends. In many states, the minimum amount that must be transferred from retained earnings to contributed capital is an amount equal to the par or stated value of the shares issued. In other states, there is no such requirement.

Because it is generally believed that most shareholders regard a stock dividend as something of value, the American Institute of CPAs, through its Committee on Accounting Procedure, recommended that in certain circumstances an amount equal to the fair market value of the shares to be issued as a stock dividend should be capitalized. Many recipients of stock dividends believe that they have received additional shares worth the market value of these shares. Such belief is especially true when the additional shares issued are small enough in comparison to the number of shares outstanding before the stock dividend to have no material effect on the stock's market price. These circumstances exist with the issuance of a *small stock dividend. A small stock dividend is defined as an increase of less than 20 percent to 25 percent of the number of shares previously outstanding.*

To illustrate the entries for the issuance of a small stock dividend, assume that the stockholders' equity of a corporation on May 1 is as follows:

Common stock, $5 par value,	
20,000 shares outstanding	$100,000
Additional paid-in capital	20,000
Total contributed capital	$120,000
Retained earnings	80,000
Total stockholders' equity	$200,000

Assume further that on May 2 the company declares a 10 percent stock dividend, or a dividend of 2,000 shares (.10 × 20,000), which is to be distributed on June 1. Assuming that the shares are selling in the market on the declaration date at a price of $20 per share, an amount equal to the fair value of the shares to be issued, or $40,000 (2,000 × $20), is transferred from retained earnings to the appropriate contributed capital accounts. The capital stock account is credited for the par value of the shares issued and the remainder is added to additional paid-in capital. The following entries are made to record the declaration and distribution of the stock dividend:

May 2	Retained earnings	40,000	
	Stock dividend distributable		10,000
	Additional paid-in capital		30,000
June 1	Stock dividend distributable	10,000	
	Common stock		10,000

If financial statements are prepared between the date of declaration and the date of distribution of a stock dividend, the stock dividend distributable account is included in the stockholders' equity section of the balance sheet. It is not classified as a liability because the corporation has no obligation to distribute cash or any other asset.

As previously indicated, the distribution of a stock dividend has no effect on either the assets or the total stockholders' equity of a corporation. In the illustration above, the only effect on the corporation was a transfer of $40,000 from retained earnings to contributed capital. The stockholders' equity after payment of the stock dividend on June 1 appears as follows:

```
Common stock, $5 par value,
    22,000 shares outstanding  . . . . . . . . . . . . . . . . . . . .    $110,000
Additional paid-in capital . . . . . . . . . . . . . . . . . . . . . . . .      50,000
    Total contributed capital  . . . . . . . . . . . . . . . . . . . . .    $160,000
Retained earnings . . . . . . . . . . . . . . . . . . . . . . . . . . . . . .      40,000
    Total stockholders' equity  . . . . . . . . . . . . . . . . . . . .    $200,000
```

The Committee on Accounting Procedure further indicated that *large stock dividends in excess of 20 percent to 25 percent would be expected to materially reduce the market value per share of stock.* Accordingly, the committee recommended that *such stock dividends should be recorded by capitalizing retained earnings only to the extent of the par or stated value of the shares issued. Under these circumstances, the entry to record the stock dividend is a debit to retained earnings and a credit to capital stock for the par value of the shares issued.* Again, there is no effect on the total stockholders' equity of the corporation..

Stock Splits

A corporation may desire to reduce the selling price of its stock in order to facilitate purchases and sales of its shares by investors. Reducing the price of shares to a reasonable amount normally increases the number of investors who are willing to purchase a corporation's stock. This may be accomplished by increasing the number of shares outstanding and decreasing the par or stated value of the stock by a proportionate amount. This procedure is referred to as a stock split.

For example, assume that a corporation has 20,000 shares of $10 par value common stock outstanding with a current market price of $200 per share. The company declares a two-for-one stock split in which each current stockholder receives two new shares with a $5 par value for each share of $10 par value stock he or she owns prior to the split. This action causes the market price to decrease to approximately $100 per share, because there are twice as many shares outstanding after the split with no change in the value of the corporation.

In a stock split there is a significant increase in the number of shares outstanding without a change in total stockholders' equity. A stock split does not require any capitalization of retained earnings. Consequently, only a memorandum entry to the common stock account to indicate the change in par or stated value and the new number of shares outstanding is required upon a stock split.

Treasury Stock

Corporations often purchase shares of their own stock from their stockholders. If the corporation does not cancel these shares but instead holds the stock, it is referred to as treasury stock. A corporation may desire to reacquire shares of its stock that have been previously issued in order to have stock available for employee stock purchase plans, for stock options, for bonuses, or for some other legitimate reason. Purchases of treasury stock are limited to the amount of retained earnings if the corporation is to maintain its legal capital, because the purchase of treasury stock results in the distribution of cash to certain stockholders. If assets are distributed to stockholders in excess of the retained earnings, the corporation is returning a portion of the invested capital. Therefore, the purchase of treasury stock reduces the amount available for subsequent distributions to the stockholders.

Although the stock of another corporation is an asset of the firm that owns it, treasury stock is generally not considered to be an asset because a corporation cannot have an ownership interest in itself. Instead, the purchase of a corporation's own shares represents a return of capital to the selling shareholder and, thus, a reduction in the stockholders' equity of the corporation.

There are basically two different methods for recording treasury stock transactions. One approach, referred to as the cost method, is the method most commonly used in practice for recording the acquisition of treasury stock. For this reason, the cost method is discussed in the paragraphs that follow.

When a corporation acquires its own shares, treasury stock is debited for the cost of the shares purchased. Neither the par (nor stated) value of the stock nor the amount originally received for the shares when they were issued is used to record the acquisition of treasury stock. If treasury shares are subsequently reissued, the difference between the cost of the shares and their selling price does not represent a gain or a loss to the corporation. Instead, the corporation has simply changed the amount of contributed capital by acquiring and reissuing treasury shares. Consequently, any difference between the acquisition cost and the resale price of treasury stock is credited to additional paid-in capital if the selling price exceeds cost. If the shares are sold below cost, additional paid-in capital is reduced. If this account is not sufficient to absorb the excess of the cost over the selling price, any remainder may be charged or debited to retained earnings.

To illustrate, assume that the stockholders' equity of a corporation appears as follows on January 1:

Common stock, $10 par value, 10,000 shares authorized, issued, and outstanding	$100,000
Additional paid-in capital	20,000
Total contributed capital	$120,000
Retained earnings	30,000
Total stockholders' equity	$150,000

Further assume that the corporation purchases 300 of its outstanding shares on January 15 at a price of $20 per share. The following entry is made to record the purchase:

Treasury stock	6,000	
Cash		6,000

The corporation subsequently sells 100 of the treasury shares on March 15 for $25 per share and another 100 shares on April 15 for $18 per share. The entries to record these transactions are as follows:

Mar. 15	Cash	2,500	
	Treasury stock		2,000
	Additional paid-in capital from treasury stock transactions		500
Apr. 15	Cash	1,800	
	Additional paid-in capital from treasury stock transactions	200	
	Treasury stock		2,000

When the treasury shares are sold, the treasury stock account is credited for the acquisition cost of the shares, or $20 per share. In the April 15 sale, the $200 excess of cost over the resale price was debited to an "additional paid-in capital from treasury stock transactions" account. If the balance in the "additional paid-in capital from treasury stock transactions" account is not sufficient to absorb the difference between the cost and resale price, any remaining amount is normally charged against retained earnings.

If a company holds treasury shares at the time financial statements are prepared, any balance in the treasury stock account is shown as a deduction from total stockholders' equity. In addition, any restriction on the amount of retained earnings available for dividends should be disclosed. Additional paid-in capital from treasury stock transactions is reported in the contributed capital section of stockholders' equity. For example, the stockholders' equity section of the balance sheet on April 15 appears as follows:

Common stock, $10 par value, 10,000 shares authorized and issued of which 100 shares are in the treasury		$100,000
Additional paid-in capital:		
From stock issuances	$20,000	
From treasury stock transactions	300	20,300
Total contributed capital		$120,300
Retained earnings (of which $2,000 is not available for dividends because of the purchase of treasury stock)		30,000
Total		$150,300
Less: Treasury stock at cost (100 shares)		2,000
Total stockholders' equity		$148,300

For various reasons, stockholders may donate shares of stock to a corporation. Since there is no cost to the corporation, no entry is required for the receipt of the donated stock. When these shares are resold, the entire proceeds are credited to the additional paid-in capital from treasury stock transactions account. An alternative treatment is to record donated treasury stock at its fair market value as of the date of donation with a corresponding credit to a donated capital account. If this procedure is followed, subsequent entries affecting treasury stock are recorded in the same manner as if the treasury stock had been purchased.

Retained Earnings

Retained earnings is the stockholders' equity portion that results from the total net earnings of the firm less any dividends paid to stockholders since its inception. If the accumulated losses, dividend distributions, and transfers to other capital accounts exceed the accumulated earnings since the inception of the business, *the debit balance in the retained earnings account is referred to as a deficit.*

The retained earnings account may be affected by a number of items. Some of these are presented in the T-account shown below.

Retained Earnings

Decreased by	*Increased by*
Net loss	Net income
Prior-period adjustments	Prior-period adjustments
Cash and property dividends	
Stock dividends	
Sale of treasury stock at a price below its cost	
Appropriation of retained earnings	

The current period's net income or loss is transferred to retained earnings. In addition, certain corrections of income related to prior periods, termed prior-period adjustments, are excluded from the determination of net income for the current period, and, instead, are debited or credited directly to the retained earnings account.

The balance in the retained earnings account normally represents the maximum amount that may be distributed to the stockholders in the form of dividends. Dividends may be paid in the form of cash or other assets (property dividends) or in shares of the corporation's own stock (stock dividends). Cash or property dividends, once declared, become a liability of the corporation and result in a reduction of retained earnings by an amount equal to the cash to be paid or the fair value of the other assets to be distributed. A stock dividend, on the other hand, is accounted for by transferring a specified amount from retained earnings to contributed capital (the capital stock and additional paid-in capital accounts).

The existence of a credit balance in the retained earnings account does not indicate that there is cash or other assets readily available for the payment of dividends. Rather, retained earnings represents a source of the corporation's equity in the various assets owned and is unrelated to the balance in the cash account or to any other specific account. Thus, a corporation with a credit balance in its retained earnings account may be either unable or unwilling to distribute cash dividends to its stockholders.

As explained previously, there are certain circumstances in which retained earnings may be reduced by the acquisition or reissuance of a corporation's own stock. If treasury stock is reissued at an amount below its cost, retained earnings may be debited under the cost method if the paid-in capital accounts are insufficient to absorb the excess of cost over the reissuance price.

Appropriation of Retained Earnings

In general, the balance in the retained earnings account of a corporation is the amount that is legally available for dividend distribution to stockholders. However, in some cases, the board of directors may restrict the retained earnings amount that can be used to pay dividends. Such restrictions may be required either by law or by contract, or they may be made at the discretion of the board of directors. For example, retained earnings available for dividends is often legally limited by the cost of any treasury stock held by the company. In addition, contractual agreements with creditors or certain classes of stockholders may also impose limitations on the retained earnings amount available for dividends. On the other hand, the board of directors may desire to voluntarily restrict dividends in order to provide for a future use of the assets represented by accumulated earnings. For example, a firm may wish to retain assets generated from profitable operations for future expansion of the business.

There are several methods that may be used for disclosing such restrictions on the amount of the retained earnings available for distribution to shareholders. The simplest, and probably the most logical method, is to indicate the amount and nature of the restriction by footnote or parenthetical disclosure in the financial statements. However, because many stockholders may not readily understand such disclosures, an alternative is to reclassify a portion of the retained earnings in order to indicate the amount that is unavailable for dividends. This reclassification, referred to as an appropriation, is accomplished by transferring the desired amount of retained earnings to an appropriation account.

To illustrate an appropriation of retained earnings, assume that the directors of a corporation with retained earnings of $300,000 decide that $100,000 of retained earnings should be restricted for future plant expansion. The following entry is necessary to record this appropriation:

Retained earnings	100,000	
Appropriation for plant expansion		100,000

This appropriation does not affect either the assets or liabilities of the corporation. The appropriation account is not an asset to be used for expansion nor does it guarantee that cash or other assets will actually be available for this purpose. Instead, it merely restricts the assets that may be distributed to shareholders. Further, the appropriation does not change the total retained earnings; it simply divides it into appropriated and unappropriated segments. Since an appropriation represents a segregation of retained earnings, no other entry may be made to this account. The retained earnings of the corporation in the example appears as follows after the appropriation is made:

Retained earnings:	
Appropriated for plant expansion	$100,000
Unappropriated	200,000
Total retained earnings	$300,000

When the purpose for the appropriation ceases to exist, the amount of the appropriated retained earnings account should be transferred back to unappropriated retained earnings. For example, assume that the corporation in the previous illustration completes the desired expansion of the business. The appropriation is restored to unappropriated retained earnings by means of the following entry:

Appropriation for plant expansion	100,000	
Retained earnings		100,000

In recent years, the formal appropriation of retained earnings has been recognized as potentially confusing or misleading to the users of financial statements. Consequently, there has been a trend to disclose both voluntary and required restrictions of retained earnings in the notes accompanying the financial statements.

STATEMENT of RETAINED EARNINGS

The periodic financial statements issued by corporations may include a statement of retained earnings as well as a balance sheet, income statement, and statement of cash flows. The retained earnings statement indicates all changes that have occurred in that account during the period. Oftentimes, the changes in retained earnings are included in a statement of changes in all of the stockholders' equity accounts; sometimes the changes in retained earnings are included with income data in a combined statement of income and retained earnings. The general form of the statement is illustrated as follows:

Red Company
Statement of Retained Earnings
For the Year Ended December 31, 19X1

Balance at beginning of the year:		
As originally reported		$200,000
Prior period adjustment-correction		
of an error applicable to 19X0		(50,000)
As restated		$150,000
Add: Net income for the year		90 000
		$240,000
Less: Cash dividends;		
$6 per share on preferred	$30,000	
$5 per share on common	50,000	(80,000)
Balance at end of the year		$160,000

Statement of Stockholders' Equity

Most companies present a statement of stockholders' equity instead of a statement of retained earnings as one of their primary statements. A statement of stockholders' equity shows the changes in all of the stockholders' equity accounts, not only retained earnings. An example of a statement of stockholders' equity is presented in Illustration 2.

Illustration 2
Statement of Stockholders' Equity

	Preferred Stock	Common Stock	Additional Paid-in Capital Preferred	Additional Paid-in Capital Common	Retained Earnings	Treasury Stock
Balances, January 1, 19X1	$50,000	$130,000	$20,000	$ 60,000	$ 80,000	($10,000)
Issued common stock		15,000		45,000		
Acquired treasury stock						(8,000)
Net income					35,000	
Dividends					(21,000)	
Balances, December 31, 19X1	$50,000	$145,000	$20,000	$105,000	$ 94,000	($18,000)

The statement of stockholders' equity has a column for each account. The beginning balances are shown on the first line. The company has preferred stock, common stock, additional paid-in capital for both the preferred and common stock, retained earnings and treasury stock. The treasury stock balance is in parentheses, because treasury stock is a deduction within stockholders' equity.

During the year the company issued common stock, thereby increasing the common stock account and the additional paid-in capital account for common stock, and acquired treasury stock. The net income for the year and the dividends declared were closed to retained earnings. The ending balance for each account is shown on the bottom line.

Book Value per Share of Common Stock

The book value of a share of stock is the stockholders' equity amount applicable to a single share of stock. Since the stockholders' equity is equal to total assets minus total liabilities, book value also represents the net assets per share of stock. Data on book value per share of a corporation's common stock are often included in corporate annual reports and in the financial press.

If a corporation has only common stock outstanding, book value per share is computed by dividing total stockholders' equity by the number of shares outstanding. When a corporation has both preferred and common stock outstanding, the stockholders' equity must be divided between or among the various classes of stock. This allocation depends on the nature of the preferred stock. Generally, if preferred stock is nonparticipating, the equity allocated to the preferred shares is an amount equal to the liquidation or redemption value of the preferred stock plus any cumulative dividends in arrears. To illustrate, assume that a corporation has the following stockholders' equity:

5% cumulative preferred stock, $100 par value, 1,000 shares authorized and outstanding (callable at $106)		$100,000
Common stock, $10 par value, 20,000 shares authorized issued, and outstanding		200,000
Additional paid-in capital:		
On preferred stock	$40,000	
On common stock	10,000	50,000
Total contributed capital		$350,000
Retained earnings		56,000
Total stockholders' equity		$406,000

If there are no unpaid dividends on the preferred stock, equity equal to the call price or redemption value of the preferred stock ($106 per share) is allocated to the preferred shares, and the remainder applies to the common stock. Thus, the book value per share of common stock is computed as follows:

Total stockholders' equity	$406,000
Less: Amount allocated to preferred	106,000
Equity to common stock	$300,000

$$\text{Book value per share of common stock} = \frac{\$300,000}{20,000} = \$15.00$$

If there are unpaid preferred dividends, an additional amount equal to the arrearage is allocated to the preferred stock. For example, assume that the preferred stock mentioned in the previous illustration has one year of dividends in arrears. In this situation, the unpaid preferred dividends of $5,000 are also allocated to the preferred stock, and the book value per share of common stock is computed as follows:

Total stockholders' equity		$406,000
Less: Amount allocated to preferred:		
Redemption value	$106,000	
Dividends in arrears	5,000	111,000
Equity to common stock		$295,000

$$\text{Book value per share of common stock} = \frac{\$295,000}{20,000} = \$14.75$$

Because the market value of the assets may differ from book values based on generally accepted accounting principles, the book value per share does not indicate the amount that would be distributed to the owner of each share of stock if the assets of the corporation are sold and its liabilities are paid. That is, any gains or losses from the disposal of assets or the settlement of liabilities and any expenses involved in the liquidation process affect the shareholders' equity. Although book value per share may have some effect on the market price, the market price is much more likely to be influenced by factors such as current and expected future earnings, dividend prospects, and general economic conditions. Depending upon the specific circumstances, book value per share may be more or less than market price per share. Therefore, book value data should be used with extreme caution in making decisions concerning the value of a corporation's stock.

SUMMARY

The simplest and most common form of business organization is the sole proprietorship. A single individual owns, controls, and usually manages the firm's assets and receives the profits from its operations.

The sole proprietorship is not considered a separate entity for income tax purposes, and the owner is taxed on all earnings of the business, whether or not the owner withdraws them. Investments and earnings are generally recorded in the capital account and withdrawals in the withdrawals account. The withdrawals account, if used, is then closed to the capital account at the end of the period.

Accounting for the partnership form of business organization is considerably more complex in that more than a single owner is involved. A partnership is an association of two or more persons organized to carry on, as co-owners, a business for profit. The partnership agreement serves as the basis for the formation and operation of the partnership and should include all essential data. Significant characteristics of a partnership include the ease of formation, the applicability of the mutual agency concept, the existence of unlimited liability of each partner and limited life of the enterprise, and the co-ownership of the assets and earnings. The partnership has certain advantages, such as the ability to combine the skills and capital of several individuals, and certain disadvantages, such as unlimited liability of the partners. These and other relevant factors should be evaluated and weighed in each case.

A separate individual capital and withdrawals account is maintained for each partner. Upon the formation of the partnership, each capital account is credited for that individual's cash contribution or an agreed-upon value of property contributions. At the end of each period, profits or losses are divided among the partners according to the terms of the partnership agreement.

A corporation is a separate legal entity permitted to engage in activities in a manner similar to those performed by a natural person. Other important characteristics of a corporation include the transferability of ownership, continuity of life, limited liability of owners, separation of ownership and management, corporate taxation, and government regulation.

Forming a corporation includes obtaining a state corporate charter, electing a board of directors, adopting bylaws, and issuing capital stock to shareholders. The expenses incurred in this process are referred to as organization costs and are either expensed in the current period or accumulated in an intangible asset account and amortized over a reasonable but arbitrarily selected period of time.

The two primary sources of the equity capital of a corporation are contributions by shareholders and earnings retained in the business. In exchange for their contributions, the shareholders receive stock certificates and certain basic rights. Common stock usually entitles its owners to vote in stockholders' meetings, to share in corporate earnings through dividends, to maintain a proportionate interest in the firm when additional shares are issued, and to share in the distribution of remaining assets upon liquidation. Preferred stock usually has limited or no voting rights but does have preference in dividend and liquidation distributions. In addition, preferred stock may be cumulative, participating, convertible, and/or callable.

Capital stock may have an arbitrary value established by the corporate charter (referred to as par value) or established by the corporate directors (referred to as stated value). This value generally has no relationship to the selling price of the stock, but a firm may be required to retain a corresponding amount in the business to protect corporate creditors. Upon issuance of stock, the corporation credits the capital stock account for the par or stated value and credits additional paid-in capital for any excess. If the stock has no par or stated value, the entire proceeds of the sale are credited to capital stock.

The retained earnings of a corporation reflects the accumulated net income and losses of the firm less all dividend distributions to shareholders.

A corporation may distribute a portion or all of its accumulated earnings to the stockholders in the form of ordinary dividends. Additionally, the firm may return a portion of the original investment in the form of a liquidating dividend. The important dates to be noted in relation to a dividend distribution are the dates of declaration, record, and payment. Although dividends are usually paid in cash, the corporation may choose to issue a stock dividend. A stock dividend has no effect on the amount of stockholders' equity, but does require a transfer of an appropriate amount from the retained earnings account to the capital accounts. Small stock dividends (less than 20 to 25 percent) are capitalized at the fair market value; large stock dividends (more than 20 to 25 percent) require the capitalization of only the par or stated value of the shares. Stockholders may also be issued additional shares in a stock split. In this case, no capitalization of retained earnings is required, although a memorandum is made to indicate the change in the number of shares outstanding and in the par or stated value of the stock.

A firm may wish to purchase its own stock from shareholders and retain the shares for future reissuance or cancellation. The purchase and resale of such stock is referred to as treasury stock transactions. Treasury stock held by a corporation when financial statements are prepared is shown on the balance sheet as a deduction from total stockholders' equity.

In reporting financial position to its stockholders, a firm may wish to indicate that the entire balance of retained earnings is not available for distribution as dividends, because certain amounts have been appropriated for special purposes. This may be accomplished by segregating the unappropriated retained earnings from the appropriated amount on the balance sheet. Additional detail regarding the retained earnings account is provided by the statement of retained earnings, which is included as one of or as a part of the periodic financial statements issued by a corporation.

The book value per share of common stock represents the amount of stockholders' equity or net assets applicable to a single share of common stock. If preferred stock is outstanding, an appropriate amount of equity must first be allocated to those shares before computing book value.

Key Definitions

Additional paid-in capital—the amount received on the issuance of capital stock in excess of its par or stated value.

Appropriation of retained earnings—the reclassification of a portion of retained earnings by transfer to an appropriation account.

Articles of incorporation—included in the application made to the state for a corporate charter and contain information concerning the corporation.

Book value per share—the amount of stockholders' equity (i.e., net assets) applicable to each share of common stock outstanding.

Capital account—the capital account of a proprietorship or a partnership consists of a separate owner or partner account that reflects the investments by the owner (partner) plus the owner's (each partner's) share of the earnings or losses from the operations of the business less any withdrawals made.

Capital stock—transferable stock shares that evidence ownership in a corporation.

Capitalization of retained earnings—an amount transferred from retained earnings to contributed capital at the time a stock dividend is declared.

Cash dividend—a distribution of cash to stockholders in the form of a dividend.

Charter—a contract between the state and the corporation. It includes the general corporation laws of the state and the specific provisions of the articles of incorporation.

Common stock—stock that has the basic rights of ownership and represents the residual ownership in the corporation.

Continuity of life—status as a separate legal entity gives the corporation a perpetual existence.

Contributed capital—capital invested directly by the shareholders of the corporation.

Controller—an officer who is responsible for the accounting function of the business.

Convertible preferred stock—stock that includes the privilege of allowing the shareholder to exchange preferred shares for a specified number of common shares at his or her option.

Corporation—an association of persons joined together for some common purpose, organized in accordance with state laws as a legal entity, separate, and distinct from its owners.

Cumulative preferred stock—backed by a provision that if all or part of the specified dividend on preferred stock is not paid during a given year, the amount of the unpaid dividends accumulates and must be paid in a subsequent year before any dividends can be paid on preferred stock for the current period and on common stock.

Date of declaration—the date on which the board of directors formally establishes a liability for a dividend of a specified amount to the stockholders.

Date of payment—the date on which the dividends are paid to the stockholders of record.

Date of record—the date on which the corporation prepares a list of stockholders who are to receive the dividends.

Deficit—debit balance in the retained earnings account.

Dividends—distributions made by a corporation to its shareholders.

Division of profits and losses—the partnership agreement determines the method of dividing partnership profits or losses among the partners. In the absence of such an agreement, the law provides that profits or losses shall be divided equally among the partners.

Incorporators—the persons who legally form a corporation.

Legal capital—a limit on the amount of assets that can be distributed to the stockholders of a corporation prior to liquidation and settlement of the corporate debts.

Limited liability—the creditors of the corporation have a claim against the assets of the corporation and not against the personal property of the stockholders.

Limited life—a partnership is legally dissolved upon the withdrawal, death, incapacity, or bankruptcy of any of its partners.

Mutual agency—each partner may act as an agent of the partnership, with the power to enter into contracts within the scope of the normal business operations.

No-par stock—stock without a par value.

Organization costs—the costs necessary to form the corporation.

Par value—an arbitrary value established in the corporate charter and printed on the stock certificate. It establishes the legal capital of the corporation in many states.

Participating preferred stock—preferred stock that has the right to participate in some specified manner with common stockholders in dividends in excess of the stated preferred dividend plus a stipulated amount paid to the common shareholders.

Partnership—association of two or more persons to carry on a business under a contractual arrangement.

Partnership agreement—this written contract of partnership sets forth the agreement between the partners as to the conditions for the formation and operation of the partnership.

Preferred as to dividends—stock that is entitled to receive a stated dividend each year before any dividend is paid on the common stock.

Preferred stock—a class of stock that has different rights from those associated with common stock.

Retained earnings—represents the accumulated earnings of the corporation, increased by net income and reduced by net losses and distributions to shareholders.

Sole proprietorship—business owned by one person.

Stock dividend—a distribution of additional shares to the stockholders in proportion to their existing holdings.

Stock split—a proportionate increase in the number of shares outstanding, usually intended to effect a decrease in the market value of the stock.

Stock subscriptions—involves an agreement by the corporation to sell a certain number of shares at a specified price to an investor with the payment at some future date(s). Upon full payment, the purchaser gains control of the stock.

Treasury stock—consists of shares that have been previously issued and are reacquired by the corporation but not formally retired.

Uniform Partnership Act—this act, which has been adopted in most states, governs the formation, operation, and liquidation of partnerships.

Unlimited liability—each partner is personally liable to the creditors of the partnership in the event that the partnership assets are insufficient to meet its obligations.

Withdrawals account—cash or other assets withdrawn by an owner (partner) during the period are reflected in the withdrawals account. Withdrawals accounts are closed to the capital account(s) at the end of the period.

QUESTIONS

1. List the three basic types of business organizations.

2. What are the primary advantages of the partnership form of organization?

3. List and describe three important disadvantages of organizing a business as a partnership.

4. What are the primary advantages of organizing a business as a corporation rather than as a sole proprietorship or partnership? The disadvantages?

5. Describe the following characteristics of a corporation:

    a. separate legal entity
    b. limited liability

    c.   transferability of ownership interest
    d.   continuity of existence

6.   Explain the meaning of the term "double taxation" as it applies to a corporation.

7.   Explain what is meant by the number of shares of stock authorized, issued, and outstanding.

8.   What are four basic rights of a stockholder?

9.   Describe the following features which may be applied to an issuance of preferred stock:

    a.   cumulative
    b.   participating
    c.   preferred as to assets
    d.   callable
    e.   convertible

10.   Explain the meaning of par value. Describe the accounting treatment of stock issued for more or less than par value.

11.   Distinguish between par value and no-par stock.

12.   What is the primary disadvantage of issuing stock for an amount less than its par value?

13.   What are organization costs? Describe two alternative accounting treatments for such costs.

14.   Indicate the nature and balance sheet classification of the subscriptions receivable and common stock subscribed accounts.

15.   What information regarding preferred stock should be disclosed in the balance sheet?

16.   How should preferred dividends in arrears be reported in the balance sheet?

17.   Describe the nature of the following three dates related to dividends: (a) date of declaration, (b) date of record, and (c) date of payment. What is the accounting significance of each of these dates?

18.   Distinguish between a cash dividend and a stock dividend.

19.   Why does a corporation normally declare a stock dividend?

20.   What is the purpose of a stock split?

21.   Why is a portion of retained earnings capitalized upon the issuance of a stock dividend?

22.   What is the difference between a stock dividend and a stock split? How does the accounting for a large stock dividend and a stock split differ?

23.   For what purposes might a company purchase shares of its own stock?

24.   What is treasury stock? How does it affect the ability of the corporation to pay dividends? How does it differ from authorized but unissued stock?

25.   What is the effect on stockholders' equity when treasury stock is reissued for (a) more than the original cost, (b) less than its cost to the corporation?

26. What is the purpose of an appropriation of retained earnings? How does a company provide for and eliminate an appropriation of retained earnings?

27. What is the significance of the book value per share of common stock? Does the book value equal the amount of assets which would be distributed to each share of stock upon liquidation? Explain.

28. How is the book value per share of common stock computed when there is preferred stock outstanding?

EXERCISES

29. Give the journal entries required to record each of the following stock transactions:

    a. Issuance of 1,000 shares of $10 par value common stock at $14 per share.
    b. Issuance of 100 shares of $100 par value preferred stock for a total of $12,000.
    c. Issuance of 500 shares of no-par common stock for $20 per share.
    d. Issuance of 2,000 shares of $10 par value common stock for land. Recent sales and purchases of the stock have been made at a price of $20 per share. The value of the land is not readily determinable.

30. Make the journal entries necessary to record the issuance of stock in each of the following independent cases.

    a. One hundred shares of $25 par value stock are sold at par for cash.
    b. Eighty shares of $15 par value stock are sold at $17 each for cash.
    c. One thousand shares of no-par capital stock are issued at $14 per share.
    d. Five hundred shares of no-par capital stock with a stated value of $10 per share are sold for $11 per share.

31. Jeffry Company was organized on March 1, 19X1. The authorized capital was 20,000 shares of $50 par value, 6 percent, cumulative preferred stock and 50,000 shares of $10 par value common stock. At the date of organization, all the common stock was issued at $20 per share and 10,000 shares of the preferred stock were sold at par.

    Required:

    Prepare the stockholders' equity section of the balance sheet for Jeffry Co. on March 1, after the issuance of the stock.

32. Niblet Corporation was organized on January 1, 19X1. On that date, the corporation issued 1,000 shares of $100 par value, 6 percent preferred stock and 20,000 shares of $10 par value common stock. During the first five years of its life, the corporation paid the following total dividends to its stockholders.

19X1	$ 0
19X2	6,000
19X3	20,000
19X4	15,000
19X5	18,000

    Determine the total dividends paid to each class of stockholders assuming that the preferred stock is:

    a. cumulative and nonparticipating.
    b. noncumulative and nonparticipating.

33. Monte Carter owns 300 of the 30,000 outstanding shares of stock in the MNX Company, which allows preemptive rights to all its existing stockholders. If MNX Company decides to issue an additional 6,000 shares of stock, how many of the new shares may Carter purchase? What would be his percent interest in the company?

34. A junior accountant for the Fetters Company is unsure as to how to complete the following stockholders' equity section of the balance sheet.

Stockholder's Equity:

5 percent preferred stock *(A)* par value, 15,000 shares authorized, 9,000 shares issues and outstanding	$ 810,000
Common stock, $20 par value, 200,000 shares authorized, *(B)* shares issued and outstanding	3,000,000
Common stock subscribed, 1,500 shares	*(C)*
Additional paid-in capital:	
Common stock issued and subscribed:	*(D)*
Preferred stock	80,000
Total contributed capital	*(E)*
Retained earnings	*(F)*
Total stockholders' equity	$4,099,000

Additional information:

Earnings for the corporation over its three-year life were $18,000 a year. No dividends had ever been paid.

Required:

Complete this stockholders' equity section by filling in amounts for the letters A–F above.

Problems

35. Consider each of the following independent cases.

a. Kanoch, Inc. issues 50 shares of $25 par value stock in exchange for land appraised at $1,500. The shares are not actively traded. Record the issuance of the stock on the books of Kanoch, Inc.

b. Red Rider Stables, Inc. acquired 100 acres of prime grazing land in exchange for 200 shares of no-par capital stock. It was found that a similar 100 acre tract had sold the previous year for $11,000. The company's stock has not been registered with a major exchange but the company's balance sheet reveals a book value of $50 per share. Record the issuance of the stock on the books of Red Rider Stables. Inc.

36. On March 15, the board of directors of Gunsmith Corporation declared a cash dividend of $1 per share to the stockholders of record on March 20. The dividend is payable on April 1. The corporation had 10,000 shares of common stock outstanding.

Required:

Prepare the journal entries required on the date of declaration, the date of record, and the payment date.

37. The stockholders' equity section of the balance sheet of Park Company on December 31, 19X1, is shown below:

6% preferred stock, $100 par value (callable at 105) 5,000 shares authorized issued, and outstanding	$ 500,000
Common stock, $5 par value, 60,000 shares, authorized and 50,000 shares issued and outstanding	250,000
Additional paid-in capital	400,000
Retained earnings	75,000
Total stockholders' equity	$1,225,000

Required:

Compute the book value per share of common stock.

38. By using the following code, indicate each transaction's effect on the respective columns.

| + = increases | 0 = no effect |
| – = decreases | ? = cannot be determined |

The market value of the company's common stock exceeds par value.

	Common Stock	Retained Earnings	Stockholders' Equity	Book Value Per Share of Common Stock
a. Common declared a cash dividend payable in the next fiscal year to persons holding shares of preferred stock.				
b. Company received shares of its own common stock, donated by a wealthy shareholder.				
c. Company purchased shares of its own common stock through a broker at the New York Stock Exchange.				
d. Company declared and issued a stock dividend on the common stock.				
e. A cash dividend was declared and paid.				
f. Retained Earnings were appropriated for plant expansion.				
g. Treasury shares of common stock were sold at an amount in excess of the purchase price to the corporation.				

39. Jones Co. had the following stock outstanding from January 1, 19X0, to December 31, 19X5.

   a. Common stock, $10 par value, 20,000 shares authorized and outstanding.
   b. Preferred stock, $100 par value with a $6 stated dividend, 10,000 shares authorized, 5,000 shares issued and outstanding.

During that period, Jones Co. paid the following dividends:

19X0	$ 0
19X1	80,000
19X2	0
19X3	30,000
19X4	70,000
19X5	20,000

Compute the amount of preferred dividends and common stock dividends in each year assuming that:

1. The preferred stock is noncumulative.
2. The preferred stock is cumulative.

40. Akens Co. was organized on January 1, 19X1. A portion of the December 31, 19X2, balance sheet of Akens Co. appeared as follows:

Stockholders' Equity:

6 percent preferred stock, $100 par		
value, 20,000 shares authorized		$ 500,000
Preferred stock subscribed		100,000
Common stock, $10 par value,		
100,000 shares authorized		400,000
Common stock subscribed		50,000
Additional paid-in capital:		
On common stock issued	$200,000	
On common stock subscribed	50,000	
On preferred stock issued	25,000	
On preferred stock subscribed	10,000	285,000
Retained earnings		330,000
Total stockholders' equity		$1,665,000

Required:

1. How many shares of preferred stock are outstanding?
2. How many shares of common stock are outstanding?
3. How many shares of preferred stock are subscribed?
4. How many shares of common stock are subscribed?
5. What were the average issue prices of the common and the preferred shares outstanding?
6. What were the average subscription prices of the common stock and the preferred stock?
7. What is the total contributed capital of Akens Co.?

41. The Auburn Corporation earned income of $33,000, $25,000, $15,000, $12,000 and $55,000 during the last five years. The common stock consisted of 200,000 shares outstanding for the first three years and 250,000 shares for the last two years. Common stock has a par value of $1 per share. The preferred stock is 7 percent cumulative and nonparticipating. There were 50,000 shares of preferred stock issued and outstanding for the first two years and 75,000 shares the last three years. Preferred stock has a par value of $5 per share.

Required:

Calculate the dividends which each class of stock would receive over each of the last five years assuming (1) the entire net income was distributed each year, and (2) only 80 percent of the reported net income was distributed in the first three years, 90 percent in the last two years.

42. The stockholders' equity of Billy, Inc. appears as follows on its December 31, 19X1 balance sheet.

Common stock, $9 par value,	
25,000 shares outstanding	$225,000
Additional paid-in capital	125,000
Total contributed capital	$350,000
Retained earnings	195,000
Total stockholders' equity	$545,000

Required:

Make the journal entries necessary to record the transactions in the following independent cases:

1. Billy, Inc. declares and distributes a 60 percent stock dividend on July 1 when the stock is selling for $30 per share.
2. Billy, Inc. declares a 3-for-1 stock split on July 1 when the market price of its stock is $60 per share.

3.   Billy, Inc. declares and distributes a 5 percent stock dividend on July 1 when the market price of the stock is $15 per share.

43.   The stockholders' equity section of the Buckeye Company appeared as follows on January 1:

Common stock, $15 par value, 20,000	
shares authorized, issued, and outstanding	$300,000
Additional paid-in capital	75,000
Total contributed capital	$375,000
Retained earnings	80,000
Total stockholders' equity	$455,000

On February 1, the company purchased 800 of its outstanding shares at $25 per share. On June 15, the company reissued 500 of these shares at $29 per share. Then, on July 15, the company resold the other 300 shares for $24 per share.

Required:

Prepare the journal entries necessary to record the above transactions on the books of the Buckeye Company. Also, prepare the stockholders' equity section of their balance sheet as of July 15.

44.   The stockholders' equity section of the Aggie Corporation as of December 31, 19X1 shows:

6% preferred, cumulative capital stock,		
$100 par value, 50,000 shares		
authorized, 20,000 shares issued		
and outstanding		$2,000,000
Common stock, no par, $10 stated		
value, 400,000 shares authorized,		
260,000 shares issued and outstanding		2,600,000
Additional paid-in capital:		
On preferred stock	$ 80,000	
On common stock	1,560,000	1,640,000
Retained earnings		1,200,000
Total stockholders' equity		$7,440,000

Note: Dividends on preferred stock are three years in arrears.

Required:

Compute the book value per share of the common stock at December 31, 19X1.

45.   The Texan Co. had the following stockholders' equity on January 1, 19X1.

Common stock, $5 par value, 100,000	
shares authorized, 50,000 shares	
issued and outstanding	$250,000
Additional paid-in capital	150,000
Total contributed capital	$400,000
Retained earnings	100,000
Total stockholders' equity	$500,000

During 19X1, the company had the following transactions related to the stockholders' equity.

Jan.	20	Issued 5,000 shares of stock for $10 per share.
Feb.	15	Purchased 3,000 shares of Texan Co. common stock for $11 per share.
May	10	Declared a $.20 per share cash dividend to the stockholders of record on May 15. The dividend is payable on June 1.
June	1	Paid the cash dividend.
	15	Sold 1,000 shares of treasury stock for $13 per share.
Aug.	15	Sold 1,000 shares of treasury stock for $10 per share.
Sept.	10	Declared a 10 percent stock dividend for the stockholders of record on September 15 to be distributed on October 1. The market price of the stock was $11 per share on September 15.
Oct.	1	Distributed the stock dividend.
Nov.	1	The Board of Directors decided to appropriate $20,000 of retained earnings for future plant expansion.
Dec.	31	Net income for the year was $35,000. The income summary and dividend accounts were closed to retained earnings.

Required:

1. Give the necessary journal entries to record the transactions.
2. Prepare a statement of retained earnings at December 31, 19X1.

46. The stockholders' equity of the National Company at December 31, 19X1, was as follows:

6% noncumulative preferred stock, $100 par value, call price per share $110, authorized 70,000 shares, issued 10,000 shares	$1,000,000
$5 noncumulative preferred stock, $100 par value, call price per share $105, authorized 100,000 shares, issued 5,000 shares	500,000
Common stock, $50 par value, authorized 100,000 shares, issued 40,000 shares, of which 1,000 shares are held in the treasury	2,000,000
Additional paid-in capital:	
On 6% preferred stock	100,000
On common stock	255,000
Total contributed capital	$3,855,000
Retained earnings (of which $60,000, an amount equal to the cost of the treasury stock purchased, is unavailable for dividends)	1,500,000
	$5,355,000
Deduct: Cost of treasury stock (1,000 shares)	60,000
Total stockholders' equity	$5,295,000

Note: Preferred dividends for 19X0 and 19X1 have not been paid.

During 19X2, National Company had the following transactions affecting the stockholders' equity:

Jan	5	Sold 11,000 shares of the common stock at $55 per share.
Feb.	1	Declared a 10 percent stock dividend on the common stock; the market value of the stock on that date was $60 per share.
	28	Paid the stock dividend declared on February 1.
May	1	Purchased 500 shares of the common stock for the treasury at a cost of $65 per share.
	5	Sold all of the treasury stock held for $70 per share.
	9	Stockholders voted to reduce the par value of common stock to $25 per share and increase authorized shares to 200,000. The company issued the additional shares to effect this stock split.
June	30	The Board of Directors declared a $1 per share dividend on common stock and the regular annual dividend on both classes of preferred stock. All dividends are payable on July 20 to shareholders of record as of July 10.

Required:

1. Prepare the necessary journal entries to record the preceding transactions.
2. Prepare the stockholders' equity section of the balance sheet at June 30, 19X2.

47. The Peterson Company was organized on January 1, 19X0, with 10,000 shares of $10 par value common stock authorized, issued, and outstanding. Journalize the following transactions which took place in 19X4:

Jan. 1   The corporation purchased 100 shares of its common stock for $15 a share.
Feb. 1   The corporation sold the 100 shares purchased on January 1 for a total price of $1,750.
Mar. 1   Mrs. Moneybags, a stockholder, donated 100 shares of the X Corporation's common stock to the corporation.
      5   The corporation sold the 100 donated shares for a total price of $2,500.
Apr. 1   The corporation purchased 100 shares of its own stock for $9 a share.
May   1   The corporation sold the 100 shares purchased on April 1 for a total price of $500.
Dec. 15 A $.50 per share dividend on common stock was declared, to be paid on January 15, 19X5.

48. The Jones Co. was organized on January 1, 19X0, with 20,000 shares of $10 par value common stock and 5,000 shares of $100 par value, 6 percent preferred stock authorized. The balances in the stockholders' equity accounts on December 31, 19X3, were as follows:

Preferred stock	$100,000
Common stock	120,000
Additional paid-in capital:	
On preferred stock	5,000
On common stock	60,000
Retained earnings	$190,000

During 19X4, the company had the following transactions that affected the stockholders' equity:

		Number	*Amount*
a.	Issuance of common stock	5,000	$ 20 per share
b.	Purchase of its own shares of common stock	4,000	$ 22 per share
c.	Reissuance of treasury stock	1,000	$ 24 per share
d.	Issuance of preferred stock	1,000	$ 102 per share
e.	Payment of dividend on common stock		$ .50 per share
f.	Payment of dividend on preferred stock		$ 6 per share
g.	Appropriation of retained earnings for future plant expansion		$100,000
h.	Net income for the year		$ 60,000
i.	Stock split on common stock with par value reduced to $5 per share	2 for 1	

Required:

Prepare the stockholders' equity section of the balance sheet for Jones Co. on December 31, 19X4.

49. O'Hare Company is considering a stock dividend.

The common stock is currently selling at $34 a share.

Common Stock, $10 Par	$ 800,000
Paid-In Capital in Excess of Par-Common	1,200,000
Retained Earnings	1,300,000
Total Stockholders' Equity	$3,300,000

Required:

Consider each event independently.

a. Make the journal entry for a 15 percent stock dividend.
b. Make the journal entry for a 40 percent stock dividend.
c. Make the journal entry for a 2 for 1 stock split.

50. The following stockholders' equity section applies to MacArthur Company on December 31, 19x4.

Common Stock, $10 Par	$30,000
Paid-In Capital in Excess of	
Par-Common	4,800
Retained Earnings	18,000
Total Stockholders' Equity	$52,800

Required:

a. Make journal entries to record the following 19x5 events.

February 14	Purchased 90 shares of treasury stock at $15 each.
March 17	Sold 30 shares of treasury stock for $17 each.
June 30	Issued 100 shares of common stock for $19 each.
October 31	Sold 30 shares of treasury stock for $12 each.

b. Assuming these were the only transactions affecting common stock during 19x5, answer the following questions about stockholders' equity on December 31, 19x5.
   1. How many shares are outstanding?
   2. If the company had profit of $6,000 and gave dividends of $4,000 in 19x5, what is the total amount of stockholders' equity at the end of 19x5?
c. Prepare a stockholders' equity section in good form.

51. Below is given the stockholders' equity section of the balance sheet of the Virginia Company as of December 31, 19X0:

6% preferred stock, $100 par value, 1,000	
shares authorized, 100 shares issued	
and outstanding, callable at $110	$10,000
Common stock, $5 par value, 20,000 shares	
authorized, 200 shares issued,	
180 shares outstanding	1,000
Additional paid-in capital:	
Preferred stock	2,000
Common stock	2,000
From treasury stock transactions	100
Retained earnings	40,000
Treasury stock, 20 shares, at cost	(150)
Stockholders' Equity	$ 54,950

Required:

a. Using the above stockholders' equity section, you are to prepare journal entries for each of the transactions which follow. Each transaction is to be treated as *independent* of all others *unless* otherwise noted.

   1. Sold 10 shares of common at par.
   2. Sold 10 shares of common at $7 per share.
   3. Sold 10 shares of common at $4 per share.
   4. Obtained subscriptions to 10 shares of common at a price of $8 per share.

5. Received cash and issued shares for the 10 shares subscribed to in (4) above.
6. Declared the annual dividend on the preferred stock and a $1 per share dividend on the common stock.
7. Date of record on the dividend in (6) above.
8. Paid the dividend in (6) above.
9. Declared a 10 percent stock dividend on the common stock; the fair market value of the common stock was $15 per share.
10. Date of record on the dividend declared in (9) above.
11. Distributed the dividend in (9) above.
12. Split the common stock 5 for 1 and changed the par value to $1 per share.
13. Sold the treasury shares for $150.
14. Sold the treasury shares for $200.
15. Sold the treasury shares for $30.

   b. Calculate the book value per share of common stock from the stockholders' equity section shown above.

52. For each of the transactions listed, indicate the effect(s), if any, on the company's year-end: (1) Balance Sheet, (2) Income Statement, and (3) Statement of Cash Flows. Your answers should be as complete and specific as possible.

   a. Sold stock at its par value.
   b. Sold stock at a price in excess of its par value.
   c. Sold stock at a price less than its par value.

53. For each of the transactions listed, indicate the effect(s), if any, on the company's year-end: (1) Balance Sheet, (2) Income Statement, and (3) Statement of Cash Flows. Your answers should be as complete and specific as possible.

   a. Declared a cash dividend.
   b. Record date for the dividend.
   c. Paid the dividend.

54. For each of the transactions listed, indicate the effect(s), if any, on the company's year-end: (1) Balance Sheet, (2) Income Statement, and (3) Statement of Cash Flows. Your answers should be as complete and specific as possible.

   a. Declared a 10 percent stock dividend.
   b. Record date for the dividend.
   c. Paid the dividend.

55. For each of the transactions listed, indicate the effect(s), if any, on the company's year-end: (1) Balance Sheet, (2) Income Statement, and (3) Statement of Cash Flows. Your answers should be as complete and specific as possible.

   a. Reacquired shares of the company's own common stock.
   b. Sold the shares (in "a" above) at a price in excess of their cost.

56. For each of the transactions listed, indicate the effect(s), if any, on the company's year-end: (1) Balance Sheet, (2) Income Statement, and (3) Statement of Cash Flows. Your answers should be as complete and specific as possible.

   a. Split the common stock, 2 for 1.
   b. Announced an appropriation of retained earnings for plant expansion.
   c. Paid cash for the plant expansion and returned the appropriation to retained earnings.

Refer to the Annual Report in Chapter 1 of the text.

57. At the end of the most recent year, what is the amount of the total stockholders' equity?

58. At the end of the most recent year, which account represents the largest amount of stockholders' equity?

59. At the end of the most recent year, where is net income reflected in the stockholders' equity section of the balance sheet?

60. Comparing the two most recent years presented, what is the increase/decrease in the capital stock (or common stock) account?

61. How much were the dividends per share in the most recent year?

62. What amount of treasury stock was issued during the current year? What amount of treasury stock was purchased?

Appendix A
Partnership Accounting

Upon the formation of a partnership, resources invested by the partners are recorded in the accounts. A capital account for each partner is credited for the amount of net assets invested (assets contributed less liabilities assumed by the partnership). Individual asset accounts are debited for the assets contributed and liability accounts are credited for any debts assumed by the partnership.

If the investments made by the partners are entirely in the form of cash, the entry required is a debit to cash and a credit to the partner's capital account for the amount of cash invested. When noncash assets such as land, equipment, or merchandise are invested, these assets are recorded at their fair market values as of the date of investment. The valuations assigned to these assets may differ from the cost or book value of the assets on the books of the contributing partner prior to the formation of the partnership. The amounts recorded by the partnership must be agreed upon by all partners. Amounts agreed upon represent the acquisition cost of the assets to the newly formed partnership. The recording of assets at their current market value as of the date they are contributed to the partnership is necessary in order to provide a fair presentation in the partnership financial statements and to assure a fair distribution of the property among partners in the event a dissolution of the partnership occurs.

To illustrate the entries required at the formation of a partnership, assume that Mantle and Maris, who operate separate sporting good stores as sole proprietorships, agree to form a partnership by combining their two businesses. It is agreed that each partner will contribute $10,000 in cash and all of his individual business assets and that the partnership will assume the liabilities of each of their separate businesses. Assuming that the partners have agreed upon the amounts at which noncash assets are to be recorded, the following journal entries on the books of the partnership are necessary in order to record the formation of the M&M Partnership:

Cash	10,000	
Accounts receivable	15,000	
Merchandise inventory	30,000	
Accounts payable		5,000
Mantle, capital		50,000
Cash	10,000	
Merchandise inventory	35,000	
Building	50,000	
Land	15,000	
Notes payable		10,000
Maris, capital		100,000

Division of Profits and Losses

The net income or loss of a partnership is divided among the partners according to the terms or procedures specified in the partnership agreement. If provisions are made only for dividing profits, any losses are divided in the same manner as profits. In the absence of any provisions for sharing profits and losses in the partnership agreement, the law provides that they must be shared equally among the partners.

The specific method of dividing profits and losses selected in a partnership situation may be designed to recognize and compensate the partners for differences in their investments in the partnership, for differences in their personal services rendered, for special abilities or reputations of individual partners, or for some combination of these and other factors. The following are examples of some of the methods that may be given consideration in the division of partnership profits or losses:

1. A fixed fractional basis.
2. A capital ratio base.
3. Interest on capital.
4. Salaries to partners.

The specific method chosen by the partners may incorporate one or more of the methods of dividing partnership profits and losses.

As a basis for these illustrations, assume that the M&M Partnership has net income of $30,000 for the year ended December 31, 19X1. The following capital accounts reflect the investments made by Mantle and Maris during 19X1.

Mantle, Capital			Maris, Capital	
1/1/X1	50,000		1/1/X1	100,000
7/1/X1	20,000		5/1/X1	60,000

Fixed Fractional Basis

Partners may agree on any fractional or percentage basis as a means of dividing partnership profits and losses. For example, assume that in order to reflect differences in their initial capital contributions, services provided, and abilities, Mantle and Maris agreed to allocate one-fourth of any profits or losses to Mantle and three-fourths to Maris. Consequently, at the end of 19X1 the $30,000 net income is allocated $7,500 to Mantle (¼ × $30,000) and $22,500 to Maris (¾ × $30,000). The division of net income is recorded with a closing entry—the income summary account is closed to each partner's individual capital account according to the terms of the partnership agreement. The entry required in order to divide the net income among the two partners is as follows:

Income summary	30,000	
Mantle, capital		7,500
Maris, capital		22,500

Additional closing entries are also necessary in order to transfer any balances in the partners' withdrawals accounts to their respective capital accounts.

Capital Ratio

When the invested capital of a partnership is a major factor in the generation of income, net income may be divided on the basis of the relative capital balances of the partners. If a capital ratio is used, the partners must agree whether the beginning capital balances or average capital balances should be used.

For example, the partners may agree to distribute net income on the basis of capital balances at the beginning of the period. Division of the $30,000 net income of the M&M Partnership on the basis of the ratio of the partners' beginning capital balances is as follows:

Partner	Capital Balance 1/1x1	Fraction of Total Capital	Division of Income
Mantle	$ 50,000	$ 50 ÷ $150 or ⅓	$10,000
Maris	100,000	$100 ÷ $150 or ⅔	20,000
Total	$150,000		$30,000

The income summary account is closed to the partners' capital accounts at the end of the year by the following journal entry:

Income summary	30,000	
Mantle, capital		10,000
Maris, capital		20,000

In order to reflect any significant capital account changes that may occur during a period in the division of income, the partners may agree to use the average capital balance ratio as a means of sharing partnership income. The average capital balance for each partner is equal to the weighted average of the different balances in their capital account during a period. In order to compute the weighted average, each balance in a partner's capital account is multiplied by the number of months until the next transaction affected the balance or to the end of the period. The sum of these amounts is divided by twelve in order to yield the partner's average capital balance during the year.

Mantle's capital balance at the beginning of the year was $50,000; Maris's was $100,000. Maris invested an additional $60,000 on May 1 and Mantle invested an additional $20,000 on July 1. The computation of the average capital balance for Mantle and Maris is as follows:

Partner	Date	Balance	×	Time		Total			Weighted Average
Mantle	1/1/X1	$ 50,000	×	6	=	$ 300,000			
	7/1/X1	70,000	×	6	=	420,000			
						$ 720,000	÷ 12 =		$ 60,000
Maris	1/1/X1	$100,000	×	4	=	$ 400,000			
	5/1/X1	160,000	×	8	=	1,280,000			
						$1,680,000	÷ 12 =		$140,000

After the average capital balances have been computed, the division of net income is based on the ratios of average capital per partner to total average capital. In the case of the M&M Partnership, the calculation is as follows:

Partner	Average Capital	Fraction of Total Average Capital	Division of Income
Mantle	$ 60,000	$ 60 ÷ $200 or 3/10	$ 9,000
Maris	140,000	$140 ÷ $200 or 7/10	21,000
Total	$200,000		$30,000

Interest on Capital

In some instances, only partial recognition may be given to unequal investments made by the partners in determining the division of income. This may be accomplished by allowing some fixed rate of interest on the capital balances and dividing remaining profits on some other basis. As in the use of capital ratios, interest may be based on beginning or on average capital balances during the period.

To illustrate, assume that Mantle and Maris agree to allow each partner interest at the rate of 8 percent on his beginning capital balance, with any remaining profit to be divided equally. Under this agreement, the $30,000 net income for 19X1 is divided as follows:

	Mantle	Maris	
Income			$30,000
Interest:			
8% × $ 50,000	$ 4,000		$ 4,000
8% × $100,000		$ 8,000	8,000
			$12,000
Remainder:			$18,000
$18,000 × ½	$ 9,000		$ 9,000
$18,000 × ½		$ 9,000	9,000
Total	$13,000	$17,000	$30,000

SALARIES TO PARTNERS

As a means of recognizing differences in the value of personal services contributed to the partnership by individual partners, the partnership agreement may provide for "salary" allowances in the division of income. For this purpose, the agreed-upon salaries are used in the allocation of income but need not actually be paid to the partners. The partnership agreement may also allow for cash withdrawals described as salaries. These withdrawals are treated like all withdrawals made by partners and debited to the withdrawals accounts; they are not salary expenses similar to those paid to employees.

To illustrate, assume that Mantle and Maris are allowed annual salaries of $6,000 and $8,000, respectively, with any remaining profits divided equally. The following division of the $30,000 profit for 19X1 is made:

	Mantle	Maris	Total
Salaries	$ 6,000	$ 8,000	$14,000
Remainder	8,000	8,000	16,000
Total	$14,000	$16,000	$30,000

SALARIES AND INTEREST ON CAPITAL

Sometimes both the investments of the individual partners and the value of the personal services contributed by each may be quite different. In these situations, partners may agree to take into consideration both salaries and interest on capital investments in determining the division of income. Any remaining profit or loss may then be allocated on any agreed-upon fractional basis.

For example, assume that Mantle and Maris agree on the following division of income:

1. Annual salaries of $6,000 to Mantle and $8,000 to Maris.

2. Eight percent interest on beginning capital balances.

3. Any remainder to be divided equally.

Under this agreement, the $30,000 net income for 19X1 is divided as follows:

	Mantle	Maris	Total
Salaries (per agreement)	$ 6,000	$ 8,000	$14,000
Interest:			
8% × $ 50,000	4,000		4,000
8% × $100,000		8,000	8,000
Remainder	2,000	2,000	4,000
Total	$12,000	$18,000	$30,000

Allowing salaries or interest on capital is simply a procedure or step in the process of dividing partnership profits. Since partners are owners, their contributions of capital and personal services are made in an attempt to earn profits. Therefore, these amounts are not considered to be expenses and do not reduce the income of the business.

Salaries and/or Interest in Excess of Income

In the previous illustrations, partnership net income exceeds the total salary and interest allowances to the partners, and the balance is divided between the partners according to the agreed-upon percentage. If net income is less than the sum of the allowable salaries and interest, or if there is a net loss for the period, the residual after the deduction of salaries and interest is negative in amount. This negative amount must then be divided between the partners according to the agreed-upon fractional basis.

To illustrate this situation, assume the same salary and interest allowances as in the previous example. Further, assume that the M&M Partnership has net income of only $20,000 for 19X1. The salary and interest allowances total $10,000 for Mantle and $16,000 for Maris. The total interest and salary allowances of $26,000 exceed the net income of the partnership for the period by $6,000. This excess must be deducted in determining the partners' share of the income as follows:

	Mantle	Maris	Total
Salaries	$ 6,000	$ 8,000	$14,000
Interest	4,000	8,000	12,000
Remainder (divided equally)	(3,000)	(3,000)	(6,000)
Total	$ 7,000	$13,000	$20,000

Partnership Financial Statements

The income statement of a partnership is very similar to that of either a sole proprietorship or a corporation. The statement does not reflect income tax expense, however, because the partnership is not subject to an income tax on its earnings. (Partners are taxed as individuals on their share of the partnership income.) In addition, the allocation of the net income among the partners is often included in the income statement as a final item below the net income figure.

The balance sheet of a partnership differs from that of a sole proprietorship or a corporation primarily in the owners' equity section. The equity section of a partnership reflects the end-of-period capital balances of each individual partner.

A statement disclosing the nature and amount of changes in the partners' capital balances during a period is often prepared for a partnership. For example, the statement of partners' capital for the M&M Partnership might appear as follows:

M&M Partnership
Statement of Partnership Capital
For the Year Ended December 31, 19X1

	Mantle	Maris	Total
Balances, January 1, 19X1	$50,000	$100,000	$150,000
Add: Additional investments	20,000	60,000	80,000
Net income	15,000	15,000	30,000
Total	$85,000	$175,000	$260,000
Less: Withdrawals	(5,000)	(15,000)	(20,000)
Balances, December 31, 19X1	$80,000	$160,000	$240,000

Thus, the December 31, 19X1, balance sheet for M&M would include capital balances of $80.000 for Mantle and $160,000 for Maris.

Admission of a Partner

Although the admission of a new partner to a partnership legally dissolves the existing partnership, a new agreement may be created without disruption of business activities. An additional person may be admitted by purchasing an interest directly from one or more of the current partners or by making an investment in the partnership. When a new partner purchases his or her share of the partnership from a current partner, the payment is made directly to the selling partner. Therefore, there is no change in either the total assets or the total capital of the partnership. When a new partner invests in the partnership by contributing assets to the partnership, however, both the total assets and total capital of the partnership are increased.

Purchase of an Interest From Current Partner(s)

When a new partner acquires his or her interest by purchasing all or part of the interest of one or more of the existing partners, the purchase price is paid directly to the selling partner(s). Therefore, the amount paid is not recorded in the partnership records. The only entry required in the accounts of the partnership is to transfer the interest sold from the selling partner's capital account(s) to a capital account for the new partner.

For example, assume that Mantle and Maris have capital balances of $80,000 and $160,000, respectively. Mantle agrees to sell one-half of his $80,000 interest in the partnership directly to Berra for $50,000. The entry to record this transaction on the partnership books is as follows:

Mantle, capital	40,000	
Berra, capital		40,000

The effect of this transaction is to transfer one-half of Mantle's current capital balance (½ × $80,000) to the new capital account created for Berra. The total capital of the partnership, $240,000, is not affected by the transaction. The entry is not affected by the amount paid by the incoming partner to the selling partner. The $50,000 payment made by Berra to Mantle reflects a bargained transaction between the two people acting as individuals, and as such, does not affect the assets of the partnership.

Purchase of Interest by Investment in the Partnership

When the incoming partner contributes assets to the partnership for his or her interest, both the assets and the capital of the partnership are increased. To illustrate, again assume that Mantle and Maris are partners in the M&M Partnership with capital accounts of $80,000 and $160,000, respectively. They agree to admit Berra as a new partner with a one-fourth interest in the partnership for an investment of $80,000. The admission of Berra is recorded by the following journal entry:

Cash	80,000	
Berra, capital		80,000

After the admission of Berra, the total capital of the new partnership is as follows:

Maris, capital	$160,000
Mantle, capital	80,000
Berra, capital	80,000
Total capital	$320,000

Berra's capital balance of $80,000 represents a one-fourth interest in the total partnership capital of $320,000. Its does not necessarily follow, however, that the new partner is entitled to a one-fourth share in the division of partnership income. Instead, the division of income or loss must be specified in the new partnership agreement.

Because balances in the asset accounts usually are not equal to their current values, the investment of the new partner may be more or less than the proportion of total assets represented by his or her agreed-upon capital interest. Since the agreement concerning the new partner's relative capital interest should be reflected in the capital accounts, adjustments to the capital accounts are necessary if the amount invested is not equal to the book value of the capital interest acquired. The adjustment required in recording the investment of the new partner is accomplished by using either the bonus method or the goodwill method.

When a new partner invests more than book value for his or her relative capital interest, a bonus or goodwill may be allocated to the old partners. To illustrate these two different methods, assume that Mantle and Maris, who share profits equally and have capital balances of $80,000 and $160,000, respectively, agree to admit Berra to a one-fourth interest in the new partnership for $120,000.

Bonus to Old Partners. The total net assets of the partnership after the $120,000 investment by Berra will be $360,000 ($240,000 + $120,000). In order to acquire a one-fourth interest in the net assets of the partnership ($90,000 = ¼ × $360,000), Berra is required to invest $120,000. The excess of the investment over the amount of capital allocated to Berra may be regarded as a bonus to the old partners. The old partners share the bonus in their agreed-upon profit and loss ratio. Each partner's share of the bonus is credited to his or her capital account. The entry to record Berra's investment in the partnership (assuming an equal distribution of profits and losses between Mantle and Maris) is:

Cash	120,000	
Berra, capital		90,000
Mantle, capital		15,000
Maris, capital		15,000

After the investment, Berra has a capital balance of $90,000 which represents one-fourth of the total capital of $360,000. The excess $30,000 investment ($120,000 – $90,000) is divided equally between Mantle and Maris.

Goodwill to Old Partners. Alternatively, if the new partner's investment exceeds his or her relative share of the net assets of the new partnership, it may be assumed that the old partnership has goodwill. The amount of goodwill is determined by the initial investment of the new partner. To illustrate, the $120,000 investment made by Berra represents a one-fourth interest in the partnership. The fact that a one-fourth interest requires an investment of $120,000 implies that the business is worth $480,000 ($120,000 ÷ ¼). The amount of goodwill is computed as follows:

Investment by Berra for a ¼ interest		$120,000
Implied value of business ($120,000 ÷ ¼)		$480,000
Net asset value exclusive of goodwill:		
Capital of old partners	$240,000	
Investment by Berra	120,000	360,000
Goodwill		$120,000

As is the case with the bonus, the goodwill is divided between the old partners in the same proportion as their profit and loss ratios unless a specific agreement is made to the contrary. The entries required in order to record the admission of the new partner (again assuming an equal distribution of profits and losses) are as follows:

Cash	120,000	
Berra, capital		120,000
Goodwill	120,000	
Mantle, capital		60,000
Maris, capital		60,000

The capital balances of the partners after the admission of Berra are as follows:

Mantle, capital	$140,000
Maris, capital	220,000
Berra, capital	120,000
	$480,000

It can be seen that Berra's share of the total capital is the agreed-upon one-fourth interest in the partnership ($120,000 ÷ $480,000).

Note that the choice between the bonus and goodwill methods results in different account balances (but the same relative capital interests). The goodwill method causes the total capital of the partners to be larger by the amount of the goodwill recorded. Thus, the choice between methods results in different financial statements.

When the new partner invests less than the book value of his or her relative capital interest, a bonus or goodwill may be allocated to the incoming partner. To illustrate, assume that Mantle and Maris agree to admit Berra with a one-fourth interest in the partnership for an investment of only $60,000.

BONUS TO NEW PARTNER. Based on this method, the excess of the new partner's share of total capital over his or her investment is allocated as a bonus to the new partner. The amount of the bonus is calculated as follows:

Total capital prior to admission:		
Mantle, capital	$ 80,000	
Maris, capital	160,000	$240,000
Investment by Berra		60,000
Total capital		$300,000
Berra's one-fourth interest		$ 75,000
Investment by Berra		60,000
Bonus to Berra		$ 15,000

The bonus may be treated as a reduction of the old partners' capital accounts on the basis of their profit and loss ratio and as a credit to the new partner's capital. The entry to record the admission of the new partner assuming an equal distribution of profits and losses between Mantle and Maris is:

Cash	60,000	
Mantle, capital	7,500	
Maris, capital	7,500	
Berra, capital		75,000

Goodwill TO NEW PARTNER. If the new partner's investment is less than his or her agreed-upon capital interest, the difference may be due to goodwill brought to the partnership by the incoming partner. This goodwill may be attributable to the new partner's reputation or special skills that might be imparted to increase the earning power of the partnership entity. The goodwill is recorded as an asset with a corresponding credit to the new partner's capital account in order to allow him or her the agreed-upon capital interest in the partnership. There is no change in the capital accounts of the old partners.

To illustrate, assume Mantle and Maris have capital balances of $80,000 and $160,000, respectively, prior to the admission of Berra with a one-fourth interest in the partnership. Since the total capital of Maris and Mantle of $240,000 represents a three-fourths interest in the total capital of the partnership after Berra is admitted, the implied value of the partnership is $320,000 ($240,000 ÷ ¾). However, the actual tangible assets of the firm after Berra's investment are $300,000, consisting of net assets of $240,000 prior to the admission of Berra plus the $60,000 investment. Therefore, the implied goodwill is $20,000 ($320,000 − $300,000). The entry required to record the admission of the new partner under the goodwill method is as follows:

Cash	60,000	
Goodwill	20,000	
Berra, capital		80,000

After his admission, Berra has the agreed-upon one-fourth interest in total capital ($80,000 ÷ $320,000).

Withdrawal of a Partner

When one partner withdraws from a partnership, he or she may dispose of his or her partnership interest in any one of several ways:

1. Sell his or her interest to a new partner.

2. Sell his or her interest to one or more of the remaining partners with the payment coming from the personal resources of the purchasing partner(s).

3. Sell his or her interest to the partnership with the payment from partnership funds.

In the first two cases, the sale and purchase is made among the partners themselves acting as individuals. Therefore, the accounting treatment is the same as for the admission of a new partner through the purchase of an interest from the existing partners. The journal entry required on the partnership books is simply to transfer the capital account balance by debiting the capital account of the retiring partner and crediting the capital account(s) of the purchasing partner(s). There is no effect on either the assets or the total capital of the partnership.

If the withdrawing partner is paid from partnership assets, both the total assets and total capital of the firm are decreased. Because the current value and the recorded book values of the partnership assets probably differ, the withdrawing partner may be paid either more or less than the amount of his or her capital balance. The difference may be attributable, for example, to the change in value of specific assets or alternatively to the existence of goodwill or to a combination of both factors. The change in the asset values or goodwill may be recorded in the accounts and shared by the partners in their profit and loss ratios.

For example, assume that Mantle, Berra, and Maris have capital balances of $100,000, $120,000, and $180,000, respectively (a total of $400,000), and share profits and losses on a one-fourth, one-fourth, and one-half basis. Further, assume that it is agreed to pay Mantle $120,000 from partnership funds upon his withdrawal from the partnership, and that the fair value of the partnership at that time is $480,000. Assuming that specific assets cannot be identified to account for the $80,000 increase in value ($480,000 - $400,000), the entries required in order to record the goodwill and the withdrawal of Mantle are as follows:

Goodwill	80,000	
Mantle, capital		20,000
Berra, capital		20,000
Maris, capital		40,000
Mantle, capital	120,000	
Cash		120,000

Instead of an increase in the value of specific assets or the existence of goodwill, the difference between the payment to the withdrawing partner and his or her capital balance may be regarded as a bonus paid to the withdrawing partner by the remaining partners. This bonus is charged to the capital accounts of the old partners in the relative profit and loss ratios of the remaining partners. Under this assumption, the withdrawal of Mantle, who is paid $120,000 for his capital balance of $100,000, is recorded as follows:

Mantle, capital	100,000	
Maris, capital	13,333	
Berra, capital	6,667	
Cash		120,000

The $20,000 bonus to the retiring partner is deducted from the remaining partners' capital balances on the basis of their relative profit and loss ratios of two-thirds for Maris (50% ÷ 75%) and one-third for Berra (25% ÷ 75%).

If the payment made to the withdrawing partner is less than his or her capital balance, the difference may be attributable either to specific assets that have fair values less than their recorded book values or to a bonus paid by the retiring partner to the remaining partners in order to retire from the partnership without undergoing a liquidation of the business. Again, the revaluation of the assets of the partnership or the bonus is divided among the partners according to their profit and loss sharing ratio.

For example, if Mantle agrees to retire for a payment of $85,000, and it is agreed that the assets of the partnership are not overvalued, the entry to record the withdrawal is as follows:

Mantle, capital	100,000	
Maris, capital		10,000
Berra, capital		5,000
Cash		85,000

Again, Maris and Berra share the $15,000 difference ($100,000 – $85,000) on the basis of their relative profit and loss ratios of ⅔ and ⅓ (as above).

Liquidation of the Partnership

When a partnership goes out of business, its assets are sold, its liabilities are paid, and any remaining cash is distributed to the partners. This process is referred to as a liquidation.

As a basis for illustration, assume that Mantle, Maris, and Berra agree to liquidate their partnership. Profits and losses are allocated one-fourth to Mantle, one-fourth to Berra, and one-half to Maris. The balance sheet of the partnership just prior to the liquidation process appears as follows:

MM&B Partnership
Balance Sheet
As of December 31, 19X1

Cash	$ 20,000	Liabilities		$ 50,000
Noncash assets	430,000	Mantle, capital		100,000
		Maris, capital		180,000
		Berra, capital		120,000
	$450,000			$450,000

Assume that all of the noncash assets of the partnership are sold for $330,000, a loss of $100,000 ($430,000 – $330,000).

Any gain or loss on the sale of the partnership assets must be divided among the partners according to their agreed-upon profit and loss ratios before any cash is distributed to the partners. Thus, the $100,000 loss on the sale of the noncash assets of the partnership is distributed among the partners as follows:

	Total	Mantle	Maris	Berra
Capital balance	$400,000	$100,000	$180,000	$120,000
Distribution of loss	(100,000)	(25,000)	(50,000)	(25,000)
Capital balance after sale	$300,000	$ 75,000	$130,000	$ 95,000

The entries required in order to record the sale of the assets and the distribution of the loss are as follows:

Cash	330,000	
Loss on sale	100,000	
Noncash assets		430,000
Mantle, capital	25,000	
Maris, capital	50,000	
Berra, capital	25,000	
Loss on sale		100,000

After the noncash assets of the partnership have been sold and the gain or loss has been divided among the partners, the cash is distributed first to creditors and then to the partners. The amount of cash distributed to each partner is reflected in the capital balances after all gains or losses on the sale of noncash assets have been recorded. The balance sheet prior to the distribution of cash appears as follows:

MM&B Partnership
Balance Sheet
January 10, 19X2

Cash	$350,000	Liabilities	$ 50,000
		Mantle, capital	75,000
		Maris, capital	130,000
		Berra, capital	95,000
	$350,000		$350,000

The distribution of the cash, first to the creditors of the partnership and then to the partners, is recorded by the following entries:

Liabilities	50,000	
Cash		50,000
Mantle, capital	75,000	
Maris, capital	130,000	
Berra, capital	95,000	
Cash		300,000

In the example above, the capital account of each partner has a credit balance after the loss on the sale of noncash assets is distributed. In some instances, one or more of the partners may have a debit balance in his or her capital account as a result of losses on the disposal of the assets. This debit balance is referred to as a capital deficit since the partnership has a legal claim against the partner. If this claim cannot be collected by the partnership, the deficit must be divided among the remaining partners' capital balances according to their profit and loss ratios.

To illustrate, assume that the MM&B Partnership has the same assets and liabilities as in the preceding example. Further assume that the capital balances prior to liquidation are Mantle, $40,000; Maris, $210,000; and Berra, $150,000; and that the noncash assets are sold for $230,000 (a loss of $200,000). The capital accounts after the distribution of the loss are as follows:

	Total	Mantle	Maris	Berra
Capital balance	$400,000	$40,000	$210,000	$150,000
Loss on sale of noncash assets	(200,000)	(50,000)	(100,000)	(50,000)
Capital balance	$200,000	($10,000)	$110,000	$100,000

After payment of the $50,000 of liabilities, the balance sheet of MM&B Partnership appears as follows:

MM&B Partnership
Balance Sheet
January 10, 19X2

Cash	$200,000	Mantle, capital	($ 10,000)
		Maris, capital	110,000
		Berra, capital	100,000
	$200,000		$200,000

If Mantle is able to pay his capital deficiency to the partnership, the following entry is made:

Cash	10,000	
Mantle, capital		10,000

At this point, Mantle has a zero capital balance and the $210,000 cash on hand is distributed to Maris and Berra in amounts equal to the balances in their capital accounts.

If the partnership is unable to collect the capital deficiency from Mantle, this loss is absorbed by the remaining partners. Since the partnership agreement provides that Maris has a one-half share and Berra a one-fourth share of profits and losses, their current interest in profits and losses is Maris's two-thirds (50% ÷ 75%) and Berra's one-third (25% ÷ 75%). The loss is written off against the capital accounts of the remaining partners as follows:

Maris, capital	6,667	
Berra, capital	3,333	
Mantle, capital		10,000

Accordingly, the distribution of the $200,000 cash is based on the amount of the partners' capital balances after allowances for the loss on the noncollection of the capital deficiency. These amounts are as follows:

	Mantle	Maris	Berra
Capital balance	($10,000)	$110,000	$100,000
Capital deficiency	10,000	(6,667)	(3,333)
	0	$103,333	$ 96,667

The entry to record the distribution of the cash is:

Maris, capital	103,333	
Berra, capital	96,667	
Cash		200,000

In the event that any cash is subsequently received from the deficient partner, it is divided between the remaining partners in their profit and loss sharing ratio, since that is how they shared the deficiency.

Appendix B
Subscriptions for Capital Stock

In some instances, a corporation may make an agreement with an investor to sell a number of shares of stock to him or her at a stipulated price. If the purchaser agrees to pay for the stock at some future date or with installment payments over a period of time, the sale of stock is referred to as a subscription. An account entitled subscriptions receivable is debited when subscriptions are accepted. Although shares are not actually issued until they are paid for, a corporation accepting stock subscriptions is committed to issue the shares upon receipt of the total specified purchase price. Accordingly, a common stock subscribed account is credited for the par or stated value of the stock subscribed. The difference between the specified subscription price and the par or stated value is credited to additional paid-in capital.

For example, assume that a corporation accepts subscriptions for 1,000 shares of its $10 par value common stock at a price of $18 per share. The subscription contract requires payment in two equal installments due in sixty and ninety days. This transaction is recorded as follows:

Subscriptions receivable	18,000	
Common stock subscribed		10,000
Additional paid-in capital		8,000

When subscribers make payments on their subscriptions, the amount collected by the corporation is credited to the subscriptions receivable account. For example, upon receipt of the first installment of the subscription, the following entry is made:

Cash	9,000	
Subscriptions receivable		9,000

When the subscription price has been collected in full, shares of stock are issued to the investor by the corporation. For example, when the second installment is collected, stock certificates for 1,000 shares of stock are issued. Collection of the installment payment and issuance of the shares are recorded as follows:

Cash	9,000	
Subscriptions receivable		9,000
Common stock subscribed	10,000	
Common stock		10,000

During the period in which subscriptions are outstanding, subscriptions receivable from investors may be reported as a contra stockholders' equity account on the balance sheet and common stock subscribed is shown as a part of contributed capital in the stockholders' equity section of the balance sheet.

FRAUD CASE: Tenants Corporation

1334 Atlantic Street is the address of an apartment building in a large southwestern city. The address became famous in the 1334 Tenants Corporation Case involving a plaintiff who brought legal action against its accounting firm for their failure to detect an embezzlement (fraud) involving the apartment house rent receipts and expenses.

The apartment house was managed by a Ms. Hattie Shipp. Ms. Shipp collected rent from the tenants, paid the bills for the 1334 Tenants Corporation [name of the company that owned the building], and remitted any remaining profits to the corporation.

Hattie did, over a period of years, embezzle approximately $256,000 from rent payments and overstating operating expenses. Her fraud was uncovered by the apartment owners. In return for a promise not to prosecute, Hattie made partial restitution and was the prime witness for the plaintiff's case. She in fact testified that the accountants should have uncovered her fraud; and the judge believed her.

The plaintiff charged the accounting firm with breach of contract and negligence for failure to discover the embezzlement. The plaintiffs claimed the accountants had been employed to perform auditing services which required them to plan and perform their engagement to detect material irregularities (fraud).

The defendant accountants contended they were engaged to perform bookkeeping work (to keep the accounting books for the Tenant Corporation) and prepare unaudited financial statements. They claimed no independent verifications were undertaken to determine the existence of irregularities. However, their actions indicated a careless approach to the $600 a year fee arrangement. For example, they had no written contract, only an oral agreement with Tenants Corporation. They frequently used words like verify and audit in their notes and they billed Tenants Corporation for audit work. Furthermore, the financial statements they prepared for the Tenants Corporation included an item on the income statement for "audit fees." Also damaging, on cross examination a partner in the accounting firm admitted that certain audit procedures were performed that were beyond the procedures of a normal bookkeeping engagement.

DISCUSSION QUESTION:

If you were aware of the actual fact that the engagement with 1334 Tenants Corporation was truly for bookkeeping services and the issuance of unaudited financial statements only, discuss which party you think should prevail—1336 Tenants Corporation or the accountants. Explain your conclusion considering the facts given in the case.

Outline

LEARNING OBJECTIVES

Chapter 13 discusses alternative methods of revenue and cost recognition. Studying this chapter should enable you to:

1. Define revenue and expenses.
2. Describe the concept of revenue recognition.
3. Describe and illustrate commonly-used methods of revenue recognition.
4. Describe and illustrate the methods used to recognize expenses.
5. Provide examples of extraordinary items and discuss the two essential characteristics of an extraordinary item.
6. Describe the situation in which prior-period adjustments are appropriate.
7. List and give examples of three types of accounting changes.
8. Compute earnings per share and explain its significance.

INCOME DETERMINATION AND EARNINGS

INTRODUCTION

Measurement, timing, and recording of revenues and expenses are complex and controversial issues in accounting. Yet they lie at the very heart of financial accounting and reporting. It is essential that the student of business has a basic understanding of these issues. The objective of this chapter is to present a concise overview of the concepts and problems involved.

REVENUE RECOGNITION

The issues relating to the measurement and the timing of revenue (the period in which revenue is recorded) have been among the most controversial problems faced by the accounting profession for many years. *The timing of revenue, generally referred to as revenue recognition, reflects the problem of determining the point or points in time when revenue should be measured and reported.* Unfortunately, from an economic perspective, the value added to the firm by productive activity is usually a continuous process. The uncertainty associated with the measurement of a continuous process has led to the adoption of a variety of specific rules for the timing of revenue.

The timing of revenue recognition is an extremely important issue, because the users of financial statements require information on a periodic basis. Revenue recognition would not be a problem if financial statements were prepared only at the termination of the life or existence of the enterprise, but, of course, this would be neither practical nor desirable.

Revenues are defined as inflows or other enhancements of assets of an entity or settlements of its liabilities (or a combination of both) during a period from delivering or producing goods, rendering services, or other activities that constitute the entity's ongoing major or central operations.[1] It is the inflow of assets (cash or other resources) that are obtained from the sale of goods or the rendering of services. Normally, the earning of revenues through sales and services is a continuous process that takes place over a period of time. For example, the earning process of a manufacturer includes the acquisition of inputs, such as materials and labor, the use of these inputs in the completion of the product, selling effort, and the collection of cash. However, because financial statements are prepared for specific periods of time (e.g., one year), some point during the earning process must be selected for use in objectively measuring the revenue earned. The accounting principle underlying revenue recognition holds that revenue should be recognized (i.e., recorded in the accounting system) in the accounting period in which it is earned or realized, which may not be the period in which the cash proceeds are received.

According to *Statement of Financial Accounting Concepts No. 5*, "Recognition and Measurement in Financial Statements of Business Enterprises," revenue is usually realized and earned at the time of the delivery of the merchandise or the performance of the service. In addition, revenues may sometimes be recognized before or at the completion of the production process. Revenues may be recognized during the production process in the case of long-term construction projects where there is a binding contract, as long as reliable measures of construction progress are available. In these situations, recognizing revenue during production is more relevant and representationally faithful than recognizing revenue at the time of delivery. In addition,

---

[1] *FASB Statement of Financial Accounting Concepts No. 6*, "Elements of Financial Statements" (Stamford, CT: FASB, 1985).

revenues may be recognized at the completion of production for products such as diamonds and silver for which prices may be determined objectively at that time, for which a ready market exists, and for which the selling effort is minimal. If cash is received in advance of production and delivery (e.g., in the case of magazine subscriptions), revenues may be recognized as production and delivery take place.

Currently, the timing of revenue is guided by the revenue recognition principle, which states that *revenue is recognized when: (1) the earning process is complete or virtually complete; and (2) an exchange transaction has taken place.*[2] In practice, many revenue recognition problems have developed because of the difficulty of determining when the criteria are met. As a result, the FASB addresses the revenue recognition problem in *SFAC No. 5*. This statement indicates that *revenue recognition involves the consideration of two factors: (1) being realized or realizable; and (2) being earned.* Revenues and gains generally are not recognized until realized or realizable. Realized means that goods or services have been exchanged for cash or claims to cash. Realizable means that assets received or held are readily convertible to known amounts of cash or claims to cash. Revenues are not recognized until earned. An entity's revenue-earning activities involve delivering or producing goods, rendering services, or other activities that constitute its ongoing major or central operations. Revenues are considered to have been earned when the entity has substantially accomplished the critical tasks to be entitled to the benefits represented by the revenues. Gains commonly result from transactions and other events that involve no earnings process such as selling an investment.[3]

In the application of these criteria, revenue is generally considered to be earned when goods are sold or services have been performed and are billable. While revenue is theoretically earned throughout the entire process of performing a service or the process of acquiring and selling merchandise, the total amount of revenue is measured and recognized at the point in time when cash or the right to receive cash in the future is received in exchange for goods sold or for services rendered. The fact that this approach results in recognizing revenue at a specific point in time even though the earning process occurs over a period of time is generally justified on the basis of the objectivity principle. That is, revenue is generally not recorded until objective evidence is available as to the existence and the amount of the revenue. However, under certain circumstances, it is acceptable to record revenue at stages of the earning process other than at the point of sale. These exceptions to the general rule of recognition at the time of sale are discussed below.

REVENUE RECOGNITION AT COMPLETED PRODUCTION

When the production process is the final revenue-generating activity, a production-based revenue recognition point may be appropriate. This situation occurs when a business sells a product for which an objective market price may be determined as soon as it is produced. Examples include certain agricultural products, precious metals, and marketable securities.

For example, if the Deep Coal Mines Company enters into a contract to sell to the Valley Power Generating Company all of the coal produced for the next five years at a price of $40 per ton, with Valley Power paying all transportation costs, recognition of revenue at the completion of production may be appropriate.

If Deep Coal Mines produces 110,000 tons of coal at a production cost of $1,100,000 in 19X1 but delivers only 100,000 tons to Valley Power, the revenue recognized on a point-of-sale basis is $4,000,000 (100,000 tons at $40 per ton). The revenues associated with the remaining 10,000 tons ($400,000, or 10,000 tons at $40 per ton) are recognized with next year's sales during the next accounting period. The production cost of this 10,000 tons appears as inventory on the balance sheet prepared at the end of the current period. If production costs of $10 per ton ($1,100,000 ÷ 110,000 = $10) remain constant throughout the year, the gross profit, calculated on a point-of-sale revenue recognition basis, and the inventory included on the end-of-year balance sheet are as follows:

[2] *APB Statement No. 4*, "Basic Concepts and Accounting Principles Underlying Financial Statements of Business Enterprises" (New York: AICPA, 1970), para. 148.

[3] *FASB Statement of Financial Accounting Concepts No. 5*, "Recognition and Measurement in Financial Statements of Business Enterprises" (Stamford, CT: FASB, 1984), para. 83.

Deep Coal Mines
Partial Income Statement
for the Year Ending December 31, 19X1

Sales	$4,000,000
Less: Cost of goods sold	1,000,000
Gross profit	$3,000,000

Deep Coal Mines
Partial Balance Sheet
December 31, 19X1

Coal inventory	$100,000

On a completed-production basis, the revenue recognized reflects revenues from all of the coal produced during the period (110,000 tons) and not just the coal delivered or sold (100,000 tons). In this example, 110,000 tons of coal are produced; therefore, the revenue recognized on a completed-production basis is $4,400,000 (110,000 tons at $40 per ton). Under the completed-production method, the income statement includes the total revenues on a production basis and the total production costs incurred in 19X1, as follows:

Deep Coal Mines
Partial Income Statement
for the Year Ending December 31, 19X1

Sales	$4,400,000
Less: Cost of goods sold	1,100,000
Gross profit	$3,300,000

It is important to note that, using the completed-production basis for revenue recognition, the gross profit for 19X1 is $300,000 greater than it would be under the point-of-sale method. Under the completed-production method, the revenues associated with the 10,000 tons produced but not delivered, less the related costs of this production, account for the additional $300,000 of gross profit (10,000 × $40 less 10,000 × $10).

Revenue Recognition during Production

Normally, revenue is recognized upon the sale of a product in the ordinary course of business. When goods are sold under contract, the delivery of the goods generally is regarded as the time when profit or loss is realized. In effect, the realization principle recognizes the total profit or loss at a single point (that is, the time of sale). However, *as the length of the earnings process increases, the potential distortion in the financial statements from this procedure increases.* For example, contractors who are engaged in the construction of buildings may require several months or even years to complete a project. The extension of these contracts over two or more accounting periods results in special accounting problems for inventory valuation and income determination. As a result, different methods of accounting for long-term construction contracts have become generally accepted. Once a method is selected, it must be used consistently, and disclosure of the method used should be made in the financial statements. If the general guidelines for revenue recognition are applied, the total revenue for each project is recognized only at the point of the final sale. This approach, which is referred to as the completed-contract method, might not result in a meaningful measure of income for various accounting periods. An alternative, the percentage-of-completion method, allows the recognition of revenue in each period as progress on the project is made.

The percentage-of-completion basis is applicable in those instances where long-term projects covering more than a single accounting period are a significant revenue-generating function. Using the percentage-of-completion method, during each period, revenues are recognized in proportion to the stage of the project's completion in that accounting period. For example, if the project is 40 percent complete at the beginning of the accounting period and 60 percent complete at the end of the accounting period, 20 percent (60% less 40%) of the total revenues on the project should be recognized for this accounting period. In actual practice, measuring the percentage-of-completion is often a problem. Ideally, the percentage should be measured on the basis of the actual amount of progress made on the project; however, in certain circumstances this estimate may be difficult to ascertain.

A comparison of the costs incurred through a given accounting period to the estimated total costs for the entire project may be used as a substitute for progress measurements. To illustrate the cost incurrence approach to revenue recognition on a percentage-of-completion basis, assume that the Building Construction Company signs a road building contract with the city of College Station to build ten miles of highway for a total price of $12,000,000. Building Construction Company's estimate of the total cost for the project is $10,000,000. If $2,000,000 in costs are incurred in 19X1, the initial year of the contract, Building Construction Company recognizes 20 percent of the revenues applicable to the contract ($2,000,000 ÷ $10,000,000). Building Construction Company's income statement for this contract reports a gross profit of $400,000 for 19X1.

Building Construction Company
Partial Income Statement
for the Year Ending December 31, 19X1

Revenues from road contract (.2 × $12,000,000)	$2,400,000
Less: Cost of construction to date	2,000,000
Gross profit on road contract	$ 400,000

The gross profit of $400,000 represents 20 percent of the $2,000,000 gross profit that is expected to result from the entire contract.

Total revenues on road contract	$12,000,000
Less: Estimated costs to complete	10,000,000
Estimated gross profit on road contract	$ 2,000,000

If, at the end of 19X2, total estimated costs on the contract are higher or lower than $10,000,000, then an adjustment is made in the estimate of the gross profit on the contract. For example, if costs incurred in 19X2 are $3,500,000 and estimated cost to complete is $5,500,000 (for a total cost of $11,000,000), then the contract is estimated to be 50 percent complete (($2,000,000 + $3,500,000) ÷ $11,000,000) and the gross profit on the contract is estimated to be $1,000,000 ($12,000,000 - $11,000,000). Revenue of $3,600,000 [($12,000,000 × .50) - $2,400,000] is recognized in 19X2. Gross profit is $100,000 ($3,600,000 - $3,500,000).

Building Construction Company
Partial Income Statement
for the Year Ending December 31, 19X2

Revenues from road contract	$3,600,000
Less: Cost of construction for year	3,500,000
Gross profit on road contract	$ 100,000

REVENUE RECOGNITION WHEN CASH IS RECEIVED

Under an installment sale, a customer makes a down payment of a portion of the purchase price and makes periodic payments on the balance to the seller under the terms of the contract. When the amount that will ultimately prove to be collectible from installment sales contracts is not reasonably predictable, the installment sales basis of revenue recognition may be appropriate. Alternatively, if the amount of uncollectible sales is reasonably predictable, the point-of-sale basis for revenue recognition should be used, even for installment sales.

Under the installment sales method for revenue recognition, all collections are considered to be comprised of two components: (1) a partial return of cost, and (2) gross profit. To illustrate the use of this technique, assume that the Small Appliance Store sells direct to its customers and uses the installment sales basis for revenue recognition. On February l, 19Xl the firm sells a washer and dryer that has a cost of $600 for a selling price of $800. The terms of the sale are no down payment and $50 per month for sixteen months, beginning March 1, 19X1. Since cost represents 75 percent of the selling price ($600 divided by $800) the gross profit percentage on this sale is 25 percent (100% minus 75%). All collections from this sale are considered to consist of a return of cost of 75 percent and gross profit of 25 percent. Revenue, cost, and gross profit are recognized as each payment is received.

	19X1 (10 Payments)	19X2 (6 Payments)
Sales (100%)	$500	$300
Cost of goods sold (75%)	375	225
Gross profit (25%)	$125	$ 75

The Small Appliance Store recognizes $500 in revenue from this sale in 19X1 and $300 in 19X2. The gross profit and cost of goods sold are recognized on a pro rata basis as cash is collected in installment payments.

The installment basis of revenue recognition avoids the problem of estimating the amount of a sale that will ultimately prove to be collectible. Revenue is recognized in the accounting period in which the cash proceeds of the sale are received, and expenses are recognized only as cash is paid. This method is often used by closely-held firms providing professional services such as attorneys, physicians, and dentists. There is little theoretical justification for the installment basis of revenue recognition, but it is simple and minimizes recordkeeping.

The installment method is widely used for income tax purposes since this method generally postpones the recognition of income and, therefore, also postpones the payment of taxes until future periods. However, the use of this method for tax purposes does not provide a basis or justification from the standpoint of theory for its use for financial accounting purposes.

RECOGNITION OF EXPENSES

Expenses are outflows or other using up of assets or incurrences of liabilities (or a combination of both) during a period from delivering or producing goods, rendering services, or carrying out other activities that constitute the entity's ongoing major or central operations.[4] Expenses are incurred to acquire goods and services that are used to generate or earn revenues. Under the matching concept (which was discussed in Chapter 3), the cost of the goods and services acquired are considered to be expenses of the accounting period or periods that benefit from their use in generating revenue. In other words, costs become expenses of the periods in which they are used or consumed in the process of generating revenues. It should be noted that the determination of an asset's cost portion that should be considered to be an expense of a particular period is usually somewhat subjective. This subjectivity is caused primarily by the concept of the accounting period, that is, determining the income earned during a specified period of time. For example, assume that a firm purchases an asset that is used in its operations for a period of ten years. The cost of that asset represents an expense to the firm over ten years, because the business will benefit from the use of the asset during this time. However, a subjective estimate is required in order to determine the expense during each separate year of that period.

In absolute terms, the earnings of a business can be determined with certainty only over its entire life span—from the date of inception of the business to its termination at the time of its liquidation. It is important, however, to measure income and financial position at various points in time throughout the life of the business in order to provide interested users such as managers, investors, creditors, and the public with relevant economic information for decision-making. Therefore, the accountant has divided the life of the business into accounting periods, which are usually defined as one year or one quarter for reporting purposes. The accountant needs to match the revenues earned and the expenses incurred during a particular accounting period, even though the actual receipt of cash relating to revenues or the payment of cash relating to expenses may take place over a number of accounting periods.

Accountants have developed procedures that may be used in order to determine the asset's cost portion that is considered to be an expense during a particular accounting period. For example, assume that a company pays cash for a building. At the time of its purchase, it is estimated that the building has a useful life of twenty-five years and will have no value at the end of its useful life. Since the building is expected to be of benefit to the company for more than one period, a portion of its cost is recognized as an expense during each accounting period that the building is used by the firm. The total expense recognized by the firm during the useful life of

---

[4] *FASB Statement of Financial Accounting Concepts No. 6*, "Elements of Financial Statements" (Stamford, CT: *FASB, 1985*).

the building should equal the cost of the asset, because it is assumed that it will have no value at the end of twenty-five years. The net book value of the building included in the balance sheet (the original cost of the building less that cost portion that has been recognized as an expense) decreases each year since a portion of the cost is charged to expense during each period.

There are certain expenditures for which the estimation of future benefit is so subjective that accountants usually make no attempt to allocate these costs to future accounting periods. Instead, costs are recognized as expenses in the period in which they are incurred because the measurement of a future benefit with any degree of accuracy is either impossible or impractical. For example, assume that Chevrolet purchases a sixty-second advertising spot during the Redskins vs. Giants football game at a cost of $25,000. It would be extremely difficult, if not impossible, to determine the periods that will benefit from this advertising expenditure. Therefore, the usual accounting treatment is to consider the outlay for advertising as an expense of the period in which the advertising is broadcast.

Two general classifications of cost are used for purposes of matching revenues and expenses: *product cost* and *period cost.* A product cost is a cost that can be directly identified with the purchase or production of goods that are available for sale. These costs are carried as assets until the goods are sold. For example, merchandise purchased by a retailer is considered to be an asset until it is sold. This inventory cost becomes an expense, referred to as cost of goods sold, in the income statement in the period in which the inventory is sold.

Period costs, on the other hand, cannot be easily identified with the purchase or manufacture of a product. Generally, the benefits associated with period costs expire with the passage of time. Examples of typical period costs include interest expense, rent expense, administrative employee salaries, and certain types of insurance expense. For a manufacturing company, period costs include all costs that will continue to be incurred if the company abandons all of its manufacturing activities and instead purchases a product for sale to its customers. Period costs are recognized as expenses in the period(s) in which the benefits associated with the cost expire or are used up in the process of generating revenues.

Nature of Earnings

A major problem of determining and reporting the net income for a period has been the treatment of unusual and nonrecurring transactions that are unrelated to normal operations. *Most accountants generally have agreed that the financial statements should disclose and distinguish clearly between those items considered to be normal and recurring and those considered unusual and nonrecurring.* For many years, the issue was how and where this distinction should be made in the financial statements.

This controversy led to a substantial variation in the handling of and definition of extraordinary items, discontinued operations, accounting changes, and prior-period adjustments both between companies and by the same company over time. Opinions issued by the APB and statements issued by the FASB have dealt with the classification and reporting of unusual items. As a result, there are four major sections of an income statement, although not every income statement includes all or any of the last three sections. These four sections are:

1. Income from continuing operations.
2. Results from discontinued operations.
3. Extraordinary items.
4. Cumulative effects of changes in accounting principles.

Each of these sections is presented net of income taxes (i.e., both the income or loss and the related tax effect should be shown). In addition, the *earnings per share on common stock should be presented on the income statement.*

EXTRAORDINARY ITEMS

The net income of a corporation includes earnings from normal operations of the business as well as certain infrequently-occurring transactions that are not related to the ordinary activities of the business. As a result of *Opinions No. 9 and No. 30* of the Accounting Principles Board, transactions that occur infrequently and that do not result from the normal operations of the business, referred to as extraordinary items, are reported separately in the income statement.

To be classified as an extraordinary item in the income statement, an item must be both unusual in nature and not be reasonably expected to recur in the foreseeable future. Unusual in nature means that the item has a high degree of abnormality and is essentially unrelated to the ordinary activities of the firm. Determining the degree of abnormality and the probability of recurrence of a particular transaction should take into account the environment in which the business operates. Examples of potential extraordinary items include the effects of major casualties (e.g., an earthquake, if rare in the area), an expropriation of assets by a foreign government, or the effects of a newly enacted law or regulation (e.g., a condemnation of property). The FASB has ruled that gains or losses from the retirement of debt are extraordinary items.

To illustrate an income statement containing an extraordinary item, assume that in 19X1 the Dolphin Company has income from normal operations of $100,000 before taxes, income tax expense of $35,000, and a $20,000 gain (net of taxes)[5] that meets the criteria for classification as an extraordinary item. A simplified income statement for the Dolphin Company appears as follows:

Dolphin Company
Income Statement
for the Year Ended December 31, 19X1

Net sales	$400,000
Cost of goods sold	100,000
Gross profit	$300,000
Expenses	200,000
Income before taxes and extraordinary items	$100,000
Income tax expense	35,000
Income before extraordinary items	$ 65,000
Extraordinary gain, net of tax	20,000
Net income	$ 85,000

Certain gains or losses should not be classified as extraordinary items because they can be expected to occur in the normal or ordinary operations of the business. For example, a loss resulting from a write-down made to recognize a decline in the value of inventory due to obsolescence should not be reported as an extraordinary item. Such an item should be included in the computation of income before extraordinary items. Other examples of items that are not normally considered to be extraordinary items include:

1. The write-down or write-off of receivables, equipment, or intangible assets.

2. The gains or losses from exchanges or translation of foreign currencies, including those relating to major devaluation or revaluations.

3. The gains or losses on the disposal of a segment of a business. (Discontinued operations are discussed below).

4. Other gains or losses from the sale or abandonment of property, plant, or equipment used in the business.

5. The effects of a strike.

6. Adjustments for accruals on long-term contracts.

---

[5] See Chapter 16 for a discussion of the allocation of income tax within a period.

Items that are either unusual in nature or occur infrequently, but do not meet both criteria, should not be classified as extraordinary items. However, if such items are material in amount, they should be separately disclosed by reporting them as separate components in income before extraordinary items or by including a description of the item and its effect in a footnote to the income statement.

For example, in its 1996 annual report PepsiCo includes among its expenses "unusual impairment, disposal and other charges" for $822 million. Some of these charges are for write-downs on assets held and used in the business and for restructuring costs due to a reorganization of business units. While unusual, these charges did not meet the criterion of infrequent of occurrence.

Discontinued Operations

The term "discontinued operations" refers to the operation of any subsidiary, division, or department that has been or will be sold, abandoned, or otherwise disposed of. The segment should be a component that represents a separate major line of business or class of customer and its assets and operations should be separable from the rest of the business. For example, a beer distributor selling an insurance company qualifies as a disposal of a segment of a business; a beer distributor in the United States deciding not to sell beer in Canada does not. In *APB Opinion No. 30*, the board concluded that the results of continuing normal operations should be reported separately from discontinued operations. Any gain or loss from the disposal of a segment of a business along with the results of operations of the segment should be reported, net of tax, in a separate section of the income statement. The purpose of reporting on the continuing operations of a business separately from the discontinued operations is that it allows financial statement users to make better judgments about the future earnings prospects of the business. Accordingly, an income statement of a firm that has discontinued operations may appear as follows:

Kingsberry Company
Income Statement
For the Year Ended December 31, 19X1

Sales		$10,000
Less: Cost of goods sold		4,000
Gross profit		$ 6,000
Operating expenses		4,000
Income from continuing operations before income taxes		$ 2,000
Provision for income taxes		800
Income from continuing operations		$ 1,200
Discontinued operations:		
Income from operations of discontinued division (less taxes of $300)	$500	
Loss on disposal of division (less tax effect of $200)	(300)	200
Net income		$ 1,400

In 1996, PepsiCo reported a charge relating to a disposal of part of its restaurant business (non-core businesses such as CPK and D'Angelo) among its operating expenses. The disposals were not considered to be part of discontinued operations, because the company was still in the restaurant business (still operating, developing, and franchising Pizza Hut, Taco Bell, and KFC).

Accounting Changes

Prior to the issuance of *APB Opinion No. 20* on accounting changes, there were various practices and procedures for reporting the effects of accounting changes on financial statements. In *Opinion No. 20*, the board clarified the different types of changes and provided guidelines for the reporting procedures to be employed. Two types of changes may be involved: (1) a change in accounting principle, and (2) a change in accounting estimate.[6] These two types of changes will be illustrated and discussed in the paragraphs that follow.

CHANGE IN ACCOUNTING PRINCIPLE

The consistency principle requires that the same accounting methods be used from one accounting period to the next. However, as exceptions to this principle, a change in accounting methods is allowed if the new method used can be justified as being preferable to the previously used method, and the effects of the change are adequately disclosed in the financial statements, or if the FASB mandates the use of a new accounting principle. Thus, a change in accounting principle results from the adoption of a preferred generally accepted accounting method that differs from the one that was previously used. An example of a change in accounting principle is a change from the sum-of-the-years'-digits method of depreciation to the straight-line method. For most types of changes in accounting methods, the cumulative effect that the use of the new method would have had on the income of all prior periods in which the old method was used must be included in the income statement in the year in which the accounting change is made.[7] The effect of this change on the current and prior years' income should be explained by a footnote to the financial statements.

To illustrate, assume that a company acquired a truck on January 1, 19X1, at a cost of $9,000. The useful life of the truck was estimated to be four years with a salvage value of $900. At the date of acquisition, the company decided to use the sum-of-the-years'-digits depreciation method. Further assume that the company decides to switch to the straight-line method at the end of 19X3. At the time of the change in methods, the cumulative difference between the old and the new methods of depreciation must be determined. The amount of this difference is computed as follows:

Year	Sum-of-the Years'-Digits	Straight-Line	Difference to December 31, 19X2
19X1	$3,240	$2,025	$1,215
19X2	2,430	2,025	405
	$5,670	$4,050	$1,620

The $1,620 difference in depreciation between the two methods is recorded during 19X3 as follows:

Accumulated depreciation	1,620	
Change in accounting principle—		
depreciation adjustment		1,620

This entry reduces the balance in the accumulated depreciation account to what it would have been had the straight-line method been used from the time the asset was purchased. The depreciation adjustment appears in the income statement in the year of the change. After the adjustment is made, the depreciation expense for 19X3 and 19X4 is recorded at $2,025 per year on the straight-line method.

In 1994, PepsiCo reported a cumulative effect of a change in accounting for postemployment benefits (related to the timing of recognizing severance benefits to terminated employees) and a cumulative effect of a change in calculating the market-related value of plan assets for computing pension expense.

CHANGE IN ACCOUNTING ESTIMATE

Changes in the estimates used in accounting may occur as additional information regarding the original estimate is obtained. An example of such a change is a change in the estimated salvage value or service life of an asset. The procedure used in adjusting for this change is to spread the remaining undepreciated cost of

---

[6] A third type of accounting change, a change in reporting entity, is not applicable to this discussion.
[7] Certain specific types of accounting changes are disclosed by revising the financial statements of prior periods to reflect the effects of the use of the new method.

the asset, less the new estimated salvage value if applicable, to expense over the unrevised or revised estimated remaining useful life of the asset. There is no effect on prior periods.

To illustrate, assume that a company decides in 19X4 that the original useful life of an asset costing $8,800 in 19X1 should have been six rather than four years and that the salvage value should have been $100 instead of $800. The amount of depreciation expense for 19X4 would be computed as follows:

Original cost	$8,800
Less: Accumulated depreciation	
to December 31, 19X3	6,000
Book value at December 31, 19X3	2,800
Less: Estimated salvage value	100
Amount to be depreciated	$2,700
Divide by: Estimated remaining useful life	3 years
Depreciation per year	$ 900

At the end of 19X4, 19X5, and 19X6, the following entry will be made to record the depreciation expense:

Depreciation expense	900	
Accumulated depreciation		900

Changes in accounting estimates may have a significant impact on the financial statements as was the case for Waste Management.

> Waste Management announced a $3.54 billion charge in 1998 to compensate, in part, for aggressive accounting techniques regarding the depreciation of its equipment. For example, while industry practice is to depreciate the cost of sanitation trucks over eight to ten years. Waste Management assigned their trucks longer useful lives, lowering the company's annual depreciation charge. In addition, Waste Management further reduced their depreciation expense by estimating the salvage value of their trucks at $25,000 (standard industry practice is to claim no salvage value on sanitation equipment). They made similar assumptions with respect to their dumpsters. These accounting maneuvers inflated Waste Management's pretax income by $716 million since 1992.[8]

EARNINGS PER SHARE

An amount referred to as earnings per share is basically the net income of a company per share of common stock outstanding for a given period. Data on earnings per share of a corporation probably receive more attention than any other single item of financial information. Earnings per share ratios is included in annual reports issued by corporations and receive extensive coverage in the financial press and the investment services. Earnings per share is often considered to be an important indicator of the market price of common stock and, in some cases, an indication of expected dividends per share. A failure to meet earnings per share forecasts often results in a decline in a company's stock price.

Because of the widespread attention given to earnings per share data, it was recognized that such information should be computed on a consistent and meaningful basis by all companies. Accordingly, the Accounting Principles Board and then more recently the Financial Accounting Standards Board provided detailed procedures for the computation and presentation of earnings per share figures under different circumstances. Further, the APB concluded that earnings per share data should be disclosed in income statements following the net income figure for all periods presented. If extraordinary items, gains or losses from discontinued operations, or cumulative effect of a change in accounting principle is included in net income for the period, separate earnings per share figures should be provided for: (1) income from continuing

---

[8] "Garbage In, Garbage Out" *Fortune* (May 25, 1998), 134.

operations, (2) discontinued operations, (3) extraordinary items, (4) cumulative effect of change in accounting principle, and (5) net income.

The computation of earnings per share is relatively simple when the capital structure of the corporation includes only common stock and the number of shares outstanding has not changed during the period. In this case, earnings per share of common stock is computed by dividing net income by the number of shares of common stock outstanding. To illustrate, assume that a company has 40,000 shares of common stock outstanding during 19X1, income before extraordinary items of $65,000, and an extraordinary gain of $20,000. Then earnings per share information is computed as follows:

$$\text{Ordinary income} \quad \frac{\$65,000}{40,000} = \$1.63$$

$$\text{Extraordinary gain} \quad \frac{\$20,000}{40,000} = \$\ .50$$

$$\text{Net income} \quad \frac{\$85,000}{40,000} = \underline{\$2.13}$$

When there are both common and preferred stock outstanding, the net income must be reduced by the preferred dividend requirements to determine the net income available to common stockholders. If the firm issues or acquires shares of stock during the period, the divisor in the calculation is the weighted average number of shares outstanding during the year. In such circumstances the earnings per share is computed as follows:

$$\frac{\text{Earnings}}{\text{Per Share}} = \frac{\text{Net Income} - \text{Preferred Dividends}}{\text{Weighted Average Number of Common Shares Outstanding}}$$

The capital structures of many corporations include convertible securities, stock options, and other securities that may be converted or exercised into shares of common stock at the option of the holder. A capital structure is considered to be complex when it includes securities and rights that could potentially decrease earnings per share by increasing the number of common shares outstanding. The existence of a complex capital structure results in significant complications in computations of earnings per share data. Essentially, they involve the calculation of hypothetical earnings per share figures that assume conversion of certain securities into common stock. The details of these considerations, however, are beyond the scope of this text.

Prior-period Adjustments

The provisions of *FASB Statement No. 16* indicate that, with one exception, all items of profit or loss recognized in a given year should be included in the determination of net income for that year. The only exception is corrections of errors in previous financial statements. Corrections of errors of prior periods are not included in the income statement of the year in which the error is discovered. Instead, these items are shown as direct adjustments to beginning retained earnings.[9] The nature of the error, the effect of its correction on income before extraordinary items and on net income, and the effects of its corrections on the related earnings per share amounts should be disclosed in the period in which the error is discovered and corrected. The financial statements of subsequent periods do not have to report the disclosures again.

Errors in financial statements can occur due to mathematical mistakes, incorrect applications of accounting principles, oversights, or misuses of the facts that existed at the time that the statements were prepared. Examples of these errors include the following:

1. Computing the percentage incorrectly for the percentage-of-completion method on long-term construction contracts.

2. Failing to make an adjusting entry for wages expense at the end of the accounting period.

---

[9] *Statement on Financial Accounting Standards No. 16*, "Prior Period Adjustments" (Stamford, CT: *FASB*, 1977).

3. Using an unrealistic useful life for an asset in computing depreciation.

4. Using an accounting principle that is not generally accepted.

5. Reporting short-term investments in debt and equity securities at acquisition cost rather than marking them to market.

The correction of the error is accomplished by computing the net cumulative effect on all prior periods and adjusting the beginning balance of retained earnings as well as any other accounts that are affected.

To illustrate, assume that equipment acquired on January 1, 19X1 for $4,000, had been incorrectly recorded as an expense rather than as an asset. This error is discovered on December 31, 19X2, at which time it is decided that the asset should have been assigned an estimated useful life of four years and a $400 salvage value. The company uses the straight-line method of depreciation. The entry at December 31, 19X2, to record the correction of the error is:

Equipment	4,000	
Accumulated depreciation		900
Prior period adjustment		3,100

This entry records the asset at its cost of $4,000, the accumulated depreciation of $900 (($4,000 − $400) ÷ 4) that should have been recorded in 19X1, and an adjustment of the prior year's earnings of $3,100 ($4,000 asset expenditure erroneously recorded as an expense less $900 depreciation expense that should have been recorded in 19X1). The prior-period adjustment is a correction of retained earnings and does not appear in the income statement. Depreciation for 19X2 is recorded in the normal manner:

Depreciation expense	900	
Accumulated depreciation		900

SUMMARY

Two basic general classifications of cost used for purposes of income determination are product costs and period costs. A product cost is a cost that can be directly identified with the purchase or manufacture of goods that are available for sale. A period cost, which is usually associated with the passage of time, is recognized on the income statement as an expense of the period in which it is incurred.

The matching concept requires that the accountant match the revenues earned during the accounting period with the expenses incurred to generate those revenues. Although revenues are usually recognized at the time the sale is made, other revenue recognition points may be used under certain circumstances. These alternative methods include recognition at the point of sale, at completed production, on a percentage-of-completion basis, and on an installment basis.

The net income of the firm is presented on the income statement in a manner that separates earnings related to the normal operations of the business from other income-related items. Such other items include extraordinary items and discontinued operations. Certain accounting changes may necessitate an adjustment of the accounting records and/or mention in the corporation's financial statements. Included in this category are changes in accounting principles and changes in accounting estimates. Prior-period adjustments are direct adjustments to the beginning balance of retained earnings resulting from error correction and other adjustments stipulated in *FASB Statement No. 16*.

The income statement also includes information regarding the earnings per share of the firm. This amount is basically the net income per share of common stock outstanding for a given period. Where preferred stock, convertible securities, or stock options are outstanding, certain adjustments must be made to either the net income or number of shares of common stock outstanding to compute the earnings per share of the firm. In addition, if there are extraordinary items, gains or losses from discontinued operations, or changes in accounting principle, it will be necessary to compute several earnings per share figures.

Key Definitions

Change due to accounting errors—may result from errors in the application of accounting principles, oversights, misuse of facts, or mistakes in mathematics.

Change in accounting estimate—occurs as additional information modifying an original estimate is obtained.

Change in accounting principle—results from the adoption of a generally accepted accounting principle that differs from one that was previously used.

Completed-production method—a method of revenue recognition whereby revenue is recognized at the time the production process is completed.

Discontinued operations—refers to the operations of any subsidiary, division, or department that has been, or will be sold, abandoned, or disposed of.

Expenses—outflows or other using up of assets or incurrences of liabilities (or a combination of both) during a period from delivering or producing goods, rendering services, or carrying out other activities that constitute the entity's ongoing major or central operations.

Extraordinary item—a gain or loss that is both unusual in nature and not reasonably expected to recur in the foreseeable future. As a result of *Opinions No. 9* and *No. 30* of the Accounting Principles Board, these items are reported as separate amounts in the income statement.

Installment sales method—a method of revenue recognition whereby revenue is recognized as collections are made. Collections are considered to be comprised of two components: (1) a partial return of cost, and (2) gross profit.

Percentage-of-completion method—a method of revenue recognition whereby revenues are recognized in proportion to the completion of the project.

Period cost—a cost that cannot be directly identified with the production of a specific product or products. It is usually more closely associated with the passage of time.

Prior-period adjustment—items of gain or loss that represent material corrections of reported earnings of prior periods and are shown as direct adjustments of retained earnings.

Product cost—a cost that is directly associated with the production or purchase of goods that are available for sale.

Revenues—inflows or other enhancements of assets of an entity or settlements of its liabilities (or a combination of both) during a period from delivering or producing goods, rendering services, or other activities that constitute the entity's ongoing major or central operations.

Questions

1. Explain the difference between product costs and period costs. Give examples of each type of cost.

2. The determination of the portion of the cost of an asset which should be allocated to expense during a period may be somewhat subjective. Explain.

3. When is revenue considered to be realized?

4. When is revenue recognition based upon production appropriate?

5. What is meant by the percentage-of-completion method?

6. Distinguish between an ordinary item and an extraordinary item on an income statement. How is an extraordinary item presented in the income statement?

7. What as a prior period adjustment? Where is a prior period adjustment shown in the financial statements?

8. Define earnings per share of common stock. Where is this information shown in the financial statements?

9. What is the effect on earnings per share presentation when a company has extraordinary gains or losses?

EXERCISES

10. Bryan Builders are in the process of constructing a new business building for Aggie University. At the beginning of 19X1, the building was 10 percent complete. At the end of the year, it was 70 percent complete. The total contract price is $1 million, and the total cost to Bryan Builders is $800,000. Prepare a partial income statement assuming revenue is recognized on a percentage-of-completion basis, if costs incurred for 19X1 are $480,000.

11. Ivy Furniture Store recognizes revenue under the installment sales method. Recently, it sold a complete set of living room furniture for $3,000. The cost of this furniture was only $2,000. If the sale was made on March 1, compute the gross margin for the first and second year. The terms of sale were no down payment and fifteen monthly payments of $200 each. The initial payment is made on April 1.

12. Assume that Ham Farm Supplies, Inc. had income after taxes from normal operations for 19X1 of $200,000. Also, the firm had an extraordinary loss of $40,000 (net of tax). The firm had 25,000 shares of stock outstanding throughout 19X1. Compute earnings per share.

PROBLEMS

13. Certain account balances of the Gobbler Company as of December 31, 19X2, are shown below:

Sales	$1,000,000
Cost of goods sold	500,000
Gain on sale of Meat Packing Division (net of tax)	100,000
Loss from earthquake (net of tax)	50,000
Operating expenses	350,000
Cash dividends:	
Common stock	250,000
Preferred stock	100,000
Correction of an error—prior period (income overstated)	100,000
Taxes on income from normal operations	75,000

The retained earnings balance on December 31, 19X1, was $850,000. The sale of the Division should be treated as a discontinued operation.

Required:

1. Prepare an income statement for 19X2.
2. Prepare a statement of retained earnings for the year ended December 31, 19X2.

14. The income statement for Bonko Company for the year ending December 31, 19X1, is shown below:

Bonko Company
Income Statement
for the Year Ended December 31, 19X1

Sales	$200,000
Cost of gods sold	100,000
Gross profit	$100,000
Operating expenses	80,000
Income before extraordinary items	$ 20,000
Extraordinary gain (net of tax)	10,000
Net income	$ 30,000

Bonko Company had 60,000 shares of common stock outstanding during 19X1.

Required:

Compute earnings per share for 19X1.

15. The Banana Computer Company sold a new computer to a customer for $4,000 on the installment basis. Terms of the sale were 20 monthly payments of $150 each plus a down payment of $1,000. Cost of the computer to Banana was $3,000. The down payment plus eight monthly payments were received by Banana in 19x3.

Required:

Compute the gross profit to be recognized by Banana in 19x3 using:

a. Revenue recognition at point-of-sale.
b. Installment basis of accounting.

16. The following data were extracted from the accounting records of Flores Flowers for the year l9x8.

Delivered Flowers in 19x8 paid for in 19x7	$ 4,000
Cash Sales in 19x8	25,000
Credit Sales in 19x8	140,000
Cash Collected on 19x7 Credit Sales	60,000
Cash Collected on 19x6 Credit Sales	15,000
Cash Collected on 19x8 Credit Sales	100,000
Cash Received for Flowers to be Delivered in 19x9	3,000
Paid Cash for 19x8 Expenses	30,000
Charged 19x8 Expenses	50,000
Prepaid 19x9 Expenses	2,000
Paid Cash on 19x7 Charged Expenses	10,000
Paid Cash on 19x8 Charged Expenses	20,000

Required:

Compute the amount of revenues, expenses and net earnings of Flores Flowers for l9x8 under the following assumptions:

a. Flores utilizes the cash basis of accounting.
b. Flores utilizes the accrual basis of accounting.

17. The following information was taken from the records of Office Builders, Inc. on a $12,000,000 contract.

	Year Ended December 31		
	19x7	19x8	19x9
Costs Incurred During the Period	$2,000,000	$4,000,000	$5,000,000
Estimated Costs to Complete	8,000,000	5.000,000	0

Required:

a. Compute the amount of gross profit to be recognized by Office Builders, Inc. during 19x7, 19x8 and 19x9 under the *percentage-of-completion* method.
b. Compute the amount of gross profit to be recognized by Office Builders, Inc. during 19x7, 19x8 and 19x9 under the *completed contract* method.
c. Compare the total amount of gross profit recognized under the two methods.

18. For each of the transactions listed, indicate the effect(s), if any, on the company's year-end: (1) Balance Sheet, (2) Income Statement, and (3) Statement of Cash Flows. Your answers should be as complete and specific as possible.

a. Sold inventory on the installment basis, receiving a down payment of 10 percent of the purchase price.
b. Received a monthly installment payment.

Refer to the Annual Report in Chapter 1 of the text.

19.   What is the net income per share (EPS) for the most recent year?

20.   On which financial statement can the EPS amount be located?

21.   In which statement would a prior period adjustment be reflected?

22.   In any year shown, was there an accounting change? If so, what type of change was it and how did it affect net income?

FRAUD CASE: Money Laundering

Money laundering is the process of converting money from illegal sources to so called clean money (laundered money) by funneling it through a legitimate business operation. The cash is disguised as sales revenue, interest or other forms of business income.

Cash is the usual medium of illegal transactions, but illegal cash can be traced just as easily as the fingerprints of a robber. Therefore, large amounts of illegally obtained currency are of little use until converted to another form, for example, by depositing it in a bank. Illegal currency, however, cannot be deposited directly in banks because it would be too obvious and would result in confiscation of the cash and conviction of those involved in the crime. Money laundering, accordingly, is a method used to change illegal, hard to use currency into useable cash on deposit in bank accounts.

Money laundering is usually detected by identifying false sources of inflated income, receivables, or other assets in business operations and then linking those business operations with a criminal element that is capable of supplying large amounts of illegal cash or other assets.

Bill Ring is the president of a local federal nonprofit credit union established to service the needs of minorities by making high risk loans that banks and other federal credit unions are unwilling to accept. Federal nonprofit credit unions operate with capital supplied by federal and state grants and gifts from various benevolent associations.

Bill Ring's credit union received a large federal grant, passed through the local municipality, for making current loans to underprivileged citizens meeting a specific financial income criterion. As a result of receiving the grant, the federal government requires the credit union to be audited by a certified public accountant.

During the audit of Ring's credit union operations to determine the appropriateness of loans and use of the federal funds, the CPAs experienced considerable difficulty obtaining the loan records and other information needed to complete their audit work. Ring, himself, was a special problem. When loan records and other documents were not available for examination, he would claim they had been lost or destroyed. When pressed by the CPAs, he eventually would produce needed documentation.

After several frustrating days, the CPAs were at a standstill, unable to complete the audit in a timely professional manner. They began to suspect Ring of mismanagement, or worse, in connection with the federal credit union.

An important item reported in the credit union financial statements was a large amount of cash donations from charitable organizations, including many local and regional church organizations. Also, the accounts showed large receivables (pledges) from these organizations.

DISCUSSION QUESTION:

Startling new evidence has come to the attention of the CPA firm regarding the integrity of Mr. Ring. A federal agent visited the accountant's office with a search warrant and examined their records for evidence of money laundering regarding the federal nonprofit savings and loan managed by Mr. Ring.

Before taking further action, such as withdrawing from the engagement, the CPA firm would like your advice on what they might do to gather evidence to confirm or refute suspicions regarding Mr. Ring's management of the savings and loans association. What would you suggest? Hint: Remember, money laundering often involves replacing legal cash with illegal cash or legal sources of cash (most likely nonexistent) with illegal cash.

Outline

LEARNING Objectives

Chapter 14 discusses common techniques of analyzing information presented in financial statements. Studying this chapter should enable you to:

1. Distinguish between horizontal and vertical analyses and discuss the type of information that is provided by each.

2. Discuss the concept of ratio analysis and identify the problems that may be inherent in its use.

3. List the most commonly-used standards against which a firm may be compared and explain the strengths and limitations associated with the use of these standards.

4. Describe and apply the basic techniques of financial analysis as they are used by common stockholders, long-term creditors, and short-term creditors.

CHAPTER 14

Financial Statement Analysis

Introduction

The financial statements of a business enterprise are intended to provide much of the basic data used for decision-making and, in general, evaluation of performance by various groups such as current owners, potential investors, creditors, government agencies, and in some instances, competitors. Because general-purpose published financial statements are by their very nature issued for a wide variety of users, it is often necessary for particular user groups to extract the information in which they are particularly interested from the statements. For example, owners and potential investors are normally interested in the present earnings and future earnings prospects of a business. Similarly, short-term creditors are primarily concerned with the ability of a firm to meet its short-term obligations as they become due and payable. Consequently, a somewhat detailed analysis and interpretation of financial statements are usually required in order to obtain the information that may be relevant for the specific purposes of a particular user. In this chapter, several selected techniques that are useful in financial analysis will be described and discussed.

Comparative Financial Statements

In general, the usefulness of financial information is increased when it can be compared with related data. Comparison may be internal (i.e., within one firm) or external (i.e., with another firm). External comparisons may be difficult to make in practice since financial statements of firms may not be readily comparable because of the use of different generally accepted accounting principles. However, some useful information may be obtained by comparison with industry averages, ratios, etc. (such as those compiled by *Moody's* and *Standard and Poor's*) or by direct comparison with the statements of another firm. Considerable caution must be exercised when making this type of analysis.

The financial statements of a particular firm are most useful when they can be compared with related data from within the current period, information from prior periods, or with budgets or forecasts. Comparative statements are useful in providing a standard that facilitates the analysis and interpretation of changes and trends that have occurred in elements of the financial statements. Generally, published annual reports of corporations provide comparative accounting statements from the previous period and often also include selected historical information for the firm for a longer period of time, such as ten years.

Assume that the income statement of a firm for the year ended December 31, 19X2, discloses net income of $100,000. This information, in and of itself, provides a user with only a single indicator of the absolute amount of income for the year. If an income statement for 19X1, disclosing net income of $80,000 is also presented, 19X2 net income becomes much more meaningful information to the user. The 25 percent increase of 19X2 income over that for 19X1 indicates a significant improvement in performance that cannot be determined from the 19X2 statements alone.

Basic Analytical Procedures

Comparisons of financial statement data are frequently expressed as percentages or ratios. These comparisons may represent:

1. Percentage increases and decreases in individual items in comparative financial statements.

2. Percentage relationships of individual components to an aggregate total in a single financial statement.

3. Ratios of one amount to another in the financial statements.

Application of each of these three methods will be illustrated by the use of the comparative financial statements of Dolbey Company. A comparative balance sheet is presented in Illustration 1, a comparative income statement is presented in Illustration 2, and a comparative statement of retained earnings is presented in Illustration 3. Selected data from the 19X0 statements are also included in Illustration 3.

Illustration 1

Dolbey Company
Comparative Balance Sheet
December 31, 19X2 and 19X1

	19X2		19X1		Increase (Decrease)	
	Dollars	*Percent of Total Assets*	*Dollars*	*Percent of Total Assets*	*Dollars*	*Percent*
Assets						
Current assets:						
Cash	$ 80,000	5.0	$ 40,000	2.8	$ 40,000	100.0
Net accounts receivable	100,000	6.3	80,000	5.5	20,000	25.0
Inventories	200,000	12.5	160,000	11.1	40,000	25.0
Prepaid expenses	20,000	1.2	8,000	.6	12,000	150.0
Total current assets	$ 400,000	25.0	$ 288,000	20.0	$112,000	38.9
Land, buildings, and equipment (net)	1,200,000	75.0	1,152,000	80.0	48,000	4.2
Total assets	$1,600,000	100.0	$1,440,000	100.0	$160,000	11.1
Liabilities						
Current liabilities:						
Accounts payable	$ 200,000	12.5	$ 130,000	9.0	$ 70,000	53.8
Notes payable	100,000	6.3	60,000	4.2	40,000	66.7
Total current liabilities	$ 300,000	18.8	$ 190,000	13.2	$110,000	57.9
Bonds payable	200,000	12.5	200,000	13.9	0	0
Total liabilities	$ 500,000	31.3	$ 390,000	27.1	$110,000	28.2
Stockholders' Equity						
Common stock ($30 par)	$ 900,000	56.2	$ 900,000	62.5	0	0
Retained earnings	200,000	12.5	150,000	10.4	$ 50,000	33.3
Total liabilities and stockholders' equity	$1,600,000	100.0	$1,440,000	100.0	$160,000	11.1

Horizontal Analysis

Analysis of increases or decreases in a given financial statement item over two or more accounting periods is often referred to as horizontal analysis. Generally, this type of analysis discloses both the dollar and percentage changes for the corresponding items in comparative statements. An example of horizontal analysis is included in the comparative financial statements presented for Dolbey Company. These statements include data with regard to income, retained earnings, and financial position for a two-year period with the dollar and percentage changes for each item listed in the final two columns.

Illustration 2

Dolbey Company
Comparative Income Statement
for the Years Ended December 31, 19X2 and 19X1

	19X2		19X1		Increase (Decrease)	
	Dollars	Percent of Sales	Dollars	Percent of Sales	Dollars	Percent
Net sales	$2,000,000	100.0	$1,500,000	100.0	$500,000	33.3
Cost of goods sold	1,400,000	70.0	1,080,000	72.0	320,000	29.6
Gross profit on sales	$ 600,000	30.0	$ 420,000	28.0	$180,000	42.9
Operating expenses:						
Selling expenses	$ 300,000	15.0	$ 240,000	16.0	$ 60,000	25.0
Administrative						
expenses	180,000	9.0	129,000	8.6	51,000	39.5
Total operating						
expenses	$ 480,000	24.0	$ 369,000	24.6	$111,000	30.1
Operating income	$ 120,000	6.0	$ 51,000	3.4	$ 69,000	135.3
Interest expense	10,000	.5	9,000	.6	1,000	11.1
Income before						
income taxes	$ 110,000	5.5	$ 42,000	2.8	$ 68,000	161.9
Income taxes	30,000	1.5	12,000	.8	18,000	150.0
Net income	$ 80,000	4.0	$ 30,000	2.0	$ 50,000	166.7

Illustration 3

Dolbey Company
Comparative Statement of Retained Earnings
for the Years Ended December 31, 19X2 and 19X1

	19X2	19X1	Increase (Decrease) Dollars	Percent
Retained earnings (January)	$150,000	$135,000	$15,000	11.1
Net income	80,000	30,000	50,000	166.7
	$230,000	$165,000	$65,000	39.4
Less: Dividends	30,000	15,000	15,000	100.0
Retained earnings (December 31) ..	$200,000	$150,000	$50,000	33.3

Data from the 19X0 statements:

Total assets (December 31, 19X0)	$1,160,000
Stockholders' equity (December 31, 19X0)	1,035,000
Net receivables (December 31, 19X0)	70,000
Inventory (December 31, 19X0)	110,000

Interpretation of the increases or decreases in individual statement items cannot be completely evaluated without additional information. For example, the comparative balance sheet discloses an increase in inventory during 19X2 of $40,000, to an amount 25 percent greater than in 19X1. This increase may have been required in order to support a higher sales volume as net sales increased by one-third during 19X2. Alternatively, this increase could have resulted from a build-up of an obsolete inventory item. The point to be made here is that additional information is often useful and sometimes absolutely necessary for meaningful interpretation.

Accounts payable increased by $70,000, more than the $40,000 increase in inventories. Selling expenses increased by $60,000; administrative expenses increased by $51,000. But these expenses may have been needed, because net sales increased by $500,000. Operating income rose by $69,000, an increase of 135.3 percent. The rise in operating expenses and cost of goods sold (29.6 percent) may have been justified.

Percentage changes included in the statements for Dolbey Company are stated in terms of the data for two years. When a comparison is made between statements of two periods, the earlier statement is normally used as a base in computing percentage changes. For statements that include more than two years, there are two methods that may be used in selecting a base year. One alternative is to use the earliest year as a base. If this alternative is selected, each amount on all succeeding statements is expressed as a percentage of the base year amount. Since this procedure results in a constant base, percentage changes for more than two years can be interpreted as trend values for individual components of the financial statements. A second alternative is to compare each statement with the statement that immediately precedes it. Adoption of this procedure results in a changing base that may make comparisons of percentage changes over a period of several years more difficult.

Vertical Analysis

The percentage relationship of an individual item or component of a single financial statement to an aggregate total in the same statement often discloses significant relationships. These relationships may be useful information for decision-making purposes. For example, in reporting income data, it may be useful to indicate the relationship between sales and other elements of the income statement for a period. This analysis of the elements included in the financial statements of a single period is often referred to as vertical analysis.

Vertical analysis is illustrated in the financial statements presented for Dolbey Company. In the comparative balance sheets, the total assets balance and the total liabilities and stockholders' equity balance for each year are used as a base. Each item in the statement is then expressed as a percentage of this base. For example, the statements indicate that current assets increased from 20 percent of total assets in 19X1 to 25 percent at the end of 19X2. An analysis of the composition of the current asset balance provides additional details of the changes in various individual categories of current assets. Liabilities increased as a percent of total assets from 19X1 to 19X2. Current liabilities are 18.8 percent of total assets in 19X2, an increase from 13.2 percent in 19X1.

Vertical analysis may also be employed in presenting a comparative income statement. In the Dolbey Company illustration, each individual item is stated as a percent of net sales for the period. Net income in 19X2 is 4 percent of sales whereas net income in 19X1 is only 2 percent of sales. Gross profit is a higher percentage of sales in 19X2 than in 19X1 (30 percent to 28 percent); operating expenses are a lower percentage of sales in 19X2 than in 19X1 (24 percent to 24.6 percent). These favorable percentage comparisons are somewhat offset by the higher percentage of income taxes to sales in 19X2 than in 19X1 (1.5 percent to 0.8 percent).

Common-Size Statements

Horizontal and vertical analyses are frequently useful in disclosing certain relationships and trends in individual elements included in the financial statements. The analysis of these relationships may be facilitated by the use of common-size statements (i.e., statements in which all items are stated in terms of percentages or ratios). Common-size statements may be prepared in order to compare data from the current period with those from one or more past periods for a firm. These statements may also be used to compare data of two or more business firms for the same period or periods, subject to the limitations mentioned previously.

A common-size statement comparing income statement data for Dolbey Company with those of Nutt Company is presented in Illustration 4. The column for Dolbey Company is prepared by using the percentage figures that are included in the comparative income statement in Illustration 2. Net sales of each firm are set as a base of 100 percent and each individual item included in the statement is shown as a percentage of net sales. Consequently, use of this statement format provides a comparison of the relationships of the income

---

Illustration 4

Dolbey Company and Nutt Company
*Condensed Common-Size Income Statement
for the Year Ended December 31, 19X2*

	Dolbey Company	Nutt Company
Net sales	100.0%	100.0%
Cost of goods sold	70.0	72.5
Gross profit on sales	30.0%	27.5%
Operating expenses:		
Selling expense	15.0%	17.5%
Administrative expense	9.0	7.5
Total operating expenses	24.0%	25.0%
Operating income	6.0%	2.5%
Interest expense	.5	1.0
Income before income taxes	5.5%	1.5%
Income taxes	1.5	.5
Net income	4.0%	1.0%

statement items for the two firms regardless of the absolute dollar amount of sales and expenses of either company. It can be seen, for example, that Dolbey Company obtained $.30 of gross profit and $.04 of net income from each dollar of net sales, while Nutt Company netted only $.275 of gross profit and $.01 of net income from each sales dollar.

Ratio Analysis

A ratio is an expression of the relationship of one numerical item to another. Significant interrelationships that may be present in financial statements are often identified and highlighted by the use of ratio analysis. A simple example of such a relationship is the ratio of cash to current liabilities for Dolbey Company at the end of 19X2. The ratio is computed as follows:

$$\text{Ratio of Cash to Current Liabilities} = \frac{\text{Cash}}{\text{Current Liabilities}}$$

$$.27 = \frac{\$80,000}{\$300,000}$$

Ratios may be expressed in several different ways. Generally, ratios are stated in relation to a base of one. For example, for the ratio computed above, it can be stated that the ratio of cash to current liabilities is .27 to 1 (which is sometimes simply stated as .27 with the "to 1" omitted). In any case, a ratio is a method used to describe a relationship between two financial statement amounts. The meaningful use of ratio analysis requires that there be a logical relationship between the figures compared, and that this relationship be clearly understood by the user.

Comparison With Standards

The analytical procedures employed in computing percentage changes (horizontal analysis), component percentages (vertical analysis) and ratios convert financial statement items into a form that may be comparable to various standards. Comparisons made among the relationships derived from the financial statements and selected standards allow the user to draw meaningful conclusions concerning the firm. Among the most commonly-used standards of comparison against which the position of a particular firm may be measured are the following:

1. Past performance of the firm.

2. Financial data of similar or competing firms.

3. Average performance of a number of firms in the industry.

A major deficiency of comparison with the past performance of the firm is that there is no indication of what *should* have occurred given the nature of the firm, the economy of the period, etc. For example, the fact that the net income of a firm increases by 3 percent from the previous year may initially appear to be favorable; however, if there is evidence that net income *should* have increased by 6 percent, the performance for the current year is regarded as unfavorable.

The weakness of comparisons with past performance of the firm may be overcome somewhat by using the performance of a similar firm or firms or an industry average as an additional standard for comparison. A problem with this approach, however, is that it is often difficult to identify firms that are truly comparable, both because of the nature of the firms themselves and because of the use of alternative "generally accepted accounting principles." In spite of these limitations, a careful analysis of comparative performance, both internal and external, often provides meaningful input for use in decision-making.

Analysis for Common Stockholders

Common stockholders and potential investors purchase securities of a firm in an attempt to earn a return on their investment through increases in the market price of the stock and by dividends. Because each of these factors is influenced by net income, the analysis of financial statements made by, or on behalf of, an investor is focused primarily on the company's record of earnings. Certain of the more important relationships that are of interest to the stockholder-investor are discussed in the following sections of this chapter.

Rate of Return on Total Assets

The rate of return on total assets provides a measure of management's ability to earn a return on the firm's assets. The income figure used in this computation is income before the deduction of interest expense, since interest is the return to creditors for the resources that they provide to the firm. The income figure is thereby the income before any distributions to those who provided funds to the company (interest or dividends). Thus, the rate of return on total assets is computed by dividing net income plus interest expense by the average investment in assets during the year.

$$\text{Rate of Return on Total Assets} = \frac{\text{Net Income (after taxes)} + \text{Interest Expense}}{\text{Average Total Assets During the Year}}$$

Although assets are continually acquired and disposed of throughout a period, an average of asset balances at the beginning and end of the period is generally used for this calculation. The calculation for Dolbey Company is as follows:

	19X2	19X1
Net income	$ 80,000	$ 30,000
Add: Interest expense	10,000	9,000
Net income before interest expense	$ 90,000	$ 39,000
Total assets:		
Beginning of year	$1,440,000	$1,160,000
End of year	1,600,000	1,440,000
Total	$3,040,000	$2,600,000
Average total assets	$1,520,000	$1,300,000
Rate of return on assets	5.9%	3.0%

This ratio indicates that the earnings per dollar of assets invested have almost doubled in 19X2. It appears that the management of Dolbey Company has increased its efficiency in the use of the firm's assets to generate income.

The rate of return on total assets can be decomposed into the return on sales ratio and the asset turnover ratio as follows:

$$\frac{\text{Rate of Return}}{\text{on Total Assets}} = \frac{\text{Net Income (after taxes) + Interest Expense}}{\text{Net Sales}} \times \frac{\text{Net Sales}}{\text{Average Total Assets During the Year}}$$

$$\text{For 19X2:} \quad \frac{\$90,000}{\$2,000,000} \times \frac{\$2,000,000}{\$1,520,000} = 4.5\% \times 1.32 \text{ times} = 5.9\%$$

$$\text{For 19X1:} \quad \frac{\$39,000}{\$1,500,000} \times \frac{\$1,500,000}{\$1,300,000} = 2.6\% \times 1.15 \text{ times} = 3.0\%$$

The rate of return on assets increased because both the return on sales and the asset turnover increased.

RATE OF RETURN ON COMMON STOCKHOLDERS' EQUITY

The rate of return on common stockholders' equity is a measure of a firm's ability to earn a profit for its residual owners, the common stockholders. Because interest paid to creditors and dividends paid to preferred stockholders are normally fixed in amount, the return on common stockholders' equity may not be equal to the return on total assets. If management is able to earn a higher return on assets than the cost (i.e., interest expense) of assets contributed by the creditors, the excess benefits the owners. This is often referred to as using debt as favorable "leverage" in order to increase the owners' rate of return or as "trading on equity." If the cost of borrowing funds exceeds the return on assets, leverage is unfavorable and reduces the rate of return to the residual owners. The rate of return on common stockholders' equity is computed by dividing net income less preferred dividends by the average equity of the common stockholders. The numerator is the income available to the common stockholders after both interest and preferred dividends have been paid.

$$\frac{\text{Rate of Return}}{\substack{\text{on Common} \\ \text{Stockholders' Equity}}} = \frac{\text{Net Income (after taxes) - Preferred Dividends}}{\text{Average Common Stockholders' Equity}}$$

Since Dolbey Company has no preferred stock, the rate of return on common stockholders' equity would be computed as follows:

	19X2	19X1
Net income	$ 80,000	$ 30,000
Common stockholders' equity:		
Beginning of the year	$1,050,000	$1,035,000
End of the year	1,100,000	1,050,000
Total	$2,150,000	$2,085,000
Average common stockholders' equity	$1,075,000	$1,042,500
Rate of return on common stockholders' equity	7.4%	2.9%

The rate of return on the common stockholders' equity is higher than the rate of return on assets for 19X2 because the cost of funds contributed by creditors is less than the rate earned on assets. Thus the company is experiencing favorable "leverage," using borrowed funds to earn a return in excess of their cost.

EARNINGS PER SHARE of COMMON STOCK

Since owners of a business invest in shares of stock, they are usually interested in an expression of earnings in terms of a per share amount. If a company has only a single class of common stock outstanding, the earnings per share figure is computed by dividing net income for the period by the average number of common shares outstanding.[1] If the firm has other securities outstanding that have certain characteristics similar to those of common stock (such as convertible bonds), the usefulness of earnings per share data is enhanced if these other securities are also considered in the computation of earnings per share. These securities are often referred to as potentially dilutive securities. While a discussion of the inclusion of potentially dilutive securities in the computation of earnings per share is beyond the scope of this text, the basic principle involved is that earnings per share figures are calculated so as to indicate the effects of the conversion of these securities into common stock.

When there is both common and preferred stock outstanding, net income must be reduced by preferred dividend requirements in order to determine net income available to common stockholders.

$$\text{Earnings Per Share} = \frac{\text{Net Income} - \text{Preferred Dividends}}{\text{Weighted Average Number of Common Stock Shares Outstanding}}$$

In the case of Dolbey Company, which has no preferred stock and 30,000 shares ($900,000 of common stock divided by the $30 par value per share) outstanding throughout 19X1 and 19X2, the earnings per share of common stock is calculated as follows:

	19X2	19X1
Net income	$80,000	$30,000
Number of common shares outstanding	30,000	30,000
Earnings per share of common stock	$ 2.67	$ 1.00

Earnings per share is frequently mentioned in the financial press in relation to the earnings performance of business firms. In addition, earnings per share data are reported on the income statement and usually in various other sections of corporate annual reports. Although the concept of earnings per share has received a great deal of attention, particularly in recent years, it should be viewed with some caution. As a minimum, it should be recognized that all of the significant aspects of a firm's performance simply cannot be reduced to a single figure. This point cannot be overemphasized.

PRICE-EARNINGS RATIO ON COMMON STOCK

Each investor must allocate his or her limited resources among various investment opportunities available to him or her. For this reason, the rate of earnings in relation to the current market price of his or her investment often provides a useful basis for comparing alternative investment opportunities. This ratio is commonly referred to as the price-earnings ratio. It is computed by dividing the current market price per share of common stock by earnings per share.

$$\text{Price-Earnings Ratio} = \frac{\text{Market Price Per Share of Common Stock}}{\text{Earnings Per Share}}$$

Assuming that the market price per common share of Dolbey Company at the end of 19X2 is $24 and at the end of 19X1 is $8, price earnings ratios are calculated as follows:

---

[1] The calculation of earnings per share was discussed in Chapter 13.

	19X2	19X1
Market price per share at the end of the year	$24.00	$8.00
Earnings per share	$ 2.67	$1.00
Price-earnings ratio	9	8

The price-earnings ratio may be interpreted as the value that investors in the stock market place on every dollar of earnings for a particular firm. An investor may compare the price earnings ratio of a firm to that of other companies in an attempt to estimate whether a firm's stock is overpriced or underpriced. A high price-earnings ratio may indicate that the stock price is too high, but not always; a low price-earnings ratio may indicate that the stock price is too low, but, again, not always. Price-earnings ratios differ among industries. Generalizations are not easy.

Analysis for Long-term Creditors

Debt-to-Equity Ratio

The debt-to-equity ratio measures the proportion of funds supplied to the firm by its stockholders as opposed to funds provided by creditors. It is computed by dividing total debt by stockholders' equity.

$$\text{Debt-to-Equity Ratio} = \frac{\text{Total Debt}}{\text{Stockholders' Equity}}$$

The debt-to-equity ratio provides a measure of the risk incurred by creditors and common stockholders. Since debt consists of fixed obligations, the larger the debt-to-equity ratio, the greater is the chance that a firm may face a situation in which it is unable to meet its obligations. At the same time, however, a high debt-to-equity ratio can increase the rate of return on stockholders' equity through the use of favorable financial leverage. This can occur because interest on debt is fixed in amount, regardless of the amount of earnings. Consequently there is no ideal debt-to-equity ratio. Rather, each investor must define a satisfactory debt-to-equity ratio based on his or her desired degree of risk.

For Dolbey Company the debt-to-equity ratios are calculated as follows:

	19X2	19X1
Total debt	$ 500,000	$ 390,000
Stockholders' equity	$1,100,000	$1,050,000
Debt-to-equity ratio	45.5%	37.1%

Number of Times Interest Earned

Bondholders and other long-term creditors, like stockholders and investors, are concerned with measures of the profitability of a business. In addition, however, long-term creditors are particularly interested in a firm's ability to meet its interest requirements as they become due and payable. A good indicator of a firm's ability to pay interest is the margin between income and interest payments. A common measure of this margin is the ratio of net income available for interest payments to annual interest expense. This ratio, which is referred to as the number of times interest earned, is computed by dividing net income before interest expense and income taxes by the interest requirement for the period. Income taxes are added back to net income because interest charges are an expense which is deducted in computing income taxes. Similarly, interest charges are added back to net income because the ratio provides a measure of the ability of the firm to pay fixed interest charges.

$$\text{Number of Times Interest Earned} = \frac{\text{Net Income} + \text{Interest Expense} + \text{Income Taxes}}{\text{Interest Expense}}$$

The computations for Dolbey Company are as follows:

	19X2	19X1
Net income	$ 80,000	$30,000
Add back:		
Income taxes	30,000	12,000
Interest expense	10,000	9,000
Amount available for interest requirements	$120,000	$51,000
Number of times interest earned	12.0	5.7

The increase in the ratio from 5.7 times in 19X1 to 12.0 times in 19X2 appears to be favorable with respect to a long-term creditor of Dolbey Company.

Analysis for Short-term Creditors

Short-term creditors are concerned with the earnings prospects of a firm. Of primary importance to the short-term creditor, however, is a firm's ability to pay its current debts on a timely basis and to meet its current operating needs. This is often referred to as the current position of the firm.

The ability of a firm to pay its current debts as they fall due depends largely upon the relationship between its current assets and its current liabilities. The excess of a firm's current assets over its current liabilities is termed working capital. Adequate working capital enables a firm to meet its current needs and obligations on a timely basis. However, an analysis of the components of working capital and the flow of working capital is necessary in order to determine the adequacy of the working capital position of a specific firm.

Current Ratio

The absolute amount of working capital may be an inadequate measure of a firm's ability to meet its obligations. As an illustration, consider the following data for two companies:

	Reed Company	Frazier Company
Current assets	$20,000	$50,000
Current liabilities	10,000	40,000
Working capital	$10,000	$10,000

In this example, both companies have $10,000 of working capital. However, the current assets of Reed Company can be reduced by 50 percent and still be equal to the current liabilities, while the current assets of Freezer Company can shrink by only 20 percent and remain equal to current liabilities.

Another means of evaluating working capital is to evaluate the relationship between current assets and current liabilities. This ratio is referred to as the current ratio.

$$\text{Current Ratio} = \frac{\text{Current Assets}}{\text{Current Liabilities}}$$

The use of the current ratio for the example given above discloses a ratio of 2 to 1 for Reed Company and 1.25 to 1 for Freezer Company. This clearly indicates the stronger current position of Reed Company.

The current ratios for Dolbey Company are calculated as follows:

	19X2	19X1
Current assets	$400,000	$288,000
Current liabilities	300,000	190,000
Current ratio	1.3	1.5

Although the working capital of Dolbey Company increased from $98,000 in 19X1 to $100,000 in 19X2, current assets per dollar of current liabilities declined from $1.50 to $1.30. This is an unfavorable trend from the viewpoint of short-term creditors because the margin of safety has declined.

A satisfactory current ratio for a particular firm depends upon the nature of its business. Although short-term creditors generally feel safer as the current ratio increases in amount, this may not be efficient from a business standpoint. For example, a firm with excess cash in relation to its current needs is inefficient since cash is a nonproductive asset. A good measure of the adequacy of a firm's current ratio is often a comparison with the current ratios of similar firms or industry averages.

Acid-Test or Quick Ratio

In analyzing the ability of a firm to meet its obligations, the distribution of current assets is also important. For example, a firm with a large proportion of cash to current assets is better able to meet its current debts than a firm with a larger proportion of inventories. This is because inventories usually require more time for conversion into cash than do other current assets. Assets with a longer conversion period are usually referred to as being less liquid. For this reason, a ratio that excludes the less liquid assets is often used as a supplement to the current ratio. The ratio of the highly liquid current assets—cash, marketable securities, and receivables—to current liabilities is known as the acid-test or quick ratio.

$$\text{Acid-Test Ratio} = \frac{\text{Cash + Marketable Securities + Receivables}}{\text{Current Liabilities}}$$

Since Dolbey Company owns no marketable securities, its acid-test ratio is calculated as follows:

	19X2	19X1
Cash	$ 80,000	$ 40,000
Net accounts receivable	100,000	80,000
Total	$180,000	$120,000
Current liabilities	$300,000	$190,000
Acid-test ratio	.60	.63

In evaluating the acid-test ratio, again the nature of the business must be considered. The .60 acid-test ratio for Dolbey Company in 19X2 may indicate a serious problem as there may not be sufficient liquid assets to meet current liabilities as they become due.

Analysis of Accounts Receivable

The rate at which non-cash current assets may be converted into cash is an important determinant of the firm's ability to meet its current obligations. Because neither the current nor the acid-test ratio considers this movement in current assets, short-term creditors should use additional tests in considering the liquidity of two significant working capital items, receivables and inventories.

An approximation of the average time required by a firm to collect its receivables may be determined by first computing the turnover of accounts receivable. Receivables turnover is computed by dividing net credit sales by the average accounts receivable balance. Ideally, a monthly average of receivables should be used, but generally only the balances at the beginning and end-of-the-year are available to the users of the financial statements.

$$\text{Accounts Receivable Turnover} = \frac{\text{Net Sales on Account}}{\text{Average Accounts Receivable}}$$

The accounts receivable turnover is an approximation of the number of times accounts receivable were converted into cash during the period. Therefore, the higher the turnover, the more liquid are the firm's receivables.

Accounts receivable turnover of Dolbey Company is computed below. Assume that all sales were made on a credit basis and that only the beginning and end-of-the-year balances of receivables are available.

	19X2	19X1
Net sales on account	$2,000,000	$1,500,000
Net receivables:		
Beginning of year	$ 80,000	$ 70,000
End-of-the-year	100,000	80,000
Total	$ 180,000	$ 150,000
Average	$ 90,000	$ 75,000
Accounts receivable turnover per year	22.2 times	20.0 times

This increase in the receivables turnover for Dolbey Company during 19X2 indicates that the average collection period for receivables has decreased as a result of more successful collection practices or a change in credit policies, or a combination of both factors.

The receivables turnover may be used to determine the average collection period, which can be readily compared with the firm's credit terms. The average number of days to collect receivables is computed by dividing 365 days by the receivables turnover.

$$\text{Average Number of Days to Collect Receivables} = \frac{365 \text{ Days}}{\text{Accounts Receivable Turnover}}$$

If the average number of days required to collect receivables significantly exceeds the credit terms of the firm, the credit department may be ineffective in its credit granting and collecting activities.

The average number of days to collect receivables is calculated for the Dolbey Company as follows:

	19X2	19X2
Days in year	365 days	365 days
Receivables turnover	22.2 times	20.0 times
Average number of days to collect receivables	16.4 days	18.3 days

Analysis of Inventories

A procedure similar to that used for evaluating receivables may be employed in evaluating the inventories of a firm. One indication of the liquidity of inventories is obtained by determining the relationship between the cost of goods sold and the average balance of inventories on hand during a period. Cost of goods sold is used because it represents the cost (rather than the selling price) of goods that have been sold from the inventories available during the period.

Inventory turnover is calculated by dividing cost of goods sold by the average inventory. Again, if possible, monthly figures should be used to determine average inventory. Usually, however, only the beginning and end-of-the-year inventory balances are available.

$$\text{Inventory Turnover} = \frac{\text{Cost of Goods Sold}}{\text{Average Inventory}}$$

A low inventory turnover may indicate management inefficiency in that excess cash has been committed to the investment in inventory. Although inventories are necessary to meet the demands of a firm, there are advantages in maintaining the investment in inventory at the minimum level necessary to service customers, thus minimizing carrying costs, risks of loss, or obsolescence.

Assuming that only the beginning and ending inventories are available, the computation of inventory turnover for Dolbey Company is as follows:

	19X2	19X1
Cost of goods sold	$1,400,000	$1,080,000
Inventory:		
Beginning of the year	$ 160,000	$ 110,000
End-of-the-year	200,000	160,000
Total	$ 360,000	$ 270,000
Average inventory	$ 180,000	$ 135,000
Inventory turnover	7.8 times	8 times

It appears that the trend of the inventory turnover for Dolbey Company is somewhat unfavorable, since inventories were turned over more slowly in 19X2 than in 19X1. Again, the analyst wants to obtain additional information before making a definitive judgment.

INTERPRETATION of ANALYSES

The user must exercise considerable caution in the use of ratios in order to analyze the financial statements of a business enterprise. Some of the problems inherent in ratio analysis are summarized below:

1. Comparisons of items for different periods or for different companies may not be valid if different accounting practices have been used. For example, one firm may use straight-line depreciation and the FIFO inventory method while a similar company may use accelerated depreciation and LIFO for its inventories.

2. Financial statements represent only one source of financial information concerning a firm and its environment. Consequently, other information not disclosed in financial statements may have an impact on the evaluation of the statements.

3. Financial statements are not adjusted either for changes in market values or in the general price level. This may seriously affect comparability between firms over time.

4. As ratio analysis has increased in popularity, there has sometimes been a tendency to develop ratios that have little or no significance. A meaningful ratio can be developed only from items which have a logical relationship.

All of the ratios and measurements developed in this chapter need not be used as input in a particular decision. In determining the financial strengths and weaknesses of a particular firm, relevant measurements need to be selected, developed, and interpreted in view of the conditions relating to the business.

SUMMARY

Financial statements provide a variety of external users with essential data regarding a firm's financial position and the results of its operations. However, most users of financial statements must make a detailed analysis and interpretation of the data presented to obtain evaluative information useful in making decisions.

The actual evaluative techniques used by an individual vary according to personal preference and the nature of the individual's relationship to the reporting firm. Most techniques involve some type of comparison with related data. The data may relate to the firm's past performance, to similar or competing firms, or to an industry average. Comparisons are often expressed in terms of percentage or ratios, although there are certain problems inherent in ratio analysis.

Firms may present a horizontal or vertical analysis of relevant data along with their regular financial statements. A horizontal analysis usually presents both the dollar and percentage changes for corresponding items for two or more accounting periods. Vertical analysis discloses the percentage relationship of an individual item or component of a single financial statement to an aggregate total included in the same statement. Presentation of these analyses may be facilitated by the use of common-size statements in which all items are stated in terms of percentages and ratios.

Since current and potential stockholders are primarily interested in earning an acceptable return on their investments through increases in the market price of the stock and by dividends, their analyses focus on the company's record of earnings. Examples of earnings relationships of interest to the stockholder-investor are the rate of return on total assets, the rate of return on common stockholders' equity, the earnings per share of common stock, and the price-earnings ratio on common stock.

Stockholders and creditors may be interested in the debt-to-equity ratio as a measure of the risk incurred by both. In addition, bondholders and other long-term creditors are concerned with the firm's ability to meet its interest requirements as they become payable. A common measure of such ability is the ratio of net income available for interest payments to annual interest expense. This measure is generally referred to as the number of times interest is earned.

Short-term creditors are primarily interested in the firm's ability to pay its current debt on a timely basis and to meet its current operating needs. Although the absolute amount of working capital available to a firm may provide useful information to a creditor, the ratio of current assets to current liabilities (referred to as the current ratio) is generally thought to provide better evaluative data. If only the more liquid current assets are used in ratio, it is referred to as an acid-test ratio. Other evaluation methods used by short-term creditors include the analysis of accounts receivable and the analysis of inventories. A summary of the financial ratios discussed in this chapter are presented in Illustration 5.

KEY DEFINITIONS

Accounts receivable turnover—an approximation of the number of times accounts receivable were converted into cash during the period. It is defined as net sales on account divided by average accounts receivable.

Acid-test ratio—a measure of a firm's ability to pay its current liabilities as they become due with its more liquid current assets. It is usually the ratio of cash, marketable securities, and receivables to total current liabilities.

Average collection period—a measure of the average time required by a firm to collect a receivable. The collection period is computed by dividing 365 days by the receivables turnover.

Common-size statements—in common-size financial statements, all items are stated in terms of percentages or ratios.

Current ratio—measures a firm's ability to pay current liabilities as they become due. It is defined as the ratio of current assets to current liabilities.

Debt-to-equity ratio—measures the proportion of funds supplied by stockholders as opposed to the funds provided by creditors. It is computed by dividing total debt by total stockholders' equity.

Horizontal analysis—the analysis of the increase or decrease in a given financial statement item over two or more accounting periods.

Inventory turnover—gives an indication of the liquidity of inventories. Its computation involves dividing cost of goods sold by the average inventory.

Number of times interest earned—this measure of a firm's ability to pay interest is computed by dividing net income before interest expense and income taxes by the interest expense.

Price-earnings ratio—the current market price of a share of stock divided by the earnings per share.

Rate of return on common stockholders' equity—this measure of the firm's ability to earn a profit for its common stockholders is computed by dividing net income after taxes and preferred dividends by the average common stockholders' equity.

Rate of return on total assets—this measure of the ability of the firm's management to earn a return on the assets without regard to variations in the method of financing is computed by dividing net income plus interest expense by the average investment in assets during the year.

Ratio analysis—the analysis of items in financial statements expressing the relationship of one numerical item to another.

Vertical analysis—the percentage relationship between an individual item or a component of a single financial statement to an aggregate total in that statement.

Illustration 5
Summary of Financial Ratios

Ratio	Method of Computation	Meaning
1. Analysis for Common Stockholders		
a. Rate of return on total assets	$$\frac{\text{Net Income (after taxes) + Interest Expense}}{\text{Average Total Assets During the Year}}$$	Measures management's ability to earn a return on the firm's assets
b. Return on sales	$$\frac{\text{Net Income (after taxes) + Interest Expense}}{\text{Net Sales}}$$	Measures the rate of earnings on each dollar of net sales
c. Asset turnover	$$\frac{\text{Net Sales (Revenue)}}{\text{Average Total Assets During the Year}}$$	Measures the efficiency of use of the firm's assets
d. Rate of return on common stockholders' equity	$$\frac{\text{Net Income (after taxes) - Preferred Dividends}}{\text{Average Common Stockholders' Equity}}$$	Measures the firm's ability to earn a profit for the common stockholders
e. Earnings per share	$$\frac{\text{Net Income - Preferred Dividends}}{\text{Weighted Average Number of Common Stock Shares Outstanding}}$$	Measures the earnings on each share of common stock
f. Price-earnings ratio	$$\frac{\text{Market Price per Share of Common Stock}}{\text{Earnings per Share}}$$	Measures the relationship of the market value of common stock to the earnings of the firm on a per share basis
2. Analysis for Long-term Creditors		
a. Debt-to-equity ratio	$$\frac{\text{Total Debt}}{\text{Stockholders' Equity}}$$	Measures the relative amount of total resources provided by creditors and owners
b. Number of times interest earned	$$\frac{\text{Net Income + Interest Expense + Income Taxes}}{\text{Interest Expense}}$$	Measures the ability of a firm to pay fixed interest charges from pretax earnings
3. Analysis for Short-term Creditors		
a. Current ratio	$$\frac{\text{Current Assets}}{\text{Current Liabilities}}$$	Measures the ability to pay short-term debt from current assets
b. Acid-test ratio	$$\frac{\text{Cash + Marketable Securities + Receivables}}{\text{Current Liabilities}}$$	Measures the ability to pay short-term debt from a firm's most liquid assets
c. Accounts receivable turnover	$$\frac{\text{Net Sales on Account}}{\text{Average Accounts Receivable}}$$	Measures the number of times accounts receivable were converted into cash during the period
d. Average number of days to collect receivables	$$\frac{\text{365 Days}}{\text{Accounts Receivable Turnover}}$$	Measures the average collection period of receivables
e. Inventory turnover	$$\frac{\text{Cost of Goods Sold}}{\text{Average Inventory}}$$	Measures the liquidity of inventory

QUESTIONS

1. How is the financial statement analysis related to the needs of the various users of financial statements?

2. Distinguish between vertical analysis and horizontal analysis.

3. What are common-size statements?

4. How are each of the following computed?

    a. Rate of Return on Total Assets.
    b. Rate of Return on Common Stockholders' Equity.
    c. Earnings per Share of Common Stock.
    d. Price-Earnings Ratio on Common Stock.
    e. Debt-to-Equity Ratio.
    f. Number of Times Interest Earned.
    g. Current Ratio.
    h. Acid-Test Ratio.
    i. Accounts Receivable Turnover.
    j. Average Number of Days to Collect Receivables.
    k. Inventory Turnover.

5. Each of the ratios (in Question 4 above) are utilized by one user group more than others. Indicate whether each item is utilized most by (1) common shareholders (or investors), (2) long-term creditors, or (3) short-term creditors.

6. What are the most commonly used standards against which to measure the position of a particular firm? What are the weaknesses inherent in these standards?

7. Business corporations usually provide comparative statements in their annual reports. What is a comparative statement? How do they enhance the usefulness of financial information?

8. What will be the effect (increase, decrease, none) on the rate of return on assets of each of the following?

    a. Cash purchase of a new machine.
    b. Increase in the tax rate.
    c. Reduction of accounts payable.
    d. Cash sale of a fully depreciated machine.

9. What is indicated if the average number of days to collect receivables significantly exceeds the credit terms of the firm?

10. What are the principal limitations that should be considered in evaluating ratios?

11. When percentage changes are given in comparative statements for more than two years, there are two methods for selecting the base year. What are they?

12. Which of the methods in Question 11 makes comparison of percentage changes over several years more difficult? Why?

EXERCISES

13. The acid-test ratio at the beginning of 19X0 was 2 to 1 for the Gilly Company.

Required:

How would the following transactions affect the acid-test or quick ratio?

1. Collection of note receivable from Silly Co. The note was due in 19X3.
2. Collection of accounts receivable.
3. Sales on account.
4. Purchase of inventory on account.
5. Payment of accounts payable.
6. Collection of an account receivable.
7. Cash purchase of common stock of ABC Co. as a temporary investment.
8. Purchase of a new machine on a credit basis, the purchase price payable in 6 months.

14. The December 31, 19X1 financial statement of Flunkart Company included the following data:

```
CA Cash  ...................................  $ 60,000
CA Accounts receivable  ....................   200,000
CA Marketable securities ...................   100,000   CA
CA Prepaid expenses  .......................    25,000
CL Accounts payable  .......................   200,000
CL Notes payable (current)  ................    85,000
CA Inventory  ..............................   115,000  CA  CL → 300
LTL Bonds payable (due in five years)  .....   300,000
CL Wages payable  ..........................    15,000
```

CA = 500

Required:

1. What is the current ratio? Acid-test ratio? Working capital?
2. Comment on the significance of this current ratio.

15. Using the information given, complete the balance sheet below.

a. The "quick" ratio is 2: 1.
b. Notes payable are long-term liabilities and are four times the dollar amount of the marketable securities.
c. Accounts receivable are $2,000 and are one-half of the "quick" assets, one-fourth of the current assets, and equal to plant and equipment.
d. Total stockholders' equity is equal to the working capital and contributed capital is twice the dollar amount of the net accumulation of earnings.

Assets		Liabilities and Stockholders' Equity	
Cash	_____	Accounts payable	_____
Marketable securities	_____	Notes payable	_____
Accounts receivable	_____		
Inventories	_____	Capital stock	_____
Plant and equipment	_____	Retained earnings	_____

16. The current ratio of Lap Co. on December 31, 19X1 was 2 to 1 ($200,000 to $100,000). In 19X2 the following transactions occurred:

   a. Payment of accounts payable, $125,000.
   b. Collection of accounts receivable, $50,000.
   c. Sales of $200,000, 3/4 of which was cash; cost of goods sold was $125,000.
   d. Purchase of goods, all on credit, $150,000.
   e. A loan for $100,000, due in 5 years.
   f. Cash purchase of marketable securities, $10,000.

   Required:

   On the basis of the preceding information, compute the current ratio at December 31, 19X2.

17. The ending inventory for each month of 19X1 is listed below for the Expo Company:

1/31	$21,998	7/31	$35,000
2/28	33,000	8/31	40,000
3/31	28,000	9/30	47,000
4/30	29,500	10/31	48,600
5/31	34,200	11/30	47,300
6/30	29,000	12/31	49,100

   During the last half of the year, the company decided to order inventory in larger quantities to take advantage of a quantity discount. The company was able to pass this discount on to its customers in the form of a price decrease. Cost of goods sold for the first half of the year was $224,000 and for the last half of the year was $410,000, reflecting an increase in demand.

   Required:

   Compute inventory turnover for both halves of the year and decide whether this new inventory policy is beneficial.

Problems

18. The comparative income statement for Joe Company and John Company is presented below.

Joe Company and John Company
Comparative Income Statement
for the Year Ending December 31, 19X1

	Joe Company	John Company
Net sales	$500,000	$250,000
Cost of goods sold	350,000	150,000
Gross profit on sales	$150,000	$100,000
Operating expenses:		
Selling expense	$ 50,000	$ 10,000
Administrative expense	10,000	7,000
Total operating expenses	$ 60,000	$ 17,000
Operating income	$ 90,000	$ 83,000
Interest expense	30,000	5,000
Income before taxes	$ 60,000	$ 78,000
Income taxes	20,000	25,000
Net income	$ 40,000	$ 53,000

Required:

Using the above information, prepare a common-size statement comparing income data for Joe Company and John Company.

19. The following information was taken from the financial statements of Maker Company on December 31, 19X2.

Cash	$ 75,000
Accounts receivable	125,000
Inventory	100,000
Fixed assets (net)	500,000
	$800,000

Accounts payable	$100,000
Bond payable (due December 31, 19X27)	300,000
Capital stock ($10 par)	300,000
Retained earnings	100,000
	$800,000

Net income for 19X2 was $ 50,000.

Required:

Compute the following:

1. Current ratio
2. Working capital
3. Acid-test ratio
4. Earnings per share
5. Debt-to-equity ratio

20. Following is the condensed common-size income statement for Francis Co.:

Francis Company
*Condensed Common-Size Income Statement
for the Year Ended December 31, 19X2*

Net sales	100.0%
Cost of goods sold	68.0%
Gross profit on sales	32.0%
Operating expenses:	
Selling expense	16.0%
Administrative expense	6.0
Total Operating Expense	22.0%
Operating income	10.0%
Interest expense	0.5
Income before income taxes	9.5%
Income taxes	2.0
Net income	7.5%

Net sales for the period were $3,000,000.

Required:

Prepare the income statement for Francis Company.

21. Given below are the balance sheets for Meyers, Inc., for 19X1 and 19X2.

Meyers, Inc.
Comparative Balance Sheet
December 31, 19X2 and 19X1

	19X2	19X1
ASSETS		
Current assets:		
Cash	$ 20,000	$ 17,000
Accounts receivable (net)	45,000	60,000
Supplies inventory	8,000	6,000
Prepaid expenses	7,000	5,000
Total current assets	$ 80,000	$ 88,000
Land	120,000	70,000
Buildings (net)	200,000	100,000
Total assets	$400,000	$258,000
LIABILITIES		
Current liabilities:		
Accounts payable	$ 10,000	$ 7,000
Taxes payable	9,000	3,000
Total current liabilities	$ 19,000	$ 10,000
Bonds payable	115,000	70,000
Total liabilities	$134,000	$ 80,000
STOCKHOLDERS' EQUITY		
Common stock ($5 par)	$ 50,000	$ 45,000
Additional paid-in capital	125,000	80,000
Retained earnings	91,000	53,000
Total liabilities and stockholders' equity	$400,000	$258,000

Required:

Prepare a horizontal and vertical analysis of the balance sheets of Meyers, Inc. for 19X1 and 19X2.

22. Shown below are partially completed comparative financial statements of Neil Company.

Required:

1. Complete the statements.
2. Compute the following for 19X2:

    a. Rate of Return on Total Assets
    b. Rate of Return on Common Stockholders' Equity
    c. Earnings per Share of Common Stock
    d. Debt-to-Equity Ratio
    e. Number of Times Interest Earned
    f. Working Capital
    g. Current Ratio
    h. Acid-Test Ratio
    i. Inventory Turnover
    j. Average Number of Days to Collect Receivables

Neil Company
Comparative Balance Sheet
December 31, 19X2 and 19X1

	19X2 Dollars	19X2 Percent of Total Assets	19X1 Dollars	19X1 Percent of Total Assets	Increase (Decrease) Dollars	Increase (Decrease) Percent
ASSETS						
Current assets:						
Cash	$ 55,000		$ 50,000			
Net accounts receivable	200,000		175,000			
Inventories	300,000		225,000			
Prepaid expenses	45,000		50,000			
Total current assets	$ 600,000		$ 500,000			
Land, buildings, and						
equipment (net)	1,400,000		1,250,000			
Total assets	$2,000,000		$1,750,000			
LIABILITIES						
Current liabilities:						
Accounts payable	$ 300,000		$ 350,000			
Notes payable	200,000		100,000			
Total current liabilities	$ 500,000		$ 450,000			
Bonds payable	500,000		500,000			
Total liabilities	$1,000,000		$ 950,000			
STOCKHOLDERS' EQUITY						
Common stock ($20 par)	$ 600,000		$ 600,000			
Retained earnings	400,000		200,000			
Total liabilities and						
stockholders' equity	$2,000,000		$1,750,000			

Neil Company
Comparative Income Statement
for Years Ended December 31, 19X2 and 19X1

	19X2 Dollars	19X2 Percent of Sales	19X1 Dollars	19X1 Percent of Sales	Increase (Decrease) Dollars	Increase (Decrease) Percent
Net sales	$3,000,000		$2,000,000			
Cost of goods sold	2,100,000		1,500,000			
Gross profit on sales	$ 900,000		$ 500,000			
Operating expenses:						
Selling expenses	$ 400,000		$ 200,000			
Administrative expenses	100,000		$ 50,000			
Total Operating Expenses	500,000		250,000			
Operating income	400,000		250,000			
Interest expense	40,000		30,000			
Income before income taxes	$ 360,000		$ 220,000			
Income taxes	90,000		45,000			
Net Income	$ 270,000		$ 175,000			

Neil Company
Comparative Statement of Retained Earnings
for Years Ended 12/31/X2 and X1

	19X2	19X1	Increase (Decrease) Dollars	Percent
Retained earnings, January 1	$ 200,000	$ 75,000		
Net income	270,000	175,000		
	470,000	$250,000		
Less: Dividends	70,000	50,000		
Retained earnings, December 31	$ 400,000	$200,000		

23. Joe Stockholder is contemplating buying stock in one of the following companies, both in the same business. Below is financial data relating to each company:

	Pirate Company	Cardinal Company
Sales	$ 6,000	$18,000
Cost of goods sold	3,800	13,884
Depreciation expense	800	1,400
Interest expense	200	800
Other expenses	44	110
Income taxes	480	600
Cash	1,000	4,000
Accounts receivable	3,500	10,000
Inventory	800	1,900
Fixed assets	10,000	38,000
Accumulated depreciation	4,000	14,000
Accounts payable	1,800	4,000
Income taxes payable	480	600
Bonds payable	200	3,600
Common stock ($20 par value)	6,000	36,000
Retained earnings	2,820	(4,300)
Current market per share	$ 33	$ 5.35

Required:

Compute the ratio that would best give the answer to each of the following questions, then answer the question. Make all necessary assumptions.

1. Which company has the best current position?
2. Which company has the most effective credit department?
3. Which company is doing the best job at keeping the most appropriate inventory level?
4. Which firm has the best ability to make their interest payments?
5. Which firm is earning the best return on the firm's assets?
6. Which stock is the best buy?

24. The following are financial statements of ZYX Corporation for 19X1.

ZYX Corporation
Balance Sheet
December 31, 19X1

ASSETS

Current assets:

Cash	$100,000	
Accounts receivable (net)	200,000	
Prepaid expenses	50,000	
Inventory	110,000	
Total current assets		$460,000

Fixed assets:

Land	$ 50,000	
Machinery (net)	100,000	
Building (net)	250,000	
Total fixed assets		400,000
Total assets		$860,000

LIABILITIES AND STOCKHOLDERS' EQUITY

Accounts payable	$ 50,000
Wages payable	5,000
Interest payable	2,000
Bonds payable (due December 31, 19X6)	200,000
Capital stock ($2 par value)	400,000
Retained earnings	203,000
Total liabilities and stockholders' equity	$860,000

ZYX Corporation
Income Statement
for the Year Ended December 31, 19X1

Sales (net)		$1,000,000
Cost of goods sold:		
Beginning inventory	$ 90,000	
Purchases	600,000	
Goods available for sale	$690,000	
Ending inventory	110,000	
Cost of goods sold		580,000
Gross profit on sales		$ 420,000
Operating expenses:		
Sales salaries expense	$ 75,000	
Depreciation expense	20,000	
Insurance expense	5,000	
Interest expense	10,000	
Total operating expense		110,000
Income before taxes		$ 310,000
Income taxes		100,000
Net Income		$ 210,000

January 1, 19X0 data:

Common shares outstanding	200,000

Required:

Compute the following:

1. Earnings per Share of Common Stock
2. Debt-to-Equity Ratio
3. Number of Times Interest Earned

    4. Current Ratio
    5. Acid-Test or Quick Ratio
    6. Inventory Turnover

25. The following information applies to River Road Products.

	19x5	19x4
Net Sales	$1,260,000	$780,000
Net Income Before Interest and Taxes	330,000	255,000
Net Income After Taxes	166,500	189,000
Bond Interest Expense	27,000	24,000
Stockholders' Equity, December 31		
(19x3: $600,000)	915,000	705,000
Common Stock, Par $50, December 31	780,000	690,000

Average number of shares outstanding were 15,600 for 19x5 and 13,800 for 19x4.

Required:

Compute the following ratios for River Road for 19x5 and 19x4.

    a. Number of times bond interest was earned.
    b. Earnings per share based on the number of shares outstanding on December 31.
    c. Price-earnings ratio (Market prices: 19x5 – per share, 19x4 – $ 116 per share)
    d. Return on average equity.
    e. Net margin.

26. Wilbur Manufacturing has a current ratio of three to one on December 31, 19x8. The following are examples of transactions the company could engage in. Indicate whether each transaction would (+) increase, (–) decrease , or (0) not affect Wilbur's current ratio. Do the same for the effect on Wilbur's working capital.

    a. Collected accounts receivable
    b. Invested in current marketable securities
    c. Paid cash for a trademark
    d. Wrote-off an uncollectable account receivable
    e. Sold equipment for cash
    f. Sold merchandise for a profit (cash)
    g. Discounted a note receivable, incurring an interest charge
    h. Declared a cash dividend
    i. Purchased inventory on account
    j. Scrapped a fully depreciated machine (no gain or loss)
    k. Issued a stock dividend
    l. Purchased a machine for a long-term note
    m. Paid a previously declared cash dividend

27. Below are the financial statements of McKeown Company.

	19x2	19X1
Revenues:		
Net Sales	$315,000	$262,500
Other Revenues	6,000	7,000
Total Revenues	$321,000	$269,500
Expenses:		
Cost of Goods Sold	$189,000	$154,875
Selling Expenses	32,000	29,000
General and Administrative		
Expenses	16,000	15,000
Interest Expense	4,000	4,500
Income Tax Expense (40%)	32,000	26,450
Total Expenses	$273,000	$229,825
Earnings From Continuing		
Operations Before		
Extraordinary Items	$ 48,000	$ 39,675
Extraordinary Gain (net of $8,000 tax)	6,000	0
Net Earnings	$ 54,000	$ 39,675

Assets

	19x2	19X1
Current Assets:		
Cash	$ 6,500	$ 11,500
Marketable Securities	1,000	1,500
Accounts Receivable	50,000	47,500
Inventories	150,000	145,000
Prepaid Expenses	5,000	2,500
Total Current Assets	$212,500	$208,000
Plant and Equipment (net)	157,000	157,000
Intangibles	30,500	0
Total Assets	$400,000	$365,000

Equities

	19x2	19X1
Liabilities:		
Current Liabilities		
Accounts Payable	$ 60,000	$ 81,500
Other	25,000	22,500
Total Current Liabilities	$ 85,000	$104,000
Bonds Payable	100,000	100,000
Total Liabilities	$185,000	$204,000
Stockholders' Equity:		
Common Stock ($3 par)	$150,000	$150,000
Paid-In Capital in Excess of Par	20,000	20,000
Retained Earnings	45,000	(9,000)
Total Stockholders' Equity	$215,000	$161,000
Total Equities	$400,000	$365,000

Required:

Calculate the following ratios for 19x1 and 19x2. When insufficient data prohibits the computation of averages, year-end balances should be used in the calculations.

a. Net margin
b. Return on investment
c. Return on equity
d. Earnings per share
e. Price-earnings ratio (market price at end of 19x2 and 19x1 was $5.94 and $4.77, respectively)
f. Book value per share of common stock

g. Times bond interest earned
h. Working capital
i. Current ratio
j. Acid-test ratio
k. Accounts receivable turnover
l. Inventory turnover
m. Stockholders' equity ratio
n. Total liabilities to total stockholders' equity

Refer to the Annual Report in Chapter 1 of the text.

28. Compute the accounts receivable turnover for the most recent year, assuming notes receivable equal zero.

29. Compute the average collection period for the most recent year.

30. Compute the current ratio for the most recent year.

31. Compute the acid test ratio for the most recent year.

32. Compute the debt-to-equity ratio for the most recent year.

33. Compute the inventory turnover for the most recent year.

34. Compute the number of times interest was earned in the most recent year.

35. Compute the return on total assets in the most recent year.

Outline

LEARNING OBJECTIVES

Chapter 15 illustrates the procedures used in preparing the statement of cash flows. Studying this chapter should enable you to:

1. Understand and give examples of the types of information an analysis of cash flows provides.

2. Identify the primary sources and uses of cash.

3. Describe the procedures involved in preparing the statement of cash flows.

4. Prepare a statement of cash flows using both the indirect and the direct methods of computing net cash flows from operating activities.

CHAPTER 15

THE STATEMENT of CASH FLOWS

INTRODUCTION

An important consideration in the decision process of many users of financial statements is the amount of, and the changes in, the cash available to a business. Comparative balance sheets indicate the cash available at the beginning and the end of a period. These statements do not, however, explain the causes of any changes in cash. While a part of the change in cash may result from the operations of the business, the net income as reported in the income statement may not be accompanied by an equivalent increase in cash. Wal-Mart's net income in 1997 was $3,056 million, but the net cash provided by its operating activities was almost twice that amount, at $5,930 million. Yet the increase in its cash for the year was only $800 million. Consequently, the combination of the balance sheet and income statement may not provide an adequate indication of the cash flows that take place during the business cycle. For this reason, a statement that discloses the analysis of the cash flows of a firm is required along with the balance sheet, income statement, statement of stockholders' equity, and related footnotes to complete the required basic financial statements for a firm.

IMPORTANCE of CASH FLOWS

Investors are interested in receiving dividends, creditors are concerned about receiving periodic interest payments and principal payments, suppliers want to be assured that they will receive payments for merchandise sold, and employees depend on being able to receive paychecks when due. The critical issue for all these groups is cash flow.

Although some information about cash flows can be derived from comparative balance sheets and income statements, neither of these statements provides a complete picture of a company's cash flows. An income statement discloses the results of operations for a period of time, but does not indicate the cash provided by operations or the cash provided by other activities. An income statement is based on the accrual method of accounting, because this method provides a better indication of future cash inflows and outflows than an income statement based on strictly cash receipts and cash payments. Comparative balance sheets show net changes in assets, liabilities, and owners' equity, but do not indicate the specific causes of these changes. For example, comparative balance sheets may show that property, plant and equipment increased, but they do not indicate how the increase was financed. Even if short-term or long-term debt increased, comparative balance sheets do not explain whether the increase was due to only new debt or if maturing debt was repaid and new debt issued. A third statement is needed—a statement of cash flows.

The statement of cash flows explains the causes of changes in cash and provides a summary of the operating, investing, and financing activities of an enterprise during a period of time. While the basic purpose of this statement is to provide information concerning the cash receipts and payments of a company, the statement also is useful in appraising other factors such as the firm's financing policies, dividend policies, ability to expand productive capacity, and ability to satisfy future debt requirements.

A BRIEF HISTORY

Prior to the 1960s, many firms voluntarily prepared statements of changes in financial position for their annual reports. The statement of changes usually provided information on the sources and uses of working capital (current assets minus current liabilities) during the accounting period. The statement of changes in financial position was not provided to replace the balance sheet or income statement, but was intended to provide information that was not available directly from the other statements.

While the basic objective of the statement of changes in financial position was to summarize the financing and investing activities of the firm, in practice the form and content of these statements varied considerably. The statement was designed to allow users to analyze the flow of funds. Funds were usually defined as working capital, but some companies defined funds as cash.

Due to increasing attention placed on funds-flow analysis, the AICPA published *Accounting Research Study No. 2*, "'Cash Flow' Analysis and the Funds Statement," in 1961.[1] This study recommended that the funds statement be presented in annual reports. In 1963, *APB Opinion No. 3*, "The Statement of Source and Application of Funds," recommended, but did not require, that a statement of sources and applications of funds be presented as supplementary information in financial reports.[2] After the issuance of *APB Opinion No. 3*, there was a substantial increase in the number of firms presenting funds-flow data; however, the nature of the funds statement varied widely in practice, because *APB Opinion No. 3* allowed considerable latitude as to the form, content, and terminology of the statement.

In 1971, the APB issued its *Opinion No. 19*,[3] which required the presentation of funds flow in annual reports. In this Opinion, the APB stated that a statement of changes in financial position is essential for financial statement users and must be presented as a basic financial statement for each period for which an income statement is presented.

The objective of the statement of changes in financial position was to provide information on all of the financing and investing activities that occurred during an accounting period. This statement did not replace the income statement or balance sheet. Rather, it was intended to provide information that the other statements did not provide concerning the flow of funds and changes in financial position.

Many companies switched from defining funds as working capital to defining funds as cash or cash plus cash equivalents (such as treasury bills, commercial paper, and money market funds). The change can be seen from data provided in the 1989 edition of *Accounting Trends & Techniques* for its survey of 600 companies. In 1985, 587 of the 600 companies presented a statement of changes in financial position, and only one company included a statement of cash flows in their annual report. In 1988, only 58 companies presented a statement of changes in financial position and 540 companies included a cash flow statement.

In 1987, the FASB issued *Statement of Financial Accounting Standards No. 95, "Statement of Cash Flows,"* requiring a statement of cash flows when both a balance sheet and an income statement are presented. The statement of cash flows should present the net cash flows from operating, investing, and financing activities.[4]

Cash Flow Concept

FASB Statement No. 95 permits preparation of the cash flow statement using a "pure cash" concept or a "cash and cash equivalents" concept. The pure cash concept reflects on the cash flow statement only those transactions that involve the direct inflow or outflow of cash. The cash and cash equivalents is a broader concept, reflecting as cash flow both cash transactions and those transactions involving highly liquid assets with very short maturity dates (usually three months or less). Cash equivalents would include U.S. treasury bills (due in 3 months or less), commercial paper, and money market funds. If the cash equivalent concept is used, it must be disclosed in the notes as an accounting policy.

---

[1] Perry Mason, "'Cash' Flow Analysis and the Funds Statement," Accounting Research Study No. 2 (New York: AICPA, 1961).

[2] *APB Opinion No. 3*, "The Statement of Source and Application of Funds" (New York: AICPA, 1963).

[3] *APB Opinion No. 19*, "Reporting Changes in Financial Position" (New York: AICPA, 1971), para. 7.

[4] *FASB Statement No. 95*, "Cash Flow Statement" (Norwalk, CT: FASB, 1987).

THE STATEMENT of CASH FLOWS

The statement of cash flows consists of three major sections: the cash effects of an entity's operations, its investing activities, and its financing activities. Grouping cash flows into these categories enables significant relationships within and among these activities to be analyzed and provides useful information to users of financial statements. The statement of cash flows can provide answers to questions such as the following:

Why is net income different from net cash flows from operations?

Why were dividend payments so low when income was so high?

How were acquisitions of plant and equipment paid for?

How much of an increase in cash during the year was due to new borrowing?

How much cash was used to buy treasury stock?

How much cash was received from selling noncurrent assets?

Previously, the statement of changes in financial position (either on a cash or working capital basis) was in the format of a listing of the sources and then the uses of cash or working capital. However, sources can include such dissimilar transactions as the issuance of bonds and the proceeds on the sale of plant and equipment; similarly, uses can include transactions such as the payment of dividends and the repayment of long-term debt. The new format required by the FASB is more useful and understandable.

The three sections of the statement of cash flows are as follows:

1. *Operating activities*—Operating activities include selling, purchasing, and producing goods; providing services; paying suppliers and employees; and interest income.

2. *Investing activities*—Investing activities include receipts from loans, acquiring and selling securities (except for cash equivalents) and acquiring and selling plant assets and land.

3. *Financing activities*—Financing activities include proceeds from the issuance of the entity's bonds or stocks, reductions of long-term debt prior to maturity, outlays to pay the maturity value of bonds, outlays to purchase the entity's stock, and the payment of dividends.

In addition, there may be a separate schedule for noncash investing and financing activities (for example, acquiring land by issuing common stock).

In preparing the statement of cash flows, cash flows from operating activities may be reported by either the direct or the indirect method. Using the direct method, cash flows from operations are computed by subtracting cash disbursements from operations directly from cash receipts from operations. Alternatively, the indirect method computes net cash flow from operations by adjusting the net income for noncash items included in the computation of net income for the period. The cash impact of any extraordinary items should be disclosed separately under either method.

A format for the statement of cash flows using the direct method is presented in Illustration 1. A format for the statement of cash flows using the indirect method is presented in Illustration 2.

Note that the only difference between the direct and the indirect methods is in presentation of net cash flow from operating activities. The remaining two sections of the statement, cash flows from investing activities and cash flows from financing activities, are identical under the direct and indirect methods.

When the direct method is used, a supplemental schedule reconciling net income to net cash flows from operating activities must be provided. The format for this schedule is presented in Illustration 3.

Illustration 1
*Statement of Cash Flows Using
the Direct Method*

Cash flows from operating activities:		
Cash received from customers	$ X	
Dividends received	X	
Cash provided by operating activities		$ X
Cash paid to suppliers	(X)	
Cash paid to employees	(X)	
Cash paid for interest and taxes	(X)	
Cash paid for operating activities		(X)
Net cash flow from operating activities		$ X
Cash flows from investing activities:		
Proceeds from sale of plant assets	$ X	
Purchase of plant assets	(X)	
Net cash provided by investing activities		X
Cash flows from financing activities:		
Proceeds from issuance of bonds payable	$ X	
Proceeds from issuance of common stock	X	
Payment of cash dividends	(X)	
Net cash provided by financing activities		X
Net increase (decrease) in cash		$ X

Illustration 2
*Statement of Cash Flows Using
the Indirect Method*

Cash flows from operating activities:		
Net income	$ X	
Noncash expenses, revenues, losses, and gains included in income:		
Depreciation and amortization	X	
Increase in receivables	(X)	
Increase in inventories	(X)	
Increase in payables	X	
Net cash flow from operating activities		$ X
Cash flows from investing activities:		
Proceeds from sale of plant assets	$ X	
Purchase of plant assets	(X)	
Net cash provided by investing activities		X
Cash flows from financing activities:		
Proceeds from issuance of bonds payable	$ X	
Proceeds from issuance of common stock	X	
Payment of cash dividends	(X)	
Net cash provided by financing activities		X
Net increase (decrease) in cash		$ X

Note that this schedule, the reconciliation of net income to net cash provided by operating activities, is almost identical to the initial section of the cash flow statement using the indirect method. This is because the indirect method normally provides a reconciliation of net income to net cash flows from operating activities for all noncash expenses, revenues, losses, and gains within the statement itself. The same amount of net cash from operating activities is reported under the direct and indirect methods.

While the FASB permits the use of either method, it encourages the use of the direct method because the board believes that it provides more useful information. The indirect method is used by over 95 percent of companies presenting a statement of cash flows. Both methods will be illustrated in this chapter.

```
┌─────────────────────────────────────────────────────────────┐
│                        Illustration 3                        │
│                  Reconciliation of Net Income                │
│            to Net Cash Provided by Operating Activities       │
│                                                               │
│                                                               │
│   Net income .........................................   $ X  │
│   Adjustments to reconcile net income to                      │
│     net cash provided by operating activities:                │
│        Depreciation and amortization ...................   X  │
│        Increase in receivables .........................  (X) │
│        Increase in inventories .........................  (X) │
│        Increase in payables ............................   X  │
│        Total adjustments ...............................  $ X │
│           Net cash provided by operating activities ....  $ X │
│                                                               │
└─────────────────────────────────────────────────────────────┘
```

CASH FROM OPERATIONS

The net income of a firm for a particular period has been defined as the excess of its revenues and gains over its expenses and losses. Revenues generally result in an increase in cash or other current assets. For example, sales usually cause an increase in either cash or accounts receivable. Similarly, most expenses require either that a current outlay of cash be made or that a current liability be incurred.

DIRECT METHOD

Under the direct method, the statement of cash flows may show cash receipts and payments from operations directly. Such a format may appear as follows:

```
Cash flows from operating activities:
    Cash received from customers ...............   $ X
    Dividends received ........................     X
    Cash provided by operating activities ..........        $ X
    Cash paid to suppliers ....................    (X)
    Cash paid to employees ....................    (X)
    Cash paid for interest and taxes ..............   (X)
    Cash paid for operating activities ............          (X)
Net cash flow from operating activities ...........     $ X
```

Cash received from customers is equal to net sales on an accrual basis plus the decrease in net accounts receivable or minus the increase in net accounts receivable. Net sales is adjusted by the change in net accounts receivable to convert sales on an accrual basis to sales on a cash basis. Assume that sales on an accrual basis are $50,000, beginning accounts receivable are $10,000, and ending accounts receivable are $8,000. Then sales on a cash basis are as follows:

```
Sales on an accrual basis ...........................   $50,000
Add:  Beginning accounts receivable ..................    10,000
                                                        $60,000
Less:  Ending accounts receivable ...................     8,000
Cash received from customers ........................   $52,000
```

The decrease in accounts receivable ($10,000 − $8,000 = $2,000) results in cash received from customers exceeding sales on an accrual basis by $2,000.

Cash paid to suppliers of merchandise is equal to cost of goods sold (1) plus the increase in inventories or minus the decrease in inventories (to convert cost of goods sold to purchases), and (2) plus the decrease or minus the increase in accounts payable and other short-term liabilities for merchandise. For example, assume that cost of goods sold is $40,000, beginning inventories are $7,000, ending inventories are $9,000, beginning accounts payable for inventories are $6,000, and ending accounts payable for inventories are $5,000. Then cash paid to suppliers is as follows:

Cost of goods sold	$40,000
Add: Ending inventories	9,000
Cost of goods available	$49,000
Less: Beginning inventories	7,000
Purchases	$42,000
Add: Beginning accounts payable	6,000
	$48,000
Less: Ending accounts payable	5,000
Cash paid to suppliers	$43,000

Cash paid for other expenses is equal to the expense on an accrual basis plus the decrease in the related payable or minus the increase in the related payable. For example, cash paid to employees is equal to salaries on an accrual basis plus the decrease in salaries payable or minus the increase in salaries payable.

Indirect Method

As indicated above, the reported net income of a firm is not always equal to the net cash flow from operating activities. Not all expenses or revenues result in a corresponding outflow or inflow of cash. Certain types of expenses enter into the determination of net income but do not affect cash. For example, depreciation on plant assets is an expense that reduces income but does not require an outlay of cash during the current period. Therefore, depreciation expense does not affect cash. Consequently, to determine the net cash flow from operating activities, it is necessary to include only those expenses that required an outflow of cash during the period. An important factor in determining net cash flow from operating activities under the indirect method is to add back to (or subtract from) net income all those items that did not result in an outflow (inflow) of cash.

Examples of items that are added to net income include depreciation expense, amortization expense, bond interest expense due to the amortization of a bond discount, and the reduction to interest revenue due to the amortization of a premium on a bond investment. Examples of items that are subtracted from net income include the reduction to interest expense due to the amortization of a bond premium and interest revenue due to the amortization of a discount on a bond investment.

Additional adjustments are required to convert revenues and expenses to cash receipts and disbursements, because income statement data are based on the accrual method of accounting. To determine net cash flow from operating activities under the indirect method, net income must be adjusted for changes in current assets (other than cash) and for changes in current liabilities (other than those not related to operations, such as nontrade notes payable and dividends payable).

These additional adjustments essentially convert the funds provided by operations from the accrual to the cash basis. Some of the more common adjustments under the indirect method to net income to obtain net cash flow from operating activities are as follows:

Add	Subtract
Decrease in net accounts receivable	Increase in net accounts receivable
Decrease in inventories and prepaid expenses	Increase in inventories and prepaid expenses
Increases in accounts payable, trade notes payable, and accrued liabilities	Decreases in accounts payable, trade notes payable, and accrued liabilities

A decrease in accounts receivable results in sales on a cash basis exceeding sales on an accrual basis. For example, if sales on an accrual basis are $100,000, beginning accounts receivable are $15,000, and ending accounts receivable are $14,000, then sales on a cash basis are $101,000.

Beginning accounts receivable	$ 15,000
Sales on an accrual basis	100,000
Cash that could have been collected	$115,000
Ending accounts receivable	14,000
Sales on a cash basis	$101,000

Therefore, a decrease in accounts receivable is added to net income to obtain net cash flow from operations. Conversely, an increase in accounts receivable is subtracted from net income to obtain net cash flow from operations.

In a similar fashion, net income is adjusted by the changes in accounts payable, short-term notes payable, and accrued liabilities to convert expenses on an accrual basis to expenses on a cash basis. A decrease in these current payables results in expenses on a cash basis being higher than expenses on an accrual basis. Therefore, a decrease in these payables is subtracted from net income to obtain net cash flow from operations. Conversely, an increase in these payables is added to net income to obtain net cash flow from operations.

The change in inventories is an adjustment to net income in order to convert cost of goods sold to purchases. An increase in inventories means that purchases exceed cost of goods sold. For example, if the beginning inventory is $7,000, the ending inventory is $8,000, and cost of goods sold is $80,000, then purchases are $81,000.

Beginning inventory	$ 7,000
Purchases	81,000
Cost of goods available	$88,000
Ending inventory	8,000
Cost of goods sold	$80,000

A decrease in inventories means that purchases are less than cost of goods sold. Therefore, an increase in inventories is subtracted from net income to obtain net cash flow from operations and a decrease in inventories is added to net income to obtain net cash flow from operations.

A firm that experiences a net loss during a period still may generate cash from its operations if: (1) the total expenses that did not require the use of cash exceed the amount of the loss, or (2) adjustments for current assets (other than cash and cash equivalents) and current liabilities convert a net loss on an accrual basis to net income on a cash basis. For example, a firm may have a net loss of $10,000 and have included depreciation expense of $15,000 among its expenses.

Additional adjustments may be required in order to obtain net cash flow from operating activities if net income includes extraordinary gains or losses. The disclosure of cash provided by operations is most useful if the effects of extraordinary items, net of tax, are reported separately from the effects of normal items. The net cash flow from operating activities may begin with the net income or loss from continuing operations. Any items that did not use or provide cash during the period and were included in the net income or loss from continuing operations should be added or deducted. Cash provided or used by extraordinary items, net of tax, should be reported immediately following cash provided or used in operations. Adjustments are necessary for any of these extraordinary items that did not provide or use cash during the period.

Similarly, other nonoperating gains or losses should be excluded from cash provided by operations. These amounts should be included as a part of the investing or financing activities. For example, if land that had an original cost of $10,000 is sold for $9,000 in cash, a $1,000 loss on the sale of land is included in the net income for the period. The $9,000 received from the sale represents the cash provided and is shown in the statement under investing activities as a separate item. The $9,000 proceeds includes the $10,000 cost minus the $1,000 loss. Therefore, to avoid double-counting, the $1,000 loss should not be included in determining the net cash flow from operating activities. Thus, to determine the net cash flow from operating activities, it is necessary to add back any nonoperating losses and to deduct any nonoperating gains.

Both the indirect and the direct methods will be used in this chapter to compute net cash flow from operating activities.

Preparation of the Statement of Cash Flows

The change in cash (including cash equivalents) during the period must be equal to the change in the noncash accounts during the period, because the accounting equation must always balance. Based on this relationship, the increase or decrease in cash may be explained by examining the changes in the noncash accounts for the period.

The primary sources of information used in preparing the statement of cash flows are comparative balance sheets, the statement of stockholders' equity or retained earnings, the income statement, and certain supplementary data concerning the transactions affecting specific noncash accounts during the period. The basic data that will be used to present the required steps for the preparation of a statement of cash flows are shown in the financial statements of the Kraton Company (Illustrations 4-6).

Illustration 4
Kraton Company
Income Statement
for the Year Ended December 31, 19X1

Net sales		$1,000
Cost of goods sold		400
Gross profit		$ 600
Operating expenses:		
Depreciation	$100	
Wage expense	100	
Other expenses	200	400
Net income from operations		$ 200
Gain on sale of land		100
Net income		$ 300

Illustration 5
Kraton Company
Retained Earnings Statement
for the Year Ended December 31, 19X1

Retained earnings at beginning of year	$250
Add: Net income	300
	$550
Subtract: Cash dividends	100
Retained earnings at end of year	$450

Illustration 6
Kraton Company
Comparative Balance Sheet

	December 31		
	19X1	*19X0*	*Change*
Assets			
Cash	$ 250	$ 100	+ 150
Accounts receivable—net	350	200	+ 150
Inventories	200	250	– 50
Building	600	400	+ 200
Accumulated depreciation—building	(200)	(100)	+ 100
Land	100	200	– 100
Total assets	$1,300	$1,050	
Liabilities and Stockholders' Equity			
Accounts payable	$ 300	$ 200	+ 100
Accrued wages payable	50	100	– 50
Bonds payable—long-term	100	200	– 100
Common stock	400	300	+ 100
Retained earnings	450	250	+ 200
Total liabilities and equities	$1,300	$1,050	

Assume that the following additional information is available:

1. During the year, a building was purchased for $200 and land was purchased at a cost of $100.
2. Land with a cost of $200 was sold at a gain of $100.
3. All common stock was issued for cash.
4. A long-term bond was retired for $100.
5. A $100 dividend was paid during the year.
6. The other expenses of $200 were paid in cash.

CHANGE IN CASH

The change in the cash account is an increase of $150 (see Illustration 6). The cash balance was $100 at the end of 19X0, but increased to $250 at the end of 19X1.

CHANGES IN NONCASH ACCOUNTS

Once the change in cash has been determined, the next step is to compute the changes in all of the noncash accounts (see Illustration 6). All changes in the noncash accounts of Kraton Company from December 31, 19X0, to December 31, 19X1, are summarized below:

Kraton Company
Changes in Noncash Accounts

	December 31 19X1	19X0	Increase	Decrease
Accounts receivable—net	$350	$200	$ 150	
Inventories	200	250		$ 50
Buildings	600	400	200	
Accumulated depreciation—buildings	200	100	100	
Land	100	200		100
Accounts payable	300	200	100	
Accrued wages payable	50	100		50
Bonds payable—long-term	100	200		100
Capital stock	400	300	100	
Retained earnings	450	250	200	

Once the amount of these changes has been determined, it is necessary to consider the effect that each change had on cash. If more than one transaction caused the change in a particular account, the effect of each transaction must be analyzed separately. Let us consider the changes in the noncash accounts of Kraton Company.

RETAINED EARNINGS. An examination of the comparative balance sheets reveals that retained earnings increased by $200 during 19X1. An analysis of the statement of retained earnings (Illustration 5) indicates that net income for 19X1 was $300 and that dividends of $100 were declared and paid during the year. These two transactions account for the net change in retained earnings. The payment of the cash dividend affected cash as follows:

Cash flow from financing activity:
Cash dividend .... ($100)

Under the direct method, net cash flow from operating activities is equal to cash receipts from operations minus cash payments from operations. Cash receipts from operations are equal to net sales less the increase in accounts receivables. Cash payments to suppliers are equal to cost of goods sold less the decrease in inventories less the increase in accounts payable. Cash payments to employees are equal to wage expense plus the decrease in accrued wages payable. Cash payments for other expenses are given at $200. Therefore, net cash flow from operating activities using the direct method is as follows:

Cash flows from operating activities:		
Cash receipts from operations ($1,000 – $150)		$850
Cash paid to suppliers ($400 – $50 – $100)	$250	
Cash paid to employees ($100 + $50)	150	
Cash paid for other expenses	200	
Cash paid for other operating activities		600
Net cash flow from operating activities		$250

Using the indirect method, the effect of the net income of the period on cash is included in the calculation of net cash flow from operating activities. As previously indicated, the net income of Kraton Company is not equivalent to net cash flow from operating activities. Depreciation expense that is included in the income statement did not require an outflow of cash. Therefore, it is necessary to add back depreciation expense of $100 to the net income of the period in computing net cash flow from operating activities under the indirect method.

A second adjustment is required to eliminate the nonoperating gain on the sale of land from net income. The $100 gain is included in the proceeds from the sale of land as an investing activity and must be excluded from net cash flow from operating activities.

The increase in accounts receivable of $150 must be subtracted from net income in calculating net cash flow from operating activities. The decrease in inventories of $50 must be added to net income in calculating net cash flow from operating activities. The increase in accounts payable of $100 must be added to net income in calculating net cash flow from operating activities. The decrease in accrued wages payable of $50 must be subtracted from net income in calculating net cash flow from operating activities. Therefore, using the indirect method the net cash flow from operating activities is determined as follows:

> Cash flows from operating activities:
> Net Income $300
> Noncash expenses, revenues, losses,
>   and gains included in income:
> Depreciation 100
> Gain on sale of land .... (100)
> Increase in accounts receivable .... (150)
> Decrease in inventories 50
> Increase in accounts payable 100
> Decrease In accrued wages payable .... (50)
> Net cash flow from operating activities $250

Accumulated Depreciation. The $100 increase in accumulated depreciation—buildings resulted from recording the depreciation expense for the year. The amount of depreciation expense is added to net income in determining net cash flow from operating activities under the indirect method and is not considered under the direct method, because it does not result in a decrease in cash.

Buildings. The increase in the buildings account was the result of a single transaction in which a building was acquired at a cost of $200. The effect of this purchase on cash is as follows:

> Cash flow from investing activity:
> Purchase of building .... ($200)

Land. The comparative balance sheet indicates that the land account decreased by $100 during 19X1. This decrease was a result of the sale of land during the year exceeding the purchase of land during the year. The cash flow from the sale of land is the proceeds received from the sale. The entry to record the sale was as follows:

> Cash 300
> Gain on sale of land 100
> Land 200

Thus, $300 of cash were provided by the sale. As indicated previously, the $100 gain on the sale must be subtracted from net income in the calculation of net cash flow from operating activities under the indirect method and is not considered under the direct method. The effect of the sale on cash is as follows:

> Cash flow from investing activity:
> Sale of land $300

The purchase of land for $100 affected cash as follows:

> Cash flow from investing activity:
> Purchase of land .... ($100)

Bonds Payable. Bonds payable decreased by $100 during the year. An analysis of the additional information provided indicates that this decrease resulted from the retirement of the bonds. The effect on cash is as follows:

> Cash flow from financing activity:
> Retirement of bonds payable .... ($100)

COMMON STOCK. The increase in the common stock account resulted from the issuance of additional stock for $100 in cash during the year. This amount is included in the statement as follows:

Cash flow from financing activity:
Issuance of common stock $100

THE STATEMENT of CASH FLOWS

All information that is necessary to prepare the statement of cash flows now has been analyzed. Kraton Company's statement of cash flows for the year ended December 31, 19X1, is shown below using: (1) the direct method in Illustration 7, and (2) the indirect method in Illustration 8 to obtain net cash flow from operating activities:

Illustration 7
Statement of Cash Flows
Using the Direct Method

Kraton Company
Statement of Cash Flows
for the Year Ended December 31, 19X1

Cash flows from operating activities:		
Cash receipts from operations		$ 850
Cash paid to suppliers	$ 250	
Cash paid to employees	150	
Cash paid for other expenses	200	
Cash paid for operating expenses		600
Net cash flow from operating activities		$ 250
Cash flows from investing activities:		
Sale of land	$ 300	
Acquisition of land	(100)	
Acquisition of building	(200)	
Net cash used by investing activities		0
Cash flows from financing activities:		
Sale of common stock	$ 100	
Retirement of long-term bonds	(100)	
Payment of dividends	(100)	
Net cash provided by financing activities		(100)
Increase in cash		$ 150

WORKSHEET APPROACH

In a relatively uncomplicated situation, such as that of the Kraton Company described above, it is possible to prepare a statement of cash flows by simply sequentially examining the changes in each account. In a more realistic situation, however, a worksheet often is used to facilitate the analysis and preparation of the statement. Although it is not necessary to use a worksheet, its use normally aids in the preparation of the statement when there are a large number of transactions and various complicating factors.

Illustration 8
Statement of Cash Flows
Using the Indirect Method

Kraton Company
Statement of Cash Flows
for the Year Ended December 31, 19X1

Cash flows from operating activities:

Net income	$ 300	
Noncash expenses, revenues, losses, and gains included in income:		
Depreciation	100	
Gain on sale of land	(100)	
Increase in accounts receivable	(150)	
Decrease in inventories	50	
Increase in accounts payable	100	
Decrease in accrued wages payable	(50)	
Net cash flow from operating activities		$ 250
Cash flows from investing activities:		
Sale of land	$ 300	
Acquisition of land	(100)	
Acquisition of building	(200)	
Net cash used by investing activities		0
Cash flows from financing activities:		
Sale of common stock	$ 100	
Retirement of long-term bonds	(100)	
Payment of dividends	(100)	
Net cash provided by financing activities		(100)
Increase in cash		$ 150

Illustration 9 presents a worksheet for Kraton Company. The direct method is used to obtain net cash flow from operating activities.

The explanations of the adjustments are as follows:

1. The payment of a cash dividend ($100) that decreased retained earnings is recorded as a financing activity.

2. Net sales ($1,000) are included in net income and retained earnings and as a component of net cash flow from operating activities.

3. The increase in accounts receivable ($150) is subtracted from net sales in determining cash received from customers.

4. The increase in accumulated depreciation ($100) is due to depreciation expense, which is included as a negative element in net income and retained earnings but is not considered in determining net cash flow from operating activities.

5. The purchase of the building for $200 is recorded as an investing activity.

6. The sale of land for $300 is shown as an investing activity; the $100 gain is included in net income and retained earnings but is not considered in determining net cash flow from operating activities.

7. The retirement of long-term bonds payable ($100) at face value is recorded as a financing activity.

8. The purchase of land for $100 is recorded as an investing activity.

9. The sale of common stock for cash is recorded as a financing activity.

10. Cost of goods sold is a negative element in net income and retained earnings and is a negative component of net cash flow from operating activities.

Illustration 9
Worksheet Using the Direct Method

Kraton Company
Worksheet for Statement of Cash Flows
for the Year Ended December 31, 19X1

	Balance December 31, 19X0	Adjustments Debit	Adjustments Credit	Balance December, 31 19X1
Debits:				
Cash	$ 100			$ 250
Accounts receivable (net)	200	$ 150 (3)		350
Inventories	250		$ 50 (11)	200
Buildings	400	200 (5)		600
Land	200	100 (8)	200 (6)	100
	$1,150			$1,500
Credits:				
Accumulated depreciation	$ 100		100 (4)	$ 200
Accounts payable	200		100 (12)	300
Accrued wages payable	100	50 (14)		50
Bonds payable	200	100 (7)		100
Common stock	300		100 (9)	400
Retained earnings	250	100 (1)	1,000 (2)	450
		100 (4)	100 (6)	
		400 (10)		
		100 (13)		
		200 (15)		
	$1,150			$1,500

Statement of cash flows:

		Debit	Credit
Cash flows from operations:			
Net sales		1,000 (2)	
Increase in accounts receivable			150 (3)
Cost of goods sold			400 (10)
Decrease in inventories		50 (11)	
Increase in accounts payable		100 (12)	
Wages expense			100 (13)
Decrease in accrued wages payable			50 (14)
Other expenses			200 (15)
Sale of land		300 (6)	
Purchase of land			100 (8)
Sale of common stock		100 (9)	
Purchase of building			200 (5)
Retirement of bonds payable			100 (7)
Payment of dividends			100 (1)
		$3,050	$3,050

11. The decrease in inventories ($50) is an adjustment to cost of goods sold to determine purchases.

12. The increase in accounts payable ($100) is subtracted from purchases in determining cash paid to suppliers.

13. Wage expense is a negative element in net income and retained earnings and is a negative component in net cash flow from operating activities.

14. The decrease in accrued wages payable ($50) is added to wage expense in determining cash paid to employees.

15. Other expenses are a negative element in net income and retained earnings and are a negative component in net cash flow from operating activities.

Illustration 10 presents an alternative worksheet for Kraton Company. The indirect method is used to obtain net cash flow from operating activities.

Illustration 10
Worksheet Using the Indirect Method

Kraton Company
Worksheet for Statement of Cash Flows
for the Year Ended December 31, 19X1

	Balance December 31, 19X0	Adjustments Debit	Adjustments Credit	Balance December 31, 19X1
Debits:				
Cash	$ 100			$ 250
Accounts receivable (net)	200	$ 150 (9)		350
Inventories	250		$ 50 (10)	200
Buildings	400	200 (4)		600
Land	200	100 (7)	200 (5)	100
	$1,150			$1,500
Credits:				
Accumulated depreciation	$ 100		100 (3)	$ 200
Accounts payable	200		100 (11)	300
Accrued wages payable	100	50 (12)		50
Bonds payable	200	100 (6)		100
Common stock	300		100 (8)	400
Retained earnings	250	100 (1)	300 (2)	450
	$1,150			$1,500
Statement of cash flows:				
Cash flows from operations:				
Net income		300 (2)		
Adjustments:				
Depreciation expense		100 (3)		
Gain on sale of land			100 (5)	
Increase in accounts receivable			150 (9)	
Decrease in inventories		50 (10)		
Increase in accounts payable		100 (11)		
Decrease in accrued wages payable			50 (12)	
Sale of land		300 (5)		
Purchase of land			100 (7)	
Sale of common stock		100 (8)		
Purchase of building			200 (4)	
Retirement of bonds payable			100 (6)	
Payment of dividends			100 (1)	
		$1,650	$1,650	

The explanations of the adjustments are as follows:

1. The payment of a cash dividend ($100) that decreased retained earnings is recorded as a financing activity.

2. Net income included in the ending retained earnings balance is reported as the initial component of net cash flow from operating activities. This amount is adjusted below in determining the net cash flow from operating activities.

3. The increase in accumulated depreciation ($100) is added to net income in determining the net cash flow from operating activities, because the depreciation expense did not decrease cash.

4. The purchase of the building for $200 is recorded as an investing activity.

5. The sale of land for $300 is shown as an investing activity; the $100 gain is subtracted from net income in determining net cash flow from operating activities.

6. The retirement of long-term bonds payable ($100) at face value is recorded as a financing activity.

7. The purchase of land for $100 is recorded as an investing activity.

8. The sale of common stock for cash is recorded as a financing activity.

9. The increase in accounts receivable ($150) is subtracted from net income in determining net cash flow from operating activities.

10. The decrease in inventories ($50) is added to net income in determining net cash flow from operating activities.

11. The increase in accounts payable ($100) is added to net income in determining net cash flow from operating activities.

12. The decrease in accrued wages payable ($50) is subtracted from net income in determining net cash flow from operating activities.

The procedures used in preparing a worksheet for the statement of cash flows are summarized below:

1. The account balances appearing on the previous year's balance sheet are entered in the first column of the worksheet. All accounts with debit balances are listed first, followed by all accounts with credit balances.

2. Adjustments are entered into the adjustment columns to account for all noncash items from the upper section and to list all of the separate increases and decreases to cash in the lower section of the worksheet. The worksheet adjustments are not entered in any journal; their purpose is solely to facilitate the analysis and classification of the data for the statement of cash flows.

3. The account balances appearing on the current year's balance sheet are entered in the last column of the worksheet. These account balances are used as a check to determine whether the change in the balance of each noncash item has been explained completely—that is, whether the beginning balance plus or minus the change equals the ending balance.

Additional Problems in the Analysis of the Statement of Cash Flows

Many of the problems that occur in the preparation of the statement of cash flows were discussed in the preceding sections of this chapter. However, additional problems may arise that require special analysis to determine the effect on cash of a change in an asset (excluding cash and cash equivalents), a liability, or an owners' equity account. Some of these special problems are examined in the following paragraphs.

Uncollectible Accounts

Under the direct method, the accounts receivable written off during the period must be deducted from sales in addition to the adjustment for the change in the receivable account, because the decrease in accounts receivable is not due to collections on credit sales. Under the indirect method, a change in the balance in the allowance for bad debts account resulting from either a charge to bad debt expense for the current period or a write-off of uncollectible accounts does not require any adjustment to net income in determining the change to cash. The allowance for bad debt account is a contra account to a current asset, accounts receivable. Therefore, the change in the allowance account is a part of the increase or decrease to net accounts receivable for the period. The debit to bad debt expense represents a deduction from revenues in determining net income. The decrease to net accounts receivable from the credit to the allowance account is added to net income in determining net cash flow from operating activities under the indirect method. Therefore, the bad debt expense is a deduction in net income and the corresponding decrease to net accounts receivable is added to net income so that there is no effect on cash. A write-off of an uncollectible account reduces both the receivable and the related contra account; it does not affect the balance of net accounts receivable. Accordingly, the write-off has no effect on cash.

Dividends

A reduction in retained earnings resulting from the declaration of a cash dividend to be paid during the following period has no effect on cash. The subsequent payment of the dividend does affect cash and is a financing activity in the period in which the disbursement is made.

INCOME TAX EXPENSE

Income tax expense must be adjusted for changes in income taxes payable. Under the direct method, income tax expense is increased (decreased) for a decrease (increase) to income taxes payable. Under the indirect method, net income is increased (decreased) for an increase (decrease) to income taxes payable.

Stock Dividends and Conversions

When a corporation declares a stock dividend, a transfer is made from retained earnings to one or more contributed capital accounts. Such a transfer does not affect either total stockholders' equity or assets. Therefore, the resulting changes in the stockholders' equity items are not included on the statement of cash flows.

Changes of substance in the individual components of owners' equity should be reported in the statement of cash flows even though these changes do not involve either a receipt or disbursement of cash. Accordingly, the conversion of long-term debt or preferred stock to common stock should be reflected in a supplementary schedule to the statement of cash flows.

Significant Noncash Transactions

The statement of cash flows should report all financing and investing activities, including those that do not involve a receipt or disbursement of cash. Among the most common of these transactions are the following:

1. The issuance of noncurrent debt or capital stock for noncurrent assets.
2. The issuance of capital stock to retire noncurrent debt.
3. Refinancing of long-term debt.
4. Conversion of long-term debt or preferred stock to common stock.

To illustrate, assume that a firm issues 50,000 shares of its $5 par value common stock in exchange for land with a fair market value of $380,000. This transaction is recorded in the accounts as follows:

Land	380,000	
Common stock		250,000
Additional paid-in capital		130,000

Although this transaction did not affect cash, the transaction should be viewed as being composed of two parts—the sale of stock for $380.000, and the purchase of a building for the same amount. Thus, the transaction is reported in the statement of cash flows as follows:

Schedule of noncash investing and financing activities:
Issuance of common stock to purchase a building $380,000

Multiple Changes Affecting Specific Accounts

Frequently, there may be several transactions that cause a net change in a noncurrent account. In these circumstances, it normally is helpful to analyze the individual transactions affecting the account in order to identify the effect of each on cash.

For example, assume that the following information is available regarding the equipment account:

	End of Year	Beginning of Year
Equipment	$212,000	$200,000
Accumulated depreciation	55,000	90,000
Depreciation expense	15,000	
Gain on sale of equipment	7,000	

Equipment with a cost of $70,000 and a book value of $20,000 was sold for $27,000 during the year. Equipment was acquired at a cost of $82,000. The individual transactions that caused the changes in the equipment and the accumulated depreciation accounts may be summarized as follows:

	Equipment	Accumulated Depreciation
Beginning of year	$200,000	$ 90,000
Acquisition of equipment	82,000	
Sale of equipment	(70,000)	(50,000)
Depreciation expense		$ 15,000
End of year.........................	$212,000	$ 55,000

The journal entries recorded at the time of each event and the resulting effect on cash are summarized below:

Sale of equipment:
Cash..	27,000	
Accumulated depreciation	50,000	
Equipment...............................		70,000
Gain on sale of equipment		7,000

      Cash inflow of $27,000 as an investing activity; the $7,000 gain is subtracted from net income in determining net cash flow from operations under the indirect method and is not considered under the direct method.

Acquisition of equipment:
Equipment	82,000	
Cash...................................		82,000

      Cash outflow of $82,000 as an investing activity.

Depreciation:
Depreciation expense	15,000	
Accumulated depreciation		15,000

      Depreciation expense is added to net income in determining net cash flow from operations under the indirect method and is not considered under the direct method.

Cash Flow Information for Analysis

Cash flow from operations is an important indicator of a company's ability to pay its debts. Some analysts believe that cash flow from operations is superior to net income in this regard, because accrual accounting can temporarily hide cash flow problems.

Free cash flow measures the cash available after capital expenditures to at least maintain the current level of production and dividend payments.

Free Cash Flow = Net Cash Flow from Operating Activities - Capital Expenditures - Dividends

For Wal-Mart in 1997, free cash flow is computed as follows (dollars are in millions):

Free Cash Flow = $5,930 - $2,643 - $481

Free Cash Flow = $2,806

The free cash flow can be used to acquire new equipment, pay debts, or other business purposes. The free cash flow figure may be understated, because not all of the $2,643 of capital expenditures was used to acquire property, plant and equipment to simply maintain current levels of production.

Cash flow adequacy is a measure of a company's debt-paying ability. Cash flow adequacy can be computed as follows:

$$\text{Cash Flow Adequacy} = \frac{\text{Free Cash Flow}}{\text{Average Amount of Debt Maturing over Next Five Years}}$$

The amount of debt maturing over the next five years can be found in the footnote pertaining to long-term debt and, if not already included, the footnote pertaining to lease obligations. For Wal-Mart in 1997, cash flow adequacy is computed as follows (dollars are in millions):

$$\text{Cash Flow Adequacy} = \frac{\$5,930 - \$2,643 = \$481}{(\$840 + \$1,340 + \$1,120 + \$2,329 + \$363)/5}$$

$$\text{Cash Flow Adequacy} = \frac{\$2,806}{\$1,198}$$

Cash Flow Adequacy = 2.3

Wal-Mart's free cash flow was over twice as large as its average debt repayments for the next five years.

Neither free cash flow nor cash flow adequacy should be examined in isolation. They should be compared with past performance of the company and with other companies in the same industry.

Summary

The statement of cash flows is included as one of the major financial statements in annual reports. This statement may be prepared using a "pure cash" or a "cash and cash equivalents" concept and provides a summary of the operating, investing, and financing activities of an enterprise during a period of time. The statement may be prepared using the direct or the indirect method. In addition, material transactions involving changes in noncash accounts must be disclosed in the statement of cash flows.

The sections of the statement of cash flows are as follows: (1) cash flows from operating activities, (2) cash flows from investing activities, and (3) cash flows from financing activities. Investing activities include collections on loans, proceeds from the sale of plant assets, and purchases of plant assets; financing activities include proceeds from the issuance of bonds and stock and the payment of cash dividends.

Key Definitions

"Cash and cash equivalents" concept—reflects as cash flow both cash transactions and those transactions involving highly liquid assets with very short maturity dates.

Cash equivalents—include U.S. treasury bills (due in three months or less), commercial paper, and money market funds.

Cash disbursement—any outflow of cash by the firm.

Cash flow—any transaction that increases or decreases the cash balance of the firm.

Cash receipt—any transaction that increases the cash account of the firm.

Direct method—computing net cash flow from operations as the difference between cash receipts from operating activities and cash disbursements from operating activities.

Financing activities—the statement of cash flows section that includes proceeds from the issuance of the entity's bonds or stocks, outlays to pay the maturity value of bonds, outlays to purchase the entity's stock, and the payment of dividends.

Funds—according to *APB Opinion No. 19*, funds were defined as either cash, near-cash, or working capital.

Indirect method—computing net cash flow from operations by adjusting net income for noncash items included in income.

Investing activities—the statement of cash flows section that includes receipts from loans, acquiring and selling securities (except for cash equivalents), and acquiring and selling plant assets and land.

Operating activities—statement of cash flows section that includes selling, purchasing, and producing goods; providing services; and paying suppliers and employees.

"Pure cash" concept—includes on the cash flow statement only those transactions that involve the direct inflow or outflow of cash.

Statement of cash flows—a statement which explains the causes of changes in cash plus highly liquid marketable securities and provides a summary of the investing and financing activities of an enterprise during a period of time.

Working capital—the excess of current assets over current liabilities.

Questions

1. Why is a statement of cash flows necessary?

2. What is the all-financial-resources concept and why is it important?

3. What are the three major sections of a statement of cash flows?

4. Give examples for each of the three major sections of a statement of cash flows.

5. Explain how income affects cash. Is reported net income always equal to the amount of cash flows from operations?

6. List items that may be included in the determination of net income but that have no effect on cash.

7. Compare and contrast the direct and indirect methods of preparing the statement of cash flows.

8. What steps are needed in preparing a statement of cash flows?

9. What is the purpose of a worksheet in preparing a statement of cash flows?

10. State how the following are presented on a statement of cash flows.

   a. Dividends paid.
   b. Conversions of bonds to common stock.
   c. Amortization of discount on bonds payable.
   d. Loss on the sale of equipment.

11. Explain how each of the following are treated in a statement of cash flows.

   a. Bad debt expense.
   b. Purchasing land by issuing common stock.
   c. Reclassifying a note payable from long-term to current.
   d. Loss on sale of current marketable equity securities.
   e. Increase in inventories.
   f. Amortization of patents.
   g. Increase in accounts payable.
   h. Conversion of bonds to common stock.

12. What are two types of financial transactions that would be disclosed under the "all-financial-resources" concept that would not be disclosed without this concept?

EXERCISES

13. *Cash Flow From Operations.* Consider the following income statement for Wills Company.

Sales		$1,000,000
Cost of goods sold		750,000
Gross margin		$ 250,000
Selling and administrative expenses:		
Salary expense	$50,000	
Depreciation expense	25,000	
Administrative expense	25,000	100,000
Net Income		$ 150,000

Additional information:

Decrease in inventories	9,000
Increase in accounts receivable	5,000
Increase in accounts payable	6,000

Required:

Compute the cash flows from operating activities.

14. *Cash Flow From Operations.* Below is the income statement for Lopes Company for the year ending December 31, 19X2.

Lopes Company
Income Statement
for the Year Ended December 31, 19X2

Sales (net)		$500,000
Cost of goods sold:		
Beginning inventory	$ 50,000	
Purchases	300,000	
Goods available for sale	$350,000	
Ending inventory	40,000	
Cost of goods sold		310,000
Gross margin		$190,000
Expenses:		
Wages	$ 35,000	
Depreciation	30,000	
Advertising	15,000	
Administrative	5,000	85,000
Income from operations		$105,000
Gain on sale of equipment		50,000
Net income		$155,000

The following balances were derived from the balance sheet.

	December 31	
	19X2	19X1
Accounts receivable	$100,000	$ 90,000
Accounts payable	30,000	50,000
Prepaid advertising expense	5,000	3,000
Wages payable	5,000	4,000

Required:

Prepare a schedule showing cash flows from operating activities.

15. *Cash Flow From Operations.* Your examination of the financial statements of Russell Company reveals the following data:

	19X2		19X1	
Sales (net)		$100,000		$75,000
Cost of goods sold:				
Beginning inventory	$17,000		$12,000	
Purchases (net)	58,000		55,000	
Goods available	$75,000		$67,000	
Ending inventory	15,000		17,000	
Cost of goods sold		60,000		50,000
Accounts payable		20,000		25,000
Accounts receivable		50,000		45,000

Required:

Compute the following for 19X2:

a. Cash receipts from sales.
b. Cash disbursements for purchases.

16. *Cash Flow From Operations.* Consider the following information for the period ending December 31, 19X1, concerning the Cey Company.

1. Net income for 19X1 was $250,000.
2. Depreciation expense on its buildings was $25,000. Accumulated depreciation on the buildings is $200,000.
3. Extraordinary (non-operating) gains and losses included a loss of $50,000 on an uninsured building destroyed by fire.
4. Dividends paid during the year in cash—$50,000.

Required:

Compute the cash flows from operating activities.

17. *Statement of Cash Flows—General Classification.* Indicate how each of the items presented below would appear in a statement of cash flows.

1. Declaration of a cash dividend.
2. Payment of cash dividend after above declaration.
3. Depreciation expense for the year.
4. Fully depreciated equipment written off the books.
5. Amortization of premium on long-term bonds payable.

6. Semiannual coupon payments on bonds mentioned in item (5) above.
7. Sale of common stock at a discount.
8. Purchase of treasury stock at a price above the original issue price.
9. Payment of wages accrued at the end of the prior year.
10. Sale of fixed assets at a loss.
11. Issuance of a 90-day note.
12. Sale of ten-year bonds at a discount.
13. Three for one (3-1) split of the preferred stock.
14. Sale of machinery at a price in excess of its book value.
15. Amortization of goodwill.

18. *Statement of Cash Flows—Preparation.* Wynn, Inc., hired you as an independent accountant to analyze the reasons for their unsatisfactory cash position. The company earned $42,000 during the year (19X1) but their cash balance is lower than ever. Your assistant prepared a worksheet providing you with the following information:

1. For 19X1, sales were $207,000, cost of goods sold was $70,000 and all other expenses totalled $98,000.
2. Additional capital stock was sold in 19X1; the proceeds of the sale were $40,000.
3. Vacant land purchased in 19X0 at a cost of $27,000 was sold in 19X1 for $30,000.
4. A payment of $22,000 was made in 19X1 on a long-term mortgage.
5. Equipment costing $89,000 was purchased during the year.
6. Included in the firm's expenses for 19X1 were depreciation charges of $7,500.
7. The firm's accounts receivable increased by $4,000, inventories decreased by $2,400 and their accounts payable decreased by $4,500 during the year.

Required:

Prepare a statement of cash flows for the year ended December 31, 19X1, which reflects the reasons for the firm's unsatisfactory cash position.

19. *Statement of Cash Flows—Preparation.* From the following information prepare a statement of cash flows for the Sabre Company for 19X1.

1. For 19X1, sales were $24,000, cost of goods sold was $9,000 and all other expenses totaled $10,000.
2. Dividends paid during 19X1 were $1,000.
3. Capital stock was sold for $2,500.
4. Depreciation for the year was $1,500.
5. Long-term bonds of $1,000 were retired at par.
6. Land was purchased for $3,000.
7. Land was sold for $6,000, resulting in a gain of $1,000.
8. A building was purchased for $4,000.
9. Accounts receivable decreased by $1,200, inventories increased by $1,600 and accounts payable increased by $800.

20. *Cash Flows From Operations.* Determine the amount of purchases, the cash disbursements for rent expense, and the cash applied to dividends for the Maple Leaf Company for the month of March from the information given below.

Cost of goods sold	$2,579
Increase in prepaid rent	864
Dividends	4,953
Rent expense	970
Increase in inventory	1,240
Decrease in dividends payable	691

21. *Statement of Cash Flows—Preparation.* Condensed financial statements for the Billy Company are as follows:

Billy Company
Balance Sheet

	December 31	
	19X2	*19X1*
Cash	$ 7,500	$ 6,000
Accounts receivable	9,000	11,000
Inventories	15,000	12,500
Fixed assets	30,000	25,000
Accumulated depreciation	(12,500)	(10,000)
	$49,000	$44,500
Accounts payable	$18,000	$15,000
Bonds payable	10,000	15,000
Common stock	15,000	10,000
Retained earnings	6,000	4,500
	$49,000	$44,500

Billy Company
Income Statement
for the Year Ending December 31, 19X2

Sales		$35,000
Cost of goods sold		17,000
Gross margin		$18,000
Depreciation	$ 2,500	
Operating expenses	11,000	13,500
Net income		$ 4,500

Required:

Prepare a statement of cash flows for 19X2.

PROBLEMS

22. *Statement of Cash Flows—Preparation.* The condensed financial statements of Buckner Corporation are as follows:

Buckner Corporation
Comparative Balance Sheet
December 31, 19X1 and 19X2

Assets	*19X2*	*19X1*
Current assets:		
Cash	$ 50,000	$ 35,000
Accounts receivable	100,000	90,000
Inventory	60,000	65,000
Prepaid expenses	10,000	8,000
Total current assets	$220,000	$198,000
Fixed assets:		
Building and equipment (net)	$200,000	$220,000
Land	50,000	50,000
Total assets	$470,000	$468,000

Liabilities and Stockholders' Equity

Accounts payable	$100,000	$ 80,000
Interest payable	10,000	10,000
Notes payable (current)	50,000	40,000
Capital stock	200,000	200,000
Retained earnings	110,000	138,000
Total liabilities and stockholders' equity	$470,000	$468,000

Buckner Corporation
Income Statement
for the Year Ending December 31, 19X2

Sales		$250,000
Less: Cost of goods sold		184,000
Gross margin		$ 66,000
Operating expenses	$ 64,000	
Depreciation	20,000	84,000
Net loss		($ 18,000)

Required:

Prepare a statement of cash flows for 19X2.

23. *Statement of Cash Flows—Preparation (Indirect).* Consider the following selected account balances for Messerschmidt. Inc.

	December 31 19X2	December 31 19X1	Increase	Decrease
Accounts receivable	$ 600	$ 400	$200	
Inventories	550	700		$150
Buildings	1,000	800	200	
Accumulated depreciation— Building	175	150	25	
Land	300	200	100	
Accounts payable	100	150		50
Bonds payable—long-term	200	100	100	
Capital stock	200	300		100
Retained earnings	300	150	150	
Sales	1,100	1,200		
Cost of goods sold	400	450		
Expenses	500	575		

Required:

Prepare a statement of cash flows for Messerschmidt, Inc., for the period ending December 31, 19X2, using the *indirect* method and assuming, where it is necessary, that the changes in the accounts are the result of cash transactions.

24. *Statement of Cash Flows—Preparation.* Given below are the balance sheets for Zahn Company for 19X1 and 19X2.

Zahn Company
Comparative Balance Sheet
December 31, 19X1 and 19X2

	19X1	19X2
Cash	$ 100	$ 300
Accounts receivable	400	350
Inventories	300	500
Fixed assets	900	1,000
Less: Accumulated depreciation	(100)	(200)
	$1,600	$1,950
Accounts payable	$ 400	$ 600
Bonds payable (due in 19X7)	400	200
Capital stock	500	700
Retained earnings	300	450
	$1,600	$1,950

Additional information:

The corporation paid a 10 percent stock dividend on January 2, 19X2, when its capital stock was selling at par. For 19X2, sales were $1,200, cost of goods sold was $550 and all other expenses totalled $450. During the year, the company sold a fixed asset with an original cost of $100 (and a book value of $25 at the date of sale) for $50. All other changes in the accounts are the results of transactions typically recorded in such accounts.

Required:

Prepare a statement of cash flows for 19X2.

25. *Statement of Cash Flows—Preparation.* The condensed comparative balance sheet for Marshall Company is presented below.

	December 19X1	
Assets	19X2	19X1
Cash	$ 80,000	$ 65,000
Accounts receivable (net)	100,000	90,000
Inventory	40,000	45,000
Prepaid expenses	12,000	10,000
Fixed assets	173,000	150,000
Accumulated depreciation—		
Fixed assets	(35,000)	(30,000)
Total assets	$370,000	$330,000
Liabilities and stockholders' equity		
Accounts payable	$ 80,000	$ 60,000
Bonds payable	150,000	150,000
Capital stock	100,000	100,000
Retained earnings	40,000	20,000
Total liabilities and		
stockholders' equity	$370,000	$330,000

Supplemental data for 19X2:

Sales	$175,000
Cost of goods sold	70,000
Expenses (other than depreciation)	80,000
Depreciation expense	5,000

A building was purchased for $23,000 cash.

Required:

Prepare a statement of cash flows for 19X2.

26. *Statement of Cash Flows—Preparation.* Following are financial statements for Brewer, Inc.:

Brewer, Inc.
Comparative Balance Sheet
December 31, 19X2 and 19X1

	19X2	19X1	Increase (Decrease)
Assets			
Current Assets:			
Cash	$ 5,000	$ 45,000	$ (40,000)
Accounts receivable	100,000	75,000	25,000
Inventories	50,000	45,000	5,000
Prepaid expenses	30,000	35,000	(5,000)
Total current assets	$185,000	$200,000	$ (15,000)
Noncurrent assets:			
Land	$100,000	$ 75,000	$ 25,000
Buildings	200,000	175,000	25,000
Accumulated depreciation—			
Buildings	(50,000)	(40,000)	(10,000)
Equipment	100,000	75,000	25,000
Accumulated depreciation—			
Equipment	(35,000)	(15,000)	(20,000)
Patents	20,000	30,000	(10,000)
Total noncurrent assets	$335,000	$300,000	$ 35,000
Total assets	$520,000	$500,000	$ 20,000
Liabilities and Stockholders' Equity			
Current liabilities:			
Accounts payable	$ 50,000	$ 40,000	$ 10,000
Notes payable	25,000	25,000	0
Accrued expenses	40,000	35,000	$ 15,000
Total current liabilities	$115,000	$100,000	$ 15,000
Long-term liabilities:			
Bonds payable	$100,000	$140,000	$ (40,000)
Stockholders' equity			
Common stock ($100 par value)	$230,000	$200,000	$ 30,000
Additional paid-in capital	40,000	30,000	10,000
Retained earnings	35,000	30,000	5,000
Total stockholders' equity	$305,000	$260,000	$ 45,000
Total liabilities and			
stockholders' equity	$520,000	$500,000	$ 20,000

Brewer, Inc.
Income Statement
for the Year Ended December 31, 19X2

Sales		$2,000,000
Cost of goods sold		$1,500,000
Gross margin		$ 500,000
Operating expenses:		
Depreciation and amortization expense	$ 50,000	
Selling and administrative expense	265,000	
Miscellaneous expense	170,000	
Total operating expenses		485,000
Net income from operations		$ 15,000
Other revenue and expense		
Add: Gain on sale of building		20,000
		$ 35,000
Less: Loss on sale of land	$ 10,000	
Interest expense	15,000	25,000
Net income before income taxes		$ 10,000
Less: Income taxes		5,000
Net income		$ 5,000

Supplementary data:

1. Depreciation and amortization of patents were as follows:

Building	$20,000
Equipment	20,000
Patents	10,000
Total	$50,000

2. A building which cost $50,000 and had accumulated depreciation of $10,000 was sold for $60,000.
3. Common stock with $30,000 par value was sold for $40,000.
4. Land with a cost of $25,000 was sold for $15,000.
5. Land was purchased for $50,000.
6. Bonds of $40,000 were retired.
7. A building was purchased for $75,000.
8. Equipment was acquired for $25,000 cash.

Required:

Prepare a statement of cash flows for 19X2.

27. *Statement of Cash Flows—Preparation.* The trial balances of Canuck Company revealed the following information.

	December 31	
Debits	*19X1*	*19X2*
Cash	$ 14,000	$ 15,400
Accounts receivable (net)	26,600	33,600
Inventory	72,800	70,000
Prepaid expenses	4,200	5,600
Permanent investments	14,000	0
Buildings	126,000	168,000
Machinery	56,000	86,800
Patents	7,000	5,600
	$320,600	$385,000

Credits

Accounts payable	$ 16,800	$ 11,200
Notes payable—short-term (nontrade)	12,600	18,200
Accrued wages	4,200	2,800
Accumulated depreciation	56,000	54,600
Notes payable—long-term	42,000	49,000
Common stock	168,000	210,000
Retained earnings	21,000	39,200
	$320,600	$385,000

Additional data:

1. For 19X2, sales were $157,200, cost of goods sold was $65,000 and all other expenses totalled $58,600.
2. Recorded depreciation on fixed assets was $11,200.
3. Amortization of patents was $1,400.
4. Machinery was purchased for $21,000; one-third was paid in cash; an interest-bearing note was given for the balance.
5. Common stock was issued to purchase machinery costing $35,000.
6. Old machinery which originally cost $25,200 (one-half depreciated) was sold for $9,800; the gain or loss was reported on the income statement.
7. Cash was paid for the building addition—$42,000.
8. Common stock was issued to pay a $7,000 long-term note.
9. Cash was received for the sale of permanent investment—$16,800.
10. Paid cash dividends.

Required:

Prepare a statement of cash flows for 19X2.

28. _Statement of Cash Flows—Preparation._ The trial balances of Islander Company revealed the following information.

	December 31	
	_19X1_	_19X2_
Cash	$ 3,200	$ 4,000
Accounts receivable (net)	4,000	7,200
Inventory	8,000	9,600
Permanent investments	1,600	0
Fixed assets	24,000	37,600
	$40,800	$58,400
Accumulated depreciation	$ 4,000	$ 5,600
Accounts payable	2,400	4,000
Notes payable—short-term	3,200	2,400
Notes payable—long-term	8,000	14,400
Common stock	20,000	23,200
Retained earnings	3,200	8,800
	$40,800	$58,400

Additional data:

1. For 19X2, sales were $75,000, cost of goods sold was $30,200 and all other expenses totalled $33,600.
2. Depreciation was $1,600.
3. Permanent investments were sold at cost.
4. Dividends of $5,600 were paid.
5. Fixed assets were purchased for $4,000 cash.
6. A long-term note payable for $9,600 was given in exchange for fixed assets.
7. Common stock was issued to pay a $3,200 long-term note payable.

Required:

Prepare a statement of cash flows for the year ended December 31, 19X2.

29. *Statement of Cash Flows—Preparation.* The 19X1 financial statements for the Alston Company are:

Alston Company
Income Statement
for the Year Ended December 31, 19X1

Net sales		$50,000
Cost of goods sold		30,000
Gross margin		$20,000
Operating expenses:		
Depreciation	$2,000	
Wage expense	7,000	
Other expenses	1,000	10,000
Net income from operations		$10,000
Gain on sale of land		5,000
Net income		$15,000

Alston Company
Retained Earnings Statement
for the Year Ended December 31, 19X1

Retained earnings at beginning of year	$25,000
Add: Net income	15,000
	$40,000
Subtract: Dividends	5,000
Retained earnings at end of year	$35,000

Alston Company
Comparative Balance Sheet

	December 31	
	19X1	*19X0*
Assets		
Cash	$ 69,000	$ 60,000
Accounts receivable	25,000	20,000
Inventories	15,000	10,000
Building	100,000	100,000
Accumulated depreciation—		
Building	(27,000)	(25,000)
Land	125,000	100,000
Total assets	$307,000	$265,000
Liabilities and Stockholders' Equity		
Accounts payable	$ 35,000	$ 15,000
Accrued wages payable	7,000	5,000
Bonds payable—long-term	130,000	120,000
Capital stock	100,000	100,000
Retained earnings	35,000	25,000
Total liabilities and stockholders' equity	$307,000	$265,000

The following information is also available:
1. Land with a cost of $25,000 was sold for $30,000.
2. Additional land was purchased for $50,000.
3. A long-term bond was issued for $10,000.
4. $5,000 cash dividends were paid during the year.

Required:

Prepare a statement of cash flows for the Alston Company for the year ending December 31, 19X1.

30. *Statement of Cash Flows—Preparation.* The trial balance of Canadiens Company revealed the following information.

| | December 31 | |
	19X1	*19X0*
Cash	$ 20,400	$ 20,700
Accounts receivable (net)	7,200	10,200
Inventory	9,600	8,400
Permanent investments	3,600	0
Fixed assets	48,000	55,800
Treasury stock	0	6,900
	$ 88,800	$102,000
Accumulated depreciation	$ 28,800	$ 23,400
Accounts payable	11,400	7,200
Bonds payable	6,000	18,000
Common stock	30,000	36,600
Retained earnings	12,600	16,800
	$ 88,800	$102,000

Additional information:

1. Sales were $42,000.
2. Cost of goods sold was $27,600.
3. The total of all expenses was $11,400.
4. Depreciation was $3,000.
5. Fixed assets were sold for $3,600; their original cost was $12,600 and two-thirds of this cost had been depreciated.
6. Fixed assets were purchased for $2,400 cash.
7. Bonds payable were issued for $18,000 to purchase fixed assets.
8. Permanent investments were sold for $5,400 cash.
9. Treasury stock was purchased for $6,900.
10. Bonds payable of $6,000 were retired by issuing common stock.
11. Unissued common stock was sold for $600.

Required:

Prepare a statement of cash flows for the year ended December 31, 19X2.

31. Following are account balances for Bangor Company for 19x8 and 19x7. Answer the following questions:

	19x8	*19x7*
Cash	20,000	25,000
Accounts Receivable	42,000	31,000
Marketable Securities (current)	40,000	35,000
Patent	15,000	13,000
Inventory	80,000	70,000
Prepaid Rent	15,000	16,000
Accounts Payable (inventory)	90,000	85,000
Dividends Payable	12,000	10,000
Salaries Payable	41,000	38,000

Consider each separately:

a. If net income were $21,000 before depreciation, how much cash was generated from operations?

b. If the income statement had included a loss on inventory of $5,000, how much cash was expended for purchases? (Cost of goods sold was $65,000.)

c. If dividends of $15,000 were declared, how much cash was expended for dividends?

d. If net income were $3,000, how much cash was generated from operations?

e. If there were patent amortization of $2,000, how much cash was expended this year for the patent?

32. The following balance sheets apply to Kleocyk Company. Prepare a statement of cash flow.

	19x7	19x6
Assets:		
Cash	$1,200	$ 800
Accounts Receivable	400	440
Inventory	1,220	740
Land	820	500
Equipment	4,600	4,140
Accumulated Depreciation	(800)	(620)
Total Assets	$7,440	$6,000
Equities:		
Accounts Payable	$1,000	$1,600
Long-Term Borrowings	1,440	1,800
Common Stock, No Par	2,000	1.200
Retained Earnings	3,000	1,400
Total Equities	$7,440	$6,000

Additional data:

a. Net income for 19x7 was $2,200.

b. During 19x7 the company sold for $740 equipment that cost $740 and had a book value of $600.

c. The company sold land for $400, resulting in a loss of $80. The remaining land change was due to the acquisition of land for common stock.

33. Following are the comparative balance sheets for Marvin Corporation. Additional information is also provided. Prepare a statement of cash flow.

	19x4	19x3
Assets		
Cash	$ 89,800	$ 82,400
Receivables	110,000	101,000
Marketable Securities	11,200	9,900
Inventory	154,500	175,500
Fixed Assets	800,000	620,000
Accumulated Depreciation—		
Fixed Assets	(228,000)	(250,000)
Total Assets	$937,500	$738,800
Equities:		
Accounts Payable	$110,500	$ 58,900
Long-Term Note Payable	0	120,000
Preferred Stock	70,000	20,000
Common Stock	500,000	400,000
Retained Earnings	257,000	140,000
Total Equities	$937,500	$738,800

Additional Data:

a. Net income, $157,000.
b. Depreciation expense, $48,000.
c. Additional equipment was purchased for $250,000 and fully depreciated equipment of $70,000 was scrapped.
d. The long-term note was paid early.

34. Below are comparative financial statements for WAC Company for the years 19X4 and 19X3.

WAC Company
Balance Sheet and Income Statements
For the Years Ending December 31, 19X4 and 19X3

	December 31 19X4	December 31 19X3
Cash	$ 6,000	$ 5,000
Accounts Receivable	14,000	18,000
Inventory	23,000	20,000
Prepaid Expense	2,000	1,000
Land	3,000	2,000
Fixed Assets	73,000	66,000
Less: Accumulated Depreciation	(28,000)	(26,000)
Total Assets	$93,000	$86,000
Accounts Payable	$13,000	$7,000
Wages Payable	3,000	4,000
Income Tax Payable	5,000	4,500
Long-Term Bonds Payable	20,000	23,000
Common Stock ($10 Par)	29,500	27,500
Additional Paid in Capital	500	0
Retained Earnings	22,000	20,000
Total Liabilities and		
Stockholders Equity	$93,000	$86,000
Sales (all credit sales)	$95,000	$89,000
Less: Cost of Goods Sold	43,000	43,000
Gross Margin	$52,000	$46,000
Less: Operating Expenses—		
Depreciation	$ 9,000	$8,000
Wages	23,000	21,000
Interest	2,000	2,000
Loss on Sale of Fixed Asset	1,000	0
	35,000	31,000
Net Income Before Taxes	$17,000	$15,000
Less: Income Taxes	7,000	6,000
Net Income	$10,000	$ 9,000

Additional Information: Sold a fixed asset with an original cost of $9,000 and accumulated depreciation of $7,000 and purchased a new fixed asset during 19X4.

Required:

Prepare a cash flow statement for the year ended December 31, 19X4.

Refer to the Annual Report in Chapter 1 of the text.

35. What was the cash flow from operating activities in the most recent year?

36. What was the cash flow from investing activities in the most recent year?

37. What was the cash flow from financing activities in the most recent year?

38. In absolute numbers, what was the largest investing activity in the most recent year?

39. In absolute numbers, what was the largest financing activity in the most recent year?

Outline

LEARNING OBJECTIVES

Chapter 16 presents a general discussion of the federal income tax. Studying this chapter should enable you to:

1. Identify the primary objectives of the federal income tax.

2. Discuss the process of determining an individual and corporate taxpayer's tax liability.

3. Recognize the important differences in the taxation of corporations versus the taxation of individuals.

4. Describe the purpose of interperiod tax allocation and the accounting procedures involved.

5. Illustrate how intraperiod tax allocation is generally accomplished.

CHAPTER 16

INCOME TAX CONSIDERATIONS[*]

INTRODUCTION

Income taxes are periodic charges levied by federal, state, and city governments on the taxable income of both individuals and business corporations. Taxable income is a statutory concept (i.e., it is defined by law) and is equal to gross income minus all allowable deductions. For businesses organized as corporations, income taxes are accounted for as an expense that is deducted in computing the net income for the period. The amount of taxes owed, but not paid, is a liability that is included in the balance sheet. Because income taxes normally represent a significant cost to a business enterprise, an awareness of the tax laws and how they are applied is essential to a complete understanding of accounting information.

Data required for the determination of income taxes are usually found in the accounting records. Taxable income, however, may not be the same as the income reported in the income statement even though both are determined from the identical set of accounting records. This difference often occurs because income tax law is not always the same as the basic concepts used for financial accounting purposes.

This chapter is devoted to a general discussion of the federal income tax and its implication for the financial reporting process of a business. Although many states and cities also impose income taxes, which may differ in application from the federal income tax, the income tax liability to all governmental units is treated similarly in the accounting records. For this reason, the following discussion is limited to the federal income tax.

THE FEDERAL INCOME TAX

The modern era of federal income taxation originated in 1913 with the adoption of the Sixteenth Amendment to the Constitution. This amendment gives Congress the power to "... lay and collect taxes on incomes, from whatever source derived, without apportionment among the several states, and without regard to any census or enumeration." Soon after the Sixteenth Amendment was adopted, Congress enacted the Revenue Act of 1913, which provided for a general yearly income tax. Since that time, Congress has passed numerous income tax statutes amending the various revenue acts so that there has been a continuous development of income tax law in the United States. In 1939, the Internal Revenue Code was enacted. This code was thoroughly revised in 1954 and extensively amended and supplemented by the Tax Reform Act of 1969, the Revenue Act of 1971, the Tax Reduction Act of 1975, the Tax Reform Act of 1976, the Tax Reduction and Simplification Act of 1977, the Revenue Act of 1978, the Economic Recovery Act of 1981, the Tax Equity and Fiscal Responsibility Act of 1982, the Deficit Reduction Act of 1984, the Tax Reform Act of 1986, the Revenue Act of 1987, the Technical and Miscellaneous Revenue Act of 1988, the Omnibus Budget Reconciliation Act of 1989, the Omnibus Budget Reconciliation Act of 1990, the Tax Extension Act of 1991, the Omnibus Budget Reconciliation Act of 1993, and the Tax Relief Act of 1997. Tax law is also supplemented by interpretations of the Internal Revenue Code by both the courts and the Treasury Department. The Treasury Department, operating through a branch known as the Internal Revenue Service, is charged with the enforcement and collection of income taxes.

---

[*] The authors would like to thank Professors Thomas L. Dickens of Clemson University, Steven D. Grossman of Texas A & M University, Bob G. Kilpatrick of Northern Arizona University, Dennis R. Lassila of Texas A&M University, Kenneth R. Orbach of Florida Atlantic University, and Sarah A. Holmes of Texas A&M University who have written and revised this chapter in its various editions.

The original purpose of the income tax was stated as simply to obtain revenues for the use of the federal government. The income tax on individuals under the 1913 Act consisted of a flat 1 percent tax on taxable income in excess of $4,000 for married persons plus a progressive surtax of 1 to 7 percent on income in excess of $20,000. A progressive tax is one in which tax rates increase as taxable income increases.

Since 1916, both the objectives of the income tax and income tax rates have undergone a significant change. The purpose of the federal income tax today includes such diverse objectives as controlling inflation, influencing economic growth, decreasing unemployment, redistributing national income, and encouraging the growth of small businesses. All of these purposes are in addition to the original objective of raising revenue to finance the operations of the government. Similarly, there have been substantial changes in tax rates. The current rates for taxpayers are presented in Illustration 1.

Illustration 1
Current Rates for Taxpayers

Selected Taxable Income Brackets

Tax Rate	Married/ Joint	Head of Household	Single	Married/ Separate
15 %	0—$ 41,200	0—$ 33,050	0—$ 24,650	0—$ 20,600
28	$ 41,200—$ 99,600	$ 33,050—$ 85,350	$ 24,650—$ 59,750	$ 20,600—$ 49,800
31	$ 99,600—$151,750	$ 85,350—$138,200	$ 59,750—$124,650	$ 49,800—$ 75,875
36	$151,750—$271,050	$138,200—$271,050	$124,650—$271,050	$75,875—$135,525
39.6	above $271,050	above $271,050	above $271,050	above $135,525

Standard Deduction

Filing Status

Married/joint	$6,900
Head of household	6,050
Single	4,150
Married/separate	3,450

The federal government's income is provided by personal income taxes (42 percent in 1996), social security and other retirement taxes (33 percent in 1996), borrowing (7 percent in 1996), corporate income taxes (11 percent in 1996), and other taxes (7 percent in 1996). Federal outlays are for social security and other retirement benefits (37 percent in 1996), national defense and foreign affairs (20 percent in 1996), social programs (18 percent in 1996), net interest payments on the national debt (15 percent in 1996), expenditures for people and community development (8 percent in 1996), and law enforcement and general government (2 percent in 1996).

Classes of Taxpayers

Income taxes are levied upon four major types of taxable entities: individuals, corporations, estates, and trusts. Business entities organized as sole proprietorships or partnerships are not taxable entities. Instead, their income is included in the gross income of the individual owner or owners, whether or not it is actually withdrawn from the business and distributed to these owners. A partnership, however, is required to prepare an information return that indicates the items of its gross income, deductions, and credits and how these are allocated to the partners. The partners then report these amounts in their own tax returns.

A corporation is treated as a separate entity for tax purposes and must pay taxes on its taxable income. In addition, individual corporate stockholders must include any dividends received from the corporation as a part of their taxable income. For this reason, it is often argued that the profits of a corporation are taxed twice—once to the corporation when the income is reported and again to its stockholders when dividends are distributed. Under limited circumstances, a corporation meeting certain qualifications may avoid this "double taxation" of corporate income by making an S Corporation election: the shareholders are then taxed on undistributed income on a current basis.[1]

An estate is a separate legal entity created to take charge of the assets of a deceased person to pay the decedent's debts and distribute any remaining assets to the heirs. A trust is a legal entity created when a person by gift or devise transfers assets to a trustee for the benefit of designated persons. The tax rules that apply to estates and trusts will not be discussed in this chapter, as they are beyond the scope of this text.

Individual Federal Income Tax

The cash basis of measuring taxable income is used by almost all individuals in preparing their tax returns. Generally, revenue is recognized upon the actual or constructive receipt of cash and expenses are recognized as cash is expended.

Individual income tax rates depend on the status of the taxpayer. There are different tax rate schedules for married taxpayers who file a joint return, married individuals who file separate returns, unmarried taxpayers, and single taxpayers qualifying as "head of household." Generally, "head of household" status applies to certain unmarried or legally separated persons who maintain the principal residence for a relative.

The amount of federal income tax that an individual must pay is generally determined by knowledge of gross income, deductions for adjusted gross income, adjusted gross income, itemized deductions (deductions from adjusted gross income), personal exemptions, tax table income or taxable income, and credits. The relationship of these concepts and the procedures for determining taxable income are summarized in Illustration 2. A more detailed explanation of the items outlined in the determination of taxable income is given in the following paragraphs.

Gross Income. Basically, gross income is defined as all income from whatever source derived, unless expressly excluded by law or by the U.S. Constitution. This includes income from sources such as wages, dividends, interest, partnership income, rents, and numerous other items. Among the more important classes of income currently excludable from gross income by law are gifts, life insurance proceeds received at the insured's death, social security benefits (up to certain amounts), inheritances (but not income from trusts and life estates), worker's compensation, and interest on certain state and municipal bonds.

Deductions for Adjusted Gross Income. The deductions for adjusted gross income are business expenses and other expenses connected with earning certain types of revenue. These include ordinary and necessary expenses incurred by the taxpayer in the operation of an unincorporated business or profession, certain business expenses of an employee, losses from the sale or exchange of certain property, net operating losses from other periods carried back or forward, expenses incurred in connection with earning rent or royalty income, payments to an individual retirement arrangement or to a Keogh retirement plan, and periodic payments of alimony made under a court decree.

Deductions From Adjusted Gross Income (Itemized Deductions). Itemized deductions include such items as a limited amount of charitable contributions, mortgage interest payments, certain taxes paid by the taxpayer, a limited amount of medical expenses, a limited amount of casualty and theft losses, and job expenses and miscellaneous deductions. These job expenses include unreimbursed employee expenses such as job travel and union dues. Miscellaneous deductions include such items as certain legal fees relating to investments, dues to professional organizations, and expenses incurred for the preparation of tax returns.

---

[1] These entities are referred to as "S Corporations." Numerous changes in the tax treatment of S Corporations were made in the "Subchapter S Revision Act of 1982." Subchapter S Corporations are now called S Corporations.

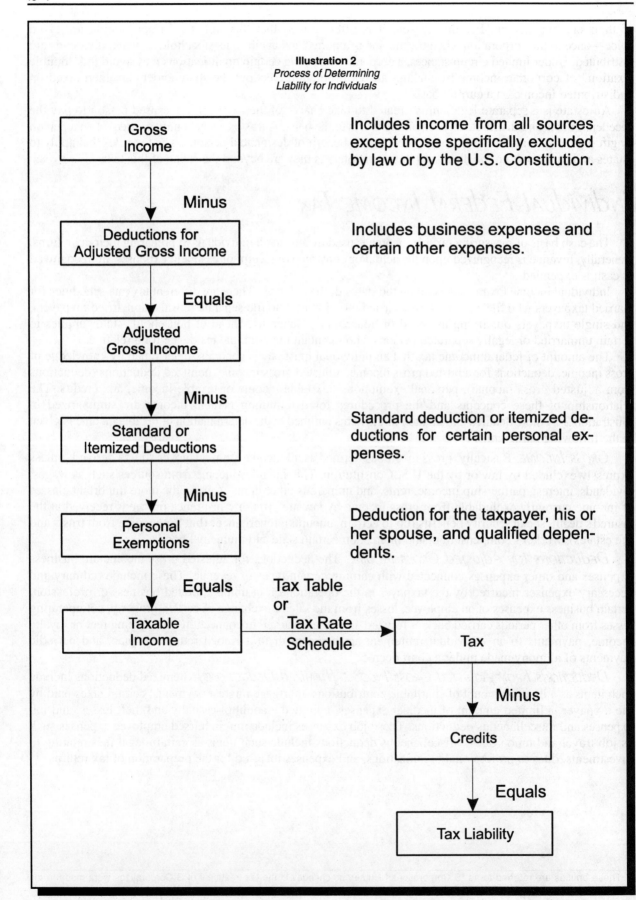

Illustration 2
*Process of Determining
Liability for Individuals*

Gross
Income

Includes income from all sources except those specifically excluded by law or by the U.S. Constitution.

Minus

Deductions for
Adjusted Gross Income

Includes business expenses and certain other expenses.

Equals

Adjusted
Gross Income

Minus

Standard or
Itemized Deductions

Standard deduction or itemized deductions for certain personal expenses.

Minus

Personal
Exemptions

Deduction for the taxpayer, his or her spouse, and qualified dependents.

Equals

Tax Table
or
Tax Rate
Schedule

Taxable
Income

Tax

Minus

Credits

Equals

Tax Liability

A taxpayer can either deduct the sum of itemized deductions or take the standard deduction, whichever is greater. The standard deduction permitted for each filing status is presented in Illustration 1.

Taxable income may now be computed. Generally, taxable income equals adjusted gross income reduced by either the standard deduction or itemized deductions and by personal exemptions.

PERSONAL EXEMPTION. A taxpayer is allowed a deduction for each personal exemption to which he or she is entitled. The amount of the deduction was $2,700 for 1998. Each year, the amount is indexed for inflation. Personal exemptions may be taken for the following individuals:

1. The taxpayer.

2. The taxpayer's spouse if a joint return is filed.

3. The taxpayer's spouse if a joint return is not filed, but only if the spouse has no gross income and is not a dependent of another taxpayer.

4. Certain dependents. A dependent is an individual who meets all five of the following requirements:

    a. *Support.* The taxpayer provides more than one-half of the individual's support.

    b. *Income.* Dependent's gross income is less than the amount of the personal exemption (unless the dependent is the taxpayer's child and is either less than nineteen years old or is a full-time student).

    c. *Relationship.* The person must be related to the taxpayer or lived in the taxpayer's home as a family member for the entire year.

    d. *Joint Return.* The dependent cannot file a joint return with his or her spouse.

    e. *Citizenship.* The person must be either a U.S. citizen or resident alien or a resident of the U.S., Canada, or Mexico or an adopted child who is not a U.S. citizen but lived with the taxpayer all year in a foreign country.

CREDITS. A credit is an amount by which the tax liability is reduced. The most commonly used credits include the earned income credit for certain workers, credit for the elderly or the disabled, credit for child and dependent care expenses, and the foreign tax credit.

WITHHOLDING AND ESTIMATED TAX. Taxpayers are generally required to make payments on their estimated tax liability during the year. This is accomplished by two principal procedures:

1. Employers withhold income tax on compensation to their employees.

2. Individuals who have income not subject to withholding (such as self-employed individuals) or who have income from which not enough is withheld file a declaration of estimated tax. This estimated tax is generally paid in four equal installments.

In either instance, any difference between the amounts paid and the actual tax liability at the end of the year is settled when the tax return is filed.

CAPITAL GAIN AND LOSSES. Prior to the Tax Reform Act of 1986, 60 percent of long-term capital gains was excluded from taxation. Gains from the sale of certain property defined by the tax law as capital assets are still given special treatment for income tax purposes. Capital assets most commonly held by taxpayers include stocks, bonds, personal residences, and land. To qualify for special tax treatment, capital gains have to be long-term. Long-term capital gains or losses result from the sale of capital assets held by the taxpayer for more than eighteen months and short-term gains or losses result from the sale of those held eighteen months or less. Short-term capital gains do not qualify for special tax treatment and are taxed as ordinary income. Net capital gains are taxed at 10 percent for taxpayers in the 15 percent tax bracket and 20 percent thereafter. Capital losses are allowed to the extent of capital gains plus $3,000. Losses may offset gains and other income (up to $3,000) dollar for dollar. Losses that cannot be used in a particular year may be carried over to succeeding years.

COMPUTATION OF INDIVIDUAL INCOME TAX—AN ILLUSTRATION. The example included in Illustration 3 details the computation of the income tax for an individual filing a joint return. This individual, who owns a pharmacy organized as a sole proprietorship, is married and has two minor children. In practice, the information is reported on standard tax forms provided by the federal government.

CORPORATE INCOME TAX

A corporation is a taxable entity that is separate and distinct from its stockholders. In general, the taxable income of a corporation is computed by deducting its ordinary business expenses and special deductions from its gross income. Although a corporation is taxed in generally the same manner as individuals, there are several important differences:

1. The concepts of itemized deductions and personal exemptions are not applicable to corporations.
2. Corporations may ordinarily deduct a percentage of all dividends received on investments in stock of other taxable domestic corporations.
3. The deduction for charitable contributions is limited to 10 percent of taxable income (before charitable contributions, before the 70% or 80% dividend deduction and before certain other deductions) in any one year.

Illustration 3
Income Tax Computation for
Married Taxpayer Filing Jointly in 1998

Adjusted Gross Income and Deductions from Adjusted Gross Income

Sales		$120,000
Less:		
Cost of goods sold	$50,000	
Business expenses	30,000	80,000
Net business income		$ 40,000
Interest on savings accounts		1,000
Rents received	$ 5,000	
Less: Expenses	2,000	
Net rental income		3,000
Net capital gain		4,000
Adjusted gross income		$ 48,000
Itemized deductions:		
Charitable contributions	$ 1,800	
Interest on home mortgage	2,900	
Property taxes	2,300	7,000
Less: Exemptions (4 × $2,700)		10,800
Taxable income		$ 30,200
Tax on ordinary income (at 15%)		3,930
Tax on capital gain (at 10%)		400
Total tax		$ 4,340
Less: Payments on estimated taxes		4,690
Amount of refund		$ 350

The corporate tax rate differs from the rate applied to individual taxpayers. A corporation pays a tax of 15 percent of the first $50,000 of taxable income, 25 percent of the next $25,000, 34 percent of the next $25,000, 39 percent of the next $235,000, 34 percent of taxable income on the next $9,665,000, 35 percent on the next $5,000,000, 38 percent on the next $3,333,333, and 35 percent on taxable income in excess of $18,333,333.

Differences Between Accounting Income and Taxable Income

Temporary and Permanent Differences

The taxable income of a corporation often differs from the net income reported in its financial statements for a particular period. Taxable income is determined by the statutory provisions of the Internal Revenue Code while accounting income is based on generally accepted accounting principles. The rules and regulations comprising the income tax laws reflect the objectives of income taxation as well as administrative rulings that have been made to implement the law. These provisions are intended to obtain revenue in an equitable manner, to operate the government and to stimulate and/or regulate the economy. Financial accounting, on the other hand, is concerned with the proper determination and matching of revenues and expenses in order to measure income and provide useful information to decision-makers.

Some differences between taxable income and accounting income occur because of special tax rules that differ from generally accepted accounting principles. Certain revenue items that are reported for financial accounting purposes are never reported on the income tax return. These are excluded by law from taxable income. For example, interest on municipal bonds is included in accounting income but not in taxable income. Similarly, certain expenses may not be treated as deductions for tax purposes. For example, premium payments on life insurance policies on key employees are an expense for accounting purposes but are not deductible under current tax regulations. Also, while percentage depletion may be taken for tax purposes, depletion based on cost is used for reporting purposes. These items represent permanent differences between taxable and accounting income and are referred to as such. Permanent differences do not give rise to deferred income taxes.

Other differences between taxable income and accounting income are not permanent. These result from temporary differences in the timing of the recognition of revenues and expenses. Temporary differences affect the determination of accounting income in one period and taxable income in another period. They may occur because, in some instances, one method or procedure may be used for tax purposes and a different method or procedure for financial accounting purposes. The underlying reason why different methods are used is because of the differences in the objectives of accounting and taxation from the viewpoint of the reporting entity. The objective of financial accounting is a fair and accurate measurement of income and financial position, while the objective of a business in selecting among allowable tax methods is usually to minimize taxable income and to postpone the payment of taxes. Although over a long enough period of time the temporary differences should "wash out" so that total taxable income and total accounting income are the same (ignoring permanent differences), the difference during any one year may be significant. Two major classes of temporary differences are as follows:

1. Current accounting income may be greater than current taxable income; therefore, the taxable income of future periods will exceed future accounting income.

   a. Revenues and gains may be included in accounting income before they are included in taxable income. For example, a firm's treatment of installment sales may recognize the entire profit at the time of sale for accounting purposes and use the installment method that recognizes profit as cash is received for tax purposes. Thus, businesses that sell merchandise on the installment basis may recognize revenue for financial accounting purposes at the time of sale but report the income for tax purposes as cash is actually received.

   b. Expenses and losses may be recognized for tax purposes before they are recognized for accounting purposes (i.e., deducted from taxable income before they are deducted from accounting income). For example, different depreciation methods may be used for tax and accounting purposes. Tax depreciation is generally calculated using the Modified Accelerated Cost Recovery System (MACRS).[2] A firm could use MACRS for tax purposes and straight-line depreciation for purposes of financial accounting. The accelerated method results in larger depreciation expense than the

[2] See Chapter 8 for a discussion of MACRS.

straight-line method in the earlier years of the life of an asset, and smaller depreciation charges in the later years. Thus, the use of the different methods may result in lower taxable income than accounting income during the early years but have the opposite effect in later years.

2. Current taxable income may be greater than current accounting income; therefore, future accounting income will exceed future taxable income.

    a. Revenues and gains may be included in taxable income before they are included in accounting income. For example, items that are considered to be unearned revenue for accounting purposes (such as cash received in advance) are taxable income to a taxpayer when the cash is received and reported as revenue for financial accounting purposes when the service is provided.

    b. Expenses and losses may be deducted from accounting income before they are deducted from taxable income. For example, a company may estimate its bad debt losses in order to match expenses with the related sales revenue for accounting purposes but use the direct write-off method for tax purposes.

INTERPERIOD TAX ALLOCATION

When one accounting method is used for tax purposes and a different method for financial accounting, revenues or expenses may be reported on the income statement and the tax return in different periods. As a result of these temporary differences, a part of the income tax liability during one year is caused by revenues and expenses reported during some other year for financial accounting purposes. Consequently, if income tax expense reported in the income statement is based on income taxes actually paid, there is a mismatching of revenues and expenses because earnings may be included in the income statement of one period and the related tax expense reported in a different period. Also, there may be a failure to report the total tax that will actually be due on the temporary differences when they reverse.

To avoid the problems discussed above, income taxes (for accounting purposes) are subject to the same accrual, deferral, and estimation concepts that are applied to all other expenses. This is accomplished using comprehensive income tax allocation procedures to calculate income tax expense for financial statement purposes. Tax allocation provides a more accurate measure of long-term earning power and avoids distortions caused by tax regulations.

Under comprehensive income tax allocation, income tax expense is affected by all transactions and events regardless of how significant and/or recurrent they may be. The tax effect of each individual temporary difference is recognized and allocated/deferred. These procedures recognize that events that create temporary differences affect cash flows in both the period of origination and the period of reversal. Since individual items do reverse, the focus is on individual items rather than on groups of items.

The liability method is used to determine the amount to be recorded. The liability method records deferred income taxes using the enacted rate that will be in effect when the reversal occurs and additional taxes will be paid (or saved). It is a balance-sheet-oriented method that reports the total taxes that will be assessed on temporary differences when they reverse. Taxes that were postponed will be paid in the future at future tax rates.

Generally accepted accounting principles require a comprehensive allocation approach using the liability method. Using this method, the deferred tax liability or asset should reflect the amount of income taxes payable or refundable in future years as a result of the deferred tax consequences of events recognized on the statements of current or past years. The entry to record deferred taxes (assuming a liability) is in the following general format:

Income tax expense	XX	
Deferred income taxes[3]		XX
Income taxes payable		XX

Interperiod tax allocation is discussed more fully in the appendix to this chapter.

---

[3] Year-end deferred tax amounts are computed as follows: (1) identity all temporary differences, (2) estimate the particular future years in which these temporary differences will result in taxable or deductible amounts, (3) calculate the amount of tax remaining by applying the enacted tax rates to the taxable or deductible amounts for each year, (4) add the amounts of tax for each future year to determine the amount of deferred tax liability or asset at the end of the current year, and (5) reduce this amount by any previously recognized deferred liability or asset.

Allocation of Income Tax Within a Period

According to Accounting Principles Board *Opinions No. 9* and *30*, the income statement should disclose separate income figures for: (1) income from continuing operations; (2) income or loss from any segment or division that has been or is to be discontinued or sold, referred to as discontinued operations; and (3) income from unusual, nonrecurring items, referred to as extraordinary items. Income from continuing operations, income or losses from discontinued operations, and extraordinary gains or losses may be included in taxable income and, hence, affect the tax liability for the period. For this reason, it is believed that allocation of the total amount of income taxes for the period among income from continuing operations, income or loss from discontinued operations, and extraordinary gains or losses provides a more meaningful income statement.

This allocation, referred to as intraperiod tax allocation, is accomplished by deducting from income from continuing operations the taxes related to that amount, and then showing income from discontinued operations and extraordinary gains net of applicable taxes and losses from discontinued operations and extraordinary losses, net of applicable tax reductions. Also, the cumulative effect of a change in accounting principle is shown net of tax.

To illustrate, assume that Cobb Company, which uses the same methods for tax purposes and for financial accounting purposes (so that there are no temporary differences), determines its income before taxes for 19X2 as follows:

Revenues	$100,000
Operating expenses	60,000
Operating income before taxes	$ 40,000
Income from discontinued operations	20,000
Extraordinary gain	30,000
Income	$ 90,000

Further, assume that the tax rate is 40 percent. The total tax liability is $36,000 ($90,000 × 40%). Of this amount, $16,000 ($40,000 × 40%) is applicable to normal operating income; $8,000 ($20,000 × 40%) is due to discontinued operations; and $12,000 ($30,000 × 40%) is applicable to the extraordinary gain. The following income statement is prepared using intraperiod tax allocation.

Cobb Company
Income Statement
for the Year Ended December 31, 19X2

Revenues	$100,000
Operating expenses	60,000
Income from continuing operations before taxes	$ 40,000
Income tax expense	16,000
Income from continuing operations	$ 24,000
Discontinued operations:	
Income from discontinued operations	
(less related taxes of $8,000)	12,000
	$ 36,000
Extraordinary items:	
Extraordinary gain (less related taxes of $12,000)	18,000
Net income	$ 54,000

INCOME TAXES AND MANAGEMENT DECISIONS

Because money has a "time value," it is rational for corporate management to defer as long as possible the incurrence and payment of corporate income taxes. Thus, a major consideration in tax planning is the timing of income and deductions. Management normally attempts to minimize the current tax liability by deferring income or accelerating deductions to the extent possible under the tax laws. Successful tax planning is dependent upon a timely selection of the most advantageous tax alternatives.

While a detailed review of management decision-making regarding corporate income taxes is beyond the scope of this text, the following are major areas of importance in tax planning:

1. Selecting the form of business organization.
2. Acquisition, use, and disposition of fixed assets.
3. Employee compensation.
4. Corporate reorganizations.
5. Financing arrangements.

SUMMARY

Income taxes represent a significant expense of doing business for both corporate and noncorporate business enterprises. The four major classes of taxpayers are individuals, corporations, estates, and trusts. Sole proprietorships and partnerships are not taxable entities; the income from these enterprises is taxed as income to their owners.

The individual federal income tax is computed by appropriately utilizing the tax tables or the tax rate schedules. Before calculating one's tax liability, an individual needs to compile or compute the amount of gross income, deductions for adjusted gross income, adjusted gross income, itemized deductions, personal exemptions, taxable income, and credits.

Although the general procedure for determining a corporation's income tax is similar to that used by an individual, the treatment of specific items may differ significantly. In addition, the tax rate structure for corporations differs from that for individuals.

Since taxable income is determined by tax law while accounting income is based on generally accepted accounting principles, the tax liabilities based on the two amounts may differ. Tax expense in the income statement should be matched against the income reported therein, regardless of when the income is included in taxable income and the tax actually paid. The process of matching tax expense to the appropriate accounting periods is referred to as interperiod tax allocation. This process is used only when the difference in tax liabilities is due to timing. If a difference is permanent, no allocation is appropriate or necessary.

An additional allocation of income tax within a period is made on the income statement to income from continuing operations, income or loss from discontinued operations, gains or losses from extraordinary items, and cumulative effect of a change in accounting principle. This is referred to as intraperiod tax allocation.

KEY DEFINITIONS

Accounting income—the amount of income determined using generally accepted accounting principles.
Adjusted gross income (for individuals)—gross income less deductions for adjusted gross income.
Capital gain or loss—a realized gain or loss incurred from the sale or exchange of a capital asset.
Deductions for adjusted gross income (for individuals)—deductions for gross income in computing adjusted gross income include business and other expenses connected with earning certain types of revenue. These include ordinary

and necessary expenses incurred by the taxpayer in the operation of his or her business or profession and certain employee expenses.

Deductions from adjusted gross income (for individuals)—legally allowable deductions that may be classified as either itemized deductions or personal exemptions.

Double taxation—the corporation is taxed on its reported income and stockholders are taxed upon the receipt of dividends from the corporation.

Estate—a separate legal entity created to take charge of the assets of a deceased person, paying the decedent's debts, and distributing the remaining assets to heirs.

Gross income—includes all income from whatever source derived unless expressly excluded by law or by the U.S. Constitution.

Head of household—the title of head of household is a tax status that applies to certain unmarried or legally separated persons who maintain a residence for a relative.

Itemized deductions—deductions for certain employee business expenses and for personal expenses and losses such as charitable contributions, taxes, interest, casualty losses, and medical expenses.

Interperiod tax allocation—a procedure used to apportion tax expense among periods so that the income tax expense reported for each period is in relation to the tax liability created by accounting income in the current year and all future years.

Intraperiod tax allocation—the allocation of the total amount of income tax expense for a period among income from normal operations, discontinued operations, extraordinary items, cumulative effects of changes in accounting principle, and prior-period adjustments.

Long-term capital gains or losses—gains or losses that result from the sale or exchange of capital assets and certain productive assets of a business held by the taxpayer for more than eighteen months.

Permanent difference—when a difference between taxable income and accounting income occurs because of tax rules that differ from generally accepted accounting principles and will not be offset by corresponding differences in future periods.

Personal exemptions—a deduction from adjusted gross income for the taxpayer, his or her spouse, and qualified dependents.

Progressive tax—this is a tax in which the tax rates increase as taxable income increases.

Tax credit—an amount by which the tax liability is reduced.

Taxable income—generally obtained by reducing adjusted gross income by the sum of: (1) the taxpayer's itemized deductions or standard deduction, and (2) the deduction for personal exemptions.

Temporary differences—these differences between taxable income and accounting income occur because an item is included in taxable income in one period and in accounting income in a different period.

Trust—a legal entity created when a person transfers assets to a trustee for the benefit of designated persons.

QUESTIONS

1. Explain how the net earnings of the following types of business entities are taxed by the federal government: (a) sole proprietorships, (b) partnerships, and © corporations.

2. The earnings of a corporation are subject to a "double tax." Explain.

3. Certain factors may cause the income before taxes in the accounting records to differ from taxable income. These factors may be either permanent differences or temporary differences. Explain.

4. Does a corporation electing partnership treatment for tax purposes (S Corporation) pay federal income taxes? Discuss.

5. What are the four major classes of taxable entities?

6. What is the objective of using the interperiod tax allocation procedures?

7. Does it make any difference in computing income taxes whether a given deduction is for computing adjusted gross income or an itemized deduction? Explain.

8. How are capital gains treated differently than ordinary income for tax purposes?

9. What are some of the differences between the tax rules for corporations and those for individuals?

10. What are some of the objectives of the federal income tax?

EXERCISES

11. Indicate the income tax status for each of the items listed below. For each item, state whether it is (a) included in gross income, (b) a deduction from gross income to determine adjusted gross income, © an itemized deduction, or (d) none of the above.

   a. Property taxes paid on personal residence.
   b. Interest paid on mortgage on personal residence.
   c. Damages of $500 to personal residence from a storm.
   d. Capital loss on the sale of stock.
   e. Insurance on home.
   f. Sales taxes.
   g. Inheritance received upon death of a relative.
   h. Interest received on municipal bonds.
   i. Share of income from partnership.
   j. Salary received as an employee.
   k. Rental income.
   l. Expenses incurred in earning rental income.
   m. Contributions to church.

12. The following differences enter into the reconciliation of financial net income and taxable income of A. P. Baxter Corp. for the current year:

   a. Tax depreciation exceeds book depreciation by $30,000.
   b. Estimated warranty costs of $6,000 applicable to the current year's sales have not been paid. (Not deductible for tax purposes until paid.)
   c. Percentage depletion deducted on the tax return exceeds cost depletion by $45,000.
   d. Unearned rent revenue of $25,000 was deferred on the books but appropriately included in taxable income.
   e. A book expense of $2,000 for life insurance premiums on officers' lives is not allowed as a deduction on the tax return. (Note: This is not a temporary difference.)
   f. Gross profit of $80,000 was excluded from the taxable income because Baxter had appropriately elected the installment sale method for tax reporting while recognizing all gross profit from installment sales at the time of the sale for financial reporting.

Required:

Consider each reconciling item independently of all others and explain whether each item would enter into the calculation of income taxes to be allocated. For any which are included in the income tax allocation calculation, explain the effect of the item on the current year's income tax expense and how the amount would be reported on the balance sheet. (Tax allocation calculations are not required.)

13. The partial tax return is shown below for Bengal, Inc. for the year.

Operating income before taxes	$ 80,000
Income from discontinued operations	45,000
Extraordinary gain (capital gain)	25,000
Taxable income	$150,000

Assume that the tax rate is 40 percent. Bengal, Inc. uses the same methods for tax and financial accounting purposes.

Required:

Reflect the application of intraperiod income tax allocation procedures as they would be reported on the financial statements.

Problems

14. For the year 19x8, Sigma Enterprises had revenue of $1,250,000 and expenses of $800,000 for an accounting income of $450,000 computed under the accrual basis of accounting. For each item listed below explain if any difference exists between accounting income and taxable income; and for any differences which are identified indicate whether they are timing or permanent differences. State the dollar difference of any permanent difference.

   a. $15,000 of the revenue recorded was due to interest on county bonds.
   b. $8,000 of the revenue recorded was due to dividends received from other corporations.
   c. For tax purposes using the cash basis of accounting, advertising of $2,000 was not paid in 19x5.
   d. An asset purchased on January 1, 19x5 with a useful life of ten years is depreciated on a straight-line basis for book purposes and the double-declining balance method for tax purposes.
   e. $150,000 of the revenue recorded was due to insurance proceeds which the company received when one of the vice-presidents died.

15. Columbia Corporation bought a capital asset for $720,000 on January 1, 19x2. The asset is expected to be useful for five years and has no salvage value. For book purposes, Columbia utilizes the straight-line method of depreciation while the double-declining balance method is used for tax purposes. The asset is classified as five year property for tax purposes. This is the only item causing a difference between accounting and taxable income. Assume the income before depreciation or taxes for years 19x2 through 19x5 is $680,000 each year and Columbia's tax rate is 34 percent.

Required:

   a. Determine the tax expense for each of the years 19x2 through 19x5.
   b. Determine the tax liability for each of the years 19x2 through 19x5.
   c. Prepare the journal entries to record the tax expense and the tax liability for each of the years 19x2 through 19x5.

16. For each of the transactions listed, indicate the effect(s), if any, on the company's year-end: (1) Balance Sheet, (2) Income Statement, and (3) Statement of Cash Flows. Your answers should be as complete and specific as possible.

   a. Recorded corporate income taxes. Income taxes based on accounting income exceeds income taxes based on taxable income.
   b. Recorded corporate income taxes. Income taxes based on accounting income is less than income taxes based on taxable income.

Refer to the Annual Report in Chapter 1 of the text.

17. What is the amount of deferred income taxes at the end of the most recent year?

18. What was the effective tax rate for the most recent year?

19. What was the income tax currently payable for the most recent year?

Appendix
Interperiod Tax Allocation

To illustrate interperiod tax allocation, assume that Marion Company agrees to rent a portion of its office space to Dean Company on a one-time basis for 19X3 and receives its annual rent of $3,600 for the year 19X3 on December 31, 19X2. None of this amount is included in accounting income for 19X2 since it will not be earned by Dean Company until 19X3. For tax purposes, however, the entire amount is included in taxable income for 19X2 since unearned rent is taxed as it is received rather than as it is earned. Assume that the income of Marion Company from all sources other than rentals is $10,000 for 19X2 and 19X3. Its taxable income is $13,600 (accounting income of $10,000 plus the $3,600 rent received) in 19X2 and $10,000 in 19X3. Further assume that the tax rate in both years is 40 percent. The entries to record income tax expense for 19X2 and 19X3 are as follows:

19X2	Income tax expense	4,000	
	Deferred income taxes	1,440	
	Income taxes payable		5,440
19X3	Income tax expense	5,440	
	Deferred income taxes		1,440
	Income taxes payable		4,000

Income tax expense in 19X2 of $4,000 is computed by multiplying accounting income of $10,000 by 40 percent. Income taxes payable of $5,440 is computed by multiplying taxable income of $13,600 by 40 percent. Deferred income taxes of $1,440 is computed by multiplying $3,600 by 40 percent.

The impact of these differences on the financial statements and the income tax return may be summarized as follows:

	19X2	19X3
Financial statements		
Income before taxes	$10,000	$13,600
Income tax expense	4,000	5,440
Deferred income taxes	1,440	0
Income tax returns		
Taxable income	13,600	10,000
Income taxes payable	5,440	4,000

In this example, the temporary difference in recognizing the rental income is eliminated by the end of 19X3.

To illustrate a slightly more complex situation, assume that Ruth Company purchases several light trucks on January 1, 19X1, for $120,000. The firm plans to use the straight-line depreciation method for financial accounting purposes and MACRS depreciation for tax purposes. No salvage value is anticipated. The trucks are assigned a four-year useful life for accounting purposes; for tax purposes, the trucks are included in the five-year MACRS class and depreciated using the 200 percent declining-balance method. Assume further that the income before taxes and depreciation remains constant at $100,000 for the years 19X1 through 19X6, and that the applicable tax rate is 40 percent. Under these circumstances, the depreciation expense on the income statement is $30,000 ($120,000 ÷ 4) each year for 19X1 through 19X4 and zero for 19X5 and 19X6. On the other hand, the deduction for depreciation on the tax return is as follows:

		Annual	Cumulative
19X1:	(2 × 20%) × ($120,000 − 0) × ½	= $24,000	$ 24,000
19X2:	(2 × 20%) × ($120,000 − $24,000)	= 38,400	62,400
19X3:	(2 × 20%) × ($120,000 − $62,400)	= 23,040	85,440
19X4:	(2 × 20%) × ($120,000 − $85,440)	= 13,824	99,264
19X5:	(2 × 20%) × ($120,000 − $99,264)	= 8,294	107,558
19X6:	$120,000 − $107,558	= 12,442	120,000

Note that only one-half year's depreciation is taken in 19X1, the year of acquisition, because of the half-year convention required under MACRS rules. In 19X6, the remaining undepreciated cost is charged to depreciation, also because of the half-year convention.

The firm's taxable income and actual tax liability are as follows:

	19X1	19X2	19X3	19X4	19X5	19X6	Total
Income before depreciation and taxes	$100,000	$100,000	$100,000	$100,000	$100,000	$100,000	$600,000
Deduction for depreciation	24,000	38,400	23,040	13,824	8,294	12,442	120,000
Taxable income	$ 76,000	$ 61,600	$ 76,960	$ 86,176	$ 91,706	$ 87,558	$480,000
Income tax paid (40%)	$ 30,400	$ 24,640	$ 30,784	$ 34,470	$ 36,682	$ 35,024	$192,000

The following income statement results if the income tax due to the government for the year is considered to be income tax expense and comprehensive income tax allocation procedures are not used.

	19X1	19X2	19X3	19X4	19X5	19X6	Total
Income before depreciation and taxes	$100,000	$100,000	$100,000	$100,000	$100,000	$100,000	$600,000
Depreciation expense	30,000	30,000	30,000	30,000	0	0	120,000
Income before taxes	$ 70,000	$ 70,000	$ 70,000	$ 70,000	$100,000	$ 100,000	$480,000
Income tax expense (as above)	30,400	24,640	30,784	34,470	36,682	35,024	192,000
Net income	$ 39,600	$ 45,360	$ 39,216	$ 35,530	$ 63,318	$ 64,976	$288,000

It should be noted that even though Ruth Company has identical operating results during each year, the tax expense and the net income figures vary if comprehensive tax allocation is not used.

To correct this improper matching of revenues and expenses, income tax expense in the income statement should be calculated using comprehensive tax allocation. Future temporary differences are determined by comparing the depreciation taken for accounting purposes to the depreciation deduction for income tax purposes. These differences are then multiplied by the tax rate expected to be in effect when the differences are reversed to determine the amount of deferred income taxes.

Future Temporary Differences	19X2	19X3	19X4	19X5	19X6
Accounting depreciation	$ 30,000	$ 30,000	$ 30,000	$ 0	$ 0
Tax depreciation	38,400	23,040	13,824	8,294	12,442
Differences	$ (8,400)	$ 6,960	$ 16,176	$ (8,294)	$(12,442)
× tax rate	.40	.40	.40	.40	.40
Deferred income taxes	$ (3,360)	$ 2,784	$ 6,470	$ (3,318)	$ (4,976)

These amounts are then used to calculate the balance in the deferred income taxes account at the end of each year.

19X1	$(3,360) + $2,784 + $6,470 + $(3,318) + $(4,976)	=	$(2,400)
19X2	$2,784 + $6,470 + $(3,318) + $(4,976)	=	960
19X3	$6,470 + $(3,318) + $(4,976)	=	(1,824)
19X4	$(3,318) + $(4,976)	=	(8,294)
19X5	$(4,976)	=	(4,976)
19X6	0	=	0

The change in the deferred income taxes account is then combined with the amount of the income taxes actually payable to determine the income tax expense for the period.

	Tax Liability	Change in Deferred Taxes (Dr.) Cr.	Tax Expense
19X1	$30,400	$(2,400)	$28,000
19X2	24,640	3,360	28,000
19X3	30,784	(2,784)	28,000
19X4	34,470	(6,470)	28,000
19X5	36,682	3,318	40,000
19X6	35,024	4,976	40,000

The entry to record income tax expense for each year is as follows:

19X1	Income tax expense	28,000	
	Deferred income taxes	2,400	
	Income taxes payable		30,400

19X2	Income tax expense	28,000	
	Deferred income taxes		3,360
	Income taxes payable		24,640

19X3	Income tax expense	28,000	
	Deferred income taxes	2,784	
	Income taxes payable		30,784

19X4	Income tax expense	28,000	
	Deferred income taxes	6,470	
	Income taxes payable		34,470

19X5	Income tax expense	40,000	
	Deferred income taxes		3,318
	Income taxes payable		36,682

19X6	Income tax expense	40,000	
	Deferred income taxes		4,976
	Income taxes payable		35,024

The deferred income taxes account appears as follows:

Date	Debit	Credit	Balance	
1/ 1/X1			0	
12/31/X1	2,400		2,400	Dr.
12/31/X2		3,360	960	Cr.
12/31/X3	2,784		1,824	Dr.
12/31/X4	6,470		8,294	Dr.
12/31/X5		3,318	4,976	Dr.
12/31/X6		4,976	0	

Using interperiod tax allocation, the following income statements for the six-year period result:

	19X1	19X2	19X3	19X4	19X5	19X6	Total
Income before depreciation and taxes	$100,000	$100,000	$100,000	$100,000	$100,000	$100,000	$600,000
Depreciation expense	30,000	30,000	30,000	30,000	0	0	120,000
Income before taxes	$ 70,000	$ 70,000	$ 70,000	$ 70,000	$100,000	$100,000	$480,000
Income tax expense (40%)	28,000	28,000	28,000	28,000	40,000	40,000	192,000
Net income	$ 42,000	$ 42,000	$ 42,000	$ 42,000	$ 60,000	$ 60,000	$288,000

Thus, under tax allocation procedures, the tax expense in the income statement is logically related to the earnings before taxes. Note that the tax expense over the six-year period is still $192,000 and the total tax liability is also $192,000.

In this example, the difference between accounting income and taxable income is eliminated over the six-year period. Therefore, the deferred income taxes account has a zero balance at the end of the six years. In practice, the differences between accounting and taxable income may last for a considerable number of years or even be created indefinitely since the company is continually replacing its assets and seldom, if ever, would all assets be fully depreciated. The balance in the deferred income taxes account may, therefore, become a significant amount. Also, in this example, there is a single temporary difference and the expected tax rate does not change during the six-year period, so the step-by-step calculations illustrated above may appear to be unnecessary. In a real-world situation, however, there are multiple temporary differences as well as permanent differences, and the tax rate(s) expected to be in effect when the temporary differences reverse change, perhaps significantly. Thus, the systematic approach illustrated above is not only helpful, but necessary.

Outline

LEARNING Objectives

Chapter 17 discusses issues relating to foreign currency transactions and translating the financial statements of a foreign subsidiary company to the currency of the parent company in the United States. Studying this chapter should enable you to:

1. Learn about exchange rates.

2. Understand the accounting procedures for foreign currency transactions.

3. Describe the procedures involved in translating the financial statements of a foreign branch or subsidiary company to the currency of the U.S. parent company.

4. Understand the reasons for the differences in accounting standards and disclosure requirements among countries.

CHAPTER 17

INTERNATIONAL ACCOUNTING *

INTRODUCTION

Many companies buy and sell merchandise in countries all over the world. From an accounting viewpoint, these transactions are more complicated than those within a country because either the importing or exporting company must be involved with a foreign currency. Gains and losses due to changes in the exchange rate of one currency for another often arise. Examples of the geographical markets for the products of several well-known companies are shown below.

American Brands:	Approximately 70 percent of its sales are to Europe and other countries.
Alcoa:	Approximately 45 percent of its sales are to Europe, other Americas, and the Pacific.
Coca-Cola:	Approximately 67 percent of its sales are to Africa, Europe, Latin America, the Middle East, and the Far East.
Kodak:	Approximately 53 percent of its revenues come from Europe, the Middle East, Africa, Asia, Canada, and Latin America.
McDonald's:	Approximately 57 percent of its total revenues are earned in Europe, Africa, the Middle East, India, Asia, Latin America, and Canada.
Phillips Petroleum:	Approximately 18 percent of its sales are to Norway, the United Kingdom, Africa, and other areas.
Kellogg's:	Approximately 43 percent of its sales are to Europe and other countries.

A company that has branches, divisions, or subsidiaries in more than one country is referred to as a multinational corporation. Examples of multinational corporations, in addition to those listed above, include Wal-Mart, Volkswagen, and Nestle. An accounting problem arises for multinational corporations when the results of operations and balance sheets of the foreign branches, divisions, or subsidiaries must be combined with the results of operations and balance sheets of the remainder of the company to obtain consolidated statements for the company as a whole.

In this chapter, we will examine the accounting problems associated with purchases from and sales to companies in other countries—foreign currency transactions—and the problems associated with combining the results of operations and balance sheets of foreign branches, divisions, and subsidiaries with those of the domestic parts of a multinational corporation—foreign currency translation. In addition, efforts to reduce the differences in accounting standards throughout the world will be discussed.

FOREIGN CURRENCY TRANSACTIONS

If a retail department store in Texas purchases inventory items from a manufacturer in Wyoming, both parties will, of course, deal in dollars. But if an American corporation purchases clothing from a British manufacturer, the American corporation may wish to pay for the inventory in dollars while the British manufacturer prefers to receive payment in British pounds. In the same manner, a British corporation that purchases electronic equipment from an American manufacturer normally wishes to pay in British pounds while the American company prefers dollars. Using different currencies complicates and may restrain transactions between countries.

---

* The authors would like to thank Steven D. Grossman of Texas A&M University who wrote this chapter.

From the perspective of an American company, a foreign currency is a foreign money commodity (such as British pounds) that has prices specified in terms of the U.S. dollar. These prices are referred to as exchange rates and express the relative values of the various currencies.

An exchange rate between two countries may be expressed in terms of the currency of either country. If a unit of foreign currency is expressed in terms of the equivalent domestic currency, the exchange rate is computed directly—or example, an exchange rate of $1.67 (U.S. dollars) per British pound. Conversely, if a unit of domestic currency is expressed in terms of the equivalent foreign currency, the exchange rate is computed indirectly—for example, an exchange rate of 0.5992 British pounds per U.S. dollar. The direct and indirect quotations are inversely related. Both direct and indirect exchange rates are published daily in the "Foreign Exchange" section of *The Wall Street Journal* and other newspapers.

Exchange rates may be either fixed or floating. Fixed or official rates are established by governments and do not fluctuate due to changes in world currency markets. Floating or free rates reflect fluctuating market prices for a currency as a function of supply and demand in world currency markets. When the demand for a particular currency exceeds the supply, the exchange rate (price) rises. Alternatively, if supply exceeds demand, the exchange rate falls. Foreign trade can be especially inhibited if exchange rates are subject to volatile short-run movements.

The supply and demand of a particular currency depend on trade (imports and exports) and investment. If an American company sells its products to foreign customers, these buyers must purchase U.S. dollars to pay for their purchases. If a foreign investor wishes to invest funds in the United States, the investor must first convert its funds to U.S. dollars. Each of these actions increases the demand for U.S. dollars and causes the exchange rate (price) for the U.S. dollar to rise. On the other hand, if an American company purchases merchandise from a foreign supplier, the purchaser must sell U.S. dollars to acquire the needed foreign currency. If an American investor desires to invest in the capital markets of another country, the U.S. investor must convert U.S. dollars to the needed foreign currency. Each of these actions reduces the demand for U.S. dollars and causes the exchange rate for U.S. dollars to fall.

A country that fixes its exchange rate may establish different rates for various types of transactions in order to further governmental policies. Such rates are referred to as multiple exchange rates. For example, a country may establish one rate for imports and a less favorable rate for exports.

The foreign exchange market is an over-the-counter market in which national currencies are exchanged. Buyers and sellers of foreign currencies are brought together by electronic transfers. This market has developed to a considerable extent due to the very large growth in international transactions. American transactions with foreign entities are facilitated by major U.S. banks that provide bank transfer and currency exchange services.

Spot and Forward Exchange Markets

Foreign currency markets may be divided into spot and forward exchange markets. The spot market involves the exchange of currencies for immediate delivery. Spot rates may be either fixed or floating. If the exchange rates are floating, the spot rate may change several times in a single day. The forward exchange market involves the trading of foreign currencies for delivery and payment at some specified future date at an exchange rate that is also specified in advance. An important function of the forward exchange market is to provide protection against the risk of an adverse movement in the spot rate. *The Wall Street Journal* publishes daily quotations of U.S. exchange rates against other currencies for both immediate delivery and for delivery in 30, 90, and 180 days. Examples of foreign exchange rates are presented as follows:

The exchange rate for the British pound was $1.5390 on May 14, 1993. About five years later, the exchange rate for the British pound had risen to $1.689. The British pound had become stronger (more valuable) relative to the U.S. dollar. In terms of the U.S. dollar, the exchange rate had fallen from £.6498 to £.5992. The U.S. dollar became weaker (less valuable) relative to the British pound. American importers had to spend more U.S. dollars to obtain British pounds; British pounds had become more expensive. On the other hand, American exporters received more dollars for each receivable denominated in British pounds. When the exchange rate was £.6498, a receivable for £6,498 brought $10,000; when the exchange rate was £.5992, a receivable for £6,498 brought $10,844.46.

Illustration 1 presents foreign exchange rates for selected countries at three different points in time. Note that some currencies are no longer in existence. Others will be eliminated if the single European currency, the euro, is introduced on January 1, 1999 as planned.

Illustration 1
Foreign Exchange Rate for Selected Countries
May 11, 1990, May 14, 1993, March 20, 1998

	U.S. Dollar Equivalent			Currency Per U.S. Dollar		
	May 11, 1990	*May 14, 1993*	*March 20, 1998*	*May 11, 1990*	*May 14, 1993*	*March 20, 1998*
Argentina (Austral)	.0002075	N/A	N/A	4820.21	N/A	N/A
Belgium (Franc):						
Commercial rate	.02943	.03017	.02648	33.98	33.14	37.760
Britain (Pound)	1.6775	1.5390	1.6690	.5961	.6498	.5992
30-day forward	1.6681	1.5352	1.6665	.5995	.6514	.6001
90-day forward	1.6499	1.5282	1.6616	.6061	.6544	.6018
180-day forward	1.6247	1.5183	1.6544	.6155	.6586	.6045
Canada (Dollar)	.8503	.7851	.7048	1.1760	1.2737	1.4189
30-day forward	.8467	.7841	.7053	1.1811	1.2754	1.4178
90-day forward	.8398	.7813	.7063	1.1907	1.2800	1.4159
180-day forward	.8313	.7783	.7076	1.2030	1.2882	1.4133
China (Yuen)	.211820	N/A	N/A	4.7210	N/A	N/A
France (Franc)	.18059	.18503	.1630	5.5375	5.4045	6.1360
30-day forward	.18038	.18425	.1627	5.5438	5.4274	6.1474
90-day forward	.18002	.18297	.1638	5.5550	5.4655	6.1041
180-day forward	.17953	.18132	.1646	5.5700	5.5150	6.0749
Germany (Mark)	.6099	.6205	.5459	1.6395	1.6115	1.8320
30-day forward	.6101	.6181	.5468	1.6391	1.6178	1.8287
90-day forward	.6104	.6141	.5487	1.6383	1.6285	1.8224
180-day forward	.6104	.6089	.5514	1.6382	1.6422	1.8135
Hong Kong (Dollar)	.12837	.12938	.1292	7.7900	7.7290	7.7420
Italy (Lira)	.0008278	.0006760	.0005548	1208.01	1479.38	1802.5
Japan (Yen)	.006542	.009027	.007666	152.85	110.78	130.44
30-day forward	.006549	.009026	.007699	152.70	110.79	129.88
90-day forward	.006561	.009027	.007765	152.42	110.78	128.79
180-day forward	.006582	.009027	.007866	151.92	110.78	127.13
Mexico (Peso)	.0003574	N/A	N/A	2798.00	N/A	N/A

N/A—not applicable; currency has changed.

Assume that an American company contracted to purchase goods from a British company and to pay 5,000 British pounds on delivery in thirty days. At the time of the agreement, the spot rate was $1.60 for one British pound. The American company expected to purchase 5,000 British pounds in the spot market to pay for the goods. But when the goods arrived, the British pound was selling for $1.6775. Consequently, the cost of the goods was $8,387.50 (5,000 × $1.6775) rather than the expected $8,000 (5,000 × $1.60). The American company had a loss of $387.50 on the transaction [($1.6775 − $1.60) × 5,000].

The American company could have eliminated the risk of an exchange rate loss on the transaction by entering into an agreement in the forward market to purchase 5,000 British pounds to be delivered in thirty days. Such an action, referred to as a hedge, would fix the dollar cost of the British goods at the forward rate. Payment for the 5,000 British pounds would have been due in thirty days. The forward rate is usually very close to the spot rate. Assume that in this case the forward rate at the time of the agreement with the British company was $1.61 for one British pound. The American company could have guaranteed itself the receipt of 5,000 British pounds in thirty days by agreeing to pay $8,050 (5,000 × $1.61) at that time. For only $50 ($8,050 − $8,000), the American company could have eliminated the risk of an adverse change in the exchange rate between the time of the agreement to purchase the British goods and the time of the payment for them.

Speculators attempt to profit in the forward exchange market by anticipating fluctuations in exchange rates. Assume that the spot rate is $1.62 for one British pound and a speculator expects it to increase to $1.70. The speculator could buy British pounds at the spot rate of $1.62 for one British pound, wait for the pound to appreciate (increase in value) against the dollar, and sell the pounds when the exchange rate has increased. If the speculator sells the pounds when the exchange rate is $1.69 per British pound, a profit of seven cents per pound would be obtained. Alternatively, the speculator could purchase British pounds for future delivery in the forward exchange market (for, say, $1.63 per British pound) and subsequently sell them in the spot market after the pound has appreciated (say, to $1.69 per British pound). Of course, if the speculator's judgment proves to be incorrect, a loss would be incurred.

An advantage of the forward market for the speculator is that no money (except a small security deposit in some cases) has to be paid at the time of the purchase of the British pounds. The speculator is required to pay dollars on the date on which the British pounds are delivered. But the dollars may be obtained by selling the British pounds. If the speculator correctly anticipated the movements in the exchange rate between the U.S. dollar and the British pound, the dollars received on the sale of the pounds will be more than sufficient to cover the obligation to purchase the pounds in the forward market. The speculator has great leverage in the forward exchange market; a positive return can be earned with no capital investment.

IMPORT-EXPORT TRANSACTIONS

When companies located in two different countries, each having its own currency, engage in transactions (purchase-sale) with each other, one company will make or receive payment in the currency of the other company's country. This foreign transaction is denominated (stated) in terms of one of the two currencies. For example, the purchase of goods by an American company from a British company can be denominated in either U.S. dollars or British pounds. A foreign currency transaction is a transaction that is stated in terms of the other country's currency. Therefore, if the purchase of goods by an American company from a British company is denominated in British pounds, the foreign transaction is considered to be a foreign currency transaction by the American company. Alternatively, if the purchase is denominated in U.S. dollars, the foreign transaction is not considered to be a foreign currency transaction by the American company. Note that the transaction may be measured in either currency. The key point is the currency in which the transaction is stated.

A receivable or payable denominated in a foreign currency is measured in the domestic currency by multiplying the amount of the receivable or payable by the spot exchange rate at the time of the transaction. By the date of payment, however, the exchange rate has probably changed. These fluctuations in exchange rates give rise to exchange gains or losses.

Foreign currency transactions for an American company are translated into U.S. dollars at the spot rate in effect at the date of the transaction. Each asset, liability, revenue, and expense account arising from the transaction is translated into dollars. If the balance sheet date occurs between the transaction date and the date of payment, the receivable or payable is adjusted to reflect the spot rate at the balance sheet date. Any exchange gain or loss resulting from this adjustment is included in income rather than being deferred until the time of payment.

There is a direct relationship between the American company's foreign currency transactions and its cash flows in dollars. Consequently, any fluctuations in the exchange rate for the company's foreign currency transactions will probably be realized at the time of payment. Therefore, exchange gains or losses are included in income for the period ending on the balance sheet date.

An exchange gain or loss arising from a purchase or sale is accounted for as a separate item rather than combined with the purchase or sale. The risk assumed on the receivable or payable is separate and distinct from the sale or purchase. The purchase or sale is recorded at the spot rate in effect at the time of the transaction. If the company decides not to pay for the purchase or sale immediately, the exchange gain or loss reflects what is. in effect. a decision to speculate in the foreign currency market.

IMPORTS—SINGLE TIME PERIOD

Assume that Amanda Company, which is located in the United States, purchases merchandise from Otto Company, which is located in Germany. At the time of the transaction, the spot exchange rate is $0.5447 per German mark. Amanda Company agrees to pay for the merchandise in thirty days. If the payable is denominated in U.S. dollars, there is a foreign transaction but not a foreign currency transaction for Amanda Company. Consequently, both the inventory or purchase and the related payable are measured and denominated in U.S.

dollars. No exchange gain or loss can occur. On the other hand, if the payable is denominated in German marks, Amanda Company is exposed to risk from exchange rate fluctuations. Assuming that the agreed upon invoice price is 10,000 marks, Amanda Company records the transaction as follows:

Inventory (or purchases)	5,447	
Accounts payable (marks)		5,447

The inventory (or purchase) is measured and recorded in U.S. dollars. The dollar amount is computed by multiplying the number of German marks (10,000) by the spot rate ($0.5447). The account payable is denominated in German marks and, therefore, is subject to remeasurement as the exchange rate changes.

If the spot rate is $0.5647 per German mark at the time of payment, Amanda Company records the payment as follows:

Accounts payable (marks)	5,447	
Exchange loss	200	
Cash		5,647

The $200 exchange loss occurs because Amanda Company has to pay $0.5647 for each German mark for a total of $5,647 rather than $0.5447 for each German mark for a total of $5,447. The loss is due to the change in the exchange rate between the date of the transaction and the date of payment.

Although the payment to Otto Company has to be made in German marks, Amanda Company simply credits cash. Amanda Company can notify its bank to send the payment to Germany in marks without actually buying marks and then making the payment itself.

Imports—Multiple Time Periods

Now assume that in the above example the balance sheet date occurs between the time of the purchase transaction and the time of payment. Amanda Company records the purchase at the time of the transaction as follows:

Inventory (or purchases)	5,447	
Accounts payable (marks)		5,447

The spot rate on the balance sheet date is $0.5347 per German mark. On the balance sheet date, the liability is adjusted to reflect the spot rate at that time. The spot rate has decreased from $0.5447 to $0.5347. Therefore, the liability is reduced by $0.01 per German mark for a total of $100 [($0.01 × 10,000) or ($0.5447 × 10,000) − ($0.5347 × 10,000)].

Accounts payable (marks)	100	
Exchange gain		100

At the time of payment the spot rate has increased to $0.5647 and an exchange loss occurs. The loss is equal to the difference between the amount required at the time of payment ($5,647) and the recorded amount of the account payable ($5,347).

Accounts payable (marks)	5,347	
Exchange loss	300	
Cash		5,647

Although the actual exchange loss is $200 ($5,647 − $5,447). an exchange gain of $100 is reported in the income statement in the initial accounting period and an exchange loss of $300 is recorded in the second accounting period. No retroactive adjustment is made.

Exports

Assume that Amanda Company sells merchandise to an Italian company for 10,000,000 liras when the spot rate is $0.0005645 for each lira. At the balance sheet date, which is before the time of payment, the spot rate is $0.0006000. At the time of payment, the spot rate is $0.0006645. Amanda records the sales transaction as follows:

Accounts receivable (liras)	5,645	
Sales		5,645

On the balance sheet date, the account receivable, which is denominated in liras, is adjusted for the change in the exchange rate. An exchange gain of $355 [($0.0006000 – $0.0005645) × 10,000,000] is recorded as:

Accounts receivable (liras)	355	
Exchange gain		355

The exchange gain occurs because the exchange rate increased and, if the exchange rate remains the same at the time of payment, Amanda Company will be able to obtain more dollars for each lira upon conversion.

On the date that payment is made, the exchange rate has increased to $0.0006645 and an exchange gain of $645 [($0.0006645 – $0.0006000) × 10,000,000] is recorded.

Cash	6,645	
Accounts receivable (liras)		6,000
Exchange gain		645

The actual exchange gain is $1,000. An exchange gain of $355 is recorded in the income statement of the initial period; an exchange gain of $645 is recorded in the income statement of the second period.

Amanda Company could have avoided the possibility of exchange rate gains or losses by setting its sales price in terms of U.S. dollars. Then, if the exchange rate changed, the Italian company would spend a greater or lesser number of liras to buy the merchandise, but Amanda Company's receipts in terms of U.S. dollars would not have been affected.

Hedging

A company may be able to avoid gains and losses on foreign currency transactions by immediately paying or receiving the amount denominated in a foreign currency or by hedging with forward exchange (futures) contracts.[1] By immediately paying the liability denominated in a foreign currency or receiving the amount due on the receivable denominated in a foreign currency, the possibility of changes in the exchange rate is avoided. Hedging is like betting with a friend on one team winning the World Series and then betting the same amount with another friend on the other team winning the World Series. One bet offsets the other; the possibility of losing (or winning) is avoided.

A forward exchange contract is an agreement to exchange currencies at a specified forward rate at a specified future date. Exchange rate gains and losses can be avoided by hedging—buying or selling foreign currency for delivery on the same date that payment denominated in foreign currency is due.

In most cases, the forward exchange rate is not equal to the spot rate. For example, the spot rate on May 11, 1990, for Canada was $0.8503, while the forward rates were $0.8467 for 30 days, $0.8398 for 90 days, and $0.8313 for 180 days. If the forward price is lower (as is the case for Canada), the difference is referred to as a discount. Conversely, if the forward price is higher (as is the case for Japan on May 11, 1990), the difference is called a premium.

---

[1] This section discusses hedging with contracts for foreign currencies. The accounting requirements for this type of hedging are not covered by FASB Statement No. 80. "Accounting for Futures Contracts."

A company with payables denominated in a foreign currency may hedge by entering into a forward contract to buy foreign currency at a specified future date. If the exchange rate increases (as it did for Amanda Company from $0.5447 per German mark to $0.5647 per German mark), a loss on a payable denominated in a foreign currency is offset by a gain in the value of the forward exchange contract. For example, Amanda Company could have entered into a forward exchange contract to purchase marks at the 90-day forward exchange rate of $0.5476 per German mark. Such a hedging transaction does not ensure the complete elimination of a loss on the payable in this example, but it does reduce the $200 exchange loss on the payable by the $171 [($0.5647 − $0.5476) × 10,000 marks] exchange gain on the forward contract to a net loss of $29.

Similarly, a forward exchange contract to hedge an account receivable denominated in a foreign currency may be used. A company could enter into a forward contract to sell foreign currency at a specified future date.

Foreign Currency Translation

The translation of foreign currency financial statements is necessary in order to record an investor's share of the income of a foreign investee and to prepare consolidated financial statements for a company with foreign branches or subsidiaries. The translation process should not alter the financial results of the component entities that report their financial information in terms of a foreign currency. Prior to the translation process, the foreign currency financial statements must be adjusted to conform with the accounting principles of the domestic company.

The development of standards for translating foreign currency financial statements has been a significant problem for the Financial Accounting Standards Board (FASB). The last two decades have been marked by the increased involvement of U.S. companies in international operations and by wide fluctuations in exchange rates. The numerous translation methods proposed over the years can yield significantly different financial statement results. Therefore, there has been a great deal of disagreement among accountants and users of financial information concerning the results produced by the various translation methods.

The translation process required by *FASB Statement No. 52*, "Foreign Currency Translation," involves the following for a U.S. parent company:

1. The functional currency of each foreign entity is identified. A company's functional currency is the currency of the primary economic environment in which the company normally operates. For example, the functional currency for a subsidiary located in London is probably the British pound.

2. Financial statement items for each foreign entity are measured in terms of its functional currency in accordance with U.S. generally accepted accounting principles.

3. Assets and liabilities are translated from the functional currency into the reporting currency (the U.S. dollar for a U.S. parent company) using the current exchange rate in effect at the balance sheet date. Equity accounts are translated using historical rates. Revenues, expenses, gains, and losses are translated at the current exchange rate in effect at the date the items were recorded; however, a weighted average exchange rate for the period may be used.

4. Translation adjustments are included in stockholders' equity rather than in income.

Translation adjustments for functional currencies that are not the reporting currency (U.S. dollars for a U.S. company) result from the process of translating financial statements from an entity's functional currency into the reporting currency. The FASB pronouncement provides that translation adjustments are not to be included in the determination of net income for the period but are to be recorded in a separate component of stockholders' equity. The FASB's rationale for this position is that translation adjustments have no direct effect on the cash flows of a U.S. parent company. The effects of changes in exchange rates are uncertain and are not realized until the disposal of the foreign entity, if then.

Basic Illustration of Translation

Dayspring Corporation has a subsidiary, Lamblight Company, that began its operations at the beginning of 19X1. The functional currency of Lamblight Company is the British pound (£) and the books are maintained in British pounds. The functional currency of Dayspring Corporation is the U.S. dollar. Lamblight Company's balance sheet at the beginning of 19X1 is presented in Illustration 2.

Illustration 2
Balance Sheet
January 1, 19X1

<u>Assets</u>

Cash	£ 76,000
Inventories	55,000
Plant assets	180,000
Total assets	£311,000

<u>Liabilities and Stockholders' Equity</u>

Accounts payable	£ 45,000
Long-term debt	132,000
Common stock	134,000
Total liabilities and stockholders' equity	£311,000

The plant assets have a ten-year life and a zero residual value. Straight-line depreciation is used. Dividends of £10,000 were declared and paid during September. The exchange rates for 19X1 are as follows:

Beginning of the year	$1.50 per pound
September	1.57 per pound
End of the year	1.60 per pound
Weighted average	1.54 per pound

The income statement for Lamblight Company for 19X1 is presented in Illustration 3.

Illustration 3
Income Statement
For the Year Ended December 31, 19X1

Sales		£445,000
Cost of goods sold		290,000
Gross profit		£155,000
Depreciation expense	£ 18,000	
Other operating expenses	102,000	
Total operating expenses		120,000
Net income		£ 35 000

The balance sheet for Lamblight Company at the end of 19X1 is presented in Illustration 4.

Illustration 4
Balance Sheet
December 31, 19X1

Assets

Cash	£ 15,000
Accounts receivable	114,000
Inventories	55,000
Plant assets, net	162,000
Total assets	£346,000

Liabilities and Stockholders' Equity

Accounts payable	£ 55,000
Long-term debt	132,000
Common stock	134,000
Retained earnings	25,000
Total liabilities and stockholders' equity	£346,000

The income statement of Lamblight Company for 19X1 translated into U.S. dollars is presented in Illustration 5.

Illustration 5
Income Statement
For the Year Ended December 31, 19X1

Sales	£445,000	× 1.54	=	$685,300
Cost of goods sold	290,000	× 1.54	=	446,600
Gross profit	£155,000			$238,700
Depreciation expense	18,000	× 1.54	=	$ 27,720
Other operating expenses	102,000	× 1.54	=	157,080
Total operating expenses	£120,000			$184,800
Net income	£ 35,000			$ 53,900

All of the income accounts are translated at the weighted average exchange rate for the year.

The balance sheet of Lamblight Company at the end of 19X1 translated into U.S. dollars is presented in Illustration 6.

Illustration 6
Balance Sheet
December 31, 19X1

Assets

Cash	£ 15,000	× 1.60	=	$ 24,000
Accounts receivable	114,000	× 1.60	=	182,400
Inventories	55,000	× 1.60	=	88,000
Plant assets, net	162,000	× 1.60	=	259,200
Total assets	£346,000			$553,600

Liabilities and Stockholders' Equity

Accounts payable	£ 55,000	× 1.60	=	$ 88,000
Long-term debt	132,000	× 1.60	=	211,200
Common stock	134,000	× 1.50	=	201,000
Retained earnings	25,000	see schedule		38,200
Translation adjustment		shown below		15,200
Total liabilities and stockholders' equity	£346,000			$553,600

All of the assets and liabilities are translated at the current exchange rate (1.60). The common stock is translated at the historical rate (1.50).

The schedule for computing the translated ending balance of retained earnings is as follows:

Beginning retained earnings	—			—
Net income	£ 35,000	see income statement		$ 53,900
Less dividends	(10,000)	× 1.57	=	(15,700)
Ending retained earnings	£ 25,000			$ 38,200

The translated beginning retained earnings is the translated ending retained earnings from the previous year (zero in this example). The translated income amount is taken from the income statement (Illustration 5). The dividends are translated using the exchange rate in effect on the date of declaration (1.57).

The translation adjustment of $15,200 shown in the balance sheet is computed as shown in Illustration 7.

Illustration 7
Computation of Translation Adjustment

	Pounds			*Dollars*
Beginning net asset balance	134,000	× 1.50	=	201,000
Increase in net assets:				
Net income	35,000			53,900
Decrease in net assets:				
Dividends declared	(10,000)	× 1.57	=	(15,700)
Ending net asset balance before adjustment	159,000			239,200
Adjusted net asset balance	159,000	× 1.60	=	254,400
Translation adjustment				15,200

The beginning net asset balance is translated at the historical exchange rate ($1.50). Individual increases and decreases are translated at the appropriate historical rates in effect at the time of occurrence (net income may be translated at a weighted average exchange rate). The ending net asset balance before adjustment does not consider the effect of the end-of-year exchange rate. The adjusted ending net asset balance takes into account exchange rate changes to the end of the year. The resulting translation adjustment (a credit of $15,200 in this example) is combined with the existing translation adjustment in the stockholders' equity section of the balance sheet (no previous translation adjustment exists in this example).

The translation adjustment is a credit in this example. The net asset position (assets minus liabilities) increased by £25,000. In addition, the exchange rate for the British pound rose. The value of the dollar decreased during the year ($1.50 was needed to purchase a British pound at the beginning of the year; $1.60 is required at the end of the year). If, for purposes of explanation in this discussion, Lamblight Company's net asset position is considered to be a receivable denominated in pounds, then the U.S. parent company (Dayspring Corporation) would receive more dollars for each British pound. Hence, there is a translation "gain" to be reported as an equity adjustment (see Illustration 6).

Uniformity of Accounting Principles

While investors can now look throughout the world for investment opportunities, financial analysis may be difficult due to differing accounting standards and requirements for disclosure. Differences arise because of varying economic, political, social, educational, legal, and environmental factors. The financial statements of companies located in different countries may be difficult to compare. Differences exist in terminology, accounts in one system do not exist in another, rules concerning revenue and expense recognition are not the same, and levels of disclosure vary considerably.

Accounting standards are not uniform from one country to another. There is no world body with the power to establish accounting and disclosure requirements.

Efforts have been made to standardize or harmonize accounting standards. To standardize accounting standards means to eliminate any differences between them (i.e., to make them uniform). To harmonize accounting standards means to lessen the differences between them.

Increased interest in standardization or harmonization is due to the need of companies to sell stock or obtain credit in foreign markets. Companies that disclose more information on their financial statements may have an advantage with international investors and creditors. Those companies not providing financial information according to standards established by the United States and United Kingdom find themselves at a competitive disadvantage in these financial markets.

Differences In Accounting Standards

Differences among countries, as well as nationalistic pride, hinder efforts at standardization or harmonization. Each country believes that its accounting system is better for itself than any other system.

Some countries have accounting standards that are set primarily by the private sector (the United States and the Netherlands); other countries have accounting standards that are heavily influenced by legal and tax regulations (Germany and Japan). The accounting practices in some countries are heavily influenced by centralized planning and decision-making (Egypt). Some countries permit a wide choice of accounting practices (France, the Netherlands, and South Africa). Some countries permit a wide variety of reserve accounts for bad debts, depreciation, and specific purposes such as overseas market development and research and development (Japan). Other countries are concerned with social accounting (Egypt and France) or inflation (Brazil). Some countries have highly uniform charts of accounts (France); others do not (Germany). Some countries are concerned with secrecy (Switzerland). Some countries are concerned with conservatism (Germany and Switzerland). Other countries have accounting systems that are similar to those of former colonial powers (the accounting systems in Ireland and New Zealand are similar to that of the United Kingdom).

In view of these differences in accounting standards and procedures, standardization is not likely to be achieved. Harmonization, especially within groups of nations, does appear to be a realistic goal, however.

Standard-Setting Bodies

The International Accounting Standards Committee (IASC) was founded in 1973 to formulate accounting standards to be observed throughout the world and to persuade the business communities and governments of all countries to secure acceptance of and compliance with these standards. The founding members of the IASC were Australia, Canada, France, Great Britain, Ireland, Japan, Mexico, the Netherlands, the United States, and Germany. Currently, 122 accounting organizations representing 91 countries are now members. The representatives to the IASC from the United States are the American Institute of Certified Public Accountants (AICPA) and the Institute of Management Accountants (IMA); the FASB has no official role.

Although the IASC has no enforcement powers and its standards are not universally applied, the organization's pronouncements have contributed to greater harmonization of accounting standards. The IASC's objective, as set forth in its *Statement of Intent* issued in July, 1990, is to remove the many alternative accounting treatments that are currently allowed so that securities commissions throughout the world will adopt the body's standards as benchmarks for generally accepted accounting principles. At the present time, there are some significant differences between IASC standards and those of some major countries. Whether these countries bring their accounting practices in line with those issued by the IASC remains to be seen.

The International Organization of Securities Commissions (IOSCO), which was established over twenty years ago, is now becoming more influential. The organization is composed of securities regulators from approximately fifty countries. The objective of the IOSCO is to improve international and domestic securities regulation by raising the quality of international accounting standards so that securities regulators can consider them for multinational securities offerings.

The European Economic Community (EEC) has made efforts toward increasing the harmonization of accounting standards among its member nations. Differences among the member countries have impeded this effort; however, some success has been achieved.

Other organizations have made contributions to harmonization. The United Nations has made recommendations for financial disclosure on annual reports for multinational corporations; the proposed code of conduct by the Organization for Economic Development and Cooperation for multinational corporations has a section dealing with financial disclosure. Wide differences of opinion exist on these recommendations between the industrialized and developing countries. Neither party had any real enforcement power to ensure compliance with the disclosure standards.

Summary

A company that buys and sells merchandise in foreign countries may have gains and losses due to changes in the exchange rates between currencies. An exchange rate is the price of one currency in terms of another currency.

Exchange rates may be established (fixed) by governments or may fluctuate (float) due to changes in the supply and demand for world currencies. Supply and demand for a particular currency depend on imports, exports, and investment. Exports to a foreign country increase the demand for the domestic currency and cause the exchange rate for the domestic currency to rise; imports by a domestic company increase the demand for the foreign currency and cause the exchange rate for the domestic currency to fall.

A foreign exchange market has both spot exchange rates and forward exchange rates. The spot rate is the rate for immediate delivery of the currency; the forward rate is the rate for delivery of the currency at some specified future date. The forward market may be used to hedge the risk of gains and losses in import and export transactions. Speculators also use the forward exchange market.

In a foreign currency transaction involving exports and imports, the spot exchange rate is used to measure the receivable or payable denominated in a foreign currency at the time of the transaction. The exchange rate at the time of payment is probably not the same as the spot rate at the time of the transaction. The resulting exchange gain or loss is not combined with the purchase or sale but instead is accounted for separately. A company may be able to avoid these gains and losses by immediately paying or receiving the amount denominated in foreign currency or by hedging with forward exchange contracts.

Foreign currency translation is needed to record an investor's share of a foreign investee's income and to include foreign entities in consolidated financial statements. Assets and liabilities are translated from the functional currency into the reporting currency using the current exchange rate in effect at the balance sheet date. Equity accounts are translated using historical rates. Income statement accounts are translated at the current exchange rate in effect at the date the items were recorded or by using a weighted average exchange rate for the period. Translation adjustments are included in stockholders' equity rather than in income.

Comparison of the financial statements of companies located in different countries is difficult due to differences in accounting standards and disclosure requirements. While efforts at standardizing accounting principles have had little success to date, several international organizations have made some impact on harmonizing accounting standards. The International Accounting Standards Committee, the European Economic Community, the United Nations, and the Organization for Economic Development and Cooperation have all made contributions toward this goal.

Key Definitions

Exchange gains and losses—Exchange gains and losses result from fluctuations in exchange rates between the time of a transaction and the time payment is made or received.

Exchange rate—An exchange rate is the price of one currency in terms of another currency.

Fixed exchange rate—A fixed exchange rate is established by the government and does not fluctuate due to changes in world currency markets.

Floating exchange rate—A floating exchange rate reflects fluctuating market prices for a currency as a function of supply and demand in world currency markets.

Foreign currency transaction—A foreign currency transaction is a transaction that is stated in terms of the other country's currency.

Foreign currency translation—Foreign currency translation is the conversion of a foreign entity's financial statements from its functional currency to the reporting entity's functional currency.

Foreign exchange market—The foreign exchange market is an over-the-counter market in which national currencies are exchanged.

Forward exchange contract—A forward exchange contract is an agreement to exchange currencies at a specified forward rate at a specified future date.

Forward exchange rate—A forward exchange rate is a specified exchange rate at a specified future date.

Functional currency—The functional currency is the currency of the primary economic environment in which the company normally operates.

Harmonization—Harmonization is the reduction in the differences in accounting standards and disclosure requirements among countries.

Hedging—Hedging is buying or selling foreign currency for delivery on the same date that payment denominated in foreign currency is due.

International Accounting Standards Committee—The International Accounting Standards Committee is an international body that was founded to formulate accounting standards to be observed throughout the world and to persuade the business communities and governments of all countries to secure acceptance of and compliance with these standards.

Multinational corporation—A multinational corporation is a company that has branches, divisions, or subsidiaries in more than one country.

Spot rate—The spot rate is the rate of exchange between two currencies for immediate delivery.

Standardization—Standardization is the elimination of differences in accounting standards and disclosure requirements among countries.

Questions

1. What is a multinational corporation?

2. Differentiate between an exchange rate computed directly and an exchange rate computed indirectly. Show the difference for the austral for May 11, 1990, and demonstrate the relationship between the two rates.

3. Differentiate among fixed exchange rates, floating exchange rates, and multiple exchange rates.

4. How do American exports affect the demand for the U.S. dollar?

5. How do American imports affect the demand for the U.S. dollar?

6. What is the foreign exchange market?

7. Differentiate between the spot and forward exchange markets.

8. Describe how an exchange loss can occur when an American company contracts to purchase goods from an Italian company and then pays for the goods in thirty days.

9. How do speculators try to make a profit in the forward exchange market? What is an important advantage of the forward market for a speculator?

10. Under what circumstances is a foreign transaction considered to be a foreign currency transaction?

11. How are the financial statements affected if the end of the accounting period occurs between the transaction date for a foreign currency transaction and the payment date? Why?

12. Why is an exchange gain or loss arising from a purchase not accounted for as part of the purchase?

13. How may a company avoid exchange gains and losses on foreign currency transactions?

14. Describe how hedging can offset an exchange gain or loss.

15. Why is the translation of foreign currency financial statements necessary?

16. What steps are needed for translating a foreign entity's financial statements by a U.S. company?

17. How do translation adjustments affect the financial statements? Why?

18. Differentiate between standardization and harmonization of accounting principles. Why might these be desirable?

19. What impediments exist in the efforts to harmonize accounting standards?

20. What is the International Accounting Standards Committee? What other organizations have made efforts toward harmonizing accounting standards and disclosure requirements?

Exercise

21. Mercy Company, located in the United States, purchases merchandise from a company located in Mexico. At the time of the transaction, the spot rate is $0.0003574 per Mexican peso. Payment is due in thirty days. The invoice price is 300,000 pesos. The spot rate twenty days later on the balance sheet date is $0.0003584 and on the date of payment is $0.0003598. Mercy Company uses a periodic inventory method. Prepare the necessary journal entries for Mercy Company on the transaction date, the balance sheet date, and the payment date.

PROBLEMS

22. Dan Corporation, located in the United States, has a subsidiary, Jeff Company, that began its operations at the beginning of 19X1. The functional currency of Jeff Company is the French franc (f). The functional currency of Dan Corporation is the U.S. dollar. Comparative balance sheets at the beginning and end of 19X1 for Jeff Company in francs are as follows:

	End of 19X1	Beginning of 19X1
Assets		
Cash	f 90,000	f110,000
Accounts receivable	320,000	
Inventories	350,000	200,000
Plant assets	450,000	500,000
Total assets	f1,210,000	f810,000
Liabilities and Stockholders' Equity		
Accounts payable	f 190,000	f 90,000
Long-term debt	410,000	410,000
Common stock	310,000	310,000
Retained earnings	300,000	0
Total liabilities and stockholders' equity	f1,210,000	f810,000

The income statement in francs for Jeff Company for 19X1 is as follows:

Sales		f2,800,000
Cost of goods sold	f1,600,000	
Operating expenses (including depreciation expense of 50,000)	700,000	2,300,000
Net income		f 500,000

Dividends of 200,000 francs were declared and paid during November The exchange rates for 19X1 are as follows:

Beginning of the year	$0.1806 per franc
November	0.1755 per franc
End of the year	0.1752 per franc
Weighted average	0.1780 per franc

Translate the financial statements of Jeff Company into U.S. dollars.

23. For each of the transactions listed, indicate the effect(s), if any, on the company's year-end: (1) Balance Sheet, (2) Income Statement, and (3) Statement of Cash Flows. Your answers should be as complete and specific as possible.

   a. Purchased inventory payable in thirty days in Mexican pesos.
   b. Paid for the purchase. The U.S. dollar now buys fewer Mexican pesos than at the purchase date.
   c. Paid for the purchase. The U.S. dollar now buys more Mexican pesos than at the purchase date.

Refer to the Annual Report in Chapter 1 of the text.

24. In what geographical areas does the company operate?

25. By how much did the currency translation adjustment increase or decrease from the previous year to the current year?

Outline

LEARNING OBJECTIVES

Chapter 18 discusses the accounting and disclosures relating to pensions, other postretirement benefits, and leases. It also examines the disclosures included as a part of comprehensive financial reports. This chapter also discusses the report of the independent auditor. Studying this chapter should enable you to:

1. Describe the basic types of postretirement benefits.

2. Explain the basic characteristics of pension plans.

3. Describe the disclosures relating to pension plans.

4. Describe the differences between pension plans and health care plans.

5. Explain the difference between a capital lease and an operating lease.

6. Explain the use of footnotes in financial disclosure.

7. Describe the independent auditor's report and its uses and limitations.

8. Discuss interim financial reporting.

9. Describe the reporting for segments of a business.

10. Explain the purpose and content of management's discussion and analysis.

Chapter 18

Accounting for Pensions, Postretirement Benefits, and Leases and Analysis of Other Disclosures

Introduction

In the previous chapters, we have discussed and examined a number of the basic principles involved in the preparation of financial reports. In the first section of this chapter, we will discuss accounting and disclosures relating to pensions, other postretirement benefits and leases. In the second part of this chapter, we will examine several disclosures included as a part of comprehensive financial reports in addition to the basic financial statements discussed in previous chapters. We will review the following types of disclosures:

1. Accounting policy disclosures.
2. Footnote and other information disclosures.
3. Auditor's report.
4. Interim reports.
5. Reporting for segments of a business.
6. Management's discussion and analysis.

PART I: PENSIONS, POSTRETIREMENT BENEFITS, AND LEASES

This section of the chapter discusses three topics relating to long-term commitments. The FASB's pronouncements dealing with pensions and other postretirement benefits are helpful to users of financial statements to understand the magnitude of these previously unrecognized liabilities. The FASB's pronouncement on leases differentiates a lease that is in substance a purchase from a lease that is merely a rental. Different accounting requirements apply to each.

Pensions and Other Postretirement Benefits

Most large companies and many smaller companies promise benefits to their employees after retirement. These benefits to be paid in the future are earned by the employees as they provide services to their companies. The basic types of postretirement benefits are:

1. *Pension benefits*—monthly payments to employees after retirement.
2. *Other postretirement benefits*—medical costs, dental costs, life insurance, and other benefits.

These costs can be quite substantial. For example, pension costs and other postretirement benefit costs totalled over $1 billion in 1992.

PENSIONS

A pension plan is a contract between a company and its employees in which the company agrees to provide benefits to the employees on their retirement. If the plan requires periodic contributions by the employee, it is called a contributory plan; if the company assumes the full cost of the plan, it is called a noncontributory plan. Pension benefits are usually paid monthly to the employees after retirement.

Pension plans create substantial long-term financial obligations. Almost all major corporations have pension plans. Most of these are noncontributory plans. Most plans allow for retirement before an employee becomes sixty-five years of age. Some plans allow employees who have at least thirty years of services to retire at age fifty-five with no reduction in benefits.

Accounting for a pension plan requires the measurement of both the current and future costs of the plan and the allocation of these costs to the appropriate accounting periods. The cost of a pension plan to a company is a function of many events (e.g., employee turnover and retirement age). The assumptions about these factors are called actuarial assumptions and have a significant impact on the amount of pension cost recognized for accounting purposes.

A pension plan has several characteristics. The company establishes the pension plan and specifies the eligibility requirements, retirement ages, amounts of retirement benefits, the method and amounts of funding, any employee contributions, and the pension plan funding agent (usually a bank or an insurance company). The company periodically transfers cash to the funding agent. These funds are invested to earn income. The funding agent makes payments to those retirees who are entitled to receive benefits.

Benefits may be vested or nonvested. Vested benefits are benefits that the employees have earned and will receive even if they leave the company. An employee must usually work for a company for a specified number of years before the pension benefits become vested.

There are two types of benefit formulas for determining retirement benefits. A defined benefit pension plan specifies the amount of the pension benefits to be received during retirement. The amount of the benefits are based on such factors as level of compensation and years of employment. A defined contribution plan specifies the amount of the periodic contributions, but the amount of the benefits are not defined.

For accounting purposes, a defined contribution plan presents far fewer problems than does a defined benefit plan. In a defined contribution plan, the pension cost for a period is equal to the amount that the company must contribute for that period. In a defined benefit plan, the pension cost is based on many estimates and assumptions. Consequently, the accounting is much more complicated.

Under a defined benefit pension plan, the pension cost for a period is a function of the following components:

1. *Service cost*—the present value of the benefits earned by employees for the current period of service.

2. *Interest cost*—a cost to reflect the increase in the pension obligation due to the passage of time.

3. *Return on plan assets*—earnings on the pension fund are used to satisfy the pension obligation and therefore reduce the pension cost.

4. *Net amortization*—an allocation over several periods of costs associated with changes in the pension obligation (e.g., amendments to the pension plan to increase benefits).

The accounting requirements, which are detailed in *FASB Statement No. 87*, "Employers' Accounting for Pensions," are very complex and a detailed discussion of them is beyond the scope of this text.

The amounts that are funded each period are not necessarily equal to the amounts charged to pension cost. If contributions are less than pension cost, a pension liability is recorded.

Pension cost	X	
Cash		X
Pension liability		X

If contributions exceed pension cost, a prepaid pension cost is recorded.

Pension cost	X	
Prepaid pension cost	X	
Cash		X

At the end of each period, a reconciliation between the funded status of a company's pension plans and the prepaid pension cost or pension liability recognized on the balance sheet must be disclosed. The funded status of the plan is the difference between the company's obligation for all future retirement benefits to be paid—called the projected benefit obligation—and the fair value of the assets of the pension plan. If the obligation exceeds the fair value of plan assets, the plan is underfunded; if the fair value of plan assets exceeds the obligation, the plan is overfunded.

The funded status of the plan does not necessarily equal the prepaid pension cost or pension liability recognized on the balance sheet, because there are unrecognized pension elements. For example, if pension benefits are increased due to a plan amendment, the increase in the obligation—called a prior service cost—is not recognized immediately, but instead is allocated to pension cost over time (part of the net amortization component of pension cost). To illustrate the reconciliation, assume the projected benefit obligation is $100, the fair value of the plan assets is $60, and there is a prior service cost of $25. Then the unfunded obligation is $40 ($100 − $60), but the pension liability recognized on the balance sheet is $15 ($40 − $25).

Projected benefit obligation	($100)
Fair value of plan assets	60
Unfunded obligation	($ 40)
Unrecognized prior service cost	25
Pension liability on balance sheet	($ 15)

The parentheses refer to a liability position, not to negative numbers. Many companies use parentheses in their pension plan disclosures.

OTHER POSTRETIREMENT BENEFITS

Spending for health care is high and is increasing. The cost for health care benefits is exceeding the cost of retirement benefits. Although this section concentrates on health care benefits, other postretirement benefits also include life insurance, housing subsidies, and legal services.

The cost of private insurance to cover health care benefits continues to rise. Reasons for this increase include the following:

1. There are more older people living in the U.S. and people are living longer.

2. Increased prices for medical services.

3. Cost shifting of medical charges due to limitations on prices for patients covered by Medicare and Medicaid and to providing services for uninsured people.

4. Significant improvements in medical technology.

5. High utilization of medical services.

6. Such reactions to the wave of medical malpractice suits as performing unnecessary operations and requesting high-priced medical tests at hospitals.

Although the portion of large companies that offer health care benefits to retirees remained steady at 72 percent between 1991 and 1992, the portion of small and medium-sized companies offering benefits declined to 37 percent. The primary reason for these cutbacks is steeply rising medical costs.

Prior to the issuance of *FASB Statement No. 106*, "Employers' Accounting for Postretirement Benefits Other than Pensions," most companies were accounting for postretirement benefits on a pay-as-you-go basis. The cost recognized for the period was equal to the cash outlay for insurance premiums or claims paid. This practice resulted in a significant understatement of the financial effects of the promises to provide these benefits.

A postretirement benefit plan is a deferred compensation arrangement in which a company promises to provide future benefits to employees in exchange for current services. *FASB Statement No. 106* requires the cost of providing these benefits to be recognized over the employees' service periods.

The requirements for accounting for other postretirement benefits are basically the same as or similar to those for accounting for pensions. Differences in accounting result from differences between the two types of plans.

Health care benefits are generally paid without limitation, have great variability, and are paid as needed. On the other hand, pension benefits are better defined and are usually paid monthly without regard to need. Health care benefits are payable to not only the retiree but also the retiree's spouse and dependents; pension benefits are usually payable to the retiree only. While pension plans are generally funded, other postretirement benefit plans generally are not.

Pension benefits usually increase the longer an employee works for the company. For example, an employee may receive a specified percentage of average annual pay for each year of service. But the amount of health care benefits received may have nothing to do with years of service. Once the employee has worked for a long enough period to meet the plan's eligibility requirements, the employee is entitled to receive full benefits whether or not he/she works for a longer period of time.

LEASES

A lease is a contract between the owner of an asset (the lessor) and the user of the asset (the lessee). The contract gives the lessee the right to use the asset for a specified period of time in return for stipulated rental payments. A lease may be a simple, short-term rental (such as the use of an Alamo rental car for two days) or a longer, more complex agreement (such as a K-Mart store leasing its retail premises). Acquiring the use of assets through lease agreements has grown considerably. Commonly leased assets include airplanes, computers, railroad equipment, and warehouses.

The primary accounting issue is whether the lease is merely a rental or the lease gives rise to property rights to the lessee. Does the lease contract represent in substance a financing arrangement for the purchase of the asset and thereby transfer many of the benefits and risks of ownership to the lessee? If so, then the lease should be treated as an acquisition; the asset and the obligation should be recognized by the lessee on the balance sheet. If not, the lease should be treated as a rental; the asset should continue to be recognized by the lessor.

In *FASB Statement No. 13*, "Accounting for Leases," the criteria for treating a lease as in substance a purchase of the asset are stated. If any one of the following conditions are met at the inception of the lease, the lessee should record the transaction as a capital lease (in substance an acquisition of the asset); otherwise, the lessee should record the transaction as an operating lease (a rental of the asset):

1. The lease transfers ownership by the end of the lease term.

2. The lease contains a bargain purchase option (i.e., the lessee has the option to purchase the asset at a sufficiently low price compared to its expected fair value when the option becomes exercisable).

3. The least term is at least 75 percent of the asset's estimated economic life.

4. The present value of the minimum lease payments at the beginning of the lease is at least 90 percent of the fair value of the asset at that time.

The lessee usually wants to classify a lease as an operating lease. No liability is recognized on its balance sheet. There is not any negative impact on working capital, the current ratio, the acid-test ratio, or the debt-to-equity ratio.

To illustrate the basic accounting differences between a lease that is treated as an acquisition (a capital lease) and a lease that is treated as a rental (an operating lease), assume that on January 1, 19X1 a company leases a machine for three years at an annual rental of $20,000. Each payment is due at the end of the year. The estimated useful life of the machine is five years and its estimated salvage value is zero. The lessee can borrow money at an interest rate of 10 percent.

The first three criteria for capitalizing the lease are not met—there is no transfer of ownership or bargain purchase option and the lease term is only 60 percent of the asset's five-year life. The classification depends on the fourth criterion (the 90% test). The present value of the minimum lease payments is $49,738.[1] If the fair value of the asset is below $55,264.44, the transaction is a capital lease; otherwise, it is an operating lease.

The journal entries for the lessee for 19X1 if the lease is considered to be an acquisition are as follows:

Jan.	1	Capitalized lease	49,738	
		Liability for capitalized lease		49,738
Dec.	31	Interest expense	4,974	
		Liability for capitalized lease	15,026	
		Cash		20,000
		Depreciation expense	16,579	
		Accumulated depreciation		16,579

Interest expense (rounded to the nearest dollar) is computed by multiplying the lease liability balance at the beginning of the period by 10 percent. Therefore, $4,974 is equal to $49,738 multiplied by 10 percent.

In addition, the lessee must record depreciation on the machine. If the leased property will be retained by the lessee, depreciation should be recorded over the economic life of the asset. Otherwise, the property should be depreciated over the term of the lease. Assume that the lessee records depreciation (rounded to the nearest dollar) over the three-year term of the lease. Each year the amount of straight-line depreciation is $49,738 ÷ 3 = $16,579 (rounded to the nearest dollar).

If instead the lease is treated as a rental, the journal entry at the end of the year is as follows:

Rent expense	20,000	
Cash		20,000

There is no journal entry to record the lease at the beginning of the year.

The differences on the income statement for 19X1 between recording the transaction as a capital lease or as an operating lease are as follows;

	Lease considered to be	
	An	*A*
	Acquisition	*Rental*
Interest expense	$ 4,974	—
Depreciation expense	16,579	—
Rent expense	—	$ 20,000

The total charges are equal over the three-year term of the lease; however, the charges are higher in the earlier years and lower in the later one for a capital lease. Therefore, capitalizing a lease rather than considering the transaction to be a rental results in lower income in the early years as well as a higher debt-to-equity ratio due to recognizing the liability for the payments to be made.

---

[1] The present value factor for an annuity of three payments at a 10 percent interest rate is 2.4869. The present value of the three $20,000 payments is $20,000 × 2.4869 = $49.738.

PART II: ANALYSIS OF OTHER DISCLOSURES

Management of each organization has considerable flexibility in selecting from alternative generally accepted accounting principles. The accounting methods selected by a firm can significantly affect the determination of financial position and results of operations. A hypothetical example of the effects of alternative accounting methods is provided in Illustration 1. In the example, earnings per share could range from $1 to $1.95, depending on accounting methods, given one set of underlying economic circumstances. Therefore, the usefulness of the financial data is enhanced if disclosure includes information regarding the methods used by the firm. When financial statements are supplemented by such information, the financial data of different firms can be adjusted for differing accounting alternatives to make them comparable.

Illustration 1
*Effects of Alternative Generally
Accepted Accounting Principles
(with identical economics events)*

	A Company	B Company
Sales revenues—net	$10,000,000	$10,000,000
Expenses:		
Cost of goods sold[1]	$ 6,000,000	$ 5,600,000
Depreciation[2]	400,000	300,000
Pension and postretirement costs[3]	200,000	50,000
Salaries and bonuses[4]	400,000	200,000
Miscellaneous expense	2,000,000	2,000,000
Total expenses	$ 9,000,000	$ 8,150,000
Income before taxes	$ 1,000,000	$ 1,850,000
Income tax expense	500,000	875,000
Net income	$ 500,000	$ 975,000
Earnings per share (500,000 shares outstanding)	$1.00	$1.95

[1] A Company uses the last-in, first-out method for pricing inventories. B Company uses the first-in, first-out method.
[2] A Company uses accelerated depreciation for book and tax purposes. B Company uses the straight-line method for financial accounting and accelerated depreciation for tax purposes.
[3] A Company accrues postretirement heath costs while B Company does not.
[4] A Company pays incentive bonuses to officers in cash. B Company grants stock options to officers.

Those accounting principles and methods of applying the principles selected by management are referred to as the *accounting policies* of the entity. *Accounting Principles Board Opinion No. 22*, "Disclosures of Accounting Policies" requires that a "description of all significant accounting policies of the reporting entity should be included as an integral part of the financial statements." Such disclosure should describe the accounting principles followed by the reporting entity and the method of applying those principles that materially affect the determination of financial position and results of operations. In general, the disclosure should identify principles and describe methods peculiar to the industry or other unusual or innovative applications of accounting principles. Accounting policy disclosure includes such items as the basis of consolidation, depreciation methods, amortization of intangibles, inventory cost-flow assumptions, income realization on long-term contracts, and recognition of revenue from franchising or leasing operations. The opinion does not require a specific format for accounting policy disclosures, but it does recommend that the disclosures could appear in a separate "summary of significant policies" preceding the notes to the financial statements or as the initial note. In recent years, most large business enterprises have included in their annual reports a separate summary of their significant accounting policies.

FOOTNOTE DISCLOSURE

The information used in financial analysis is basically derived from the financial statements. Normally, however, the statements alone cannot provide all the information needed to understand the subtleties impounded in the financial position and results of operations. Consequently, *footnotes* are an important means of disclosing additional quantitative and qualitative information required for a proper interpretation of the statements. These footnotes are considered an integral part of the financial statements. Although footnote disclosures tend to be detailed and lengthy, they generally represent a vital input to the analysis process. Some of the more important topics covered by footnotes are the following:

1. Significant accounting policies.
2. Changes in accounting principles and retroactive adjustments
3. Contingent assets and liabilities.
4. Description of liabilities outstanding and credit agreements.
5. Information regarding stockholders' equity.
6. Long-term commitments.
7. Subsequent events.
8. Other useful disclosures.

These subjects are discussed and illustrated in the following paragraphs.

SIGNIFICANT ACCOUNTING POLICIES

As indicated previously, *APB Opinion No. 22* requires that the accounting principles followed and methods of applying those principles be described within the financial statements, preferably as the initial footnote or as a separate summary preceding the notes to the financial statements. Frequent disclosures concern the consolidation basis, depreciation methods, interperiod tax allocation, inventory cost flow assumptions, translation of foreign currencies, and revenue recognition. The accounting policies footnote from the most recent annual report of Wal-Mart includes the following information:

1. The consolidated financial statements include the accounts of subsidiaries.
2. Wal-Mart has stores throughout the United States and in Argentina, Canada, and Puerto Rico.
3. Inventories are stated principally at cost using the retail method.
4. Interest costs are capitalized during construction.
5. Straight-line depreciation is used.
6. Earnings per share is based on the weighted average number of common shares outstanding.

CHANGE IN ACCOUNTING PRINCIPLE

APB Opinion No. 20, "Accounting Changes," concludes that a change in accounting may significantly affect the financial statements, and therefore disclosures should be made to facilitate financial analysis. For changes in accounting principle, footnotes to the financial statements should disclose the nature of and justification for the change as well as the effect of the change on net income and the related earnings per share. Also, footnotes are frequently used to disclose the effect on income of a change in estimate.

CONTINGENCIES

A contingency involves circumstances shrouded in a considerable degree of uncertainty that may result in gains or losses through potential effects on asset or liability balances. Contingent liabilities arise from current or prospective litigation against the company, guarantees of indebtedness, and tax reassessments. Contingent assets may arise from loss carryforwards, claims for tax refunds, and patent infringement suits against other parties. The usual means of disclosing contingencies is in the footnotes to the financial statements.

In the 1996 annual report, PepsiCo discloses contingencies relating to lawsuits, taxes, environmental and other matters. PepsiCo was contingently liable under guarantees for $338 million in 1996.

DESCRIPTION OF LIABILITIES OUTSTANDING—CREDIT AGREEMENTS

Typically, footnotes are used to disclose supplementary information regarding the nature of current liabilities, long-term debt, and loan commitments for future loans or extensions of existing loans. In addition, footnote disclosure is often used to describe imputed interest on long-term payables not bearing interest or bearing an interest rate lower than the prevailing rate.

INFORMATION REGARDING STOCKHOLDERS' EQUITY

Companies present in the body of the balance sheet some information regarding the nature of equity securities; however, additional disclosure is usually presented in footnote form. The need for disclosure in connection with the capital structure of a corporation is stated *APB Opinion No. 15*, "Earnings Per Share" as follows:

"... financial statements should include a description in summary form, sufficient to explain the pertinent rights and privileges of the various securities outstanding. Examples of information which should be disclosed are dividend and liquidation preferences, participation rights, call prices and dates, conversion or exercise prices or rates and pertinent dates, sinking fund requirements, unusual voting rights, etc."

This disclosure should also include a description of stock options or purchase plans outstanding. In addition, it is important to disclose the nature of any restrictions such as the amount of retained earnings available for cash dividends.

LONG-TERM COMMITMENTS

Many businesses make various types of commitments for future performance. Such commitments include long-term lease agreements and pension and retirement plans. Some of these events are typically not reflected in their entirety in the accounts, but they are sufficiently important so that disclosures should be made in the notes to financial statements. Certain disclosures are required for pension plans and for long-term leases. Wal-Mart's footnotes report aggregate minimum annual rentals under operating leases of $4.744 million beginning in 1998.

SUBSEQUENT EVENTS

Events or transactions that occur subsequent to the end of the accounting period but prior to the issuance of financial statements and that have a material effect on the financial statements should be disclosed in the statements. Examples of subsequent events that may require disclosure are business combinations pending or affected, litigation settlements, issues of bonds or capital stock, and catastrophic loss of plant or inventories. In its 1996 annual report, PepsiCo stated that it planned to spin off its restaurant businesses (Taco Bell, Pizza Hut, and KFC) to its shareholders as an independent publicly-traded company.

Other Useful Disclosures

Footnote disclosure is often used to provide any other information relevant to the understanding and interpretation of the financial statement data. Examples of such information relate to foreign operations, product lines, sales backlogs and inventory profits.

The Auditor's Report as an Information Disclosure

Financial statements are representations of the management of an entity to interested parties. Although management has a responsibility to disclose sufficient information to ensure that financial statements are not misleading, an independent auditor may evaluate these statements to express an opinion to third parties about the fairness of presentation of the statements. This independent audit provides confidence to readers of the financial statements about the quality of information provided to them. Consequently, the report prepared by the auditor may serve as an important input to the financial reporting process. However, readers must understand the meaning of the auditor's opinion and the implications of the opinion for financial statement analysis.

The *auditor's report* is written after the auditor has undertaken an extensive and objective study of the accounting process and the financial statements prepared by management. Auditors indicate in a report to the stockholders the scope of their examination and then express an opinion regarding the fairness of the financial statements. The standard format of a report that indicates no qualification as to the fairness of the financial statements is presented in Illustration 2. This report is referred to as an *unqualified (clean)* opinion because the auditor has not qualified his or her opinion in any way.

Illustration 2
Independent Auditor's Report

[Date]

INDEPENDENT AUDITOR'S REPORT

We have audited the accompanying balance sheets of X Company as of December 31, 19X2 and 19X1, and the related statements of income, retained earnings, and cash flows for the years then ended. These financial statements are the responsibility of the Company's management. Our responsibility is to express an opinion on these financial statements based on our audits.

We conducted our audits in accordance with generally accepted auditing standards. Those standards require that we plan and perform the audit to obtain reasonable assurance about whether the financial statements are free of material misstatement. An audit includes examining, on a test basis, evidence supporting the amounts and disclosures in the financial statements. An audit also includes assessing the accounting principles used and significant estimates made by management, as well as evaluating the overall financial statement presentation. We believe that our audits provide a reasonable basis for our opinion.

In our opinion, the financial statements referred to above present fairly, in all material respects, the financial position of X Company as of [at] December 31, 19X2 and 19X1, and the results of its operations and its cash flows for the years then ended in conformity with generally accepted accounting principles.

[Signature]

Scope of the Audit

In the second paragraph (referred to as the scope paragraph), the statement "We conducted our audits in accordance with generally accepted auditing standards" relates to both general standards and standards of field work. Conformance to general standards implies that the examination was performed by adequately trained, proficient auditors who maintained an independent mental attitude and who exercised due professional care.

Conformance to field standards implies that the work was properly planned, that assistants were adequately supervised, and that a sufficient study and evaluation of the internal control (of the business) was made. The audit includes an examination of evidence supporting reported dollar amounts and an assessment of accounting principles used and significant estimates made by management. The audit must have a sufficient basis upon which to form an opinion concerning the financial statements.

THE OPINION

The opinion paragraph of the auditor's report requires the auditor to express an opinion on the financial statements; or if he or she cannot express an opinion, to clearly indicate so and state all the reasons. The four reporting standards are listed below:

1. The report shall state whether the financial statements are presented in accordance with generally accepted principles of accounting.

2. The report shall state whether such principles have been consistently observed in the current period in relation to the preceding period.

3. Informative disclosures in the financial statements are to be regarded as reasonably adequate unless otherwise stated in the report.

4. The report shall either contain an expression of opinion regarding the financial statements, taken as a whole, or an assertion to the effect that an opinion cannot be expressed. When an overall opinion cannot be expressed, the reasons therefore should be stated. In all cases where an auditor's name is associated with financial statements, the report should contain a clear-cut indication of the character of the auditor's examination, if any, and the degree of responsibility he or she is taking.

Thus, if an auditor's examination is made in accordance with generally accepted auditing standards, and if the financial statements are fairly presented in conformity with generally accepted accounting principles, applied on a consistent basis, and include all necessary disclosures, the auditor will issue a "clean" (unqualified) opinion. In all other circumstances, the auditor must give either a qualified opinion or an adverse opinion or disclaim an opinion.

In a *qualified opinion*, the auditor expresses certain reservations in his or her report concerning the scope of his or her examination and/or the financial statements. When the auditor's reservations are more serious, an adverse opinion or a disclaimer of opinion is given. In an adverse opinion, the auditor indicates that the financial statements do not present fairly the financial position and results of operations of the company. A disclaimer of opinion indicates that the auditor is unable to express an opinion. The inability to express an opinion usually occurs because of limitations in the scope of the audit.

The five major types of conditions that require the auditors to express an opinion other than an unqualified opinion are as follows:

1. The scope of the auditor's examination is limited by:

    a. Conditions that prevent the application of auditing procedures considered necessary in the circumstances.

    b. Restrictions imposed by the client.

2. The financial statements do not present fairly the financial position or results of operations because of:

    a. Lack of conformity with generally accepted accounting principles or standards.

    b. Inadequate disclosure.

3. Accounting principles are not consistently applied in the financial statements.

4. Uncertainties exist concerning the future resolution of material matters whose effects cannot be reasonably estimated.

5. There is doubt about the entity's ability to continue operations as a going concern.

The auditor's report shown in Illustration 3 shows a qualified opinion based on litigation and going concern problems.

Illustration 3
Example of Qualified Opinion

1991 Annual Report
USG Corporation

REPORT OF INDEPENDENT PUBLIC ACCOUNTANTS

To the Stockholders and Board
    of Directors of USG Corporation:

We have audited the accompanying consolidated balance sheet of USG Corporation (a Delaware corporation) and subsidiaries as of December 31, 1991 and 1990 and the related consolidated statements of earnings and cash flows for each of the three years in the period ended December 31, 1991. These financial statements are the responsibility of the Corporation's management. Our responsibility is to express an opinion on these financial statements based on our audits.

We conducted our audits in accordance with generally accepted auditing standards. Those standards require that we plan and perform the audit to obtain reasonable assurance about whether the financial statements are free of material misstatement. An audit includes examining, on a test basis, evidence supporting the amounts and disclosures in the financial statements. An audit also includes assessing the accounting principles used and significant estimates made by management, as well as evaluating the overall financial statement presentation. We believe that our audits provide a reasonable basis for our opinion.

In our opinion, the financial statements referred to above present fairly, in all material respects, the financial position of USG Corporation and subsidiaries as of December 31, 1991 and 1990, and the results of their operations and their cash flows for each of the three years in the period ended December 31, 1991, in conformity with generally accepted accounting principles.

The accompanying consolidated financial statements have been prepared assuming that the Corporation will continue as a going concern. The Corporation is in default of various of its loan agreements and does not expect to fund its debt service requirements in 1992 without restructuring its debt. Management's plan to restructure its debt is discussed in the financial restructuring footnote to the consolidated financial statements. As discussed in the litigation footnote, U.S. Gypsum is funding certain asbestos property damage defense costs until resolution of its coverage litigation against its insurance companies. In view of the current financial circumstances of the Corporation and the limited insurance funding currently available for property damage cases, management is unable to determine whether an adverse outcome in the asbestos litigation will have a material adverse effect on the financial condition of the Corporation. These conditions raise substantial doubt about the Corporation's ability to continue as a going concern. The consolidated financial statements do not include any adjustments relating to this uncertainty.

ARTHUR ANDERSEN & CO.

Chicago, Illinois
February 11, 1992

It should be apparent that information very relevant to the process of financial analysis may be revealed in the auditor's report. Consequently, the user of financial statements should carefully examine the auditor's opinion in relation to the other financial data in the annual report.

INTERIM REPORTING

Interim financial reports, usually issued on a quarterly basis, are designed to provide more timely information than annual reports. Interim financial information may include data on financial position, results of operations, and cash flows, and it may take the form of either complete financial statements or summarized financial data. The publication of interim reports is required by companies listed on both the New York Stock Exchange and the American Stock Exchange. The Securities and Exchange Commission also requires all listed companies to file quarterly reports on Form 10-Q.

Because the ultimate results of operations cannot be known with certainty until the business is finally liquidated, many problems are incurred when allocating costs and revenues to relatively short time periods. Consequently, interim reports are subject to even more significant limitations than annual reports. Given the problems inherent in determining interim financial results, it is important that the user fully understand the limitations of such data. Despite these limitations, however, interim financial results are very important.

The two most significant measurement issues created by interim reporting are the estimation of annually determined items and the seasonality of operating activities. Typically, the determination of income for a year includes several items that are not directly measurable until the end of the year. For example, with graduated tax rates, the income tax expense is a function of the total taxable income for the year. Also, if inventory levels are decreased during the interim reporting period, the cost of goods sold under the LIFO inventory method depends upon whether or not the inventory levels will be increased by the end of the year. These types of problems generally cause interim computations to be even more subjective than the annual figures. As a result of such problems, information available at the year end may be substantially modified from previously reported interim data.

Another problem that affects interim computations is that many companies experience seasonal variations in their operating activities. For example, book publishers sell most of their books at certain times of the year. Such seasonality creates a problem in the allocation of operating costs that may be incurred at a different rate than the revenues. For example, even if sales are highly seasonal, such costs as property taxes, insurance, and executive salaries may be incurred relatively evenly throughout the year. A similar problem exists with the allocation of fixed costs (that is, depreciation) among interim periods.

The Accounting Principles Board attempted to establish consistent guidelines for interim financial reporting by issuing *APB Opinion No. 28* in 1973. The APB's objectives were to develop accounting principles and disclosure requirements that are appropriate for interim statements and to specify minimum guidelines for information to be reported by publicly-held companies.

The same principles and practices followed in the annual period should generally be followed in the interim periods. However, the Board also concluded that certain modifications in accounting principles or practices followed for annual periods are necessary at interim dates.

Revenues should be recognized as earned during an interim period on the same basis as recognized for the full year. Any significant seasonal variations in the activities of the business should be disclosed in the interim report. Costs associated directly with, or allocated to, products should be recognized from those products as revenue is earned. The gross profit method for estimating inventories is allowable for interim reports. All other nonproduct costs and expenses should be charged to income as incurred or be allocated to interim periods based on an estimate of time expired or activities associated with the periods. Businesses incurring costs or expenses subject to seasonal variations should disclose the seasonal nature of their activities in their interim financial statements.

Income tax provisions should be determined at the end of each interim period based on an estimate of the effective tax rate to be applied for the full fiscal year. To illustrate, assume that a company has pretax income of $60,000 in the first quarter of the year and pretax income of $100,000 in the second quarter. The income tax expense for the first quarter is $10,000. If the effective tax rate for the fiscal year is now estimated to be 34 percent, then income tax expense for the second quarter is computed as follows:

Pretax income for the first and second quarters	$160,000
Estimated tax rate	.34
Income tax expense for first and second quarters	$ 54,400
Income tax expense for first quarter	10,000
Income tax expense for second quarter	$ 44,400

There is no retroactive correction for incorrectly estimating the effective tax rate for the fiscal year in any quarter. Therefore, in the above example, there is no retroactive correction for estimating the effective tax rate for the fiscal year as 16.67 percent in the first quarter and then 34 percent in the second quarter.

Typically, interim reports include summarized financial data that have considerably less detail than are included in annual financial reports. Information required in interim financial reports includes sales, provision for income taxes, extraordinary items, cumulative effect of a change in accounting principle, net income, earnings per share, and the seasonal nature of revenues or expenses. The opinion also encourages publicly-traded companies to include balance sheets and cash-flow data. When analyzed with the proper caution, it appears that the information contained in interim reports can be used to improve the user's decision-making process.

Reporting for Segments of a Business

In the 1960's, conglomerates were formed. These are companies that operate in several lines of business. For example, Tenneco has operations in pipelines, heavy and farm equipment manufacturing, ship building, and agricultural products. The purpose of the diversification is to hedge against downturns in any one area of business activity. Such diversified companies are required to disclose financial information concerning the activities of individual segments of the business. The term segment generally is used to describe a component of an entity whose activities relate to a separate major class of customer or product. Individual segments of a diversified company may be uniquely affected by economic conditions and have different rates of profitability, degrees of risk, and opportunities for growth. Therefore, segment financial data can help financial analysts and other users of financial statements learn about and make informed decisions regarding such companies. Some of the more important specific uses of segmented data include the following:

1. To provide information regarding the nature of the businesses a company is involved in and the relative size of the various segments.
2. To use the sales and contributions toward profit as an input to the evaluation and projection of corporate earnings.
3. To appraise the ability of management in making acquisitions.
4. To make credit decisions by using information concerning the cash flows of the various segments.

Problems in Providing Segment Data

There are several potential problems in providing financial data for diversified companies on a segment basis. The three main problems that occur in developing financial data on a segment basis are: (1) allocation of common costs to two or more segments, (2) pricing transactions between segments, and (3) determining segments to be used for reporting purposes. Each problem must be addressed if meaningful information is to be reported.

Disadvantages to the Reporting Company

Concern has been expressed by corporate management that disclosure of segment financial information may cause difficulties harmful to the reporting company. The disadvantages cited often include confidential information is revealed to competitors, technical problems inherent in the preparation of the data might result in misleading information users, and the cost of providing the data can be significant.

Determining Reportable Industry Segments

In recognition of the perceived importance of segment information, the FASB in 1976 issued *Statement No. 14*, which required a diversified company to disclose certain information concerning its operations in different industries, its foreign operations, its export sales, and its major customers. Then in 1997, the FASB issued *Statement*

No. 131, which requires companies to report in their annual and quarterly financial statements information pertaining to operating segments, products and services, geographic areas of operation, and major customers.

FASB Statement No. 131 requires disclosure of financial activities for the company's operations in different industries. In general, separate disclosure must be made for each industry segment that is a significant corporate component providing products or services to unaffiliated customers.

FASB Statement No. 131 does not provide detailed rules and procedures that must be followed in defining industry segments because of the inherent differences among businesses by the nature of their operations. Instead, segment information is determined using a management approach. The segments are evident from the structure of the company's internal organization, because they are based on the way segments are organized for purposes of making operating decisions and assessing performance. Consequently, segment reporting is aligned with internal reporting.

Once the products and services have been grouped into industry segments, the segments that are reportable must be selected. A test is made on an annual basis to determine a company's reportable segments. In order to be classified as a reportable segment, the segment must satisfy at least one of the following tests.

1. Industry revenue of the segment is at least 10 percent of total company revenue.

2. Operating profit or loss of the segment is 10 percent or more of the greater of:

   a. The total of all the company's industry segments that have operating profits.

   b. The total of all the company's industry segments that have operating losses.

3. Identifiable assets of the segment are 10 percent or more of the combined industry segments' identifiable assets.

In addition, the statement provides two overall tests to be made:

1. Combined revenue from sales to unaffiliated customers of all reportable segments should amount to at least 75 percent of combined revenues from unaffiliated customers. Additional industry segments should be reported until this test is met.

2. No more than ten segments needs to be reported. Segments may be reexamined and possibly combined to avoid an excessive number of reportable segments.

A reconciliation should be provided for the total of the reported segments' revenues, profit or loss, and assets to the respective consolidated figures.

As an illustration of the application of these tests, assume that a company has the following data available:

Segment	Revenue	Operating Profit (loss)	Identifiable Assets
A	$ 700	$ 75	$ 250
B	400	30	190
C	90	15	130
D	80	(10)	50
	$1,270	$110	$ 620

All sales are to unaffiliated companies.

REVENUE TEST. Total revenue equals $1,270. Reportable segments are A and B. Segments C and D do not meet the test because neither has revenue of at least $127 ($1,270 × .10).

OPERATING PROFIT OR LOSS TEST. Operating profits total $120 ($75 + $30 + $15), which exceeds the total of the operating loss ($10). Therefore, the test is based on the operating profit of $120. Reportable segments are A, B, and C; each has an operating profit of at least $12 ($120 ×.10). Segment D does not meet the test, because the absolute value of its operating loss is less than $12.

IDENTIFIABLE ASSETS TEST. Total identifiable assets are $620. Reportable segments are A, B, and C. Segment D does not meet the test, because its identifiable assets are less than $62 ($620 × .10).

The reportable segments are A, B, and C as long as their combined revenues from sales to unaffiliated companies equal at least 75 percent of total sales to unaffiliated companies. Sales to unaffiliated companies for Segments A, B, and C total $1,190 ($700 + $400 + $90). Total sales to unaffiliated companies total $1,270. The 75 percent test is met.

FOREIGN OPERATIONS

A company should provide information on revenues and long-lived assets in the country in which it is located and all applicable foreign countries in total. If revenues or assets in an individual foreign country are material, they should be disclosed separately.

USEFULNESS OF SEGMENT DATA

Diversified companies present special problems in financial analysis and decision-making. Since these companies may have varying degrees of profitability, uses, and growth potential for individual components, the analyst needs financial information regarding the components to make meaningful decisions. Despite the potential usefulness of segment information, however, the analyst must use extreme caution in assessments and evaluations of the data.

MANAGEMENT'S DISCUSSION AND ANALYSIS

An important element of disclosure in financial reporting is management's discussion and analysis. The purpose of this analytical disclosure is to assist investors and creditors in identifying underlying trends in a company's operations in order to enhance predictions of future financial performance.

In *FASB Statement of Financial Accounting Concepts No. 1*, the FASB addressed the importance of management explanations and interpretations.

> Financial reporting should include explanations and interpretations to help users understand financial Information provided.... [T]he usefulness of financial information as an aid to investors, creditors, and others in forming expectations about a business enterprise may be enhanced by management's explanations of the information. Management knows more about the enterprise and its affairs than investors, creditors, or other outsiders and can often increase the usefulness of financial information by identifying certain transactions, other events, and circumstances that affect the enterprise and explaining their financial impact on it ... Moreover, financial reporting often provides information that depends on, or is affected by, management's estimates and judgment Investors, creditors, and others are aided in evaluating estimates and judgmental information by explanations of underlying assumptions or methods used, including disclosure of significant uncertainties about principal underlying assumptions or estimates.[2]

Management's discussion and analysis has been required by the SEC since 1974. The content of the information to be contained in Form 10-K was restructured in 1980. Additional guidance was provided by the SEC in 1989. Management's discussion and analysis should include information on the following items:

1. Short-term and long-term liquidity.

2. Capital resources.

3. Results of operations.

4. Favorable and unfavorable trends, demands, commitments, events, or uncertainties.

5. The causes for material changes in line items.

---

[2] *FASB Statement of Financial Accounting Concepts No. 1*, "Objectives of Financial Reporting by Business Enterprises" (Stanford, CT FASB, 1978), para. 54.

An example of management's discussion and analysis is presented in the Wal-Mart annual report included in this text.

SUMMARY

A pension plan is a contract between a company and its employees to provide benefits on their retirement. The plan may specify the amount of benefits to be received or the contributions to be made. Accounting for a pension plan requires that the current and future costs of the provided benefits be measured and allocated to the appropriate accounting periods.

A postretirement benefit plan, like a pension plan, is a deferred compensation arrangement in which future benefits are promised in exchange for current services provided. The largest component of these postretirement benefits is health care benefits.

A lease that is in substance a purchase should be recognized as an asset by a lessee. The liability for the payments on the lease should also be recognized. If the lease arrangement is not in substance a purchase, it should be accounted for as a rental with no recognition of the asset or liability.

Footnotes are an integral part of the financial statements. They provide information that is essential for developing an understanding of the information presented in the statements. The footnotes contain information on specific accounting methods or policies adopted by the company, details regarding account information, and information regarding commitments and contingencies. The auditors' report indicates the scope of the auditors' investigation and their opinion regarding whether the financial statements are a fair presentation of the results of operations and the financial position of the company. Management's discussion and analysis aids users to form expectations about a company.

Interim financial reports provide information on a more timely basis than annual reports. Generally, the same principles and practices followed for the issuance of annual reports should also be used for interim reports.

Segmental reporting helps users of financial statements to make more informed decisions regarding diversified companies. Segment information provided includes revenues, operating profit or loss, and identifiable assets.

KEY DEFINITIONS

Accounting policies—the particular accounting methods adopted by a company in preparing its financial statements.
Accumulated postretirement benefit obligation—the obligation for future postretirement benefits to be paid.
Auditors report—the auditor's letter that indicates the scope of his or her audit and his or her opinion regarding the fair presentation of the financial statements.
Capital lease—a lease that is in substance a purchase of an asset; both the asset and liability are recognized on the financial statements.
Defined benefit pension plan—a plan that specifies the amount of pension benefits to be received during retirement.
Defined contribution pension plan—a plan that specifies the amount of the periodic contribution, but not the amount of benefits to be received.
Interest cost—a cost to reflect the increase in the pension or postretirement benefit obligation due to the passage of time.
Interim reports—the quarterly financial reports that are issued during the time period between the annual reports.
Lease—a contract between the owner of an asset (the lessor) and the user of the asset (the lessee).
Operating lease—a lease that is not in substance a purchase of an asset; the transaction is recorded as a rental.
Prior service cost—the increase in the pension obligation due to a plan amendment.
Projected benefit obligation—the company's obligation for all future pension benefits to be paid on retirement.
Qualified opinion—an audit opinion that has reservations regarding the scope of the audit, uncertainties or going concern.
Return on plan assets—earnings on the pension or postretirement benefit fund used to satisfy the obligation.
Segment information—information presented in the footnotes to the financial statements regarding specific product lines and/or customers.
Service cost—the present value of the benefits earned by employees for the current period of service.
Vested benefits—benefits that employees have earned and will receive even if they leave the company.

QUESTIONS

1. What are actuarial assumptions?

2. What are the characteristics of a pension plan?

3. Differentiate between accounting for a defined benefit pension plan and a defined contribution pension plan.

4. If pension cost for the period does not equal the contribution made to the pension fund, to what account(s) is the difference recognized in a defined benefit plan?

5. What is the funded status of a pension or postretirement benefit plan?

6. What are the differences between pension plans and postretirement benefit plans?

7. How has the issuance of FASB Statement No. 106 changed the accounting requirements for postretirement benefits?

8. If a company rents a chain saw for two days, would this be considered a capital lease or an operating lease? Explain.

9. What are the criteria for determining whether a lease is a capital lease or an operating lease?

10. Why might a company want to classify a lease as an operating lease rather than a capital lease?

11. What are the differences on the financial statements between classifying a lease as a capital lease or an operating lease?

12. What disclosures and reports, besides financial statements, are large businesses (such as large publicly held corporations) required to prepare or publish?

13. Describe the accounting policies section of footnotes found in financial statements.

14. Why are accounting policies required to be disclosed?

15. What kind of information should be included in the footnotes to the financial statements?

16. List some topics commonly covered in the footnotes to the financial statements.

17. Is the management of a firm responsible for preparing the auditor's report on that firm's financial statements?

18. What kinds of opinions may an auditor express in an auditor's report regarding the fairness of a firm's financial statements?

19. Of what use is the auditor's report to the financial statement user?

20. How does an interim financial report differ from the annual financial report?

21. Why do the major stock exchanges require corporations listed on those exchanges to publish interim financial statements?

22. What limitations exist to the preparation and use of interim financial statements?

23. Define the term business segment.

24. Of what benefit is it to a financial statement user to be provided with financial reports that separately report business segment activities for diversified businesses?

25. Providing financial data for segments of a business is more complex than providing data for the whole business. List some additional accounting problems associated with segment reporting.

EXERCISES

26. For each of the transactions listed, indicate the effect(s), if any, on the company's year-end: (1) Balance Sheet, (2) Income Statement, and (3) Statement of Cash Flows. Your answers should be as complete and specific as possible.

    a. Funded pension costs. The amount funded is less than total pension costs.
    b. Funded pension costs. The amount funded is more than total pension costs.

27. For each of the transactions listed, indicate the effect(s), if any, on the company's year-end: (1) Balance Sheet, (2) Income Statement, and (3) Statement of Cash Flows. Your answers should be as complete and specific as possible.

    a. Signed a lease agreement and made a lease payment. The lease is treated as a rental.
    b. Signed a lease agreement and made a lease payment. The lease is considered to be an acquisition.

Refer to the Annual Report in Chapter 1 of the text.

28. What are the future minimum commitments for capital leases?

29. What is the present value of the future minimum commitments for capital leases?

30. What are the future minimum commitments for operating leases?

31. By how much did net sales increase or decrease in the most recent year?

32. Why did cost of sales as a percentage of net sales increase or decrease in the most recent year?

33. Did interest expense increase or decrease in the most recent year and why?

34. By how much did inventories increase or decrease in the most recent year and why?

35. What was capital spending in the most recent year?

36. By how much did other liabilities increase or decrease in the most recent year and why?

37. What was the increase or decrease in stockholders' equity in the most recent year?

38. In which quarter in the most recent year are net sales the largest?

39. In which quarter in the most recent year is the operating profit the greatest?